KEN SCHULTZ'S

Fishing Encyclopedia

Worldwide Angling Guide

VOLUME 4

KEN SCHULTZ'S

Fishing Encyclopedia

Worldwide Angling Guide

Ken Schultz

IDG Books Worldwide, Inc.
An International Data Group Company
Foster City, CA • Chicago, IL • Indianapolis, IN • New York, NY • Southlake, TX

IDG Books Worldwide, Inc.
An International Data Group Company
919 E. Hillsdale Boulevard
Suite 400
Foster City, CA 94404

For general information on books from IDG Books Worldwide's in the U.S., please call our Consumer Customer Service department at 800-762-2974. For reseller information, including discounts and premium sales, please call our Reseller Customer Service department at 800-434-3422.

For information on a multimedia version of this book, available from Tricom Intrtactive, Inc., please go to this Web site: intellipedia.com

To contact the author, please visit: www.kenshultz.com

Library of Congress Cataloging-in-Publication Data

This edition of *Ken Schultz's Fishing Encyclopedia,* which is published in 7 volumes, contains the entire contents of the work as previously published in a single volume: *Ken Schultz's Fishing Encyclopedia,* ISBN 9780028620572

This is Volume 4 of 7

Schultz, Ken, 1950–
Ken Shultz's fishing encyclopedia: worldwide angling guide/ Ken Schultz. — 1st ed.
p. cm.
ISBN 0-02-862057-7
Volume 4: ISBN 9781684427697 (hardcover) | ISBN 9781684427703 (paperback)

1. Fishing—Encyclopedias. 2. Fishes—Encyclopedias. I. Title.
SH411.S38 2000
799.1'03—dc21 99-033719
CIP

Manufactured in the United States of America

First Edition

Table of Contents

Introduction

"Ah, the gallant fisher's life! It is the best of any;
'Tis full of pleasure, void of strife, And 'tis beloved by many."

—IZAAK WALTON

"All men are equal before fish."

—HERBERT HOOVER

WHILE PRODUCING THIS FISHING ENCYCLOPEDIA I SPOKE TO MANY HUNDREDS OF informed anglers. Nearly all of them thought the compilation of all things piscatorial was too overwhelming to contemplate because the angling universe is so enormous and diverse.

Certainly a modern fishing encyclopedia—if it truly provides a full field of knowledge—runs counter to the short and specialized tenets of today's journalism. Yet it is precisely because there is so much to the sport of fishing, plus an increasing profusion of specialized equipment and confusing terminology, that it was necessary to bring order and perspective to all of this in one definitive book.

Ken Schultz's Fishing Encyclopedia & Worldwide Angling Guide has been a long time in the making. I started thinking about it in 1991. Since work began in earnest in 1995, the project became even more expansive than expected, and indeed there were times when it was nearly overwhelming. As a result, the book (now a series of books) grew much bigger than originally planned, becoming 50 percent larger than any fishing encyclopedia that has heretofore been published.

As a result, however, this encyclopedia contains the equivalent of thirty standard-length books, meaning that there is ample space to devote to the species, equipment, techniques, locations, and ancillary matters that encompass the angling universe. Consider that nearly one-third of the encyclopedia series is comprised of the most comprehensive information on worldwide angling opportunities ever assembled. There is absolutely no place to find these details together; indeed, some elements of the *Worldwide Angling Guide* cannot be found anywhere else at all.

Likewise, the coverage of angling methods and equipment has never been addressed more comprehensively between the covers of any other book. In fact, *Ken Schultz's Fishing Encyclopedia* contains the most modern, illuminating, and extensive discourses on the basic elements of fishing tackle—baitcasting, big-game, conventional, flycasting, spinning, and spincasting—ever found in one place. Each of these entries undoubtedly contain more than all but the most scrupulous person will want to know.

Great lengths were also taken, however, to make sure that the less obvious subjects in the angling universe were included and reviewed in comprehensive fashion. For example, nowhere else is there a more extensive review of the principles, methods, and pros and cons of catch-and-release—perhaps the most important angling conservation development of the twentieth century.

Topics like fisheries management, angling-related travel, choosing guides and charter boats, and the care and preparation of fish for consumption, which are among many unglamorous subjects taken for granted elsewhere, receive complete explanation and review here. Likewise the otherwise oft-ignored subjects of ethics and etiquette—increasingly important issues as human pressures increase—are included.

Although there's an enormous amount of information in this series of books, every topic was approached with the intent to take nothing for granted and to present information in straightforward language. Angling is not like nuclear physics, and if it was half as complicated as some people try to make it, no one would enjoy it or have success. The extensive insertion of cross references is thus intended to direct you through a continuing stream of appropriate topics, so you can take any subject as far as you want to go. Some cross references appear within entry text next to topics that are more thoroughly reviewed elsewhere; many cross references appear at the end of entry text, either to direct you to the appropriate subject entry or to note related topics.

We've tried to make things easy to find and to place subjects where you're most likely to look for them, even if you're unsure of the proper terms or spelling. As an example, you'll find rainbow trout under the "T" entries (trout, rainbow) rather than under the "R" entries. Also, at the back of each book is a weights and measures conversion chart; this will be convenient for many readers since there's a liberal mix of metric and U.S. customary weights and measures throughout this book, just as there is at boat docks, fish camps, and tackle shops throughout the world.

Because the text is encyclopedic in format, however, it does not provide a full sense of the joy or spirit of sportfishing—the pleasure that makes it "beloved by many," as Izaak Walton said. Perhaps the accompanying photos help convey this. Photos and line art, incidentally, were planned and selected to reflect the broad, eclectic places and situations that so many anglers experience, as well as to reflect the great diversity of its participants. Angling is a very democratic recreation; as the quotation from President Hoover implies, the fish don't care who hooks them.

It is a special delight to publish this encyclopedia at the close of the twentieth century—a period with the most phenomenal sportfishing growth in the history of mankind—and at the advent of a new millennium. Knowing that the decades ahead will require proper stewardship of aquatic resources—something that anglers in particular have always demonstrated personal and financial support for—this text has been written and edited with sensitivity to conservation issues while also being realistic about the role that humans play as the highest predators and the diverse motivations they bring to angling.

In a sense, the sport of fishing is like a book with as many footnotes as main text. It is full of variables, especially individual skills, weather issues, peculiarities among species, habitat differences, and so forth. You may notice that the words "usually" and "generally" occur often in portions of the text. This isn't meant to be vague; it's because there are often no hard-and-fast rules in catching fish, no matter what you may have heard to the contrary. There are norms, but straying from norms is common for one reason or another, as any angler who has been humbled at a "hot" site at the "best" time of the season can attest.

While there is a wealth of reliable information here, a caveat is in order with regard to the contents of the *Worldwide Angling Guide.* Many of the countries profiled have not in the past provided, or do not currently provide, or may not in the future provide stable travel environments, especially to tourists of certain nationalities. Jungle fishing opportunities are especially among those that may present danger. Angola, Colombia, and Zambia come immediately to mind in this regard. Civil unrest can likewise make travel in certain places dangerous; recent troubles in Kenya, Indonesia, Russia, Uganda, and the Balkans serve as examples. The adventurous angler needs to use good judgment.

Things change the environmental order and aquatic resources, too. Yugoslavia hadn't been wrecked by bombs when that entry was written; Nicaragua and Honduras were leveled by Hurricane Georges right after those entries were written. Environmental changes sometimes radically alter the presence or availability of certain gamefish species, and in the more remote pockets of the world only native people and intrepid explorers are likely to know it.

On a final note, it is tempting to say, as marketers and publicists are wont to do, that this book contains everything an angler will ever need to know about fish and fishing. But new developments in fishing tackle will surely come along, changes in some habitats or in fish populations will alter the techniques and equipment used, and certainly natural changes will take place in some of the world's best angling spots. However, a lot of the fundamentals—the underlying principles of fish behavior, the function of basic equipment, and angling methodology—will be constant, making most of the information in this book relevant to the discerning angler even in years to come.

I expect to add to this body of knowledge in time, so if you think there's something that should have been included, if you have knowledge about fishing in a country that wasn't covered, or if you can suggest an improvement to any aspect of this book, please visit my website—www.kenschultz.com—and post a message about it.

Now, turn to any page and become absorbed.

—Ken Schultz

"If I fished only to capture fish, my fishing trips would have ended long ago."

—ZANE GREY

Acknowledgments

PRODUCING A BOOK OF THIS MAGNITUDE REQUIRED THE INVOLVEMENT OF A tremendous number of people and a great array of talents. This encyclopedia would not have gone beyond a mere suggestion, however, had it not been for the endorsement and encouragement of Natalie Chapman, a former publisher at Macmillan General Reference, now IDG Books Consumer Reference, whose confidence and vision made this book possible, and who gave me free rein to produce it as necessary. I'm also indebted to publisher Marie Butler-Knight, who took this project over in mid-stream, marshaled all the resources, and fervently shepherded the book to completion. Sincere appreciation is also extended to Renee Wilmeth and Kristi Hart, who directed the publisher's nitty-gritty editorial and production work with outstanding dedication and professionalism, plus a reassuring enthusiasm; to Pamela Benner, who paid excellent attention to details in the copyediting process and made good suggestions; and to many other directly involved personnel, particularly Beth Jordan, Faunette Johnston, and Jeanine Bucek.

This book could also not have been completed without the special assistance of my wife, Sandy, and my daughters, Alyson, Megan, and Kristen. They each helped in a variety of ways, especially by being patient. Sandy's assistance with a host of matters was very beneficial, and Kristen was particularly vital, pitching in for a second time during a desperate period with important research and writing assistance.

In order to make this encyclopedia truly comprehensive and of worldwide significance it was imperative to involve a host of contributors with expertise in technical fisheries matters, regional angling opportunities, and specialized sportfishing topics. I'm grateful for their participation and excellent contributions, the bulk of which made up the *Worldwide Angling Guide*. In particular, appreciation is extended to the incomparable Ed Migdalski, who provided technical scientific fisheries advice and vetted all of the fish art.

I'm also indebted to the late, and incomparable in his own right, A. J. McClane. His fishing encyclopedia of 1965 and 1974, though now outdated, was not only a phenomenal reference work, but a monumental achievement in an era before personal computers, electronic mail, fax machines, scanners, laser printers, and the various modern technology that made putting this book together far easier than it was in his time. Unlike me, he was unable to write and edit on a laptop computer in cars, planes, airports, hotel rooms, and other places, or receive electronically transmitted text. More significantly, McClane set a very high bar for what a real fishing encyclopedia ought to be, and provided a template for such a book for the twenty-first century. Without his accomplishment, it would have been much more difficult to plan and publish this book. (Aside to historians: four contributors to this project—Ed Migdalski, George Reiger, Jack Samson, and Bill Scifres—were also contributors to McClane's encyclopedia.)

Just as McClane, the contributors to this book, and the people at IDG Books Worldwide are the best in their fields, so is *Field & Stream* the largest and best fishing and hunting magazine in the world, and I've been privileged to be part of this publication continuously since 1973. I appreciate the confidence and opportunities provided me over that time by its editors. Those opportunities laid the groundwork for this encyclopedia. I'm especially grateful to Editor Slaton White and Managing Editor Mike Toth for allowing me leeway over the last several years that I've been working on this project.

Information, suggestions, encouragement, technical advice, reference paraphernalia, reviews and critiques, and assorted material assistance were received from so many individuals and organizations that some will likely be overlooked in these acknowledgments, for which I apologize.

I'm very grateful to the following individuals:

Blaine Anderson
John Anthon
Dick Ballard
Ron Ballanti
LaVerne Barnes
Cameron Baty
Susan Baumgartner
Gene Bay
Dick Bengraff
Virginia Benoit
Walt Boname
Toby Bradshaw
Eric Burnley
Cyril Calendini
Bill Chapman, Jr.
Jim Chapralis
Larry Columbo
David Cosby
Gary Dollahon
Lou Duarte
Todd DuPuis
Jack Erskine
Mike Fine
Paul Fuller
Riccardo Galigani
Ken Gangler

Guy Geffroy
Lois Gerber
Alessandro Giangio
Barry Gibson
Gary Giudice
Fred Golofaro
Jerry Gomber
George Gowen
Garry Gurke
Judy Hammond
Bill Hilts, Jr.
Bruce Holt
Dr. James Imai
Jimmy Kano
Nick Karas
Glenda Kelley
Gary King
Jason Klein
Bob Lang
Steen Larsen
Mike Leech
Bill Liston
Chun Liu
George Loechl
Paulo Loes
Frank Longino
Jim Matthews
John Mazurkewicz
Tom Melton
Paul Merzig
Ed Mesunas
Bill Miller
Gail Morchower
András Nagy
Andy Newman
Stuart Newman
Donald J. Orth
Tom Pagliaroli
Sheldon Pasternack
Dennis Phillips
Stanko Popovic
Norville Prosser
Jim Reist
Al Ristori
Milt Rosko
Gail Ross
Sharon Rushton
Pat Salimeno
Marty Salovin
Glenn Sapir
Christine Moore Serrao
Vin Sparano
Ron Speed, Sr.
Roy Stiner
Mick Thill
Roger Tucker
Jerry Valentine
Mike Walker
Ben Wechsler
Mark Weintz
Fenner Weller
Jim White
Anthony M. Williams
Dick Wood
Peter Yaskowski

I'm also grateful to the following companies and organizations (and specific people where noted in parenthesis):

American Sportfishing Association (Mike Hayden)
American Wire (Michael Shields)
Arkie Lures
The Atlantic Salmon Federation
Bay de Noc Lure Co.
Bead Tackle (Peter Renkert)
Bear Advertising (Dick Bear, Mark Malkin)
Big Jon (Jerry Livingstone)
Bullet Weights (Douglas Crumrine)
Bushnell Sports Optics (Barbara Mellman)
Cabela's Inc. (Tony Dolle)
Classic Fishing Products (Mike Richards)
C-Map USA (Pam Oldham)
Computrol, Inc.
Cossack Bait Products (Garry Shaw)
Cuba Specialty Mfg. Co. (Craig Osterhus, Dana Pickup)
Daiwa Corp.
Earie Dearie Lure Co. (Helen Galbincea)
EZE Lap Diamond (Donna Long)
Fin-Nor (Niels Stenhoj)
Flambeau Products Corp. (Jason Sauey)
Florida Keys and Key West Visitors Bureau
Flow-Rite of Tennessee (Don Zielinski)
Furuno
Future Fisherman Foundation
Garmin International (Steve Featherstone)
G. Loomis (Gary Loomis, Steve Rajeff)
Gudebrod
International Game Fish Association (Jim Brown)
Hudson River Foundation
Interphase Technologies
K-C Tackle (Raymond Packer)
L. L. Bean (Mary Rose MacKinnon)
L&S Bait Co. (Eric Bachnik)
Lowrance Electronics (Darrell Lowrance, Steve Schneider)
Luhr Jensen & Sons (Phil Jensen, Barry Ternahan)
Magellan Systems Corp. (Don Meyer)
Mann's Bait Co.
Marado Inc.
Old Town Canoe (Jim Kaiser)
O. Mustad & Sons USA (John DeVries)
National Freshwater Fishing Hall of Fame
Nomadic Expeditions (Denise Gogarty)
Normark Corp. (Ron Weber, Craig Weber)
The Orvis Company
Outdoor Technologies
Owner America Corp. (Kat Shitanishi)
Penn Fishing Tackle
Pradco (Joe Hughes, Bruce Stanton)
Scientific Anglers
Shakespeare Fishing Tackle (Mark Davis)
Sheldon's Inc.
Shimano American Corp.
Si-Tex Marine Electronics
Storm Lures (Sharon Andrews, John Storm)
Sufix USA, Inc.
Techsonics Industries
Len Thompson Lures (Richard Pallister)
Top Brass Tackle (Eric Cosby)
Tru-Turn Hooks (Wes Campbell)
Wisconsin Pharmacal
H. D. Wood Advertising
Worden's Lures
The Worth Co.
Wright & McGill Co. (George Large)
Yakima Bait Co. (Rob Phillips)
Zebco Corp. (Jenni Foster)

Gratitude is also due the following government agencies and government-funded programs (and the people noted in parenthesis), which provided research and reference materials, and, in some cases, other forms of assistance:

Alabama Cooperative Extension Service (Richard Wallace)
Alabama Department of Conservation and Natural Resources (Stan Cook)
Alabama Sea Grant Extension Program
Alaska Department of Fish and Game (Jon Lyman)
Alaska Sea Grant College Program (Kurt Byers)
Alberta Department of Environmental Protection

Arizona Game and Fish Department
Arkansas Cooperative Extension Program, Univ. of Arkansas (Nathan Stone)
Arkansas Game and Fish Commission (Keith Sutton)
Auburn University Marine Extension (Richard Wallace, William Hosking, Stephen Szedlmayer)
Brazil Embratur
British Columbia Ministry of Environment, Fisheries Branch
California Department of Fish and Game (A. Petrovich)
Canada Department of Fisheries and Oceans
Canadian Consul General
Cayman Islands Department of Tourism
Colorado Department of Natural Resources
Connecticut Department of Environmental Protection
Delaware Division of Fish and Wildlife
Florida Department of Environmental Protection, Marine Research Institute and Division of Marine Resources (Jim Lewis)
Florida Game and Freshwater Fish Commission, Division of Fisheries (Henry Cabbage)
Georgia Department of Natural Resources (Chris Martin)
Great Lakes Fishery Commission
Guam Department of Agriculture (Gerry Davis)
Hawaii Department of Land and Natural Resources, Division of Aquatic Resources
Idaho Department of Fish and Game (Jack Trueblood)
Illinois Department of Natural Resources
Indiana Department of Natural Resources (Jon Marshall)
International Center for Living Aquatic Resources Management/Food and Agriculture Organization of the United Nations
Iowa Department of Natural Resources (Steve Suman)
Kansas Department of Wildlife and Parks (Mike Miller)
Kentucky Department of Fish and Wildlife Resources (J. Beth Garland)
Louisiana Department of Wildlife and Fisheries
Louisiana Sea Grant College Program
Maine Department of Inland Fisheries and Wildlife (V. Paul Reynolds)
Manitoba Department of Natural Resources, Fisheries Branch (Carl Wall)
Maryland Department of Natural Resources (Eugene Deems, Jr.)
Maryland Sea Grant College Program (Jack Greer)
Massachusetts Division of Fisheries and Wildlife
Michigan Department of Natural Resources, Fisheries Division
Michigan Sea Grant College Program (Martha Walter)
Minnesota Department of Natural Resources (Tom Dickson)
Mississippi Department of Wildlife, Fisheries and Parks (Jim Walker)
Missouri Department of Conservation (John McPherson)
Montana Division of Fish, Wildlife, and Parks
Nevada Department of Conservation and Natural Resources
New Brunswick Department of Economic Development and Tourism
New Brunswick Department of Natural Resources, Fish and Wildlife Branch (Peter Cronin)
Newfoundland Department of Natural Resources
New Hampshire Fish and Game Department (Patricia Fleurie)
New Jersey Division of Fish, Game and Wildlife (Dave Chanda)
New Mexico Department of Game and Fish (Ruth Anderson)
New York Department of Environmental Conservation (Robert Brandt)
New York Sea Grant Program (David MacNeill, Mark Malchoff)
NOAA/Gray's Reef National Marine Sanctuary (Beth Kostka)
NOAA/National Marine Fisheries Service
NOAA/National Weather Service
North Carolina Division of Boating and Inland Fisheries (Fred Harris)
North Carolina Sea Grant
North Dakota Game and Fish Department (Terry Steinwand)
Nova Scotia Department of Fisheries (Murray Hill)
Nova Scotia Department of Lands and Forests (Barry Sabean)
Ohio Department of Natural Resources
Ohio Sea Grant College Program
Oklahoma Department of Wildlife Conservation (Nels Rodefeld)
Ontario Ministry of Economic Development, Trade & Tourism (Tom Boyd)
Ontario Ministry of Natural Resources
Oregon Department of Fish and Wildlife (Randy Henry)
Oregon Sea Grant (Pat Kight)
Parátur, State of Pará, Brazil
Pennsylvania Fish and Boat Commission
Portuguese National Tourist Office (Maria Joáo Ramires)
Prince Edward Island Department of Environmental Resources
Quebec Department of Recreation, Fish and Game
Rhode Island Division of Fish and Game
Rhode Island Sea Grant
Saskatchewan Department of Environment, Fish and Wildlife (Bruce Howard)

South Carolina Department of Natural Resources (Greg Lucas)
South Carolina Sea Grant Consortium (John Tibbetts)
South Dakota Department of Game, Fish and Parks
Spain Ministry of Commerce and Tourism
Tennessee Wildlife Resources Agency (Dave Woodward)
Texas Parks and Wildlife (Steve Lightfoot)
Tourism British Columbia
Tourism New Brunswick
Tourism Newfoundland and Labrador
Tourism Nova Scotia (Randy Brooks)
Tourism Prince Edward Island (Carol Horne)
Tourism Quebec (Siegfried Gagnon)
Tourism Saskatchewan (Gerard Makuch, Nadine Howard)
Travel Alberta (Peter Gregus)
Travel Manitoba (Dennis Maksymetz, Colette Fontaine, Gord Richardson)
University of Connecticut Sea Grant Marine Advisory Program (Nancy Balcom)
University of Delaware Sea Grant College Program
University of Florida Cooperative Extension Service
University of New Hampshire and University of Maine Sea Grant College Program
U.S. Fish and Wildlife Service
Utah Department of Natural Resources (Gerry Schlappe)
Vermont Department of Fish and Wildlife (John Hall)
Virginia Department of Game and Inland Fisheries (Mitchell Norman)
Washington Department of Fish and Wildlife (Nina Carter, James Chandler)
Washington Sea Grant Program (Kris Freeman)
West Virginia Division of Natural Resources (Hoy Murphy)
Wisconsin Department of Natural Resources (David Kunelius)
Woods Hole Oceanographic Institute (Tracey Crago)
Wyoming Game and Fish Department
Yukon Territory Department of Renewable Resources (Susan Thompson)

Finally, I'm also grateful to four student interns, whose early work compiling and organizing research materials was of much help—Kristen Schultz of Oberlin College, Alyson Schultz of Boston University, Mathew Kane of Hamilton College, and John Kuhner of Princeton University—and to Megan Schultz of Ithaca College, for website development and advice.

—Ken Schultz

About the Author, Artists, and Contributors

PRINCIPAL AUTHOR AND EDITOR

Ken Schultz has been a staff fishing writer and editor for *Field & Stream* since 1973. His feature articles and columns for that publication appear monthly, and he contributes to the magazine's nationally syndicated weekly radio show and to its website. Schultz is a frequent author of the outdoors column of the *New York Times*, and he previously was a syndicated newspaper columnist for Gannett. He has authored a dozen books on sportfishing and angling travel topics, has been a featured guest on CNBC, ESPN, and The Nashville Network, and appears regularly in assorted fishing segments for the Outdoor Life Network. A widely traveled angler, Schultz is a former holder of seven line-class world records and was inducted into the Fishing Hall of Fame in 1998. He lives in Forestburgh, New York.

THE ARTISTS

Steve T. Goione is a rising star in the world of fishing and boating art, working in mixed mediums to present his lifelong passion for angling in a dynamic and realistic style. Although he drew the distinctive pen-and-ink illustrations for this book as well as the cover, Goione is primarily a creator of fine art. From his studio in Toms River, New Jersey, he produces commissioned fishing scenes for private collections and limited-edition prints, and he has created original artwork for Sea World in Florida. Goione has also made a mark among boat builders and owners for commissioned renderings of big-game sportfishing craft, and he recently created original artwork for the latest products of Hatteras Yachts. A frequent guest artist on the big-game fishing tournament circuit, Goione appears at exclusive contests each year from Nantucket to Venezuela, and his work is regularly featured at fund-raising events for prominent conservation organizations.

David Kiphuth, whose renderings of fish appear in this book, has had a varied career in the field of art, having been a professional illustrator since 1969. His work has included portraiture, architectural renderings, maps, and book illustration. Kiphuth has created archaeological and scientific book and exhibit renderings for the Yale Peabody Museum, the Yale Department of Anthropology, and Yale University Press. He formerly maintained a studio and gallery in Branford, Connecticut, where he created and sold wildlife and nature art and animal portraits. Since 1989, he has been the staff illustrator for the *Gazette Newspapers* in Schenectady, New York. He lives in Saratoga Springs, New York.

THE CONTRIBUTORS

Brett Albanese of Virginia is a Ph.D candidate at the Department of Fisheries and Wildlife Sciences at Virginia Polytechnic Institute; he formerly worked at the Mississippi Museum of Natural Sciences.

Ken Allen of Maine is Associate Editor of *Maine Sportsman* and a prolific writer, photographer, newspaper columnist, book author, and guide.

Michael Babcock of Montana is Outdoors Editor of the *Great Falls Tribune*.

Ken Bailey of Alberta is Manager of Field Operations in central Alberta for Ducks Unlimited Canada; he is a prolific writer and President of the Outdoor Writers Association of Canada.

Dick Ballard of Missouri is President of Dick Ballard's Fishing Adventures and a foremost authority on Amazonian angling; he's sent anglers fishing around the world for 18 years, and established the first travel service for Bass Pro Shops.

Scott Bannerot of Pennsylvania and Florida has a Ph.D. in fisheries science and has worked in marine biological research and consulting; he is a photojournalist and a charter boat captain.

John A. Barnes of Bermuda is the Director of Agriculture and Fisheries for Bermuda; he authors a weekly fishing column in the Bermuda *Mid Ocean News*, and is an IGFA representative.

Rob Barraclough of Indonesia and England works in the oil industry and is a charter boat captain and freelance writer.

Carlos M. Barrantes of Costa Rica established the first two sportfishing camps in Costa Rica; he is an IGFA representative and was the first President of the Costa Rican Fishing Federation.

Cody Beers of Wyoming works for the Wyoming Game and Fish Department as Associate Editor of *Wyoming Wildlife* magazine and Editor of *Wyoming Wildlife News and Wild Times*; he is also a freelance writer and photographer.

Bob Berry of California is one of the world's top fish carvers and sculptors, and swept all divisions of the 1986 world championship of fish carving; he is a foremost competition judge, a former professional taxidermist, and author of the book *Fish Carving*.

Mike Bleech of Pennsylvania is a writer and photographer whose work has appeared in most major U.S. fishing and hunting magazines.

Larry Blomquist of Louisiana is Publisher of *Breakthrough*, the world's largest taxidermy trade magazine, and one of the top competition judges in North America; he is a retired award-winning taxidermist, and former President of the National Taxidermists Association.

Fred Bonner of North Carolina is Editor of *Carolina Adventure* magazine; he is also a syndicated newspaper columnist, fisheries biologist, and an IGFA representative.

Judith Bowman of New York has been a foremost sporting books dealer for over twenty years; she produces two sporting book catalogs a year, with special emphasis on fishing.

John Brownlee of Florida is Senior Editor of *Salt Water Sportsman* and a former charter boat captain; he has served on the South Atlantic Fishery Management Council, is former Chairman of the Florida Conservation Association, and is an IGFA representative.

Eric B. Burnley of Virginia is the author of *Surf Fishing the Atlantic Coast* and a radio show host; he is a charter boat captain and Regional Editor of both *Salt Water Sportsman* and *The Fisherman* magazines.

Erwin Bursik of South Africa is Publisher of *Ski-Boat* and *Flyfishing* magazines of Durban, a member of the executive board of the South African Deep Sea Angling Association, and an IGFA representative.

Mac Campbell of Great Britain works for *Angling Plus*, a match fishing magazine, and has previously worked for *Sea Angler*, *Trout Fisherman*, and *Angling Times*.

Jim Casada of South Carolina is the author of many books, including *Modern Fly Fishing*; he is Senior Editor of *Sporting Classics* magazine, and outdoor columnist for the Rock Hill *Herald* and Greensboro *News and Record*.

Göran Cederberg of Sweden has been Editor of several international fact-packed large-format angling books, including *The Complete Book of Sportfishing*; he contributes regularly to north-European publications and has been chief editor of a Swedish sportfishing magazine.

Matthew D. Chan of Virginia is a Ph.D candidate at the Department of Fisheries and Wildlife Sciences at Virginia Polytechnic Institute; he formerly worked as a fisheries biologist for the U. S. Army Corps of Engineers.

Dawn Charging of North Dakota is Outdoors Director for the North Dakota State Tourism Department; she is also a writer and photographer whose family owns a successful fishing resort on Lake Sakakawea.

Homer Circle of Florida has been Angling Editor of *Sports Afield* magazine for 34 years; the dean of American outdoor writers, he is the recipient of numerous media and achievement awards, a former member of the Arkansas Game & Fish Commission, and a renowned television and video host.

Barry Ord Clarke of Norway is a professional photographer and writer and the author of several books on fly fishing and fly tying; he contributes regularly to most European fishing magazines, and is fishing consultant to Norway's largest private sporting estate.

Soc Clay of Kentucky is an accomplished and prolific fishing writer and photographer whose work has appeared in every major outdoor periodical in North America.

Angelo Cuanang of California is a Pacific Regional Editor for *Salt Water Sportsman* and a freelance writer and photographer.

Paula J. Del Giudice of Nevada is Outdoor Columnist for the *Las Vegas Sun*; a freelance writer, photographer, and book author; and former President of the Nevada Wildlife Federation.

Arthur De Mello of Uganda is a representative for the IGFA in Uganda.

Hansjörg Dietiker of Switzerland is Editor of the Swiss Anglers Magazine *Petri-Heil*, and an IGFA representative.

Philippe Dolivet of France is the Chief Editor of the French fly fishing magazine *Plaisirs de la Pêche* and a professional photographer; he is a fly fishing instructor and competitor, an ichthyologist, and an IGFA representative.

Gary Edwards of Wyoming is a longtime fishing guide and a television show host; he is the former Editor and Publisher of *Salmon Fever* magazine, and a former fly rod world record holder.

D'arcy Egan of Ohio has been a sportswriter for *The Cleveland Plain Dealer* for over 20 years; he authored the book, *Guide to Ohio Fishing*, and is host of the American Outdoorsman Radio Network.

Bill Ensor of New Brunswick works for the Fish & Wildlife Branch of the New Brunswick Department of Natural Resources; he was formerly marketing manager of fishing and hunting for the New Brunswick Department of Tourism, and is a longtime fishing guide.

Jack Erskine of Australia is a foremost big-game tackle designer and technical innovator who has helped design many of the modern rods, reels, and drag systems in use today.

Stan Fagerstrom of Oregon is one of the world's best known trick and accuracy casters, and has been featured at sport shows worldwide for half a century; he is also a book, magazine, and newspaper writer.

Jan Fogt of Florida is Editor of *The Bahamas Sportfishing Guide* and was the founding editor of *Bahamas Blue Water Magazine*; she is a contributing editor for *Sport Fishing* and *Marlin* magazines, and is also a book author.

Frank Fry of the Yukon Territory has worked with the Yukon Territory's Department of Natural Resources on various fishing projects.

Mike Garzillo of New Hampshire has been a newspaper columnist for 24 years; he is a regular contributor to various publications and a former regional editor for *Outdoor Life*.

Alessandro Giangio of Italy writes for Italy's premier fishing magazine, *Pesca in Mare*, and has been published worldwide; he has authored five books, is owner and master instructor of the Fishbuster Trolling School and Sportfishing Travel, and has a charter boat in Huatulco, Mexico.

Jerry Gibbs of Vermont is Fishing Editor of *Outdoor Life*, where his career as a staff writer has spanned three decades and made him one of North America's most respected angling authors; he has written several books and has been inducted into the Fishing Hall of Fame.

Barry Gibson of Massachusetts is Editor of *Salt Water Sportsman* and a longtime Maine charter boat captain; he is a former member of the New England Fishery Management Council, and former advisor to the International Commission for the Conservation of Atlantic Tunas.

Jerry Gomber of New Jersey has over twenty-five years of experience in design, development, and marketing of fishing rods and reels; during that period he has been responsible for several successful product innovations.

George Gruenefeld of Quebec and Saskatchewan is Editor of *Canadian Outdoor Publications*; he has written for many magazines in Canada and the U.S., is a book author, and was formerly Outdoors Editor for the *Montreal Gazette*.

Chris Hanks of the Northwest Territories is an anthropologist, freelance writer, and author of the book *Fly Fishing in the Northwest Territories*.

Steve Harper of Kansas is the Outdoors Editor of the *Wichita Eagle* and author of the book *Kansas Day Trips*; in 1995 he was named Conservation Communicator of the Year by the Kansas Wildlife Federation.

Dan Heiner of Alaska is an advertising agency executive and former editor and writer for *Alaska Outdoors* magazine; he is the author of four books on Alaska fishing, including *Fly Fishing Alaska's Wild Rivers*.

Bob Hodge of Tennessee is the Outdoors Editor of the *Knoxville News-Sentinel*; he was named the state's Best Outdoor Writer for 1996-97 by the Tennessee Sportswriters Association.

Grant Hopkins of Ontario is the outdoor columnist for the *Ottawa Citizen*, a frequent contributor to *Ontario Out of Doors*, and retired from the Royal Canadian Air Force.

John Husar of Illinois is the longtime outdoors columnist and general sportswriter of the *Chicago Tribune* and co-host of a Chicago radio show; he has worked for newspapers in Kansas, Texas, and New Mexico, and has covered the last nine Olympics.

Jim Imai of California has a Ph.D in physics and is Professor of Physics at California State University, Dominguez Hills; he is a Consulting Physicist for the Daiwa Corporation, and a leading authority on the design and performance of fishing reels and rods.

James Kano of Ontario is the Marketing Director of Japan Communications in Toronto and Outdoor Coordinator for the Press and Tourism division of the Ontario government; his articles have appeared online and in newspapers, guide books, and magazines.

Nick Karas of New York is the retired outdoor columnist for (New York) *Newsday* and a charter boat captain and ichthyologist; he has written for many national magazines and authored a dozen books, including *The Striped Bass* and *Brook Trout*.

Lee Kernen of Wisconsin is the retired Director of Fisheries for the State of Wisconsin; he is also a writer, fishing guide, and fisheries consultant.

Ronnie Kovach of California is a radio and television show host, educator, magazine writer, guide, and author of five books, including *Bass Fishing in California*, *Trout Fishing in California*, and *Saltwater Fishing in California*.

Steen Larsen of Denmark is one of Europe's leading sportfishing writers and photographers; he is a book author and lecturer, and contributes widely to many European angling publications.

Dick Lewers of Australia is Technical Editor of *Encyclopaedia of Australian Fishing*, author of seven books on angling, a former IGFA representative, 35-year columnist for *Modern Fishing Magazine*, and past President of the Australian National Sportfishing Association.

Bill Loftus of Idaho is the Outdoors Editor of the *Lewiston Morning Tribune* and the author of two guidebooks to Idaho.

Maurice Loustau-LaLanne of Seychelles is the Principal Secretary in the Ministry of Tourism and Transport for the Seychelles, and an IGFA representative.

Carl. F. Luckey of Alabama is a writer specializing in antiques and collectibles; he has authored ten books, including his best-selling, 618-page work, *Old Fishing Lures and Tackle*.

Joe Macaluso of Louisiana is an award-winning outdoors sportswriter/editor for the *Baton Rouge Advocate;* his weekly fishing reports have appeared in Louisiana newspapers since 1976.

Rosanne Macfarlane of Prince Edward Island recently received her Masters degree in Biology at

Acadia University; she works for the Department of Fisheries and Environment.

Dennis Maksymetz of Manitoba is Manager of Tourism Marketing for the Industry, Trade and Tourism division of the Manitoba government.

Don Mann of Florida is a longtime contributor to *Florida Sportsman*, a record-holding big-game angler, and book author; his articles and photographs have appeared in many publications.

Al Marlowe of Colorado has written numerous articles for outdoor magazines; he authored a trail guide for the Flat Tops Wilderness area and a fly fishing guide for the Colorado River.

Peter B. Mathiesen of Missouri is Executive Editor and Producer of the *Field & Stream Radio Hour*; he is also a magazine writer, photographer, and video and television show producer.

John McCoy of West Virginia is Outdoors Editor for the *Charleston Daily Mail*, Regional Editor for *Field & Stream*, and a frequent contributor to regional and national magazines.

Tom Meade of Rhode Island writes about the outdoors for the *Providence Journal-Bulletin*; he is the author of *Essential Fly Fishing*, and writes for various magazines.

Ed Migdalski of Connecticut is the retired Director of Yale University's Outdoor Education and Club Sports Programs, retired Ichthyologist for the Yale Peabody Museum, and holder of the current world record for the largest strictly freshwater fish (piraruçu) ever caught on rod and reel.

Kent Mitchell of Georgia has covered outdoor sports for the *Atlanta Journal-Constitution* for three decades; he has received the Communicator of the Year Award from the Georgia Wildlife Federation, and has authored three books on martial arts.

Bill Monroe of Oregon has covered the outdoors for his state's largest daily newspaper, *The Oregonian*, for 18 years.

Gary W. Moore of Vermont is a freelance writer and photographer; he is former Commissioner of the Vermont Fish and Wildlife Department and former Chairman of the Vermont Water Resources Board.

Sam Mossman of New Zealand is Special Projects Editor for *New Zealand Fishing News* magazine; he is the author of three books and hundreds of magazine articles, and has held five world and numerous New Zealand fishing records.

Perry Munro of Nova Scotia is a writer and artist who contributes to *The Atlantic Salmon Journal* and various other magazines; he is also an outfitter, master guide, operator of Maple Mountain Lodge, and a Director of Trout Unlimited Canada.

Iain Nicolson of Angola is an IGFA representative and has a Ph.D. in molecular genetics; he and his family pioneered fishing for blue marlin in Angola and collectively established six world fishing records.

Chris Niskanen of Minnesota is the Outdoors Editor of the *St. Paul Pioneer Press*.

Donald J. Orth of Virginia is a Professor of Fisheries Science in the Department of Fisheries & Wildlife Sciences at Virginia Polytechnic Institute.

Tom Pagliaroli of New Jersey is an advertising agency executive, freelance writer, and photographer whose work has appeared in various regional and national publications.

Ali Pasiner of Turkey is an attorney, the author of two fishing books, and a consultant to the Turkish version of the *Encyclopaedia Britannica*; he is also a writer, editor, and representative of the IGFA.

C. Boyd Pfeiffer of Maryland is a longtime journalist and photographer, a regular columnist for many angling magazines, and the author of numerous books on fishing topics, the latest of which is *Fly Fishing Salt Water Basics*.

Larry Porter of Nebraska has been on the sports staff of the *Omaha World-Herald* for over three decades and their outdoors writer since 1990; he has been named Nebraska Sportswriter of the Year three times, and is a former professional tournament angler.

Steve Price of Texas is a longtime Senior Writer for *Bassmaster* magazine and contributor to a wide variety of national sporting magazines; he is an accomplished photographer and author of several books.

Gareth Purnell of England is Editor of Britain's leading angling magazine, *Improve Your Coarse Fishing*, and former News Editor of *Angling Times*; he has fished annually in the World Freshwater Angling Championships since 1993.

George Reiger of Virginia is Conservation Editor of *Field & Stream* and *Salt Water Sportsman* magazines and the most widely respected conservation writer in North America; he has been a staff writer for *Field & Stream* since 1972, is the author of seven books on angling and marine ecology, and the recipient of numerous honors and awards.

Tim Renken of Missouri has been the outdoors writer for the *St. Louis Post-Dispatch* since 1963; he previously worked for the Nebraska Game Commission.

Len Rich of Newfoundland is the author of two books and many outdoor magazine articles; he operates Awesome Lake Lodge in Labrador, is a former Hunting and Fishing Development Officer for Newfoundland and Labrador, and is a past representative of the Atlantic Salmon Federation.

Tom Richardson of Massachusetts is Managing Editor of *Salt Water Sportsman* magazine, as well as a freelance writer and photographer.

Al Ristori of New Jersey is Saltwater Fishing Editor of the *Newark Star-Ledger*, Regional Editor of *Salt Water Sportsman*, Conservation Editor of *The Fisherman* magazine, and the author of several books;

he is also a charter boat captain and has served on the Mid-Atlantic Fishery Management Council.

Jim Rizzuto of Hawaii is Hawaii Editor for *Salt Water Sportsman* and *Western Outdoors*, a longtime columnist for *West Hawaii Today* and *Hawaii Fishing News*, and the author of the books *Modern Hawaiian Gamefishing* and *Fishing Hawaii Style*.

Nels Rodefeld of Oklahoma is an avid angler and hunter who frequently covers Oklahoma's hunting and fishing scene.

Milt Rosko of New Jersey is a writer for *Big Game Fishing Journal* and various other publications and a longtime authority on saltwater sportfishing; he is a photographer, book author, magazine feature writer, and lecturer.

Terry Rudnick of Washington has been writing articles on Northwest fishing subjects for more than 25 years; he is the author of the book *Washington Fishing, the Complete Guide*, and co-author of *How to Catch Trophy Halibut*.

Bob Sampson, Jr. of Connecticut is a writer, photographer, science teacher, and fisheries biologist; his work has appeared in numerous national and regional magazines.

Jack Samson of New Mexico is the retired Editor-in-Chief of *Field & Stream* and a former Associated Press columnist; he is Saltwater Editor of *Fly Rod & Reel* magazine, author of twenty books, and the first angler to catch both Atlantic and Pacific sailfish and all five species of marlin on a fly.

Ray Sasser of Texas is the Outdoor Editor of *The Dallas Morning News* and a freelance contributor to various magazines; he has been writing about outdoor sports for over 25 years.

Carl Werner Schmidt-Luchs of Germany is a contributor to *Blinker*, the largest angling magazine in Europe; he is a photographer, writer, and author of a dozen angling books.

Kristen Schultz of Massachusetts is a writer who recently graduated from Oberlin College; she works for an engineering consulting firm.

Bill Scifres of Indiana has been the Outdoor Editor of the *Indianapolis Star* since 1953; he is a book author, freelance writer, and photographer.

Eric Sharp of Michigan is Outdoor Editor of *The Detroit News*, and was formerly Outdoor Editor of *The Miami Herald*.

Luis Sier of Argentina is a newspaper columnist, a former magazine publisher, and an outfitter who operates several Argentinian fishing camps.

Jeff Simpson of South Dakota is an information officer for the State of South Dakota, a book author and freelance magazine writer, and former project developer for Cowles Creative Publishing.

DeWayne Smith of Arizona is an information officer for the Maricopa County Parks and Recreation Department; he covered the outdoors for over 30 years for *The Phoenix Gazette*.

Ryan Smith of Virginia is a research assistant with the Department of Fisheries and Wildlife Sciences at Virginia Polytechnic Institute.

Michael Snook of Saskatchewan is a freelance writer, conservationist, outdoor educator, and television producer.

Frank Sousa of Massachusetts is a writer for the *Springfield Sunday Republican* and the *Union News*, Editor/Publisher of *Northeast Woods and Waters*, and a freelance writer and photographer.

Vin T. Sparano of New Jersey is Senior Field Editor and retired Editor-in-Chief of *Outdoor Life*, for whom he worked for over three decades; he is a former syndicated columnist for *Gannett Newspapers*, and the author/editor of fourteen books, including *The Complete Outdoors Encyclopedia*.

Vladimir Stakic of Yugoslavia is Deputy Editor-in-Chief of the Yugoslavian angling magazines *Ribolovacka Revija* and *Ribolovacke Novine*, a freelance writer, and the author of three books of short stories.

Bob Stearns of Florida has been the staff boating/saltwater fishing writer of *Field & Stream* for 20 years and is the Electronics Editor of *Salt Water Sportsman*; the author of two books, he is a renowned fly fishing and light tackle expert, and has held two fly rod world records for sailfish.

Larry Stone of Iowa has been a writer and photographer for over three decades, and writes about the outdoors for the *Des Moines Register*.

Keith Sutton of Arkansas is Editor of *Arkansas Wildlife magazine*, a conservation publication of the Arkansas Game & Fish Commission, and a prolific freelance writer and photographer.

Ferenc Szalay of Hungary is Editor-in-Chief of *Magyar Horgász*, Hungary's premier fishing magazine; he is also President of the Hungarian National Committee for Match Fishing and Executive Board member of the Federation Internationale de la Pêche Sportive en Eau Douce.

Allan Tarvid of Texas is a contributing editor for *Sport Fishing* magazine and has authored hundreds of articles on electronics for sporting and commercial fishing and emergency service use; he has been a fishing guide and search and rescue diver.

Rikk Taylor of British Columbia is Editor and Publisher of *British Columbia Sport Fishing* magazine.

Mick Thill of Illinois and England is one of the world's top professional match fishing anglers and the first and only person to medal in the open water and ice fishing World Freshwater Fishing Championships; he is also a prominent float designer, and coach of the U. S. World Championship fishing teams.

Albert A. W. Threadingham of Fiji is an IGFA

representative for the Fiji Islands and Governor of the Hawaiian International Billfish Association and the Pacific Ocean Research Foundation; he is a former world-record fish holder.

Raj Tilak of Maryland and India is co-author of the book *Game Fishes of India and Angling,* and author of more than 200 research publications; he is experienced in fisheries and wildlife management, with extensive knowledge of gamefishes and their ecology in India.

Anssi Uitti of Finland works for the Finnish outdoor magazine *Metsästys ja Kalastus*, and his articles have appeared in *Urheilukalastus* (Sportfishing) and *Perhokalastus* (Flyfishing) magazines.

Luis Umpierre of Puerto Rico is a physician, Editor of *Notipesca* (Fishing News), President of the Puerto Rico Sportfishing Association, and advisory member of the Caribbean Fishery Management Council.

Rudy Van Duijnhoven of Holland is a freelance photographer and author; his work appears monthly in *BEET-Sportvissers* magazine, and he is European Correspondent for Fly Fishing in *Salt Waters* magazine.

Carlo Vernocchi of Italy and Zanzibar introduced modern big-game fishing to the Zanzibar archipelago of Tanzania in 1992; he is an IGFA representative and charter boat captain.

Victor Villavicencio of Manila is a representative for the IGFA in the Philippines.

Tsutomu Wakabayashi of Japan is the General Manager of the Japan Game Fish Association; he has written for several Japanese fishing magazines, and is an IGFA representative.

Steve Waters of Florida is the outdoors writer for the *Fort Lauderdale Sun-Sentinel* and occasionally writes for national magazines; he was formerly a newspaper writer and video executive in New York.

Tom Wharton of Utah has been Outdoor Editor of the *Salt Lake Tribune* since 1976; he has co-authored five books, and is past President of the Outdoor Writers Association of America.

Jesse E. Williams of New Mexico is the retired Chief of Public Affairs for the New Mexico Department of Game and Fish, and a former Colorado wildlife manager and environmental education supervisor.

Juergen Willms of the Yukon Territory has worked with the Yukon Territory's Department of Natural Resources on various fishing projects.

Jorge Xifra of Paraguay operates El Pescador, a sportfishing outfitting service; he is a writer, television show host, IGFA representative, and holder of four world fishing records.

Photo Credits

ALL PHOTOGRAPHS BY KEN SCHULTZ EXCEPT FOR THE FOLLOWING:

Cabela's 926, 927
Gary and Robin Edwards 1043
Alessandro Giangio 850, 973
Steve Goione 975
Steen Larsen 853
Storm Lures 937
Al Ristori 943, 947, 970

J

JACK

(1) A young, sexually mature male salmon that returns to freshwater rivers during the spawning run.

(2) Jacks are among the most important sport and commercial fish and are distributed worldwide in the temperate and tropical waters of the Atlantic, Indian, and Pacific Oceans. They are among 140 species that constitute the Carangidae family of jacks and pompano, which include such prominent sportfish as amberjack *(see: amberjack, greater; amberjack, lesser),* yellowtail *(see),* and permit *(see),* as well as many others. Jacks are almost exclusively saltwater fish, although some species occur rarely in brackish water. They are strong, fast swimmers and virtually all fight like a bulldog when caught on rod and reel, regardless of their size. Some jacks, but not all, are good table fare, although a few species have been associated with ciguatera poisoning.

These fish are distinguished by a widely forked caudal fin and a slender caudal peduncle. The body is generally compressed, although the shape (and color) varies considerably, from very deep to fusiform. Some jacks resemble mackerel *(see)* and are equally swift, but they lack the distinguishing rows of finlets. Many have extremely small scales, but at the end of the lateral line these are enlarged to form a keel. There are usually two spines in front of the anal fin.

Although young jacks travel in schools, adults of most species are usually solitary or travel in small groups. Some are generally caught in water of moderate depth, some are caught in relatively deep waters, and some are pursued on shallow flats and reefs.

See: Jack, Almaco; Jack, Bar; Jack, Crevalle and Pacific; Jack, Horse-eye; Jack, Yellow; Lookdown; Moonfish; Palometa; Pilotfish; Pompano; Pompano, African; Pompano, Florida; Roosterfish; Runner, Blue; Runner, Rainbow; Trevally.

A jack crevalle from the Caribbean waters of Costa Rica.

JACK, ALMACO *Seriola rivoliana.*

Other names—amberjack, greater amberjack, longfin yellowtail; Afrikaans: *langvin-geelstert;* Arabic: *gazala;* French: *seriole limon;* Hawaiian: *kahala;* Japanese: *songoro, hirenaga-kanpachi;* Malay/Indonesian: *chermin, aji-aji;* Portuguese: *arabaiana, xaréu limao;* Samoan: *tavai, tafala, palu-kata;* Spanish: *pez limon, palometa, medregal, huayaipe, fortuno, cavallas.*

A deep-bodied amberjack and a member of the Carangidae family, the almaco jack is an excellent and widely distributed sportfish. It is a fine food fish, although it sometimes has tapeworms in the caudal peduncle area, which can be cut away so that the meat can be eaten safely, and it has been associated with ciguatera poisoning in the Caribbean, especially during spawning season.

Identification. The body and fins can be a uniform dark brown, a dark bluish green, or a metallic bronze or gray, with the lower sides and the belly a lighter shade, sometimes with a lavender or brassy cast. A diagonal black band usually extends from the lip through the eye to the upper back at the beginning of the dorsal fin; young fish sometimes display five or six bars. The front lobes of the dorsal and anal fins are high and elongated and have deeply sickle-shaped outer edges. There are seven spines in the first dorsal fin. The almaco jack is similar in appearance to the greater amberjack *(see: amberjack, greater)* but has a deeper, more flattened body than the greater amberjack and a more pointed head; the greater amberjack

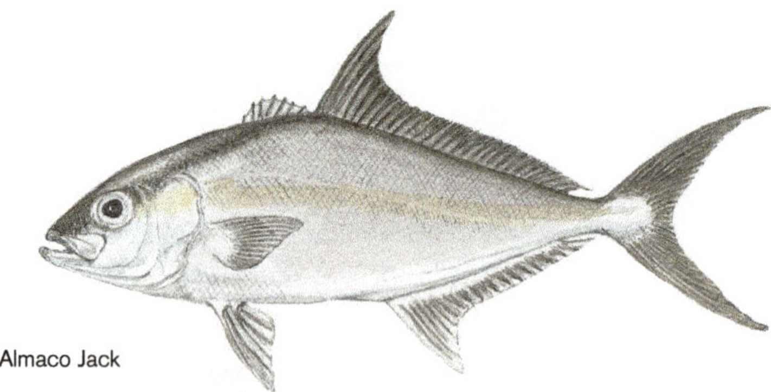

Almaco Jack

J

has a more elongated body, a lighter band, and a shorter front dorsal fin.

Size/Age. A large species, the almaco jack is known to grow to 3 feet in the Atlantic, although it is commonly between 1 and 2 feet long and weighs less than 20 pounds. In the Pacific, it grows to almost 5 feet and 130 pounds but usually weighs 50 to 60 pounds. In the Atlantic, the all-tackle world record is a 78-pound fish taken off Bermuda in 1990, whereas the Pacific all-tackle world record is a 132-pound fish taken off Baja California in 1964.

Distribution. Found around the world, almaco jacks occur in the Indo-West Pacific from eastern Africa to the Mariana and Wake Islands, as well as north to the Ryuku Islands and south to New Caledonia; they are absent from the Red Sea and French Polynesia. In the eastern Pacific, they occur from Southern California to Peru, including the Gulf of California and the Galápagos Islands. In the western Atlantic, almaco jacks range from Cape Cod to northern Argentina, and they are present in the eastern Atlantic, although distribution is not well established.

Habitat. A warmwater species, almaco jacks prefer deep, open water and inhabit the outer slopes of reefs, but they rarely swim over reefs or near shore. Young fish are often associated with floating objects and sargassum. Almaco jacks often travel alone and occasionally in schools at depths of 50 to 180 feet.

Spawning. Almaco jacks spawn offshore from spring through fall.

Food. An offshore predator, the almaco jack feeds mainly on fish but also on invertebrates.

Angling. Like other jacks and especially amberjack, the almaco is a tenacious fighter, but it is caught less frequently than its amberjack cousins, probably because it is a generally deeper and more oceanic species. Almacos are usually caught around buoys, wrecks, or natural reefs, usually incidental to general offshore trolling for various species, or fishing for assorted reef dwellers, rather than as a deliberate target. Trolling with deep-running plugs or bottom fishing with cut baits are both effective.

See: Inshore Fishing; Jack; Offshore Fishing.

Bar Jack

JACK, BAR *Caranx ruber.*

Other names—runner, skipjack; Spanish: *cojinua carbonera, cojinua negra, negrito.*

A member of the Carangidae family, the bar jack is small and more like a saltwater panfish, but it is a scrappy species and a good food fish.

Identification. The bar jack is silvery with a dark bluish stripe on the back that runs from the beginning of the soft dorsal fin and onto the lower tail fin. Sometimes there is also a pale-blue stripe immediately beneath the black stripe that extends forward onto the snout. The bar jack bears a resemblance to the blue runner *(see: runner, blue)* but has fewer and less prominent large scales along the caudal peduncle than the blue runner does. The bar jack has 26 to 30 soft rays in the dorsal fin and 31 to 35 gill rakers on the lower limb of the first arch. When feeding near bottom, it can darken almost to black.

Size. Usually 8 to 14 inches in length, the bar jack reaches a maximum of 2 feet.

Distribution. In the western Atlantic, bar jacks are found from New Jersey and Bermuda to the northern Gulf of Mexico and southern Brazil, as well as throughout the Caribbean.

Habitat. Bar jacks are common in clear, shallow, open waters at depths of up to 60 feet, often over coral reefs. Usually traveling in spawning schools, they sometimes mix with goatfish and stingray, although they are occasionally solitary.

Food and feeding habits. Opportunistic feeders, bar jacks feed mainly on pelagic and benthic fish, some shrimp, and other invertebrates.

Angling. Bar jacks are usually caught on light spinning outfits and a small jig or small baited hook.

JACK, CREVALLE *Caranx hippos.*
JACK, PACIFIC CREVALLE *Caranx caninus.*

Other names for the crevalle jack—common jack, crevally, toro, trevally, horse crevalle; Spanish: *cavallo, chumbo, cocinero, jurel común.*

Other names for the pacific crevalle jack—toro, crevally, cavalla, jiguagua; Spanish: *aurel, burel, canche jurel, chumbo, cocinero, jurel toro, jurelito, sargentillo.*

These two members of the Carangidae family are almost identical in appearance and were formerly thought to be Atlantic and Pacific versions of *Caranx hippos.* Differences documented by scientists have led to the classification of the Pacific crevalle jack in recent years as a validly separate species from

Crevalle Jack

J

the crevalle jack. These jacks are popular sportfish and are among the toughest of all inshore fish, although they are not highly valued as table fare. In addition, jacks in general have been associated with ciguatera poisoning. The Pacific crevalle jack is marketed fresh, frozen, smoked and salted/dried and may be utilized as fish meal and for its oil.

Identification. Both the crevalle jack and the Pacific crevalle jack are bluish green to greenish gold on the back and silvery or yellowish on the belly. They are compressed, and the deep body has a high rounded profile as well as a large mouth. The tail and anal fin may be yellowish, and the ends of the dorsal and upper tail are occasionally black. There is a prominent black spot on the gill cover and another black spot at the base of each pectoral fin. Young fish usually have about five broad, black bands on the body and one on the head. The soft dorsal and anal fins are almost identical in size, and there are 18 to 21 soft rays in the dorsal fin and 16 to 19 gill rakers on the lower limb of the first arch. The two species are distinguished externally from each other only by the presence of a larger maximum number of scutes, up to 42 on the Pacific crevalle jack, as opposed to 26 to 35 on the crevalle jack. The crevalle jack bears a resemblance to the Florida pompano but has a larger mouth. It can be distinguished from the similar horse-eye jack *(see: jack, horse-eye)* by a small patch of scales on the otherwise bare chest, whereas the chest of the horse-eye jack is completely covered with scales.

Size. Averaging 3 to 5 pounds in weight and 1 to $2^1/_2$ feet in length, the crevalle jack can regularly weigh as much as 10 pounds; the Pacific crevalle jack is usually smaller. The all-tackle world record for the crevalle jack is a 57-pound, 5-ounce fish taken off Angola, and the record Pacific crevalle jack is a 29-pound, 8-ounce fish taken off Costa Rica.

Distribution. In the western Atlantic, crevalle jacks occur from Nova Scotia south throughout the northern Gulf of Mexico to Uruguay, including the Greater Antilles. In the eastern Pacific, Pacific crevalle jacks occur from San Diego, California, to Peru, including the Galápagos Islands.

Habitat. Both species can tolerate a wide range of salinities and often inhabit coastal areas of brackish water and may ascend rivers, frequenting shore reefs, harbors, and protected bays. Small fish are occasionally found over sandy and muddy bottoms of very shallow waters, as in estuaries and rivers. They are common in depths of up to 130 feet and often move into cooler, deeper water during the summer.

Life history/Behavior. Spawning occurs offshore from March through September. Young fish occur in moderate to large fast-moving schools, and crevalle jacks occasionally school with horse-eye jacks, although larger fish are often solitary.

Food and feeding habits. Voracious predators, they feed on shrimp, other invertebrates, and smaller fish. Crevalle jacks will often corner a school of baitfish at the surface and feed in a commotion that can be seen for great distances, or they will chase their prey onto beaches and against seawalls. Fish of both species often grunt or croak when they are caught.

Angling. Like other jacks, the crevalle and Pacific crevalle are tenacious fighters and excellent candidates for light-tackle fishing. The crevalle jack is most often caught by anglers casting and trolling for other species, commonly using artificial as well as natural baits. This superb light-tackle species can be taken by spinning, fly fishing, trolling, or surf casting, and with such live baits as mullet or pinfish. Anglers should retrieve lures and flies at a fast pace without pausing or stopping, as jacks tend to lose interest in anything that doesn't act normally.
See: Inshore Fishing; Jack.

JACKFISH

A term, often derogatory, used for northern pike and sometimes for chain pickerel, especially common in parts of Canada.

J

JACK, HORSE-EYE *Caranx latus.*

Other names—big-eye jack, goggle-eye, horse-eye trevally; French: *carange moyole;* Portuguese: *guarajuba;* Spanish: *jurel, jurel ojo gordo, ojón, xurel.*

Like other jack species, the horse-eye is a member of the Carangidae family and a strong-fighting fish suitable for light-tackle angling. Unlike some jacks, it is not highly esteemed as a food fish, although the quality of horse-eye jack meat can be improved by cutting off the tail and bleeding the fish directly after it is caught. This and other jacks have been implicated in cases of ciguatera poisoning.

Identification. The horse-eye jack is silvery, with yellow tail fins and usually dark edges on the dorsal and upper tail fin. There is often a small black spot at the upper end of the gill cover, and it usually has blackish scutes. The body is compressed, and the entire chest is scaly. There are 20 to 22 soft rays in the dorsal fin and 14 to 18 gill rakers on the lower limb of the first arch. The horse-eye jack is similar in shape to the crevalle jack, although it has a less steep forehead and is either lacking the dark blotch at the base of the pectoral fins of the crevalle jack, or the blotch is more poorly defined. It can also be distinguished by its scales, which the crevalle jack lacks except for a small patch.

Size. This species is commonly found up to 30 inches and 10 pounds. The all-tackle world record is 24 pounds, 8 ounces.

Distribution. In the western Atlantic, horse-eye jacks occur from New Jersey and Bermuda throughout the northern Gulf of Mexico to Río de Janeiro in Brazil. In the eastern Atlantic, they occur off the northwest coast of Africa, throughout the Ascension Islands, and scarcely in the Gulf of Guinea.

Habitat. Horse-eye jacks are most common around islands and offshore, although they can tolerate brackish waters and may ascend rivers. Adults prefer open water and may be found over reefs, whereas young are usually found along sandy shores and over muddy bottoms. Schooling in small to large groups at depths of up to 60 feet, horse-eye jacks may mix with crevalle jacks.

Food and feeding habits. Horse-eye jacks feed on fish, shrimp, crabs, and other invertebrates.

Angling. This is a good light-tackle gamefish that can be taken with live baits such as mullet, pinfish, and other small fish, as well as with plugs, jigs, spoons, flies, and other small artificial lures. They are often encountered in fast-moving schools. Lures should be retrieved at a fast pace without slowing or stopping.

See: Inshore Fishing; Jack.

JACK PLATE

A device that raises an outboard motor up on the transom and also moves it away from the transom, increasing speed and fuel economy. Also known as a transom jack, it provides some of the benefits of a bolt-on transom bracket without its greater weight, higher cost, and sometimes engine-immersing problems.

Jack plates are popular on many high-performance boats, particularly bass boats, because they increase speed. Raising the engine 3 to 6 inches lifts that much more of the lower unit out of the water, reducing critical drag and thereby allowing an increase in speed. The higher you can raise the engine, the greater the increase. But you cannot raise the engine unless it is also moved back from the transom far enough to allow water running out from under the bottom to rise sufficiently to keep the required amount of the propeller in the water and ensure that adequate water gets to the motor's cooling system.

Besides increasing speed and fuel economy (some V6 outboards get as much as a 20 percent increase in speed and fuel economy), jack plates also permit shallower water operation at planing speed, shaving several inches off what could be obtained

Horse-eye Jack

J

Yellow Jack

with a plate. These extra inches can make a big difference to some anglers, especially those on unfamiliar water who might otherwise nick their propeller or lower unit at an unexpected time.

Jack plates are available in manual and hydraulic electric versions. Adjusting the jack plate's height for optimum performance merely requires trying different elevations.

See: Boat.

JACKSMELT *Atherinopsis californiensis.*
Other names—silverside, horse smelt, blue smelt, California smelt.

The jacksmelt is a member of the Atherinidae family of fish known as silversides *(see)* and not a true smelt *(see)*. It is an important forage species for predator fish, is a major component of the Pacific smelt commercial catch, and is one of the most common fish taken by pier anglers.

Identification. The body of the jacksmelt is elongate and somewhat compressed. The head is oblong and compressed, and the eyes and mouth are small. The color is greenish blue above and silver below. A metallic stripe bordered with blue extends the length of the body.

Size/Age. Jacksmelt can attain a maximum size of $17^1/_2$ inches and a little more than a pound. When 13 to 15 inches long, they are 8 or 9 years old, and they may live at least 11 years.

Distribution. This species occurs from Santa Maria Bay, Baja California, to Yaquina, Oregon.

Habitat. Jacksmelt are found in bays and ocean waters throughout the year. They are schooling fish that prefer shallow water less than 100 feet deep and are most common in 5- to 50-foot depths.

Spawning behavior. The spawning season extends from October through March, and jacksmelt spawn first when two years old and about 6 inches long. Large masses of eggs, about the size of small BBs, are attached to shallow-water seaweeds by means of long filaments.

Food. Jacksmelt feed on small crustaceans.

Angling. These fish are often caught from piers but may also be taken in the surf. Sometimes a number of coiled-up worms are found in the flesh. These are intermediate stages of spine-headed worms, the adults of which are harmful to sharks, pelicans, and other fish predators. The worms are harmless to humans when the fish is thoroughly cooked.

JACK, YELLOW *Caranx bartholomaei.*
Other names—French: *carangue grasse;* Spanish: *cojinua amarilla, cibi amarillo.*

This small and spunky member of the Carangidae family is an occasional catch by anglers. Its flesh is considered fair to good eating.

Identification. Silvery with a yellow cast, the yellow jack has a bluish back and strongly yellow sides, which grow even more strikingly yellow after the fish dies. The fins are also yellowish, as is the tail. It lacks the black spot near the gill cover that the similar horse-eye jack has, and has a less steep head. There are 25 to 28 soft rays in the dorsal fin, and 18 to 21 gill rakers on the lower limb of the first arch. Young fish are more brassy in color and have many pale spots.

Size. Averaging less than 2 pounds in weight and 1 to 2 feet in length, the yellow jack can reach a maximum of 3 feet and as much as 17 pounds. The all-tackle world record weighs 19 pounds, 7 ounces.

Distribution. In the western Atlantic, the yellow jack is found from Massachusetts to the Gulf of Mexico, including Bermuda, and south throughout the Caribbean and the West Indies to Maceio in Brazil. In the eastern-central Atlantic, they are also found off the northwest coast of Africa.

Habitat. Common on offshore reefs, yellow jacks are usually solitary or travel in small groups in depths of up to 130 feet. Young typically roam inshore in mangrove-lined lagoons, often in association with jellyfish and floating sargassum.

Angling. Anglers usually catch yellow jacks incidentally, often while trolling.

See: Inshore Fishing; Jack; Offshore Fishing.

J

JAMAICA

At 144 miles long, Jamaica is the third largest island in the Caribbean and about the size of Connecticut. It lies 90 miles south of Cuba's eastern shores and is situated on the southern boundary of the deep Cayman Trench. A lack of shallow flats limits inshore fishing opportunities, but the quick drop-off to deep water provides fertile grounds for marlin, which are influenced by the flow of the Caribbean Current through the Windward Passage between Haiti and Cuba and through the Cayman Trench.

Proponents of Jamaican big-game angling proudly point out that you can fish suitable water for the highly coveted Atlantic blue marlin when you're just a few minutes from the dock, especially if the dock is at San Antonio or Ocho Rios on the north coast.

And it's true. The water drops to 100 fathoms very close to shore, and the marlin in these waters are abundant. Local boats, accustomed to raising a good number of fish per outing, rarely travel more than a few miles offshore. Anglers pursue their quarry from the near-shore drop-off to the 3,000-foot contour; this is a run of just $^1/_2$ mile to 3 miles from the island, depending on departure point.

The blue marlin in Jamaica are not particularly large as a rule. The normal range is between 100 and 350 pounds. An occasional larger fish is caught (the island record is a 590-pounder), and there is speculation that the bigger blues in these waters are holding well offshore, 30 miles or so, around banks that are hardly touched by anglers embarking from Jamaica.

Nevertheless, this is a great place to be in the fall. In a fall tournament in the late 1980s, 105 marlin were caught in four days, setting a local record. A double-header and a triple-header occurred during the event, and this is not a run-of-the-mill experience with blue marlin.

Blue marlin are reportedly here year-round, although the better fishing is from August through October. This is the breeding season and a period of peak abundance, when smaller males from 100 to 150 pounds are prominent. This doesn't quite overlap with the presence of white marlin in winter; although a few are caught prior to winter, they are most likely to be landed in February and March. In June, the larger female blues (300 to 350 pounds) are present, and they remain through the fall. They are, however, overshadowed by the more abundant smaller marlin, which provide good light-tackle opportunities.

It has been reported that in colonial days England gained more wealth through fish products from the Americas than Spain obtained in gold.

Dolphin, king mackerel, yellowfin tuna, and wahoo round out other year-round possibilities, but dolphin are most abundant from March through May, and wahoo and tuna peak both in spring and fall. Sailfish, skipjack tuna, rainbow runners, and sharks also frequent these waters.

The important fishing ports are Port Antonio, Ocho Rios, and Montego Bay on the north shore, Kingston on the south shore, and Negril on the west end. Well-equipped charter boats with experienced crews are available, and beautiful Port Antonio—situated on the northeastern coast and relatively sheltered from southeast trade winds—is a prominent hub.

Inshore anglers have some opportunities as well, although these have not been widely explored or developed. Such reef species as barracuda, amberjack, yellowtail snapper, and various grouper are available. The coastal rivers hold tarpon and snook.

The Rio Grande, west of Port Antonio, has fair-size snook and tarpon. The Black River, in the southwest, is reported to have produced snook up to 20 pounds and tarpon to 100 in the past.

JAPAN

A small island nation in the western Pacific, Japan is surrounded by saltwater and blessed with freshwater in nearly every valley of its mountainous main islands. It borders the Sea of Okhotsk on the north, the Pacific Ocean on the east and south, the East China Sea on the southwest, and the Korea Strait and Sea of Japan on the west. With its more than 1,000 islands, Japan boasts nearly 30,000 kilometers of coastline.

Japan's waters are influenced by the warm Black Current *(Kuroshio),* which moves northward from Taiwan, by the Black Current's offshoot, the Tsushima Current, and by the cold Okhotsk Current, which moves southward along the Kamchatka Peninsula. These opposing currents meet near the northern part of the largest Japanese island of Honshu (known as the mainland), making this region one of the world's most fertile saltwater fishing grounds. These are also among the influences that give this small country a diverse climate. The southernmost islands of Okinawa, and the Ogasawara chain, have a subtropical climate; the northern island of Hokkaido has a subarctic climate.

Because of these environmental conditions, Japan is blessed with abundant varieties of fish, and fish have been a food staple for the Japanese since long before recorded history. Both commercial and recreational fishing have a lengthy tradition as important components of Japanese society.

Japanese anglers pursue approximately 30 species of freshwater fish. The most prominent of these are several species each of carp, salmon, and trout, as well as landlocked charr. All of these are native and found throughout Japan except in the southern islands. Prominent introduced species include rainbow trout, brown trout, largemouth bass, and bluegills. Since 1992, however, the introduction of largemouth bass and bluegills has been banned by law to protect native species.

In recent times, Japan's freshwater fisheries have suffered from pollution, the absence of possession limits, unfamiliarity with the practice of voluntarily releasing fish, and an increasing angler population.

These conditions have contributed to the depletion of most native fish populations, and freshwater fishing sites and fish populations are primarily maintained through cultivation efforts and stocking.

Ocean fishing, however, is a different story. The popularity of shore and boat fishing in Japan is among the highest per capita anywhere in the world. Shore fishing is most popular, and almost every harbor and its surrounding area becomes a fishing spot. Fishing from rocky shores is usually practiced only by veteran anglers, and these areas have become top angling locations throughout Japan. Nevertheless, shore fishing has been steadily declining in recent decades due to overharvesting, especially by commercial interests.

Although anglers can pursue more than 80 saltwater species, they completely ignore sharks and fish that are not suitable for eating, even though these species may provide good sport on rod and reel. Furthermore, in Japan, sportfishing is limited to protect commercial fishermen; local regulations throughout most of the country, for example, ban trolling.

Popular small near-shore species of fish include Japanese horse mackerel *(ma-aji),* Japanese whiting *(shirogisu),* Japanese common sole *(karei),* rockfish *(kasago),* and brown rockfish *(mebaru).* All weigh less than 1 kilogram on average, but this doesn't detract from their popularity, as most Japanese boat and shore anglers tend to fish for the purpose of catching fresh fish to eat.

Other popular fish include black sea bream *(kurodai),* greenfish *(mejina),* Japanese parrot bass *(ishidai),* spotted parrot bass *(ishigakidai),* and moara grouper *(kue).* Except for the moara grouper, which can grow to more than 50 kilograms, the average size of these fish is 0.5 to 5 kilograms.

There are 37,000 boats for hire throughout Japan. These and private boats all strictly bottom-fish with fresh natural baits; fishing with lures and trolling are not practiced, as they are in North America and Europe. Hired boats may include charter boats as in North America, but most are party boats for which individuals pay a per person fee for eight hours of fishing.

In Japan, freshwater sportfishing is not controlled by the government but is managed by local city organizations or local angling cooperatives. Therefore, to obtain a sportfishing certificate or license, or to pay an entry fee to a fishing area, you must deal directly with the local manager of the area.

Hokkaido

Trout. With its generally cold climate, the northernmost island of Hokkaido is well suited to salmon and trout. The predominant species caught with lures and flies here include mountain trout or cherry trout, known as *yamame* (the freshwater-dwelling form of masu salmon); landlocked or whitespotted charr *(Salvelinus leucomaenis),* known as *ezo-iwana;* Japanese huchen, or *itoh;* Dolly Varden, or *oshoro-koma;* and rainbow trout, or *niji-masu.*

The Japanese huchen is the largest of the salmonids in Japan and should not be confused with taimen. The range of the Japanese huchen is only Hokkaido and Saghalien; it can reach a length of 1.5 meters and weight of 20 kilograms. These large fish, however, have declined in number as a result of overfishing and development, which has destroyed their natural river habitats. Large Japanese huchen are rarely caught these days; the average catch is less than 80 centimeters (31 inches) long.

Lake Akanko in eastern Hokkaido is the most popular spot for trout fishing. From May through September, landlocked charr, Japanese huchen, rainbow trout, and brown trout can be caught on lures and flies. Dry-fly fishing is possible beginning in June. These fish are wild and put up a spectacular fight. The lakes have an abundance of pond smelt *(wakasagi),* a favorite food of trout. Streamer flies, which imitate the smelt, are thus used to land big trout here. Boat operators line the shores of the lake to take anglers out, and many people fish around the shores while wading.

Salmon. The most common species of salmon in Hokkaido is the chum salmon *(shirozake).* The average fish weighs 2 to 4 kilograms, and the largest is in the range of 8 kilograms. Until just a few years ago, salmon sportfishing in rivers, as well as within 500 meters of river mouths, was prohibited, although commercial fishermen could fish in these places because salmon were viewed as a vital source of food for the Japanese nation. Since 1995, however, when abundance brought down the price of salmon, some rivers were opened to anglers on a trial basis.

Currently, salmon sportfishing is permitted in three rivers: the Churui and Charo Rivers in eastern Hokkaido, and the Motoura River in Hidaka. Anglers commonly fish with spoons and streamer flies.

Saltwater. Charter boats and party boats exist for chum salmon fishing near Nemuro and Funka-wan Bay from the end of August to the end of November. By the river mouth on the eastern side of Hokkaido, and in the Okhotsk Sea, anglers can catch pink salmon *(karafutomasu)* migrating upriver to spawn. The best time is August and September; mooching with cut baits, and fishing with metal jigs and spoons, are common tactics.

There is fishing for charr around the shores of Otaru and Shimamaki in Hokkaido from December through May, and this obviously requires appropriate warm clothing. Lure anglers cast spoons or metal jigs. Fly anglers use minnow or shrimp patterns on slow-sinking 8- to 12-weight fly lines. The fish average about 1 kilogram but can be caught to 3 kilograms.

Around Matsumae at the southernmost tip of Hokkaido, bluefin tuna *(kuromaguro)* weighing between 5 and 20 kilograms are caught on lures from July through November. Specimens in excess of 50 kilograms are possible. Here anglers use minnow-imitating lures on 8- to 9-foot spinning rods equipped with 30- to 50-pound line.

Anadromous masu salmon *(umimasu)* are found around the south shores of Hokkaido; a particularly good place is along the shores of Tomakomai. The best time is December through April. The average size is 1 to 3 kilograms, but there are occasionally larger specimens, some exceeding 5 kilograms. This area also produces chinook salmon *(masunosuke)* in the 10-kilogram class.

Other ocean fish around Hokkaido that are caught from a boat or from shore are flounder *(karei),* greenling *(ainame),* and ribbed greenling *(hokke),* which are all relatively small fish.

Farther offshore there are Pacific cod *(madara)* in the 7- to 10-kilogram class; these are pursued from charter and party boats, which are available at most harbors.

Honshu, Shikoku, and Kyushu

Trout. The long and narrow mainland island of Honshu features a mountain range that runs from north to south. Because the island is less than 300 kilometers wide at its widest point, no part of it (nor any other part of Japan, incidentally) is more than 150 kilometers from the sea. The rivers that run off mountains with a height of about 3,000 meters all have a steep incline and therefore run fast. The upper watersheds contain native landlocked charr and mountain trout (freshwater masu salmon).

Throughout all regions of Japan, there are also rainbow trout, which first came from North America. Rainbow trout do not fare as well as mountain trout and landlocked charr in the upper fast-flowing water, however, so they are mostly stocked in fish farms or fishing ponds. The season for all three species is generally from March through September. They may be caught only in fishing ponds after September.

The trout in these rivers, especially those dwelling upstream, are extremely small, averaging 20 to 25 centimeters in length. Due to large numbers of anglers, and no catch-and-release ethic, all of the stocked fish are caught, leaving no holdovers of larger fish for the following year.

Anadromous masu, or cherry, salmon migrate into the larger rivers that flow to the Japan Sea. Although they are few in number, they are targets for lure and fly casting. Their average size is 1 to 4 kilograms, and the occasional 5-kilogram-class fish is a prized catch. The Yoneshiro River in Akita Prefecture, the Aka River in Yamagata Prefecture, and the Kuzuryu River in Fukui Prefecture are known for these fish.

Lakes known for trout include Lake Ashino-ko in Hakone, Lake Kawaguchi-ko at the foot of Mt. Fuji, and Lake Chuzenji-ko at Nikko. Lake Chuzenji-ko is famous as the birthplace of trout fishing in Japan, and even today you can catch brown trout, rainbow trout, lake trout, and landlocked masu salmon in its waters.

Large rainbow trout are stocked in Lake Ashino-ko, and some exceed 70 centimeters and 5 kilograms in size. In Lake Kawaguchi-ko, emphasis has been placed on stocking rainbow trout, and the numbers have been increased in recent years. There are rental boats and lodging facilities around all of these lakes. Perhaps because of their proximity to Tokyo, these lakes host a large number of anglers every weekend.

Bass. In 1925, largemouth bass were imported from the state of Oregon in the United States and first released in Lake Ashino-ko in Hakone. They have since been spread to other lakes.

Since about 1970, fishing with lures has increased in popularity in Japan, and largemouth bass were released in lakes throughout Honshu, Shikoku, and Kyushu, and fishing for this species has increased in popularity. Popular lakes for bass are Biwa-ko (northeast of Kyoto and the largest lake in Japan, covering about 672 square kilometers), Kasumiga-ura (northeast of Tokyo), Kita-ura, and Hachirogata, all on Honshu. As noted, however, further stocking of largemouth bass has been prohibited by law to protect native species, although fishing for bass is allowed.

These lakes all have northern-strain largemouth bass, but Ikehara Reservoir in Nara Prefecture has Florida largemouths. Although the numbers caught there are small, specimens in excess of 4 kilograms are taken around the month of June. The lake record, caught in 1998, is 6.86 kilograms.

Sweetfish. Fishing for sweetfish *(ayu)* is a tradition that is unique to Japan. Throughout most rivers in Honshu, Shikoku, and Kyushu, as well as some rivers in Hokkaido, sweetfish fishing continues from the beginning of summer to the end of autumn every year.

There are two common fishing methods. One is Dobuzuri style. This is a type of wet-fly fishing in which two or three wet flies are rigged dropper style on a line attached to an 8- to 10-meter-long pole. Reels are not used. The other is Tomozuri style, in which live sweetfish are used as decoys to attract other fish. The quarry is lured close by and then snagged with a 9-meter-long telescopic pole that has a line just a bit longer than the rod. Reels are not used. A live sweetfish is placed on the line via a metal ring attached to its nose. A treble snag hook is attached to a leader 5 to 6 centimeters in front of the decoy. The average sweetfish is 18 to 25 centimeters long, and any specimen exceeding 30 centimeters is considered large.

Other freshwater fishing. Other freshwater fishing in Japan is centered on members of the carp *(koi-zoku)* family. Since olden times the common carp *(koi)* and the Crucian carp *(funa)* have been representative catches, and both exist throughout Japan. Other cyprinids are pursued as well. Fishing for carp in Japan usually involves a telescopic rod without a reel for small specimens, and a 5-meter spinning rod with reel and 16- to 20-pound line

for individuals that weigh more than 10 kilograms.

Since the Edo period of the eighteenth century, the Japanese have fished for a particular small fish that is normally less than 5 centimeters (2 inches) in size. Known as *tanago,* these fish, even when big, are no larger than 10 centimeters long. They are found mainly in the Kanto area of east-central Honshu in small rivers and ponds, especially during cold winter months. The specialized fishing equipment used is traditional, handmade, and expensive. The rod is 1.2 to 1.5 meters long and comprises six to eight pieces that are each about 25 centimeters long. The rod is used with a small float made from peacock feather and a specially designed small hook that is approximately 4 millimeters long. The best bait is the innards of moth cocoons, but kneaded egg yolk is also used.

Tanago fishing is rare and unique because the fish are so tiny. But the focus required to catch these small fish is the game.

General saltwater. For the most part, saltwater sportfishing in Japan developed from commercial fishing. The majority of present charter boat captains are former commercial fishermen or people who still work in the commercial fishing industry. The species of fish sought are almost always those that are preferred as food. The species pursued for sportfishing vary according to location, but red sea bream *(madai),* flounder *(hirame),* yellowtail *(buri),* and sea arrow *(surumeika)* are popular throughout Japan.

Red sea bream and flounder are the prize catches. The former are common from 0.5 to 8 kilograms, but specimens from 8 to 10 kilograms are also possible. Traditional methods of catching sea bream are governed by location, but most people jig with prawn as baits. Red sea bream fishing is particularly popular throughout Honshu, Shikoku, and Kyushu.

Angling for flounder occurs throughout Japan except in subtropical areas. Although the largest of these can reach 15 kilograms, the average weight is 1 to 3 kilograms, and a specimen exceeding 5 kilograms is considered big. Live sardines are used as baits in bottom fishing efforts. The fishing season is from October through April. Flounder are also caught on plugs and metal jigs.

The common seabass *(suzuki)* is a popular catch for ocean lure anglers throughout Japan except in the southern islands and Hokkaido (the south shore of Hokkaido is the northerly limit for these species). Angling for these fish is prevalent from the shore, as well as in bays and river mouths; it is most prevalent in Tokyo and Osaka Bays. The median length is 30 to 50 centimeters, but occasionally specimens can reach 80 centimeters in length and 4 kilograms in weight; some grow as large as 1 meter long. Most fishing is done with a metal jig and a minnow-shaped plug. Charter and party boats specializing in common seabass fishing are available from almost any harbor. Spring and fall the prime seasons to pursue these fish.

Similar to the common seabass is the blackfin seabass *(hirasuzuki),* which live around the rocks near shore. This fish is popular among lure anglers and is usually caught by experienced enthusiasts. Its size is similar to that of the common seabass, and the season lasts throughout the year, although this fish is scarce in midsummer.

Billfish. Various billfish *(kajiki)* occur on the Pacific side of Honshu from February through October in areas washed by the Black Current. This includes striped marlin *(makajiki)* from 20 to 80 kilograms, Pacific blue marlin *(kurokajiki)* from 60 to 250 kilograms, black marlin *(shirokajiki)* from 80 to 250 kilograms, and sailfish *(bashokajiki),* which average 20 to 35 kilograms. Occasionally, shortnose spearfish *(fuulaikajiki)* from 15 to 30 kilograms are also caught.

Billfishing centers around the islands offshore of the Izu Peninsula, southwest of Tokyo. Charter boats for billfishing depart from Katsuura in Sotoboh, Shimoda in Izu, Miyake-jima in Izu-shichitoh, Nishiki in Kiihantoh, and Kushimoto. The Japanese-style boats usually have an outrigger but no fighting chairs or rod holders. The season begins in June, but July is best for blue marlin and black marlin. Angling success is sporadic, however, as commercial fishing pressure is heavy in this area.

Amami-ohshima and Okinawa

This subtropical area of Japan is part of the Ryukyu Islands and is popular as an ocean resort destination. It has convenient access as well as lodging and is a great place for gamefishing. English is seldom spoken, other than in the hotels, however, so non-Japanese-speaking visitors must be accompanied by an interpreter.

At Amami-ohshima, anglers catch giant trevally *(ronin-aji),* dogtooth tuna *(isomaguro),* and amberjack *(kanpachi)* weighing from 10 to 50 kilograms, plus yellowfin tuna *(kihada),* by casting or jigging. Because the winter months are affected by seasonal winds, the best time to fish for these species is from mid-May through November.

Charter boats for casting and trolling leave from the following islands: Amami-ohshima, Okinawa Hontoh, Kume-jima, Miyako-jima, Ishigaki-jima, Kohama-jima, Iriomote-jima, and Yonaguni-jima.

Casters here use a 7- to 9-foot-long spinning rod with a 2- to 4-ounce popping plug and 20- to 50-pound line. Jiggers use a 6- to 7-foot-long spinning or baitcasting rod with 20- to 80-pound-test line; a 4- to 12-ounce metal jig is fished at depths of between 30 and 200 meters.

Blue marlin are the primary marlin species. Commercial fishermen catch them to 400 kilograms here, but the largest caught by angling usually weigh around 200 kilograms. The average fish is in the 80- to 150-kilogram range. Sailfish are also abundant and are caught from 20 to 40 kilograms on average. Black marlin and striped marlin are small in number.

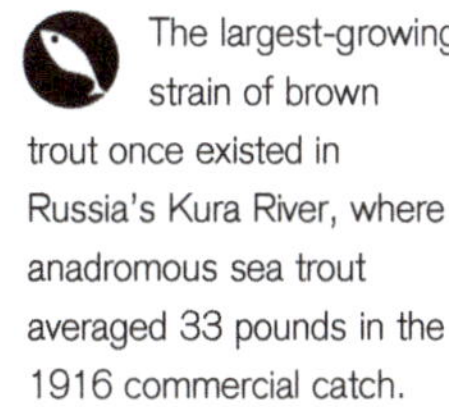
The largest-growing strain of brown trout once existed in Russia's Kura River, where anadromous sea trout averaged 33 pounds in the 1916 commercial catch.

J

Among the tuna family, yellowfins in the 20- to 60-kilogram class are possible, but the average fish weighs less than 20 kilograms. The main methods of tuna fishing are jigging with a metal jig and fishing with baits. Fly fishing has been successfully tried, but only by a few anglers.

Dolphin *(shiira)* are also caught throughout this area, starting in May. The largest weigh from 28 to 30 kilograms, and the average fish weighs between 7 and 10 kilograms. In addition, reef fishing, which in Japan is unique to subtropical areas, is also popular.

Ogasawara (Bonin) Islands

The subtropical Ogasawara chain of islands, also known as the Bonin Islands, are located in the Pacific Ocean roughly 1,000 kilometers south of Tokyo, and north of the Mariana Islands.

This mid-ocean chain is roughly divided into three sections, the northerly Muko-jima islands, the Chichijima islands, and the southerly Hahajima islands. Access is limited to a weekly ferry from Tokyo; there is no air service. This limited access has helped keep these islands well preserved. The presence of steep cliffs all around the islands, as well as fast currents, has also prevented development, as has occurred at Okinawa. Rocky shore fishing, however, is more abundant here than in Okinawa and is especially good at Hahajima. Ferries run between the various islands.

From the rocky shores, anglers catch grouper *(hata)* up to 30 kilograms, two-spot red snapper *(barafuedi)* from 10 to 20 kilograms, amberjack and giant trevally from 10 to 50 kilograms, and dogtooth tuna and yellowfin tuna from 10 to 30 kilograms.

The best season for shore fishing is June through August. Fishing lasts until November, but in late summer and fall typhoons may result in ferry cancellations, requiring two-week ferry schedules. The tackle used for shore fishing is an 11- to 14-foot rod with 15- to 130-pound line and conventional reels. Frozen mackerel scad *(muroaji)* are used for dead baits, and small fish that can be caught around the rocks are used as live baits. Casting with lures and flies is also possible from rocks, but because the fish are large and powerful, heavy tackle is necessary.

Boat anglers can catch all of the aforementioned species and in larger sizes than do shore-bound anglers. They also catch wahoo *(kamasu-sawara)* that exceed 30 kilograms, and amberjack exceeding 50 kilograms, by casting or jigging.

Some areas in the open seas of the Ogasawara Islands remain undeveloped, and Japanese records are being set in these waters. Charter boats leave from Chichijima and Hahajima. Tackle for jigging and casting from boats is the same as that used in Amami-ohshima and Okinawa. Billfish are abundant in this area, but none of the local charter operations specialize in fishing for them or have the appropriate equipment.

JAÚ

A large South American catfish.

See: Catfish.

JERKBAIT

A specially balanced plug or soft worm without a built-in swimming action, fished fairly shallow beneath the surface in a twitching motion. This term once applied only to certain large wooden plugs used in muskie fishing, but today includes many hard- and soft-bodied lures that manifest these characteristics. Strictly used in casting, jerkbaits are mainly freshwater lures and are often grouped within other lure categories, especially plugs and soft worms.

Plugs. Jerk plugs are floating/diving lures that do not have surface fishing merit and do not dive and swim like normal plugs on a steady retrieve. Most are lipless, and the majority are wooden and are usually fished just under the surface. They are very buoyant and are retrieved in a series of pull-pause jerking motions, which makes them dart and roll in short bursts. Large models in 6- to 10-inch sizes are used in muskie fishing; some have rounded broom-handle-like bodies, others are flattened and rectangularly shaped, and some are homemade. One of the most popular muskie standbys has a small metal lip and metal tail, strictly for balance.

Other jerk plugs are in the 3- to 6-inch range and meant for bass, northern pike, and walleye. Some of these are called jerk plugs or jerkbaits mostly because of the manner in which they are best retrieved, which is in a ripping, jerking motion rather than in a straight swim, but they are otherwise similar to shallow-running minnow-shaped plugs. Some also have a suspending characteristic, which is beneficial when they are used around cover.

Worms. Soft worms that are fished in a similar manner to these hard plugs are also called jerkbaits, or jerk worms. The great majority are used in freshwater for largemouth bass, but some are suitable for

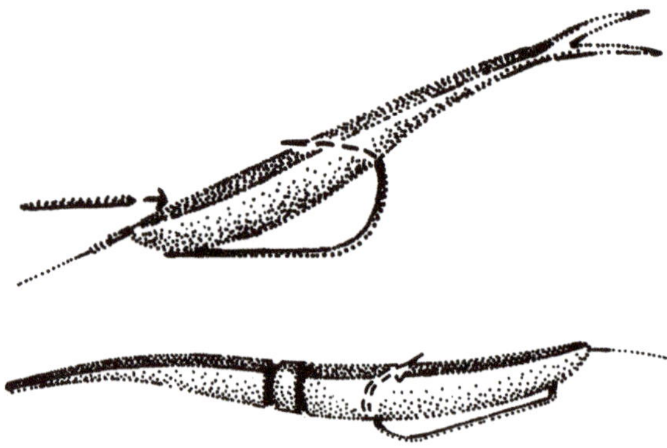

Shown are two common types of soft jerkbaits. Note that in rigging, the point of the hook is pushed through the soft lure, then retracted to just under the surface. Some models are weighted for balance or depth, often with a slender lead weight (top).

saltwater casting in estuaries and shallow flats for striped bass, redfish, and seatrout.

Soft worms that suspend or sink slowly under the surface and that are deliberately erratic upon retrieval have been part of the freshwater bass angler's repertoire since the mid-1980s. Many of these lures are vaguely wormlike in appearance but could imitate eels, small baitfish, or other creatures in a general way.

These lures are not as supple as conventional soft worms, and they are usually fished suspended or just under the surface in a pull-pause, slow-jerking type of retrieve. This is different from the way most other soft lures are worked. Most soft worms, for example, are known for their slithering, shimmering, undulating type of action, worked primarily on or close to the bottom.

Unlike jerk plugs, jerk worms have a lackluster appearance, and it takes a little use to get accustomed to their rolling, disoriented-fish-like action. Actually, these soft plastics do look a lot like a wounded darting fish when jerked or when paused, because they descend slowly like a dying fish. Like conventional plastic worms, they are rigged with a single hook embedded inside, which makes them reasonably snag-resistant and very capable of being fished amidst heavy cover, especially vegetation. Lily pads, with their frequent openings on the surface and ample clearance below it, are very good locales for these lures.

Soft jerkbaits or jerk worms are usually rigged without a conventional sinker. They may be fished unweighted for shallow use or may be fished with a thin-diameter 1-inch-length lead stick or nail segment inserted into the head for deeper use, longer casts, and less erratic action. The hook should be deployed in a semi-Texas rig manner, with the point slightly protruding through the wider top (or back) of the bait for better hookups. Hook point placement, and style of hook shank, varies with different baits.

Some jerk worms dart well from side to side, and others have more of a slightly canted darting-rolling action. You should experiment a bit with hook size and placement to achieve the desired effect, and you should also be attentive to proper rerigging after a fish has been caught.

When fishing either of these types of jerkbait, you typically have to keep your rod tip down and pointed at the water. You can work them quite well on a raised rod (angled at a 10 to 11 o'clock position) but only when the lure is a long distance away. A low rod angle also aids hooksetting.

See: Plug; Soft Worm.

JET BOAT

A boat propelled by a jet-drive motor and used for navigating in extremely shallow areas, primarily rivers. Jet boats, which are also referred to as jet sleds, are popular with river anglers who travel considerable distances and who at times need to run in mere inches of water. Jet boats are especially popular in the Pacific Northwest and in Alaska but are also used in other areas.

The advantage of a jet boat is obvious to the angler who must traverse shallow rivers and has limited time to fish. It's easy to fish along very shallow rivers via drift boats, canoes, and inflatables, but only in one direction: downstream. It's difficult to cover much distance upstream, even in a canoe, if there is any significant current to beat against. Float trips are a fine way to see and fish a river, if you have the time. But, if you have only a few hours to do your angling, or have a lot of upstream distance to cover rapidly, then jets are the way to go.

A good jet rig is fast. It will even quickly ascend rapids and long stretches of white water if the boat is properly designed and the engine has sufficient horsepower. Some top-end jet boats can cover 50 miles of river, much of it upstream, in little more than an hour.

Jet boats are overwhelmingly aluminum models with flat-bottom hulls, but newer versions include fiberglass models and versions with tunnel hulls. Inflatables also can be used, although they are not as efficient as well-designed aluminum hulls, probably mostly due to air entrainment under the hull that mixes with water in the jet's intake.

Jet-drive motors are not efficient unless they can keep the boat, when fully loaded, easily on plane. A hull that is on plane draws much less water than one that is plowing through the water at displacement speeds. Since the jet unit does not project significantly below the bottom of the boat, it will work just fine as long as there is barely enough water for the boat to plane through.

The lowest point of a jet-drive motor, either outboard or inboard, is the intake; when properly installed, the intake projects only an inch or so lower than the bottom of the boat. When the rig is on plane, the rear nozzle directs a high-velocity stream of water backward through the air, much like a fire hose. Only the skimming intake grill touches the water.

Driving a jet boat is different from driving a conventional boat. When designed for skinny river work, the hull has no significant keel. The jet unit itself has no "rudder" in the water (the skeg and lower unit of a conventional outboard lower unit or stern serve as a rudder) and thus can steer by thrust only. It's more like an airboat, which means a certain amount of planning ahead is required when underway. When making a quick turn, it's sometimes necessary to reduce power a little, momentarily, to prevent sliding. It's also necessary to start each turn a little early, since the boat will slide into turns.

See: Jet Drive.

JET DRIVE

A jet-drive motor is one in which the lower unit

Tests have shown that a fish weighing 20 pounds upon capture will lose 1 pound 4 ounces through dehydration after being left in the open air for 12 hours.

features a propeller-less water-intake propulsion system, rather than having a traditional propeller immersed in the water below the boat hull. The intake is covered by a screen and is flush to the hull; an impeller pulls great volumes of water in and

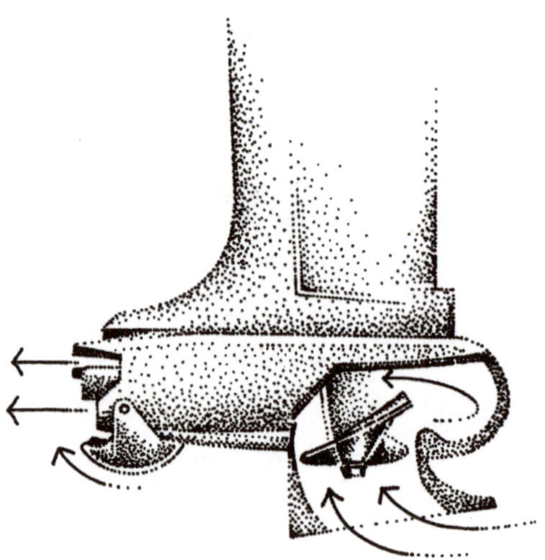

In a jet drive, water is drawn into a pump by an impeller, then forced out at high velocity to provide forward momentum. A gate closes over the outflow area to provide neutral and reverse modes.

expels it out a rear discharge, resulting in forward momentum. To maneuver in reverse, which is not done well in a jet boat, a clam-shaped deflector cups over the discharge area.

Boats equipped with a jet drive are usually called jet boats (including the small and popular vessels called "personal watercraft"), and fishing boats with jet engines in the Pacific Northwest are called jet sleds. Jet-drive motors accelerate quickly, turn sharply, and feature shallow draft when used on appropriate boats. Anglers typically use jet drives on flat-bottomed boats, enabling them to run in just a few inches of water, which is especially useful when navigating many rivers. They also use them on tunnel-hulled boats, which puts the transom in the so-called tunnel and at the transom line for an unimpeded pickup of water and the ability to run in whatever little water the skimming transom can handle.

Jet-drive motors come in basically inboard and outboard versions. The inboard version is rigged more like a stern drive than a regular inboard, with the jet nozzle protruding from the transom where the outdrive unit would be for an inboard/outboard (I/O). The outboard version is either manufactured in whole or fashioned from conventional outboards via a conversion unit; in the latter case, a jet housing is bolted onto the bottom of an outboard exhaust housing, right where the lower unit was before it was removed to make room for the jet pump. It's possible to buy conversion units for almost all of the popular makes of outboards, from 18 to 235 horsepower (hp), and to find manufactured units in a similarly wide range of power.

In the higher ranges, a jet-drive boat can move very fast. When matched with the right hull, it may be actually somewhat faster than a similar size prop-driven inboard with the same horsepower.

With a jet drive, a flat-bottomed boat can run in the skinniest water, and a semi-V can run in just a few inches. Jet-drive motors use more fuel than conventional engines, cut horsepower by up to a third, and have very "loose" steering. They are noisier than a propeller-equipped motor and require some getting used to for steering, especially in rough water and windy situations. They are not suitable for areas with heavy vegetation, which is sucked into the impeller and clogs it. But shallow-water operation

The bottom of the propeller-less jet drive aligns with the bottom of the hull.

is a great advantage in some places. Plus a jet drive is good for fighting strong fish because there is no propeller in the water to cut the line, and a jet drive is safer than a propeller when there are people in the water.

Jet-drive motors do not have a neutral gear, and when operating they are always in forward or reverse movement, primarily the former. When the key is turned on a jet drive, even with the throttle in neutral position and with the boat at rest on a boat trailer or tied to a dock, the motor is pulling in water and pushing the boat forward. This can be a disadvantage in docking and at some launch ramps. To depart, especially when the motor is cold, it may be wise to turn the boat around, facing the open water for boarding. This is also a drawback when trying to control a boat slowly, where you might otherwise put the motor in and out of forward, neutral, and reverse. That type of manipulation is not as effective with a jet drive, perhaps making it less desirable for some anglers.

See: Jet Boat.

JETTY

A man-made structure, usually of concrete or stone, projecting into the water from the shore to protect a sandy beach from erosion, funnel current from an inlet, or protect a harbor or pier. Jetties may be constructed of wood and stone, or all stone, and form a perpendicular wall-like extension from a rocky or sandy shore into the water. They are primarily found in saltwater along the coasts.

Technically, a jetty is a structure that extends from inlets and harbor mouths. Its purpose is to protect those places by impeding wave and current action and to keep the entrance to them open for boat traffic; it is also meant to stabilize the beach or shoreline and help prevent erosion. Inlet and harbor jetties support various navigational aids.

Structures extending from a beachfront are technically called groins *(see)* but are commonly referred to as jetties. Groins are intended to impede the action of waves and current and to prevent erosion by stabilizing the sand in the immediate vicinity; they do not usually have navigational aids.

Jetties also exist on large bodies of freshwater, such as the Great Lakes, where they are primarily intended to aid boat passage and protect harbor entrances; freshwater jetties are often called piers *(see)*, especially if they are topped with a surface that allows easy pedestrian access.

A jetty is slightly different from a breakwater *(see)* in that a jetty is usually narrower, shorter, and in some cases higher; it serves the same purpose, however. Some breakwaters are detached from shore, not accessible by foot, and may not be perpendicular to the beach or shoreline. Jetties always protrude above the water except under extreme water conditions, and they are a favored place for angling for diverse species.

See: Jetty Fishing; Surf Fishing.

JETTY FISHING

Fishing Coastal Jetties, Groins, Rockpiles, and Breakwaters

For the shore-bound coastal angler, the area close to the beach holds diverse fishing opportunities. These are available along the expansive shoreline, which requires fishing along the shore directly in the surf or fishing around and near various accessible structures. Some of the popular structures that exist are piers, bridges, docks, and bulkheads *(see: pier fishing)*. The most commonly fished structures are the assorted formations of rock, concrete, wood, and rubble that protrude into the water. Such formations include groins *(see)*, inlet jetties, rockpiles that may or may not have been deliberately placed, and accessible harbor breakwaters *(see)*. Though slightly different, these are all commonly referred to by anglers and the general public as jetties *(see)*, and they provide a wealth of angling possibilities.

Fishing these jetties often develops into a lifelong challenge. It is a challenge that depends solely on the angler and the skills and experience that are developed. It can be enjoyed at nominal cost and can provide a wide range of species and angling experiences, as well as some of the sea's most challenging fishing. Jetty fishing is actually among the most physical types of angling you can experience, especially if you move about, visit several jetties, and work along the length of each of them.

Striped bass, shown here, and many other species are found among the rocks of jetties or in the turbulent water nearby.

Jetty fishing is unlike other types of saltwater angling in that there is no comfortable platform like a boat, or secure location like a beach, to fish from. Angling from jetties requires dexterity to move about the moss- and mussel-covered rocks, sometimes in the darkness of night; an ability to present a lure or bait properly to gamefish that are often tough adversaries; and the temerity to land fish from a promontory that is often cascaded

An angler fishes from the head of the jetty at Barnegat, New Jersey.

with crashing waves and flying spray. Jetty fishing aficionados, known as "jetty jockeys," are a breed of anglers who find excitement, challenge, and reward in an activity that tests their skills every second they are on the rocks.

The testing is worth the discomfort endured and the energy expended, however, not only because of the exciting situation, but because of the great variety of species that are caught from rockpiles and jetties on all coasts. Mid-Atlantic and New England jetty anglers, for example, find such bottom feeders as both summer and winter flounder, tautog, sea bass, pollock, and cod around these locations, as well as striped bass, bluefish, weakfish, and the occasional little tuna.

In the Southeastern United States and along the Gulf Coast, flounder, grouper, croaker, sheepshead, and a variety of snapper are caught among the rockpiles and coral outcroppings, as well as more prized species like redfish, bluefish, tarpon, snook, barracuda, and spotted weakfish (trout). Along the Pacific Coast, surf perch, rockfish, Pacific halibut, and sand bass, as well as Pacific barracuda, yellowtail, and Pacific bonito, succumb to those who cast from the many rocky outcroppings.

Other species also are encountered, some less often than others. Jetty anglers who cast from coral breakwaters in the Bahamas, for example, are known to regularly catch bonefish while working a bait on the bottom, and big cobia are occasionally landed from breakwaters in Alabama's Mobile Bay.

The variables of how, where, and when you fish these locations all affect your success, no matter what the geographic location or the species likely to be encountered.

Tackle. The types of tackle used on jetties vary widely, from heavy-duty surf outfits with levelwind reels, all the way down to light spinning gear and fly rods. Some of the lighter outfits are used by occasional jetty anglers, and they may have success under favorable conditions for smaller species. Generally you need to match the tackle to the water conditions, the lures or bait that need to be fished, and the size of the species. Although room exists for a wide range of equipment under optimum conditions and in certain situations, keep in mind that when the water gets rough, the conditions get difficult, and the species get large, your equipment must be up to the demands.

Rods and reels. Spinning tackle is by far the most popular gear for jetty fishing, but some anglers use conventional or baitcasting equipment and there are opportunities for flycasters as well.

Two types of outfits are necessary for most jetty fishing. A near-universal choice for small fish is a 6- to 7-foot rod with a fairly stiff action, coupled with a reel capable of holding 200 yards of 10- or 12-pound-test line. This will handle the smaller bottom-feeding species that are found within reasonable casting range.

To deal with gamefish species in the 5- to 20-plus-pound category (like tarpon, snook, redfish, striped bass, bluefish, cobia, and yellowtail), larger lures and baits and heavier gear are in order. Here, you need a 7- to 8-foot rod with a stiff action, ca-pable of casting a 3- or 4-ounce sinker, bucktail jig, metal squid, or large and heavy plug. This rod should be coupled with a medium-heavy spinning reel that can hold 200 to 250 yards of 12- to 17-pound line on conventional or levelwind reels with similar capacity. Veteran jetty anglers feel that if a fish cleans you out of line when you are using such an outfit, it deserves to get away.

Admittedly, fly fishing from jetties is difficult, but it is manageable when using a stripping basket *(see)*. A 10-weight outfit with a sink-tip shooting head line is a good choice; the reel should have between 150 and 200 yards of backing for the time when a bruiser takes a streamer and heads for the horizon.

Bottom bait rig. Use a basic bottom-fishing bait rig for fishing natural bait around jetties. This is constructed via a three-way swivel, with a sinker on a 3- or 4-inch-long loop of monofilament line attached to one eye of the swivel, and a snelled hook on a 3-foot length of line attached to the other eye. The line to the hook should be 20- or 30-pound test. Use a pyramid sinker for holding qualities if the surf near the jetty is rough, and a bank or dipsey sinker if it is light. Weight varies from 2 to 4 ounces.

You can tie in a dropper loop about a foot from the swivel and place a second hook there. It may be useful to place a Styrofoam float, a half inch in diameter and between 1 and 2 inches long, on the leader where it meets the hook. This strategy suspends the hook and bait off the bottom, within range of cruising fish yet away from pesky crabs on the bottom. When targeting summer flounder, weakfish, striped bass, redfish, rock bass, and species that average a couple of pounds or more, use a 2/0 or 3/0 Beak, Claw, or Wide Gap hook, particularly with seaworms, shrimp, squid, killies, or other small baits. When fishing with large, 2- to 4-inch-long chunks of menhaden, mullet, mackerel, or other fish, or whole squid or clams, use 4/0 through 6/0 hooks.

Work such a rig on the bottom in the waters surrounding the structure you're fishing. Assuming you're fishing from a rockpile that extends several hundred feet seaward, make your initial casts from along the side of the jetty just outside the surf line. Often the churning surf exposes sand fleas, crabs, shrimp, sand eels, and other forage, and the fish move in to feed. Patience is important, but if your bait rests on the bottom in prime water and doesn't receive a strike in 10 to 15 minutes, move farther out on the jetty and make another cast into new water. Keep repeating this procedure until you receive strikes; this way you're covering the entire bottom surrounding the structure.

It's usually not essential to cast great distances

while fishing from a jetty or rockpile, since the natural forage is often in close. A good practice is to make a cast of nominal distance, perhaps 100 to 150 feet, and periodically reel in the bait several feet, thus bracketing the entire area.

Freelined live bait. Live baits are often used when targeting some bigger gamefish. These should be freelined without a sinker so that the bait can swim out and away from the jetty. For this, tie a tiny barrel swivel to the end of the line and then a 3- or 4-foot leader of 20- to 30-pound test. The leader is heavier than the main line because fish often ingest part of the leader when taking the bait, and this helps prevent leader breakage. This basic terminal rig will work for the majority of species found around coastal jetties. The key is tailoring the size of the hook and bait to the species being sought.

Beak and Claw style hooks are favored for live bait; some anglers employ the O'Shaughnessy or Chestertown style, and circle hooks are becoming more popular. If targeting 1-pound winter flounder and using bloodworms as bait, you should try a No. 8 or 9 Chestertown hook with a 2-inch-long piece of sandworm bait, since the flatfish have very small, rubbery mouths. If line-shy Pacific bonito are the quarry, try a No. 4 or 5 Beak-style hook and anchovy.

Anglers who fish live crabs for tarpon often use 5/0 through 7/0 hook sizes; these are honed needle sharp, with the hook placed through the crab's hard shell so that the crab can swim about freely, and with the pincer claws clipped off to prevent getting nipped while handling. Anglers targeting striped bass employ menhaden, mackerel, and herring; they lightly hook the bait just beneath the dorsal fin, cast it out, and permit it to swim away from the jetty. Live eels are fished in a similar manner, except that they are usually hooked through the lips or eyes. Live mullet are also used to tempt strikes from tarpon, snook, and redfish. Some anglers add a sliding float to their line, positioning it so that their bait works from 3 to 5 feet beneath the surface, with the float signaling precisely where the bait is.

Properly hooked, a live baitfish will swim about for a half hour or more, quickly becoming excited as a large gamefish zeroes in on it. Live baits such as these are transported to jetties in 5-gallon buckets, placing just a couple of baits in the bucket so that all of the oxygen in the water isn't quickly consumed. This is just about the only practical way to bring live bait onto jetties and departs from the rule that buckets should not be carried onto rockpiles. When the bait is no longer useful, save it and use it in chunks or strips later, after you've used up all your live ammunition.

Lures. The most popular lures at the disposal of the jetty fraternity include metal squids, plugs, and bucktail or soft-bodied jigs. Within these three lure categories are dozens of combinations.

Metal squids include the time-proven molded-block tin squids, hammered stainless steel jigs, chrome- and gold-plated jigs, and assorted variations of the diamond jig. Some of these are fished plain and others by adding a plastic tail or tube to the hook, or feathers, bucktail skirt, or pork rind strip. The lures are available in sizes ranging from 1/4 ounce to 3 or 4 ounces. The key is matching lure size and color to the baitfish in residence.

Dozens of plugs also have merit around jetties. Perhaps the most popular one is the swimming minnow version with a side-to-side swimming action. Shallow, intermediate, and deep-diving models come in one-piece or jointed versions and in various sizes and every color imaginable. Matching size is important here also. Other possibilities include an assortment of popping, darting, and skipping surface plugs. All are fun to use, and each requires a different technique when retrieved to maximize its action and draw strikes. These work best when there is a lot of activity around the jetties and competition for food.

A bucktail or plastic-bodied jig may be the best all-around lure for jetty fishing. Various sizes, colors, and soft body styles are possible. With the soft tails, you simply select the size and look that seems best and slip the tail onto the hook. The soft bodies are made to exactly replicate many baitfish, include such important jetty forage as sand eels, herring, and mullet.

Perhaps the oldest ancestor of today's plugs was the Phantom Minnow, an English lure made around 1800 consisting of a metal head, metal fins, three treble hooks, and a silk body.

Jetty anglers regularly employ some of these lures in combination; they'll use a plug or metal squid as the primary lure at the end of the line and put a hooked soft-tail bait 24 to 30 inches ahead of that as a teaser. This combination is deployed by tying a small barrel swivel to the end of your line, followed by a 30- to 36-inch leader for attaching the main lure. The teaser, which can also be a streamer fly or even just a strip of pork rind on a hook, is then tied off the barrel swivel on a 6-inch dropper line. Sometimes the teaser gets strikes, and sometimes the primary lure. It's not unusual to hook a double, with a fish on each lure; this often happens when a lot of bluefish, seatrout, and striped bass are around.

Live eels are used effectively for striped bass, weakfish, cobia, and other species found around rockpiles, although many anglers employ dead rigged eels with great results. These common eels, ranging in length from 6 to 18 inches, are killed in salt brine. They are then rigged on metal squids designed expressly for this purpose. The metal squid's hook is placed in the head of the eel, and a second hook is run through the eel with a rigging needle so that it comes out near the eel's vent. Rigged in this manner, the eel is a combination lure and bait. It is cast and retrieved much the same as a plug or metal squid and is very effective.

Anglers generally keep six to a dozen eels rigged and stored in Kosher or sea salt brine in 1-gallon plastic jars. These jars, used for mayonnaise, are easily obtained at most delicatessens. Rigged and stored in this manner, the eels are tough and keep for months at a time.

It's easy to make the mistake of carrying a massive lure selection with you and constantly changing. The better tactic is to select two or three lures of each basic type and build confidence in using them, matching the lure to the specific situation. When the surf adjacent to the jetty is running high and the wind is onshore, for example, it's appropriate to break out a heavy metal squid to reach into the stiff wind, whereas on a calm, windless night a small swimming plug worked in close to the rocks may be just right.

Footwear. Safety underfoot is unquestionably the most important consideration for accessory equipment when jetty fishing. You'll be walking on a variety of surfaces, from solid rock to concrete and wood, all of which may be wet, covered with slippery marine growth, or sheathed in mussels. Peculiar configurations are the norm, and you must sometimes have the dexterity of a mountain goat to negotiate angles and crevices to reach a spot that is flat enough to cast from and that also provides a decent chance at landing your quarry. Be careful as you move about the rockpiles, and make safety a primary concern.

Wearing ordinary footwear while fishing from jetties, such as sneakers or shoes, or even rubber-soled boots or waders, is sheer folly, and only practical when the jetty is high and dry—which is usually when the fishing is poor. This type of footwear does not give you traction when you're negotiating peculiar angles, nor does it hold securely on slippery, slimy marine growth.

Wet moss and slippery rocks on jetties make walking hazardous; most regulars use cleated soles to improve traction.

A variety of jetty footwear is available, with the term "jetty creepers" most often used to describe soles designed to secure your footing. Ordinary golf soles, such as those found on golf shoes, which have replaceable aluminum cleats, are ideal, although they do not last long. The golf shoes can be worn as is, especially when fishing from jetties where you're situated well above the water and don't have to wear boots or waders to gain access. You can also wear golf rubbers, which, if large enough, can be slipped over regular boots or waders.

Another option is to have a shoemaker carefully remove the rubber sole from a pair of boots or waders and then cement golf soles to the bottom. This method is used extensively by veteran jetty anglers. Over time, the aluminum golf cleats wear down from the abrasion of the rocks, but they are easily replaced using a wrench made expressly for that purpose. Always lubricate the threads of the cleats when inserting them; this prevents them from becoming corroded and makes replacement easier.

Manufactured strap-on creepers are also used by jetty jockeys, but they are less desirable, because the straps tend to bind and the creepers may be tough to put on and uncomfortable to wear. The creepers have spikes on the soles for gripping; they can be slipped over canvas boat shoes in warm climates or over wader boots but must be sized accordingly. There are also jetty creepers made to slip on over boots and footwear. Some anglers even use felt-soled boots and chainlike slipovers on their boots. None of these options are as effective, safe, or comfortable as the golf soles.

Depending on where you fish and the type of structure you'll be fishing from, select basic footwear as light as you can go. Golf shoes are ideal, followed by knee boots if you'll be sloshing through ankle-deep water, followed by hip boots and waders, the latter as a last resort. You will need boots or waders on jetties or breakwaters where the surf has eroded the beaches, requiring that you wade through water to gain access.

Other gear. A storm suit is still another piece of indispensable gear. In most jetty fishing situations, waves crash against the rocks, producing wind-blown spray. In cold weather, a breeze can be chilling. The suit provides warmth, dryness, and comfort, especially during cold weather.

Mobility is essential while jetty fishing, so carrying a tackle box or bucket is usually not an option. Newcomers who carry a tackle box often suffer the consequences of placing it on a rock: slipping into a crevice and losing its contents, or being showered with a crashing wave. A shoulder bag is the only way to go. Carry a minimum of essential gear and use plastic sealable pouches to keep gear in the bag readily accessible and dry. Many good shoulder bags are available, some compartmented with plastic tubing and sleeves for inserting plugs, metal

Jetty fishing offers the opportunity to fish at various levels and with various techniques, depending on water conditions and likely species.

squids, and bucktails. Store the bag in a well-ventilated spot after each jetty fishing excursion; if you place a wet shoulder bag in a damp place and come back a week later, your lures will be a rusty mess.

If you elect to fish from jetties at night (which is often when the angling is superior as the fish move in close to feed), you'll need a headlamp. This can easily be strapped loosely around your collar, so that the light hangs under your chin. The headlamp makes changing lures, moving around the rocks, or putting your beam on a fish about to be landed relatively easy. Forget penlights and regular flashlights because you need hands-free lighting and mobility.

Veteran jetty jockeys who target large gamefish of a size that can't be lifted with their outfit generally employ a long-handled gaff to land their catch. The gaff handle is usually the same length as the rod you're using, with a 2-inch gaff hook. The long handle enables you to reach the fish without getting too close to the water, an important consideration when heavy surf is working across the rocks. Make sure that you can legally gaff a gamefish that is under an established minimum size restriction. Even when there are no prohibitions on gaffing but still a minimum size limit, only employ a gaff if you're absolutely certain the fish is well beyond the minimum size restriction, and you intend to keep it.

If you'll be keeping fish, you should have a 6-foot length of plastic-covered clothesline with you. This makes an excellent stringer, especially for small and medium-size fish.

General Jetty Tactics

Tidal influence. Tides play an important role when fishing from jetties. High tide may bring 8 or 10 feet of water where only a sand flat existed at low tide. At some jetties, the rockpile isn't even accessible at high tide, and you can get onto the rocks only after the tide has ebbed for a couple of hours. Experience is the best teacher. Visit the spots you plan to fish; if you're new to an area, visit the local tackle shops and ask their advice about tides. Keep in mind there are no set rules, for many of the species move about with the tides, taking up station to feed for just a short while and then moving on. The key is learning which jetty locations produce results at a given tide stage and planning your strategy accordingly. It's not unusual for a jetty jockey to visit several jetties in the course of a tide, capitalizing on the movements of the fish.

Because erosion and the ravages of the ocean often displace rocks and tumble them about away from the jetty, you will at times foul your rigging on them. It's a good idea to pre-visit the jetties you plan to fish when the tide is low; then you can make a visual observation of spots to avoid later when the water is higher and more favorable for fishing. Often the fronts of jetties are in disarray; at high tide the jetty appears straight and intact, whereas on the ebb tide you'll notice that the front of the jetty actually has boulders tumbled about. Scouting your locations at a time when you can learn about their characteristics is very useful.

Cover it all. No two jetties are alike, and it takes a while to master the techniques of fishing each. Keep in mind that fish are attracted to a jetty because forage species often seek the protection of the rocks; thus, crabs, lobsters, sand fleas, and shrimp are readily available. Since you have no way of knowing precisely where the fish will be feeding, it is very important that you thoroughly cover with your lures all the water surrounding the jetty.

This is best accomplished by making your first cast shortly after you walk out onto the jetty, placing your lure just outside the curl of the breakers

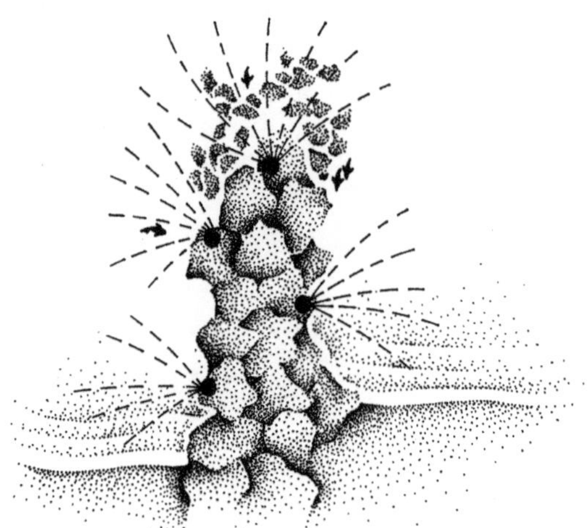

From each casting location on a jetty, an angler should bracket the area with casts to properly cover all water where fish may be feeding.

working in toward the beach. Often the churning action of the waves there exposes sand fleas, crabs, and shrimp, and fish will move into the heavy water to feed. After several casts, move out onto the jetty and bracket your casts, making a cast in toward the beach, so that the retrieve almost parallels the jetty. Next place a cast at a 45-degree angle from where you're standing, then straight in front of you, out 45 degrees, and finally almost paralleling the jetty. Then move out and repeat the procedure.

As you approach the end of the jetty, you'll often find that the seas are crashing onto the rocks and that it's difficult to cast over the submerged rocks and to work your lure. But this is a spot where the fish often feed, so you should work it carefully. Among the tumbled rocks of the jetty front there could be feeding striped bass, redfish, and snook.

Complete the circuit, and work the remaining side of the jetty to the beach. Over time you'll find that each jetty will produce strikes at different spots. Sometimes it's the location of submerged rocks and the way currents swirl around them that results in fish taking up station to feed. With experience, you'll accumulate a wealth of information about each jetty, and instead of working the entire rockpile, you'll be able to concentrate your efforts in the spots, and with the lures, that regularly produce strikes.

Fish in the rocks. Although casting away from the jetty works for most species, there are exceptions, for example, tautog (blackfish), sea bass, grunts, snapper, and sheepshead. These species often crowd the rocks, even swimming into crevices as they search for crabs and shrimp or rip mussels from the rocks. To catch them, you've got to present your baits in close, with the rig resting among the rocks. These fish will never find the bait if it's 10 or 15 feet from the jetty.

It's easy to snag your rig in the rocks, so when targeting these species simply tie a loop into the end of your line, onto which you slip a $^1/_2$- or 1-ounce dipsey or bank sinker. Tie in a dropper loop a foot or so above the sinker, and put a 10- to 12-inch leader with a No. 1 or 2 Claw or Beak style hook on it. This is a small, compact rig that is less apt to get snagged than a multihook rig with a swivel.

Bait the hook with small pieces of seaworm, shrimp, squid, clam, mussel, snail, or cut mullet, and cast out just far enough that the bait rests on either the rocks or the sand immediately adjacent to the rocks where these species are searching for a meal. Most species that feed among the jetty rocks are quick to take a bait, so be alert and strike the fish immediately; delaying often results in a lost bait or a hooked fish that dives into a rocky crevice and cuts your line or leader.

Casting/landing tips. Try to make each cast count. If a fish is feeding in a pocket adjacent to a jetty, it will often strike on your first cast, since it is actively searching for a meal; as your lure comes into range, it's onto the lure in a flash.

Make sure that you work every lure to the very edge of the rocks before lifting it from the water. People often reel fast as their lure approaches the rocks to avoid getting fouled. This is a big mistake, because the greatest number of strikes will come in close. Sometimes the fish are feeding in close; more often they are attracted to and follow the lure and realize that it appears to be seeking the sanctuary of the rocks, so they make a last-second strike lunge to prevent it from getting away. Huge stripers, tarpon, and snook often startle anglers as they crash a lure within a rod's length, an exciting experience that gets the adrenaline moving.

When fishing for smaller fish, you can usually reel them within range of where you're standing and work them in close with the assistance of a wave, or you can simply lift them onto the rockpile. With bigger specimens, once the fish is hooked, permit it to move well away from the jetty, where it can't get the line caught on the rocks and mussels. Let the fish have its head, take drag, and tire itself out. As the fish tires, work it in close and position yourself so that you can get it within range of your gaff or, if someone is with you, within range of their position. Avoid spots where tumbled rocks or pilings or other debris are in front of you; this limits your control, especially when you have a big fish doing its best to get away.

Inlet jetty tactics. Technically, a jetty is a structure that extends from inlets *(see)* and harbor mouths, although the word "jetty" is also commonly used to refer to coastal structures that extend from a beach where there is no inlet (these are actually groins). The purpose of an inlet jetty is to impede wave and current action and thus to protect those places and keep the entrance to them open for boat traffic. It is also meant to stabilize the beach or shoreline to help prevent erosion and to prevent shifting sands from causing the inlets to shoal.

The inlet entrance usually has a pair of parallel jetties or rockpiles on each side of it. These jetties may provide excellent fishing. However, the conditions at inlet jetties vary considerably from other coastal jetties. For one thing, the area between inlet jetties may be a couple of hundred feet wide and over a quarter-mile long. Where most coastal jetties have currents working up and down the beach adjacent to them, in the inlets the tidal flow, moving into bays and rivers or emptying into the ocean, presents a different set of conditions, requiring different tactics.

Tidal influence. The tidal flow in and out of inlets ranges from just a few feet to 10 feet or more. As this water moves, strong currents develop, often carrying huge quantities of bait with it. This typically occurs on the ebbing tide, when forage species found in bays and rivers are carried along with the tide, as well as quantities of crabs, shrimp, and other food. Gamefish and bottom feeders often take up station in the inlets, usually along the bottom, in areas where they can place themselves out of the heaviest current and wait for a meal to be swept their way.

This presents a different, yet challenging, set of circumstances for the angler casting from inlet rockpiles. The techniques of casting and retrieving, whether with natural baits or lures, are different because of the current. Often the currents are so swift that any lure or the heaviest sinker and bottom rig is just swept along.

Bait presentation. The jetty angler who uses natural baits with a bottom rig must constantly cast out a rig, permit the current to carry it along, and then retrieve and cast again. Bottom fishing is usually best within an hour or so of either high or low tide; current moves with less velocity just before the slack, and the fish that have taken up station in the quiet water behind or ahead of rocks, ledges, or depressions in the bottom may begin to move about in search of a meal.

Lure presentation. Many of the lightweight lures that are customarily fished from coastal jetties, especially surface and intermediate-depth plugs and metal squids, don't work as effectively in the swift and often deep water adjacent to inlet jetties. The depth of many inlets ranges from 20 to 25 feet or more, and fish holding at the bottom, where they try to avoid fighting heavy currents, rise only infrequently to the surface for a lure. In fact, they may not even realize it's there, because it's so far above them.

The single best lure in inlets is a leadhead jig, with either a bucktail or a soft plastic body, or a combination of both, perhaps also with a strip of pork rind. These lures get to the bottom quickly in even the heaviest current and can then be worked

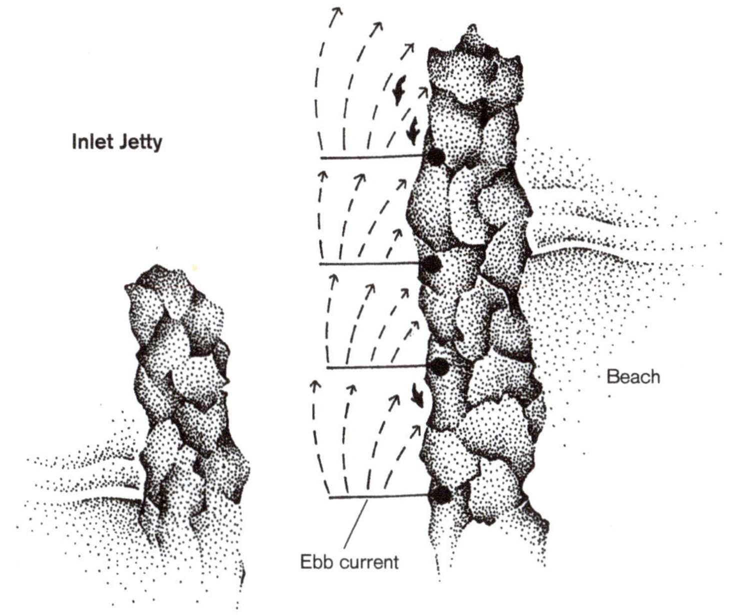

This scenario depicts an inlet jetty with an ebb current heading seaward. Jetty anglers here should work toward the end of the jetty; at each location begin with short casts and extend outward; then move 20 or 30 feet out and repeat.

along the bottom as the current carries them along.

When you start lure fishing at an inlet jetty, you should position yourself low to the water on the rocks and cast out and across the current, beginning with a short cast of perhaps 25 to 40 feet. As the lure enters the water, permit it to settle on a slack line. As soon as the jig touches bottom, the line will pull taut, and you should close the bail or engage the gears. Let the lure be lifted off the bottom and carried by the current; it will often lift off the bottom again, move some more, and then bounce. As it moves along, it is being carried in toward the rocks; and as it nears the end of the swing, the current will sweep it off the bottom. This is where the strikes most often occur. Frequently the strike feels as though you've snagged bottom, as a tarpon, snook, redfish, striped bass, bluefish, or weakfish moves up and engulfs the jig as it lifts off the bottom.

Lengthen each succeeding cast by 15 or 20 feet; this action enables the bucktail jig to bounce and sweep across a progressively longer stretch of bottom. Continue extending the distance of your casts as far as you can. If you receive no strikes, move out along the jetty rocks 20 or 30 feet and repeat the same procedure. In this way you'll cover all of the bottom. What often happens is that you'll receive the first strike and then you'll get multiple strikes on successive casts, as your jig works into an area where a pod of fish are schooled up, waiting for a meal to be carried to them.

Getting the feel of a bucktail jig bouncing bottom correctly is best accomplished by getting low to the water and keeping your rod tip pointed downward. Play it safe and don't get too close if a sea is running in the inlet. As the tide begins to slack, especially on the ebb—which is when the bulk of the forage is in the inlet—you'll find the jig moving more slowly. You can enhance its action by working your rod tip, causing the jig to dart ahead, then falter, and be again carried by the tide. At the end of the sweep, you can work the jig back to you, alternately lifting your rod tip, hesitating, then sweeping it upward, reeling, and repeating until you've completed the retrieve.

As the tide slackens in the inlet, you can often get strikes on metal squids, rigged eels, and plugs, but most often the intermediate or deep-running models will bring more strikes than surface lures.

An occasional exception to this deep-fishing/deep lure scenario occurs when the tide is swiftly ebbing and rips are formed to the seaward end of the inlet jetties. Tarpon, jack crevalle, snook, redfish, striped bass, weakfish, and bluefish may take up station in these rips and feed on the baitfish that become trapped in the whirlpool-like eddies. Often this activity is accompanied by sea gulls and other sea birds picking baitfish from the water. This is when a big surface swimming plug cast out into the rips and just held in the current, where it swims as the current pushes against it, may bring exciting surface strikes.

See: Surf Fishing; Tide.

JEWFISH *Epinephelus itajara.*

Other names—spotted jewfish, southern jewfish, junefish, Florida jewfish, esonue grouper; Fon (spoken in Benin): *tokokogbo;* French: *mérou géant;* Portuguese: *garoupa, mero;* Spanish: *cherna, cherne, mero, guasa, meroguasa.*

The largest of the grouper and a member of the Serranidae family, the jewfish is an important gamefish and an excellent food fish. Marketed fresh and salted, the meat is of excellent quality, finely grained, white, and with a strong flavor. The jewfish has been overfished, mainly through spearfishing and particularly in Florida, where it is completely protected from harvest. Larger fish exhibit a great deal of curiosity, leaving their caves to investigate and interfere with diving operations, sometimes even trying to eat divers.

Identification. The jewfish is yellowish brown to olive green or brown. Dark brown blotches and blackish spots mottle the entire body, including the head and fins; these markings are variable and more prominent on the young. Irregular dark bands run vertically along the sides of the jewfish, although these are usually obscure. The body becomes darker with age as the blotches and spots increase and become less noticeable in contrast to the body. The first dorsal fin is shorter than, and not separated from, the second dorsal fin. The jewfish is differentiated from the giant sea bass by its dorsal fin soft rays, of which it has 15 to 16; the giant sea bass has only 10. Distinctive features of the jewfish also include a very small eye, a rounded tail fin, and large rounded pectoral fins. Jewfish smaller than $1^1/_2$ feet long bear a strong resemblance to spotted cabrilla but can be distinguished by the number of dorsal spines, of which the jewfish has 11 and the spotted cabrilla 10.

Jewfish

Size/Age. Jewfish can reach 8 feet in length and 700 pounds in weight. Although the average fish weighs roughly 20 pounds, weights of 100 pounds are not unusual, nor are 4- to 6-foot lengths. The all-tackle world record for jewfish is a 680-pounder taken in Florida in 1961. They have been known to live for 30 to 50 years.

Distribution. In the western Atlantic, jewfish occur from Florida to southern Brazil, including the Gulf of Mexico and the Caribbean, although they are rare in Florida, the Bahamas, and the Caribbean. In the eastern Atlantic, they occur from Senegal to Congo, though they are rare in the Canary Islands. In the eastern Pacific, jewfish occur from the central Gulf of California to Peru.

Habitat. Jewfish inhabit inshore waters, and juveniles are common in mangrove areas and estuaries, especially around oyster bars. Both juveniles and adults frequent bays and harbors. Usually found in shallow water at depths between 10 and 100 feet, jewfish prefer rocky bottoms, reefs, ledges, dock and bridge pilings, and wrecks, where they can find refuge in caves and holes. Extremely territorial, jewfish seem to have limited home ranges, where they stay for years at a time.

Life history/Behavior. There is some indication that the jewfish starts out as a female and undergoes a sex change later in life, as occurs in certain grouper. Spawning takes place over summer months.

Food and feeding habits. A sluggish but opportunistic feeder, jewfish feed chiefly on crustaceans, especially spiny lobsters, as well as turtles, fish, and stingray.

Angling. Despite its poor fighting ability (mostly strong pulling through massive weight), the jewfish's great size and weight, and its habit of swimming into a hole or between rocks when hooked, make it difficult to land. It can be taken on live or dead baits fished on the bottom from boats, bridges, or shore. Slow trolling also works on occasion. Baits include crabs, spiny lobsters, mullet, grunts, mackerel, conch, clams, fish heads, and cut baits. Extremely heavy tackle is necessary, given the jewfish's large size.

See: Grouper; Inshore Fishing.

J

Jigs come in a variety of weights, bodies, and colors.

JIG

An artificial lure with a metal head molded to a single hook. The hook shank is never fished plain and may be dressed with fur, feathers, rubber, soft plastic, pork rind, or other synthetic materials, and occasionally with live or dead natural bait. In some cases these materials are permanent; in others they're removable and easily replaceable. The shape of the head varies widely (primarily variations of oval, ball, bullet, pancake, and angled designs) as does the color of the head and body. Various metals may be used for the head, although lead is by far the most common and its use is partly why many people refer to this type of lure as a leadhead. Head size primarily determines weight, which is normally between $^1/_8$ ounce and 2 ounces but can be several ounces more and can be found down to $^1/_{64}$ ounce.

A jig is one type of lure that cuts across species, since some type or size of jig has near-universal appeal to the widest possible range of gamefish. Its other virtues include the fact that a jig is aerodynamic and casts very well, it sinks quickly so it gets down in the water column fairly fast, and it can be effective in cold and warm water alike. As with any lure, however, its successful use depends largely upon skillful manipulation by the angler.

Although jigs are a preeminent North American type of lure, they do not enjoy quite the international freshwater use that spinners *(see)* or spoons *(see)* do. In fact, in some places, terminology and language differences have confused the act of fishing a jig, called jigging, with the act of deliberately snagging *(see)* or foul-hooking a fish. Deliberately snagging a gamefish is generally illegal and is always unsporting; in fact, the design of a true jig makes snagging difficult to do, and even accidental snagging is an unusual occurrence. Furthermore, true jigs have only a single hook, which is easier to remove from a fish that will be released than the treble hooks found on lures.

Most true jigs have hair, synthetic, or soft-plastic bodies, and smaller sizes see a lot of crossover use, especially in freshwater fishing; if an angler has a decent selection of these lures, some can be pressed into duty at any time for a particular fish or angling circumstance. Many of the same $^1/_8$-ounce marabou or soft-plastic curl-tail jigs that catch smallmouth bass, for example, can also be employed to catch walleye, bluegill, yellow perch, trout, and white bass, and they can contribute to the unintended catch of such fish as pike or pickerel. The same jigs that will catch big striped bass in freshwater or saltwater will also catch large, deep-dwelling lake trout in freshwater as well as bottom-dwelling groupers in saltwater. Perhaps the preferred colors will differ, but they don't always. When you consider the crossover value, plus the fact that jigs are inexpensive enough that you don't fret over losing one (which happens fairly often, especially when using light tackle), it seems that carrying along a few jigs ought to be as routine as filling your fishing reel with line.

Components. Head design, body dressing, and hook style are the major components of all jigs.

Head design, or shape, influences not only the weight but also the sink rate, action, and ability to avoid getting snagged. There are many shapes of jig heads, as well as variations of stan-

Jig Head Styles

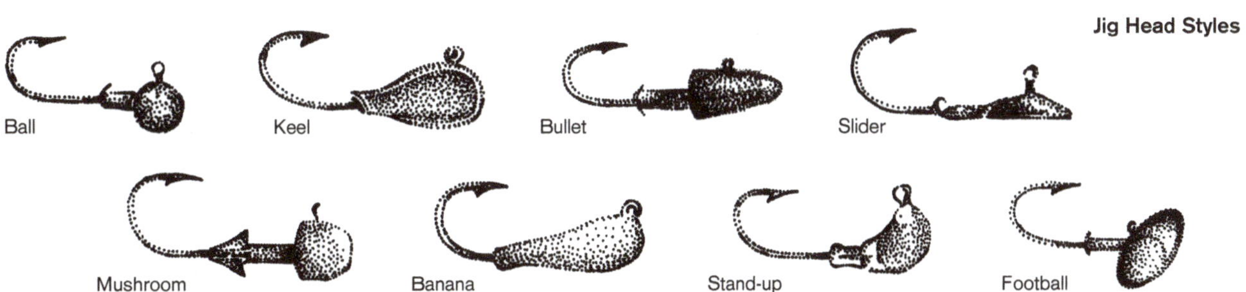

J

dard shapes. The most common shape is the ball head, which sinks fast and has near-universal use. Another popular and fast-sinking style is the bullet head, which is good in current and resists snagging somewhat better than a ball head. The football head is a compact, heavy head that is good with big bodies, sinks fast, and holds bottom well. A keel head is somewhat flattened on the sides and rounded on the bottom; it sinks fast and is especially suited for heavy current. A mushroom head is somewhat of a cross between the bullet and the ball, with a flat inside head that allows a plastic body to fit flush to the head; it usually has a body-holding barb. Other fairly common designs include the slider, a flat slow-sinking head; the pancake, a flat-sided design with little drag and wide action; the banana, a vertical-fishing head with a forward-most line tie (hook eye) and forward weighting; and the stand-up, also a weight-forward design and one that is fairly snag-free.

Just as there are many types of jig heads, so are there many body dressings. Hair jigs, primarily sporting bucktail, are old favorites, durable and active in the water. Some also feature marabou feathers, which have good action but lack durability. Soft bodies, primarily of plastic, but also a mix of plastic and natural organisms, are very popular; these slow the sink rate and have both excellent feel and action, and the appearances of some imitate natural foods. Soft bodies feature curl-tail, grub, fishtail, and paddletail configurations, and though they have good action they lack durability. Various pork rind or soft-plastic products adorn the jigs used by black bass anglers for casting and flipping. Jigs tipped with natural or dead bait, including earthworms, minnows, leeches, chunks of fish flesh, or other items have merit for many freshwater fish, and jigs in saltwater are routinely fished with sandworms or chunks or strips of fish or squid.

In 1996, an angler was about to land a huge marlin when his wire leader wrapped around the rod. The fish lunged away, pulling him overboard, stripping the guides off the rod, and breaking the line. The angler suffered only scratches and a dislocated finger.

The style of hook on a jig also varies. Lighter, smaller jigs have fine-wire hooks that penetrate easily; the lighter models are easily straightened (and freed from snags) when heavy pressure is applied. Thicker hooks, some forged, are used with heavier jig heads in more demanding situations.

In addition to these basic components, some jigs incorporate a very small spinner blade on them. The spinner blade is usually attached to a small stub under the lead head or is affixed to the bend in the hook. The flash and the movement of the blade help attract fish, making this a versatile jig that can be fished conventionally or fished on a slow but steady retrieve and a stop-and-go manner. Some anglers refer to these as spinner-jigs, and they are overlooked by most jig users. Small versions are good for yellow perch, white bass, crappie, and small bass.

Small jigs are also used in conjunction with a spinner blade that is attached to an overhead wire arm. Technically this turns the lure into a spinnerbait *(see)*, although the arm is removable and the lure can be used as a jig or as a spinnerbait on a quicker retrieve if circumstances warrant.

As a category, jigs have the simplest appearance of all artificial lures, but they are a bit of an anomaly in that, at rest, they don't closely resemble fish, insects, or other aquatic forage. Also, for a lure type that catches such a wide range of species, a jig is not a cast-and-crank product. For an item with such productive potential, many anglers do not use jigs because they find working these lures hard to master. At the heart of such anomalies is the key to catching fish with jigs: Success is directly proportional to your ability to impart action to the lure, effect a proper style of retrieval, and detect strikes. These issues are detailed in the entry on jigging *(see)*.

Although jigs may be broken down by size for categorizing as panfish jigs, bass and walleye jigs, saltwater jigs, etc., the basic categories are simple: jig and pork/eel combinations, which are popularly used in freshwater bass fishing; and jigs with hair, synthetic, or soft-plastic bodies, which are available in all sizes and used widely in both freshwater and saltwater. These types are fished differently and have distinct characteristics and applications, however.

True jigs as described here are sometimes confused with, and categorically lumped with, jigging spoons, which are fished in a vertical manner *(see: spoon)*. There is also a trolling lure known as a feathered jig or simply feathers, which has no true jigging application *(see: trolling lures, salt-water)*. In order to distinguish true jigs from other types of lures that can be jigged, many anglers call these lures leadheads, although lead is not the only material used in the construction of the head.

Jig and Pork

Pork rind has been used for years as a jig garnish, starting with strips and continuing with shaped chunks. These combinations have proven versatile and especially effective in freshwater fishing for largemouth and smallmouth bass. Pork strips are made of pork rind that has been stripped of fat. Chunks have a layer of fat on them, giving them bulk and weight in addition to different action.

A jig with a strip of cured pork rind on its hook is an old-time bait, known as a jig and eel. A jig with a chunk of pork on its hook became popular in the 1980s, and is variously called jig and chunk, jig and pig, jig and frog, etc. Pork baits and similar soft plastics to be used with jigs are available from several manufacturers and in a wide variety of forms.

Whereas the jig and pork combination of yesteryear was principally thought of as a cold-weather, semideep bait, today it's a hallmark of versatility, being fished for bass almost anywhere. With a weedguard, it penetrates the most imposing tangles. Without, it is very effective in open-water sanctums. Fish it deep, shallow, or in between.

The most successful application of this jig is probably in the bushes, brush, and submerged treetops. In the springtime, the shallow bushes along banks often hold bass. The fish are deep in the middle of these bushes, which may be located in 5 to 10 feet of water. Few anglers toss a lure into the heart of these tangles, and a plastic worm, cast from a good distance away, often scours only the periphery of the bush and may not be effective unless bass come out after it. By getting close to these objects, an angler can flip or pitch a jig right into this brush, work it through and out of the entanglement, and snake a hooked bass out with less difficulty than would otherwise be possible. The same is true for logjams and the roots of stumps or trees and other thick hard-to-fish spots. This is why the technique of flipping *(see)* is so effective, and why these lures are part of that bass fishing method.

Rocky banks can be another strong jig and pork locale, particularly if they have a very steep dropoff and possess a lot of craggy, ledgelike rock formations. Bass will usually seek refuge in the crags and under the ledges but are often not susceptible to lures like diving plugs or falling-away plastic worms. On rocky banks jigs can be flipped or cast. In both cases, present the jig close to the edge of the rock and allow it to fall vertically as close to the bank as you can. Crawl it off each ledge, over each rock, swimming it along as unobtrusively as possible, and working it under the boat or as deep as your cast will permit. Always work the lure slowly, keeping light tension on the line, and be prepared to set the hook the instant a strike is detected.

Yet another prime application for these jigs is a situation in which bass are holding tightly in very dense cover, such as milfoil, hyacinths, floating mats of hydrilla and debris, grassy shoals, or bridge pilings and boat docks. Some of these objects can be very difficult to fish with conventional casting techniques, but by getting close and by quietly (and accurately) flipping a jig around them, you can achieve some highly effective results. In thickly matted clusters of vegetation, drop the jig in any hole that is visible, and jig it up and down repeatedly therein. In some cases you may even have to make your own holes.

The weight of jig and pork that you use depends primarily on the depth of the water, but also upon wind and current conditions. For deep-bank work, a $^1/_4$-ounce lure on light line might do the trick, but more likely you'll need a $^5/_{16}$-ounce jig and may even have to go up to $^1/_2$ ounce. For flipping the bushes and such, size may vary from $^3/_{16}$ ounce to as much as $^3/_4$ ounce. The color is usually dark, with black, brown, or purple being best. It's good to also have some jigs with a weedguard (the forked style seems best). For pork chunks, a pork rind that weighs $^1/_4$ ounce and measures 1 inch by $2^1/_2$ inches is favored, in black, brown, or multiple colors. The chunk, incidentally, can be trimmed with a knife to make it fall faster.

To care for the pork baits after use, keep them in the container of brine that they came in. After you're finished with a pork chunk, put it back in the manufacturer's jar or some other wet container. While fishing, keep the pork wet; otherwise, it will dry and shrivel up and become useless. One way to keep it wet when it's not being used is to toss the jig and pork into a boat livewell.

To attach pork to a lure, locate the slit at the head of the bait and insert the hook point through it. To remove the pork, turn it sideways at a right angle to the hook point, grab the hook with one hand and the pork with the other, and carefully exert pressure to pull the pork down while pulling the barb out.

These are, obviously, big baits. Even a $^1/_4$-ounce jig with a twin-tailed strip trailer or frog chunk weighs closer to $^1/_2$ ounce. Specifically what they represent is speculative, though crayfish and salamanders seem plausible. Unquestionably, these unobtrusive baits ring the chow bell in both cold and warm water for largemouth and smallmouth bass, and they constitute one of the better big-bass baits in use today.

Soft Plastic and Hair Jigs

Conventional jigs come in various head styles, featuring bucktail or synthetic hair bodies, or soft-plastic bodies. Jigs with a bucktail dressing are commonly called bucktails or bucktail jigs, and are popular in large sizes, especially in saltwater, because they have good bulking characteristics and display movement well. Soft-plastic bodies are more abundant and can be attached to the hook of a jig for use as is or in combination with a hair or synthetic body. They come in many

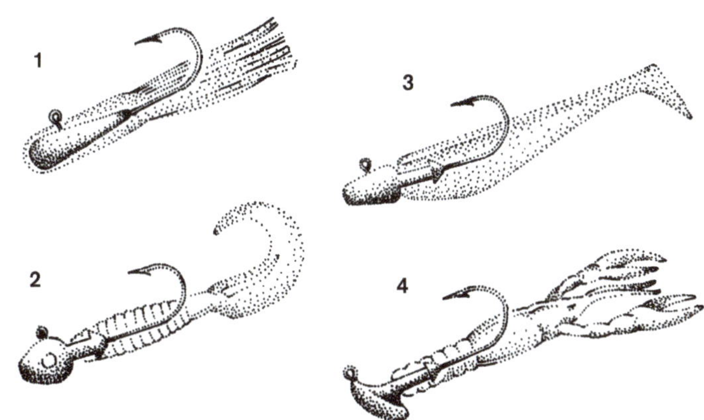

Different soft bodies are rigged on appropriate styles of jig head as shown. Common arrangements from top to bottom include: tube jig (1), grub jig (2), shad-body jig (3), and crayfish (4).

styles. Some are in the form of hellgrammite, crayfish, or shad imitations; others are spider-legged or shaped like a tube or grub. Many are simply long and curly, somewhat like a worm, snake, eel, leech, and so on.

Grubs and tubes are probably the top soft-plastic body forms for jigs used in freshwater fishing; in saltwater these and longer eel-like bodies are equally popular. Grub bodies are solid and either flat-tailed or curl-tailed; they are threaded onto the hook from the head and have a tight, well-defined action if rigged properly. Tube jigs are hollow with many squidlike legs in lieu of a tail; a tube jig head is worked through the body from back to front with only the line-tie hook exposed; the jig has an erratic action when fished on a drop-and-fall.

The weight of the jig itself is the most important aspect in fishing it, and this may vary from $^1/_8$ to $^1/_2$ ounce for freshwater bass fishing, from $^1/_{16}$ to $^3/_{16}$ ounce for panfishing, and from $^1/_2$ to 3 ounces for saltwater fishing, although this is just a broad characterization. Choice should be dependent upon the depth of the water, its clarity, the wind conditions, the strength of the line used, and the type of jig. This may sound involved, but it really isn't.

Use the lightest jig that you can under the circumstances. You don't want a jig to sink too fast, which would appear unnatural, yet you need the appropriate size to attain necessary depth. When fishing in a lake with current or when fishing in flowing water like a stream or river, you'll need to use a heavier jig than you would if the current were not present. Another influential factor is wind. The harder the wind blows, the more difficult it is for the unanchored angler to hold bottom with a light jig.

Jigging depth is also influenced by the size of your line; the heavier the line, the greater its diameter and the more drag it has in the water, which obviously reinforces the fact that light jigs fall more slowly than heavier ones. Then, too, the clearer and shallower the water, the more you should be using light jigs for less obtrusive presentations. These considerations all add up to interpreting the effects of the elements and selecting the best size of lure according to the conditions.

Light hair jigs, grubs, and tube jigs are usually better fished with spinning tackle than baitcasting gear. They cast better with spinning tackle, where the bail remains open and the lure falls relatively straight once it hits the water. With baitcasting gear, you usually have to pay out line by hand after the cast to get the jig to fall straight. With heavier jigs, of course, this is not a factor.

Flat-tailed grubs should be placed on the shank of the jig in such a way that their tails ride flat, or horizontal, to achieve a good side-to-side falling action. When rigging curl tails, use the side seam as a guideline, and rig it so that the curl tail rides up vertically in the same direction as the hook. The length of these flat-tailed or curl-tailed soft plastics varies from $1^1/_2$ to 3 inches. There are many successful colors for soft-plastic bodies; gray (or smoke), green, black, purple, white, and chartreuse are traditional, but pumpkinseed, Junebug, and assorted combinations with embedded metal flecks are very popular. For hair bodies, the best colors are black, brown, yellow, and white.

To work hair-bodied and grub jigs, you must first let them settle to the bottom wherever you've cast. When fishing a moderately sloping shoreline or point, you should slowly pull the lure a little bit off the bottom, let it settle down while keeping in contact with the lure, take up the slack, and repeat this. When working a ledge or a sharply sloping shoreline, slowly pull the lure over the structure until it begins to fall, let it settle, and then repeat. Don't hop the jig up quickly here, because it will fall out and away from the bottom, most likely missing a good deal of the important terrain.

A good technique with grubs is to make them jump quickly off the bottom rather than make short hops. You can also swim a grub on the edges of cover by reeling it slowly across the bottom and giving it occasional darting movements by manipulating your rod tip. The majority of strikes while jigging with these lures will come as the lure falls back down, so be alert for a strike then, and keep both a good feel and an eye on your line to detect this. Tube jigs are better if fished more in a hopping motion than a crawling one. Hop a tube jig off the bottom and let it flutter back. These lures spiral downward rather than dive, and they're often used on lighter jig heads (like $^1/_{16}$ ounce) than other lures, as well as on light or ultralight spinning gear, which has led some to refer to their use as "finesse" fishing.

These lures can also be fished in a vertical manner, and this is common in all sizes depending on the circumstances. Crappie, for example, can be caught on light jigs fished vertically over cover such as a brushpile; bottom-dwelling saltwater species can be caught on heavy jigs worked just over a reef or wreck. Vertical jigging is discussed further in the entry on jigging.

See: Lure.

JIG AND EEL

See: Jig.

JIG AND PORK

See: Jig.

JIGGERPOLING

Jiggerpoling is an old-time method of making a quiet, sneaky presentation of a lure close to cover, primarily used in fishing for largemouth bass. Jiggerpoling is done with a minnow-shaped float-

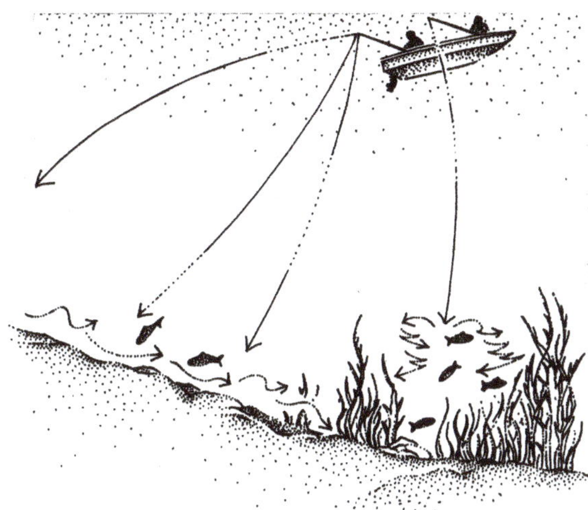

Depending on circumstances, anglers can fish by casting toward shore and jigging a lure back along bottom, or by vertically fishing a jig or jigging spoon on or just slightly above bottom or objects.

ing plug or a hooked piece of fish belly or pork strip attached to the tip of a long cane pole via a short length of line. The angler sits in the bow of a boat (often a pirogue or small jonboat), prowls shallow cover, and rapidly jiggers or dapples the lure in and around grassy banks and stumps. The angler usually fishes directly in front of the boat, which is paddled or poled by someone in the stern. This is effective where the water is murky and where bass are likely to be close to cover, especially along the bank.

JIGGING

One thing that a jig is not is a throw-it-out-and-reel-it-back-in kind of lure, one that can catch fish in spite of the abilities of the person using it. An angler has to put some work into making a jig catch fish and into being able to detect strikes. There is a knack to jigging. Good jig users have a feel for what is happening to their lure and they have a razor-sharp ability to detect and respond to strikes.

The key to jigging success is establishing contact with your lure, getting and keeping it where the fish are, and using the right rod to feel a strike. The greatest concerns are often how deep you need to fish a particular jig and how effective you are at doing that. Jigs excel at being on or close to the bottom, which is where the majority of jig-caught fish are found. They also are productive for covering the area between the bottom and upper levels via vertical presentations.

Covering bottom. When fishing on or close to the bottom, many anglers do not have success because they fail to reach and keep their jigs on the bottom. The simplest way to get a jig to reach the bottom is to open the bail of your spinning reel or depress the freespool mechanism on a baitcasting, spincasting, or conventional reel; let the lure fall freely until the line goes slack on the surface of the water and no more comes off the spool. If the water is calm and the boat still, you can readily detect when you're on the bottom. If it is somewhat windy or if current is present, you have to watch the departing line carefully to detect the telltale slack and to differentiate between line that is leaving the spool because the lure has not reached bottom and line that is being pulled off by a drifting lure or boat. If you're fishing from a boat, a depthfinder can help you determine when your lure has reached the bottom because you will have some idea of the local depth.

The lighter (and thinner) the line and the heavier the lure, the easier it is to reach the bottom. The stronger the line, the greater its diameter will be and the more resistance it will offer in the water. A quarter-ounce jig will fall more quickly on 8-pound line than it will on 14-pound line, for example. The advantage here (the magnitude of which depends on fishing conditions) is that you will more easily get your lure to the bottom and keep it on the bottom with 8-pound line than with 14-pound line.

A typical scenario for jigging the bottom is to let the jig fall freely until the line goes slack. Reel up slack and lift the jig off the bottom. Once you're on the bottom, you need to maintain contact with it. Assuming that you have cast your jig some distance away, have let it settle to the bottom, and are now

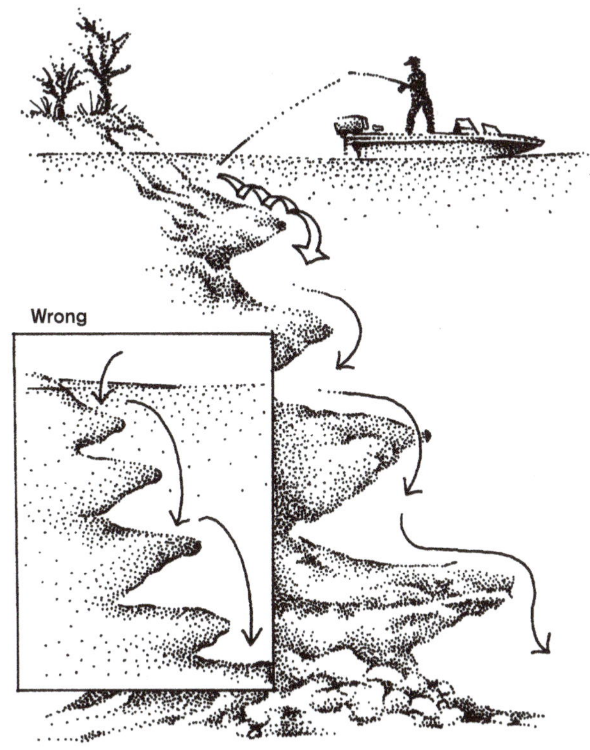

When jigging along a steep shoreline, such as this ledge, retrieve the jig in short, slow hops to crawl the jig along and let it flutter to the next ledge below. Long sweeps of the rod bring the jig out and away (inset), missing some of the best cover.

J

retrieving it toward yourself, you should keep it working in short hops along the bottom as long as the terrain and length of paid-out line enable you to do so. If you are in a boat and drifting, the jig will eventually start sweeping upward and away from you and the bottom as you drift, unless it is very heavy; so you need to pay out more line occasionally until the angle of your line has changed significantly and then reel in and drop the jig back down again.

Choosing the right weight lure to use is critical to most types of jigging. The ideal is to have a lure that gets to the bottom and stays there under normal conditions but that is not too large to intimidate the fish. Most anglers who fail to reach bottom don't use the right retrieval technique or don't compensate for wind or current; in addition, they may use too light a jig for getting down to the bottom under the conditions that they face.

Sometimes you need to swim a jig by pumping it slowly and reeling, never actually letting it hop along the bottom. Other times you may need to slowly drag it. When fishing a moderately sloping shoreline or point, for example, you should slowly pull the lure a little bit off the bottom, let it settle down while keeping in contact with it, take up the slack, and repeat this. When working a ledge or a sharply sloping shoreline, slowly pull the lure over the structure until it begins to fall, let it settle, and then repeat. Don't hop the jig up quickly here, because it will fall out and away from the bottom and likely miss a good deal of the important terrain. With some jigs, such as grubs, a good technique is to make them jump quickly off the bottom rather than make short hops. You can also swim a jig on the edges of cover by reeling it slowly across the bottom and giving it occasional darting movements by manipulating your rod tip. The majority of strikes while jigging come as the bait falls back down, so be alert for a strike then and concentrate on the feel of your line to detect it.

Scientists have answered the age-old question "do fish sleep?" affirmatively. Fish have no eyelids, so their eyes remain open, and many assume sleeping postures and positions.

Jigs also have value in rivers and where there is current. In a fair amount of current, you should cast upstream or up-and-across-stream, engage the line-pickup system as soon as the lure splashes down, reel up slack, and try to keep the line taut by letting the jig drift or by reeling in slack to achieve a natural drift. You virtually fish a jig in quick water the same way a fly angler works a nymph, keeping slack out and rod tip up and feeling the lure as it bounces along. In deep, swift current, you actually need to swim the jig a bit by pumping the rod tip.

Vertical jigging. Jigging vertically, of course, is useful, especially when fishing through the ice in freshwater, when angling on the bottom in deep water, and when angling for suspended fish in open water. Here, both leadhead jigs and metal or lead spoons are used and you needn't maintain bottom contact, though you might start at the bottom and jig your way upward. Sometimes you'll need to get to a particular depth and regularly jig at that spot.

If you know what depth to fish, you can let the desired length of line out and commence jigging, never reeling in any line and paying out line only if you begin to drift. Here's one way to know how much line you're letting out: Reel the jig up to the rod tip, stick the rod tip on the surface, let go of the jig, and raise your rod tip to eye level; then stop the fall of the jig. If eye level is 6 feet above the surface, your jig will now be 6 feet deep. Lower the rod tip to the surface and do this again. Now you've let out 12 feet of line. Continue until the desired length is out. With a levelwind reel having a freely revolving line guide, you can measure the amount of line that is let out with each side-to-side movement of the line guide; multiply this amount by the number of times the guide travels back and forth. If you use a reel that doesn't have such a guide, you can strip line off the spool in 1-foot (or 18-inch) increments until the desired length is out. Another method is to count down the lure's descent. A falling rate of 1 foot per second is standard and may be accurate for medium-weight jigs, but you should check the lure's rate of fall in a controlled situation first to ensure accuracy.

For some vertical jigging, you may need to let your lure fall to the bottom and then jig it up toward the surface a foot or two at a time. Bring the lure off the bottom, and reel in the slack; then jig it there three or four times before retrieving another few feet of line and jigging the lure again. Repeat this until the lure is near the surface. The only problem here is that you don't usually know exactly how deep a fish is when you do catch one, and you can't just strip out the appropriate length of line and be at the proper level.

Detecting strikes/hooksetting. Discerning a strike when jigging can be difficult because so many fish don't slam a jig when they take it. Certainly some do, and there's no question then that a fish has struck, but in most light-jig usage where small fish are sought, something just a little "different" happens that signals a strike. That difference is often barely perceptible. The job of detection is made even less obvious by the fact that most strikes come when a jig is falling, which is often when the line has a slight amount of slack. If you fail to detect the strike quickly enough, the fish may reject the lure or you may be too late to set the hook properly.

In a sense, it's good to tight-line a jig backward as the jig falls, but don't use so much tension that the jig falls unnaturally and stiffly. You need to slightly lower your rod tip as the jig falls; when you feel something take the jig, set the hook quickly, keeping the rod tip high and reeling rapidly at the same time. A lot of jig-struck fish are lost because the angler, in reacting to a strike, raises the rod high but never gets the hook to penetrate the mouth of the fish. So the hook pulls out after a moment, or the fish jumps and throws the hook easily. A forceful hookset that eliminates slack, coupled with constant pressure and rapid reeling, is the way to avoid losing fish on a jig.

Having the right rod is also a big factor, especially in freshwater where jigs are usually fairly light. Light jigs are rarely fished well on stiff, heavy rods, and vice versa; wimpy super-flexible rods don't make good jigging rods, nor do the pool-cue versions. This is where that elusive quality of sensitivity comes into play. A well-tapered rod with a fast tip is preferable, and it's good to keep the tip angled upward. In some types of jigging, a low-stretch line is helpful. Great depths, very heavy jigs or jigging spoons, and fishing for large bottom fish that can quickly get into cover and break off are instances where lines with little or no stretch may be beneficial.

Two conditions that make strike detection more difficult when jigging are fishing jigs under windy conditions and fishing them in and around weeds. These conditions also make it more difficult to maintain jig depth and control. Many anglers tip their jig hooks with bait; for fishing around vegetation, the best bait is a leech. The leeches work better for weed fishing than nightcrawlers because worms get torn up too easily through constant contact with weeds and the constant contact makes it hard to detect a strike, especially if the wind is up.

Developing a keen feel, especially in weeds, takes patience and practice. Realizing that the "tick" you feel is a fish (often a walleye or perch) sucking in your offering, takes some adjustment, although detection is usually easier with larger fish because they take in more water when they inhale a lure and thus the effect you feel is more pronounced. You will lose a number of fish, including a few good-sized ones, that you have momentarily hooked because you don't realize quickly enough that you have a strike instead of contact with a weed. Most of the time you feel the strike as you pull on the jig. Detecting that strike is made easier by using light jigs and light (6- or 8-pound) line on a spinning outfit.

If you must fish a jig in weeds when there is wind, try using a bobber with the jig in the weeds to counter the detection problem. An alternative is to use a split shot and jig, which will keep the lure down but is very hard to feel.

See: Jig.

JIGGING SPOON

See: Spoon.

JONBOAT

The term "jonboat" is used to refer to nearly any rectangularly shaped boat that has a flat bottom, a square bow and stern, and low straight sides. Also

Perfect for small waters and calm conditions, the jonboat is widely used in North America.

referred to as a flat-bottom boat, and frequently called a rowboat, this is one of the most common and oldest types of fishing craft.

Jonboats are frequently used with low-horsepower outboard motors or electric motors, as well as with oars, poles, and paddles. Because of their low draft, they are especially useful in shallow-water fishing, particularly small lakes, ponds, and rivers. In rivers, when shallow sections are encountered, jonboat users simply tilt up a motor if they are using one, get onto the gravel bar, and walk the boat down to deeper water to continue on. Jonboats are primarily used in freshwater but are not meant for big bodies of water or places that might experience heavy wave and wind conditions.

These simple-design boats feature a fair amount of interior room, and they are quite stable if properly loaded, although the shorter and narrower versions can be tipsy. They are light and easily maneuvered and are preferred over canoes by many anglers because of their ruggedness, roominess, and standup fishing stability. Anglers can easily stand up and fish in jonboats, including those 14 feet or longer, as well as some 12-footers; they can also readily transport a jonboat to the water, which is an asset in many places where access is unimproved. Many anglers use 12- to 14-foot jonboats, which can be toted atop a car or on a trailer. Long and narrow jonboats are used in stream and river float fishing, especially in the Ozarks; they sport small outboards placed on a high-backed transom for shallow-water running.

Most jonboats today are made of aluminum, although older models were wooden, which made them heavier and in more need of maintenance; some jonboatlike vessels are made from various plastics. The flat-bottom jonboat hull has been used on boats with more complex interiors, in effect, putting consoles, decks or raised platforms, livewells, and similar options on them, and making them into a form of bass boat or at least a more advanced jonboat.

Many anglers have customized basic jonboats, especially in 14- and 16-foot lengths, with fishing and boating accessories including fore and aft decks, bow-mount electric motors, rod holders, fixed-mount sonar, and other items. Many of these customized boats are used on slightly bigger waters but still require avoidance of rough conditions because of their low freeboard. They also produce a tooth-rattling, rump-aching ride if they have to be taken through rough water. In smaller, less souped-up jonboats, savvy anglers carpet the bottom to deaden sounds, or make a flooring of wooden slats or plywood supported by wooden slats or aluminum braces.

See: Boat.

J

JUG HOOK

A single hook and line attached to a floating jug rather than to a hand-operated mechanical reel. The hook is usually baited, and it may or may not be attended. A jug hook, also simply called jug or a jugline, is prohibited in some places; where legal, its use and location may be regulated. A jug hook may also be called a setline *(see)*, or set hook *(see)*. Although using a jug hook may be considered fishing, and such usage may be covered under established regulations, a jug hook is not a sportfishing instrument, and jug fishing is not sportfishing.

JUMP BAIT

A term for small, easy-to-cast metal lures that are used in quick-casting to schools of surface-feeding white bass, largemouth bass, and striped bass.

See: Spoon.

JUMP FISHING

Spotting, chasing, and fishing for schooling fish that are feeding on the surface; this term is generally used in freshwater for striped bass.

See: Schooling.

JURUPOCA

A South American catfish.

See: Catfish.

K

KAHAWAI *(Australian Salmon)*

Other names—Australian salmon, sea trout (New Zealand), bay trout, salmon trout, black-backed salmon, cockie salmon, sambo, colonial salmon.

This is one of the finest light-tackle gamefish in the world but one known to relatively few people and the subject of confusion. *Kahawai* is a Maori word for fish of the Arripidae family that are found in the inshore waters of New Zealand and Australia. Confusion exists over whether there are two or three species in this family, and the proper terminology; kahawai are also widely known, especially in Australia, as Australian salmon, although they are not a true salmon.

The Arripidae family is believed to consist of two kahawai and possibly one smaller relative, the Australian ruff (*Arripis georgianus;* also known as tommy rough, sea herring roughy, and Australian herring), which occurs off the southern coast of Australia.

The two kahawai consist of the eastern *(Arripis trutta)* and western *(A. esper)* species. Confusion over identity arises between the two species because adults of the eastern species are chiefly plankton feeders, whereas the western species feed mainly on small pilchards, anchovies, garfish, and squid. To compound the problem, in Australia the eastern species rarely moves across to the West Coast, whereas the western species is well known in East Coast waters as far north as Eden on the South Coast of New South Wales. Because eastern Australian salmon are predominately plankton feeders, individuals caught by surf and rock anglers using pilchards, garfish, or lures are most likely to be the western Australian salmon.

Identification. Both species have a moderately rounded elongate body and are difficult to differentiate. The dorsal fin has nine spines and 15 to 19 rays, and the anal fin is much shorter. The caudal fin is forked, and pectoral fins are bright yellow. The back and upper sides are olive green to steel blue with small dark spots, the color changing to pale yellow green to silvery white below. The western species has 25 to 31 gill rakers, and the eastern species 33 to 40. It is doubtful that anglers can distinguish between the two species without counting the gill rakers, which only the rarest angler will bother to do.

Size. Kahawai are known to reach 10.5 kilograms and a length of 80 centimeters. A land-based capture of the all-tackle world record, weighing 8.74 kilograms, was made in Australia in 1994, but the average specimen weighs from 3 to 4 kilograms.

Distribution. The eastern species of kahawai are generally confined to New Zealand, and in Australia to the waters of Bass Strait and along the East Coast of Australia as far north as Brisbane, Queensland, and across to Norfolk Island, Lord Howe Island, and New Zealand. Rarely do they find their way across to Western Australian waters. The western species ranges from Kalbarri in Western Australia, around the bottom of Australia to Tasmania, and as far north as Eden on the south coast of New South Wales. Strays may find their way northward, but they are rarely taken much farther north than Sydney.

Habitat. These fish inhabit estuaries, bays, inlets, and the open sea, especially over reefs and around rocky headlands, and in gutters along surf beaches. They tend to remain well out from the beach, necessitating casts in excess of 50 meters by surf anglers. Juveniles often inhabit the upper reaches of estuaries, where water salinity is low.

Life history/Behavior. The western species spawns from February through June in waters off the southwest corner of Western Australia. Juveniles migrate across the Great Australian Bight to South Australia, Victoria, southern New South Wales, and Tasmania, progressively appearing in bays and inlets from July through October as they travel eastward. Some (western populations) mature in their third or fourth year, and others (eastern populations) in four to six years. Maturing fish eventually return to the Western Australian spawning grounds to complete the cycle.

The eastern species spawns between November and February off the southeast coast of Australia. Juveniles migrate to Tasmanian and Victorian waters, with some dispersing northward along the New South Wales coast. They mature in their fourth year. In Victorian and Tasmanian waters, schools of both western and eastern species are known to mix.

Food and feeding habits. Juveniles of both

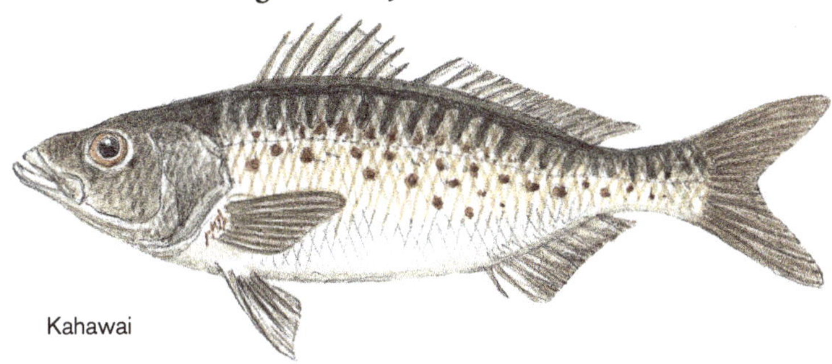

Kahawai

species feed on small fish, crustaceans, squid, and worms. On reaching maturity, the eastern species feeds mainly on zooplankton such as krill and other small crustaceans, and the western species feeds chiefly on pilchards, anchovies, garfish, and squid. Both are known to eat beach worms, which are often used as baits by surf anglers.

Angling. The kahawai challenges surf, rock, and boat anglers, and is considered by most people to be the finest light-tackle sportfish found in Australian and New Zealand waters. It is superior to the tailor (bluefish) in its fighting qualities.

Surf anglers, using 3- to 4-meter surf rods and spinning, conventional, or side-cast reels spooled with 5- to 7-kilogram monofilament line, resort to high-speed spinning or baitfishing. Favored baits are whole pilchards and garfish, and strip bait, rigged on four or five linked 4/0 hooks. Because these fish rarely venture closer than 50 meters from shore, sinkers up to 113 grams are used to ensure that the necessary casting distance is achieved. Since kahawai tend to be timid, hesitant takers—and will often drop a bait if they feel a weight attached to it—the sinker is rigged so that the line runs freely through it. This also serves to prevent the fish, during a head-shaking run, from using the weight of the sinker to dislodge the hook.

Rock-based anglers use tackle similar to that of the surf angler, but favor high-speed spinning reels. Where bait is used, it is suspended under a float cast to gutters and reefs, or it is cast unweighted and retrieved. Lures are usually metal minnow- or pencil-shaped hexagonals with treble hooks. For productive fishing, both surf and rock anglers must be experienced in the identification of the channels, gutters, and reefs the salmon frequent.

Boat anglers find trolling especially effective, and use pilchards and garfish rigged on linked (ganged) hooks, trolled slowly 15 to 20 meters behind the boat. Lures, including feathered jigs, metal lures, plastic minnow-type lures, and interior-weighted plastic squid (pink is good) are also used. Wire is seldom employed. Fly anglers use large streamers dressed with white, orange, blue, or red feathers (or a combination of these), which they cast from a boat to schooling salmon. Lure casters do likewise, using spoons, jigs, and plugs.

The kahawai is a spectacular fighting fish that head-shakes and tail-walks along the surface when hooked. Fish should not be pressured unduly, as hooks are easily torn from their soft mouth.

Although kahawai can be taken from most southern waters in Australia year-round, the best times to fish for them in southeastern Australia are during the autumn/winter months (March through August). In Western Australia, anglers prefer late summer and early autumn (February through May).

KANSAS

Although Kansas has only one natural lake, the state is a remarkably fine place to fish. Angling opportunities in its 83,000 square miles are provided largely by public impoundments, specifically 24 reservoirs, 46 state fishing lakes, and hundreds of city and county lakes, but also by thousands of privately owned watershed ponds where largemouth bass and panfish reign supreme.

Kansas has an ample array of species; some of the more popular and currently prominent ones are introduced species. Native fish include Kentucky (spotted) bass, channel catfish, flathead catfish, blue catfish, bullhead, several species of panfish, gar, paddlefish, drum, carp, and buffalo. Since the reservoir system was started in the 1950s, introduced species have included striped bass, wipers (hybrid striped bass), smallmouth bass, largemouth bass, white bass, walleye, sauger, saugeye, crappie, rainbow trout, and northern pike.

The most sought-after species statewide is crappie. White crappie are most abundant, primarily because of this fish's ability to do well in environments that vary from the clearer waters of the western and central reservoirs to the murkier impoundments of eastern Kansas.

For folks who enjoy river and stream fishing, Kansas also has hundreds of small and large tributaries to its three primary public river systems. The Arkansas River, the longest in Kansas, enters from Colorado and then travels east and southeast to Oklahoma, eventually joining the Mississippi in Arkansas. The Kansas River system, which begins as a public waterway at the confluence of the Smoky Hill and Republican Rivers near Fort Riley at Junction City, travels east, connecting with the Missouri River at Kansas City, Kansas. The Missouri, which is the largest and most powerful of the state's major rivers, cuts a jagged edge off the northeast corner of Kansas; those who fish from the middle of the river west need a Kansas fishing license; others require a Missouri license.

The Kansas and Missouri Rivers offer a plethora of gamefish species, largely because of the diverse fisheries in reservoirs along their lengths. The primary and most sought-after river species are flathead and channel catfish, but walleye, saugeye, white crappie, wipers, largemouth and smallmouth bass, and the usual mix of bottom feeders and gar also inhabit these waters.

In Kansas, only 1 percent of the state is available to the public for recreation of any form. Ninety-seven percent of the land is privately owned, and the remaining 2 percent consists of roads and right-of-ways. Although the Kansas, Arkansas, and Missouri Rivers are public waters, the land anglers must cross to fish them is often privately owned. Virtually all of the tributaries to the major rivers, save for the state- or federal-owned wildlife areas above and below reservoirs, are accessible to the public "by permission only."

There are, however, numerous public access points along the important rivers, and more continue to be developed. The Kansas Department of Wildlife and Parks produces a guide to Kansas fishing that lists all of the public access points as well as the exact locations of all public fishing areas, reservoirs, state fishing lakes, and city and county lakes.

The state fishing lakes in Kansas are intensely managed and consistently produce more angling success than other fisheries in the state. Each lake is managed individually by district fisheries biologists and each is subject to site-specific regulations that are posted at each lake.

Northwest/Central Region

This region, which incorporates the High Plains and the Smoky Hills, includes 8 reservoirs, 7 state fishing lakes, 10 community lakes, and 8 river access points. It is also the finest region in Kansas for largemouth bass, smallmouth bass, white crappie, black crappie, wipers, and walleye.

Norton Reservoir is a small, relatively clear impoundment with a high density of largemouth bass. Also known as Sebelius Reservoir, it is one of the state's finest saugeye, wiper, and black bass fisheries. Partially submerged tree lines and old roadbeds on the south edge of the lake provide ample fish cover. A deep sand pit at the upper end, on the south side, is a popular hangout for wipers, particularly in May.

Kirwin Reservoir is part of Kirwin National Wildlife Refuge near Phillipsburg. Because half of the lake is on the refuge, the fish are, in essence, protected from angling pressure. Like Norton, Kirwin is relatively clear and has large amounts of flooded trees and aquatic vegetation to provide nursery habitat for young fish. It is regarded as the finest Kansas lake for lunker white and black crappie, and its largemouth bass population is one of the best.

Webster Reservoir is famous for its walleye and wiper populations, and holds its own with black crappie. The lake has flooded timber at the upper end and plenty of rocky shoreline to hold largemouth bass.

Cedar Bluff Reservoir is one of Kansas' few east-west impoundments and has high limestone bluffs along a portion of its south side, a real bonus when battling the prevailing southwest winds. Almost dry in 1992, it was 50 feet below conservation pool and slowly filling with trees and shrubs when floods in 1993 and 1995 refilled the reservoir. An explosion in largemouth bass, walleye, channel catfish, wiper, and white bass populations followed. Cedar Bluff could well be the best fishing lake in Kansas, and, situated just 13 miles south of Interstate 70, it is a great stop for visitors.

Glen Elder and, to a slightly lesser degree, Lovewell Reservoir are excellent walleye fisheries, particularly during the spawn, when anglers "walk-troll" the face of dams. Fed by the Solomon River,

White bass are among the various panfish that provide good fishing at many Kansas lakes and ponds.

Glen Elder also produces high numbers of channel catfish, flatheads, white bass, and crappie. During high inflow periods, anglers routinely take large catfish at the upper end of the reservoir. In June, surface-feeding white bass become the hot ticket as anglers follow gulls feeding on the abundant gizzard shad under attack by white bass near the surface. In October, many anglers fish directly below cormorant roosting sites, a popular hangout for feeding channel catfish. And when Glen Elder ices over, it provides very good crappie fishing.

Wilson Reservoir, only 8 miles north of Interstate 70, is a blue-water gem. It is the clearest, coolest, and deepest public impoundment in Kansas, and certainly one of its finest striper, walleye, and smallmouth bass lakes. Even though stripers don't reproduce at Wilson, the high salinity provided by the inflow from the Saline River seems to enhance the lake's ability to growing large stripers. Although state records come and go, the three that Wilson seems to virtually own are for stripers, walleye, and smallmouth bass. The lake has productive dropoffs, long points, deep areas below the dam, and especially productive river and creek channels. White bass anglers also do well in June, when the whites are on top.

Kanopolis Reservoir, near Lindsborg in the Smoky Hills, is Kansas' oldest reservoir and remains a consistent producer of white crappie, walleye, white bass, and channel catfish. Anglers do well over roadbeds along the eastern edge and in an area known as the humps, an old borrow pit between two boat ramps on the southern shore.

Northeast Region

The densely populated northeast region contains five reservoirs, including the three largest in the state. It also has 13 state fishing lakes and significantly more community lakes and river access points than any other region in Kansas.

Tucked into the Flint Hills is Milford Reservoir, which, at 16,200 surface acres, is Kansas' largest impoundment. Fed by the Republican River, Milford is best known for consistently producing white crappie. But it also has a growing walleye and white bass population and, through a Wildlife and Parks stocking effort, some surprisingly large smallmouth bass.

Just a stone's throw to the east of Milford is Tuttle Creek Reservoir, the state's second largest at 15,800 surface acres. This long, narrow impoundment is embraced by the Flint Hills and is filled with hefty white crappie, flatheads, and channel catfish. The Rocky Ford area below the dam is a well-known hotspot for catfish anglers.

Located between Topeka and Lawrence is Perry Reservoir, the third largest impoundment in the state at 12,600 acres. It is well established as Kansas's best white crappie fishery. In spring, anglers head up into the Delaware River to take advantage of the crappie and white bass spawn, then they follow both species back into the main lake during the summer and winter months. The most famous fishing hole on Perry is the "Hog Trough," a channel cat–rich series of breaks just off the western shore about midway up the lake. Sometime in the 1980s a group of anglers, some say they were farmers, started chumming the area with spoiled, rank-smelling soybeans. The beans attracted the channel cats, and other anglers soon followed suit. Now, every day, rain or shine, scores of boats anchor up over the popular spot. To find it, just follow your nose. And it doesn't hurt to bring a 5-gallon bucket of nasty-smelling soybeans. Stinky cheese baits are the preferred hook bait.

The oldest complete-fish fossils were discovered in central Bolivia in the mid-1980s and have been dated at 450 million years old; the fish possessed armor and rounded head plates.

Clinton Reservoir, just under the gaze of the University of Kansas at Lawrence, is another fine crappie lake, and its white bass and channel cat aren't bad either. The stickups at the upper end, where the Wakarusa River enters, offer good opportunities for anglers to jig crappie at just about any time of year.

Hillsdale, the newest reservoir in Kansas, is still a 6,000-surface-acre work-in-progress located south of Olathe. However, it has already established itself as a promising largemouth and crappie fishery.

Southwest Region

Without a doubt the most arid region of Kansas, the southwest has no reservoirs but does hold 11 state fishing lakes, more than a dozen community lakes, and two access points to the Ninnescah River. But that doesn't mean you won't find good fishing as well as a few geological surprises.

Clark State Fishing Lake may hold only 337 surface acres, but all of them are in an area known as Fatty Evans Canyon, located at the upper end of the Gypsum Hills Region. Unseen until you reach the rim of the canyon, Clark not only offers a good angling experience, it does so in a beautiful setting. Good numbers of largemouth bass, walleye, and channel catfish thrive here.

Another scenic surprise is Scott State Fishing Lake, a 115-acre gem fed by four large springs and tucked into Ladder Creek Canyon, a few miles north of Scott City. The lake has largemouth bass and particularly nice bluegills and redear sunfish. Due to 56°F spring water, Scott also holds rainbow trout.

Encompassing only 80 acres, Meade State Fishing Lake is just a wet spot in the road, but it does offer good largemouth bass angling, especially along the cattails at the northwest end. The lake is near one of the four state fish hatcheries, but it's the only state hatchery that produces largemouth bass.

South-Central Region

South-central Kansas is the focal point for many anglers who fish the Arkansas River drainage. Located in the region are 4 reservoirs, 5 state fishing lakes, 15 community lakes, and several excellent river access points along the Arkansas, Chikaskia, Cottonwood, Little Arkansas, Neosho, and Walnut Rivers, as well as Grouse Creek.

Cheney and El Dorado Reservoirs are on either side of Wichita, Cheney being 20 miles to the west and El Dorado 30 miles to the east.

Cheney is well known for its walleye and striper populations, and for its white bass run each spring as the fish move into the North Fork of the Ninnescah to spawn. It is also a fine white crappie fishery and has been a consistent producer of lunker channel and flathead catfish. Like virtually all Kansas lakes, Cheney is relatively flat-bottomed; most anglers achieve success by jigging over old roadbeds, borrow pits, and submerged tree lines.

With 8,000 surface acres, El Dorado is 1,500 acres smaller than Cheney, but it has thousands of stickups left by the Army Corps of Engineers when the lake was impounded in the early 1980s. Once a powerhouse for largemouth bass, El Dorado has struggled as a bass fishery in recent years because of its lack of nursery habitat. This is primarily due to loss of shoreline vegetation from wind and water erosion. A program to reestablish aquatic vegetation has begun, and biologists are hopeful that the bass population will rebound once the habitat spreads along the shoreline. What El Dorado does have, however, is an ample supply of big walleye, a fish that seems to have found its niche in the windswept environment. The lake also has good white crappie and white bass populations, and the smallmouth bass have found homes in the riprap and borrow pits along the dam, as well as in other areas with rocky shorelines.

Marion Reservoir, about 50 miles north of Wichita, is a south-central Kansas hotspot for walleye, white crappie, white bass, wipers, and largemouth bass. And the catfishing is superb. Consistently ranked in the top five Kansas lakes for three to four species of gamefish, Marion is one of many Kansas reservoirs to reap fish population-explosion benefits from 1993 floods.

At the northeast corner of the south-central region is Council Grove Reservoir, a 3,500-acre impoundment on the north edge of Council Grove, the last pit stop on the Santa Fe Trail. Council Grove, fed by the Neosho River, is another white crappie mecca, and, along with Norton, is one of the two best saugeye lakes in Kansas. The main lake is a popular spot for boat anglers, but the spillway and seep stream are heavily fished by bank anglers, who pull in 40- to 60-pound flatheads as well as lunker saugeye. The saugeye get into the seep stream after spilling out of the reservoir.

An excellent river access area is at Grouse Creek, below Silverdale and some 6 miles east of Arkansas City. Located in the KAW Wildlife Area, Grouse Creek is one of the many fine Flint Hills streams that have Kentucky bass, green sunfish, bluegills, channel catfish, and flathead catfish. It also holds good numbers of long-nose gar, which provide entertainment for fly anglers who catch this species while fishing from float tubes. Of the three access points to Grouse Creek, only one has a boat ramp; it is roughly 50 yards above the spot where the creek flows into the Arkansas River.

Southeast Region

The southeastern portion of Kansas is an ecologically diverse area made up of hardwoods, streams, rivers, hills, and farmland. It holds seven reservoirs, and at least two towns on the Neosho River proclaim to be the Catfish Capital of Kansas.

Pomona and Melvern Reservoirs sit at the top of the region. Pomona is best known for producing the 90-pound state-record flathead, a feat that should stand for several years. Like so many reservoirs, Pomona has good numbers of white crappie and white bass. Melvern is the only Kansas impoundment with a viable sauger population. Sauger were introduced by the state in the 1980s to provide eggs and milt that would be combined with similar ingredients from walleye. The resulting saugeye hybrid are hatched and raised in a state hatchery adjacent to Milford Lake. Melvern is also a good walleye, white crappie, and largemouth bass fishery.

Down the road is John Redmond Reservoir, best known for its white bass. Crappie fishing in the Neosho River above the reservoir is rated as very good by the anglers who jig the "jam," an enormous clot of deadfall trees and limbs that span the river for up to a half mile.

Within eyesight of Redmond is Wolf Creek Reservoir, a 5,000-acre cooling lake for the Wolf Creek Nuclear Generating Plant. Closed to the public until 1995, this gem-quality lake has an incredible 70-30 predator-prey mix, the result of front-loading the lake with an enormous predator population of largemouth and smallmouth bass, walleye, wipers, stripers, white bass, and panfish, to keep the gizzard shad population in check. Wolf Creek is the finest smallmouth fishery in Kansas, and although these fish aren't huge, they are plentiful. Tight regulations ensure that Wolf Creek will be a premier lake for many years.

La Cygnes Lake is situated along Kansas' eastern edge. It doesn't officially count as a reservoir, but it certainly fits nicely into that category. Created as a cooling lake for a coal-fired electric generating plant, La Cygnes is the only Kansas lake with an established population of Florida-strain largemouth bass. It holds virtually every other species of fish found in Kansas, but it is the prospect of 9- and 10-pound largemouths that draws bass anglers here. Wipers are another favored species at La Cygnes.

The southern tier of the region has four reservoirs: Toronto, Elk City, Fall River, and Big Hill. In this part of the state it's not hard to find a flathead angler, especially at Toronto, a 2,800-acre lake that many flathead aficionados believe will yield the next state record. Fed by the slow-moving Verdegris River, it could be harboring a fish in excess of 90 pounds. Elk City, at 4,450 acres, is another fine fishing hole for anglers with a preference for white bass and white crappie. During the spawn it's not hard to run into a lunker largemouth or Kentucky bass if you follow the whites up into the Elk River.

Fall River, with 2,550 acres, offers the same mix as Elk City, but it has more angling access to the river above and below the reservoir. The areas above the reservoir are well known to crappie and white bass anglers. Big Hill has a sizable population of largemouth bass, as well as a 21-inch length limit; that limit makes the chance of a bass reaching 5 to 8 pounds better here than in other Kansas lakes. Clotted with stickups and deadfalls, the upper end of Big Hill has more than enough cover to provide ambush points for big bass.

KAWAKAWA *Euthynnus affinis.*

Other names—wavyback skipjack, eastern little tuna, mackerel, tuna, Pacific little tunny, false albacore, dwarf bonito; Cantonese: *to chung;* Hindi: *suraly;* Japanese: *hiragatsuo, obosogatsuo, soda, suma;* Malay: *ayu, bakulan, kayu;* Tagalog (Philippines): *katsarita, manko, pidlayan;* Turkish: *yazili.*

A member of the Scombridae family of mackerel, the kawakawa was classified as *Euthynnus alletteratus affinnis* when it was thought to be a subspecies of the Atlantic little tunny *(Euthynnus alletteratus)*. It is now considered a separate species. This good gamefish is a prominent commercial spe-

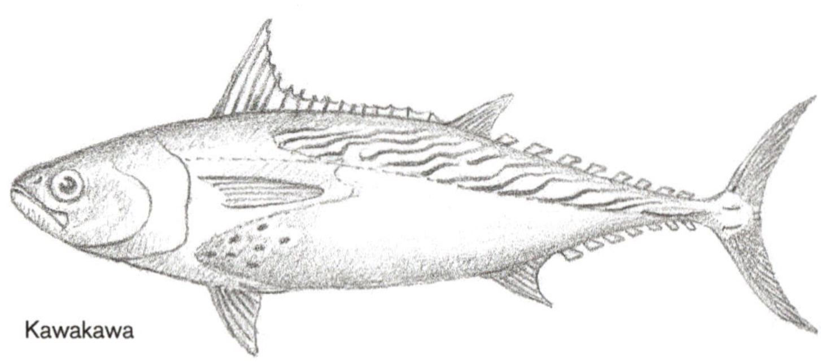
Kawakawa

cies in the Philippines, Malaysia, and India. Its flesh is dark red, and in some places it is highly valued as food. In Hawaii it is often prepared as sashimi.

Identification. The first dorsal fin of the kawakawa has 14 to 16 spines, and the second dorsal fin has 12 to 13 rays. The anal fin has 12 to 14 rays. There are no scales on the body, except on the corselet and lateral line. There are 29 to 34 gill rakers on the first arch, compared to 53 to 63 in the skipjack tuna *(Katsuwonnus pelamis)* and 32 to 41 in the black skipjack *(E. lineatus).* On the back, beginning near the midpoint of the dorsal fin, are a number of oblique, wavy lines over a turquoise background. These squiggly lines run from the lateral line back toward the dorsal fins. Some live specimens may display dark, prominent longitudinal stripes on the venter. These stripes tend to disappear quickly once the fish is removed from the water, leaving only a number of dark spots showing between the pectoral fins and the ventral fins.

Size. Kawakawa are reported to attain a maximum length of 40 inches and a weight of 30 pounds. The all-tackle world record is a 29-pound specimen.

Distribution. This species is widespread in tropical and temperate waters of the Indo-Pacific, from the Red Sea and South Africa east to Indonesia and Australia, and from Japan and the Philippines throughout Oceania to the Hawaiian Islands. It is accidental in the eastern Pacific, where it is replaced by the closely related black skipjack *(see: skipjack, black).*

Habitat. This pelagic and migratory species stays fairly close to land. It may be found near reefs and in estuaries, as well as in open waters, and sometimes forms multispecies schools by size with other scombrids consisting of between 100 and several thousand individuals.

Food and feeding habits. More than half of the food ingested by the kawakawa consists of crustaceans, although squid and pelagic fish also form a large part of its diet. It is a highly opportunistic feeder.

Angling. Fishing methods include trolling lures or whole or cut baits, live-bait fishing, and casting. Some effective baits include squid, herring, sauries, mullet, anchovies, mackerel, halfbeaks, and yellowtail.

See: Mackerel.

KAYAK

The term "kayak" usually conjures up an image of someone ensconced in a small, tipsy, canoelike craft negotiating the whitewater of a roiling river. This is not exactly a fishing scene, and a kayak is not the type of craft that often comes to mind for fishing. Yet, anglers are using kayaks to a limited extent, and although kayaks are not about to clog the angling waterways, they do appeal to some people for certain common fishing activities (as canoes do) and, in a few cases, for some extreme activities.

The craft primarily used in saltwater fishing are sea kayaks, made of polyethylene and with raised seats that have a center of gravity near water level. These are very stable and not excessively prone to capsizing (or rollover). In freshwater, kayaks used by anglers include touring models, which are used by adventurers on long-distance forays but not really set up for a lot of fishing, and general-purpose kayaks. The latter are models used for calm rivers (not whitewater) and small lakes and ponds. They range roughly from 12 to 15 feet in length.

Like canoes, kayaks draft hardly any water, so they have obvious benefits for shallow-water fishing and quiet movement; they are eminently portable and less expensive than many boats with trailers, motors, and other accessories. However, most models are not suitable for rough water fishing, require a bit of exertion (not everyone is up to this exercise), can be difficult to get through coastal inlet waves, are short on storage (including fish storage), and have some safety concerns that are not posed by other boats. Moreover, it is not possible to stand up in many kayaks (although it is possible in catamaran-hulled versions, and some agile anglers do stand up in shallow, warm waters, such as tidal flats), and the low level of position changes fishing perspective for people who are used to higher vantage points, although this may be compensated by a quiet, stealthy approach for getting close to fish.

Some anglers are using kayaks to fish shallow waters and get to places that are otherwise hard to access.

Some anglers using kayaks in coastal waters paddle many miles to fish (a few even going offshore to blue water), and others go short distances, but in all cases anglers must pay attention to tides, current, wind, and wave direction when planning the day's activities. Most fishing-related kayaking is done in warm tropical waters, but those who fish in cold water and in cold weather require enclosable cockpits and need to wear wetsuits. Models with scupper holes to drain water are preferred, as are those with waterproof hatches.

A variety of specialized kayak fishing accessories are available, including rod holders and padded high-backed seats. Sea anchors, a folding anchor, dry bags, appropriate PFD, and some standard safety items are among the other items used, as well as portable sonar. Creative anglers have found ways to troll as well as to fish live bait from kayaks, in addition to casting and jigging, and have been expanding the applications for this craft, particularly in saltwater.

See: Boat.

KEDGE

A type of anchor, seldom used on recreational boats, with opposing flukes and used on rocky bottoms.

See: Anchor.

KEEL

The backbone of a boat, the main structural element; also, the lateral fore-to-aft area at the bottom of the hull that provides stability.

See: Boat.

KEEL HOOK

A hook with a raised shank, or keel.

See: Fly; Hook.

KEEPER

A term for a fish that meets legal length limits.

See: Regulations.

KEEPER RING

A small, usually folding, ring ahead of a rod handle; the keeper ring holds a hook that is attached to the fishing line.

KELP

Large varieties of brown algae, or brown seaweeds. Kelp grows in large structures called macrocysts, which may be up to 200 feet long, or grows as elaborately branched mats. Concentrations are known as kelp forests, and they harbor an entire food chain of sea life, which makes them prominent places to locate many species of gamefish.

KELT

A term for sea-run Atlantic salmon that have overwintered in a river and returned to saltwater in the spring. Also called "black" salmon, or spring salmon, these fish are thinner and somewhat darker than fresh bright-silver migrants but lose this darkness as they descend toward the sea. Kelts begin to feed in the spring, the only time when Atlantic salmon do so in freshwater, and can be hungry, aggressive, and thus more eager to take a fly. Some anglers disparage fishing for kelts, in deference to their condition, although there are spring kelt fisheries in some places, and these fish can be good sport.

See: Salmon, Atlantic.

KENTUCKY

"The Happy Hunting Ground," a term Native American Indians used two centuries ago to describe the game-rich landmass that would become the commonwealth of Kentucky, probably took the region's excellent fishing into account as well.

Kentucky is blessed with a wide diversity of fisheries. These range from wild brook trout in the eastern highland region along the Virginia border to world-class crappie and bass fisheries in the lake country of the western lowlands. In between, some 86,000 miles of rivers and streams course the landscape. This is more running water than exists in any other state, and it provides a smorgasbord of flowing-water opportunities for the likes of white bass, smallmouth bass, rock bass, spotted bass, muskellunge, and catfish, plus it offers almost untapped crappie and panfish populations.

Numerous state-owned lakes are scattered throughout the commonwealth, and these provide excellent opportunities to catch bass, crappie, channel catfish, and other species from small boats or by fishing from the banks. A host of large and small impoundments offer outstanding angling as well.

Beginning in the 1940s, when Dale Hollow Reservoir and Kentucky Lake were completed, and extending into the 1970s, when many flood-control reservoirs were constructed across the state, Kentucky anglers underwent a transformation. Having almost exclusively fished streams and rivers, they began to try their luck in the newly formed reservoirs. Some Kentucky anglers now do nothing but fish the lakes, especially the larger ones.

Several small reservoirs provide good fishing in the eastern highland region. Among the better ones are Yatesville, Paintsville, Dewey, Buckhorn, Cave Run, and Carr Fork. In central Kentucky, such famous and larger waters as Lake Cumberland and Dale Hollow receive much of the fishing pressure and publicity. Numerous smaller reservoirs like Barren River, Rough River, Green River, and Nolin contribute a combined 23,000-plus acres of additional angling opportunity.

The greatest attractions for bass and crappie

anglers continue to be huge Kentucky Lake and nearby Lake Barkley. Kentucky Lake, a 184-mile-long reservoir that straddles the Kentucky-Tennessee border at the western end of the state (50,000 acres in Kentucky), grows tackle-rattling largemouth, big smallmouth, and football-shaped Kentucky (spotted) bass. Rod-bending flathead, channel, and blue catfish are so plentiful in Kentucky Lake that it supports a fairly large commercial fishing operation, and the crappie fishing is nearly legendary. Lake Barkley, just across the nearby ridge line, adds 58,000 acres of prime bass and crappie habitat to the already bountiful opportunity of the far western region.

In addition to great bass, crappie, and catfish angling in various waters, Kentucky boasts some of the finest muskie fishing in the South, rockfish (landlocked stripers) up to 60 pounds, and record-size walleye and sauger. It also supports an astonishing number of trout fisheries for a so-called "Southern" state.

K

Eastern Region

No one really knows if brook trout were ever native to the highlands of eastern Kentucky, but this species has been successfully introduced to some of the region's most remote streams, where they not only survive hot low-water summers, but where they have also been showing strong evidence of natural reproduction. The bulk of the brook trout streams exist in the highlands of the easternmost areas of the state and inside the vast reaches of the Daniel Boone National Forest. Brook trout fishing isn't promoted highly by the state fish and wildlife agency because of the species' delicate habitat, yet more than a dozen streams offer challenges in pursuing these beautifully colored fish, some of which range to 14 inches and more in length. Specific information about this remote fishery is available from the state fish and wildlife agency's regional office at Williamsburg.

There are 19 streams in the hilly to mountainous eastern region of Kentucky that support good numbers of native muskellunge. Heading the list of the top muskie streams are Tygart Creek in Carter and Greenup Counties, the Kinniconick in Lewis County, and the Licking River, which begins in Morgan County and empties into the Ohio River at Covington.

Fish from these streams and others in eastern Kentucky were used to develop one of the finest muskie rearing and stocking programs in America. Minor Clark Fish Hatchery, at Cave Run Lake, annually produces many 10- to 14-inch-long muskie fingerlings for planting in various streams and rivers, and in three lakes. Cave Run Lake, an 8,500-acre standing-timber-infested reservoir in Rowan and Menifee Counties, is not only rated as the finest muskie fishing lake in Dixie, it is also one of the top sites in North America for this species.

Some eastern Kentucky lakes also hold good populations of walleye. Laurel River Lake, a 5,000-acre clear-water mountain gem surrounded by the Daniel Boone National Forest in Laurel County, has large numbers of walleye, some of which have grown to 20 or more pounds. Some believe these giant walleye are remnants of the old river walleye that grew to world-class proportions in the upper Cumberland River system after Lake Cumberland impounded the river in the early 1950s.

From 1955 to 1959, anglers who fished the famed walleye spawning runs in Laurel River and the Big South Fork of the Cumberland during February and March reported catching limits of heavy walleye—10 to 20 pounds and more. Those big walleye virtually disappeared from the rivers by the early 1960s. Whether their gene pool is still in the Laurel Lake population is uncertain, but the fish in that body of water today are still large.

Two lakes in eastern Kentucky—180-acre Greenbo in Greenup County and 700-acre Woods Creek in Laurel County—may contain the biggest largemouth bass in the state. Tiny Greenbo has surrendered two state-record largemouths; the bigger one weighed $13^1/_2$ pounds. Biologists believe that this small clear-water reservoir, which forms the hub of Greenbo Lake State Resort Park, has more trophy-size largemouths per acre than any other body of water in the commonwealth.

Woods Creek Lake, which borders Interstate 75 near London, produced a record largemouth weighing 13 pounds, 10.4 ounces. Poor water clarity makes both lakes difficult to fish during the day. The record fish here, and the two at Greenbo, were caught at night—two on 7-inch plastic worms and one on a spinnerbait.

Rainbow and brown trout are widely spread over this eastern third of Kentucky thanks to a cooperative effort between the state fish and wildlife agency and the U.S. Fish and Wildlife Service. Wolff Creek Federal Fish Hatchery, located below the dam at Lake Cumberland, provides hundreds of thousands of catchable-size rainbow trout, and some brown trout, for stocking throughout Kentucky.

In the hilly and mountainous regions, approximately 30 streams provide good trout fishing for at least six months of the year. This is the result of a mostly put-and-take program. Streams are stocked beginning in April and running through September—provided there is adequate flowage—with a supply of 9- to 12-inch trout each month.

The U.S. Forest Service stocks an additional 15 streams inside the boundaries of the Daniel Boone National Forest beginning in March and extending through June in most instances. In McCreary County, Rock Creek—the state's premier small-stream trout fishery—receives stockings of both rainbow and brown trout through October, with one planting of sub-adult-size fish each fall.

Laurel River Lake is the best lake fishery for trout in the state. This deep, exceptionally clear reservoir provides ideal habitat for rainbow trout, some of which have grown to 8 pounds. Each year, the lake is stocked with about 125,000 catchable-size trout during February. Most of the fish are caught by anglers who troll small spinners and crankbaits just off the shore early in the season. By May, hundreds of night anglers invade Laurel River Lake during weekends, using battery-powered lights attached to the sides of their boats to attract fish close to their offerings of organic baits and vertically jigged artificials.

In addition to these fisheries, eastern Kentucky offers great float fishing opportunities for smallmouth bass, Kentucky bass, and muskies. Tygarts and Kinniconick Creeks are popular for this in the northern end of the region; the remote reaches of Rockcastle River in Rockcastle County is a favorite farther south. Little access development along the streams keeps fishing pressure to a minimum, making a float trip for energetic anglers even more rewarding in the form of more and larger fish.

Central Region

Sprawling Lake Cumberland is a 55,250-acre flood-control and power-generation lake that provides anglers with nearly 1,300 miles of rocky shoreline from Somerset to Jamestown and has long attracted the bulk of fishing attention in the center of Kentucky.

Cumberland has a variety of notable species, with bass being of foremost interest. During its heyday in the 1950s and 1960s, Lake Cumberland was regarded by many bass fishing authorities as one of the best largemouth lakes in the world. That is not the case today, but the big lake still surrenders abundant quality bigmouths, as well as smallmouth bass, to anglers who fish the lake yearround. Rockfish are plentiful in the lower reaches of the lake and offer anglers a good chance to tangle with a powerful swimmer that may weigh in at 50 pounds or more.

Lake Cumberland is the state's best walleye producer. Biologists have reported a huge population of walleye ranging from 20 to 28 inches in the lake. Found throughout the reservoir, walleye are mostly caught incidentally by anglers in pursuit of bass and crappie, although interest in this so-called northern species has been growing among locals.

The Lake Cumberland tailrace, which extends for 55 miles from the base of Wolff Creek Dam at Jamestown south past Burkesville to the Tennessee border, is considered by Kentucky fisheries managers as a blue-ribbon trout producer. Each year, more than 80,000 catchable-size rainbows and 30,000 similar-size brown trout are released into the tailrace below the dam and downstream for about 5 miles. Trout thrive in the cold water released from the bottom of the lake and grow to record-setting sizes. Browns in the 18-pound class have been caught here, as well as rainbows upward of 14 pounds. Trolling, casting, drifting live baits, and fly fishing are all popular means of taking these wild fish from the underpressured environment.

Dale Hollow Lake straddles the Kentucky and Tennessee border and offers one of the best opportunities in the country to catch a truly large smallmouth bass. An 18-inch minimum size limit and a two-fish-per-day creel limit have contributed significantly to the large number of sizable bronzebacks in the lake.

Dale Hollow also has a good population of walleye, even though few anglers target the species. The 27,000-acre lake is also stocked with rainbow trout and lake trout, which are more numerous in the lower reaches near the dam.

The three river lakes—Barren River (Barren County), Rough River (Grayson County), and Nolin (Edmonson County)—also provide good fishing for largemouth, panfish, and crappie in the central area of the commonwealth. The tailrace below each of these lakes is stocked regularly with several hundred 9- to 12-inch rainbow trout.

Farther north, in Spencer County, 3,300-acre Taylorsville Lake has good numbers of largemouth bass, crappie, and hybrid striped bass. Unfortunately, the relatively small Taylorsville is close to large population centers in Lexington and Louisville, resulting in the heaviest fishing pressure of any lake in the state, much of which comes from organized clubs that hold numerous bass tournaments here. Catch-and-release is practiced almost exclusively among this group, but as one state fisheries biologist noted, every bass in Taylorsville has been caught and released many times.

Tarpon have been known to leap as high as 10 feet vertically and 20 feet horizontally, making them one of the most spectacular showboats an angler could want.

Less pressured are several streams and rivers that offer excellent populations of smallmouth bass for floating and wading anglers. Foremost among these streams is the South Branch of the Licking River, running between Cynthiana and Falmouth. This wide but shallow limestone-bottomed stream has good numbers of smallmouth bass up to 3 pounds; these are usually taken with both live minnows and artificials, either by casting or fly fishing.

Elkhorn Creek, the state's most historic smallmouth stream (which was once stocked with king salmon), flows into the Kentucky River at Frankfort and offers ideal float fishing conditions on its North Fork. Numerous spots along the river are conducive to wading and fishing with lightweight spinning or fly fishing tackle.

Western Region

Huge Kentucky Lake and Lake Barkley overshadow all other fisheries in the western third of the state. When it comes to largemouth bass, crappie, and catfish, few other lakes in Kentucky can match up in sheer numbers as well in size.

Fisheries biologists believe that Kentucky Lake holds more 4- to 6-pound largemouths per acre than any other lake in the commonwealth. Lake Barkley, no more than a few miles to the east, continuously challenges its sister lake in numbers of

Early-morning fog doesn't stop bass and crappie anglers on Kentucky Lake.

K

bass as well as the size of its crappie. Both reservoirs are famous for their world-class crappie fisheries during spring and autumn.

In recent years, Kentucky Lake has developed a trophy smallmouth bass fishery. Smallmouths moved downstream from Pickwick Lake, a stronghold for the species in southern Tennessee (the Tennessee River, which forms Kentucky Lake, flows north to meet the Ohio River near Paducah). Presently, anglers are landing smallmouths in all areas of the lake, but the eastern shore, bordering the Land Between The Lakes recreation area, is most productive.

Lake Barkley, which was formed from the lower reaches of the Cumberland River, is shallower than nearby Kentucky Lake. It has copious bottom structure in the form of submerged stump fields, numerous sunken treetops, and stake beds, created to afford concentrated cover for the lake's large crappie population.

Anglers who test their fishing skills for bass and crappie on Kentucky and Barkley Lakes divert their attention during various seasons to the tailraces. Situated no more than 3 miles apart, both tailraces have large populations of sauger and white bass, as well as striped bass, some of which run up to 25 pounds. Huge flathead catfish, channel cats, and Mississippi blue cats are also plentiful in the tailraces, which are well developed for both bank anglers and boaters.

Anglers traveling to this part of Kentucky typically visit and camp in the 170,000-acre Land Between The Lakes recreation area. This uncommercialized area separating Kentucky and Barkley Lakes has lakeside campgrounds, a nature center, an elk and bison range, and many other recreational facilities.

Lake Malone, a 700-acre lake in Muhlenburg County, has long been a producer of supersize largemouth bass. According to one fisheries biologist, anglers report catching more 10-pound bass from this lake than from any other lake in Kentucky.

Swan Lake, a 300-acre flooded lowland in Ballard County, is the state's only natural lake. It is a part of the large oxbow system that borders the Ohio and Mississippi Rivers in the far western tip of the state. These oxbow lakes are flooded by nearby rivers during winter and spring, bringing in fresh stocks of crappie, spotted bass, and other species. The Kentucky Department of Fish and Wildlife Resources owns many of these lakes and manages the fishery, which includes bluegills, crappie, bass, and catfish.

Ohio River

The Ohio River flows along some 600 miles of Kentucky's northern border and is one of the strongest fisheries in this area of North America. Along this stretch of the Ohio are seven large pools formed by high-lift navigation dams. These pools form lakes as large as 20,000 acres or more, which force the Ohio's waters into every bordering lowland and up the mouths of tributaries, creating numerous backwater areas that offer excellent habitat for largemouth bass and crappie.

The main stem of the river affords countless miles of catfish habitat and good fishing for Kentucky spotted bass during spring and again in autumn. It also has one of the best white bass runs in the world. In recent years, striped bass as well as hybrid stripers have been stocked in the river.

With the exception of bass angling and fishing from the banks near the mouths of tributaries for "anything that bites," most fishing along the Ohio River occurs in the tailraces below the big dams. Here, giant schools of white bass, hybrid stripers, rockfish, and sauger feed on plentiful gizzard shad, emerald shiners, and herring (skipjacks). Action can be fast-paced during late spring and through the early autumn months for white bass and hybrids. In summer, catfish anglers come out in force in the tailraces, using a variety of organic and live baits to catch large numbers of channel and flathead catfish at night.

As the water temperature falls off in autumn, tens of thousands of sauger swim into the tailraces. Blocked in their pre-spawn, upstream migration, the fish mill about the tailrace throughout the winter months, providing late-season anglers with one of the best fisheries for the species in America.

Smithland Pool, near Paducah, is currently one of the top places on the river to take flathead, channel, and blue catfish. Anglers use boats to access and negotiate the turbulent currents beneath the dams, where they slow-bounce organic and live-bait presentations off the bottom. An outboard holds the boat in place against the strong current.

Each of the pools on the Ohio River has excellent access via launching ramps. A reciprocal agreement between states that share the Ohio as a border permits anglers who hold a resident or nonresident angling license to fish both sides of the river.

KENTUCKY REEL

Term for the original multiplying reel, crafted between 1800 and 1810 in Kentucky by watchmakers George Snyder and Jonathan Meek. This was a multiple-action revolving-spool casting reel, developed at a time when a single-action revolving- spool reel was the only reel available for sportfishing, and anglers exclusively used natural bait or artificial flies. The single-action reel was primarily employed to store and retrieve line, and had no casting function, whereas the revolving-spool multiplier was used for casting—paying out line with the object being cast—and one turn of the crank caused more than one full turn of the spool.

Between 1835 and 1840, Jonathan Meek and his brother started the first commercial manufacture of Kentucky Reels. These and later multipliers would lead to casting with objects other than unweighted flies, and eventually to the development and popularity of artificial lures, including spoons, spinners, and plugs.

See: Antique Fishing Tackle; Baitcasting Tackle; Conventional Tackle; Multiplying Reel.

KENYA

Most often associated with four-legged wildlife, safaris, high mountain peaks, the Masai Mara savanna, Amboselli and its view of Mt. Kilimanjaro, and abundant tourist facilities, Kenya is also one of Africa's best sportfishing destinations. It offers diverse and notable offshore angling opportunities, as well as high-mountain trout fishing. Along the coast these fisheries are more accessible and developed than those in most other countries, especially central and northern Africa, on this continent.

Situated on the eastern coast of Africa and facing the Indian Ocean, Kenya is virtually bisected by the equator. Its coastal region is on the southeast, and to the east lies Somalia, to the north Ethiopia, to the northwest Sudan, to the west Uganda, and to the south Tanzania.

The southwestern border of the country is marked by a small portion of Lake Victoria, the second largest lake in the world.

While much of northeastern Kenya is a flat, bush-covered plain, the remaining geography encompasses pristine beaches, scenic highland and lake regions, the Great Rift Valley, and magnificent Mount Kenya. Although Kenya's varied topography experiences a wide variety of climatic conditions, the coastal temperature remains comfortably warm year-round. Much of Kenya experiences heavy rainfall from mid-April through June and, to a lesser extent, from mid-September through November.

The best time for most outdoor activities (including safaris and fishing) is during the dry season, from November through March. Kenya's saltwater fishing season typically starts as early as August and continues until as late as the end of April. During this time the calm northerly wind, the Kaskazy, provides friendly seas.

One of Africa's top spots for tourists, Kenya is still one of the world's foremost safari destinations. Although its warm climate, exotic animal life, and lush flora and fauna certainly help attract this attention, Kenya's attitude toward its resources may be more responsible for its popularity among nature lovers. Kenyans regard the environment as a primary resource for a wide variety of "clean" incomes, an example ignored by the great majority of African countries. For anglers, this philosophy has resulted in an ocean free of ravaging commercial longlining operations and boasting pristine lagoons and mangrove breaks protected by hundreds of miles of untouched coral reefs.

Saltwater

For all practical purposes, waters within some 30-odd miles of the 300-mile-long Kenya Coast are the main local fishing grounds. This is essentially an area of sea lying above the continental shelf. The seabed here does not plunge to its greatest depths, but it still reaches down in places to about 3,000 feet. The 100-fathom contour, however, roughly marks the landward edge of the coastal current, and, in general terms, is where big-game offshore fishing efforts are focused.

Despite its warm climate and diverse undersea environment, Kenya and other African fisheries formerly had a reputation in international fishing circles for short fishing seasons and limited offshore species, namely sailfish. In the 1960s and 1970s, a primitive infrastructure limited Kenya's billfishing seasons and catches. Captains of small, poorly equipped boats would fish only in the best of seasons, and even then they rarely ventured past the calm "sailfish alley" to search for other species. Of course, at the time there was little reason for them to do so.

Much of this fishing took place out of Malindi, whose prime location near the Sabaki River allows skippers to take advantage of the remarkable color change just a few miles offshore, where river runoff meets the cobalt blue water of the Indian Ocean. This clear area of demarcation has historically been prolific, offering excellent numbers of dolphin, wahoo, kingfish, tuna, snapper, jacks, and sailfish.

In succeeding decades, Kenya's leading charter operators made huge strides in catching up to international standards in boats, tackle, electronics, and fishing techniques, notably so at Malindi and nearby Watamu, and 50 miles south of Mombasa at Shimoni, which borders Tanzania and accesses the promising year-round fishery of the Pemba Channel. As a result, the country's skippers began to explore the far-off rips and banks that had previously been ignored. They found surprisingly productive angling spots and caught not only sailfish, but good numbers of striped, blue, and black

A view of the beach, sportfishing boats, and the Indian Ocean from Watamu.

K

marlin, as well as the occasional spearfish.

But the biggest surprise for Kenya's skippers was a prolific fishery for swordfish. In 1992, overnight trips to the North Kenya Banks, an undersea chain of mountains 55 miles northeast of Malindi, began producing excellent swordfishing. Another hotspot for broadbills, The Rips, was just 14 to 22 miles from Watamu. Since these discoveries, offshore fishing has diversified along the length of Kenya's coast, although some ports are more focused on gamefishing than others.

Today, Malindi, Watamu, and Mombasa are main ports for offshore excursions. Sophisticated, although limited operations (in terms of the number of boats available) work out of Lamu in the north; out of Kilifi, halfway between Mombasa and Malindi; out of Mtwapa Creek, about 8 miles north of Mombasa; and out of Diani and Funzi Island on the south side of Mombasa.

Off Mombasa are good catches of sailfish, as well as wahoo, barracuda, dorado, tuna, and jacks, and it is not unusual to encounter a marlin. This is also a main site for bottom fishing.

Boats departing from Shimoni commonly fish in the water of the famous Pemba Island Channel. The main fishing areas here extend from Chale Point in the north all the way down to Zanzibar, although it is rare for boats to venture more than 15 to 20 miles south of Shimoni.

The Pemba Channel proper is very deep. The seabed on either side drops abruptly like great escarpments, and these must rival in size the famous Rift Valley hundreds of miles inland. Thus, really deep water is very close to shore and is a main factor in attracting marlin to this area. They may also be attracted by an abundance of food, given the rich pickings along the almost sheer escarpment walls. The many rips here are also significant in this respect.

About 20 miles offshore, Pemba Island is a 15-mile-wide obstruction in the path of migrating billfish. When they reach it, some turn and swim down the channel, whereas others pass the island farther out to sea. This results not only in a good local population of marlin, but also the diversion of many marlin into the sea. The local Pemba Channel Fishing Club (phone: 254-11-313749; fax: 254-11-316875) has good boats for charter.

Ten miles north of Mombasa lies Mtwapa Creek, a site highly favored by many anglers and offering boats that have helped pioneer big-game fishing locations and techniques in Kenya waters. Kilifi, nearly 40 miles north of Mombasa, lures many private boats, and visitors congregate here to fish from the rapidly expanding Mnarani Club. This is an excellent area for tuna and many other species.

About 70 miles north of Mombasa, Watamu and Malindi have become the most popular ports for big-game fishing off Kenya, in terms of scale of operation and tourist notoriety. Malindi and Watamu fall more or less into the resort category. They are famous for sailfish, striped marlin, blue marlin, black marlin, and swordfish (which, in season, are found and caught in very large numbers). Runs of yellowfins, kingfish, and other species are common as well. Watamu and Malindi host prominent international fishing competitions. At Malindi, the Kingfisher Charter Fleet (phone: 254-123-21168; fax: 254-123-30261) is highly respected, as is Hemingway's Hotel & Sportfishing Resort (phone: 254-122-32624; fax: 254-122-32256) in Watamu.

Freshwater

Trout. There's nothing that takes the breath away like creeping up to a likely trout pool at 9,500 feet in the Aberdare Mountains—especially when keenly aware of nearby populations of buffalo, elephants, lions, and leopards.

The origin of trout fishing in Kenya dates back to the turn of the twentieth century, when Lord Delamare and friends imported the first fish for release into the waters of Mt. Kenya and the Aberdares. Nearly all fish caught today are natives from naturally evolved stock; only a few streams and lakes are planted with hatchery-reared fish. Both rainbow and brown trout thrive, and in some cases inhabit waters fairly close to each other.

Trout fishing in Kenya is restricted to those regions above 5,200 feet altitude. The enthusiastic angler could undertake a trout fishing safari lasting several weeks and still not have fished all the available trout-bearing waters.

The most popular locations for fly anglers are among the slopes of Mt. Kenya, the Aberdare Mountains in the center of Kenya, and in the Mt. Elgan area near the western border. Excellent sites are incongruously tucked away between the tea fields of Kericho, off the track in the Nandi Hills and just a 40-minute drive from Nairobi. Part of the attraction of trout fishing in Kenya lies in the tremendous geographic variety within a practical radius of travel. The real magic, however, is standing knee-deep in a rushing mountain stream, as monkeys peer down from the acacia trees, and giant forest hogs and bushbuck slip down to drink at the water's edge.

Fishing is allowed in Mt. Kenya and Aberdare National Parks, and anywhere outside the smaller Mt. Elgan National Park. An impressive band of Forest Reserve encircles all three mountains, preserving the quality of trout habitat within. A specific trout license is required and can be bought for either 48 hours or a year at the park gates. The only legal offering for trout within Kenya is an artificial fly. Kenyan anglers have designed numerous fly patterns dedicated to meeting the appetites of local trout, two prominent local examples being the Kenya Bug and the Mrs. Simpson. Both are available from local suppliers.

Lakes. Although Kenya has a variety of lakes and a few major rivers, few organized opportunities for other types of freshwater fishing exist. Warm-water species inhabit these, however, and some provide angling for tigerfish and Nile perch, as well as coarse species. Visitors bringing their own equipment may find boats (and drivers) at some sites.

One of these is Lake Turkana. Formerly known as Lake Rudolf, Turkana lies in the Great Rift Valley, where the Ethiopian highlands give way to the northern Kenya desert. It was near the northeastern shore of this lake, in Sibiloi National Park, that anthropologist Dr. Richard Leakey discovered the 26-million-year-old remains of early man.

Turkana is 180 miles long, between 6 and 30 miles wide, and covers 6,400 square kilometers. It contains three main islands. The word *Turkana* means "Jade Sea," so named for the color of its water, which is fed from the highlands by the River Omo, entering the lake on its northern tip. Situated in the middle of the Chalbi Desert, at 1,200 feet above sea level and quite far inland, this site is always very hot, although often a strong wind blows.

Lake Turkana has an abundant population of Nile perch and reputedly harbors monsters that have grown to 300 pounds. Ample tilapia, catfish, barbel, tigerfish, and other species reside here as well. Casting, trolling, and live-bait fishing are popular. The Lake Turkana Angling Club has a lodge on the west side of the lake; Turkana Fishing Safaris (phone: 254-122-312234; fax: 254-122-32266) can arrange a mobile fishing camp with boats for adventure anglers. Be prepared for scorching heat, perennial high winds, and wildlife viewing, which includes crocodiles.

Two other notable lakes are Victoria and Naivasha. Situated at an altitude of 6,200 feet in the highlands 60 miles northwest of Nairobi, Lake Naivasha is the highest lake in Kenya. It has an area of approximately 75 square miles and an average depth of 20 to 30 feet, except around Crescent Island, where the water drops off sharply to depths of up to 45 feet.

Before the 1920s, the only fish native to Lake Naivasha was one species of carp. Theodore Roosevelt unsuccessfully proposed introducing black bass here in 1909. One strain of tilapia was introduced in 1926, another strain was transplanted from Lake Victoria in 1956, and still another was introduced in 1965. Tilapia today are mainly caught in nets by native commercial fishermen, but it is possible to catch them on a rod with a very small spinner.

Fifty-six black bass were imported here in 1928, and these were plentiful by the mid-1930s. With the introduction of crayfish from North America in the 1970s, the supply of food for bass improved immensely, and subsequently there was a boom in largemouth bass fishing. The inner rim of Crescent Island is known for excellent bass, and various techniques work throughout the lake, which has abundant weed growth. Two of the largest bass caught in the lake are displayed at the Lake Naivasha Club, and each weighed approximately 10 pounds; fish up to 13 pounds have been caught in the past.

Access to this fishery is principally through Safariland and the Lake Naivasha Country Club (Lake Hotel), which provides luxurious lakeside accommodations. Camping facilities are located at Fisherman's Camp and Burch's Farm. Good angling can be combined with superb wildlife viewing.

Enormous Lake Victoria is situated 200 miles west of Nairobi and is the second largest freshwater lake in the world (after Lake Superior in Michigan). Lake Victoria borders on the countries of Kenya, Uganda, and Tanzania. Its waters host the voracious Nile perch, which reputedly can grow up to 500 pounds here and has only the giant crocodile as a natural enemy. Other gamefish present are tigerfish and giant catfish, and the lake harbors tilapia and scores of other native species.

Anglers at Lake Victoria favor varied methods, including trolling with a boat, casting with lures or flies from shore or a boat, and bottom fishing with live baits (especially for the biggest fish). Several local fishing clubs organize angling excursions to Victoria from Kisumu; a list can be obtained at the local sportfishing magazine, *The Rainbow Runner,* in Nairobi.

KICK BOAT

A term for self-propelled dual-pontoon float tubes.
See: Float Tubes.

KICKER

A term for a small outboard motor used for trolling (it saves gasoline and permits slow operation of the boat); also a term for a small auxiliary outboard available for emergency purposes if the main engine fails.
See: Outboard Motor.

K

KIDNEY HARNESS

See: Harness, Fighting.

KILLIFISH

Also called topminnows and toothed carps, these fish are members of the large Cyprinodontidae family of small fish. They are most abundant in warm climates, but a few species occur in temperate regions. The fins are soft rayed, as in cyprinid minnows, but killifish have scales on their head and have no lateral line. Typical family members have a flattened head, and the mouth opens upward, an adaptation for feeding at the surface. Some species are used as baits, and many tropical species are kept in aquariums.

Killifish travel in schools, generally in the shallows, and are an important link in wetland and estuarine food webs. They are important prey for shorebirds, crabs, and larger fish, and many species are valued for mosquito control, as they feed on the surface and consume whatever insect larvae and small invertebrates are available. Killifish are also among the species most tolerant of high turbidity and low oxygen.

Species

Many killifish live in brackish water as well as freshwater. The best known of these is the mummichog *(Fundulus heteroclitus),* a robust 3- to 5-inch species found along the Atlantic coast from Florida to Labrador. It can tolerate salinities to 35 parts per thousand. The mummichog is noted for its habit of burrowing into the silt on the bottom, sometimes to depths of 6 inches or more in winter.

A rather fat-bodied fish compared to other members of the family, the mummichog varies in color depending on the chemistry of the water from which it is taken. Generally, however, the female is brownish green on the back and sides and light below. The sides are barred with a dark color. Males are brighter and have a much more pronounced contrast between the dark bars and the lighter body color.

Mummichogs are popular bait minnows in some regions, often going by the name of hardheads. They are hardy, remaining alive and vigorous on the hook for a long time. They can also be kept successfully in aquariums, adjusting quickly to freshwater and not demanding a constant high temperature, as do many of the more sensitive tropicals. On the Pacific coast, the California killifish *(F. parvipinnis)* is similar in size and habits to the mummichog, and occupies the same ecological niche.

Mummichog

The banded killifish *(F. diaphanus)* has many narrow vertical dark bars on its sides. It is a slimmer fish than the mummichog and usually shorter, rarely exceeding 3 inches in length. Also ranging into brackish water (preferring salinities of less than 5 parts per thousand), it occurs from South Carolina northward to the St. Lawrence River and westward through the Mississippi Valley. It is sometimes used for bait, but is not as hardy as the mummichog.

Another well-known species is the gold topminnow *(F. chrysotus),* which inhabits freshwater and brackish estuaries and streams from Florida to South Carolina. Its greenish body is covered with gold or reddish dots that are almost metallic, and the female is duller than the male.

Other common species of *Fundulus* include the banded topminnow *(F. cingulatus),* which has a red belly, red fins, and red dots on its bluish body; the striped killifish *(F. majalis),* a hardy species sometimes as much as 6 inches long, with a metallic-brown body striped with a darker color; the plains topminnow *(F. sciadicus),* a strictly freshwater species found in the Mississippi and its tributaries, primarily in headwaters; and the saltmarsh topminnow *(F. jenkinsi),* a mainly brackish water species of Florida and adjacent states.

Florida has the greatest representation of cyprinodonts in North America. Notable among these is the flagfish *(jordanella floridae),* a short-bodied, almost sunfishlike species attaining a maximum length of 3 inches, and the pygmy killifish *(Leptolucania ommata),* a slender fish that rarely exceeds $1^{1}/_{2}$ inches in length.

KILLING FISH

See: Fish Preparation—General Care.

KINGFISH

A term for king mackerel *(see: mackerel, king),* and yellowtail *(see).*

KIRIBATI

The Republic of Kiribati ("ti" is pronounced like the letter *s*) consists of 33 low-elevation coral atolls flung across some 3,800 kilometers of the equatorial South and North Pacific Ocean, organized into three significant island groups: The Gilbert Islands (Tungaru), the Phoenix Islands, and the Line Islands. Kiribati's total land area is only 817 square kilometers, yet the well-spaced geography of tiny landmasses allows 3,550,000 square kilometers of surrounding ocean to fall within the jurisdiction of the country's 200-nautical-mile Exclusive Economic Zone (EEZ). The majority of the mostly

Micronesian population of 80,000 lives in the Gilbert Islands, centered around Tarawa, the capital. Although English is the official language, and enough is understood and spoken by locals for most visitors to effectively communicate, Kiribati is the most widely spoken.

A former British colony, Kiribati gained independence in 1979. It is the poorest nation in the Pacific, with a $32 million gross national product derived from a simple agricultural/fishing economy. With its former phosphate deposits exhausted, the primary exports are copra and fish. Most of the native population lives by subsistence seafood gathering from the reefs and lagoons, fishing, and farming. These are supplemented by part-time cash-generating activities, often copra production. Tourism is only lightly developed.

The country's richest resource is the EEZ. It encircles a vast area of both the equatorial North and South Pacific, on either side of the International Dateline. Ichthyologists estimate that more than 1,000 inshore fish species exist within these bounds. This zone also features particularly prolific offshore tropical fishing grounds. Biological productivity is elevated due to a persistent oceanographic phenomenon called equatorial upwelling, whereby nutrient-rich seawater is drawn from the depths to sunlit surface layers by the spiraling action of opposite-flowing surface currents near the equator. Various Asian and American commercial fishing corporations have been long aware of the area, contributing millions annually to Kiribati for fishing rights.

Sportfishing interests have been slower to gain access to this remote cornucopia of both inshore and offshore angling opportunities due to the overall lack of facilities and promotion. Where facilities do exist, native friendliness, and expertise derived from the strong role fishing plays in local culture—combined with the extremely productive waters—have induced results that are nothing less than spectacular.

Line Islands

The Line Islands extend in a loose, 2,300-kilometer northwest-to-southeast arc from 750 kilometers north of Tahiti to 1,120 kilometers south of Hawaii. Eight of the 10 islands belong to Kiribati, with Jarvis Island and Palmyra Atoll being U.S. possessions. The six members of the group south of the equator are uninhabited.

Christmas Island. The undisputed sportfishing capital of Kiribati is Christmas (Kiritimati) Island, which has the largest landmass of any atoll in the world at 388 square kilometers (nearly half the dry land area of the country). With an estimated population of only 4,000 inhabitants organized into three main villages, nearly the entire 160-kilometer perimeter of the island comprises deserted beaches, fringed by a narrow band of coral-reef flat that seldom falls away to blue water farther than a long surf cast from the shore.

An albatross is undisturbed by a nearby Christmas Island caster.

This long, relatively narrow landmass encloses a large complex of lagoons, some landlocked. Many are connected to the main lagoon, however, which features a nearly 5-kilometer-wide pass to the open ocean on the western side. The lagoon complex is generally shallow and features vast, white and light-colored sand flats, many bordered by beaches, deeper channels, and open bottom sometimes dotted with coral heads and rubble, small islets, and shallow tidal creeks and basins.

The government operates a small hotel at Christmas Island, complete with guide services specializing primarily in outstanding lagoon and reef fishing pursuits. The local private sector now features alternative accommodations and guides, including opportunities to sample the somewhat lightly tested offshore fishing. Most vessels are locally crafted wooden punts and outrigger canoes powered by outboard motors, uniquely suited to the shallow lagoon areas that must be traversed regardless of fishing destination. Anglers can choose between wading or boat fishing, guided or unguided. Vehicles with or without a guide are available for access to lagoon areas via land.

Outstanding flats fishing for bonefish initially put Christmas on the sportfishing map. Visiting anglers drawn by bonefish, however, quickly discovered unparalleled shallow-water opportunities to target bluefin and giant trevally on light tackle, particularly fly fishing, resulting in numerous line-class and fly-rod world-record catches for both species.

The growing number of anglers fishing offshore have experienced consistent action for yellowfin tuna and wahoo. Other species here include mahimahi, rainbow runners, skipjacks and other small tuna, and, less commonly, dogtooth tuna and African pompano. Sailfish and blue marlin have been landed, but very little effort has been expended specifically targeting billfish potential. Hefty giant trevally, and a myriad other species, including various other jacks, queenfish, grouper, snapper, sharks, barracuda, emperors, and sweetlips may all enter the catch along the outer reefs and around coral-head-studded areas of the pass and lagoon.

Inshore and reef species are generally caught year-round. Bonefish (averaging 3 to 6 pounds, with larger fish caught frequently) aggregate monthly at specific locations, apparently to spawn, one to four days after the full moon. The best-known aggregation at Christmas Island is in the vicinity of Paris, located on the point of land due south across the lagoon pass from the main village of London. Fish coming from outer reef areas as they enter the lagoon tend to concentrate here. Most larger fish aggregate in deeper water over gravel-like rubble bottom. Guides position anglers to target these fish as they move along shallower flats en route to other spawning areas. Although this situation can afford stationary anglers a fairly continuous parade of sight-casting opportunities, especially on the middle to top of the incoming tide, actively wading in numerous areas at other times can regularly yield nearly as many bonefish sightings as when fishing near an aggregation. Bonefish are also widespread on the reef flats between outer perimeter beaches and the reef crest, but they are more difficult to land due to abundant sharp coral.

Giant trevally between 30 and 80 pounds are common and are caught in a variety of habitats, including lagoon flats and channels, in the surf near the reef crest, and in deeper water near steep dropoffs to the open ocean around the outside of the atoll. Anglers sight-cast, usually with fly or spinning gear, fish blind in the surf, or troll outer reef margins. Large surface poppers and plugs deployed from the boat, or cast from the beach or while wading, work well, as do a variety of subsurface presentations, most using fast retrieves.

Swordfish, which use their bill to slash and maim, are known to rest on the surface and to cruise the ocean's depths; one was photographed by a research submarine at 2,000 feet.

Milkfish, an elopiform species closely related to tarpon and bonefish, are extremely abundant in most lagoon habitats, as well as along the outer reef slopes. These fish feed on benthic algae and sediment and associated invertebrate fauna, and can also be seen in large schools feeding near the surface along windrows and slicks outside the pass. They can be taken on imitation "algae flies," commonly reach 8 or more pounds at Christmas, and are reported to be hard fighters.

Stronger seasonal trends are more evident for some offshore fishing. Wahoo averaging 40 to 65 pounds can be caught all year but are noticeably more abundant during times of cooler sea-surface temperatures (less than 84°F). Yellowfin tuna, particularly school fish under 40 pounds, are available year-round, as are skipjacks and sizable rainbow runners (averaging 6- to 8-pounds). The largest concentrations, as well as bigger individual yellowfins (from 50 to more than 100 pounds), however, occur more frequently during the summer months, from April through November.

This period coincides with the most frequent blue marlin sightings and hookups, often in the vicinity of tuna schools, although at least some seem to be present year-round. The bigger blue marlin (500-pound-class and over) have been encountered in summer. Sailfish are not consistent or abundant; they tend to show up between August and November, and have been seen and caught while showering ballyhoo near the reef shallows. Small packs of larger yellowfin tuna (50 to more than 80 pounds) frequently do the same, most often in the early morning or late afternoon in the sandy shallows just outside the surf between London and the small village of Tabakea to the north. Mahimahi show up occasionally, usually small groups of large fish (more than 20 pounds) during summer.

Most offshore fishing consists of trolling lures on relatively light tackle. Guides also maneuver the boat for casting to bait showers, to mixed surface schools of skipjacks and yellowfin tuna in order to tease or draw direct strikes from the larger individuals, and to selected surf breaks for giant trevally. Lures worked closely along the outer reef slopes, by trolling and deep jigging, catch a large variety of species, including a large, cubera-like red snapper and a colorful Pacific grouper called coral trout, which is bright crimson and covered with electric blue dots. Beware of ciguatera *(see)* poisoning, and seek local advice before consuming any reef-associated fish at Christmas Island.

Other Line Islands. Other inhabited islands in this group belonging to Kiribati are Fanning (Tabuaeran) and Washington (Teraina), both difficult to access except by irregular government freighters or voyaging sailboats. Fanning Island, 285 kilometers northwest of Christmas, is an 18- by 11-kilometer atoll with a beautiful lagoon harboring a significant population of bonefish, and good flats for pursuing them. Subsistence gillnetting activities in the lagoon for milkfish, mullet, and bonefish by the estimated native population of 2,000, however, are more pervasive here than at more sportfishing, tourism-oriented Christmas Island. Rugged Washington, the next island to the northwest, has no lagoon or not even a tenable vessel anchorage.

Palmyra Atoll, 1,600 kilometers south of Honolulu, is the northernmost Line Island. It is a privately owned, unincorporated territory of the United States, claimed by the Kingdom of Hawaii in 1862 and annexed by the U.S. in 1912, later serving as a naval air station during World War II. The owners maintain a single manager on the island. Palmyra periodically makes the news, when various investors investigate purchasing it for all manner of business schemes, including tourism. The U.S. government has recently enacted a major cleanup of war-era fuel tanks and debris, even reactivating the overgrown airstrip.

In the meantime, the only recreational visitors are maritime, mostly traveling sailors and occasional American commercial fishing boats in transit, who enter the lagoon via the pass blasted out of the reef during wartime by the navy. The state of the lagoon and reef-fish populations is nearly pristine. Bonefish feature prominently, with fly-rod catch rates exceeding those reported from various world hotspots. Large giant trevally patrol the edges of the flats, attracted into the shallows along with numerous blacktip reef sharks by the struggles of hooked bonefish. Yellowfin tuna schools are active outside the pass, and wahoo, big giant trevally, and a host of other species are caught by anglers trolling on or near the reef edge. The billfish potential is unknown.

Kingman Reef, an atoll entirely submerged except for a 40-meter sand spit, also belongs to the U.S. and lies 53 kilometers northwest of Palmyra.

Phoenix Islands

The Phoenix Islands lie in a cluster below the equator, just over 1,000 kilometers north of American Samoa and nearly 1,000 kilometers southeast of the Gilbert Islands, slightly more than halfway from the Line Islands to the Gilbert Islands. Kanton Island represents the only realistic sportfishing opportunity within this group of atolls, and it has air service but no tourist facilities.

The lagoon at Kanton is 14 kilometers long, in the shape of an irregular, elongated diamond. Thirteen Gilbertese families totaling 84 people inhabit this government outpost. They are caretakers of vacated facilities, including a substantial wharf left from Kanton's former roles as a stopover for Pan American Airways trans-Pacific seaplanes in the 1930s, a U.S. Air Force base in World War II, and a NASA tracking station in the 1960s. The Kiribati government has studied the possibility of opening a Christmas Island–style sportfishing operation on Kanton.

Like other atolls in Kiribati featuring appropriate lagoon habitat and light fishing pressure, Kanton has a robust population of bonefish and an adequate flats area to support a recreational fishery, but not enough space to support the pressure sustained by Christmas Island's much larger lagoon. Larger inshore species are abundant and similar in composition to those at Christmas Island. Offshore fish activity, most obviously tuna, appears to be at least commensurate with other areas of the tropical Pacific Equatorial Upwelling Zone.

The Gilbert Islands

The Gilbert Islands are the population center and political capital of Kiribati, yet they have relatively few tourist facilities and no business interests specifically serving anglers full-time. Nevertheless, the 16 atolls of this island group, distributed nearly equally above and below the equator in an 800-kilometer-long swath just west of the International Dateline, as well as western outlier Banaba, are in exceptionally productive waters. Fishing plays an intimate role in the fabric of the local culture. Lagoon fish populations in general are depressed in particularly crowded areas, but bonefish do occur in and around the lagoons and reefs, and regular spawning aggregations exist. Migratory pelagics are less affected by local dense human populations and are intensively sought, but mostly on a subsistence basis. Most of the relatively small amount of locally applied modern methods and gear are directed toward commercial fishing.

Some visitors say that the Gilbert Islands remind them of other areas in the tropical Pacific as they were decades ago. Many natives still fish from unpowered, home-built canoes, using traditional techniques such as drop-stone fishing for large yellowfin tuna near the reef edge. With a handline specially knotted to a specific shape and weight of stone, they are able to lower the bait (often a milkfish or bonefish) and drift it at very specific depths. Night fisheries employing coconut-frond torches to attract and net flyingfish still operate. Trolling using an outboard is considered relatively "new," and many trollers use handcrafted lures made of indigenous pearl oyster shells or various materials with fish skin sewn over them. A relatively large proportion of the population is still closely attuned to a vast array of environmental cues and the implications these have for fishing—nuances of wind and current, atmospheric conditions, moon and tide, subtle changes in seasons—and confluences of which can substantially impact the catch.

Where these talents have been focused on sportfishing pursuits, most notably at Christmas Island, the result has been a growing number of sharp, capable young guides. In the absence of a similar arrangement in the Gilbert Islands, hotel and guest-house operators in, for example, Tarawa and Abemama, regularly arrange for visitors to be taken fishing. A flexible, open-minded angler could likely learn a great deal from a day spent with a skilled Gilbertese angler.

At the Chicago World's Fair in 1893, William Steinway, of piano fame, and Gottfried Daimler introduced a gasoline engine for boats.

KITE FISHING

Fishing with kites is a tactic employed in saltwater, primarily by offshore anglers fishing for sailfish, but it can be used for many species in both inshore and offshore environs. The main purpose is to work a live bait far from the boat, but kite fishing also offers the clear water advantage of presenting the bait without an obvious fishing line. Although baits fished off kites can be presented at various levels, they are typically fished on or close to the surface and are worked both while trolling or while drifting.

The principle of kite fishing is similar to that of using sideplaners *(see)* or planer boards *(see)* in that the kite carries the fishing line and bait away from the boat at distances that can be varied and, via a release clip, the line is freed from the kite to allow an angler to play a fish unimpeded.

Kites for fishing come in versions suitable for different wind conditions, and they are attached

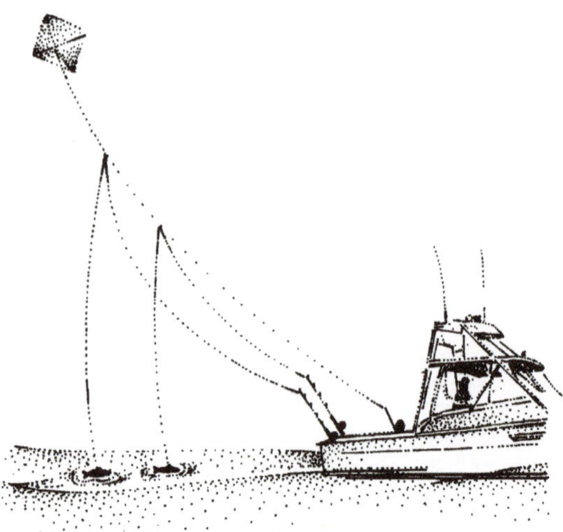

By using a kite, you can get bait an adjustable distance away from the boat and also keep them active on top of the water.

by tow line to a retrieval device; this may be an old 6/0 or 9/0 conventional reel and short rod, or a large-wheeled direct-drive manual retriever with a swiveling clip, similar to the devices used for retrieving sideplaners. The tow line is usually Dacron, at least 50-pound strength, which may be subject to fraying but which has the benefit of not stretching. When two kites are fished together, they are kept away from each other by attaching split shot to the kite edges (on opposite sides), and they may be labeled left or right fliers.

In operation the kite is set out a reasonable distance and then the fishing line is attached to it via a release clip on the tow line (running it through a ceramic guide attached to the clip keeps the line in the right position). Multiple baits may be fished via multiple release clips, though few people fish more than two baits from one kite. Baits are fished so that they frantically circle near the surface, which attracts the attention of fish. It's important to keep monitoring the kite lines to make sure that the baits are properly positioned; colorful markers on the line help make the position of the baits visible. If changes in the wind raise or lower the kite, the bait will be affected, and the line has to be adjusted to keep the bait on the surface.

When a fish strikes, the angler grabs the appropriate rod, reels the line until it comes tight to the release clip, and then waits until the striking fish has swallowed the bait and moved enough to pull the line out of the release clip. The angler points the rod at the fish and reels in slack until the line gets tight, setting the hook several times.

Kites are used in drifting when there is ample wind, and in trolling when there is not enough wind, or even when there is wind in conjunction with trolling baits or lures on flatlines and off downriggers. In the latter scenario, kites help round out the offerings and the breadth of water covered.

KNIFE

See: Fish Preparation—Cleaning.

KNOCKER

A device used to free a lure snagged in deep water; also called plug knocker.

See: Unsnagging.

KNOTS, BOATING

Any angler who uses a boat must sometime or other have to tie the boat to a dock or pier, either temporarily or long-term. The security of the boat may depend on how well you tie it up, how quickly you can get it untied if you have to, and whether you take into consideration that the boat's position may be affected by wind, tide, waves, boat wakes, and so forth.

Dedicated boaters, like Boy Scouts, take pride in their knowledge of knots for boating applications. In the boating community, a knowledge of knots is viewed as an indicator of good seamanship.

The majority of anglers are not seamen nor are they rabid boating enthusiasts. They consider the boat a fishing tool, and they know little about knots. This attitude is fine, as long as they make mostly temporary moorings, are attentive to changing conditions, and avoid using an overhand knot (which is extremely difficult to undo after pressure has been applied). The following are commonly used boat knots and ones that all boaters should be familiar with.

Cleating

Almost everyone who uses a boat has had occasion to tie a line to a cleat, usually in a temporary situation, such as at a launch ramp or fuel dock. Each end of a cleat is called a horn. The proper way to tie to a dock cleat is to put the strain on the base of the cleat by bringing the line around both horns at the base and then make no more than two figure-eights around the cleat. Finish it off and bind it by turning the last hitch over on itself so that the tag end is under the cleated line. More turns around the cleat do not hold better and take longer to undo. The line from the boat should come in at an angle.

Cleating

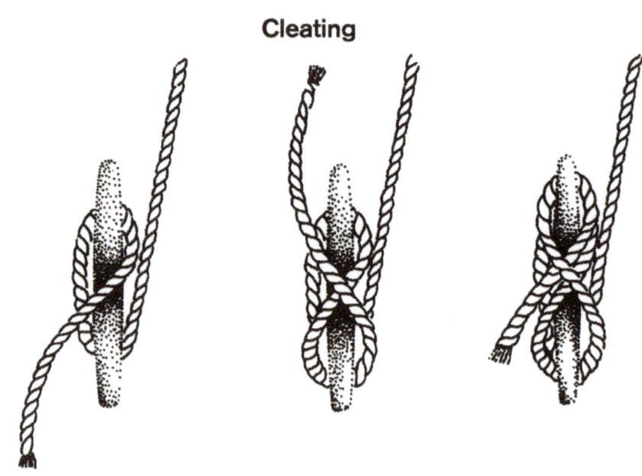

When cleating make sure to tuck the final wrap under (right) and pull tight.

A form of no-knot cleating that is useful for mooring small boats in calm or protected locations (ponds, small lakes, boathouses) is the use of a line-gripping device that lies flush to the dock. These feature an S-configuration through which the line is woven. They hold very well and can be used properly by anyone, but they are best in situations where the boat gunwale is fairly close to the dock so that the line from the boat doesn't come down at a steep angle.

Clove Hitch

A Clove Hitch is commonly used to tie a boat to a piling. Although easy to form, it has a tendency to slip, especially with nylon lines. To avoid slippage, leave plenty of line at the tag end and make one or two half hitches with the tag end around the standing line.

Clove Hitch

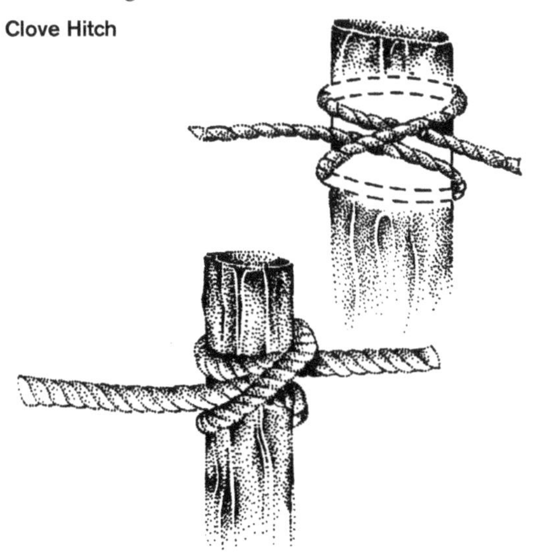

Rolling Hitch

The Rolling Hitch can be used to tie a line to a piling or to tie a bumper to a guardrail without the bumper slipping sideways. The turns should be firmed up close and tight, and you should pull on the tag end to help secure it.

Rolling Hitch

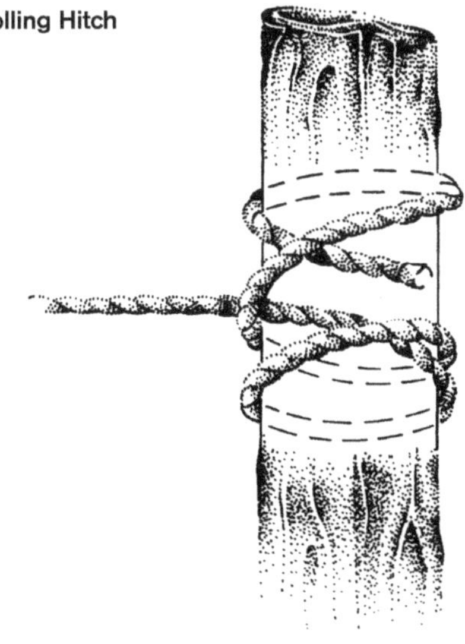

Bowline Knot

The Bowline Knot is a customary all-purpose boating knot that doesn't slip or jam when properly tied.

Bowline Knot

Sheet Bend

The Sheet Bend is a good knot for connecting two ropes together, as might be done for towing. It works with lines of different diameter and does not slip.

None of these boat knots retains 100 percent of the breaking strength of the unknotted line or rope, so if your rope is weakened (frayed or cut), be careful. Under maximum-stress conditions, you may get only 60 to 70 percent of the normal breaking strength.

Sheet Bend Knot

K

KNOTS, FISHING

Just as a strong fishing line is essential in sportfishing, so, too, is a strong knot essential in connecting the fishing line to the object being fished.

Putting a knot in a line changes its breaking strength because the knot is usually the weakest section. Thus, anglers should tie the strongest, most reliable fishing knots they can to achieve the maximum strength possible from their fishing lines. Many people use inferior or poorly tied knots and get away with it because they seldom test their tackle in extreme situations (for example, where ultralight gear is being used or huge fish are being battled).

The ideal knot is one that retains the full breaking strength of the line as if it never had a knot in it. In the ideal scenario, every time that there was breakage, the split occurred at the section of line above the knot. That would be as good as you could possibly hope for. Unfortunately, this scenario seldom happens, partly because anglers use inadequate knots or tie good knots improperly. It is also because there are different knots for different applications, and for some applications no knot yields 100 percent strength.

If you use a knot that regularly achieves only 75 percent of the strength of your line in maximum stress situations, the knot will break before the line. If, however, you tie a knot that achieves 100 percent of the breaking strength of the line, the line will usually break before the knot. Of course, you don't want either one to break, but the important point is that under extreme circumstances your line did as much as it was capable of doing. Perhaps the line was too light for the conditions, the fish was too big, the drag was set too loosely, or the rod was too soft—nevertheless, the line did what it was supposed to do.

However, knot performance varies from one angler to the next. People vary in the way they form their knots, how many wraps they make, how fastidious they are in tying, and so forth. A knot is only as good as the angler tying it. Much can be said regarding the virtue of practice for achieving uniform knot tying, so that once you have mastered a given knot and its use, you can expect it to perform reliably time after time.

Certain lines seem to accommodate particular knots better than others. This may be due to differences in the fiber, material, coating, or molecular structure. Nylon monofilament manufacturers say that knot strength is a characteristic that is built into fishing line and manipulated in the finishing process, so this quality may be stronger in some brands than in others. With nylon, knot failures are usually due to improper tying rather than to the properties of the line itself. With braided and microfilament lines, knot failures are usually due to using the wrong knot.

Here are some pointers for effective knot tying:

1. Learn to tie a knot at home; don't practice on the water. Practice tying it with several different strengths (diameters) so that you can do it uniformly time after time with confidence.
2. Be neat. Keep your wraps and other steps uniform so that when you draw a knot closed, it is neat and precise. Make sure that wraps don't cross over each other.
3. Don't twist a line that is meant to be wrapped. Knots that create a jam do not form as well if the line is twisted, instead of being wrapped over itself.
4. Snug all knots up tightly with even, steady pressure. Knot slippage under pressure can cut the line, so watch the knot for evidence of slippage and redo it if necessary. Don't pop the knot to tighten it. With heavy line, you may need to use pliers to pull on the tag end.
5. Moisten the line as an aid to drawing it up smoothly. If your hands are wet and will wet the line, fine; if not, place the knot and line in your mouth momentarily. Saliva doesn't hurt it. Or dip the entire knot-tying portion of line into the water. Moistening should be done for every knot, especially prior to drawing it.
6. Be careful that you don't nick the knot with clippers or pliers when you cut off the protruding tag end. A nick is a potentially serious and weakening defect. Clip the knot as close as you can; a properly tied knot won't slip. Avoid biting the line with your teeth; this will eventually damage the crown.
7. Check every knot after it is finished by looking at it and by hand-pulling on it in both directions. If a knot breaks repeatedly when you tighten it, check your hook eye or lure connection for rough spots that are cutting the line. If it continues to break, the line may be defective and may need replacement. Try pulling off several feet and retying the knot; often the first few feet of a line are weakened but not the remainder. When you test a knot, you may want to use a glove on your hand or wrap a cloth around your hand before you pull hard on the line.
8. Use plenty of line to complete tying steps without difficulty and to avoid malformed knots. Wetting the line is also helpful. A relaxed line is easier to knot than one that is stiff and coiled or twisted.
9. When using double lines, keep them as parallel as possible and avoid twisting them as the knot is being tied.
10. Test your knots occasionally with a scale to see if they're delivering top performance. You can do this by tying the line to the hook of a reliable spring scale. Have someone wrap the unknotted line around his or her hand several times, using a towel or cloth to keep from getting cut. While your accomplice pulls on the line, you hold and watch the scale, noting the amount of pressure at which the line or the knot breaks. If it is the line that breaks, your knot held.

Using a scale is also a good way to monitor the basic strength of your unknotted line, although this test should be conducted when the lines and knots are wet. Don't be too alarmed if your knot breaks before the line, as long as the breaking point reached is still quite high. A typical top-quality 12-pound-test nylon monofilament line will break in a wet, unknotted condition when roughly 12.8 pounds of pressure are applied. A wet knot delivering 95 percent strength will break when 12.2 pounds of pressure are applied, and one delivering 90 percent will break at 11.5 pounds. If a knot delivers consistent breakage at or near the labeled strength of the line, then you can be satisfied with it until you can find a better knot. Generally, a fishing knot is considered good if it breaks at or above 85 percent of the line's unknotted strength in a wet condition.

If you are experiencing strength or holding problems with an otherwise reputable knot, there are several possible causes. You may be weakening the line by drawing the knot down too roughly or by failing to moisten it first; wetting the line and knot before drawing the knot down smoothly is very important. Another cause may be the type of line; the same knot will not perform as well when tied on some lines as on others. Super thin lines, for example, are more problematic than conventional diameter lines. Try making more wraps or more turns around the hook eye than you might otherwise. When all else fails, try a different knot for the line you're using.

In using a particular knot, you need to consider more than just its maximum breaking strength. Likewise, just because a knot is easy to tie—and some are much easier than others—it is not the best choice in every circumstance. Some knots are very bulky and would not be useful on a small hook or wouldn't easily pass through rod guides when you are casting or—more importantly—when a big fish is pulling the leader or backing off a reel and through a bunch of rod guides at phenomenal speed. By knowing a number of knots, you can adapt to changing circumstances.

Fishing knots are primarily terminal connections and line-to-line connections, but they are also a means of creating double-line leaders. Terminal connections are knots used to tie a line directly to a lure or hook. Line-to-line connections join two lines of similar or dissimilar diameter, including fishing line to a leader or tippet.

Terminal Knots

Improved Clinch Knot. Sometimes referred to incorrectly as a "cinch" knot, the Improved Clinch is probably the most popular terminal connection, especially in freshwater and with nylon monofilament line. It is best used for lines under 20-pound-test. Tied properly, this knot has a strength of 90 to 100 percent; poorly tied, it may yield only 75 to 85 percent, which is insufficient, especially for a light line. It is not a good knot to use on lines with a slick finish or on microfilaments.

Improved Clinch Knot

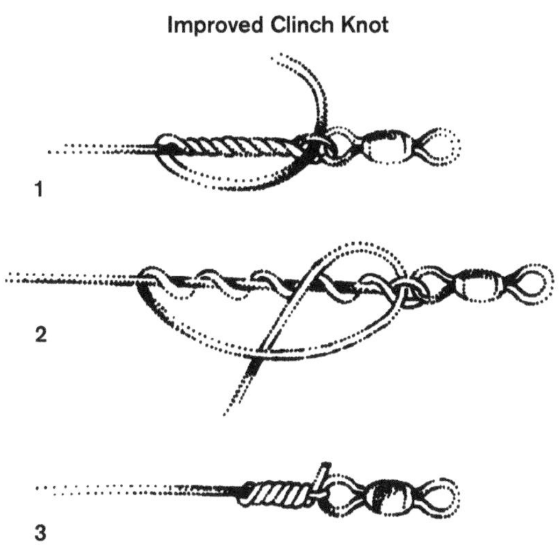

To tie the Improved Clinch Knot, pass the line through the eye of the hook and then make five turns around the standing part of the line. Thread the end through the loop ahead of the eye, and bring it back through the newly created large loop. Moisten the knot with saliva, and check that the coils are spiraled properly and not overlapping one another. Pull firmly to tighten. Test the knot with moderate tension, and clip off the loose end.

Depending on the type and diameter of line being used, six spirals may be best for line through 12-pound test and five spirals for 14- to 17-pound test. For 20-pound test and over, make four spirals and use a pair of pliers to pull on the loose end and snug up the knot.

If you experience slippage with this knot, try running the line through the hook eye twice before completing the other steps. This is a Double Loop Improved Clinch Knot. A variation on this is the Double Loop Clinch Knot, sometimes called a Trilene Knot, which also features two turns around the hook eye but the tag end comes back through both turns and then is snipped off.

Palomar Knot. Line manufacturers say this knot is easier to tie than the Improved Clinch and more consistent. Because it is easier to tie, fewer anglers experience difficulty with its use. Tied properly, it yields a strength of 90 to 100 percent and is meant for terminal connections. Some anglers use it mainly for tying leader tippets to flies, since it is a smaller profile knot than the Improved Clinch. It is an especially valuable knot when used with braided and fused microfilament lines, provided that two or three turns are made around the eye.

To tie the Palomar Knot, double about 6 inches of line and pass the loop through the eye of the hook. Tie an overhand knot in the doubled line, and pass the loop over the entire hook. Moisten the knot, pull on both ends, tighten, and clip the tag end.

The only problem encountered with this knot

occurs when it is used for large, multihooked plugs, where a longer loop must be created to allow the

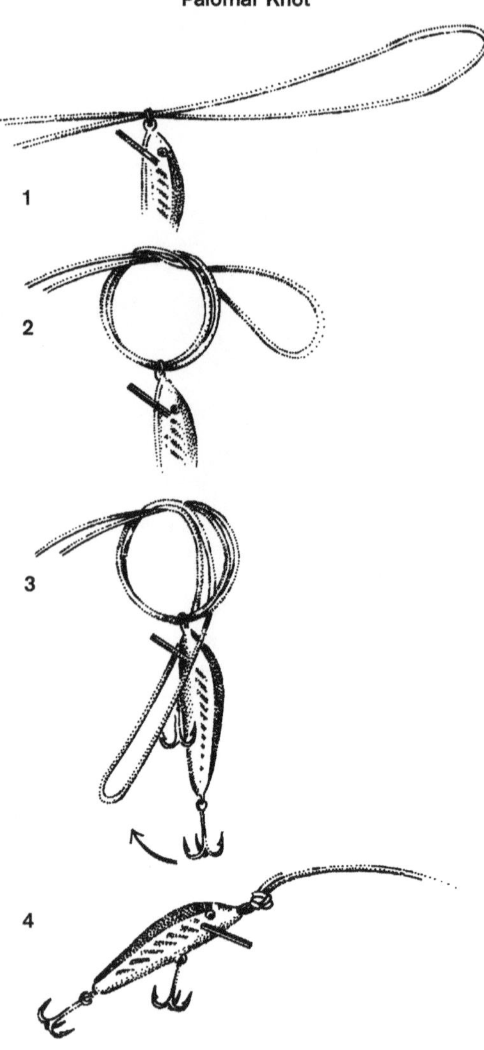

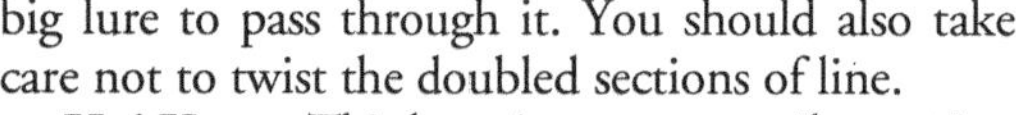

big lure to pass through it. You should also take care not to twist the doubled sections of line.

Uni Knot. This knot is a very versatile creation applicable to most fishing situations. The Uni Knot is actually a do-it-all system and can also be used in line-to-line connections. It can give 90 to 100 percent strength as a terminal tackle connector. When doubled, it can be used with braided and fused microfilament lines.

To tie the Uni Knot as a terminal connector, pass at least 6 inches of line through the eye of the hook and make a circle with the tag end. Bring the tag end around the double length and through the circle six times, moistening and then pulling snugly after the last turn.

World's Fair Knot. This knot is not as popular as the previous terminal connections, but it is simple to tie, holds line strength fairly well, and is similar to a common, unnamed knot used in sewing.

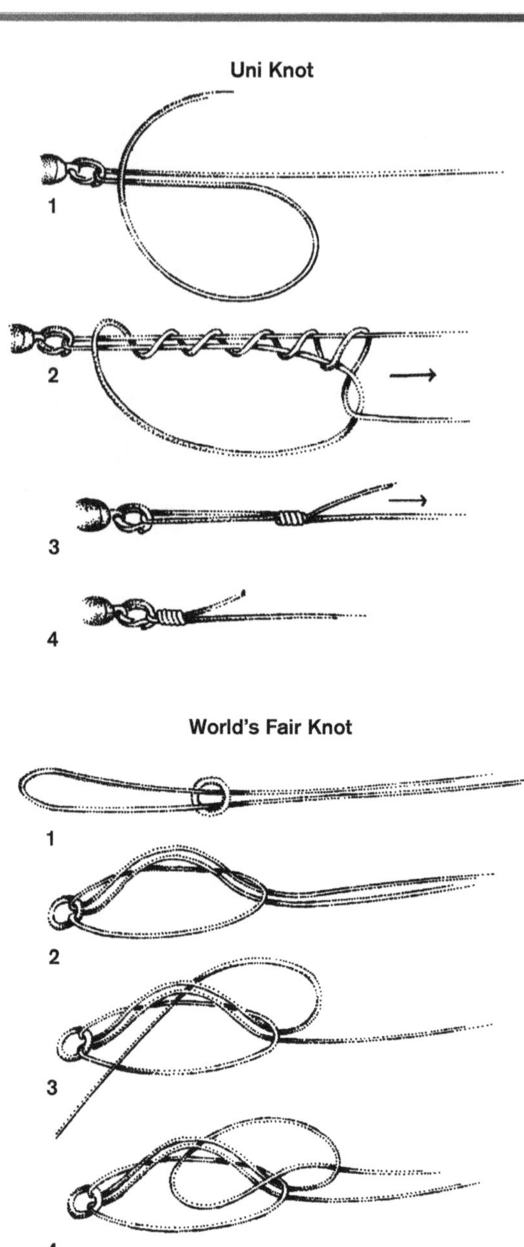

To tie the World's Fair Knot, double a 6-inch length of line and pass the loop through the hook eye. Bring the loop back over the standing doubled line, and pull the double line through the loop. Pass the tag end through the double-line loop and then back through the new single-line loop. Moisten, pull snug at both ends, and clip excess.

Nonslip Loop. Loop knots are useful terminal connections when you want to get more action out of a lure and you prefer not to use a snap. These knots are also helpful with some jigs and weighted flies, allowing them to appear more natural on the fall, swim, or drift. Anglers have devised a number of loop knots, and many work fairly well, although some slip under extreme pressure and few hold a high percentage of line

Nonslip Loop Knot

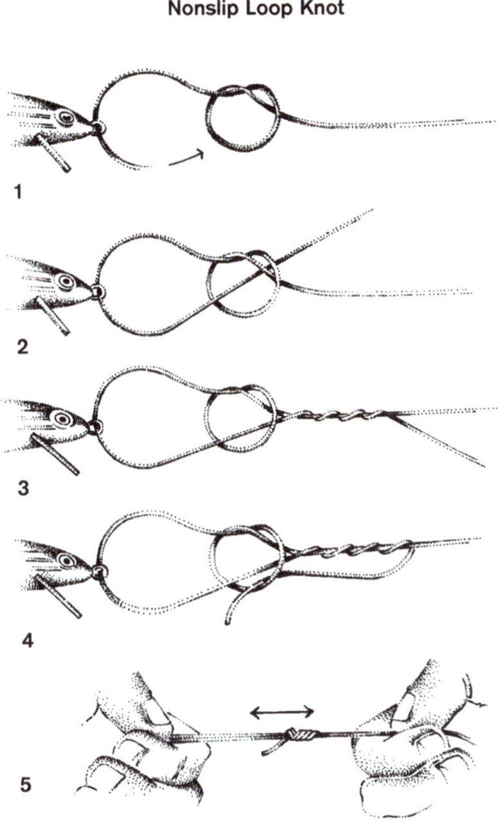

strength. Loops can be made with the Uni and Improved Clinch Knots by using pliers to grasp the tag end and pull it tightly without pulling firmly on the standing line. However, these knots will slip down under extreme tension and will need to be retied, plus the friction caused by that slipping makes the knot and the line just above it suspect. Therefore, it's better to use a good loop knot that will not slip.

The Nonslip Loop Knot has had several names in the past. Primarily used with nylon monofilament, it is not as difficult to tie as it seems and has very good strength. To tie it, make an overhand knot in the line, leaving about 6 inches at the tag end. Pass the tag end through the hook eye and then back through the overhand knot the same way that it came out. The size of the overhand knot determines the size of the loop; for most situations, keep it small.

Hold the overhand knot softly with one hand, and pull on the tag end of the line to bring the overhand knot down toward the eye. Wrap the tag end around the standing line the proper number of times. (Manufacturers recommend seven wraps for line under 10 pounds, five wraps for 10- to 14-pound line, four wraps for 15- to 40-pound line, three wraps for 50- to 60-pound line, and two wraps for heavier line, but you may need to experiment with this on thin-diameter lines.) Bring the tag end back through the loop of the overhand knot the same way that it exited. Moisten, pull on the tag end to form the final

Offshore Swivel Knot

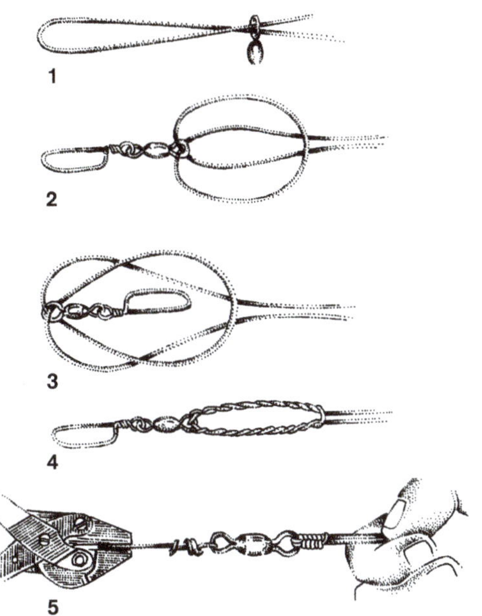

knot, and then pull from both ends to snug up completely.

Offshore Swivel Knot. This knot is a very strong terminal connection for use with a doubled line leader (formed with a Bimini Twist or Spider Hitch), primarily employed in saltwater and by big-game anglers. It is mainly tied on a swivel or a snap but can be tied to a hook or an eyelet, and it will continue to hold if one of the two lines is cut.

To tie the Offshore Swivel Knot, bring the loop end of the doubled line through the eye of the swivel and make one twist in the loop beyond the swivel eye. Bring the end of the loop back against the standing double line, and hold the two together with one hand. With your other hand, slide the swivel to the opposite end of the loop and rotate the swivel through the center of both loops six times. Hold the double line tightly, and release the end of the loop while pulling on the swivel. Grip the swivel with pliers, and pull on both the swivel and the standing double line with even pressure. Push the loops toward the swivel as necessary.

Conventional Snell Knot. Many anglers do not know how to tie a Snell Knot, but it is an important, and very strong, knot when properly formed. A Snell Knot is applied only to hooks with a turned-up or turned-down eye and has the advantage of a direct pull for increased hooksetting efficiency. It is used in fishing with bait and is an especially popular knot with salmon and steelhead anglers, which is why it is sometimes called a Salmon Hook Knot.

To form the Conventional Snell Knot, bring at least 6 inches of the tag end of the line through the hook eye, lay it along the shank, and form a loop. Pinch both sections to the shank with one

K

Conventional Snell Knot

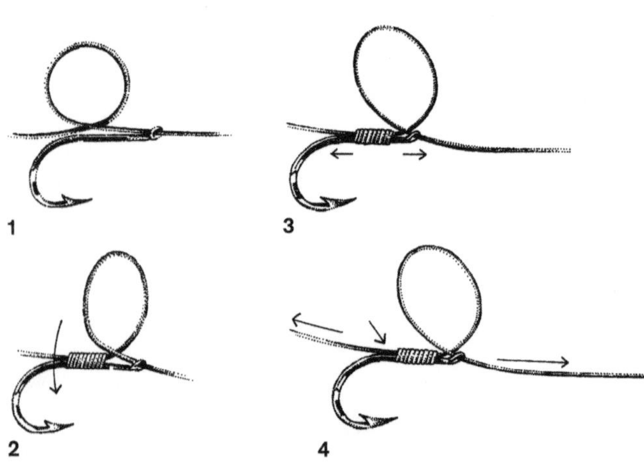

hand, and with the other hand wrap the looped line tightly and closely without overlays toward the eye. After making 10 wraps, snug down the knot. Slide the snell toward the eye if it is not going to be used to hold bait and to the midshank if it is to be looped to hold bait (primarily it is used to hold an egg or spawn sack to the shank). Pull the line with equal pressure in opposite directions, and trim the tag end. Unless you have taken pliers to the tag end of the snell and pulled it extremely tight, you can usually move this knot along the shank of a bait hook. If you move it to the middle, hold the shank of the hook in one hand and with the other hand push the standing line in through the eye until a loop forms. The loop can now be tightened around bait, especially a cluster of salmon eggs or a spawn sack, and these can be readily replaced.

Uni Snell. For many people the Uni Snell is an easier method of snelling a hook and, once mastered, is quicker to tie than the conventional knot.

To tie the Uni Snell, pass 6 inches of line through the hook eye, pinch the line against the shank, and form a circle. Make five to seven turns

Uni Snell Knot

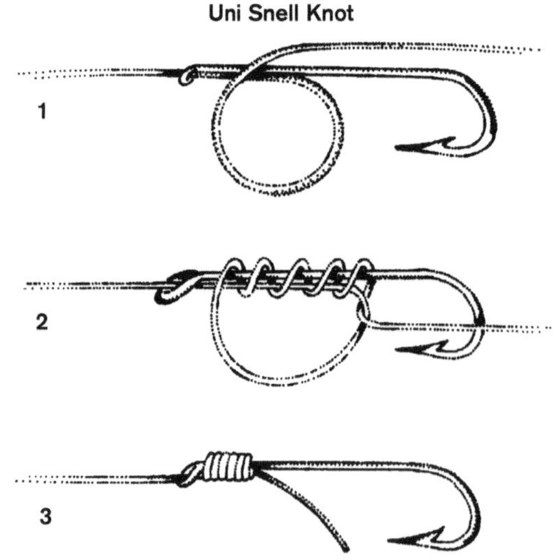

(fewer for stronger line) through the loop and around the standing line and hook shank. (Locate the knot on the midshank if it is to be looped to hold bait or close to the eye if it will not hold bait.) Snug the knot tightly by pulling in both directions, and trim the tag end. See the previous instructions for making a bait-holding loop.

Double Turle Knot. This knot is a terminal connection that has long been popular with fly anglers. It is easy to tie, has moderate strength, permits a direct pull through a turned-up or turned-down eye, and may help a dry fly sit better on the water.

To tie the Double Turle Knot, pass the tippet end of the leader through the turned-up or turned-down hook eye, going from the eye toward the point. Make a loop, wrap the tag end around twice, and snug up. Open the loop and slip the fly

Double Turle Knot

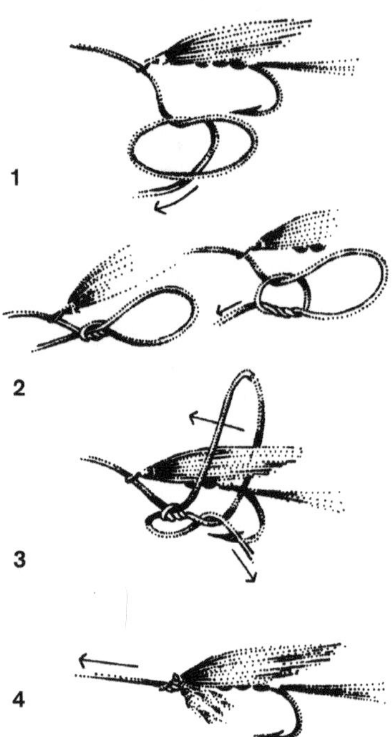

through; then place the loop around the neck of the fly just behind the eye. Pull on the standing line until the knot is tight against the neck.

Figure Eight Knot. The Figure Eight Knot is used for connecting a braided wire leader to a hook or lure and is popular for quick-changing lures. It is principally used by saltwater anglers who are fishing deep for toothy species and is not recommended for use with nylon monofilament, braided, or microfilament lines. It is primarily shown here to help illustrate the Improved Figure Eight.

To tie the Figure Eight Knot, pass the tag end of braided wire through the hook eye and bring it back toward the standing end. Pass the tag end under the standing end, up and over it, and through the loop in front of the hook eye. Use

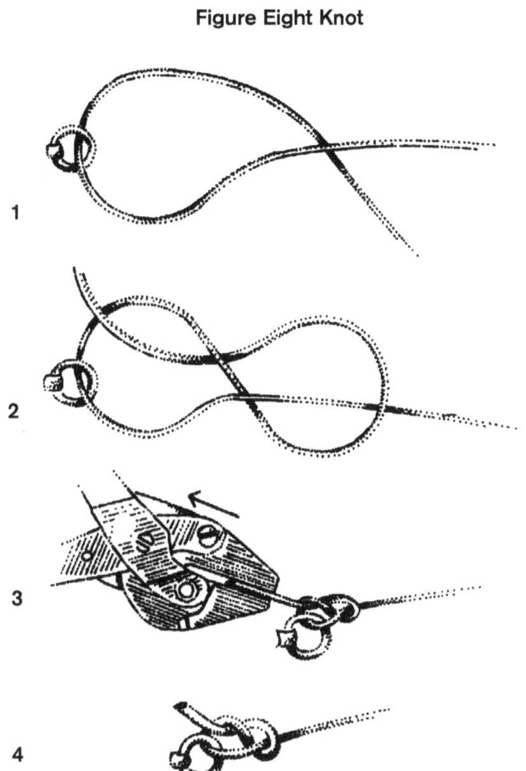

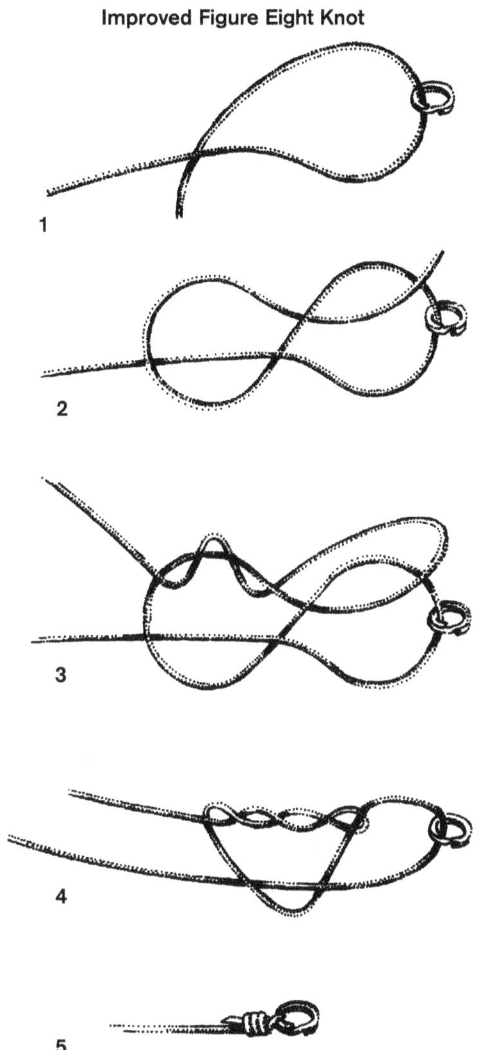

pliers to pull on the tag end and tighten the knot. Do not pull on the standing end; this may cause a crimp that could affect lure action.

Improved Figure Eight Knot. Sometimes referred to as the Orvis Knot, this is a strong variation of the Figure Eight Knot. The Improved Figure Eight Knot is useful with nylon monofilament line and leaders, and is easy to form.

To tie the Improved Figure Eight Knot, pass the tag end of the line through the hook eye and bring it back toward the standing end. Pass the tag end under the standing end, up and over it, and through the loop in front of the hook eye. Wrap the tag end twice through the loop farthest from the hook eye, and pull on both the hook and standing line to snug the knot.

Haywire Twist. The Haywire Twist is an important means of connecting a single-strand wire leader to a swivel or hook. For tying instructions, *see: Wire Leader.*

Line-to-Line Knots

Line-to-Line Uni. This knot is excellent for joining two lines and is perhaps the easiest line-to-line connection to make. Quicker and easier to tie than the time-honored Blood Knot, the Line-to-Line Uni is equally reliable. It is best for joining lines of similar diameter, especially in strengths up to 20 pounds, but can also work on those of different but not hugely disparate diameter by decreasing the number of wraps on the stronger line. It can also be used to join nylon monofilament and microfilament or braided lines.

To join two light lines of fairly similar diameter, overlap each at least 6 inches. Hold these in the middle of the overlap with your left hand, and make a circle with the line extended to the right. Bring the tag end around the double length six times, pulling snugly after the last turn. Repeat the process in reverse direction on the other side. Moisten the lines and knots, and pull the two sections away from each other to draw up the knot; then pull the lines firmly and clip both loose ends. Use five wraps for 10- to 17-pound line, four wraps for heavier line.

To tie the Line-to-Line Uni with lines of different diameter, use the appropriate number of wraps for each line. For example, when joining 12-pound to 20-pound, as might be done for a short leader, make five turns in the lighter line and four turns in the heavier line. With heavier lines, you may need to use pliers to pull on the tag ends and snug up. For lines of different material or vastly different diameter, consider doubling the lighter or more slippery line; in other words, when joining 6-pound line to 20-pound line, make a Uni Knot with a double length of 6-pound line, tying it to a single length of 20-pound. You do not

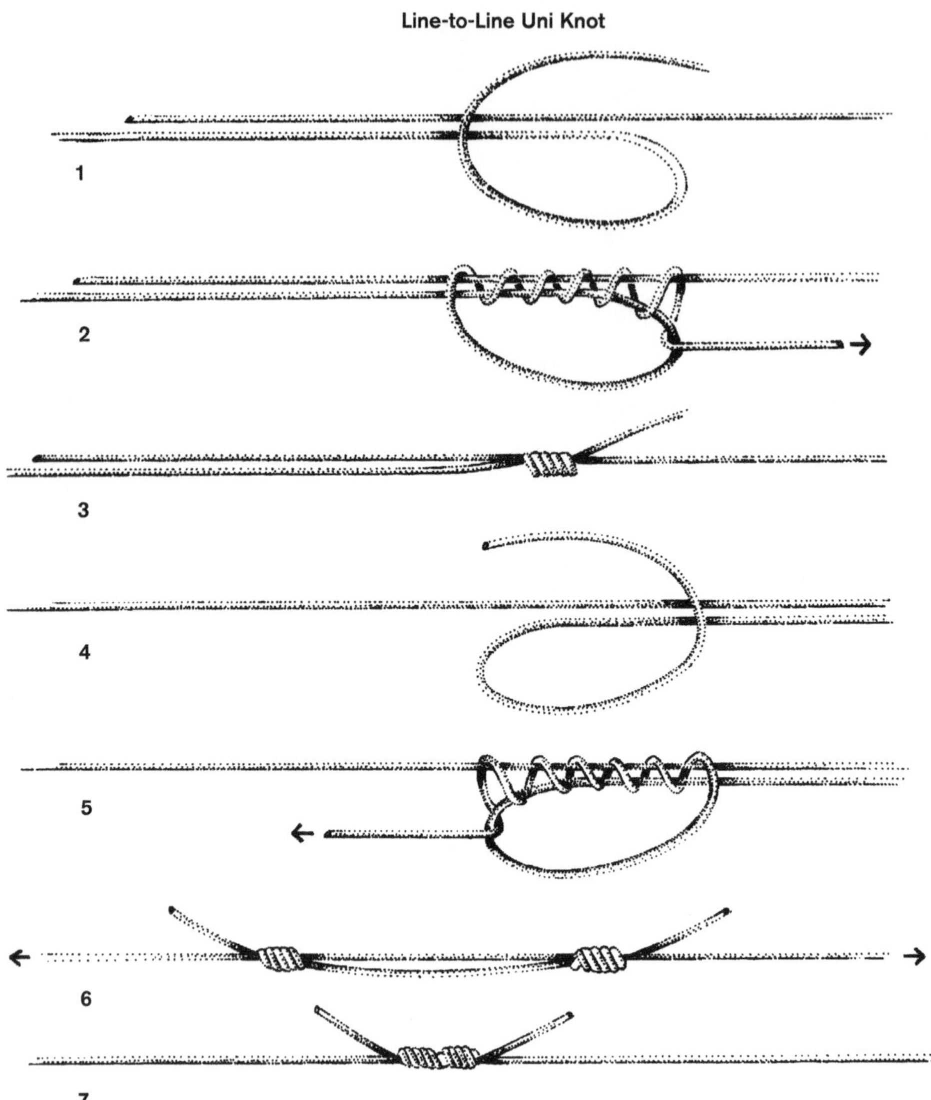

need a double-line knot to do this because adding another knot to the equation is not an advantage. Simply fold the lighter line back over itself, and make the same wraps with two strands as you would with one.

Albright Knot. Also called an Albright Special, this knot is excellent for joining two lines of unequal diameter but is moderately difficult to tie. It is useful for connecting nylon monofilaments to each other or to microfilament or wire, for making shock leaders, for connecting fly line to braided backing, and for tying a Bimini Twist in the end of the lighter casting line.

To tie the Albright Knot, make a loop in the tag end of the heavier line (or fly line) and hold the loop between the thumb and forefinger of your left hand. Pass 8 to 10 inches of lighter line (or fly-line backing) through the loop from the top, and pinch it tightly against the two loop strands. With your right hand, wrap the lighter line back over itself and the loop strands. Make 10 to 12 tight wraps, starting next to your fingers and working toward the loop end. Pass the tag end of the lighter line through the loop from the bottom, and exit out the top; both strands of the lighter line should be on the same side of the loop. With the left hand still holding the knot, move the knot gently toward the loop and then pull on both the standing and the tag ends of the light line. Pull tightly on the standing and tag ends of all lines, and trim tag ends.

Surgeon's Knot. This is a good knot for tying a leader with lines of different diameter and is popular with fly anglers for connecting a tippet and leader, especially when using a shock tippet. This is a very simple knot to tie, and people who fish in cold weather love it.

To tie the Surgeon's Knot, bring the tippet and leader lines parallel to each other and overlap about 6 inches. Make a loose overhand knot, bringing the tippet completely through the loop. Bring both lines through the loop a second time, keeping the strands together. Hold both lines at both ends, and

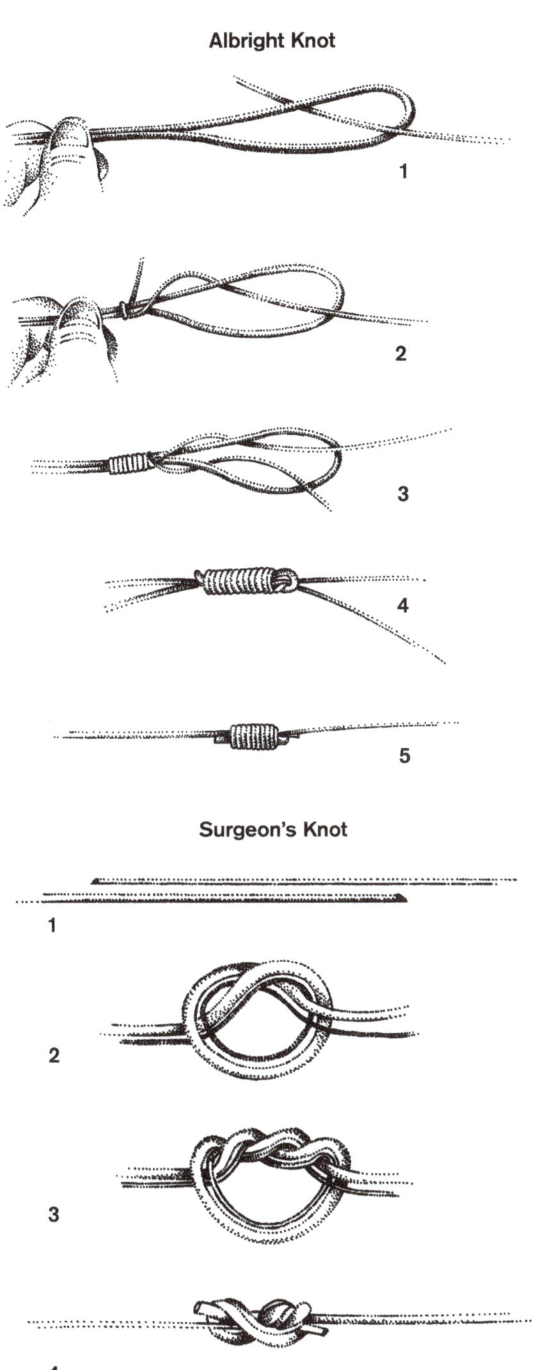

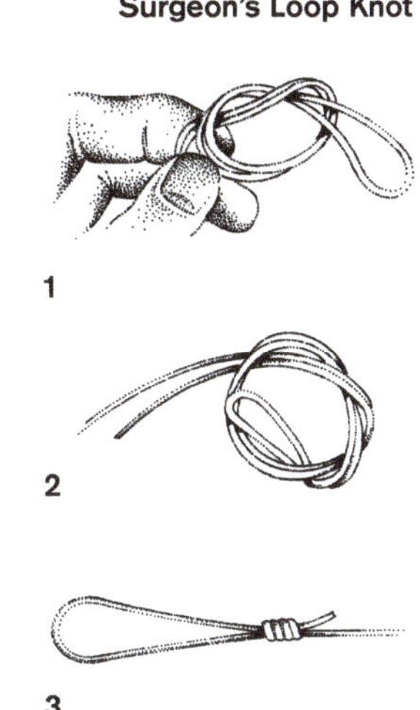

K

pull the knot tight. Trim closely because this knot is slightly bulky and any protrusion could catch in the rod guides.

Surgeon's Loop. A common and easy-to-tie knot, a Surgeon's Loop is used to put a loop in the end of a line for connecting other lines. It is primarily used in fly fishing for loop-to-loop leaders but is slightly bulky and can snare the rod guides.

To tie the Surgeon's Loop, double the end of a line and make an overhand knot at the point where the line is doubled. Leave the loop open and pass the end of the double line through it a second time. Hold the single standing line and adjust the loop size; then pull on the loop to tighten it, and clip the excess.

Blood Knot. The Blood Knot is a strong knot if tied properly, and it has long been a popular connection for two nylon monofilament lines, although some anglers prefer the simpler Uni Knot for tying one line to another. However, the Blood Knot has a low profile if properly formed and if the tag ends are trimmed close, and it runs through rod guides nicely. Some anglers consider the Blood Knot an easy knot to tie, but the plethora of tools invented over the years to aid in tying it seems to disprove this statement. It isn't really difficult to tie, and regular users can tie it virtually blindfolded, but some attention to detail is required when it is being learned. The Blood Knot is primarily used by fly anglers for connecting different lengths of line when making their own multipiece tapered leader, and it is best when tied with lines of the same or generally similar diameter. For tying to dissimilar diameters (such as 30-pound line connected to 12-pound line to make a shock leader), double the tag end of the smaller-diameter line and wrap it around the thicker-diameter line by using the same general instructions that follow but making just three wraps in the thicker-diameter line. This variation is called an Improved Blood Knot.

To tie the basic Blood Knot, cross two lines and wrap one five times around the other, bringing the tag end back and between the strands. Pinch this section to keep it from unraveling. Wrap the second line over the first five times in the opposite direction, bringing the tag end of the second line back and into the center loop in the opposite direction of the other tag end. Slowly pull on both of the joined lines to draw the wraps together; then tighten firmly and trim.

A modification of the knot is the Extension Blood Knot, which provides a short length of trailer line for a dropper fly. It is tied in the same manner as an ordinary Blood Knot, except that a longer length of line is used on one section and

K

Blood Knot

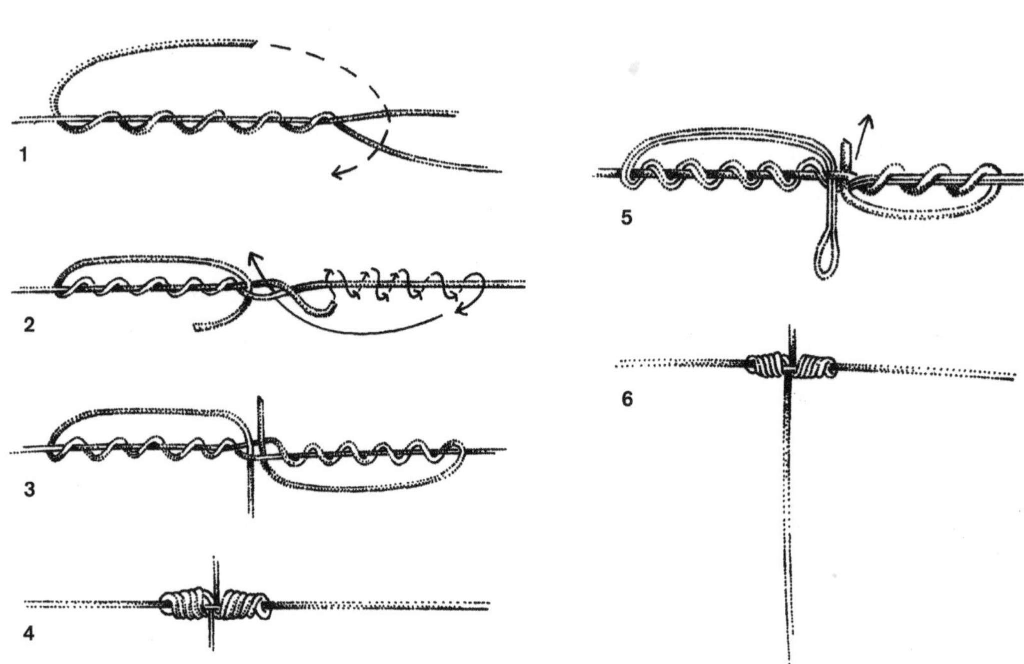

drawn completely through the middle loop. Leave between 8 and 12 inches of this line extending from the knot; too little will not be enough to tie a fly to it, and too much will encourage tangling. This extension should be used whenever you plan to fish a dropper fly; it provides the best and strongest connection to the main line (or leader).

Common Nail or Tube Knot. Known primarily as a Nail Knot, but also a Tube Knot, this knot is meant for joining lines of dissimilar diameter. It has long been a preferred method of connecting the butt end of a leader to a fly line, as well as reel backing to a fly line. It is formed with the use of a smooth instrument like a nail, small tube, piece of straw, straightened paper clip, or sewing needle. The Tube or Nail Knot is a nicely compressed knot that moves through rod guides well and does not pull out. Although experienced anglers can tie this knot fairly readily, many people who have infrequent occasion to join lines find it troublesome and time-consuming, usually having to make a couple of attempts until they get it right. The fact that an accessory like a nail or tube is needed (but often unavailable on the water) is also a drawback.

To tie a Tube Knot using a tube (a short piece of rigid plastic from the tube used in a ballpoint pen is great), lay the tube, the butt end of the leader, and the tip end of the fly line alongside each other with the fly line headed left and the leader headed right. Pinch all three in the middle with your left thumb and index finger, and allow 8 to 10 inches of leader overlap. With your right hand, wrap the leader snugly five or six times around the fly line, leader, and tube. Working

Nail/Tube Knot

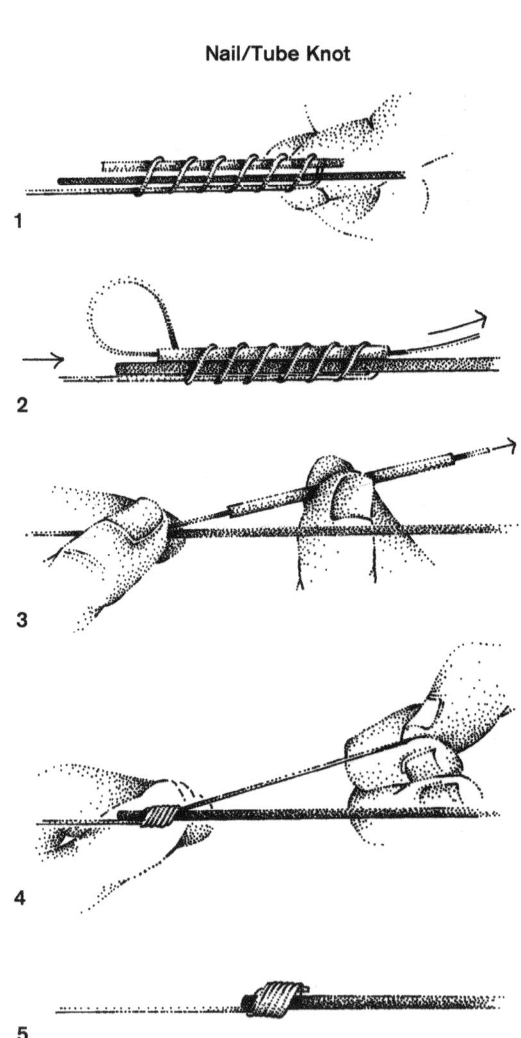

from right to left, line the wraps up against each other and pinch the entire assemblage in with the left fingers. Pass the butt end of the leader through the tube from left to right. Pull both ends of the leader tight and remove the tube. Tighten both ends of the leader again, and simultaneously pull on the leader and fly line tightly before clipping off the ends.

To tie a Nail Knot, place a nail between the two lines and follow the same instructions as for a tube with the following exceptions: Make the wraps less snug, and run the tag end of the leader down alongside the nail. Using a small-diameter tube is actually easier.

Double Nail Knot. The Nail or Tube Knot has a number of variations. One of these is a Double Nail Knot in which two nail knots are tied in opposite directions; it can be used to tie similar-diameter lines together, although the Line-to-Line Uni is far easier to tie and just as useful if you are simply putting more line on a reel. The Double Nail Knot is used with heavy monofilament leaders by some fly anglers because of its lesser bulk; it is used by some big-game anglers for connecting a shock leader to a double line, in part because it can be easily wound through guides and onto a reel.

To tie the Double Nail Knot, overlap both lines with an ample length, form the first knot, remove the nail, and gently draw the knot together without tightening; then form the second knot in the opposite direction, remove the nail, and pull this knot snug. Finally pull both together and tighten firmly.

Double Nail Knot

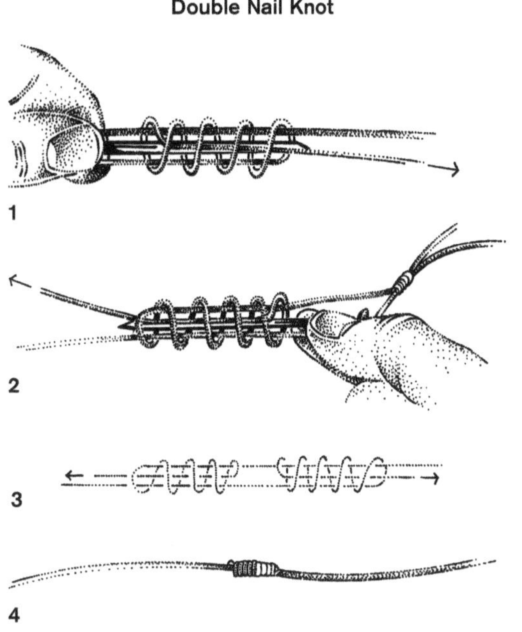

Speed Nail Knot. The Speed Nail Knot, also called an Instant Nail Knot or Fast Nail Knot, is an interesting version of the Common Nail Knot. More like a snell, this knot originated with steel-

Speed Nail Knot

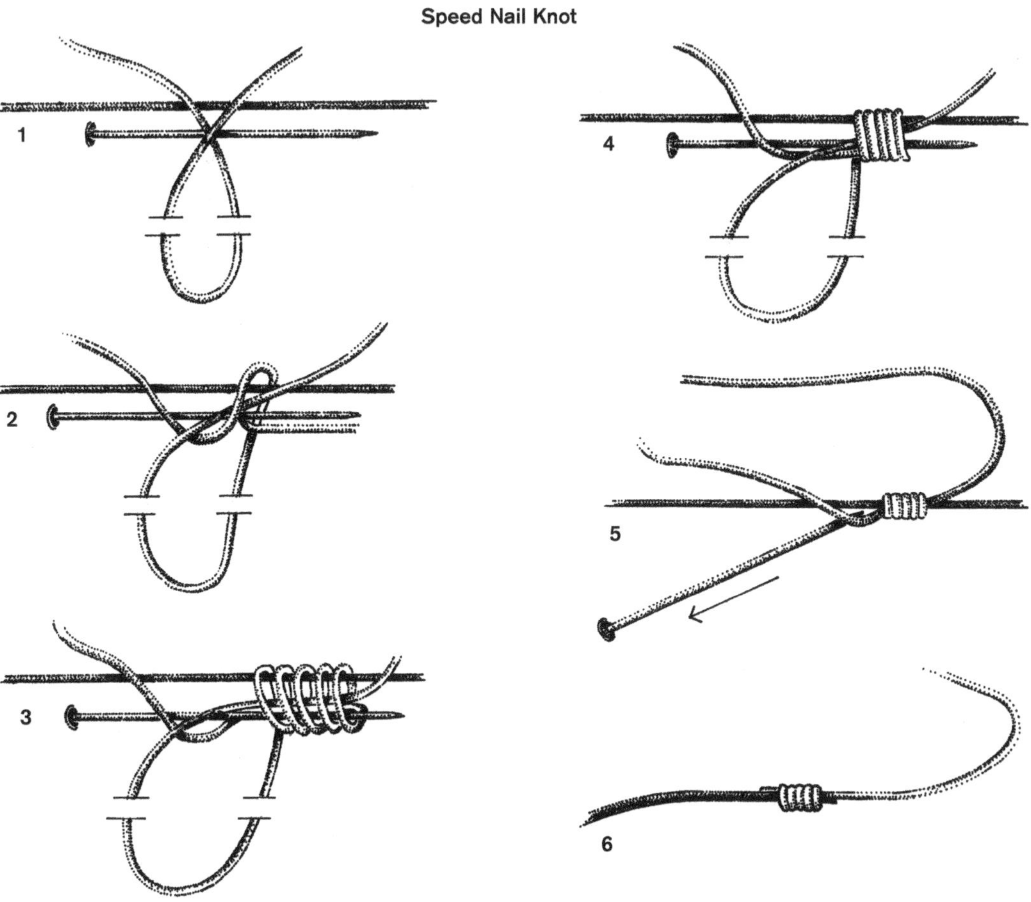

K

head anglers who used it for snelling bait hooks. It looks much more difficult to tie than it is and with a bit of practice can be whipped up in mere seconds.

To tie the Speed Nail Knot to a fly line, use a nail or something smooth and rigid. Hold the nail parallel to the fly line with the end facing right and extending no farther than the edge of the nail. Take whatever length of leader you want to make, cross the ends, and place the crossed portion against the nail and fly line; pinch all three in your left thumb and first joint of your index finger. Keep the tag end of the leader a short distance from the nail, in effect creating a very large loop that dangles below. Take the upper right side of the loop in your right hand, and wrap only that portion of the loop around the tag end of the leader, the fly line, and nail five or six times, using the tip of your index finger to keep the wraps in place. With the wraps secure in your left hand, let go of the loop with your right hand and grab the tag end of the leader, pulling until the loop dissolves and the knot snugs. Gently slide the nail out, and pull on both ends of the leader to tighten, then on the leader and fly line. Clip the excess.

With practice you can tie this knot in under 20 seconds, and you can do it without the use of a nail. Honest.

Other Line-to-Line Connections

In addition to the knots already described, other knots can be used for line-to-line connections, particularly for big-game wind-on leaders and shock leaders; and for situations where tremendous stress is put on terminal tackle (especially near the boat), where lines of greatly different diameter are coupled for special situations, and where light tackle is employed for big fish. Many of these variations are offshoots of existing knots and hybrid combinations of knots. An example is making a dissimilar-diameter line-to-line connection by using a few wraps of a Uni Knot with heavy leader material and a Blood Knot with lighter material; another example is connecting a fly leader with a Bimini Twist on the class tippet and a Nail Knot on the shock leader. Many of these knots are in some way related to the use of double-line leaders or require doubling lighter line to bulk it up for connecting to a heavier (thicker) line. Experiment with other connections, looking for ease of tying, maintenance of full line strength, and bulkiness of the final knot.

Double Line Knots

A double line in essence is a leader, though one made from the actual fishing line by virtue of a Bimini Twist or Spider Hitch Knot. If properly tied, these knots, especially the Bimini Twist, hold the full 100 percent breaking strength of a line and knot, offer more resistance to abrasion, and offer added breaking protection in the event (which is relatively unlikely) that one of the two strands breaks.

Bimini Twist. The Bimini Twist, once also known as the Twenty Times Around Knot, has such an intimidating reputation that many anglers have avoided learning to tie it. It is a knot primarily associated with saltwater fishing, especially the use of heavy leaders and big-game angling; however, its usefulness extends much further than that, especially for making a double-line leader in light tackle fishing, where a lot of stress might be applied to the last section of the line. This knot is difficult at first to tie, but you can tie it in under a minute once you've got it mastered. If you can walk, chew gum, and think at the same time, you can tie it.

To tie the Bimini Twist, follow these steps, which are keyed to the illustration:

1. Measure a little more than twice the footage you'll want for the double-line leader. (First-time tiers should use shorter lengths.) Bring the end back to the standing line and hold together. Rotate the end of the loop 20 times, putting twists in it.
2. Spread the loop to force the twists together about 10 inches below the tag end. Step both feet through the loop, and bring it up around your knees so that you will be able to place pressure on the column of twists by spreading your knees apart.
3. Grasp the tag ends firmly, and force the twists as tightly together as possible by spreading your knees. Hold the standing line in your left hand, which is just slightly off a vertical position, and keep the line taut. With your right hand, move the other end to a position at a right angle to the twists, keeping it taut as well. Keeping tension on the loop with your knees, gradually ease the tension of the tag end in your right hand so that the tag end line will roll tightly over the column of twists, beginning just below the uppermost twist.
4. Spread your legs apart slowly to maintain pressure on the loop. Steer the tag end into a tight spiral coil as it continues to roll over the twisted line. Keeping a balance of constant tension without slack is critical to this process.
5. When the spiral of the tag end has rolled over the column of twists, continue keeping knee pressure on the loop and move your left hand down to grasp the knot. Place a finger in the crotch of the line where the loop joins to prevent slippage of the last turn; take a half-hitch with the tag end around the nearest leg of the loop, and pull up tight.
6. With a half-hitch holding knot, release knee pressure but keep the loop stretched out. Using the remaining tag end, take a half-hitch around both legs of the loop but do not pull tight.
7. Make three more turns with the tag end around both legs of the loop, winding inside the bend of the line formed by the loose half-hitch and toward the main knot. Pull the tag end slowly, forcing the three loops to gather in a spiral.

Bimini Twist Knot

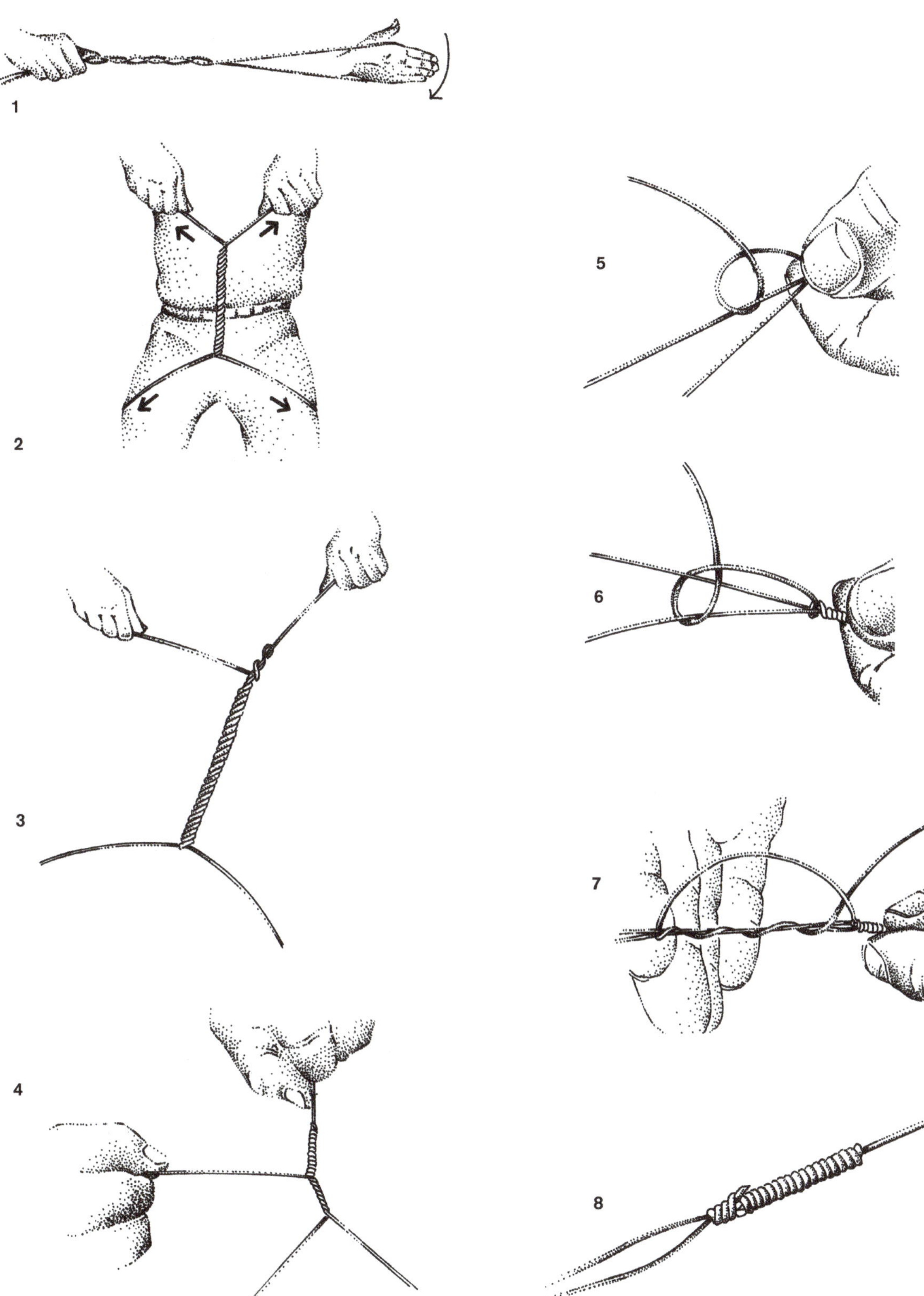

Small, slender fishes with bony spines in front of all their fins existed and disappeared eons ago; some types had bony armor as well.

Spider Hitch Knot

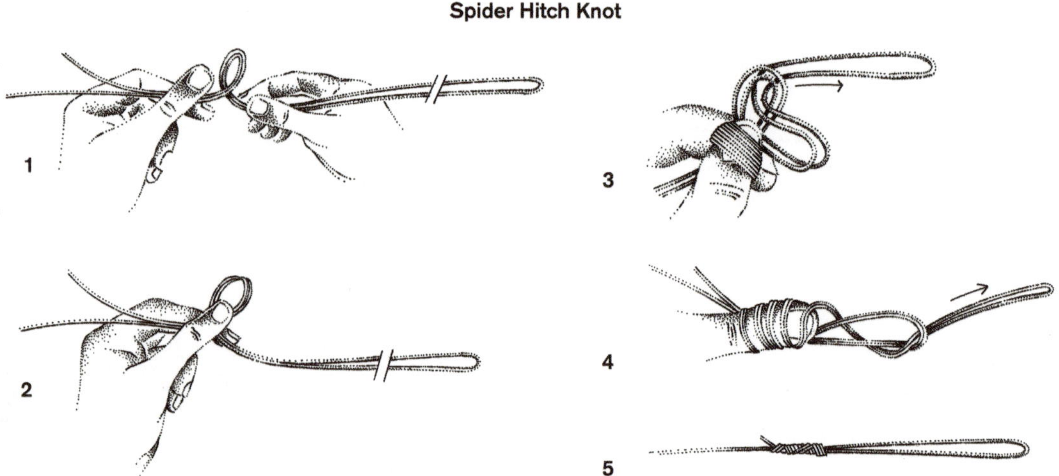

K

8. When the loops are pulled up nearly against the main knot, moisten and tighten to lock in place. Trim the end.

These directions apply to tying double-line leaders of 5 feet or less. For longer double-line sections, two people may be required to hold the line and make initial twists. Or the line could be looped around a firm object, like a cleat, and the twisting done at the tag end. It is also possible to use a Bimini Twist to tie short lengths of double line by placing the loop over one knee that has been tucked underneath your thigh.

Spider Hitch. The Spider Hitch is a very good knot that is an alternative to the Bimini Twist. Although not as well known as the Bimini Twist, it is much easier to tie, especially with cold hands. This knot is very useful in lighter-strength line, particularly as a leader in freshwater fishing.

To tie the Spider Hitch, make a loop of whatever length of line you want to use as a leader, and hold the ends between thumb and index finger at the first joint of the thumb. Make a small loop in the line, tuck it between the fingers, and extend it directly in front of the thumb. Wrap the doubled line around the thumb and small loop five times, working toward the tip of the thumb. Then pass the doubled line through the small loop, making the five wraps unwind off the thumb and using a steady draw. Pull firmly on all ends to snug the knot.

See: Leader.

KOKANEE

The landlocked form of sockeye salmon *(see: salmon, sockeye).*

KRILL

Small pelagic shrimplike crustaceans with bristled tails. Krill range from about 1/2 inch to 3 inches long. Most are transparent, and many have light-producing organs. They migrate vertically and are plentiful enough to be a major food source for seabirds, fish, and whales.

KYPE

The curved or hooked lower jaw of male salmonids.

L

LABRADOR

See: Labrador; Newfoundland.

LACTIC ACID

Acid produced in muscle tissues after strenuous exercise. This occurs in fish, sometimes to their detriment, when being landed by anglers.

See: Catch-and-Release.

LACUSTRINE

Having to do with, or living in, a lake.

LADYFISH

Ladyfish are members of the small Elopidae family. They occur worldwide and are related to tarpon *(see).* They are similar in appearance to tarpon, although far smaller. Ladyfish are excellent light-tackle sportfish commonly found in schools prowling shallow nearshore and brackish waters. They are known for their habit of skipping along the water and jumping energetically when hooked. Ladyfish are pursued commercially in some parts of their range, although a plentitude of bones discourages human consumption; most commercial captures are used as fish meal, and most angler captures are released.

There are at least six species of ladyfish in the genus *Elops,* all of which are similar in average size, behavior, and characteristics. In the western Atlantic, the ladyfish *(E. saurus)* ranges from Cape Cod and Bermuda to the northern Gulf of Mexico and southern Brazil, although it is most common in Florida and the Caribbean. It is also known as tenpounder, as *ubarana* in Portuguese, and as *malacho* in Spanish.

In the eastern Atlantic, two species are found off the African continent and are often confused with each other. These are the West African ladyfish *(E. lacerta),* which occurs from Senegal to Angola and is also known as the Atlantic ladyfish, ninebone, and Guinean ladyfish, and the Senegalese ladyfish *(E. senegalensis),* which occurs from Mauritania to Zaire and is also known as ninebone.

In the eastern Pacific, the Pacific ladyfish *(E. affinis)* occurs from Southern California to Peru, although it is rare in northern Baja California. It is also known as machete, and as *chiro* and *malacho del Pacifico* in Spanish.

The Hawaiian ladyfish *(E. hawaiensis)* occurs throughout the west-central Pacific and is known as *awu'awu* in Hawaiian. In the Indo-West Pacific, the tenpounder or springer *(E. machnata)* occurs from South Africa to the Red Sea and eastward to India and the western Pacific, and is reported from New Caledonia and Taiwan.

Identification. Ladyfish have an elongated, slender silvery body with a blue green back and small scales. They look very much like a juvenile tarpon, although they can be distinguished from tarpon by the lack of an elongated last ray on the dorsal fin. Their head is small and pointed, the mouth is terminal, and the tail is deeply forked.

Size. Some species of ladyfish may reach weights from 15 pounds to 24 pounds and a length of 3 feet; such specimens are extremely rare, and in general these fish most commonly weigh 2 to 3 pounds. The all-tackle world records are a 5-pounds, 14-ounce *E. saurus* (from South Carolina), a 12-pound, 9-ounce *E. senegalensis* (from Guinea-Bissau), and a 23-pound, 12-ounce *E. machnata* (from Mozambique).

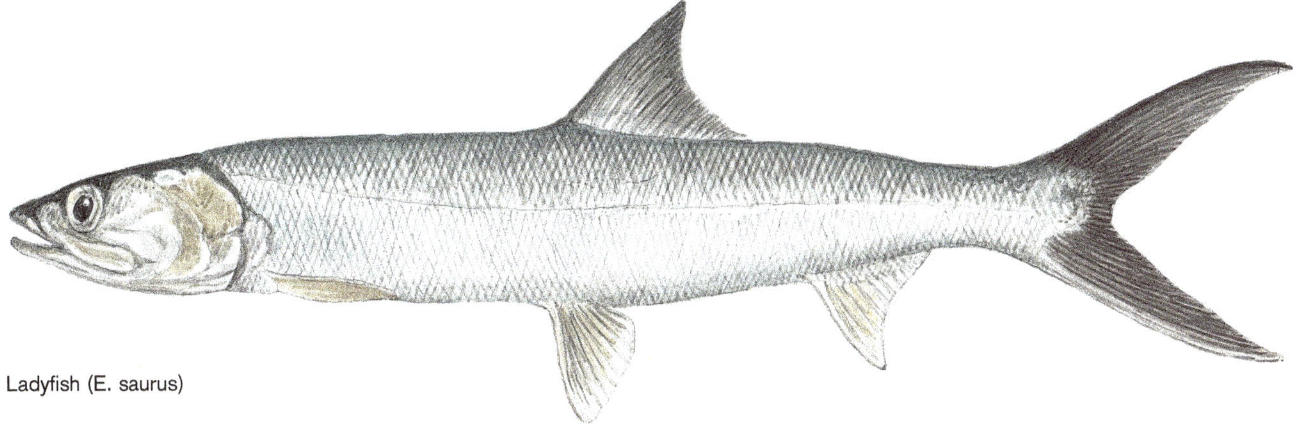

Ladyfish (E. saurus)

Habitat. Ladyfish are inshore species that prefer bays and estuaries, lagoons, mangrove areas, tidal pools, and canals. They occasionally enter freshwater and are rarely found on coral reefs.

Life history. These fish form large schools close to shore, although they are known to spawn offshore. Their ribbonlike larvae is very similar to that of bonefish and tarpon.

Food and feeding habits. Adults feed predominantly on fish and crustaceans. Ladyfish schools are often seen pursuing baits at the surface.

Angling. Ladyfish take baits, flies, and lures readily and are caught by anglers fishing from boats, piers, bridges, the surf, and on flats. They strike swiftly enough to surprise many anglers, so that the fish often isn't hooked. Nevertheless, multiple opportunities to catch these fish are common when large schools are encountered.

The fight of a ladyfish is disproportionate to its size, as it can make searing bonefish-like runs and also leap repeatedly across the surface. Small spoons, shallow-running plugs, and streamer flies are the best artificial offerings, and a leader is necessary to avoid chafing the line. Ladyfish are not often a deliberate pursuit of anglers owing to their generally small size, and thus do not get the attention that is bestowed upon such prized angling targets as bonefish and tarpon. Most anglers encounter ladyfish incidental to other pursuits.

LAMPREY

Other names for the sea lamprey: lamprey eel, stone sucker, nannie nine eyes (UK); Danish: *havlampret;* Dutch: *zeeprik;* Finnish: *merinahkiainen;* French: *lamproie marine;* Italian: *lamprea di mar;* Norwegian: *havnioye;* Portuguese: *lampreia do mar;* Russian: *morskaja minoja;* Spanish: *lamprea de mar.*

Overview

Lampreys are one of two groups of jawless fish (the other being hagfish), which are the most primitive true vertebrates. They are members of the Petromyzontidae family. Jawless fish are fishlike vertebrates that resemble eels in form, with a cartilaginous or fibrous skeleton that has no bones. They have no paired limbs and no developed jaws or bony teeth. Their extremely slimy skin lacks scales. Fossils of lampreys have been dated back 280 million years.

The jawless, eel-like lampreys are just as ugly as their hagfish *(see)* cousins in form and feeding habits; they differ in other respects, however. Hagfish are strictly marine, whereas lampreys are either totally freshwater inhabitants or, if they live in the sea, they return to freshwater rivers to spawn.

Sea Lamprey

Lampreys have a large sucking disk for a mouth and a well-developed olfactory system. The mouth is filled with horny, sharp teeth that surround a filelike tongue. A lamprey's body has smooth, scaleless skin, two dorsal fins, no lateral line, no vertebrae, no swim bladder, and no paired fins. Lampreys have no prominent barbels on their snout; their eyes are well developed in the adult and visible externally; there are seven external gill openings on each side; and the nasal opening is on the upper part of the head.

Whereas hagfish scavenge dead or dying fish and secure their nourishment by entering the body cavities of their victims, literally consuming them from inside outward, lampreys are usually parasitic. The lamprey attaches itself to the side of a live fish by using its suctorial mouth; then, by means of its horny teeth, it rasps through the victim's skin and scales and sucks the blood and body juices. The lamprey's mouth glands produce anticoagulating secretions, thereby assisting the flow of blood. After exhausting the blood supply of its weakened or dying host, the lamprey seeks another fish to attack.

There are reportedly 31 species of lampreys worldwide. Not all are parasitic, however. Sixteen are small, inconspicuous, nonparasitic filter feeders in freshwater streams. Of the parasitic species, nine are anadromous, living as adults in the ocean and returning to freshwater to spawn. Most parasitic types attain a length of roughly 12 inches. The marine, or sea, lampreys *(Petromyzon marinus),* are the largest, some capable of reaching a maximum length of 36 inches.

Lampreys spawn in the spring. They ascend streams where the bottom is stony or pebbly and build shallow depressions by moving stones with the aid of their suctorial mouths. Usually, the male and female cooperate in constructing the nest. When ready to spawn, the pair stir up the sand with vigorous body movements as the milt and eggs are deposited at the same time. The eggs stick to particles of sand and sink to the bottom of the nest. The pair then separate and begin another nest directly above the first, thereby loosening more sand and pebbles, which flow down with the current and cover the eggs. The procedure is repeated at short intervals until spawning is completed. The adults die after spawning.

After a period of several days, depending on the species and water temperature, the young appear and drift downstream until they are deposited in a quiet stretch of water where they settle down and burrow into the bottom to spend several years as larvae (called ammocetes). In this stage, they feed on materials strained from the bottom ooze. When they reach a few inches in length (this varies with the species), the ammocetes transform during late summer or fall into adultlike lampreys, complete with a sucking disk and circular rows of horny teeth.

The sea lamprey is most notorious as a despoiler of valued sport and commercial fish. It ranges the eastern Atlantic from Iceland and northern Europe (including the North Sea and the Baltic, western Mediterranean, and Adriatic Seas) to northern Africa. It ranges the western Atlantic from southern Greenland, Labrador, and the Gulf of St. Lawrence south to the Gulf of Mexico in Florida. It is landlocked in the Great Lakes, the Finger Lakes, Oneida Lake, and Lake Champlain. It breeds exclusively in freshwater.

Young lampreys, when in saltwater or en route to saltwater, are white underneath and blackish blue, silvery, or lead-colored above. Large specimens approaching maturity are usually mottled brown or dressed in different shades of yellow brown and various hues of green, red, or blue. Sometimes they appear black when the dark patches blend with each other. The ventral surface may be white, grayish, or a lighter shade of the ground color of the dorsal surface. Colors intensify during the breeding season.

Mature sea lampreys are from 2 to $2^1/_2$ feet long. The maximum recorded length is nearly 4 feet, and the maximum weight 5.4 pounds. Reproductive activity is the same as in other lampreys. A single female may contain 236,000 small and spherical eggs.

Little is known of lamprey habits in the sea, except that they are extremely aggressive in their attacks on other fish and are capable of swift travel by body undulations similar to that of an eel. Lampreys do not take the angler's lure or baits but may be accidentally caught in freshwater; they are often seen by trout anglers in shallow water, and are sometimes attached to the bodies of trout or salmon that are caught by anglers. Although lampreys are usually close to land during their stay in the sea, they sometimes stray far offshore to water hundreds of fathoms deep. The sea lamprey is tolerant of a wide range of temperatures and water salinities, ranging from freshwater to that of full oceanic saltiness.

Sea lampreys were considered a delicacy in Europe during the Middle Ages. Also, at one time, large numbers were caught for human consumption in New England, especially in the Connecticut and Merrimack Rivers. Today a few are eaten as table fish, but in general the only value the lamprey has is in its larval form as a bait for anglers.

Commonly, but erroneously, lampreys are known or referred to as "lamprey eels." They are not true eels *(see)* of the family Anguillidae. For easy differentiation, eels possess jaws and pectoral fins; these are lacking in the lamprey.

Sea Lampreys in the Great Lakes

Several different types of native lampreys (including the silver lamprey, the American brook lamprey, and the northern brook lamprey) exist in the Great Lakes, but the exotic sea lamprey *(Petromyzon marinus)* is far larger and more predaceous than native lampreys. None of the Great Lakes lampreys have traditionally had any economic value.

A lake trout from Lake Michigan bears a scar made by a lamprey.

Sea lampreys are native to the Atlantic Ocean and Lake Ontario but not to the upper Great Lakes. Sea lampreys entered the Great Lakes system in the 1800s through man-made locks and shipping canals. Prior to the opening of the Welland Canal in 1829, and prior to its modification in 1919, Niagara Falls served as a natural barrier to keep sea lampreys out of the upper Great Lakes.

Sea lampreys were first observed in Lake Ontario in the 1830s. They did not invade Lake Erie prior to the improvements of the Welland Canal in 1919; sea lampreys were first observed in Lake Erie in 1921. After spreading into Lake Erie, sea lampreys moved rapidly to the other Great Lakes, appearing in Lake St. Clair in 1934, Lake Michigan in 1936, Lake Huron in 1937, and Lake Superior in 1938. By the late 1940s, sea lamprey populations had exploded in all of the upper Great Lakes, causing severe damage to lake trout and other critical fish species.

Sea lampreys attach to fish with their sucking disk and sharp teeth, rasp through scales and skin, and feed on the fish's body fluids, often killing the fish. During its life as a parasite, each sea lamprey can kill 40 or more pounds of fish. Sea lampreys are so destructive that under some conditions, only one out of seven fish attacked by a sea lamprey will survive.

Of the 5,747 streams and tributaries of the Great Lakes, 433 are known to produce sea lampreys. Adult sea lampreys move into gravel areas of tributary streams during spring and early summer. They build nests and lay eggs before dying. After the eggs hatch, small, wormlike larvae are swept downstream from the nest and burrow into sand and silt. The larvae feed on bottom debris and algae carried to them by stream currents. During this stage, which can range from 3 to 17 years, larvae grow to about 6 inches. After the larval life stage, sea lampreys enter their parasitic phase and migrate into the open waters of the Great Lakes. Sea lampreys spend the next 12 to 20 months there (not migrating to saltwater) feeding on fish. The sea lamprey's life cycle, from egg to adult, averages about 6 years, and may last as long as 20 years.

The Jitterbug, a classic American surface lure, was first made by Fred Arbogast in 1937 and named after the popular dance of that era. worth about $500 today.

Sea lampreys have had an enormous negative impact on the Great Lakes fishery. Because they did not evolve with naturally occurring Great Lakes fish species, sea lampreys' aggressive, predacious behavior gave them a strong advantage over native fish. Sea lampreys prey on all species of large Great Lakes fish such as lake trout, salmon, rainbow trout (steelhead), whitefish, chub, burbot, walleye, and catfish.

Sea lampreys were a major cause of the collapse of lake trout, whitefish, and chub populations in the Great Lakes during the 1940s and 1950s. These fish were the mainstay of a vibrant and important fishery. Before the sea lamprey's spread, the United States and Canada harvested roughly 15 million pounds of lake trout in the upper Great Lakes each year. By the early 1960s, the catch was only about 300,000 pounds. In Lake Huron, the catch fell from 3.4 million pounds in 1937 to almost nothing in 1947. The catch in Lake Michigan dropped from 5.5 million pounds in 1946 to 402 pounds by 1953. The Lake Superior catch dropped from an average of 4.5 million pounds to 368,000 pounds in 1961. During the time of highest sea lamprey abundance, up to 85 percent of fish somehow not killed by sea lampreys exhibited sea lamprey wounds. The once thriving fisheries were devastated.

L

In 1958, scientists discovered that TFM (3-trifluoromethyl-4-nitrophenol) was selectively effective in controlling sea lampreys without significantly impacting other species. Since its discovery, TFM has been used to suppress populations of sea lampreys in the Great Lakes (and also in other areas) by killing their larvae. As a result, sea lamprey populations in the Great Lakes have been reduced by 90 percent from their historic high numbers of the 1940s and 1950s. Decades of exhaustive tests have shown that at the dose needed to kill sea lampreys, TFM is nontoxic or has minimal effects on aquatic plants, fish, and other aquatic organisms, and is nontoxic to humans and other animals.

Despite this success, due to the high cost of TFM and in response to concerns about the use of chemicals, the Great Lakes Fishery Commission and its agents are reducing reliance on the lampricide by 50 percent by the year 2001. The lampricide is being applied more selectively, and alternative control methods, such as traps, barriers, and sterile-male release, are being employed.

See: Exotic Species.

LANDING FISH

Landing is the act of taking a fish into possession once it has been played close to the angler. In a broader sense, landing also involves the act of setting the hook as well as playing or fighting a fish until it is able to be captured, but these actions are treated separately in this book *(see: hooksetting; playing fish).*

Landing is accomplished in a number of ways, the most common being hand-holding, netting, or gaffing. The circumstances, species, size of fish, type of terminal tackle used, strength of line or leader, and other considerations affect the decision to use one method or another. An especially important factor is whether the fish will be kept or released *(see: catch-and-release).*

Many fish are lost at, or close to, the boat because of the actions of the angler or the person attempting to land the fish. Sometimes, even when everything is done right, a fish manages to get free just when it is almost landed; this usually happens when the hook pulls out even though the angler has kept a tight line. However, in most cases, when fish are lost at or near the boat, either just prior to being landed or while in the act of landing, the cause is a mistake or series of mistakes.

Perhaps the greatest mistake made by inexperienced anglers is reeling a fish right up to the tip of the rod when a fish is at boatside—as if they were going to spear it with the tip of the rod. It's better to leave a few feet of line between the rod tip and the fish so that you can direct the fish or lift/swing it onboard. A common mistake made by many people is applying too much pressure on an active fish that is near the boat, as if the game were a tug of war; finesse, not muscle, is the solution. To properly land fish, especially large, strong, and active specimens, the key is to employ common sense, anticipation, and finesse.

Many of the fish caught in freshwater are fairly small, being a pound or two at most in size. Few people have much trouble landing such fish on any type of equipment. Since the majority of all fish caught are small, most freshwater anglers do not often get to experience difficult fish-playing or fish-landing situations, and unfortunately they are ill-prepared to handle them when they do occur. That partially explains why some large freshwater fish are lost after being hooked. Salmon, large trout, steelhead, and large striped bass will fully test the average freshwater angler's playing and landing skills, and anglers who frequently fish for these creatures learn to handle their tackle and use the proper methods to make landing more of a sure thing.

Fish that are caught in saltwater, on average, are larger than those in freshwater, in terms of both length and weight, and many are not as easily landed by hand as a result. Boats for saltwater use typically have a higher freeboard than those used in freshwater, so the distance to a fish in the water next to the boat is different and is more of a factor in how fish are landed. On the other hand, the tackle used in saltwater, especially for bottom fishing and weighted bait, is generally stout, so some fish can be lifted out in saltwater that could not be lifted out in freshwater or with lighter gear.

When a fish is close to the boat, you can take several actions that will greatly improve your chances of landing it, regardless of how it will actually be landed. Often, a fish that is fairly close to you is still energetic. This is a time to cautiously direct the fish. If you're in a boat and the fish streaks toward it (perhaps to swim under it), you could be put at a disadvantage, particularly when using light tackle. You must reel as fast as possible to keep slack out. If the fish gets under the boat, stick the rod tip well into the water to keep the line away from objects and prevent it from being cut.

You should anticipate that a fish will rush the boat and should be prepared to head it around the stern or bow. In some cases a companion can manipulate the boat (especially with an electric motor or with a pushpole) to help swing the stern or bow away from the fish, which is a smart maneuver. If possible, go toward the bow or stern to better follow or control the fish. Whenever possible, fight the fish on the side that it wants to go; don't try to make it come to the side you are on when it wants to go the other way. Also, when there is wind or current, try to get the boat below the fish, so that it is landed on the upstream or upcurrent side. Try to maneuver the fish around the boat at some point in the fight so that this happens. If it is on the wrong side of the boat prior to landing, it may try to dive under the boat and head upcurrent or upriver, and you will be in a terrible position.

The best tactic is usually to move with the fish around the boat according to what the fish is doing. Never hang back in a tug-of-war with a large, strong fish; use finesse rather than muscle.

When the fish swims around the boat, keep the rod tip up (sometimes out, too) and apply pressure to force its head up and to steer it clear of the outboard or electric motor and the propellers. (Sometimes it's best to tilt motors out of the water.) At times it may be necessary to change the angle of pull on a strong and stubborn fish, perhaps to help steer it in a particular direction or away from some obstruction, or to make it fight a little differently. Apply side pressure then, bringing the rod down and holding it parallel to the water, and turning your body partially sideways to the fish. Fight it as you would if the rod were perpendicular to the water.

With very large fish that get near the boat but are still energetic, or with big fish that stay very deep below the boat and can't be budged, the boat may need to be quickly moved a fair distance away so that line peels off the drag. This changes the angle of pull on the fish and usually helps bring it up from the depths. This situation is common in saltwater but does not happen very much in freshwater, except occasionally with big salmon and big striped bass.

In current, a big fish that gets downriver and through rapids where you are unable to follow, may return upriver if you release line from your reel and allow slack line to drift below the fish. The line below the fish acts as a pulling force from downstream (instead of ahead) and may cause the fish to head upstream again.

With some species of jumping fish (Atlantic salmon, for example), and when using fly fishing tackle, you may have to slacken the tension when the fish jumps by bowing the rod toward it so that the jumper cannot use taut line as leverage for pulling free of the hook. Sometimes you can stop a fish from jumping by putting your rod tip in the water and keeping a tight line, which change the angle of pull and may stop a fish from clearing the surface. These and other aspects of fish playing are discussed in more detail in that section *(see: playing fish).*

Eventually the fish is next to you and may be ready for landing. Most fish, especially large ones, will make at least one final effort at freedom, and this will be a crucial moment. Because of the short distance between you and the fish, there will be a lot of stress on your tackle. You must act swiftly when the fish makes its last bolt for freedom. As it surges away, don't pressure it. Let it go. Point the rod at the fish at the critical moment so there is little or (preferably) no rod pressure. A large fish will peel line off the drag, which, if set properly (and if it does not stick), will keep tension on the fish within the tolerance of the line's strength and provide the least amount of pressure possible. As the surge tapers, lift up the rod and work the fish back.

Now it's time to land the fish. But first, a decision has to be made: Are you keeping it or not? If the answer is not, then consider not landing it at all but unhooking it in the water to minimize injury to the fish. You can do this by holding the line with one hand or gripping the fish around the lower jaw with a jaw-gripping tool and using a pair of pliers, a hook gripper, or a hook puller to get the hook out; then let the fish go immediately. In this manner, the fish is never or minimally touched and is least likely to be injured.

However, whenever a fish is on the surface or its head is removed from the water, there is the danger that it will flip, spin, thrash, lunge, or take other action to escape, and this may result in injury to you or the fish or result in a fish that escapes. You have to be very careful when you lift a fish to unhook it, and you should remember that when landing a fish, by whatever means, you should leave the head of the fish in the water to minimize problems (although when you net a fish, it's best to get the head up to the surface). Many fish react instinctively when their heads are lifted and the buoyancy of being supported by water is gone; they'll use their tails to take some type of action. If you keep its head in the water, a fish may be less inclined to do this; and if you can grab it by the tail, its main source of power is gone and it usually can't take action.

Hand-landing. When you grab or hold a fish with your hands, you may potentially harm yourself or the fish, so do it carefully. If a fish is going to be released, handling should be reduced to a minimum *(see: catch-and-release)* to avoid external damage to the fish or damage to internal organs or to the protective mucus coating (the loss of which increases the possibility of infection). If the fish will be kept, then it doesn't have to be handled as carefully, the major concern then being to avoid personal injury. The sharp fin rays, gill covers, and teeth of some fish, as well as the barbels and pectoral spines on others, can easily cause a cut or stab wound that is likely to be very sore for a while and may become infected.

In addition, the landing of fish that are still green, or fresh, or that are very powerful has the potential for causing more serious bodily harm, as well as for damage to equipment. Large saltwater species, for example, if brought into a boat without being subdued properly, can writhe and thrash and do extensive damage. A big fish that flops around in a boat is capable of knocking equipment loose; in a worst-case scenario, it could throw itself against the boat's occupants or get hooked in the tail by loose lures and lash against those in the boat, causing a life-threatening situation. This is extreme, but it has happened. Being careful is mandatory whenever you are handling a fish, especially one that is hooked.

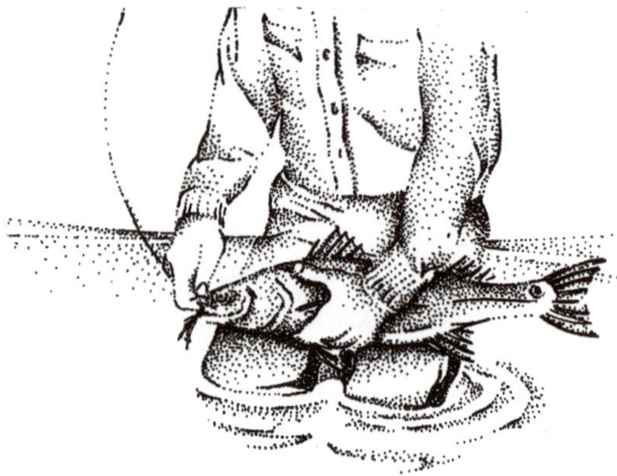

Wading anglers may need to pin a large, strong, or frisky fish to their wet legs, as shown, to land and unhook the fish.

Grasping. There are several locations on a fish that should be avoided if you are going to release them but that make good holding spots if you are keeping them. The foremost location is under the lower edge of the gill; this is a secure, but deadly, place to grasp a fish. A specimen that is tired and on its side may be grabbed under the lower gill cover for landing, and this location usually keeps your hands away from the hooks in a fish's mouth.

Many fish can also be grasped one-handed under the upper gill cover by the back; place the thumb under the upper edge of the gill cover and place the tip of the middle finger under the edge of the opposite gill cover. Another secure but fatal grasping spot for small and medium-size fish is by the upper edge of the eye sockets.

Grabbing by the jaw is a possibility with some fish; the characteristics of their mouths, lack of teeth on the jaws, and size make them quite easy to grasp in this manner. Such species as largemouth bass, panfish, and small stripers can be landed by grasping the lower lip, provided the fish is well tired before the attempt is made.

Simply insert the thumb inside the lower jaw and pinch the jaw against the bent forefinger, which is outside and pressing against the lower jaw. If you'll be landing a lot of fish, you can wear a leather thumb guard to keep from raking your thumb and the skin in the crease between thumb and forefinger. This method of grasping immobilizes the fish and is good for unhooking as well as landing, and has no adverse effect on releasing a fish. It may, however, be hard to accomplish when the mouth opening is covered with one or two treble hooks from the lure.

Larger and stronger fish that lack teeth on the jaws can also be held by the jaw in reverse fashion. For such fish, keep the thumb outside and below the jaw, and put the other four fingers inside the jaw—preferably you are wearing a wet glove when you do this. Gloves, especially versions with a sure-grip surface, aid you in grasping the fish and holding it for unhooking. Wet cotton gloves are best for fish that will be released.

Most fish cannot be held by hand in the mouth, usually because of teeth. One way to hand-land and hand-hold species by the mouth is with a jaw-gripping tool. These clamp over the lower jaw to secure the fish and do not require that you touch the jaws by hand; these tools don't harm the fish, although many models work best on smaller fish.

Some small fish can be gently lifted with a hand

The largemouth bass is one species that can be easily grabbed by the lower lip, but be careful to avoid hooks.

placed under the belly. This may be a good alternative when a fish has been caught on a lure with multiple hooks; however, it is really a technique for small fish. Proper balance cannot be supplied to larger fish this way, a lot of pressure can be placed on internal organs, and a lot can go wrong if the fish squirms and escapes your grasp. Some fish can be calmed by turning them over and holding them upside down. This technique is more useful for a fish that will be unhooked and released than for a fish that will be kept.

A lot of fish, especially small- to medium-size specimens in freshwater, and smaller specimens in saltwater, are hand-grasped behind the mouth and the head in the "neck" or nape area. Holding too tightly here can damage internal organs if the fish is to be released, but bigger fish, with more meat in this area, can be held firmly without problem. Fish with prickly spiny rays may be a problem to land this way; instead, run your hand from head to tail with thumb on top and other fingers on the belly. Depress the dorsal fins with the thumb; now you can safely hold the fish around the middle of the body.

Catfish must be held properly to avoid a puncture from their sharp pectoral fins. The best way to do this is to grab behind, and at the base of, the pectoral fins in order to keep them pointed sideways.

Lifting and swinging. An easy way to boat small fish that are well hooked is simply to lift them aboard with your rod. This method is practical only for small- to medium-size fish caught on sturdy tackle. Bass anglers often bring a fish into the boat by swinging it in because the fish is small and the line and tackle are heavy enough to handle this. Fish under 3 pounds are the usual candidates. Landing is best accomplished by working the fish to the surface and leading it toward the boat; when the head clears the surface near the boat, continue the momentum and lift the fish up, swinging it in. Small fish that are swung into a boat then have to be grabbed by hand, and obviously they may wind up flopping on the floor. Such treatment is not conducive to proper handling and release but is probably all right for fish that are to be kept.

In saltwater, many fish that are taken from party boats, as well as some of the smaller ones caught on other craft, are lifted right out of the water and over the gunwale onto the floor of the boat. Most of these fish are being kept. Lifting and swinging are suitable when fish are well hooked and when a rod and line of appropriate strength are used.

Billing. The long bills of sailfish and small marlin provide a good handle for landing, or at least for holding while the fish is unhooked. That bill is used as a weapon when the fish chases prey, and it can become a weapon used against you if you're not careful enough. To avoid this, try to grab the bill with both hands when it's just below the surface. On small boats, billfish are usually landed on the starboard side so that the operator can see what is happening, but on larger boats they may be landed on either side or at the stern.

In any case, grab the bill with both hands, with your thumbs facing each other but slightly apart. Be prepared to push away from the bill and head if the fish suddenly lunges up and ready to hold on if the fish thrashes moderately.

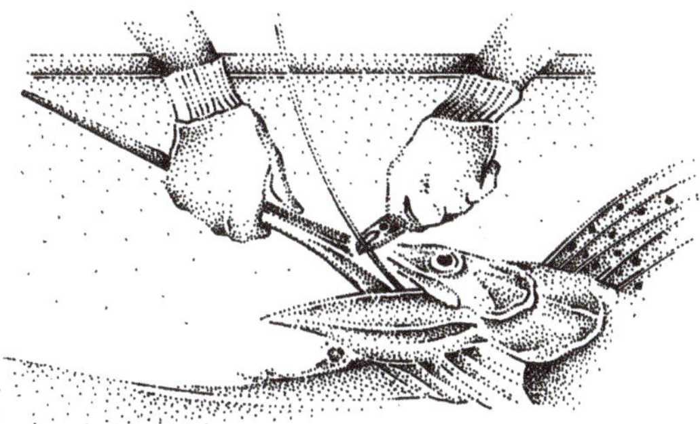

To secure a billfish for unhooking and releasing, grab the bill close to the mouth, using one or two hands, depending on the size of the fish.

Tailing. The tails of some fish are rigid enough to permit you to grab them by placing your hand over the caudal peduncle just ahead of the tail fin. You can grab a jack or a tuna this way, and you can grab large salmon and pike by the tail. Smaller fish usually can't be grabbed by the tail, and the tails of many bigger fish are not rigid enough. You can't grab a big largemouth bass securely enough by the tail, nor can you grab most trout (except really large ones) this way. But for some fish, the tail provides a good handle for landing, and it is far enough from teeth or hooks to be an attractive gripping point.

When you do grab a fish by the tail, you can do it either by hand for fish that will be released, or with a tailer for fish that will be kept. A tailer, also called a tail rope or loop, is a nooselike device that slips over the fish and cinches down on the caudal peduncle (the stem just forward of the tail fin). A tailer is best for fish with a stiff rather than flexible caudal peduncle.

If the boat is moving, as is the case when trolling or fishing in open waters for offshore species, a fish can be tailed pretty easily while it is alongside and moving with you. If the boat is drifting or is anchored, or if you are wading and playing a fish to you, then you have to pick the moment to grab the tail. Usually a fish will try to bolt when touched, so you want to get the first try right; otherwise, the fish may sprint off and lengthen the fight, possibly getting free. When the fish is tired and just lying by you, you can grab it easily. If it is still moving a little, bring it around in a circular manner if possible and grab the tail when the fish is headed away from you. When using a tailer, you have to get the noose partway up the body and then quickly draw it tight; after the tail is secured, you have to lift it out of the water or you may have a tiger by the tail. Once the fish's tail is raised out of the water, its powerful leveraging agent is gone.

Netting. The three rules of netting should be to avoid netting if you plan to release the fish, *or* if the net is a standard hoop-style, *or* if the fish has been caught on a multihooked lure. Fish that have been hooked with a multihooked lure and then netted may be easily damaged. The hooks inevitably grab the webbing of the net, and the fish thrashes and rips itself while pulling violently against the embedded hooks. If the fish rolls in the net with treble hooks, untangling becomes a real problem; a lot of time is lost before the fish can be unhooked, and the fish's skin, jaws, or eyes may be damaged.

Obviously the decision to release a fish has to be made before the fish is in the net. Cotton mesh nets are softer and don't seem to hurt the fish as much, but hooks are harder to get out, and the cotton nets are not as widely available as nylon or rubber nets.

Fish that are netted usually can be released alive if they have not been handled excessively and have not spent too much time out of water. One way to facilitate the release of netted fish is to keep the net in the water while unhooking the fish. Those who wade, such as stream trout anglers who use flies or single-hook lures, can do this quite easily. Once the hook has been removed, the net can be turned over and the fish gently jiggled out. Obviously, to release the fish alive, you have to be careful how you do this, so that damage is minimized.

How to net. Proper netting technique is as much a matter of knowing what not to do as it is knowing what to do. Under most circumstances, you shouldn't put the net in the water and wait for the fish to come close. Nor should you wave the net overhead where a fish might see it. A net lying in the water or moving above it is foreign and alarming to fish. Moreover, a net in the water cannot be turned or moved swiftly. It's best to keep the net solidly in hand and at the ready, either motionless or out of sight, until a fish is almost within reach.

Don't attempt to net a fish unless it is within reach, and don't try to net it if it is going away from you or appears to be able to go away from you. Ideally, the fish should be heading toward you so that it must continue moving forward, or so that you can move the net in front of it if it turns. As a rule, don't try to net a fish unless its head is on the surface or is just breaking to the surface. A fish that is on the surface has little mobility and cannot be as active as one that has its entire body in the water.

Don't try to net a fish from behind. If a fish is completely exhausted, you may be able to net it from the side, but the most desirable position is from the front. And don't touch the fish with the rim of the net until it is well into the net. Touching fish, particularly if they are still lively, often initiates wild behavior. If the fish acts wild, it could roll on your line and break the line or simply snap the line from the force of its getaway rush. Therefore, resist taking a stab at a fish that may be technically within reach of your extended net but is not in the best position for capture.

The angler has to keep the head of a big, strong fish up and guide it toward the net, and the netter shouldn't stab at or chase the fish.

Snagging a multihooked lure on the net webbing is a major problem when anglers try to net a fish that is in a poor position or when the fish doesn't come squarely into the middle of the net. Snagging like this is one of the surest ways to lose fish, particularly those that are heavy and cannot be readily hoisted into the boat or scooped up in the now-tangled net.

You can help the netter by making an effort to get the fish's head up so that it is near or on the surface and not deep in the water. When the fish comes up and is being worked toward the net, you should back up in the boat, put more pressure on the fish to gain line, raise the rod high to keep the fish's head up, and tell the netter that the time is right, attempting to lead the fish closer as the netter goes into action. Be prepared for miscues. When a strong fish, and especially a green one, is brought to the net, try to back off a bit on the reel drag, or perhaps open the bail of the reel or put it into freespool, keeping a finger on the line to maintain tension. If the fish flops out, runs through the net (it happens with lousy nets), or charges away, there may be a lot of pressure on your tackle, so anticipate this possibility and let the fish go in the manner noted previously. When it stops, reengage the reel and work the fish back. Don't count the fish as caught until it is solidly in hand.

Netting a fish by yourself is often a tricky chore, made more difficult by the influence of current, wind, and tide. Bringing a fish to net or boat as quickly as possible may not be feasible when you are alone and have a large fish, and often you must play the fish out thoroughly before you can slip the net under it. Try to get the fish to within several feet of the tip of the rod; then raise the rod high over and behind your head while you reach for the fish with net extended in your other hand. Keep the line taut, and don't let your rod hand come down to create slack.

Netting efforts are sometimes more arduous in fast-moving waters because fish are usually below you, and it is hard to get big fish back upcurrent and positioned for proper netting. Another problem is that when you don't gain on fish in current, they rest momentarily and recoup enough strength to prolong the battle or give that last extra kick just when you think you have them. For this reason, those who are netting a big fish for someone else in swift water should usually be a reasonable distance downriver, in a position to land a tired fish as it wallows near the bank, still resisting the angler but unable to swim off with vigor.

If landing the fish isn't feasible—because the net is too small or because you are without a net—you always have the option of landing it by hand or beaching it. In either case, the fish must be thoroughly whipped and under your control before you can do so.

Release cradling. Perhaps the best method of netting a fish that will be released is to use a type of net called a cradle, or release cradle. This is not a net in the traditional handle-and-dipping sense, but it has similarities and is a benign way of landing and subduing a large or long fish that will be unhooked and released. The most popular release cradles have two long narrow wood boards connected by 1/4-inch soft-mesh knotless netting that is closed at the ends; the netting droops into the water to envelop the fish. The cradle is laid alongside a boat, and the netting droops into a trough below. The angler leads a captured fish alongside the boat and over the netting, and the net is folded up like a purse to enclose the fish, which remains full-length and in the water. Perhaps most important, the cradle supports the full body of the fish in a horizontal position. Another version, usually homemade and intended for shorter fish, is smaller, with open ends and open-grip handle. In both cases, the fish stays relaxed in the net while the hook is removed and can be released without having to be handled. Moreover, you can rig up the cradle for weighing, keeping the fish in the cradle and providing excellent horizontal support for the fish. A cradle is difficult to use when fishing by yourself; in that case, it is better to avoid a cradle or net altogether and try to unhook the fish while it is in the water.

Gaffing. Gaffing is a fish-landing option that is primarily used in saltwater and, with one exception, is not recommended for fish that are to be released. That exception is when a fish is gaffed in the mouth through the lower jaw.

Like netting, gaffing isn't terribly difficult,

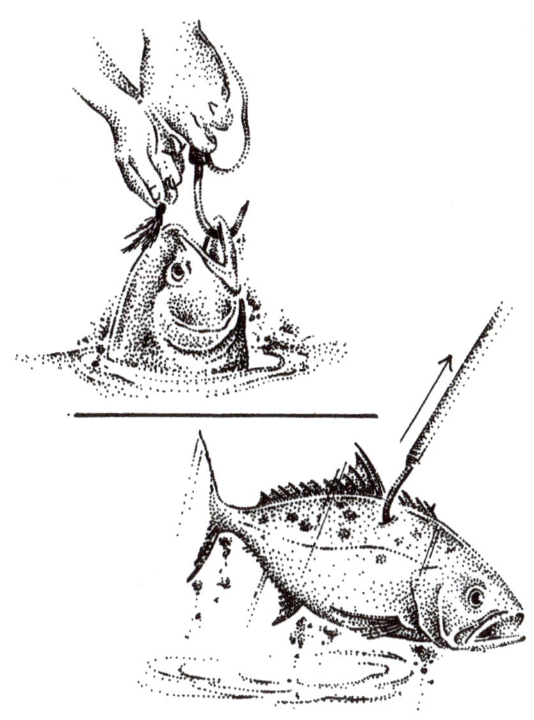

A hand gaff can be used on some fish that will be released, especially those having large mouths (top); the best place to gaff small- and intermediate-size fish that will be kept is in the upper back, as shown (bottom).

although anglers sometimes have trouble executing a proper gaff. In essence, you gaff a fish by getting the point of the gaff in the water beneath the fish and then strike upward sharply. Being too excited or being careless can cause problems. When gaffers flail wildly, they often miss the fish, strike it in a spot that makes control and lifting difficult, or, worse, strike and break the angler's line. Poking the fish with the gaff instead of ramming it home is likely to make the fish act wild, perhaps causing it to surge enough to break free.

The location where you gaff a fish is not critical if you plan to keep the fish, but the gaff is often in the upper back muscle of the midsection of the fish. This may damage some meat, but it is a good secure spot. Gaffing a fish in the belly may cause the fish to react violently and either shake free, pry the gaff out of your hand, or break the gaff. It also contributes to a heavily bleeding fish that makes a mess in the boat or in a fish box.

Gaff the fish with a firm, sure motion and follow through with the upward motion by lifting the fish out of the water if it is small enough to lift; otherwise, a second gaff (or tail rope) or two people hauling will be necessary to get the fish in. To gaff a fish when a boat is moving and the fish is swimming or is being towed alongside the boat, reach across the back with the hook down and pointed at the side of the fish facing away from you. When the handle is close to the back of the fish, smoothly and sharply drive the point all the way to the bend and keep the gaff coming to you.

1 

2 

3 

4 

In these photos, a big dolphin is skillfully gaffed and brought aboard a large sportfishing boat. Note how the mate uses one leg to brace himself as he extends far out, sticks the gaff hook into the fish and instantly grabs it with two hands as the fish starts to thrash, begins to lift up as the fish is under control, and then swiftly lifts the fish over the high gunwale.

The technical procedure is the same when gaffing from a boat that is at anchor or drifting, the difference being that your target is moving and you have to plan the strike well. Try to plant the gaff hook when the fish has just turned and is facing away from the boat rather than when it is headed toward the boat; if you miss, the fish will probably steam away from you rather than go underneath.

Flying gaffs and bridge gaffs are used in big-game and bridge fishing, respectively. The procedure is similar, although a bridge gaff is used more like a snagging tool and is less precise.

Fish to be released can be gaffed in the lower jaw with a hand gaff, preferably by driving the point through the inside of the mouth and out the lower jaw (rather than coming from outside to inside). This is done when the fish is thoroughly played out.

Obviously, the point of the gaff must be razor sharp to do the most effective job. The point should be covered when the gaff is not in use.

What the angler can do. It is worth reaffirming the role of the angler in the fish-landing process, especially during the acts of netting, gaffing, cradling, and tailing.

The angler can do a lot to help the person who is actually landing the fish, or the angler can make those efforts much more difficult. An inexperienced angler can be talked through the process by the person doing the landing. A good mate or captain on a charter boat will tell the angler what to do when the moment of truth draws near. On the other hand, a good angler can play a big fish and still get a successful landing effort out of a totally inexperienced lander if the angler tells the person what to do and when to do it.

Generally, however, when the fish is near, the angler can help a lot by keeping up the fish's head

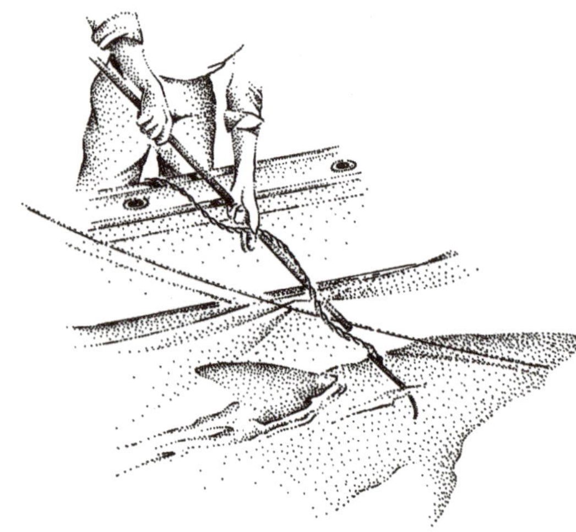

When a flying gaff is used on big-game species, the pole detaches from the hook, and the rope is left attached to the gaff hook in the fish.

so that it is near or on the surface and not deep in the water. When the fish is coming in close, the angler should put more pressure on the fish to gain line by continuing to pump and reel; as the fish is about to be landed, the angler should raise the rod high (keeping it there and not allowing slack), forcing the fish's head to stay up. If a long leader is used, or if there is a lot of hardware on the terminal end (like a dodger and a 6-foot leader to the lure), the angler may need to step back in the boat so that the fish can be reached for landing. If that is not the case, then the angler should remain close to the gunwale in order to see what the fish does and react accordingly.

An angler should be prepared for miscues and ready to lower the rod tip and point the rod at a fish if it streaks away after being touched by a net or gaff or hand. Even if battling the fish of a lifetime, a good angler stays calm and doesn't try to force the results. If the fish is not landed on the first attempt or if something goes wrong in the landing process, the angler stays with the fish and keeps the line away from obstructions. An experienced angler anticipates a problem and prepares to counter it without applying tug-of-war force and thus is often able to bring the fish back for another landing attempt.

Unusual measures. Some situations in saltwater fishing call for more unusual measures for landing fish. Monster-size Pacific halibut and big sharks, for example, can be dangerous fish if they are not killed before being brought into the boat; a knock on the head, which is used to dispatch most fish once they are landed, or hanging from a gin pole, does not do it for these creatures.

Shooting and harpooning are sometimes used by charter boat captains to dispatch a fish before it is actually brought into the boat. A shotgun loaded with bird shot and aimed at the head, and a harpoon whose metal tip is attached to a buoy, are the instruments used for halibut; sometimes, heavy-duty gaff hooks, attached by rope to a cleat, are also used. In the past, large sharks were shot with rifles, shotguns, and pistols, but the wisdom of doing this and concerns for firearms safety have more or less relegated this method to yesteryear status. However, some captains do keep a handgun available for emergencies, including the dispatching of a large shark; others use a 12-gauge bang stick for killing a shark, a device that has to be treated with extreme caution.

LANDING NET

A net with a handle used by anglers to capture hooked fish.

See: Catch-and-Release; Landing Fish; Net.

LANDINGS

The number or poundage of fish unloaded at a dock by commercial fishermen or brought to shore by recreational fishermen. This term refers primarily to saltwater fisheries. Landings are reported at the points at which fish are brought to shore. This term differs from "catch," which is all fish that are caught, including those released or discarded.

See: Fisheries Management.

LANDLOCKED

A term for anadromous *(see)* fish that have adapted to a completely freshwater existence, spending the greater portion of their life in a lake and returning to natal rivers or streams to spawn. Any fish—usually salmon but also striped bass—with such behavior and without access to saltwater is landlocked.

LARVAE

The early life forms of a fish or other animal between the time of hatching and transforming to a juvenile.

LATERAL LINE

A series of sensory cells, usually running the length of both sides of the fish's body, that perform an important function in receiving low-frequency vibrations.

See: Anatomy.

LAUNCH

(1) To put a boat in the water, usually the act of easing a boat off a trailer and into the water at some type of access site.

(2) A place to put a boat into the water, as in boat ramp or boat launch *(see).*

(3) A multiple-rod-holding device at the back of a seat or backrest, usually found on a center console boat and referred to as a rocket launcher *(see: sportfishing boat).*

LAUNCHING

Launching primarily refers to the act of getting a boat off a trailer at an access site, but it can also refer to carrying lightweight craft to the water's edge. Many of the same factors that are important when launching a boat are also important when retrieving it (loading it on a trailer).

Fishing boats on trailers are launched at many places, primarily at official and designated access sites called boat ramps or boat launches *(see).* Launch sites may be improved (paved and maintained) or unimproved. Launching is easier at improved sites with paved ramps, and such sites are mandated when launching large and heavy craft. Small, lightweight boats on trailers, as well as some midsize boats, can be launched at unimproved sites, although care must be taken to judge the firmness of the ground at the site, the depth of water, and the firmness of the bottom near shore. At unimproved sites, getting a boat out is often harder than getting it in, and much depends on how far the trailer (and tow vehicle) have to be backed into the water, the strength of the towing vehicle in relation to the weight of the boat and trailer, and existing ground conditions.

Whether improved or not, launch sites vary in important ways: steepness or angle of incline, width, depth of water, extension of pavement into the water, docking space, amount of time that a boat may be docked, availability of adjacent parking, fees, and hours of operation.

The best access sites for launching trailered boats are those with moderate inclines and a gradual dropoff to deep water, rather than a steep dropoff or long shallow one. At sites with an immediate steep dropoff, the trailer cannot be backed very far into the water, and this situation places a lot of pressure on the bow when the stern is floating. When the boat is retrieved, the angle is insufficient for it to be winched onto the bow support, especially if the trailer is at a steeper angle than the tow vehicle. For retrieval you need to be able to get the boat onto the trailer far enough that it is centered properly; side bunks or guides if the trailer is so equipped are aids here. An unguided boat floats freely and may not get centered on the trailer when it is winched on. In the worst cases, it may take several attempts to center the boat, a chore made more difficult by wind or current. The assistance of others is welcome when you're trying to position the boat for retrieval.

Access sites with little or no change in the bottom near shore require you to back the trailer and tow vehicle a long way into the water and perhaps push the boat off the trailer if it will not float itself off. The heavier the boat, the more of a problem this is, not to mention that you can wind up with a vehicle whose front and rear tires are in the water and a tailpipe that is submerged. When retrieving a boat in these situations, you usually don't have to put the trailer as far into the water as you do when launching because the motor can be used to push the boat all or part of the way onto the trailer. If you expect to launch in this condition all or most of the time, consider a trailer that cradles the boat lower and thus floats it sooner than one that sits high. Drive-on trailers, incidentally, provide the easiest launching and retrieval at improved sites.

Anglers who keep boats on trailers for portability do not always have an option in picking launch sites, so they have to make do with conditions as they find them. It is tougher to launch at narrow ramps than at wide ones, which accommodate multiple simultaneous launchings. However, the latter are also more crowded, especially at prime days and hours, so if you're new to trailering and launching, practice backing up a trailer beforehand (lay out cardboard boxes at an empty mall parking lot), and try to launch at off-peak hours. Anyone who has watched a busy boat launch knows what a comedy (and tragedy) it can be.

Backing Up

Backing up with a trailer is a problem for many people, and the only way to get good at it is through practice. If you keep your hand on top of the steering wheel, the rear of the trailer heads left when you turn the wheel to the right, so in effect you need to steer in reverse. You may prefer to keep your hand on the bottom of the steering wheel so that when you move your hand to the left, the trailer goes to the left. When you first start, it's a good idea to turn your body sideways and look at the trailer as you turn the wheel and back up. When you get proficient, you won't need to turn around at all but can simply use both side mirrors to watch your progress. Always back up slowly and try to position the trailer as straight as possible in the water.

How to Launch

The first thing to realize about launching is the need for courtesy. Prepare your boat for launching in the parking lot, not while blocking the ramp. Put everything you need into it, and make all installations before you launch, not when you are backed onto the ramp or tied up at the dock or pier.

If you've never been to the launch site before, or if it has changed since your last use, it's wise to inspect the ramp and the area nearby. Look at the length of the pavement into the water, and check to see if there is a drop after the pavement that might be an impediment to trailer wheels. Many boaters have been stuck at ramps when they could not pull trailer wheels over the back lip of a paved ramp, so don't get your wheels in so far as to allow that to happen. Check to see whether the ramp is nonskid or whether conditions have made it slippery (grass and moss can do this). You may need to make sure that the tow vehicle's wheels don't get into the water if that part of the ramp is slippery. Also check or ask about nearby hazards and current, and note the direction of the wind, which may have an effect on launching or retrieving.

Before launching, make sure that the drain plug is in the boat, remove tiedowns, raise the motor or outdrive so it doesn't strike anything, make sure that nothing is sticking out of the boat, disconnect the trailer lights, and, if the ramp is gradual, remove the safety chain on your trailer.

If you are proficient at backing up, try to get the trailer fairly close to the dock or pier. If the ramp slopes properly, you shouldn't have to completely submerge the trailer. The degree to which you put the trailer in the water will depend in part on the trailer design. Roller-type trailers can be backed up so the bottom of the tires are partly in the water and

L

then the boat is pushed off. Drive-on or bunk-style trailers should be backed in until the wheel hubs are almost submerged; this should give some float to the boat and allow it to back off under power without much effort. Back the trailer into the water only until the boat begins to float or can be easily pushed off, or until the trailer tilts.

With the trailer in position, keep the motor of the tow vehicle running. Put an automatic transmission in parking gear and a standard transmission in neutral, and apply the emergency brake. For some vehicles and some ramps, it's not a bad idea to put a chock behind two wheels; cars and trucks have been dunked at ramps. Now disconnect the bow of the boat from the trailer winch cable and push it into the water; a long rope should be tied to the bow or to both the bow and the stern so that a companion can guide the boat to the dock and secure it. If you're alone and cannot push the boat off by yourself or drive it off, tie a long bow rope to the front of your trailer, back far enough into the water to float the boat backward, and then slowly pull forward until the trailer is halfway out of the water. Untie the rope from the trailer, and pull the boat to the dock and secure it.

Depending on the site, boat, and trailer, and the wind, wave, and current conditions, this is the basic launching procedure. Try to avoid getting the trailer hubs in the water unless they are meant for submersion; if you have to submerse the hubs, let them cool down first. Take your time, and launch safely. Don't loiter on the dock or leave your vehicle on the ramp; get it out of the way and leave room at the dock for someone else to come in.

Retrieval

Retrieving your boat at a boat launch is not just the reverse procedure of launching, although many of the same precautions are necessary. It is especially important that you get the boat positioned perfectly on your trailer, and loading a boat on a trailer can be difficult if the trailer is on a bad angle or is not placed into the water at the right depth. Keep in mind that conditions for retrieving your boat may be different than when you launched it; the main differences include tidal fluctuation, presence of wind, presence of wave action from boaters, changes in visibility, and more activity at the launch site. At times when a sudden storm comes up and everyone heads into the launch ramp, there can be near pandemonium, especially if temporary docking space is at a minimum; it's important to watch out for other boaters and to be able to retrieve your boat quickly and get out of the way.

Drive-on trailers are the best for quickness, and if a ramp has a moderate angle, you can usually drive right up onto the trailer to the bow chock (not too fast) if you have the boat centered right at the outset, being careful not to dig the lower unit of the motor into the ramp if the ramp is shallow. You may want to tilt the motor up a bit if you are unsure of the depth. If you can't drive the boat all the way onto the trailer, you may be able to drive it up enough that the boat is firmly on the trailer and then get out and hook up the winch cable to bring it up the remaining distance.

Anglers load a bass boat onto a drive-on trailer at Lake Sam Rayburn in Texas.

Winch-on trailers provide many chances to get things wrong, usually because the stern of the boat sways to one side (because of wind, current, waves, or bad luck). If you don't get the bow positioned properly along the centerline of the trailer, and centered on the keel rollers, it will not be aligned properly when fully winched up and you'll need to do it all over again, so be sure to get it lined up right. When it is windy, someone on the dock or shore could hold a stern line to help keep the boat centered, with another person pulling the stern in or pushing it out as needed.

Whenever you retrieve your boat, it's a good idea to drain water out of the bilge, livewell, or baitwell so that you don't have to put extra weight on your trailer or crank extra weight out of the water if you're using a winch. Trim the motor or outdrive so it doesn't strike anything. Do not drive away with a boat that is cockeyed on the trailer; back it down into the water and get it positioned properly. Before you pull the boat and trailer off the ramp, fasten the safety chain and make sure the boat is attached to the winch cable. Unload away from the immediate ramp area, fasten tiedowns to the trailer, and reconnect the trailer lights. If you have an outboard motor transom-saver bracket (a device attached to the trailer that supports the weight of the lower unit of the motor), put that on. If not, tilt the motor up, put the motor bracket lock down, and lower the trim, leaving the throttle in forward gear. Secure the electric motor so that it can't bounce. Stow or secure rods, coolers, PFDs, and anything that might blow out of the boat (like containers and cans so you don't become a litterbug). Make sure you turn off all electronics in the boat; turn the engine key to the off position, or you'll have a dead battery. A final safety check,

especially of the hitch connection, safety chains, bow tiedown, rear tiedown, tires, and lights, should be made before you depart. If a brake light or turn signal is out, you may not be able to do anything about it at the launch site, but you should be aware of the problem so that you can take it into account while on the road. Lastly, before you leave, take your vehicle out of four-wheel-drive if you put it in that position for hauling your boat out of the launch site, as many people do.
See: Trailer.

By far the oldest fishing record on the books is that of a 4-pound 3-ounce yellow perch caught in Bordentown, New Jersey, in May 1865.

LAWS
See: Regulations.

LCD
Acronym for liquid crystal display.
See: Sonar.

LCR
Acronym for liquid crystal recorder.
See: Sonar.

L

LEAD
See: Sinker.

LEAD-CORE LINE
See: Weighted Line.

LEADER
A length of nylon monofilament or wire at the end of a fishing line. Also known as a trace, a leader is intended either to have low visibility so that it does not appear to be connected to a lure, hook, or fly or to protect the line from cutting or breaking. No leader material is able to do both of these simultaneously, which would be the ideal. Low-visibility leaders are mainly employed in freshwater fishing, especially for trout and salmon in streams, and in some saltwater situations, like bonefishing.

Leaders are of varying lengths; the terminal end is connected directly to a lure, fly, hook, snap, or swivel, and the butt is connected directly to the fishing line. Sometimes a leader is used from a swivel to a weight, baited hook, diving planer, or bottom rig.

A leader may be lighter or heavier in strength than the main fishing line, depending upon its application, and level or tapered in both diameter and strength. Nylon monofilament leaders are always used in fly fishing because they aid the delivery of a fly and, in most situations, are relatively imperceptible; such leaders are lighter than the fly line, and the terminal end is generally tapered to a fine diameter and a lighter strength. Most leaders used for other applications have a greater breaking strength than the main fishing line because their primary purpose is to protect against abrasion, cutting, or shock that would cause breakage.

Leaders may be employed in casting, trolling, and baitfishing, and while using all types of tackle. They are more common in saltwater angling than in freshwater, owing to the greater number of nasty fish encountered in the marine environment and some of the different techniques employed; some type of leader, for example, is virtually always used in offshore big-game fishing and shark fishing. Leaders are most likely to be used for fish with sharp teeth, scales, or gill covers; for fish that are very big and powerful; for fish that are hard to land or unhook and release near the boat; and for species that live in places where line-damaging obstructions are frequently encountered.

Tapered Fly Leaders
In fly fishing, using nylon monofilament leaders of varying lengths (up to 9 feet) is a necessity. This is because the fly line is too thick to be attached directly to the fly, and its size would alarm fish if it were attached directly to the fly; the lighter line, when tapered down, is important for turning over and quietly presenting a fly as well as getting it to float or sink naturally. Fly leaders are nearly all tapered from a heavy butt end (which is usually 20- to 30-pound test) through the midsection to a light end, with or without a tippet *(see)*. However, in some situations, a short length of level leader (one length of the same diameter) can be used; this is most common when using sinking lines and leaders under 6 feet long, and when angling for fish that are not highly selective or leader-shy.

In other circumstances, and especially in stream trout fishing and fishing with dry flies, a progressive taper is important to a leader for transmitting the rolling energy from the line throughout the leader. Thus, the butt should have enough stiffness (and usually from two-thirds to three-quarters of the diameter of the fly line) to transfer the rolling energy from the fly line through the rest of the tapered leader to a fine tippet that will allow it to settle lightly and move naturally.

Fly leaders are available in premanufactured knotless tapered versions, or they can be constructed by the angler in knotted compound tapered sections that successively taper down in strength and diameter. The butt is similar in diameter to the fly line, to which it is tied; the midsection continues the taper, and the tip or terminal end tapers still further and is attached to the fly. When using small flies and light leaders, tie a separate light tippet to the end of the leader and then to the fly in order to minimize its visibility; the tippet also helps to turn the leader and fly over with a well-executed cast, and it helps the fly act naturally with less line drag. When using large flies, such as bugs or poppers for bass fishing or big streamers for salt-water species, use a short but heavier tippet, known as a shock tippet *(see)*.

Lengths and strengths of fly leader vary with fish and conditions. Although traditionalists tie knotted compound tapered leaders, most anglers, especially in freshwater, use knotless tapered leaders, since the former take time to construct properly; require an assortment of lines for making the full leader; and can be troublesome when the knots catch on guides, surface debris, grass, or other objects. However, being able to tie your own knotted leader can be helpful when delicate circumstances require a fine leader; in any event, the tip of a knotless leader usually has to be replaced eventually with a newly knotted section of tippet.

Fly leader lengths typically range from 7$^1/_2$ feet to 10 feet, but also run to either extreme down to 4 feet and up to 16. As a generality, longer leaders (over 7 feet) are used with floating lines, and shorter leaders with sinking lines. Shorter lengths of nylon monofilament leader are preferable with sinking lines because this material is only slightly more dense than water and thus sinks slowly. Fluorocarbon material, however, is more dense and sinks faster, allowing for longer leader lengths when sinking fly lines are used.

The length of leader varies with fishing conditions and species. Most stream trout anglers use a leader that is about 9 feet long, and many use a longer leader for wary and selective fish if a proper back cast can be made. The problem with long leaders in tight quarters is that the angler often cannot get enough fly line in the air (because of brush and trees) to carry the long leader, or to roll cast enough fly line to unfurl a long leader. This has led to a general belief in using a leader that is about the overall length of the fishing rod, but this is just a convenient guideline, since some anglers are very successful with longer leaders and some with shorter ones. In fact, shorter leaders are preferred by many people who are very capable casters, since they can put the fly where they want it without getting the fly line near or over the fish. Shorter fly leaders are also favored in situations where fish are less wary or generally aggressive.

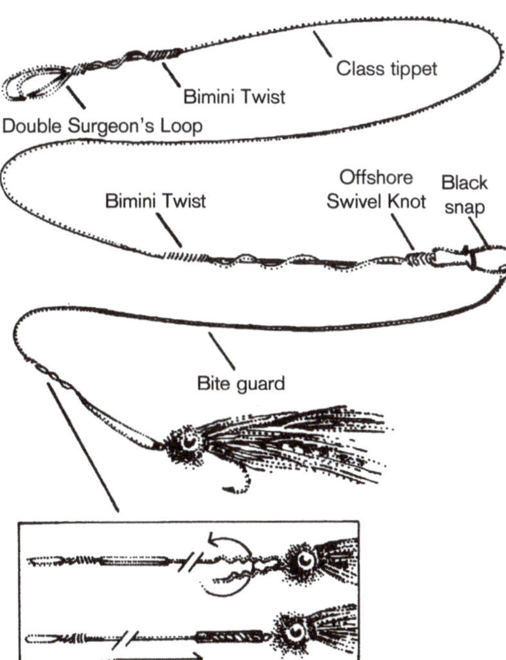

Depicted here is a fly tippet and wire bite guard used to avoid breakoffs by fish with sharp teeth or rough mouths. The end of the guard that attaches to the fly has a reformable Haywire Twist that gets covered by a plastic tube (inset).

Fly leaders are typically much stronger for saltwater fishing applications than for freshwater, and they start with heavier butts that commonly taper to 12- or 16-pound-test tippets, although they can be much lighter. Many are constructed with loops in both ends to facilitate quick changing of the leader or of the shock tippet (also commonly used for bigger species). Some shock tippets also employ a short length of braided or single-strand wire ahead of the fly; this is helpful for sharp-toothed fish like barracuda and bluefish.

Many fly anglers, especially those after tarpon, keep a set of shock leaders prepared and ready to fish when the need arises to interchange leaders. They use heavy monofilament, which also takes some work to straighten, so prestraightened line is tied to a fly and kept in traction for use as a spare if needed.

Level Monofilament Leaders

In non-fly-fishing applications, level leaders may be used with any type of tackle and with a variety of techniques. A level leader has one unknotted section of line of the same strength and diameter throughout; this is distinguished from a tapered leader, which is used with flycasting tackle to help present a fly. When casting with other types of equipment, there is no benefit to a tapered leader for presentation, since the weight of the object being cast carries the line.

Whether a leader is necessary or desirable at all depends on the situation and the species. Most freshwater bait and lure anglers seldom use a leader; they tie their nylon monofilament fishing line (the overwhelming favorite) directly to the lure, hook, snap, swivel, or rig because the fish they catch and the circumstances do not endanger the terminal end of the fishing line, or they periodically cut off a small piece of the line as necessary and retie it. Consistent fishing in areas where the terminal fishing line is likely to be abraded might call for a heavy nylon monofilament leader, provided that doing so doesn't alert the fish; the clearer the water, the more you have to be sensitive to the visibility of the end of the line (because of diameter and possibly color). In freshwater, species that often require a leader are pike, muskies, and payara; however, most anglers use a short wire leader for these toothy species rather than a nylon monofilament leader.

In saltwater, a nylon monofilament leader is used for many species but not on others. Line can be tied directly to a hook or to a lure when fishing for striped bass, for example. Most anglers using light spinning tackle for bonefish can tie the fishing line directly to a shrimp hook or to a jig. However, a heavy monofilament leader is desirable for some species because of their sharp teeth or gill covers, or because the act of landing them puts a lot of stress on the terminal end of the line (which is often grabbed in landing fish, whether they are kept or released). Tarpon are a species that require a heavy mono leader; this is called a shock leader, similar to the shock tippet used in fly fishing, but it is simply a nylon monofilament leader, from 60 to 100 pounds in strength, that is tied to a lighter, usually 20-pound, main line. Heavy mono shock leaders may be useful for some toothy species, but a wire leader (also called a bite leader) is preferred in many other instances. As in freshwater, a nylon monofilament leader used in saltwater is almost always heavier than the main line and meant to provide extra strength and/or abrasion resistance.

The length of a nylon monofilament leader is usually short for freshwater fishing and for general casting purposes. As a rule when casting in freshwater, it should be a little less than the length of the rod, or just enough so that the knot connecting the leader and main fishing line doesn't reach the reel when the lure or bait is reeled to the top of the rod. This shorter length is meant to keep the knot off the reel and lessen the chance of it hanging up and impeding casting or freespooling, which it is more likely to do on the smaller baitcasting and spinning reels used in freshwater. However, where big reels and light fishing line are used, a longer leader, which can be wound onto the reel, may be employed; this puts all of the close-to-the-boat pressure on the leader, with the main line wound onto the reel.

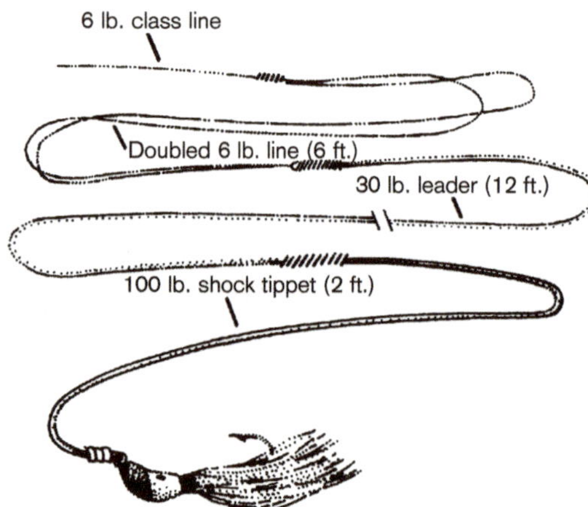

Using double line and line-to-line knots, you can create a heavy shock tippet for a light line. This example depicts lengths that conform to record-keeping rules.

To qualify for a freshwater world record, a leader may not be longer than 6 feet; if a double line is used, the combined length of leader and double line may not exceed 10 feet. For practical purposes, most freshwater fishing doesn't require a leader that is even 6 feet long, and many anglers use a leader that is no more than 4 feet long.

To qualify for a saltwater world record, a leader may not be longer than 15 feet on line classes up to 20 pounds, and the combined length of a leader and double line may be no more than 20 feet. The leader may be no longer than 30 feet on line classes over 20 pounds, and the combined length of the leader and double line may not exceed 40 feet. The greater lengths are geared more to tuna and billfish and to use with conventional tackle *(see)* or big-game tackle *(see)*.

Keep in mind that you need only a short leader to provide protection from teeth, scales, gill covers, and the like. Also, you can combine a short heavy leader with a section of double line, if necessary. Light-tackle anglers in both freshwater and saltwater can use a combination approach to very effectively fish light line with a heavy leader. The most extreme example of this, and primarily for saltwater, is to make a double length of the light main fishing line, connect it to a heavy leader, and then connect this to a short shock tippet. In some cases, the shock tippet is unnecessary. To qualify for a world record, make sure that the respective lengths of each section and the overall length conform to requirements.

In both environments, there are no restrictions regarding the strength of the leader or the material used, and this fact allows wire to be used as leader material under the same stipulations. The strength of the leader, however, should generally be only enough to provide the toughness or protection needed. For leader strength, stronger isn't always better; greater strength often also means greater diameter, which can mean greater visibility, which may translate into fewer strikes.

Nylon monofilament leaders are tied to the double line by using a number of knots *(see: knots, fishing)*, with a line-to-line Uni Knot being especially useful. Two important points to consider are making a connection that retains the full breaking strength of the line—this is essential where great pressure, big fish, and light line are involved—and tying a neat knot that flows readily through the rod guides (and in some cases onto the reel spool).

Some reasons for using a nylon monofilament leader are not as obvious as the main issues of resistance to abrasion and cutting. For example, when the fish are very selective and spooky, it might be useful to fish with a leader that is lighter than the main fishing line, or to use one that is less visible (perhaps fluorocarbon). When using a Dacron or microfilament line *(see: line)* for its low stretch and high sensitivity, tying in a nylon monofilament leader may be best because it is less visible and aids in repeated retying. Likewise, using lead-core line calls for a nylon monofilament leader to overcome the visibility of the main line.

Catching large fish on light and ultralight lines is definitely aided by having at least a heavier leader (or a double line or both). And any time there is a lot of stress on the terminal end of the line (especially when landing fish), a leader or a double length of line should be a consideration.

When fish have repeatedly cut off your line or leader, or when the likelihood is high that they will, consider using a wire leader. However, the action of wire leaders is not as good as more supple nylon monofilament, no matter what the strength or diameter, and they are subject to some problems—kinking and curling—that most nylon monofilament doesn't have.

Wire Leaders

The purpose of a wire leader is to prevent the terminal line from being cut. It is generally used in circumstances where nylon monofilament is apt to fail, such as when the teeth, bill, or other portions of a fish will slice or abrade the line. There are essentially preformed and self-made wire leaders, all are level in diameter, and they come in bright or dark brown versions, with the latter preferred by most anglers (the brighter wire is more noticeable and subject to being struck by fish).

Premanufactured wire leaders from 6 to 36 inches in length are mainly used in freshwater lure casting and trolling, primarily for toothy species like northern pike, muskellunge, and payara, occasionally for lake trout, and also for peacock bass and striped bass in rough-and-tumble environs. They are also used in saltwater for some casting and inshore trolling activities, but not for heavy-duty big-game or offshore work, or when fishing bait.

The most common of these leaders are nylon-coated multistrand stainless steel leaders, which have a barrel swivel at the butt end, to which the fishing line is tied, and a snap swivel at the terminal end for connection to the lure. Some versions, however, are uncoated single-strand stainless steel and the newest and most durable ones are titanium coated. They're available in various strengths, primarily from 20 to 75 pounds, and should be used in a strength that at least meets, and preferably exceeds, the breaking strength of the main line. For casting purposes, a short wire leader is preferred, and this can be combined with a nylon monofilament leader or a section of double line. As with all wire, these leaders are subject to kinking and coiling, and you should discard them when they reach this condition because they will impair lure action and may be weakened. Titanium-coated leaders, however, resist kinking and coiling and have a much longer life.

You can make this type of leader with coated multistrand wire, wire sleeves, snaps, and snap swivels, using good crimping pliers. You can also

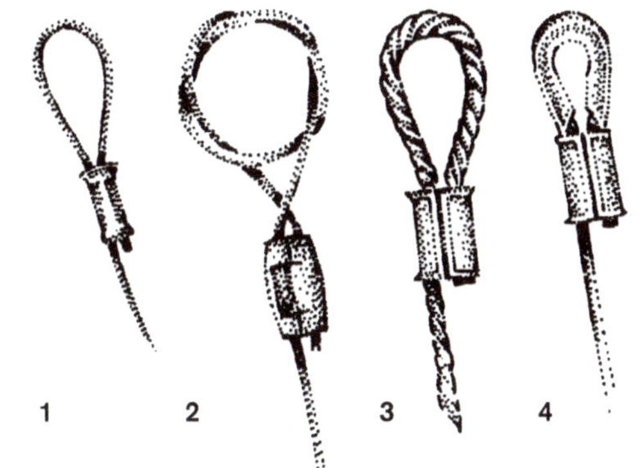

Shown are crimps of nylon monofilament: coated wire (1) cable (2) and wire with stainless steel thimble (3).

make a less-complicated wire leader with uncoated single-strand wire by connecting it directly to the lure or fly with a Haywire Twist *(see)* and then forming another Haywire at the other end, which is tied to the main line with an Albright Special knot. Twist-making and wire-straightening tools are available to assist with this, but the drawback is that this permanent wire-to-lure connection precludes quick changing of the lure or fly.

Still another option is a multistrand (braided) stainless steel wire that is flexible enough to be knotted. This has use for both fly and nonfly anglers. Likewise, short preformed light wire leaders with a preformed line tie are available from fly tackle suppliers; known as bite guards, they are available in 4- and 8-inch lengths, with one bent open end that the angler attaches to the eye of a fly by using a clever prefabricated retwistable Haywire Twist that is covered with a plastic tube. The other end is preformed into a closed loop. You can prerig these to be available for instant use as needed.

In saltwater, a heavy-duty system is used to prerig a class tippet to this wire leader, with a bunch of these stored and ready for instant use, as shown in the illustration on page 885. Using a class tippet, tie a 6-inch Bimini Twist in the butt end and then a Double Surgeon's Loop, which will loop onto the monofilament leader (connected to the fly line); tie a 3-inch Bimini onto the tag end of the tippet, then connect that to a black interlocking snap equal in strength to the weakest part of the whole system. The closed loop of the bite guard is attached to the snap.

For offshore trolling and big-game activities, it's necessary to use a longer leader made from single- or multistrand wire, which may or may not be coated with nylon. Coils of such wire are available from under 20-pound strength up to at least 250-pound strength in some varieties, and over 300 pounds in others, and in ample lengths for making numerous leaders.

Single-strand wire, also known as piano wire, is made of stainless steel and is comparatively cheap. It is nearly bulletproof when it comes to resisting cutting by a fish, but it is highly prone to kink-

L

ing. This causes both minor and severe bends, the latter of which change the molecular structure of the wire and greatly weaken it. Thus, while single-strand wire with a minor kink can be straightened and reliably used, wire with a major kink should be discarded, and a new leader should be used.

Multistrand wire, referred to as cable, is more supple and does not kink as readily, but it has a thicker diameter, creates more drag, and is subject to weakening when thin individual strands are nicked or cut, even though the other strands may be unaffected. It needs to be run over a stainless steel thimble when it is bent or looped to prevent kinking. Cable is more often used in short lengths and for casting, and is often available with a nylon coating, which can be a nuisance because the coating is subject to shredding and fraying by fish teeth, requiring frequent replacement of the cable.

Although premade offshore leaders of different lengths and strengths are available, most expert offshore and big-game anglers prefer to make their own. The length depends on the application, but for offshore trolling and shark fishing, wire leaders are commonly from 12 to 18 feet long but up to 28 feet long in accordance with International Game Fish Association (IGFA) record specifications. Such lengths are necessary where long fish are caught; keep in mind that a big billfish, tuna, or shark, when it swims away, is capable of thrashing its tail repeatedly against the line, which is a major reason why the wire needs to be long enough to withstand this abrasion instead of the fishing line. However, a long wire leader means that the angler can reel the fish only so far to the boat and that crew mates must "wire" the fish by grasping the wire to get the fish close enough to land—preferably the fish will be tagged and released (by cutting the line if the fish has just a bait hook in its mouth, or by unhooking and retrieving a trolling lure). Skilled mates usually do a great job of wiring a fish, but it's dangerous and problematic for a variety of reasons.

Shorter lengths are more common for most applications, with inshore and bottom fishing lengths being from a few feet long up to 10 feet. It is obviously desirable in some situations to use lighter-strength wire, which has a smaller diameter, to enhance bait or lure presentation and minimize detection, and the wire choice should be in accordance with the strength of the main fishing line.

The actual rigging of a single-strand wire leader in its simplest form requires making a Haywire Twist in the butt end that will be attached to a heavy-duty snap swivel at the end of the fishing line (which is most likely doubled); the other end is then run through the eye of a bait hook or through the connection for a prerigged natural bait or lure, and another Haywire is made. The rigged leader is neatly coiled and stored for use as necessary.

Many rigs for trolling, bottom fishing, or baitfishing require other uses of wire (and also heavy monofilament line) that involve crimping with a heavy-duty hand crimper, using single- or double-oval sleeves (which are squeezed and are better than round sleeves, which are crushed), and using nylon or stainless steel thimbles for holding a loop. Crimps should squeeze the line instead of crushing it, and in some cases two crimps are employed instead of one, but that is usually because an inferior crimping tool or sleeve is used.

See: Knots, Fishing; Line.

LEADHEAD

A jig with a lead head.

See: Jig.

LEAN

To "lean" on a fish is to bring as much pressure as the tackle and drag setting can withstand in order to land it.

See: Landing Fish.

LEDGERING

A North American spelling variation of legering *(see)*.

See: Carp.

LEE

Being sheltered from the wind, as in the lee side of an island, which is the side that is protected from the wind and where many anglers find themselves fishing on rough days.

LEFT BANK

The left side of a river as viewed when facing downriver.

LEGERING

A European term for bottom fishing with bait rigs without floats, also known as ledgering. This is primarily a shore-based technique in which baits are cast a fair distance from the angler and allowed to rest on or near the bottom, generally using the lightest amount of weight or sinker possible to avoid alarming the fish yet also allowing proper presentation and positioning. Rod rests and bite indicators may be used. When the angler does not leave the rod in a rest but holds it, with the reel bail open and the line between the fingers, it is called touch legering.

See: Carp.

LENOK *Brachymystax lenok.*

A member of the Salmonidae family, the lenok is a nonanadromous troutlike species endemic to northern Asia that has some commercial value and is

Lenok

caught by a few adventurous anglers in remote areas.

There is believed to be just one species of this genus, found in river basins ranging from the River Ob in Siberia eastward and south to the Amur River drainage, as well as in the mountainous sections of the Yellow, Lo, and Han River drainages of China. Two forms of lenok—sharp- and blunt-snouted—have been reported from the Amur basin, however, and may be different species.

Lenok evidently do not grow large; they are reported to attain 16 pounds, and the all-tackle world record is 5 pounds, 6 ounces. They feed mainly on invertebrates, and strike lures and flies readily, including large lemming imitations fished on the surface.

LESSER ANTILLES

The Lesser Antilles are part of the West Indies archipelago and extend from Puerto Rico to the northeastern coast of South America. They include the Virgin Islands *(see)*, Windward Islands, Leeward Islands, Netherlands Antilles, Barbados, and Trinidad and Tobago, and form a demarcation of sorts between the Caribbean Sea and the Atlantic Ocean. Some parts of the Lesser Antilles are independent nations (Barbados, and Trinidad and Tobago); others are dependencies, territories, or possessions of Great Britain, France, the Netherlands, the United States, or Venezuela.

The Leeward Islands are at the northern end of the Lesser Antilles and include Antigua, Guadeloupe, Montserrat, and Saint Kitts and Nevis. The Windward Islands are at the southern end of the Lesser Antilles and include Dominica, Grenada, Martinique, Saint Lucia, and Saint Vincent. The Netherlands Antilles include Curaçao, Bonaire, and Aruba, which are northwest of Caracas, Venezuela, as well as Saba, Saint Eustatius, and the southern half of Saint Martin (Maarten), which are southeast of Puerto Rico. Numerous islets near these main islands are also part of the Lesser Antilles.

Most of the noncoral islands in the Lesser Antilles are volcanic vestiges of submerged mountains. Deep ocean trenches are fairly close offshore and parallel to many of the islands, making some of them conducive to offshore sportfishing for pelagic gamefish. Many feature coral reefs that attract various inshore and bottom fish, and some have shallow flats conducive to sight casting or baitfishing for nearshore gamefish such as bonefish, snook, permit, and tarpon.

Many of the islands have few facilities that cater to angling, and sportfishing as a tourist attraction is lightly developed or undeveloped; boats and knowledgeable guides/captains are limited or scarce. Some have a small number of established guide and charter boat services and are slightly more developed seasonally, usually the result of individual entrepreneurial efforts. Sportfishing at a few islands has developed only lately and is still maturing. Typically, the emphasis is on big game because the deep blue water that exists on both the Atlantic and Caribbean sides of these islands (closer to some than to others), and the currents that flow past them, bring migratory species like blue marlin, Atlantic sailfish, and yellowfin tuna in particular. Islands without charter boats or inshore guide services do not necessarily lack local species or seasonal angling opportunities.

Well-equipped marinas catering to transient boaters exist at many of the islands in the Lesser Antilles, and it may be possible to find a charter service at such facilities. Resorts at the more popular islands may be able to make recommendations, but this information—particularly regarding availability and seasonal fishing opportunities—should be explored well in advance. In the Lesser Antilles, the independent nations are most likely to have some level of organized and experienced sport-fishing effort.

Barbados, one of the two independent nations and also the easternmost island in the Antilles, is an island with top-flight sportfishing boats. Wahoo and dolphin are the most prevalent species caught from boats departing this 166-square-mile island, although anglers do land some blue marlin, white marlin, and sailfish.

The blue marlin are generally small, but large fish are present. One angler landed a 910-pound blue in April of 1996, and a 970-pounder was reportedly taken around the same time on a handline by a native bait fisherman. December through April or May is the blue-water season. The island is primarily surrounded by coral reefs, but inshore fisheries are limited. Local shore casters land occasional jack species and the odd permit, usually at night.

Roughly 130 miles southwest of Barbados, Grenada has the same offshore species fairly close to the island, although interest in them is low. Grenada waters harbor snook and tarpon along the east coast, however, where there are several freshwater streams.

Westward in the Netherlands Antilles, a lack of reefs and shallows minimizes inshore fishing potential, but a surfeit of yellowfin tuna, wahoo, dolphin, sailfish, white marlin, and blue marlin makes up for this. Blues are the primary target of the sportfishing fleet; nearly a dozen charter boats make them the primary quarry. They practice catch-and-release only. An 803-pounder is the biggest sport-caught blue marlin reported from Curaçao.

Similarly, eastward and at the southernmost end of the Lesser Antilles off the coast of Venezuela, the independent nation of Trinidad and Tobago offers excellent sportfishing that has garnered attention only since the mid- to late 1990s. Just a few modern sportfishing boats regularly ply its waters, which have a veritable potpourri of species, from tarpon to tuna and barracuda to blue marlin.

Tobago, the smaller of these two islands, is about 20 miles northeast of Trinidad and farther out in the deep blue water of the Atlantic. This makes it an especially attractive spot for blue marlin and yellowfin tuna, as well as dolphin and wahoo. Baitfish are plentiful here, especially in late winter and early spring. Dolphin are abundant from winter through spring, and the average fish weighs between 10 and 15 pounds, but specimens over 50 pounds have been caught. Winter through spring also yields yellowfin tuna, some weighing more than 100 pounds, 10- to 20-pound blackfin tuna, and lots of wahoo. In addition, king mackerel, cero mackerel, mutton snapper, cubera snapper, African pompano, and big barracuda inhabit the waters closer to shore.

Blue marlin are sporadic Tobago catches, although this may reflect marginal effort; huge blues have reportedly been encountered and lost here, and the potential for blue marlin is allegedly strong. Tobago is situated such that the Guiana Current, which flows northwesterly along the top of South America, pushes directly into and around this island, making it a natural for the presence of bait and pelagic species.

The first jawless fishes appeared between 510 and 438 million years ago; the first fishes with jaws appeared between 438 and 410 million years ago.

Blue marlin and yellowfin tuna are not in the mix at Trinidad, but sailfish and numerous other species are present. Loads of wahoo, sailfish, blackfin tuna, and dolphin frequent these waters. The wahoo often stay close to the northern rocky and steep shoreline, and the others stay a few miles offshore. Sailfishing is good from December through April; wahoo, dolphin, and tuna are good to excellent from October through May.

Relatively large as Caribbean islands go, hilly Trinidad has numerous small islets, mostly along its northern and northwestern coasts (where swift current provides superb wahoo action), and is fortuitously situated 11 miles north of the Orinoco Delta across Boca de la Serpiente. South America's second largest river, the Orinoco produces one of the world's most impressive deltas, a mangrove jungle some 160 miles across. It floods prodigiously every year as a result of interior rains from May through November, and it has a significant influence on this coastal region.

The main influx of the muddy Orinoco is a good distance from Trinidad; borne by currents, however, it turns the water around the island murky. Perhaps pushed out of the delta by increased flows, tarpon appear near the island in increasing numbers sometime in April. Although they are reportedly here year-round, they are most abundant from June through September and are predominantly caught in the passes that separate the islets. So far, tarpon are weighing in at up to 100 pounds, but larger fish are likely. They are also likely to be present in other areas of the island that are seldom fished. King mackerel are available when the tarpon are abundant. Other prevalent species include Spanish mackerel, cubera snapper, pompano, and various grouper and jacks.

Both Trinidad and Tobago have a small number of well-equipped and experienced sportfishing charter boats. Tourism is an important industry, and facilities and services are abundant.

All of the Lesser Antilles islands lie within the Tropical Zone and are influenced by trade winds. There is a dry season from roughly November through May, and a wet season from roughly June through October, although this may vary in certain years due to diverse influences. Like all islands in the Caribbean, the Lesser Antilles are susceptible to hurricanes, some of which do great damage, between July and October.

LEVEL LINE

A taperless fly line with the same weight and diameter throughout.

See: Flycasting Tackle.

LEVELWIND

A mechanism on some conventional reels and most baitcasting reels that automatically disperses line evenly across the spool when line is retrieved.

See: Baitcasting Tackle; Conventional Tackle.

LEVER DRAG REEL

A type of reel used in big-game fishing, and also known as a big-game reel, in which the drag adjustment mechanism is separate from the reel handle and doesn't turn with the handle as the star wheel drag control on a conventional reel does.

See: Big-Game Tackle.

LICE

A common external parasite on marine fish.

See: Diseases and Parasites.

LICENSE

See: Regulations.

LIE

The station or home habitat used for rest or feeding by a fish, primarily salmonids, in a river or stream. Such a location provides feeding opportunity and often shelter. Fish in stillwater adopt specific locations for the same reasons, but these are rarely referred to as lies.

LIFE JACKET

A common term for a Class III personal flotation device *(see)* that is worn by an individual. It usually resembles a vest, and is sometimes called a life vest, but may be jacket style.

LIFE PRESERVER

A common term for a personal flotation device *(see),* usually referring to a article that is worn by an individual, but also sometimes to a buoyant cushion, ring buoy, or horseshoe buoy that is thrown to someone in the water, who holds onto it until help arrives.

LIFT BITE

The upward lift of a properly balanced float *(see)* indicating that a fish has taken the hookbait.

LIFTING

A manner of taking fish by rod and reel in which the fish is hooked in the mouth without having struck the lure or bait. Lifting is viewed by some (including law enforcement officials) as a manner of snagging *(see),* except that fish are hooked inside of the mouth, although they did not actively strike the offering. The lure, fly, or bait (generally bait) is repeatedly floated near a resting fish in such a way that it passes across the open mouth of the fish; when the offering is inside the mouth area, the rod tip is raised to set the hook point into the inner mouth of the fish, thus giving the appearance of hooking a fish fairly.

This activity is practiced by unscrupulous anglers on Great Lakes tributaries, primarily for steelhead and salmon, and in close situations where holding fish can be observed and presentations can be deliberately and repeatedly made. It is often difficult to detect a person who is doing this, although repeatedly lifting the rod tip up at the end of a bait's drift may be a giveaway. Inexperienced anglers have unknowingly watched crafty lifters repeatedly catch fish using this method when others were unable to hook a fish. It is a difficult activity to police, and unfair and unethical to practice.

See: Ethics and Etiquette.

LIGHTHOUSE

A prominent aid to navigation supporting a light that is visible for a long distance and that marks a prominent point of the mainland, a harbor entrance, an offshore hazard, or islands and shoals. Technically known as primary seacoast and navigational lights, lighthouses may also issue a fog signal or radar beacon.

LIGHT METER

A portable electronic device used by a relatively small number of freshwater anglers to measure the light intensity of prospective fishing water at various levels as a guide to using the most visible color of lure for the species they seek.

Manufacturers of light meters for anglers maintain that, as a rule of thumb, the depth at which the available light drops to 50 percent is a good point at which to start fishing. Smaller, more natural-colored lures may work best under brighter conditions, whereas larger lures in more reflective colors may work better where light penetration is less. A light meter is primarily of use in situations where vision is the primary sense that fish rely upon for locating prey.

A greater discussion of light, lure color, and fish behavior is contained under the subheading of color in the lure entry.

See: Lure.

LIGHT STICK

A chemiluminescent stick that glows in the dark or in low light conditions and is used in conjunction with bait or some lures to draw attention to them. Light sticks are most often used with deep night-time angling for swordfish *(see).*

LIGHT-TACKLE FISHING

Anglers often talk about using light tackle, which is a vague term that means different things to different people. There is no established standard for what constitutes light tackle, since the species, size of average catch, angling circumstances, and other factors all vary on a case by case basis in both freshwater and saltwater. Furthermore, some tackle that would be considered heavy in freshwater is considered light in certain saltwater situations. For example, 4- to 8-pound line on spinning tackle is light for largemouth bass and northern pike, but 12-pound test on baitcasting tackle used for the same species is not. Yet, 12-pound baitcasting tackle is light for muskellunge, and lighter spinning gear is inappropriate for that species. The same 12-pound baitcasting tackle would be light for casting to saltwater stripers and ultralight if used on tarpon.

Although most people directly associate light tackle with the breaking strength of the line, this is not an absolute criterion. Generally, the use of any gear that calls upon above-average efforts to hook, play, and land a fish is light. If even greater effort or more extreme skill is needed to do these things, it is ultralight.

Thus, the hallmarks of using lighter than average fishing equipment are a good bow in the rod, a lot of stress on the line, a good scrap by small fish and a real battle for larger ones, and the need to take extra steps to keep a moderate-size fish from getting free. They also include taking more than

Using a long rod with light line, an angler can cast great distances but faces the challenge of delicately working a fish; this scene is in the Beaufort Sea at Victoria Island, Nunavut Territory.

a few seconds to land even a small fish and using skills and finesse more often than brawn.

Since ultralight fishing is just an extension of using light tackle, and in some cases may be nearly the same thing, it will be considered the same for purposes of reviewing the basic aspects of light-tackle fishing.

Advantages. In addition to the obvious elements of fun and challenge, there are practical advantages to using light gear, especially line that is lighter in strength than might ordinarily be employed. One of these advantages is producing more strikes. In many circumstances—including when fish are spooky, heavily pressured, or generally turned off—using a fine-diameter line and a lighter lure will induce more strikes, and the lighter tackle is especially beneficial when angling in very clear water. Also, a light line can make a strike easier to detect and make your cast go farther.

Casting distance is an overrated aspect of angling *(see: casting)* because there are downsides to making long casts (it is more difficult to set the hook when a fish strikes a long distance away). However, when you must fish in a stiff wind, a lighter and finer-diameter line offers less wind resistance.

Necessary components. No matter how you define light tackle or what you fish for, the elements of using it are the same. Rods used for light tackle fishing tend to be a bit limber in order to provide more of a cushion for the lightness of the line. They can be short for small fish like stream trout or panfish, but a longer rod is a distinct advantage for landing big fish. Long rods (7 to 9 feet is the norm but 10- to 14-footers are used by some anglers) give you more leverage to pressure a fish, putting less strain on your arms and wrists, and they're very helpful when a hooked fish is near the boat and you need to steer around obstacles.

An important aspect of light tackle use is having fresh line in top condition. Using light line, fishing in demanding circumstances, and playing large fish require the most from your line *(see: line)*. Light line must be checked periodically for nicks and abrasions, and replaced more often if severely stressed. Only the best knots, tied consistently perfect, will do for light tackle, since more is demanded of these critical connections.

Hooksetting *(see)* can be more difficult with light line if you're timid, but you must be able to set the hook with authority no matter what tackle you use, and this requires confidence in the condition of your line and the ability of your knots. Hooksetting is enhanced by having the sharpest hooks. Maintaining ultrasharp hooks *(see: hook sharpening)* also helps minimize losing fish.

Another aid to successful fishing with light tackle is using a doubled length of line or a heavier leader, both to ensure greater strength in the knot and to help minimize the effects of abrasion. Some fish writhe a lot in the water near the boat and can easily wrap themselves up in the first few feet of line. They can snap it under the right circumstances, or at least abrade it. The doubled line or heavier leader makes dealing with strong fish on light tackle easier at the boat, which is where a lot of good fish are lost. Depending on the species and the circumstances, you may want to double the last 3 to 5 feet of light line used on casting tackle with a Bimini Twist or Spider Hitch knot *(see: knots, fishing)*, keeping it just short enough that the knot doesn't reach the spool of the reel. You should have no trouble casting these knots through the rod guides if you make them correctly, especially with smaller lines.

When angling for big fish with light line on a spinning outfit, it can be worthwhile to first make a 3- to 4-foot section of doubled line and then add a 2- to 3-foot heavier leader to it using a Uni Knot. Tying good knots is obviously very important here, but this setup really helps avoid abrasion and overcome near-the-boat stress. For some toothy species, add a short wire leader to the heavier monofilament leader or to the doubled line.

Another key component of light-line fishing is using drag *(see)* properly. You should have a reel with a smooth-operating drag, one that doesn't stick when initially needed and doesn't jerk or hesitate during use. Setting the drag properly is critical when tangling with strong fish on light tackle because the drag will be used often. Do not set the drag too loose, which impedes hooksetting (the drag slips) and puts too little pressure on a fish; and don't set it too tight, which might cause the line to snap under the extreme pressure of a surging fish. Knowing your limits, based on the line strength, the effectiveness of your knots, and the type of tackle that you're using, will determine how you play a fish caught on light tackle.

Playing and landing fish. Under ideal conditions of little boat traffic or few anglers nearby, you can play a strong fish in open water without too much difficulty because the line has nothing to snag on. The deck can be cleared and the boat maneuvered to your advantage. If the drag is set properly, the fish can take plenty of line and do its stuff. But if there are obstructions beneath the surface, or if you hook a big fish unexpectedly in a place having plenty of snags, then you have to be very aggressive and take the fight to the fish as quickly and as well as you can.

Fish captured on any tackle are easier to release if they are landed as quickly as possible. Since a quick landing is a little more difficult with light tackle, an extra effort must be made to play the fish correctly; if the landing takes too long, the fish may be so thoroughly exhausted that it cannot recover when (if) it is released.

By pumping and reeling and keeping pressure on the fish at all times, you tire it out. When you rest on a big fish, it rests and the battle is prolonged. So you must work the fish constantly *(see: playing fish).*

If you use good equipment, including a quality line with a knot that retains full strength and a rod with backbone, you can pressure a fish very well with light tackle. Depending on whether you're in a boat in open water or on a river bank, you'll probably be unable to land a really big fish by playing tug-of-war. You'll have to pump and reel whenever possible to gain on the fish, but you'll almost certainly have to change your position to work the fish more effectively. You may have to walk the bank or wade downstream after a big river fish because you won't have the muscle to coerce it back upstream. You may have to get below the fish or at least get into a section of river that has less current. On a lake, you may need to move the boat in order to change the angle of pull on the fish.

With light tackle it's important to pressure a fish from the very beginning and to periodically change the angle of tension from vertical to horizontal (left and right), which directs the fish away from obstructions and keeps it disoriented. When the fish swims off, let the drag do the work; otherwise, try to gain line at every chance. If the drag is a bit too loose and the line slips when you pump, use some extra tension (place your thumb on a bait-casting spool, palm on a spinning-reel spool, and fingertips on the inside of a fly-reel spool).

Disadvantages. Using light tackle does have a few disadvantages. It's possible that you might lose a few more fish with light tackle than you would ordinarily. If you can lose a good fish and not be upset about it, if you can lose a good fish and still enjoy the moment, if you can lose a good fish and feel good for the fish—then you have the right attitude for using light (and especially ultralight) gear. You'll definitely lose more lures and hooks with light tackle than with heavier gear; light line is frayed and weakened more easily, mistakes are magnified, and hangups on the bottom are harder to free. Also, since you generally can't use large, heavy lures, casting and hooksetting may pose problems.

These are minor issues, however. Light tackle under the right circumstances is very appropriate for freshwater and saltwater, and more people should gear up for fish of average size than for extreme size. However, some circumstances are inappropriate for light tackle, so be practical. Largemouth bass, for example, are caught in some areas where you can't work an appropriate lure if your tackle is too light; it would not be good sportsmanship to hook a large bass in a field of lily pads by using a wimpy rod and super-fine line, only to have the fish break off with a hook in its mouth and probably trailing a stream of nylon line. Ditto for when you're steelhead fishing in a deep swift pool and have to use many ounces of lead to get a bait or lure down; there you need a heavy rod to muscle fish away from snags, other anglers, anchor lines, and the like.

You can catch big fish on light tackle, as well as more fish of average size, if you know what you're doing. The seriousness and the effect of making mistakes when using ultralight gear is greatly magnified. The margin of error is slim, and there's no gimme even if you use perfect knots, have good reel drag, and skillfully battle fish. Therefore, it takes a more complete angler, with well-rounded skills, to be consistently effective.

LIMBLINE

A line that is anchored at one point, often to the limb or trunk of a dead or overhanging tree, and that is not connected to a hand-operated mechanical reel.

See: Setline.

LIMESTONE STREAM

A stream that flows through a bedrock of limestone or through land laced with varying degrees of limestone deposits. Also known as chalk streams because of their whitish, chalk-colored complexion, limestone streams are extremely rich in aquatic insects and plant life and are a favorite of trout anglers, although they are much fewer in number than freestone streams *(see)*. Their pristine, clear waters produce trout that some anglers consider to be larger, wilier, and often more brightly colored than trout living in most freestone streams.

Whereas freestone streams flowing off mountains or hillsides are fed from a single watershed, limestone streams may collect water from several watersheds through a far-ranging network of underground channels. The limestone aquifers in which the water gathers can carry a large quantity of water over some distance through underground solution channels. These channels usually are no more than 1 or 2 feet in diameter. Several of these channels may come together where they cut through the ground surface to spew cold waters to the outside. These springs are often quite large, with flows of 2,000 to more than 15,000 gallons of water per minute.

Limestone streams generally are meadow streams emanating from calcium-rich rock on the valley floor. Often, these valleys are bounded by sandstone ridges. As sinkholes develop and solution channels and caverns form, limestone is dissolved into the water. The water is gin-clear, but boiling it in a tea kettle will prove that there's a great deal of dissolved limestone present, since the water leaves a residue behind.

Limestone streams have an advantageous ability to neutralize acid precipitation. This natural buffering effect is due to high levels of calcium carbonate, which provides naturally high levels of alkalinity (in many cases from 7.5 to 8.0 year-round). With high alkalinity, these streams are extremely fertile. They hold abundant populations of such aquatic insects as mayflies and midges, and large populations of crustaceans like scuds and sowbugs.

Limestone streams can be shallow or deep, sometimes deceptively deep because of their clarity, and can have a thick growth of aquatic vegetation, which may include waterweed and watercress. They are often bordered by high grasses, rich bogs, and overhanging willow trees.

Most limestone streams support a much heavier food base than freestone streams. The even temperature of these spring-fed waters allows aquatic life to feed and grow throughout most of the year.

L

LIMIT

A restriction on the size or number of fish that can be taken, caught, or killed. Limit refers to regulations that have been established, usually with reference to recreational fishermen but in some cases also to commercial fishermen. Regulations pertaining to numbers of fish are called bag, creel, daily, and possession limits; regulations pertaining to size are called minimum length, total length, or slot limits.

See: Bag Limit; Creel Limit; Possession Limit; Minimum Length Limit; Slot Limit; Fisheries Management; Regulations.

LINE

Line is the element of fishing tackle that delivers a lure or bait from a rod to the water. In its simplest form, a piece of thread tied to the tip of a willow branch and used to dangle a worm-baited hook in the water constitutes a fishing line. Indeed, horsehair, cotton, and silk are among the materials that were once used as fishing line. Today, fishing line is synonymous with synthetic and technologically engineered products possessing attributes conducive to the various types of angling and manufactured to provide specific performance features, whether cast, trolled, or merely dangled.

Often overlooked and usually unappreciated, especially by freshwater anglers, line is a necessary and important component of fishing. It plays arguably *the* prominent role in the three most important aspects of catching fish: presentation, hooking, and landing. When all facets of fishing technique and fishing tackle use are taken into consideration, line becomes the single most important equipment item. To get the most out of your equipment, and to be more successful on the water, every angler should understand the types of line available, the properties of fishing line, and fundamental aspects of line use.

Fishing line is an angler's most critical connection, and it sometimes undergoes a lot of stress.

History of Modern Line

Today's angler is incredibly spoiled when it comes to fishing line. Ask contemporary anglers what kind of line was used a century ago and they will be hard-pressed to answer. This is a credit to the role that modern lines—especially nylon monofilament—have come to occupy in sportfishing.

Most fishing line in the early 1900s was made of linen, silk, and even cotton. As natural fibers, those lines required a lot of attention and tender loving care from the angler. Most lines then, for example, had to be rinsed and unspooled periodically to dry off and to deter line rot. And the lines of that time had nowhere near the performance properties of today's lines, much less the early monofilaments.

Although braided Dacron lines came into prominence for casting and trolling purposes, and were a step up from other products, especially in terms of maintenance, they, too, were problematic. However, the real change in line usage that led to today's products occurred in the period from 1934 to 1958. It started with the discovery of synthetic super-polymers, which is credited to the brilliant DuPont research chemist Dr. Wallace H. Carothers, who perfected their development in the mid-1930s. The turning point that came to benefit virtually all anglers happened in 1935 in a chemist's laboratory about 100 yards from Brandywine Creek in Wilmington, Delaware, when researchers succeeded in spinning a synthetic fiber with a high melt point.

In October of 1938, DuPont announced the discovery of a "group of new synthetic superpolymers" from which textile fibers could be spun with a strength-elasticity factor surpassing that of cotton, silk, wool, or rayon. DuPont called this group nylon, a play on the suggested name "no run," with respect to its value as a replacement for silk in the manufacture of stockings. In 1939, DuPont began the first commercial production of nylon monofilament fishing line; that same year, nylon stockings were introduced at the New York and San Francisco World's Fairs. Although both were significant developments, the value of fishing line was not as apparent as that of hosiery; 64 million pairs of all-nylon hose were sold in the first 12 months of production until halted by the advent of World War II.

For nearly 20 years, nylon monofilament fishing line would grow in popularity but not supplant the older fishing lines, particularly braided Dacron. By comparison with today's nylon monofilament, the early nylon line was primitive. Nevertheless, for its time, the early nylon line was durable, resisted abrasion, and didn't break readily; unfortunately, it also was thick and lacked uniformity.

The emergence of spinning reels and later spincasting reels *(see: spincasting tackle; spinning tackle)* caused line to undergo changes, since the nylon monofilament then was too limp to come off these reels properly. The era of modern lines began when a high-quality product called Stren was introduced in 1958 by DuPont, becoming the first line to be marketed with the DuPont name (previously, DuPont had made the line for others). This product had properties that allowed it to be used with different types of reels for varied fishing activities, and it became known as a premium line. In the vernacular of the modern age, it would be called a "super line."

The development of a thin and uniform-quality line with balanced properties was certainly an evolutionary milestone that made nylon monofilament the dominant (and at times nearly universally used) fishing line. And the uniformly embraced nylon monofilament became a catalyst for other tackle development and for a boom in sportfishing popularity because it helped make the various acts of fishing much easier.

Types

Line is made from different materials in varying strengths, diameters, and colors. It is manufactured in strengths ranging from 1 pound to 200 pounds, with 6- through 20-pound strengths being most popular. Some heavier strengths are made, but these are used only in special applications. Line is supplied on spools of varying but continuous lengths, from 100 yards up to many thousands of yards. The largest spools, with 6,000 yards of line or more, are called service spools and are used by retailers for filling many reels, by fishing clubs, and by some record-seeking anglers who change line often. Bulk spools range in size from 600 to 2,000 yards and may be useful to anglers who fish often. Most anglers use 250-yard spools.

Although there are many hybrid products, line is essentially characterized as being monofilament, braided, or having a core. Nylon monofilament accounts for more than two-thirds of all fishing lines sold, the remainder being essentially braided microfilament, fused microfilament, braided Dacron line, weighted line, wire line, and fly line.

Weighted, wire, and fly lines are distinctly different in principal usage than most other lines. Weighted and wire lines are trolled rather than cast. Fly line is cast but is used to carry nearly weightless objects; other lines that are cast are carried by the weight of the object being cast. These three types of line are discussed elsewhere *(see: flycasting tackle; weighted line; wire line).*

Monofilament. "Monofilament" is a word that means a single strand of line, but in sportfishing the name has become synonymous with nylon line. Nylon monofilament, also referred to as mono, was first introduced as leader material in 1939, and it became popular as fishing line in the 1950s. It became extraordinarily popular with the introduction and refinement of top-quality spinning and spincasting tackle.

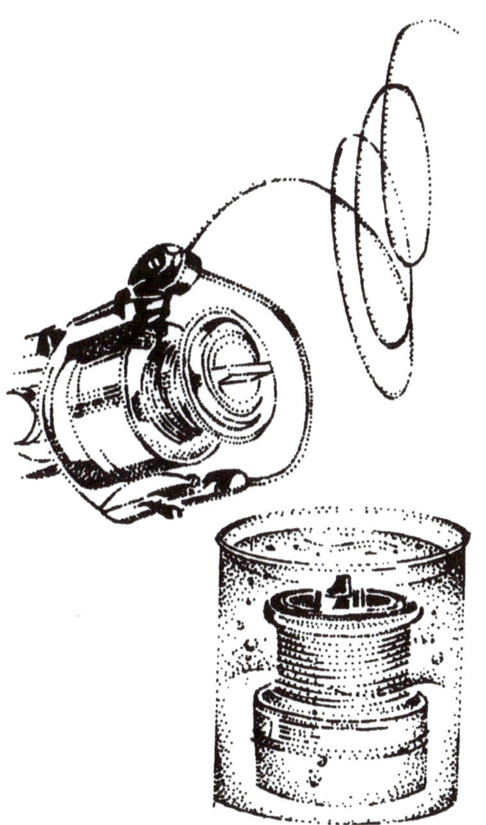

One way to remove coils from nylon monofilament line is to take the spool off the reel and soak it for a while (an hour for line that hasn't been used in a long time); the line absorbs water, relaxes, and becomes limp.

Nylon monofilament line, as the name suggests, is a single-component product. It is formed through an extrusion process in which molten plastic is formed into a strand through a die. Nylon monofilament lines are polymeric by-products of crude oil processing. Nylon alloys, a mixture of various types of nylon, are also used to form fishing line; fluorocarbon *(see)* is such a product. Although various brands of nylon monofilament line possess the same derivatives, the way they are processed and extruded and the way their molecules are compounded determine the different characteristics of the line and its properties. Additionally, premium-grade lines receive more quality-control attention, more additives, and more attention in the finishing processes than nonpremium line. As a result, they cost more.

Braided. Braided lines consist of intertwined strands of material, technically making them a multifilament product. Today that material is Dacron, gel-spun polyethylene fiber, or aramid fiber.

Braided line was once synonymous with Dacron, and before the discovery of nylon it was a primary line for fishing. However, nylon monofilament proved to be so superior to braided Dacron (which possessed poor knot strength, low abrasion resistance, and little stretch) that Dacron nearly disappeared in fishing, and today it has an infinitesimally small niche in the marketplace. It remains in use primarily as a backing material on fly reels; for a very few anglers, it is used as a big-game trolling product or a baitcasting reel product.

In the early 1990s, braided lines made from high-tech fibers became available. Because these lines featured great strength with small diameter, and because the fiber and no-stretch characteristics enhanced sensitivity, they became known as "super lines" or "microfilaments." Also called performance lines, microfilaments are braided from gel-spun polyethylene fiber (different grades or generations of Spectra, Dyneema, or Tekmillon) or from aramid fiber (Kevlar). The synthetic fiber itself, which is 10 times stronger than steel, has been used in industrial, aerospace, and military applications, and is incredibly strong yet very thin. Individual strands of fiber are married through an intricate, time-consuming, and costly braiding process. The result is an ultrathin, super-strong, and very sensitive line.

Fused. Braided microfilaments were popular for a while but yielded to a superior product made by fusing, rather than braiding, the same fibers. In this process, multiple microfilaments of gel-spun polyethylene fibers are fused together to produce what appears to be a single-strand line that is also ultrathin, super strong, and very sensitive, yet highly castable. Fused microfilament is a relatively new category of high-performance fishing line that has the same characteristics as its braided predecessor but a more affordable price (fusing is cheaper than braiding). It has garnered a section of the fishing line market, mostly for specific applications rather than all-around use.

Properties

The ultimate test of a fishing line is how it performs when used in all aspects of angling. That performance is based upon the properties that are engineered into the line. Until recently it was believed that a good line was one that had a proper balance of characteristics, primarily being strong, relatively thin, and durable. To a large degree, that is still true, although technological advancements have allowed manufacturers to manipulate properties to improve certain performance features. This has resulted in a wider variety of products than ever, some confusion among consumers, and also much better fishing line.

The most significant advancement in fishing line technology has been the evolution of thinner-diameter products. Anglers have always wanted a line that was strong and thin. Thin-diameter lines enable lures to work better and are less visible to fish. Thin-diameter lines have changed the complexion of line discussions; previously anglers spoke of line in terms of the rated strength, knowing that lines of similar strength also had similar diameter. But with the emergence of lines of conventional strength but unconventional diameter, the game has changed and anglers often unwittingly find themselves comparing apples to oranges.

Most anglers do not take the time to learn about the properties of line; if they did, they would purchase line more wisely and evaluate it more closely when using it. The properties include the following:

Breaking strength. The most prominent feature of any line is its strength, that is, how much pressure must be applied to the unknotted line before the molecules part and the line breaks. Unfortunately, this is an area with a great deal of disparity between products, and one that is poorly understood by many anglers.

All spools of line are labeled to indicate their breaking strength. Some are labeled with the customary United States designation in pounds, some with metric designation in kilograms, some with both. Those that are labeled with both are often not quite accurate; an 8-pound designation may be followed by a small-print designation of 4 kilograms, which actually equals 8.8 pounds.

There are two breaking strength categories: "test" and "class."

Class lines are predominantly used by saltwater big-game tournament anglers, by anglers specifically interested in establishing line-class world records (world records are kept for all species based on strength of line used as well as in all-tackle designations; *see: records),* and by fastidious anglers who want to know exactly what their line strength is. Class lines are guaranteed to break *at or under* the labeled metric strength in a wet condition, in order to conform to the metric world-record specifications of the International Game Fish Association (IGFA), which is the repository for world-record fish. Lines that conform to this guarantee are labeled on the packaging as "class" or "IGFA class." Class line is more expensive than test line and is primarily differentiated from test line in the wet breaking strength feature; its other properties should be similar to those of test lines.

The reason for fishing with a class line is partly to ensure that a fish that might be a record would meet the criteria. If line is tested and found to be slightly stronger than it should be for the parameters of a specific category, then it would be disqualified or bumped into a higher strength category for consideration. Line is tested by the IGFA in a wet condition because line is wet when it is fished and because the wet breaking strength of some lines—most notably nylon monofilament—is weaker than the dry breaking strength. There may be as much as a 20 percent difference in strength among some lines, and a negligible percentage in others. Another reason for fishing with class line is the certainty of knowing the basic strength of your line; the actual breaking strength of similarly labeled test lines varies greatly.

Any line that is not labeled as class line is, by default, test line. Perhaps 95 percent of all line sold is categorized as test, even if the word "test" is not used on the label. Despite the labeled strength, there is no guarantee as to the amount of force required to break the line in either a wet or a dry condition. The labeled strength may not reflect the actual force required to break the line in a wet condition. Since there are no guarantees with test line, they may break at, under, or over the labeled strength. An overwhelming number break above the labeled strength, some just a little above, some very far above.

To illustrate the breaking strength difference, anglers fishing with a class 12-pound line are fishing with a product that will break at slightly less than 12 pounds in a wet state, whereas those fishing with a good-quality test 12-pound line are using a product that will probably break at somewhere between 13 and 14 pounds in a wet state. This difference between labeled and actual breaking strength may not sound like much, but there are situations when it is considerably different. In an extreme example, a poor-quality test 12-pound line may break at 15 or 16 pounds in a wet state, making it a deliberately mislabeled product.

Since there is a great deal of difference in the actual breaking strength of various test lines, and since people only know what the label tells them, many anglers fish with line that is much stronger than what they think it is. And many are mislead into believing that some lines are stronger than others because they physically feel that way. It is meaningless to take a piece of nylon monofilament, wrap it around your hand, tug on it, and proclaim it has great strength. This is dry strength, which is irrelevant.

To determine the actual fishing strength of a line, you have to soak it in water for a while and then test it. Since few anglers have the machinery

All kinds of line are tested for world-record fish certification by the International Game Fish Association; here, a sophisticated machine tests a line sample and records results on a computer.

to calibrate exact breaking strengths, they are usually in the dark as to the actual strength of a line, although some independent analyses (with widely varying results) have been published.

The difference between labeled breaking strength and actual breaking strength exists in braided and fused products as well. Microfilaments technically do not absorb water and do not change in strength from dry to wet. However, tests indicate that their breaking strength varies a good deal from what is labeled (usually being lower) and that they may not break at the same strength consistently. Fluorocarbon line is one in which there is no discernible weakening in a wet state, although there may be some inconsistency in actual versus labeled breaking strength.

To many anglers, who do not push their tackle to the limits and who do not catch large fish or do not angle under difficult circumstances, the amount of difference between labeled strength and actual strength and between wet strength and dry strength is largely nit-picking. However, for anglers who need top performance and who fish to exacting specifications, an understanding of actual breaking strength is vitally important.

Diameter. It used to be that the breaking strength of a line was directly related to its diameter. The greater the breaking strength, the larger the diameter. However, in recent years nylon monofilament line manufacturers have found a way to produce ultrathin lines that have the same performance characteristics as conventional mono but that are markedly thinner. The newer microfilaments are exceptional in regard to thin diameter; a line with 24-pound breaking strength may have a diameter equivalent to a conventional 10- or 12-pound-strength line. Therefore, the diameter of a line is no longer necessarily a corollary to its breaking strength.

This creates some confusion between anglers discussing the merits or demerits of certain prod-

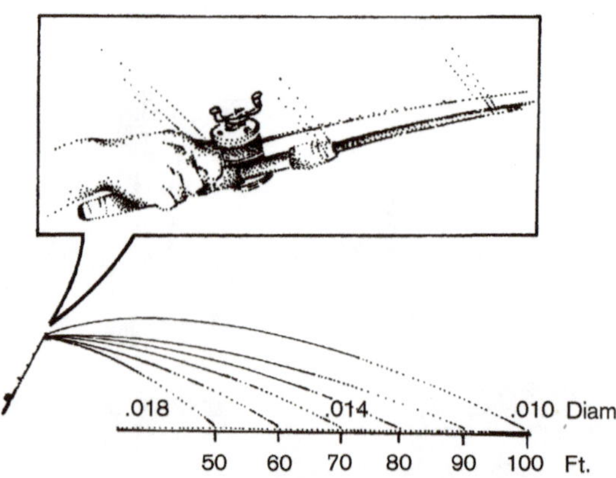

There is a clear relationship between casting distance and line diameter when using the same weight lure.

ucts or strengths of line, as well as confusion in anglers doing comparison shopping. There is some concern among anglers that thin-diameter lines are more susceptible to abrasion, since it once was true that thicker-diameter lines were better at resisting abrasion. In some conventional lines, and in poorer-quality lines, that is still true; however, many thin-diameter lines also have a high-degree of abrasion resistance as well.

Line diameter has some bearing on the amount of line that will fit on a spool—and therefore on the amount of line that is available for fighting strong fish. This is of special concern to light-tackle anglers who need plenty of line on a reel. It also impacts the size of knots, especially line-to-line knots, and may affect how well they sit on a reel spool or flow through a reel or rod guides. It is also a factor in achieving distance when casting and in getting lures to work effectively; thinner line has less drag and can be cast farther, and it allows lures to dive or sink deeper or faster. In some cases, it even enhances the action of lures. Because thin-diameter lines are less visible to fish, they are also conducive to getting more strikes, especially in clear water.

Perhaps one day anglers will have to become better attuned to thinking in terms of diameter in order to make valid comparisons between line. Only fly anglers, basically because of their use of fine leaders *(see)* and tippets *(see)*, have some understanding of numerically based line diameter, some going to the extent of using a micrometer to measure diameter. To really compare products, you have to know what the diameter is as well as what the actual breaking strength is. Some manufacturers are providing diameter information on their nylon monofilaments but not on braided or fused microfilaments. Solid, round, single-strand nylon monofilament provides a uniform diameter and is easy to evaluate, but other products do not provide consistent or necessarily accurate diameter measurements.

Abrasion Resistance. Abrasion resistance is one of the most difficult qualities of line to measure because no laboratory test has yet been devised that accurately reflects the abrasive contact that line is subjected to during fishing conditions. Some lines are more abrasion resistant than others due to greater diameter, the composition of the line, or a coating that is applied to it. Determining the differences among brands is subjective, although some lines do seem to be considerably more resistant to abrasion than others. However, you can make this judgment only through use.

Fishing line manufacturers have often showcased the alleged abrasion-resistant property of their line by mechanically scraping it and competitive lines, all in a dry state, repeatedly over sandpaper. This is irrelevant and unrelated to actual fishing situations, where a wet line is making contact with rocks, fish teeth and gill covers, barnacles, propellers, and all sorts of objects.

Some lines, particularly premium nylon monofilaments and fluorocarbon, have excellent abrasion resistance. Some are just barely adequate. Lack of abrasion resistance was braided Dacron's biggest drawback when it was a commonly used line, and microfilaments, though better than braided Dacron, do not seem to be remarkably good in this area either. Manufacturers claim that fused microfilament lines have better abrasion resistance than nylon monofilament lines, but this has not been proven on the water. Their claim has to do with the fact that because of the high number of filaments used in the manufacturing process, there can be some abrasion without sacrificing the integrity of the line. The experience of some anglers, however, is that the abrasion resistance of microfilament lines is actually poorer than that of good-quality nylon monofilament lines.

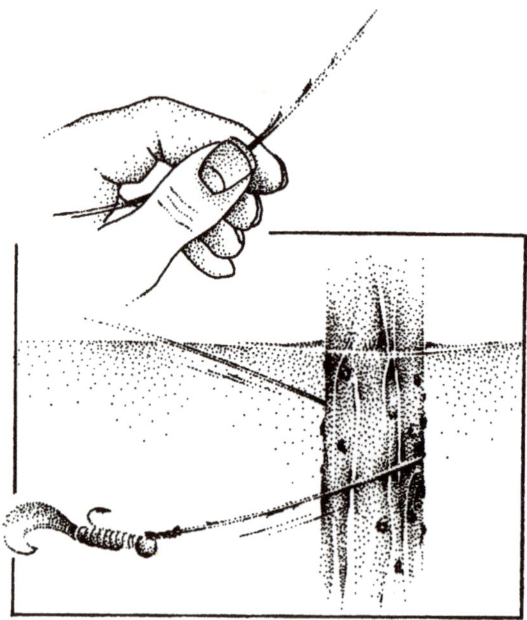

It's a very good idea to periodically run your fingers over the terminal end of fishing line to check for nicks and abrasions because some circumstances are more likely than others to cause abrasion.

Many anglers have to contend with abrasion. Sometimes you have to cut off nicked line every half hour or so while fishing because the conditions are so tough on line. The thinner the diameter of line, the more damaging abrasion can be. Contact with rocks, trees, stumps, vegetation, and fish can wear heavily on line, so selecting one with satisfactory abrasion resistance is important, but not so easy. Keep in mind that no castable line completely withstands abrasion, but some withstand it better than others. The key is to find a line that resists abrasion adequately while still having other properties important for fishing performance.

Stretch. Most lines stretch. The issue is how much they stretch and how this impacts your fishing. Stretch, which is also referred to as elasticity and elongation, is both good and bad. It allows for mistakes in fighting a fish, inadequate drag setting, or countering sudden close-to-the-angler surges by strong fish; yet it hampers the inattentive angler who forgets to keep all of the slack out of the line when setting the hook or who is inexperienced at detecting strikes, especially at long distances.

The average percent of stretch in nylon monofilaments was once around 30 percent in a wet state but now has been reduced in better products to a range of 10 to 25 percent. Nylon monofilament line has slightly more stretch in a wet state than in a dry one. Lines that have high stretch are great for casting, but they are terrible for hooksetting and playing fish because they have the elasticity of a rubber band. The cushioning effect that has been provided by lines with controlled stretch has been important to many anglers, and they are accustomed to it.

On the other hand, having low stretch should increase an angler's ability to detect strikes, aid hooksetting, provide more control in playing a fish, increase the sensitivity of the line so that the angler can feel what a lure or bait is doing, and theoretically help catch more fish. These have been the most important attributes of microfilaments, which have virtually no stretch (or up to 4 percent).

A simple way to detect the difference as it relates to a typical angling situation is to take a 40-foot length of wet microfilament and a similar length of wet nylon monofilament, and connect one end to a firm object and the other to identical fishing rods. Set the hook on each. The lack of stretch and the greater hooksetting ability of the fiber line will be immediately apparent.

A similar way to test this, using the same length of wet line, is to measure the lengths of these lines when you apply an equal amount of pulling tension on them. For instance, if you take a 40-foot length of wet microfilament, connect it to a good scale, and pull on it until only 1 pound of pressure is exerted, you'll see that it doesn't stretch. Take a wet 40-foot length of a good-quality nylon monofilament, do the same thing, and it will stretch a long way.

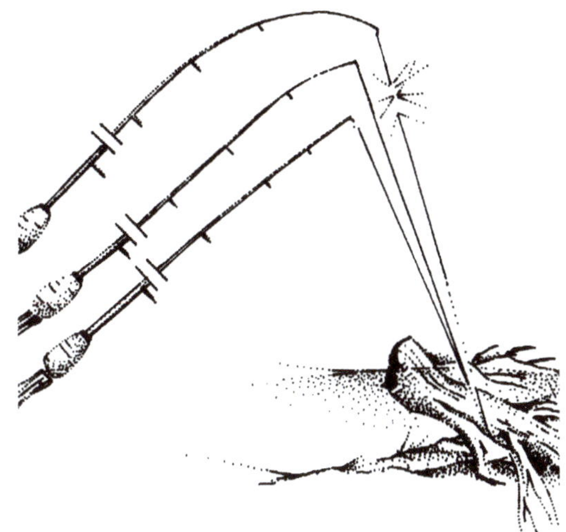

When a line is stretched too far, it reaches a breaking point or is damaged beyond usefulness, which can compromise its strength when you later fight a strong fish.

Stretch is a feature that directly relates to sensitivity. You may have seen film of fish sucking in a lure and then spitting it out, without the angler knowing that he or she had a strike. This illustrates the difference that stretch and sensitivity make. The less stretch, the more sensitivity; the more sensitivity, the better you should detect fish.

Although you would think that it would be best to fish with a line that had virtually no stretch, such as the different microfilaments, many anglers have tremendous difficulty with these products precisely because they have no stretch and are unforgiving. Anglers set the hook too hard or pull too intensely on a hooked fish and yank the hook out of the fish. Because of low stretch, anglers have to use these products differently than nylon monofilament, and they need to make adjustments (such as decreasing the reel drag and using a more limber rod).

It is worth noting that line-pulling tests and demonstrations notwithstanding, a fair amount of stretch in a line may not be as significant a factor in your fishing as it would seem, depending upon the circumstances. For example, a line that has 15 percent wet stretch may not impair your ability to detect a strike or set the hook if it is used at fairly short angling distances and the fish are not especially large or tough. If you go by the numbers, a 40-foot section of line with 15 percent stretch should elongate another 6 feet. But this simply does not happen at the moment you set the hook, say when using a 10-pound line on a jig while fishing the bottom for a 3-pound walleye. Stretch doesn't enter the equation until an appropriate amount of force is applied to the line. If the fish is extremely large, it may, after the hookset and while you are fighting it, stretch the line up to that 15 percent margin, but not before you set the hook. If you fish at closer distances, as you would, for example, when dabbling a minnow for crappies 15 feet below your boat, there is no concern. If you are fishing

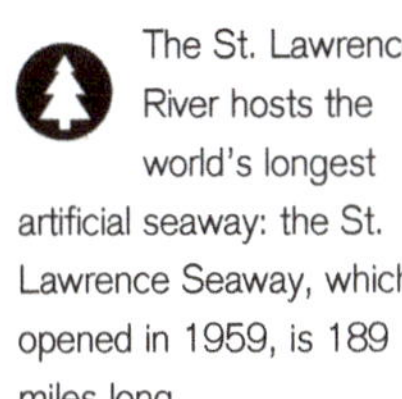

The St. Lawrence River hosts the world's longest artificial seaway: the St. Lawrence Seaway, which opened in 1959, is 189 miles long.

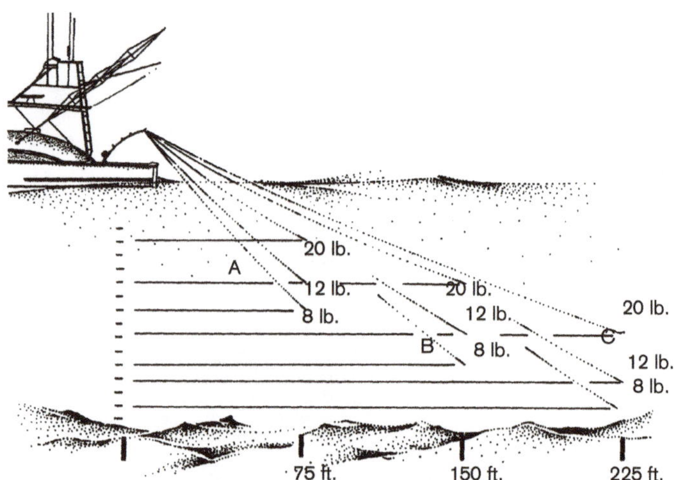

This representation of trolling a deep-diving plug with different strengths (also diameters) and lengths of lines depicts the differences that exist. Longer lines (C) take lures deeper than shorter lines (A and B), and lighter/thinner lines (8 lb.) get lures deeper than heavier/thicker lines.

in places where a strong fish could peel off a lot of line and cut you off on some obstruction, then you do need to think about stretch very seriously; when a bottom-caught fish applies a lot of pressure to the line, it will cause that line to stretch, and that stretch may allow a fish (like an amberjack or grouper, for example) to get to an object that will cut the line. This happens often to anglers.

At longer distances, there is also reason to be concerned about stretch, which, compounded with the action of the rod, absorbs some amount of energy and does make both strike detection and hooksetting more difficult. For example, if you have 120 feet of line out, which might be common when trolling, and even if you're using a line that stretches only 10 percent, mathematically you might receive 12 feet of undesirable stretch when pressure is applied. Even if the amount is much less than 12 feet, say just 5 feet, that's still a lot to overcome.

The final point on this subject that you should know about is ultimate elongation. Ultimate elongation is the amount of stretch that a line will take before breaking. This does not apply to microfilaments, where ultimate elongation and breaking point are virtually the same. Good-quality nylon monofilament lines have an ability to return to their normal state after severe pressure and stretching and to maintain basic strength. Stretch is not a permanent condition under average fishing conditions. However, lines that have seen the severest stress warrant close examination. It is difficult to determine when a line has been stretched to the maximum—the point where it cannot recover and is no longer serviceable—other than checking whether it holds knots well and can be broken in your hands. If in doubt about the continued serviceability of your line, replace it.

Flexibility. Fishing line has to perform a lot of functions, and in order to fulfill each function it must have the right blend of limpness and stiffness. Somewhere between a limp piece of cooked spaghetti and a rigid piece of uncooked spaghetti is the proper amount of flexibility that will allow an angler to cast a line, spool it, detect strikes, and absorb sudden impacts.

A limp, or very flexible, line is advantageous for achieving casting distance, in part because the line comes off the reel spool easily in smaller coils and straightens out quickly. It can be managed on a reel, especially a spinning reel, more easily than a stiff line, but it lacks some of the sensitivity of the latter. Stiff lines tend to spring off the spool of spinning reels in large coils, which flap against the rod guides, decrease distance, and increase the likelihood of developing a tangle. Stiff lines can affect the appearance or workings of lures, especially light objects such as flies (when used as tippet material), and some types of bait.

The flexibility of a line is hard to judge by observation, although in some instances you can feel that a line is very stiff or very limp. Braided lines are limper than nylon monofilaments, which vary a great deal in flexibility. The molecular structure of nylon is such that nylon monofilament line forms a memory when placed in a certain position (such as being spooled) for an extended period of time. Nylon lines with less memory are considered limp and are more castable than stiff lines, a factor that is important in light-line angling. Nylon lines with a lot of memory are considered stiff, which con-

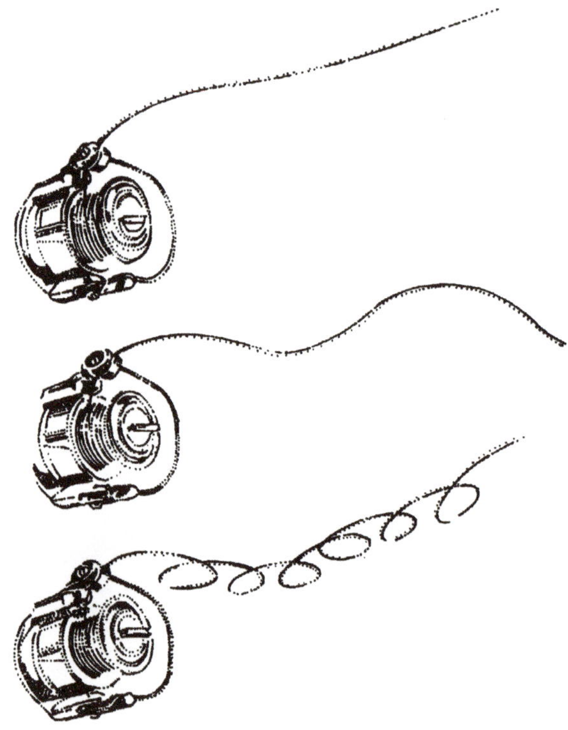

The flexibility of a line depends on its manufactured characteristics, as well as the condition in which it has been stored for a long time. The worst scenario is a very wiry, stiff line that is tightly coiled (bottom). The limpest lines (top) have virtually no memory and come off a reel with almost no coiling.

tributes to spooling and twist problems and makes casting more difficult.

Castability is affected not only by limpness but also by water absorption in lines that absorb water; wet lines usually cast better than dry lines. It is also affected by line diameter. The greater the diameter, the harder it is to cast. With nylon monofilament, the stiffer the line, the less stretch it has but the more difficult it is to cast. Thus, there is a dramatic trade-off between castability and stretch in nylon monofilament. It's a good idea to wet nylon monofilament line (place the spool in the water) before you start using it on a given day, to help the molecules to relax.

Braided and fused microfilaments are different in this respect. They have low stretch, good limpness, and high castability, wet or dry.

Knot strength. Generally, once you tie a knot in a fishing line, it becomes weaker. Furthermore, knots tied in nylon monofilament that are tested in a wet condition (as they would be when fished) are weaker than when in a dry condition. Nylon monofilament line manufacturers claim that their technological processes produce molecular formations that result in specific knot-strength abilities for their line. Since the same knots are tied with various levels of expertise by different individuals, this is hard to verify when comparing knots tied by one angler with those tied by another. Nonetheless, if you are tying knots carefully and uniformly, and they're not holding, it could be because the knot strength of the line is deficient.

It could also be that the knot you are using isn't well suited to the type of line. The same knots that are used for nylon monofilaments are not as good with braided lines and fused microfilaments, although they may just need some minor adaptation. Braided lines tend to cut themselves when knotted improperly and tend to break at the knot when only moderate pressure is applied, so the proper knot is essential. Braided and fused microfilament lines tend to be slick and don't hold many of the conventional knots used with nylon monofilament, and thus may require different knots. In general, however, microfilament lines lose some of their strength even when tied with a proper knot. That percentage could be as high as 25 percent, a factor that you must take into consideration when evaluating the actual breaking strength of the product being fished.

Uniformity. It is reasonable to expect that what you get at one end of a line spool you should get at every point along that spool to the end. With premium lines you generally do. Sometimes, however, the manufacturing processes may alter the diameter of the line in certain spots or may in some way alter the characteristics in unidentified areas. You may find a spot that is thicker than the rest of the line. Here, the molecules have not been well oriented, and this part of the line will be weaker than the rest. Conversely, a thin spot will be stronger. With the premium lines on the market today, you should encounter none of this. With bargain-basement specials—those lines selling for a few dollars for a 2,000-yard spool—you get what you pay for: junk.

Visibility. The visibility of a fishing line has no effect on its basic performance and generally has nothing to do with the other properties. Line visibility, or color, is one perceptible property of fishing line, yet it is also a highly subjective feature. Fishing line is available in many colors and shades as well as in fluorescent versions. How the line looks above the water is less of a factor than how it looks on or in the water where it is used. Since only the fish know for sure what they think about that, we're left to speculation and trial-and-error fishing. Because so many variables affect angling success, it is usually difficult to blame line color or visibility alone for a lack of fishing success.

It is known, of course, that some colors are more visible in the water than others. Anglers who fish in shallow clear water have more reason to be concerned about the visibility of line than those who fish in murky water. The background can have something to do with the visibility as well, and most anglers would like their fishing line to be invisible in the water, and highly visible above the water.

High-visibility line, particularly fluorescent line, is of great value to anglers whose eyesight isn't as keen as it used to be. It is also useful to anglers who bottom bounce, troll, fish with jigs or plastic worms, and otherwise have reason to watch their lines for an indication of a strike. Sometimes, high visibility to the angler outweighs high visibility beneath the surface because the angler fishes more effectively by virtue of being able to see the line better. Fluorescent line, which was first introduced by DuPont, was highly successful for them but denigrated by their competitors until the patent ran out; then the competitors eagerly introduced fluorescent lines.

Today there are dark lines and light lines, dull lines and shiny lines, and an assortment of colors picked by enterprising marketers. The so-called clear color remains the distinct favorite of most anglers, with a light-green color perhaps running a distant second in popularity. Fluorescent lines, incidentally, lose some of their brightness after long use because of ultraviolet exposure. And some microfilaments lose their color as well, in part because the color has been added after manufacture and does not hold well.

Anglers should recognize that some lines may absorb light and be more visible, and thus alarming, to some fish under some circumstances. Some lines may alarm fish by casting a greater shadow on the water or by exhibiting flash due to a shiny surface. The trouble is that most anglers use their tackle to angle for different fish in varying circumstances, clear water one moment, cloudy water the next. And those situations are always changing. Sometimes the diameter of the line is more important than the color. And sometimes having the right lure and retrieving it properly is more important than line color.

Durability. There are many significant properties of fishing line, and their function and importance are interwoven. Some manufacturers emphasize the durability of fishing line as being the most important property; durability is actually a function of all the properties. Although the definition of durability varies, it is agreed that a fishing line should be durable enough to withstand a reasonable amount of hard fishing. However, some of the most durable lines are not the best-performing lines because they are weak in certain properties. For example, a line that is especially resistant to abrasion, perhaps because of its thickness or a coating, may not be as castable because it is stiff. Generally, anglers need a line with a balance of properties, including the ability to hold up to obvious environmental influences as well as specific angling needs.

Line Use

Modern fishing line is so superior to the line available just a few decades ago that anglers are easily lulled into thinking that their line needs no attention. This lack of attention to line, especially in freshwater, also stems from the fact that the average angler seldom catches fish large enough to really test even the poorest line or the angler's own abilities. This is a mistake. Proper care, use, and attention to line pays dividends over and over again in ordinary day-to-day fishing situations.

Controlling line twist. Probably the greatest problem that most anglers experience in relation to line is twisting. Many anglers incorrectly blame their line for twisting problems. If your line twists and you think it's because the line is no good, take a brand-new consumer spool of that line, lay out the amount you want, and wait for it to twist. You'll be waiting forever. The point is that you have to do something to make line twist; it doesn't twist by itself. Line twist can occur as a result of various factors, including improper spooling, improperly playing a fish, having too loose a drag, using certain lures without a swivel, fishing in swift current, and using a lure that isn't running properly.

If the problem is a faulty lure, you'll need to adjust the lure so that it runs without spinning or else try using a split-ring, snap, or snap swivel, all of which aid in preventing spinning and twisting. Certain lures, such as most spinners used in flowing water, require the use of a snap swivel to prevent twisting. Almost all lures that revolve or turn over, including most spinners and spoons, will put twist in your line and should be used with a snap swivel, preferably a ball-bearing one.

If your drag is too loose, it will slip while you are fighting a fish and reeling in. This results in line twist. Similarly, if you crank a fish by forcefully reeling it in with spinning gear, instead of pumping, retrieving line, etc., you will put a bad twist in the line, since every turn of the rotor puts a full twist in the line.

When line on a reel is twisted, you can straighten it out by trolling it behind a boat, without any objects attached to the line. Rewind the line under tension.

When you retrieve a lure, you can tell whether your line is twisted by watching how the lure dangles from the tip of your rod. If it begins to rotate, the line is twisted. Another indication is the development of coils in the line when you give it slack. Often an angler will be retrieving a lure, let it momentarily rest, and not notice that a coil develops near the reel. The angler continues retrieving, only to pile up line on the reel arbor on top of the loose coil. During a subsequent cast, the angler is likely to get a bird's nest, the severity of which will depend on how twisted the line has become.

Twisted line is not difficult to cure when you're in a boat or near running water. Line will untwist itself if you let a long length of it out behind your boat, with nothing attached to the end of it (no snap, swivel, split-shot, hook, lure, etc.), and drag it along for a few minutes. The faster your boat travels, the quicker the line unravels. Reel the line back in, and you're ready to attach terminal gear and fish. You can achieve the same effect on moderate- to fast-flowing water by letting the unweighted line float downstream and then holding it in the current for several minutes. This has the same effect as dragging it behind the boat.

Line twist can be impossible to cure if the problem is not recognized until the line is a mass of twists and curls. When line twist is this serious, cut off the problem section and start anew, being careful to correct the cause of the twist before fishing again.

Filling a reel. Many problems associated with line actually begin at the first step of line use: putting new line on a reel spool. How you put line on and how much of it you put on are keys to minimizing twist and enhancing casting.

Spool Filling

Under

Over

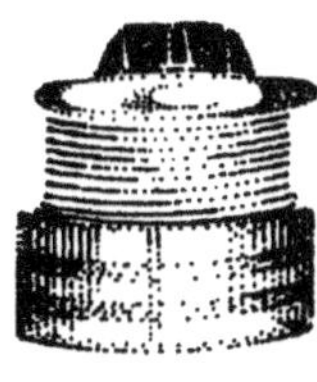
Proper

The best performance of a line and reel is achieved when the reel has been spooled properly. This means filling it almost to the edge, within $^{1}/_{8}$ to $^{3}/_{16}$ inch. If you overfill a spinning reel, line will fall off loosely when slack is given, causing a snarl to develop; several loops of line will pile up and jam in the spool or in a rod guide. Also, line can become pinched in the side flanges of the spool of an overfilled baitcasting or levelwind reel.

A properly filled reel allows you to achieve good distance in your casts, particularly with light lures. An underfilled reel hampers your casting range, since more coils of line (causing more friction) must come off the spool. After a period of time, through cutting frayed line, tying knots, and experiencing breakoffs, the level of line on the reel will become too low. In addition to hampering casting in some fishing situations, too little line might cost you a big fish if you hook one that takes all the remaining line off the reel. Additionally, drag pressure increases as line on the reel arbor decreases, creating a sometimes difficult situation for the angler when fighting a strong, surging fish.

You can put twist in the line by improperly spooling it, which happens often to inexperienced anglers. Unlike microfilaments, nylon monofilament has a memory factor, and it returns to its "memoried" state after being used. Line thus develops a set in the position in which it has been placed for a long time, such as the plastic spool on which it is wound for packaging.

On a consumer spool, not only has the line taken a set, but it actually is slightly coiled already, which is an inherent part of the manufacturer's spooling process. The manufacturer has huge bulk spools of line from which the smaller retail spools are filled. Line that comes off the extreme periphery of a full bulk spool has less coiling than the line that comes off the core of the bulk spool.

You and a friend could conceivably possess the same brand of line in the same strength, and one would be noticeably more coiled than the other. The reason is probably that they came from different locations on the bulk spool, or that they were produced at different times (when one batch of line was more coiled than the other). In any event, the longer that line stays on the retail spool, the more its coils conform to the diameter of the spool. Coiling is less pronounced in top-grade lines and lines that come off large-diameter bulk or service spools.

On baitcasting reels, which are aptly called levelwind reels, line is fairly free of the twisting problems caused by spooling. This is because the line is wound straight onto the reel arbor in a direct, level, overlapping manner. The spooling suggestions that follow can also be applied to baitcasting reels.

Open-faced spinning reels and spincasting (closed face) reels pose many problems in line spooling for beginning anglers. The reason is that these systems actually put a slight twist in the line as it rotates off the bail arm and onto the arbor. If the line is of poor quality or if it already has a fair degree of manufacturer-instilled coiling and the angler improperly spools it onto a spinning reel, the result can be twisting, curling, coiling line—endless trouble unless it is run out behind the boat and rewound.

The first secret to successful spooling is watching how the line comes off both sides of the manufacturer's spool. Take line off the side with the least apparent coiling. Then apply moderate pressure on the line before it reaches the reel.

Follow this technique for proper spooling: Place the supply spool on the floor or any flat surface. The line should balloon or spiral off the spool as you pull it up. After you've threaded line through your rod guides and attached it to your reel, hold the rod tip 3 to 4 feet above the supply spool. Make 15 to 20 turns on the reel handle and stop. Now check for line twist by reducing tension on the line.

Lower the rod tip so that it is a foot from the supply spool, and check to see whether the slack line twists or coils. If it does, turn the supply spool upside down. This will eliminate most of the twist as you wind the rest of the line onto the reel. If the other side has more of a coiled or twisted nature to it, go back to the first side and take line off while it is face up. The trick here is to take line from the side that has the least amount of coiling. In effect, this method counter-spools the line on your spinning reel and cancels the curling tendencies that would otherwise exist.

Although manufacturers have recommended placing a pencil or other object inside a spool to let it run freely while you put on line, this is not as good a method as the one previously described. Although the pencil method may suffice for direct spooling of levelwind reels, it seems to compound the spooling problem on spinning and spincasting reels.

Keeping moderate tension on the line with one hand as you reel with the other is important when filling a reel. Do this by holding the line between your thumb and forefinger with your free hand. A loosely wound reel results from not applying spooling tension and causes loops of line to develop on the reel spool. Excessive tension, however, may bind up the line and allow more line to be spooled than necessary—a fact that you will discover later after the used line starts to bunch up as you begin to spool it naturally by reeling. So you have to find the right medium.

For some strengths and types of line and some types of fishing tackle, it is important to spool line

Idaho's Snake River sockeye traverse up to 897 miles to and from the Pacific, making them the sockeye migration champs in the lower 48 of the United States.

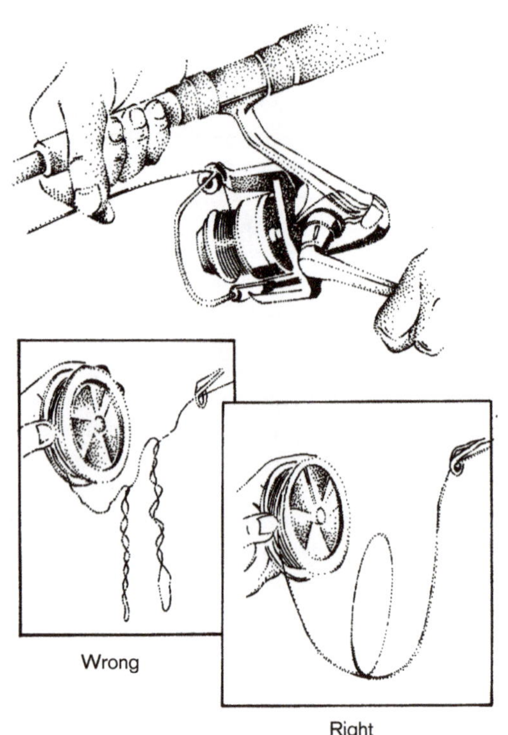

Always put line on a reel while applying a moderate amount of tension (top), and be sure to take line off a filler spool from the side that produces the least coiling.

very tightly onto the reel. Large conventional reels *(see: conventional tackle)* and big-game reels *(see: big-game tackle),* for example, require that line be wound tightly on them so that the pressure of fishing or of fighting a large fish does not cause wraps of line to become buried into a loosely packed spool. A similar issue holds for using braided or fused microfilament lines; when spooled onto the reel, these types of line need more tension than a comparable nylon monofilament.

Removing coils. Nylon monofilament develops coils because the line has memory and takes a set that conforms to the spool of the reel. This tendency can be troublesome, especially on spinning reels. To remove these coils, relax the line by soaking it in lukewarm water. Dipping it momentarily in water before use may help a bit as well.

Another way to ease coiling is to put a lot of tension on the line. You can apply tension in a controlled way by tying the line to a fixed object, backing off a reasonable distance, raising the rod as if you were playing a fish, and then applying moderate tension to it about 10 times. Don't strain the rod too hard or you risk breaking it, and don't apply so much tension that you break or severely stretch the line.

Changing line. In a sense, new fishing line is like a new automobile. When you purchase a new car and drive it off the dealer's lot, it becomes a "used" or old car. When you put new line on your reel and fish with it, it's used. A new automobile that is driven frequently but is garaged and taken on only the best roads is likely to stay in top condition longer than one that is used daily, constantly exposed to the elements, and subject to every type of road condition. Line is very much the same. The age of the line is much less important than how much and under what conditions it has been used.

The primary reasons for changing line are that it is too low on the spool, it's very old, or it has had such extensive, stressful use that a cautionary replacement seems warranted.

When line becomes too low, it hampers casting and reduces effective drag settings, and it needs to be refilled. Many reels have large line capacities, so even when a reel has too little line left on it for good casting, usually it still has half of its capacity left. If the line has not been on the reel very long, it is still worth using. You should consider taking off this leftover line by tying the end to a tree or a post in an open area (or on the water) and backing away so that the line does not bunch up or become tangled. Take off the line, put on a suitable amount of stronger line for backing, and then take the end of the monofilament that you hitched to the post and tie this to the backing. When your spool is full, you have the fresh, unused back section of old line for fishing.

If you have a large-capacity reel but will need only a third or half of it for fishing, and you will not need it for other kinds of fishing, attach a backing to the spool before putting on new line. The backing should be of equal or greater strength than the main line.

If you wish to replace the full capacity of line on a reel, simply strip it all off and discard it in the garbage or in a recycling bin at a tackle shop. You can do this fairly quickly by giving it the old clothesline palm-to-elbow wrap. Another method is to use an electric drill. Affix an old consumer spool or some large-capacity object in the drill bit head, set the reel on freespool or reduce the drag setting to the least amount of tension (this is also a way to break in a drag), and run the drill until the line is off. A third method is to use a battery-operated line stripper.

Old nylon monofilament line needs to be replaced completely, as does line that has been used often in punishing fishing conditions. Some anglers have had nylon monofilament line on their reels for years—so long that they have no idea how old the line may be.

How long line may be used before being replaced is a question with no set answer. This depends on how much fishing you do, the strength of the line, how large and hard-fighting the fish are that you regularly catch, how much care or abuse your tackle receives, and the original quality of the line. An angler who fishes only a few times a year would be well advised to change line at least once a year, preferably before the start of each season. A slightly more frequent angler should change it at least twice a year. And anglers who fish regularly should change their line every few weeks. If your line is exposed to the elements for long periods of time (such as sitting in a sunlit boat or lying on a dock), you may need to change it more frequently than if it had been put away. Line should not be exposed to sunlight or to heat for days or weeks on end.

The type of fishing circumstance can also serve as a guide. Fishing in unobstructed water puts less demand on a line than does fishing around rocks, logs, timber, docks, and the like. Light line, because of its thin diameter, requires more frequent changing than heavy line. Microfilaments may need to be changed much less frequently than conventional line because they are more resistant to light and extremely durable.

Inspecting line. You can't tell much about the thickness of line by feeling it, since variations are generally in thousandths of an inch. You could use a micrometer to measure the diameter, but very few anglers have reason to own or regularly use this costly piece of equipment.

You can detect abrasion by feel, and this is quite important. A nick, cut, or fray in nylon monofilament can weaken it, sometimes by as much as 50 percent or more. A 10-pound-test line, which would ordinarily need 10 or more pounds of pressure to break it, may need only 5 or 7 or 8 pounds if it is abraded. Microfilaments are said to be weakened less by cuts and frays, but it's not worth taking a chance. The only way to assure 100 percent strength is to cut off abraded sections.

Line breakage as a result of undetected abrasion leads many anglers to question the quality of their line, when in fact the anglers are to blame for not checking the line. Therefore, periodically running your fingers over the first few feet (more if necessary) of line to detect nicks or frayed areas is a good idea. When you do find such spots, cut off the damaged section of line. If, for some reason, you find it hard to detect abrasion by feeling the line, try running it through your lips.

Abrasion usually results from underwater contact with objects and fish, though it can happen after a portion of your line contacts tree limbs or stumps when a lure hangs up. Occasionally, however, imperfections in your rod or reel cause abrasion. A nick or burr on a rod guide, reel pickup arm or levelwind guide, or spool edge can be the culprit. If line abrasion occurs regularly throughout the line or when you're fishing in unobstructed water, you should check the tackle and correct the problem.

Another sign of old line, and possibly well-worn line, is the visibly faded look, which may be the result of age or extensive exposure to sun. With nylon monofilament, this is a result of the fluorescence evaporating from exposure to ultraviolet light. Sometimes anglers find that the line on their reel suddenly seems to have lost its strength. The reason usually remains a mystery. Old nylon line does, however, become stiff as the result of the seepage of its plasticizing agent (monomer, which is the white chalky buildup that you sometimes get when spooling line on a reel) and thus is brittle and weaker. This condition is evidenced in lighter lines by failure to hold knots well or by the easy breaking of unknotted sections. In some cases, this old line is still serviceable once it is soaked in water, but it's best to consider fading as an indication of wear and to plan on replacing the line.

Care of line. A lot remains to be learned about the effect of outside elements and substances on microfilaments, so caution is still advisable. Nylon monofilament, however, has a longer track record and is definitely not ageless. Its effective life depends on how it is treated and to what it is subjected. Long exposure to sunlight can affect nylon, so don't store it, either on a consumer spool or a fishing reel, in a position where sunlight falls on it daily. The ultraviolet elements of the sun's rays are very strong, and to diminish their effect, premium lines feature an ultraviolet retardation element, which prolongs the effective life of the line. The fluorescent characteristic of some line is especially vulnerable to ultraviolet light and will fade in time. The best storage for line is in a cool, dry environment, away from extremes in temperatures, water saturation, and sunlight. A garage, closet, or basement might provide suitable storage. Examples of how not to treat line include leaving a spool on the dashboard of your automobile or a reel by a window where sunlight regularly reaches it.

The first rod meant for use with multiplying reels was created in the early 1880s by James Henshall and manufactured by the Orvis Company. It was wooden and 8 feet 3 inches long.

Many anglers lose track of the strength of line on a particular reel or can't recall when they put it on. Sometimes they are mistaken about which brand they are using. This can all be solved by marking the reel. Some line manufacturers supply gummed labels with each spool of their product, so that an angler can jot pertinent information on the label and affix it to the reel.

You should also be careful about what substances come into contact with your line. Some can alter the characteristics of line in unsuspected ways. WD-40, for instance, which is commonly used on reels to inhibit rust, may leach out some of the plasticizers of nylon monofilament, resulting in stiffer line. If the line was in contact with water soon after contact with WD-40, there would be no effect. More effect would be incurred if the reel full of line was sprayed with this substance (and some got on the line) after fishing and then was stored.

Suntan oils can pose a problem, too. Their active ingredients can plasticize nylon monofilament and increase elongation, and the lines become excessively stretchy. Gas and motor oil can also be detrimental to line if there is contact for an extended period of time. In extreme cases of contact (or soaking) with gasoline, a 50 percent reduction in line strength can occur. Motor oil is not as potent as gasoline.

The most harmful substance to line, even for short contact, is battery acid. This sulfuric acid attacks nylon line properties almost immediately and advances oxidization. Light lines in particular are very vulnerable.

Perhaps more serious is the possibility that these substances may imprint an odor on the line that is not noticeable to humans but is detectable by fish. What effect this may have on fish behavior is unclear. It surely cannot be positive.

It is not far-fetched to imagine that you might spray yourself liberally with bug repellent and then touch your line while tying a knot; or that coils of line might fall on an uncovered battery when you laid down your rod; or that gasoline or oil might be inadvertently spilled on your reel. Just take care to keep such substances off your line for extended periods.

Line disposal. Although it does not have a direct relationship to line care, line disposal is an important element of use. Fishing line can have a long residual life and can be harmful to wildlife if discarded outdoors. No type of line should be discarded anywhere but in the garbage or in recycling bins at retail stores.

See: Baitcasting Tackle; Knots, Fishing; Leader; Spincasting Tackle; Spinning Tackle; Tippet.

LINE-CLASS WORLD RECORD

The largest individual of a given species of sportfish that is caught on a specific breaking strength of line, and within parameters established by the International Game Fish Association *(see),* the certifying organization.

See: Records.

LINE DRESSING

The coating or treatment that is used to help float and/or clean a fly line.

See: Flycasting Tackle.

LINE GUIDE

See: Guide, Rod; Rod, Fishing.

LINEN LINE

Fishing line made from linen, primarily popular with saltwater anglers and replaced by Dacron and nylon monofilament in the mid-twentieth century. Linen line was braided or twisted and had to be removed periodically from reel spools and dried to avoid rotting.

See: Line.

LINEWINDER

An electrically powered device for putting line on, and taking it off, a fishing reel spool; it is usually found in fishing tackle shops.

LINGCOD *Ophiodon elongatus.*

Other names—cultus cod, blue cod, buffalo cod, green cod, ling; Finnish: *vihersimppu;* French: *terpuga;* Japanese: *ainame;* Portuguese: *lorcha;* Swedish: *grönfisk.*

The lingcod, a Pacific marine species, belongs to the family Hexagrammidae. Its name is misleading because it is not a true cod. A local term for lingcod is "cultus cod"; the word "cultus" is an Indian term meaning "false."

Table quality. The lingcod is an important and highly prized commercial and sportfish, and many consider it one of the finest table fish in the West. Its white, firm flesh is often deep-fried as the main ingredient in fish and chips, but it may also be smoked, baked, grilled, or poached with excellent results. The flesh of the lingcod may be greenish blue, depending on diet.

Identification. The lingcod has a large mouth, large pectoral fins, a smooth body, and a long, continuous dorsal fin divided by a notch into spiny and soft parts. Adults have large heads and jaws, and long, pointed teeth. Juveniles have slender bodies. Its coloring is usually brown or gray with blotches outlined in orange or blue but is closely associated with habitat.

Size. Lingcod may grow to 50 inches or longer. Males are smaller than females, usually reaching no longer than 3 feet in length or 20 pounds in weight. Basically mature by eight years, the male will weigh about 10 pounds and the female about 15. Commercial catches for lingcod sometimes include fish of 50 to 60 pounds. The all-tackle record is 69 pounds.

Distribution. The lingcod occurs in North American waters from Southern California to Alaska but is most abundant in the colder waters of the north.

Habitat. Lingcod inhabit colder waters in intertidal zone reefs and kelp beds that have strong tidal currents. They prefer depths from 2 to more than 70 fathoms over rock bottom.

Life history/Behavior. The spawning season is in winter, from December through February, when the eggs are released in large pinkish white masses into crevices in rocks. Egg masses can contain more than a half million eggs and are frequently found in the intertidal zone. The male protects the eggs, which hatch in one to two months. The young stay at the surface for three to four months before dropping to the bottom.

Food and feeding habits. Adults feed on herring, flounder, cod, hake, greenling, rockfish, squid, crustaceans, and small lingcod. Juveniles consume small crustaceans and fish.

Angling. The aggressive lingcod is as rough and rugged as the jagged, rocky bottom structure it inhabits. When the mood strikes it, the ling may viciously attack any potential meal unfortunate enough to come within striking range, including other lingcod nearly the size of the attacker. Most West Coast bottomfish anglers have stories about lingcod that grabbed hooked fish and hung on, often long enough to be gaffed or netted at the surface. Just

Lingcod

as often, though, lingcod will lose interest in feeding, and these apparent fasts may last hours or even days.

Slack tides usually afford the best opportunity to hook lingcod because that's when it's easiest to work a bait or lure straight down to the rocky, snaggy bottoms where this big predator is found; too much current or wind results in a flat line angle and constant hookups on the rocky bottom.

Metal slab jigs that imitate smaller fish work well for lings, as do big leadheads with large, plastic grub bodies or pork-rind strips. Many bait anglers use herring, and live baits work much better than dead ones. The ultimate lingcod bait is a live greenling, about 10 inches long, fished with a large, single hook through both lips to pin its mouth shut. Live-bait anglers must use a sinker large enough to take the offering down but have to exercise care in keeping it just off bottom, or the bait will dodge into a hole and become snagged before a lingcod finds it.

Lingcod also have a habit of diving for a rocky crevice when hooked, so anglers should try to turn them toward the surface and reel them as far off the bottom as possible after setting the hook. Snubbing that first dash toward the rocks is often the difference between landing and losing a big ling. For this reason, many anglers use rather stout tackle for lingcod, including stiff boat rods, large conventional reels, and low-stretch braided line of 40- to 80-pound test. A tough monofilament leader of 50-pound test or larger also helps avoid abrasions and breakoffs.

The largest lingcod are females, and serious West Coast anglers have, in recent years, gotten into the habit of releasing these bigger fish in favor of the smaller males. Keeping smaller lingcod not only provides somewhat better table fare, it also allows the important mature females to continue spawning and providing lings for the future. Slot limits in some areas require anglers to release both smaller lingcod and the big females.

LINING

Spooking a fish when false casting a fly line over it or landing the fly line on the water over or near the fish.

LIQUID CRYSTAL DISPLAY

A sonar device, also known by the acronym LCD.

See: Sonar.

LIQUID CRYSTAL RECORDER

A sonar device, also known by the acronym LCR.

See: Sonar.

LITTLE TUNNY

See: Tuna; Tunny, Little.

LITTORAL

Living in or related to nearshore waters; the intertidal zone of the marine environment that is exposed at low tide and covered at high tide.

LIVE BAIT

Whole live fish or other natural organisms used to catch predatory fish in both freshwater and saltwater.

See: Natural Bait.

LIVEWELL

A containment device for keeping fish or bait alive; also called a baitwell when used exclusively for holding bait. Livewells may be compartments integral to the interior construction of a boat or may be external containers that are situated within a boat or outside of it on the water's surface. External versions often take the form of insulated coolers or large round plastic wells and should not be confused with bait buckets *(see)* or small bait containers *(see)* that have no means of aeration. It is also possible to fashion a livewell out of a food and beverage cooler, if you have a pump to use for aeration and a battery to power it. Livewells feature a pump that aerates the water, either recirculating it or introducing fresh raw water. This oxygenation of the water and the maintenance of appropriate (usually cool) water temperature are key elements to keeping fish and bait alive.

The primary element in effective livewell containment of either sportfish or bait is a quick, preferably continuous, turnover of water. The problems that develop with livewell containment are due to numerous factors, especially warm water, a pump that does not turn over enough volume, poor positioning of the water pickup, pumps that fail or that lose their prime, inferior drainage, lack

L

Livewells, such as the one that this largemouth bass is being lowered into, must be big enough and well aerated to properly care for fish.

of top-to-bottom turnover, crowding of bait, and rectangular wells.

Sportfish containment. Livewells are primarily used to hold bait for saltwater anglers and to hold both bait and sportfish for freshwater anglers. The only reasons to keep captured sportfish alive for any period of time are to keep them fresh until you get them home to be cleaned or to keep them alive until they are released at the end of the day in a tournament. The only good way to keep fish alive and reasonably fit is to use some type of aerated livewell. Fish kept on stringers and dragged around for a long time are seldom suitable for release, even though they may still be alive. However, if a fish is to be released alive, then it should be released alive immediately after being captured and unhooked; putting it in a livewell is seldom better for the fish than returning it immediately to its own environment. Nearly all fisheries agencies advise against confining fish that are intended for release.

Many built-in boat livewells are good for keeping a few sportfish alive, but most are not designed to hold many fish or to hold large specimens. There is some question about the effect of daylong holding in this environment, as well as the subsequent handling and weighing that fish undergo prior to release. Sportfish kept in a livewell not only have been hooked, played, landed, and handled, but have also suffered long- or short-term captivity in a restricted place, have been bounced around during travel, have been confined with other fish, and then have been released at a later time in a foreign place. Some hardy fish will make it, and some won't. This treatment is not doing the fish any good other than keeping it alive. To retain fish in a livewell that you want to keep for consumption is fine; to retain them to show off at the end of the day and then make a heroic release is false sport and is quite likely to be harmful to the fish.

Largemouth and smallmouth bass and walleye are primary targets for livewell containment, largely because of the popularity of tournaments and the necessity to keep fish alive for weighing and then later release. However, freshwater anglers also use livewells to contain these fish for nontournament purposes and also to contain various panfish species, as well as pike, pickerel, and white bass. Few saltwater anglers keep their catch in livewells because they either release it right away or kill it and put it in a fish box *(see)*; many saltwater species are too large for proper containment in a livewell or would require a livewell so large as to be impractical.

Many fish, and large fish in particular, are not suited for holding in most standard built-in boat livewells, although this varies with the species, the temperature of the water, the size of the well, and the abilities of the pump. In freshwater, small striped bass, trout, and salmon may be kept alive under the best of conditions, but usually larger members of these species are not suitable for containment outside of very large tanks. The size of the livewell is often a factor in keeping fish; the larger the livewell, the better the chance of releasing healthy fish.

Keeping sportfish alive for later release requires frequent if not constant aeration; otherwise, a "livewell" will become a "deathwell." Many freshwater boats, especially bass boats and general-purpose craft, have aerator timers that automatically activate the pump and shut it off at variable intervals. This saves battery power, especially if the main engine battery is also used for powering electrical accessories, including the livewell pump and bilge pump. However, if the water is very warm, it may be necessary to override the timer for frequent manual use, or leave the pump on continuously. Lacking a timer, you have to leave the livewell pump on constantly or manually turn it on and off repeatedly.

Most sportfish survive best in cold or at least cool water. They are hardest to keep alive in a well when the outside temperature and the surface temperature of the water are warm. It is possible to cool livewell water by adding small blocks of ice; however, you cannot take fish from warm water and put them into much cooler water; they must get acclimated to it. Furthermore, if the ice has come from a source that has been treated with chlorine, the content of chlorine in the water may be sufficient to kill the fish or to require the addition of a dechlorinating powder to the livewell water. It may be helpful, incidentally, to add uniodized (rock) salt to livewells to help reduce stress in fish.

Chemicals are available for livewell use that somewhat tranquilize sportfish and keep them from banging around in the well, lower their requirements for oxygen, and provide some antifungal protection. These measures all require that the livewell system contains a means of recirculating existing water, rather than strictly adding outside (raw) water and discharging used water, which will cause a loss of temperature as well as chemical additives. There is concern, however, about the effect of using chemicals on confined fish that are to be released back into the water, where they might be recaught and consumed by others.

Since boats sometimes move a great deal during a day of fishing, a livewell that will hold sportfish should be capable of operating both when the boat is at rest (taking in fresh outside water) and when it is running from one place to another (recirculating and aerating the existing water). A recirculating system accomplishes this. It is also preferable to have an aerator spray nozzle that delivers water in a sharp showerlike stream, rather than in a faucetlike stream because the former provides better aeration. However, overhead aeration may only aerate the surface and not adequately aerate the lower portion of a livewell, especially if the well is deep, so there are trade-offs. Incidentally, when the boat is moving any distance in rough water, fish should be held in a rear livewell to minimize pounding, if there are forward and aft livewells from which to choose.

Many freshwater boats, especially bass boats, have two small livewells; others have a single large one with a divider. The large ones are preferable, especially if you can remove or retain the divider to give the fish more freedom. Many also have cutoff valves that prevent water from entering or exiting. Leave this valve shut most of the time to keep water out of the livewells because a full livewell contributes a lot more weight in the boat (water weighs roughly 8 pounds to the gallon). When you catch a fish to be kept, open the valve to allow fresh water into the livewells. If the boat does not have a recirculating system and you have a fish in the livewell, you should shut the valves (or plug the drain), since the livewell water will flow out and the fish will be dry if you have to travel any distance. If you have to fill a boat livewell quickly, open the valve or plug, put the engine in reverse, and drive backward. This forces water to come in, filling the livewells.

Make sure that your livewell lines are clean and free of debris for best aeration performance. Be careful about using sportfish livewells for storage of small baitfish unless you have the proper size screens on the outlets. If not, small baitfish will get into drain lines and clog up the aerator. Don't try to keep small baitfish and larger gamefish in the same livewell at the same time. It's a good idea to clean the livewell(s) once in a while because a coating of dirt and scum gathers if you use it enough. You can wash out the drain lines with pressurized water from a garden hose. Be careful about transporting water in a livewell (or bilge) from one place to another, since this can be a means of spreading undesirable and perhaps harmful exotic aquatic life.

The keys to keeping sportfish alive and healthy are cool temperatures, adequate space, and plenty of aeration. Most built-in livewells by manufacturers do not have the water-volume capacity or the pumping ability to treat many fish, so you have to recognize the problems associated with livewell containment; you may need to modify the existing setup with a more powerful pump, or with larger intake and discharge lines to move plenty of fresh water through. Generally, it is best to have a flow-through system that constantly brings in outside (raw) water and constantly flushes the livewell.

Bait containment. Live bait is most effective when it is energetic and frisky. Some gamefish will not take live bait that is lethargic, especially if other anglers are in the area and there is a choice of food available. Fresh, lively bait is important, and keeping it this way depends on the bait, the size and shape of the well, the amount of aeration, and the water temperature. Some baitfish are very difficult to keep alive. Those that are purchased at bait shops for sums exceeding several dollars apiece represent a considerable investment that has to be protected with the right kind of livewell and good aeration.

The type of livewell and the size are dictated by the bait. Most livewells are circular or oval shaped because many baitfish, especially any member of the herring family, will gather motionless in corners and die. They need to keep moving, and in round or oval wells you can create a stream of current that forces the bait to keep swimming. Ideally there should not be any devices sticking into the well because they are likely to become hideouts and death traps. Obviously wells have to be watertight and hold a sufficient volume of water. The larger the size of the individual bait to be stored, the

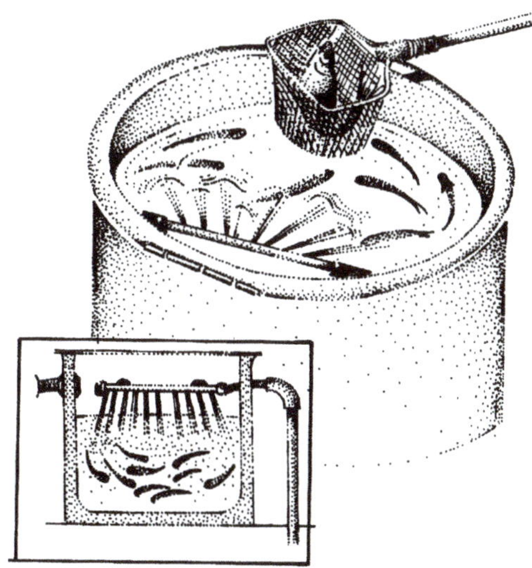

When keeping bait alive, proper aeration is important; some baitfish survive only in oval or round wells, as depicted here.

greater the diameter of the well; ditto for numbers and volume.

The most desirable livewell systems are those that pump raw water from outside and deliver it to the well, usually spraying it into the well from above to help aerate it, constantly flushing the old water and removing debris and body waste and maintaining the temperature, which should conform to the surface of the outside water. Some systems merely recirculate existing water, which retains debris and waste matter and usually raises the temperature; this is true for some portable systems, including ice chest livewells, and with these it may be a good idea to occasionally scoop out some of the water with a bucket and replace it with fresh water. However, if the livewell empties its water while the boat is running from one place to another, you should have a shutoff valve or drain plug to stop water from draining out and to allow the pump to recirculate and oxygenate the water while you are underway; after you've reached the destination, you can switch back to outside water intake. In large-volume systems without outside raw water circulation, high-quality filters should be used to draw out bacteria and waste.

In order to process this water efficiently, you need an adequate pump. You can make do with a pump that is also used for other purposes (like washdown), but it's best to have a pump devoted solely to the livewell; have a backup available because if the pump breaks down, there go your bait and maybe your fishing. In a pinch, you may be able to switch over a washdown pump or a bilge pump, or to use one of these or a backup to handle excess bait that aren't making it in an overtaxed main well (a large plastic pail or a cooler can be turned into temporary bait housing if necessary).

If the pump is rated at 300 gallons per hour (gph), it will theoretically turn over a 30-gallon well 10 times per hour, assuming that the drainpipe is of sufficient diameter to accommodate an even exchange. Some gravity-flow drains are too small and become clogged easily and cannot handle the influx of water; this situation leads to overflowing in the well and insufficient aeration when the inflow line is submerged. Overflowing will cause water to spill into the sump or possibly onto the deck or into storage compartments; the bilge pump will then need to be used. Drain lines should be two to three times the diameter of the inflow line but in most cases are not; to achieve this you may have to make some modifications.

Many freshwater anglers use pumps in the 300- to 600-gph range, but greater-capacity models are available and are usually necessary for serious bait maintenance. Some saltwater bait users employ a 2,000-gph pump for larger fish. By talking with other anglers, you can figure out the turnover rate you need for the most demanding bait that you'll use, and make a choice accordingly. For small baitfish and small numbers of bait, pumps with a lower rating are adequate. A 500-gph pump is adequate for holding shrimp and small pinfish, for example, in a 20-gallon-capacity well. If your fishing takes you to extremes in the bait-use spectrum, you might be wise to employ a dual-pump system where either a higher- or a lower-capacity model is used as necessary. No matter what capacity pump you use, if the water gets murky, then your system needs some adjustment. It may be necessary to use a higher-volume pump. Check the baitfish for signs of stress, like loss of scales or color.

Make sure you remove the lower layer of water in the well from time to time if it appears stagnant or does not seem to get mixed with the rest of the water on its own. Stirring the water occasionally may help if you have a large flow-through volume and no standpipe to keep the well water at the proper height. A bottom drain in the tank will help, but you need to have an adjustable riser or standpipe, or else you have to periodically remove the standpipe to flush out bottom water from a bottom drain (and that may cause some problems with the bait). At the very least, remove bottom water when you're finished fishing, and flush all water out of the well at the end of the day. Be aware that flushing bottom debris, especially scales, can lead to clogging the system. Switching between normal and short standpipes allows you to flush out most of the water without trouble, if the short standpipe is covered with a screen. A short pipe is also useful for those times when you want only a small amount of water in the well and want to get at bait easily. An alternative is an adjustable pipe. To fashion it, drill some small holes at the base of the standpipe, and then cover the pipe with tight-fitting PVC tubing that has an inside diameter closely matching the outside diameter of the standpipe. When you need to flush bottom well water, raise the outside tube to expose the holes and lower it back when you're done. Make sure that the outer tube fits snugly so that water doesn't flow out when you don't want it to.

See: Bait; Boat.

LIVIES

A term for small live fish used as bait in saltwater.

LOBWORM

A term for nightcrawler *(see)*.

LODGE

See: Fishing Lodge.

LOG

A nautical term for a record of the events that occur while boating, usually detailing course, speed, and other details of navigation or the voyage; it is also applied to a record of fishing activities, usually detailing location, success, weather, and other matters.

LONGLINE

A commercial fishing line of considerable length, bearing numerous baited hooks and usually set and drifted horizontally in the ocean. This line is supported in the water column by floats, and baited hooks are suspended from it. Sections of line may be attached to one another, depending on the size of the fishing boat and number of crew, and the total length of connected sections may extend for miles.

Longlines are used in snapper, grouper, cod, haddock, ling, swordfish, and bluefin tuna fisheries, among others, but may catch nontarget species as well as other animals. They are set for varying periods, up to several hours, on the sea floor or, in the case of tuna, in surface waters before being retrieved. Commercial fishing with a longline is a controversial practice that has contributed to overfishing of some primary species and has had a detrimental influence on others.

See: Commercial Fishery.

LONG-RANGE BOAT

A party boat *(see)* that makes excursions lasting from several days to two weeks to distant fishing grounds.

LOOKDOWN *Selene vomer.*

Other names—Portuguese: *galo de penacho, peixe-galo;* Spanish: *caracaballo, joro bado, papelillo, pez luna.*

A member of the Carangidae family of jacks, the lookdown is so called because of its habit of hovering over the bottom in a partly forward-tilted position, which makes it seem to "look down." The flesh of the lookdown has an excellent flavor and is commercially marketed fresh.

Identification. Bright silver and iridescent, the lookdown has a deep and extremely compressed body that may have goldish, greenish, bluish, or purplish highlights. One of its most striking features is the unusually high forehead, as well as the low placement of the mouth on the face and the high placement of the eyes. The first rays of the second dorsal fin and the anal fin are long and streamerlike; in the dorsal fin, they may extend to the tail, whereas in the anal fin they do not extend as far. The lookdown may also have three or four pale bars across the lower body. On young fish, there are two very long, threadlike filaments that extend from the dorsal fin.

Size. Ordinarily 6 to 10 inches long and weighing less than a pound, the lookdown may reach 1 foot in length and weigh 3 pounds. The all-tackle world record is a Brazilian fish that weighed 4 pounds, 10 ounces.

Distribution. Endemic to the western Atlantic, lookdown are found from Maine and possibly Nova Scotia in Canada to Uruguay, as well as in Bermuda and the Gulf of Mexico.

Lookdown

Habitat. Lookdown favor shallow coastal waters at depths of 2 to 30 feet, generally over hard or sandy bottoms around pilings and bridges and often in murky water. Occasionally occurring in small schools, lookdown hover over the bottom. Small fish may be found in estuaries.

Food. Lookdown feed on small crabs, shrimp, fish, and worms.

Angling. *See: Inshore Fishing; Jacks.*

LOOP KNOT

Usually a type of terminal connection in which the line is attached to the hook or lure with a free-swinging loop rather than a snug attachment. There are various types of loop knots.

See: Knots, Fishing.

LORAN

An acronym for LOng RAnge Navigation, Loran is a land-based electronic navigation system that was widely employed in coastal areas of North America in the latter part of the twentieth century. Its use and popularity faded in the late 1990s because of the prominence of the far-reaching and satellite-based Global Position System *(see: GPS);* Loran will eventually be obsolete in North America when government-supported transmitting stations are decomissioned.

The current generation of Loran is known as Loran-C. It operates via a network of shore-based transmitting stations covering the coastal areas of North America and the Great Lakes, but not extending to other inland areas; it's even somewhat marginal in the northwestern part of the Bahamas and does not reach down through the rest of the islands.

A Loran unit (white) on this boat's console provides navigational information.

Active Loran-C systems are in use in other countries, however, and primarily employed for shipping purposes. In fact, while Loran-C use has been decreasing in North America because of increased GPS use, it is becoming more widely used in other countries where more transmission stations are being constructed. There are European, Far-Eastern, Russian, and Mediterranean Loran-C networks.

Loran-C is the modern form of Loran and followed the original version, which was known as Loran-A. In a basic sense, Loran is a sophisticated radio receiver that obtains signals from two transmission sources, known as stations, that are situated on the ground along a coast. Loran measures the time differences between these signals to obtain a Line of Position (LOP) for each signal, which, when intersected, provides a "fix" to ascertain position. Loran-A required time-consuming plotting with a navigational chart and was subject to a lot of operator error. Loran-C eliminated the need for charting and provided quick electronic depiction of current position.

In operation, land-based stations transmit signals that are obtained by Loran receivers installed on boats. When everything is working right, the best Loran-C receiver can update its position every second, but most do not update that frequently.

Loran-C receivers determine position based on time differences, or time delays; these are commonly called TDs or numbers. They display location information in a set of TDs and in corresponding latitude and longitude coordinates, which correspond to lines connecting TDs of the same value that are overprinted on marine navigational charts. Loran-C receivers are capable of providing such important navigational information as course heading, elapsed time and distance traveled, course necessary to navigate to specific locations (which are called waypoints), time to reach those waypoints at present course, and estimated arrival time; and they can store waypoints in permanent memory to recall for return navigation. Many Loran-C units can also be interfaced with other electronic devices, especially autopilot; the ability to use autopilot can mean significant fuel savings for boaters traveling long distances.

Although Loran-C is useful to anglers for pure navigational purposes, it is more useful for its ability to guide a boat back to a fishing hotspot (reef, wreck, etc.) at any time of the day or night, and with accuracy that under the best conditions—where reception is good and the crossing angles for the TD signals are close to 90 degrees—can be as close as 50 feet. As long as it is being used in an area where reception is reliable and the signals are of good quality, Loran offers great benefits. However, it does experience occasional interference due to severe electrical weather disturbances, and it may be down temporarily when a transmitter goes off-line for maintenance. A distant line of thunderstorms, even out of sight far over the horizon, can sometimes knock out the signals from a critical Loran station.

The advantages offered by GPS navigation are significant: GPS is unaffected by weather and atmospheric conditions, is transmitted via a series of orbiting satellites, can determine position and provide navigational information anywhere (land or water, inland or coastal) in any country, and is capable of greater accuracy.

Nevertheless, Loran is an excellent navigation system. However, any navigation system, like any electronic device, is subject to failure; with Loran this could be because of signal loss or receiver malfunction, so it is best to be prepared with a good chart and reliable magnetic compass, or to be able to revert to dead reckoning basics.

See: GPS; Maps; Navigation.

LOUISIANA

Louisiana has the resources to back up its claim that it is a "Sportsman's Paradise." Its maze of waterways, for example, offers anglers the rare opportunity to tangle with red drum and trophy largemouth bass on the same day. Within easy reach is the Gulf of Mexico and a chance to battle record blue marlin, white marlin, wahoo, yellowfin tuna, and king mackerel. A full range of warmwater species exists inland, including striped bass, crappie, and big catfish; in saltwater the mix is even broader, including not only pelagic species but also tarpon, seatrout, flounder, amberjack, barracuda, pompano, cobia, and many more. Among the Gulf of Mexico states,

Louisiana has the most liberal catch-limit regulations for freshwater and saltwater species.

Abundant water resources are the reason for Louisiana's rare blend of quality and quantity. The state has an estimated 200,000 miles of fishable coastal banks and shorelines, and 41 percent of the coastal wetlands in the United States. This vast, warm shallow-water habitat stretches from Louisiana's eastern boundary with Mississippi to its western boundary with Texas. The National Marine Fisheries Service estimates this ecosystem makes up as much as 80 percent of the finfish in the Gulf of Mexico dependent on Louisiana waters at some time in their life cycle.

The state's importance in fish production closely relates to its status as the terminus of the Mississippi River, which, over thousands of years, has carved four distinct paths to the Gulf of Mexico. The present route takes the Mississippi through New Orleans, where it winds 120 miles south and east, then courses through five passes, and finally empties into the Gulf of Mexico. This terminus, where freshwater mixes with saltwater, creates an "edge" effect, a nutrient-rich, brackish water ecosystem that makes Louisiana a vital nursery for finfish and shellfish.

The Mississippi is in effect Louisiana's marsh builder. The rich silt deposits from America's heartland attract freshwater and saltwater species to the same area, making it possible to catch largemouth bass, red drum, and spotted seatrout on the same fishing trip.

The geological effects of the Mississippi River's flow put Louisiana closer to the continental shelf than any gulf state and explain the proximity of blue-water species. Depths of 400 feet are within 12 miles of South Pass, the southernmost of the five passes in the Mississippi River Delta; 1,000-foot depths are within an hour's ride from this pass.

In its never-ending quest to find a shorter route to the Gulf of Mexico, the Mississippi River has graced Louisiana with 14 fishable oxbow lakes. The scouring effect of millions of gallons of sediment-laden water cut these sharp bends off from the river's main flow. Six of the state's rivers still receive water from the Mississippi during spring floods, which also restock the oxbow lakes.

The Mississippi's quest for a shorter passageway to the gulf has also produced in Louisiana the largest overflow swamp in the U.S. When the Mississippi River began to cut through to the smaller Red and Atchafalaya Rivers early in the nineteenth century, U.S. Army officer Amos Stoddard noted that the Atchafalaya River provided a shorter route to the gulf. He concluded that the Mississippi would likely change its course within 100 years. When Captain Henry Shreve searched for a shorter route along the Mississippi River to New Orleans, a canal was dug that cut off a section of the Mississippi at Turnbull's Bend. This canal routed the Mississippi River back into the Red River's channel, which flowed directly into the Atchafalaya. A logjam in the Mississippi then reduced the Red's flow, thereby averting the immediate threat of Mississippi waters running directly into the Atchafalaya.

Over the following century plus, the U.S. Army Corps of Engineers produced further documentation that the Mississippi River was indeed meandering toward the Atchafalaya. In 1959, at a cost of $47 million, the Corps of Engineers constructed the Old River Control Structure. When completed in 1962, the massive project allowed 30 percent of the Mississippi River's flow into the Atchafalaya River and maintained 70 percent of the Mississippi's flow along its present course. The project also sent the river's flow down the Atchafalaya. The structure was upgraded in the early 1990s to further alleviate the hydrological pressure of the Mississippi River's migration toward the Atchafalaya.

Responsible for flood control, the Corps of Engineers earlier in the twentieth century constructed or refurbished levees along the Mississippi River's course through Louisiana and also leveed the 60-mile-long Atchafalaya. The latter project created the expansive Atchafalaya River Floodway, a maze of bayous and lakes that comprises a 5- to 25-mile-wide swamp. The area between the levees holds the Atchafalaya River's flood waters, a vast ecosystem that is one of Louisiana's most productive and visited recreational fishing areas, and a vital commercial fishing location as well. The flow down the Atchafalaya has created one of few expanding river deltas in North America.

This new land is much needed. Levee and jetty projects, along with massive canal digging for oil production and navigation since the 1930s, have put Louisiana's marshlands in a precarious predicament. Hydrologists estimate that Louisiana is losing an acre of land per day, or between 35 and 50 square miles per year.

Several marsh-enhancing projects have been designed. One is operating in the Caernarvon area south of New Orleans along the Mississippi River, and restoration of this brackish water marsh has been documented. Another project is designed to restore the marshlands in the Barataria area southwest of New Orleans, an area made famous as the home of buccaneer Jean Lafitte. Other projects are pointed toward restoration of dozens of barrier islands, a fish-rich string of sandy outcroppings that not only attract anglers but also give the state needed protection from hurricanes.

These natural areas have inherent problems, not the least of which is access. Because the coast is marshland, all roads must be built over water. Although coastal land routes have been improved since 1980, access is mostly over two-lane roads. Because high, dry ground is at a premium along the coast, boat launches and angler accommodations are limited. These factors have stifled the expansion of Louisiana's recreational fishing populace and pose problems that nonresident anglers find difficult to overcome.

Nevertheless, Louisiana's vast natural saltwater, brackish water, and freshwater areas, as well as its 12 inland reservoirs, offer variety to suit the taste of any angler. As many as 1 million anglers annually take advantage of these opportunities.

Freshwater

As previously detailed, bountiful bayous, swamps, rivers, oxbow lakes, large and small reservoirs, and brackish water marshes give Louisiana's freshwater anglers a wealth of choices. There are no closed seasons here, so these opportunities can be enjoyed year-round.

Extensive environmental cleanup efforts have induced the return of sea-run striped bass to Louisiana's important rivers: the Mississippi, the lower Atchafalaya, the Pearl, and the Mermentau. In addition, state-run hatchery programs have introduced striped bass, hybrid striped bass, and Florida-strain largemouth bass to various waters. Florida largemouth fingerlings placed in oxbows, reservoirs, and city lakes brought trophy bass fishing to a state more well known for its quantity of freshwater fish than their size.

To the nonresident angler, the striking difference between Louisiana's freshwater and that elsewhere in the U.S. is that with the exception of large reservoirs, Louisiana waters are cloudy, murky, or muddy. This makes lure selection a problem for anglers accustomed to fishing clearer environs. As a result, gold- and copper-colored blades are commonly used on spinnerbaits and buzzbaits, and brightly colored crankbaits, and soft lizards or worms are the rule rather than the exception. Gold-sided crankbaits and jerkbaits are popular with bass anglers here because of the water color.

Atchafalaya Basin

Because the 60-mile-long expanse of swamps, bayous, man-made canals, and small lakes is connected at its source to the Mississippi and Red Rivers, the Atchafalaya River Basin is subject to springtime flooding; it is an angler's paradise only after the annual floods recede. During the late winter and early spring, commercial crawfishing holds sway and produces 35 to 100 million pounds annually.

When flows settle down and banks reappear—usually in late May or June—this basin truly is a fishing paradise. Catches of 60 to 100 bass a day are common in the first eight weeks after the floods. Crappie (called sacalait), bream (meaning bluegills, green sunfish, pumpkinseeds, and redear sunfish—the latter called chinquapin), and catfish are highly sought then as well. These species take a variety of artificial lures and live baits, notably small baitfish, crickets, and nightcrawlers. Anglers also land less desirable species like freshwater drum (called gaspergoo), buffalo, and bowfin (called choupique).

Crawfish are an important food source for all predator species, especially bass. As a result, crawfish-colored jigs with pork or soft-plastic trailers, crankbaits, and spinnerbaits, along with soft-plastic lizards, are preferred offerings for bass. During the postflood period, the prime bass areas are runouts, which drain swamps that provide post-spawn bass and other species with a ready food source, mostly crawfish.

After the water levels stabilize, usually in August or September, the next four to five months are when bass and other species search out deep-water canals and bayous. Except for the Atchafalaya River, the basin is shallow throughout its expanse, and summertime water temperatures can reach the upper 80s. This places a premium on early morning and late afternoon, the most active feeding periods.

The basin's fish stocks were severely depleted by Hurricane Andrew in 1992, when fisheries biologists estimated 175 million fish were killed; but extensive restocking efforts along with significant annual river flooding has replenished stocks of gamefish and other species.

In 1998, the state and the Corps of Engineers joined forces in a 15-year, $335-million-dollar program to enhance access to, and implement water-quality projects, in the Atchafalaya Basin.

Mississippi River and Oxbow Lakes

Because the Mississippi River has continually changed its course over the years, Louisiana is littered with oxbow lakes. The largest accessible and fishable oxbows are Yucatan, Bruin, St. John, Concordia, Deer Park, and Old River. During spring floods, to a greater or a lesser degree, the Mississippi River still flows into St. John, Deer Park, and Old River Lakes. These oxbows, so named because they resemble the "bows" that pioneer farmers used on oxen, can vary from 8 to 14 miles long and from 100 to 300 yards wide.

Lake Concordia, near the communities of Vidalia and Ferriday, is one of Louisiana's "trophy lakes" and has been extensively stocked with Florida-strain bass. Catches of 9- to 12-pound bass are a weekly occurrence from January through April.

Although most oxbows were once lined with fishable cypress, tupelo, and willow trees, development of waterside homes and camps has cut into these tree stands, and most of the structures in the oxbows are now piers and brushpiles planted by anglers. These are suitable holding locations for bass, crappie, and bluegills. The best bass fishing is from late winter through early summer, when topwater lures, jerkbaits, soft lizards, and jigs are top producers. Worms and crankbaits take over in early summer, and crankbaits and Carolina-rigged worms work best from midsummer into fall.

Crappie catches are best in the fall and early winter. Shiners and 2-inch-long black-and-chartreuse, orange-and-brown, and blue-and-white tube baits on a 1/16-ounce jig consistently take large numbers of fish daily. Crickets and worms work for bream throughout the spring and summer.

Natural Lakes

Most of the productive natural lakes outside the Atchafalaya Basin are in Louisiana's south-central and southeastern areas. The notable exception is cypress-lined Lake Bistineau in the northwest near Shreveport.

The southeast lakes—Verret, Grassy, Palourde, DeCade, Penchant, and Des Allemands—are productive year-round for bass, crappie, and bream. Because crawfish flourish in these environs, jigs and other crawfishlike lures are especially good for bass. Crappie and bream also thrive on smaller crawfish.

These lakes are popular with fly anglers, who use popping bugs to catch bass and bluegills. Lined with cypress and tupelo, these lakes offer excellent topwater and artificial frog action, although spinnerbaits and soft-plastic lizards and worms hold sway most of the year. In spring, when crawfish are most numerous, black-and-blue and brown-and-orange jigs are most often fished near runouts and around stands of cypress. On hot summer days, working soft-plastic frogs over patches of floating duckweed is a solid technique.

The brackish water chain of Maurepas, Pontchartrain, Borgne, and St. Catherine provide launching pads for bass in nearby rivers, bayous, and grassy marsh ponds. Bass action here is subject to tidal movement, water levels, and wind direction. Spinnerbaits with chartreuse-and-white skirts, small spinnerbaits, and soft jerkbaits, lizards, and worms are the most productive lures.

The Lake Larto-Saline Lake complex in east-central Louisiana is the most productive crappie lake in the state. Crappie weighing over 3 pounds are common here, with March through May and September through December considered prime.

Reservoirs

The king of the hill in Louisiana is 186,000-square-mile Toledo Bend, which straddles the border with Texas. Smaller lakes like Caney Creek, Grand Bayou, Cleco, Indian Creek, and Chicot have been stocked with Florida-strain bass and hold the promise of trophy specimens.

Caney Creek, a smallish 5,000-acre impoundment near Jonesboro in north-central Louisiana, had produced 19 of the top 20 recorded largest bass in the state as of 1998. A state-record 15.97-pound largemouth came from these waters.

These reservoirs are the deepest-water fishing holes in Louisiana; bass, crappie, and bluegills react here as they do in most other lakes throughout the South. The bass tend to hold along points, creekbeds, and humps during late spring, summer, and early fall before moving up to pre-spawn staging areas along the upper reaches of creekbeds in late winter. Because Louisiana is a warm-weather state, even during winter, bass tend to spawn earlier here than elsewhere. They have been known to start preparing spawning areas as early as mid-January.

These lakes also hold large schools of white bass, striped bass, and hybrid striped bass. Crappie and bluegill numbers are highest in Toledo Bend and Indian Creek. These fish move to the old riverbeds in 60- to 80-foot depths in early summer and stay there through the fall and early winter.

Bass respond best to deep-running crankbaits and worms in late spring, summer, and early fall, after which spinnerbaits and buzzbaits take over. Jigs are best in winter and early spring, when jerkbaits and lizards begin to attract bass strikes.

Freshwater Marshes

Other than the Atchafalaya River Basin, Louisiana's bass-rich marshes can be the most confounding and confusing fishing areas for a newcomer. The vast marshes stretch from state line to state line, from the mouth of the Pearl River on the east to the mouth of the Mississippi River, and west nearly 250 miles to the Sabine River. The maze of waterways and mix of freshwater, brackish water, and saltwater provides the state with a nursery ground for countless finfish, shrimp, oysters, and crabs, all of which are food sources for predatory fish. The dividing line is usually the Intracoastal Canal, which spans the entire state.

These inland marshes are dotted with lakes, small bays, and freshwater or brackish water ponds, and are crisscrossed with bayous and canals. They have become a prime target for an increasing number of bass anglers. Increasingly powerful and reliable outboards have opened this area to small-boat owners since the early 1980s. Freshwater diversion projects have helped stabilize several areas, notably the Caernarvon and Delacroix Marshes on the east side of the Mississippi River south and east of New Orleans, and increased largemouth bass numbers such that these are preferred big-bass sites. Small numbers of crappie and bream inhabit these waters, and blue and channel catfish thrive even in areas considered to be brackish.

Because of the wide range of food, bass react to various offerings, including jigs in the winter and early spring, and lizards, worms, and spinnerbaits during late spring, summer, and fall. Crankbaits work best as bass congregate on points in the fall and early winter, when they move from the cooler water in the bayous and rivers into the canals. Topwater lures and soft jerkbaits work best in areas with extensive grassbeds, which occur most often in ponds and shallow canals.

Coastline and Saltwater

Of the five Gulf of Mexico states, Louisiana boasts the most productive nursery ground, thanks to the Mississippi River. It may in fact be the most productive in all of North America. Deposits of nutrient-rich soils and the Louisiana coast's proximity to the Gulf of Mexico create a fertile area that supports entire life cycles for as many as 300 species of finfish, shrimp, oysters, and crabs.

Among the marshes and throughout the state's

L

The largest specimen of whale shark, a rare plankton-feeder found in warm oceans, was 41 1/2 feet long and 23 feet around, and weighed more than 16 tons. It was captured near Pakistan in 1949.

3-mile territorial limit out into the gulf are food and sportfish like spotted seatrout (speckled trout), red drum (redfish), southern flounder, Spanish and king mackerel, black drum, sheepshead, white trout, Atlantic croaker, spot, gray (mangrove) snapper, tarpon, and gafftopsail catfish, all of which use the maze of brackish- and saltwater marshes to spawn and/or raise young.

The two most highly prized and sought-after species are speckled trout and redfish. These, along with flounder, black drum, and sheepshead, move into shallow marshes during the fall and winter, making them available to small-boat anglers. During these months, smaller speckled trout and redfish follow shrimp into marshes, and also find minnows and small crabs to feed on; most of them later move out into the bays and lakes near the gulf to spawn with larger sea-run members of their species. Trout larger than 3 pounds seldom frequent inland waters, yet redfish up to 15 pounds are taken on light tackle in the same areas.

Soft-plastic minnow imitations in a wide array of colors, gold spoons, shad-colored crankbaits, and live minnows and shrimp are the best offerings for "inside" fish. Add a great variety of topwater lures to that list, and your tackle box is complete for fishing coastal bays, lakes, and barrier islands. Sheepshead prefer fresh shrimp. Most anglers also use corks for artificial and live baits, and employ a jerking method called "popping" to trigger strikes.

The best areas to find trout, redfish, and flounder are around rock jetties; in runouts, where shallow ponds empty into deeper canals and bayous; and over oyster beds in bayous, lakes, and bays. Beds of oysters tend to attract schools of baitfish. Tidal movement, either rising or falling, triggers feeding.

Most tackle stores are well stocked with the local maps and information needed to navigate the extensive series of canals and bayous.

Mississippi River Area

Breton Sound and its barrier island hold large numbers of trout, redfish, and Spanish mackerel during late spring, summer, and early fall. Oil platforms serve as artificial reefs for trout and redfish, while passes tend to hold redfish and white trout.

Barrier islands, notably Breton Island and the Chandeleur Island chain, are destinations for anglers looking for the largest trout and redfish. These are accessible only by boat. Wade fishing is the norm at these islands, which also attract particularly large shallow-water sharks swimming in the western gulf. Topwater lures are useful to anglers wading the islands, and fly anglers use topwater poppers along with shrimp imitations to take trout up to 8 pounds and redfish up to 40 pounds. The rock jetties at South and Southwest Passes hold large redfish and trout.

During fall and winter, smaller trout and redfish move into the marshes, even up into the Mississippi River, and provide opportunities to catch these saltwater fish along with largemouth bass, white bass, and striped bass. Shad-colored diving crankbaits and chrome-finished lipless crankbaits are the two most widely used lures. It's possible to catch a largemouth with one cast, a redfish with the next, and a striper with the next in the Mississippi River as far north as the Fort Jackson area, between New Orleans and Venice, which is the southernmost terminus of road travel along the river.

Other treasured spots are the Wagon Wheel, a series of oil-field location canals dug in a spoked-wheel pattern west of Venice; California Bay; Yellow Cotton Bay; Spanish Pass; Fast-Water Canal; and East Bay. The Pointe à la Hache canals, and small lakes and canals near Buras and Port Sulphur, also offer fall, winter, and early-spring trout and redfish action.

To the east, the Delacroix area has first-rate fall/winter bass, trout, and redfish angling. The starting point for most trips is the intersection of the Oak River and the Twin Pipeline Canals, about a 30-minute boat ride from the nearest launches at Delacroix and Pointe à la Hache.

Grand Isle-Fourchon-Cocodrie

Bayou Lafourche, which was a bed of the Mississippi River thousands of years ago, teams up with Barataria Bay and marshes and bays in Terrebonne Parish, to form an expanse of marshes, bayous, lakes, bays, and barrier islands highly favored among Louisiana anglers.

In Grand Isle, Elmer's Island, Fourchon Beach, and Belle Pass provide the only seaside fishing area with roads near the beaches. Local anglers use these three locations extensively to wade for trout, redfish, and Spanish mackerel.

To the east, Grand Terre Island and Four Bayous and Grand Bayou Passes are havens for summertime tarpon and redfish anglers. These areas are reached only by boat.

To the west of Fourchon, notable fishing areas include rock-studded East Timbalier Island and a chain of sandy barrier islands that once made up Last Island, or Isle Dernieres as found on some maps. The latter islands are reached only by boat.

Wade fishing for trout and redfish, and nighttime "gigging" for flounder are favorite pastimes at all islands except East Timbalier, which is ringed by underwater rocks to prevent erosion. Huge boulders here draw anglers for the largest speckled trout in this area of coastal Louisiana. The favorite tactic is to pitch a live 4- to 8-inch-long menhaden (called pogey) into the rocks. No weight or cork is used, and the baitfish is allowed to swim free around the boulders. This method also works on redfish and trout at the rock jetties at Belle Pass.

Redfish action concentrates near the passes from Four Bayous on the east end of this area, to Barataria and Caminada Passes on the east and west ends of Grand Isle, over to Little Pass and Whiskey Pass near Last Isle. Here, anglers use cracked or whole crabs on a 30-pound or heavier leader, with a 1-ounce or larger sinker 30 to 40 inches above the hook, to take "bull" reds, which can run up to 60 pounds (the state record is 61 pounds). They cast the rig into the pass and allow it to sit for 10 to 20 minutes. Because so many smaller fish inhabit these waters, the hook must be rebaited several times an hour.

Speckled trout and white trout are scattered throughout the area, even into Barataria, Timbalier, and Terrebonne Bays and Pelto and Barre Lakes. Numerous oil platforms and oil/gas pumping stations hold the fish, as do the barrier islands. Larger trout and redfish also stake out territory at the close-in oil platforms in the Gulf of Mexico. These fish prefer live baits to artificials. Boat launches are available at Grand Isle, Fourchon, Cocodrie, Dulac, and Theriot.

During fall and winter, speckled trout and redfish migrate into marshes as far north as the cities of Golden Meadow and Chauvin, which are 40 miles by road from the coast. Spots to check out during this time are Lake Laurier just north of Grand Isle; Bully Camp Sulphur Mine Lake and Catfish Lake west of Golden Meadow; Wonder Lake and Boudreaux and Robinson Lakes near Chauvin; Terrebonne, Petit Caillou, and Sale Bayous; Madison Bay near Cocodrie; and the extensive series of canals off the Houma Navigational Canal near Dulac.

A redfish is landed at Calcasieu Lake in western Louisiana.

Calcasieu Lake

Called Big Lake by locals, this area stretches southward 40 miles from south of Lake Charles to the Gulf of Mexico and offers the best chance to tie into a big speckled trout. Because of its much deeper and cooler water, the adjacent Calcasieu Navigational Canal holds trout and redfish during summer months. Trout up to 10 pounds are common in late spring and early summer, and 6- to 8-pounders show up in catches well into the fall.

Like marshes to the east, this area also holds the promise of first-rate late-fall and winter catches of smaller trout and redfish. Although smaller fish will attack gold spoons, jigs sporting soft-plastic minnow imitations, and topwater baits, anglers mostly cast live shrimp and minnows to oyster beds, small islands, runouts, and rock jetties.

Offshore

For variety of species and proximity to ports, Louisiana is without peer among the five Gulf of Mexico states with respect to offshore fishing.

Two factors influence the state's offshore catches: the Mississippi River and the oil platforms constructed off the state's coast after World War II. The river provides nutrients that concentrate baitfish, the first building block of the food chain, and the numerous oil platforms serve as artificial reefs to attract species like snapper, amberjack, grouper, cobia, tripletail, king mackerel, barracuda, Atlantic croaker, triggerfish, rainbow runners, and little tunny. They also attract tarpon, blackfin and yellowfin tuna, and, on occasion at the deeper oil rigs, sailfish, blue and white marlin, mako sharks, jewfish, and large pelagic sharks.

Tarpon is a prized species. From the mouth of the Mississippi River west to the Ship Shoal area south of Cocodrie, large schools of silver kings feed on a wide variety of baitfish. Striped mullet and menhaden are their favorite foods, and huge schools of these species show up in offshore waters during the summer and early fall.

Tarpon fleets from Houma, New Orleans, Golden Meadow, and Baton Rouge go after their quarry with trolled spoons and have taken to casting locally made jigs into schools of rolling tarpon. Since 1990, the hot tarpon spots are near West Delta block 58, the Grand Bayou Pass area, and the Midnight Lumps near the Mississippi River's South Pass. The state-record tarpon is a 230-pound specimen.

The waters south of the Mississippi River hold the best promise of tangling with marlin, yellowfin tuna, mako sharks, sailfish, and an occasional giant bluefin tuna. It is in this area that the river lies nearest to North America's continental shelf and its 1,000-plus-foot depths. Bottom areas east and west of the river tend to flatten out and thus do not have the depths needed to attract these blue-water species.

Anglers can reach blue water by traveling as few as 12 miles south of South Pass, or as many as 80 miles south of the popular launching/docking spot on Grand Isle, which is approximately 40 miles west of the river. Its proximity to this prolific area explains why Venice, on the Mississippi River, has become the busiest blue-water port in Louisiana.

Lake Charles also has its share of blue-water anglers, who travel 100 miles south to the Flower Gardens, the only living coral reef in the western Gulf of Mexico that is located in U.S. waters. Once in blue water, and usually around rips, big-game anglers begin by trolling offshore lures in various colors.

Even though the allure of an offshore blue-water adventure is high on most anglers' lists, trips to the oil platforms in West Delta, Grand Isle, South Timbalier, Ship Shoal, and Eugene Island fill charter bookings and most hours of recreational fishing. The abundance of baitfish is evident around the rigs, and most anglers use stout rods and 4/0 conventional reels filled with 50- to 80-pound line to take a variety of species in depths from 60 to 250 feet. Live, fresh, and freshly frozen baitfish are used, either on drift lines or heavily weighted drop lines.

Patterning selected species is often the most difficult task, and anglers drop baited hooks to several different levels, usually at 10-foot intervals and starting at depths of 40-feet, to find species like snapper, grouper, and amberjack. The drift lines are usually reserved for cobia and king mackerel.

The flows of the Mississippi and Atchafalaya Rivers usually suspend a murky layer of freshwater over the gulf. This doesn't stop experienced anglers, who know that under this layer is clean greenish or blue saltwater. They also know, however, that under these conditions live baits or brightly colored jigs must be used to attract strikes. Otherwise, when offshore waters clear—usually by late summer—fresh and freshly frozen bait can be used with equal success.

Louisiana has also enhanced its offshore fishing through its Rigs-to-Reefs Program, a plan that sinks retired oil platforms on the bottom of the gulf to provide additional artificial reefs, which attract many of the same species that converge on standing platforms.

LOWHEAD DAM

A concrete structure in rivers that is designed to maintain a minimum water level above the dam. Because a lowhead dam obstructs fish movement in the river and there is turbulent, highly oxygenated water just downstream of the dam, fish such as shad, walleye, and smallmouth bass may congregate there. However, a lowhead dam is a deceivingly dangerous structure that can claim lives.

The typical dropoff at a lowhead dam is deceptively small, yet the power of the water going over the dam is great. Boaters heading downstream, especially those in nonmotorized craft like canoes or jonboats, can be tempted to shoot over the dam but risk capsizing when they do so. Boaters approaching a lowhead dam from below are tempted to get too close when placing or retrieving an anchor, for example, and they risk instability that causes capsizing as well.

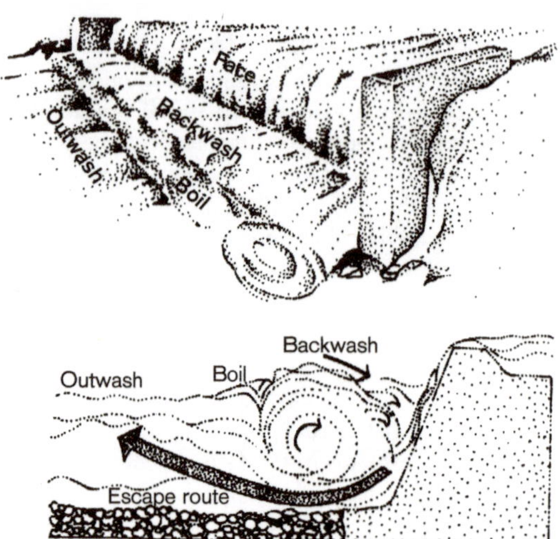

The powerful backwash below a lowhead dam is dangerous; it can pull a person back to the face of the dam, trapping the victim beneath the falling water.

The real danger lies in the powerful backwash that exists behind these dams; its hydraulic effect pulls a person back to the face of the dam, trapping them beneath the falling water without chance of rescue. Wearing a personal flotation device is of no help. It is necessary to stay well away from the upstream and downstream sides of a lowhead dam. See: Boat; Safety.

LUDERICK *Girella tricuspidata.*

Other names—blackfish, black bream, darkie, bronzie.

It has been said that any angler who can master the art of luderick fishing has the necessary skills to catch any fish that swims. Certainly, angling for "loo-drik" has captured the hearts of most Australian saltwater anglers, and the affection shown this species, by old and young alike, is akin to the devotion demonstrated by their freshwater counterparts who angle after the legendary trout. For its mass, the luderick is one of the most determined fighters in the sea, and ranks as high as some of the top gamefish for its extraordinary stamina and fighting strength.

Although luderick anglers are convinced that its edible qualities are improved if it is bled as soon as possible after capture, there is a significant commercial fishery for the species along the East Coast of Australia.

Identification. The luderick's body, which is moderately elongate and moderately compressed, is generally dark brown on top to silvery gray below. Depending on the habitat, this coloration can change to silvery gray on top to silvery white on the belly, or pale olive brown above with a beautiful bronze sheen extending to the belly. There can be 8 to 12 narrow, vertical, dark bars across the back and sides. The mouth is small, with flattened tricuspid teeth. There is a single, unnotched dorsal fin, and the caudal fin is large and emarginate or concave. Fins are a uniform grayish green.

Size. The largest size recorded stands at 5.2 kilograms, but the average size taken by anglers is around 500 grams to 1 kilogram. An Australian angling record is listed at 2.43 kilograms.

Distribution. Luderick range from South Australia, along the Victorian coastline, and up the East Coast as far north as Hervey Bay in southern Queensland. They are also found on the northern, eastern, and western coasts of Tasmania.

Habitat. Luderick live in estuaries, bays, and inlets, and along rocky coastal shores. They prefer areas where seagrass is prolific but can be found around algae-covered bridge and jetty pylons, rock walls, and submerged reefs. They live close to weed-covered rocks and feed along the edges where the wash dislodges small weed growths.

Life history/behavior. The luderick is a very fecund fish, capable of spawning up to 400,000 eggs. Spawning is a lengthy process and occurs during the months of July through March, the timing depending on location. Eggs are released in the surf and in the estuary mouths, and the larvae find their way into the seagrass beds from where they move well up into the estuaries and coastal lakes. They are schooling fish that hide in the weed-beds, where they are fairly safe from predatory fish.

Food and feeding habits. Luderick are essentially herbivorous, although they are sometimes taken on a prawn. Estuary luderick feed chiefly on green, filamentous algae, and those fish living along rocky shores feed on a lettucelike plant (colloquially called lettuce or cabbage) that grows prolifically on the ocean rocks as far up as the high-tide mark. They will also feed on small crustaceans, marine worms, and the flesh of the cunjevoi, a tunicate that lives on the rocks at about low tide level.

Angling. The tackle of the estuary luderick angler consists of a light, flexible 2.5- to 3-meter rod and a reel spooled with 2- or 3-kilogram-strength line. The line is usually greased so that it floats on the surface, ensuring that there is no slack to interfere with the angler's strike when the float disappears. Accurate timing of the strike is an empirical skill. Hooks are small (No. 10 or 12), suspended beneath a quill or pencil float with near-neutral buoyancy (weighted by sheet lead or split shot to achieve this state), and baited with a twist of green weed. Sometimes small pieces of fresh green prawns are used when the angler runs out of weed. Lures are not used for luderick fishing, nor are flies.

Rock-based anglers use a stouter rod to 3.5 meters, and a larger, sturdier reel. Hooks are No. 8 or 10, suspended beneath a heavier float and usually baited with sea lettuce. Lines are heavier, to 5 kilograms, and may or may not be greased. Although conditions are more boisterous than those experienced in estuary situations, accurate timing of the strike is still required.

Tides and currents are carefully considered, with flood and ebb tides affecting the feeding patterns of the fish. Chumming is considered essential, and a chum of finely chopped weed mixed with sand for estuary fishing, or torn sea lettuce leaves scraped into the wash by the rock plates on the boots of the rock angler, is the ideal. Some anglers mix other ingredients with their chum in order to attract other species to a bottom bait while they concentrate on the luderick.

When hooked, luderick refuse to give up, and patience is essential at all times until the fish is safely in the net. They frequently dive for the bottom, and have been observed rubbing their cheeks along rocks in an attempt to dislodge the hook. The action of the sensitive rod will cushion most of these runs, but the angler must be on guard, especially when the fish reaches the surface, to counter a sudden surge in which the fish dives back to the bottom.

LUMPFISH *Cyclopterus lumpus.*

Other names—lump, lumpsucker, nipisa, kiarkvarrey; Italian: *ciclottero;* Spanish: *cicloptero.*

One of the largest members of the Cyclopteridae family of lumpfish and snailfish, the unusual-looking lumpfish is not a quarry of anglers, but it is known as a food fish in Europe and is reportedly valued for its eggs as an inexpensive substitute for caviar.

Identification. The lumpfish is a stout-bodied, almost round fish with a humped upper profile. It has a warty appearance due to a ridge of prominent tubercles running along the middle of the back, as well as three other rows of tubercles on the side, the uppermost of which extends from the tip of the snout to the base of the tail. Another distinctive feature is the way the pelvic fins are fused to form a round suction disk, which enables the lumpfish to attach itself to rocks. Of variable coloration, it is usually olive green or bluish gray with a yellowish belly; this grows red on males during breeding. The pectoral fins are broad and fanlike, and lower rays start at the throat region. The first dorsal fin is apparent only in the young.

Size. The lumpfish can grow to 2 feet and 21 pounds, although it is usually smaller.

Distribution. In the western Atlantic, lumpfish occur from Hudson Bay to James Bay and from Labrador to New Jersey; they are rarely found from the Chesapeake Bay south or in Bermuda. In the eastern Atlantic, lumpfish occur from the Barents Sea to Iceland and Greenland and south to Spain.

Habitat. Lumpfish generally inhabit rocky bottoms of cold waters but may also occur among floating seaweed.

Life history/Behavior. Female lumpfish may lay 20,000 eggs or more, which sink to the bottom and stick. They are guarded by the male until they hatch. Lumpfish are solitary rather than schooling fish.

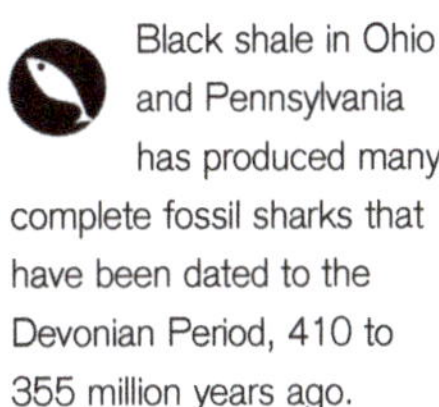
Black shale in Ohio and Pennsylvania has produced many complete fossil sharks that have been dated to the Devonian Period, 410 to 355 million years ago.

Lumpfish

Food. The lumpfish feeds on small crustaceans and small fish.

LUNATE

Used to describe a caudal fin that is shaped like a crescent moon.

LUNKER

A big fish of any of the larger species.

See: Trophy Fish.

LURE

The generic definition of the word "lure" as a noun is "a thing used to entice," and as a verb is "to attract, tempt, or entice." Thus, in the broadest sense related to sportfishing, a lure might be construed as any natural or artificial object with a hook that is used to catch a fish. However, this all-encompassing definition is accepted and referenced only by nonanglers and language purists. Anglers have a narrower view of what constitutes a lure, and it excludes any live or dead natural organism. Thus, an earthworm, a minnow, and an insect aren't lures, even though they're used to tempt or attract fish.

The distinction between broad types of objects used to catch fish has long been clearly delineated between natural organisms, called natural bait *(see)*, and objects that are not natural but imitate natural foods consumed by fish. The latter became known as "artificial lures," but since the mid-twentieth century the word "artificial" has been decreasing in common usage.

Today most anglers classify objects used to catch fish as being either natural bait or lures. Thus, a simple twenty-first century definition of a lure is any nonnatural object with a hook that is used to catch fish. These nonnatural objects are made from a variety of materials, primarily wood, metal, lead, and hard and soft plastic, but also including feathers, fur, yarn, and combinations of materials.

History

The history of lures as described in print dates back to artificial flies, which were used at least in the late fifteenth century, if not earlier. The first published description of artificial flies appeared in the second edition of Dame Juliana Berners' *Boke of Saint Albans,* printed in 1496. Included in the book was her essay *Treatyse of Fysshynge with an Angle,* in which she mentioned a dozen flies. Nearly 200 years later, Izaak Walton's famous book *The Compleat Angler* listed 65 artificial fly patterns for trout. Little progress had occurred in the interim, and lightweight fly patterns for angling with reelless rods continued to be the only known fishing lures until the nineteenth century, when modern fishing reels evolved and gradually created a means for dispensing, retrieving, and storing line; after this period, fishing horizons began to expand.

Lures made of metal appeared in the nineteenth century, perhaps starting in England around 1800 with the Phantom Minnow, which had a metal head, metal fins, three treble hooks, and a silk body. Julio T. Buel, an American, is credited with inventing the metal fishing spoon; he reportedly had fished with his own invention since 1821 and began the commercial manufacture of spoons in 1848. The first patent for a wooden lure was granted to Americans David Huard and Charles Dunbar in 1874, yet James Heddon of Michigan is credited with creating and manufacturing the first wooden fishing lure in the early 1900s.

The types, categories, and variations of artificial lures mushroomed exponentially every decade thereafter, greatly fueled by the development of plastic molding technology after World War II, fiberglass fishing rods, nylon monofilament fishing line, and the development of both spinning and spincasting reels.

General Information

Lures catch fish because of their appearance and the manner in which they are deployed, which are interrelated factors. Even though some lures don't specifically imitate or suggest food through their physical appearance, they imitate or suggest food in the way that they're used. Thus, in one sense or another, all lures represent some form of food, either mimicking it closely, as is true of artificial flies or minnow-style plugs, or suggesting it broadly, as is true of jigs, spinners, and spoons.

Even though lures represent food, they are not only or always struck by fish that are feeding. Fish strike lures for many reasons. Hunger is a prime motivation. Instinctive reflex, aggravation, competition, and protection are others. Fish refuse to strike lures at times for many reasons, too. Predatory fish, which are of major sportfishing interest, spend varied portions of their time feeding; some species, especially many in saltwater, are necessarily eating machines and constantly forage, whereas others, especially many in freshwater, feed less frequently and are often more selective.

Certainly the range of food consumed by fish

is extremely wide, varying with different environments, different species, and different seasons. Thus, some fish are more susceptible to lures, and certain types of lures and fishing techniques, than others, and there is great variety in the types of lures that have evolved and that are appropriate at a given time. A visit to a well-supplied tackle store, with a mind-boggling array of lures, will verify this.

To put the situation into perspective, consider a midsize lure manufacturer. When specific models are taken into account, then multiplied by the various sizes and assorted colors in which the models are produced, the number of different lures that the manufacturer makes may swell to a staggering 1,500 plus. And there are dozens of large and medium-size lure manufacturers, plus many more smaller ones, making fishing lures out of plastic, wood, and metal, not to mention all of the commercial and home tyers of artificial flies.

Either as the cause or the effect of this situation is the fact that anglers have a deep fascination with the objects that they use to dupe fish, and as a group anglers are obsessed with finding, creating, or trying new lures in the never-diminishing hope of increasing success. This not only fuels the array of individual products, but leads to extensive regional preferences in types and colors of lures used for various fish species.

Almost invariably the first question someone asks a successful angler is, "What type of lure did you use?" and this fact underscores the interest that anglers take in items that have caught, or will catch, fish. Some avid anglers possess so many lures that they could open up their own tackle emporium.

Function/design. No lure, no matter how appealing it is to the human eye, will catch fish of itself. How the angler uses it—in other words, where it is fished and how skillfully it is retrieved—are key factors in its success, although some lures are inherently better than others owing to their design, swimming action, and appearance.

There are two elements to being consistently effective with lures. The first is knowing the quarry: knowing something about the behavior of the food it most often consumes and then matching lure selection to the habits of that fish and the prevailing conditions. The second is being completely familiar with the characteristics of each lure you use: being able to make each work to its maximum designed ability. The more you know about your lures and the fish you seek, and the better you understand the conditions in which you seek them, the better prepared you'll be to make a knowledgeable lure selection.

Categories. Many lures overlap in application and technique, but others are suitable only to particular conditions and require specialized usage. All lures are designed to perform a specific function, however, and thus can be reviewed in a general manner according to type or category. The category is, in part, a function of the materials that are used to create the lures. Flies, for example, are extremely lightweight lures primarily made of feather and fur that is wrapped around a hook. By comparison, spinners and spoons are comparatively heavy sinking lures that are made of metal. Plugs are wooden or molded hard-plastic lures with a lot of buoyancy and built-in swimming action. A detailed review of each category is contained under their respective entries.

All lures are somehow meant to imitate natural food; here, a 5-inch-long alewife is contrasted with wooden (top) and plastic minnow-imitating plugs.

See: Antique Fishing Tackle; Buzzbait; Crankbait; Fly; Jerkbait; Jig; Jigging Spoon; Plastic Worm; Plug; Soft Lure; Spinner; Spinnerbait; Spoon; Stickbait; Surface Lure; Surgical Tube Lure; Tailspinner; and Trolling Lures, Saltwater.

Lure Color

How we see color, how we think fish see it, and how this relates to the way we make lure color selections is an intriguing aspect of fishing. Successful anglers are routinely quizzed about what type and color of lure they used, and no other topic fascinates anglers more.

Size, action, vibration, and color complement each other and are all critical to a lure's success. But perhaps the most common modification to lures has nothing to do with their working action. It has to do with changing the lure's color.

You cannot discuss color without discussing light. Color is the result of reflecting (or absorbing) light of different wavelengths: The shortest wavelength visible to humans produces violet, and the longest produces red. Shorter (ultraviolet) and longer (infrared) wavelengths are invisible to the human eye—it is not clear whether fish can see them. Furthermore, colors are perceived differently above water than in the water, and their visibility is greater if they fluoresce. (Fluorescent objects absorb short wavelengths of light, particularly ultraviolet, and re-emit longer, visible wavelengths of light at a higher energy level.)

Although we know a great deal about how humans are affected by light and how we perceive

A potpourri of plugs and spoons adorns an angler's Styrofoam "tackle box."

colors, we can't say unequivocally that what we know applies equally to fish. Therefore, anglers form theories and opinions based on experience and information provided by limited research.

It was once thought that fish were color blind and that they perceived colors as gradients of gray. Over the last century, that opinion has changed, however. More than 60 years ago, researchers reported that some fish could definitely perceive colors. Then it was thought that some species of fish could see color and some couldn't. Now it is conceded that most fish see color; only cave fish and extremely deep-dwelling ocean fish do not. Over the past 50 years, various researchers have reported that the vision of some species of fish is tinted yellow, red, blue, or orange. Some had postulated that the most important sense of a fish is its hearing, especially in turbid water; others believe that fish may see far better than we think, even in turbid water.

Anglers have been influenced greatly by scientific studies and by their own attempts to analyze natural conditions. But many anglers still behave as if fish perceived colors exactly as we do; that is why it's said that some lures are designed to catch anglers, not fish. Some anglers completely disregard the color perception of fish in making lure color selections; some work strictly on the basis of natural forage imitation—if baitfish aren't chartreuse, why use a lure that color? And others are ambivalent, vacillating between what looks good to them and what other anglers seem to be successful with.

Despite the fact that we know more about our quarry and its sensory abilities than ever before, there still are some perplexing, fascinating, and unresolved questions. Perhaps the greatest puzzler is this: Why do fish strike a lure that bears no physical resemblance to any natural food item? It happens all the time, of course. Some effective lures act unlike any known forage, some have a form unlike natural food, and some are colored unlike anything we know or see. Yet at times they are more productive than another lure that in every way seems more representative of real prey. The answer must be that, for some reason, these lures suggest food to that fish. What drew the fish's attention in the first place still begs for an answer.

Another mystery: How important is it to use a lure that we assume is most visible to the fish? At issue here is whether fish are acting principally on the basis of visual stimuli, whether vision is secondary to the fish's other senses, or whether it's important under some conditions but not others. Researchers think they have some clues to the answers to these questions and some insight into how fish perceive color and what makes them respond to our offerings. But we may never really know about these matters—and perhaps we never should, because angling will cease to be a sport when the puzzles have been solved.

Nonetheless, some fish appear to be sight-feeders almost exclusively, and a confirmed way to appeal to them is to use lures that have very high visibility under given water and light conditions at particular depths.

An overlooked and underexplored mystery is where the most prominent color should be located on a lure, especially a plug. Most predator and prey fish are dark on the top and light on the bottom. Did nature make them light on the bottom to be less conspicuous from below? Are they dark on the top so that they will blend in with the environment when viewed from above? Many anglers maintain that gamefish strike their prey (and lures) predominantly from below. If they are coming from below, should your aim be to imitate nature and have a light color at the bottom of your lure? If so, what difference does it make what the top color is? On the other hand, should your aim be to contrast nature and thus have the most visible color on the bottom of the lure? This coloring system, known as countershading, has been tried (with modest success) by manufacturers from time to time.

When someone reports that fish are taking a chrome plug with green ladderback tape on the top, you have to think about this. Fish seldom go down to chase a lure, so how could the ladderback tape atop the plug be influencing the catch? If the ladderback extends onto the sides of the lure, it may offer a bit of visual appeal to a fish. For this reason, when you add prism, luminescent, or ladderback tape to plugs, avoid the top of the lure and place it on the sides or bottom.

Should lure color be based on light intensity? Dark days/dark lures, light days/light lures has been an angling dictum for decades, though it is occasionally admitted that fish sometimes break the rules. There is good reason to use light-colored lures on dark days and dark-colored lures on light days. That might mean, for example, trolling a black spoon for salmon when it is very sunny, for example, especially in the early part of the season and when the fish are shallow. The dark color contrasts well with the brightness from above.

However, many good anglers disagree with this.

There are a few facts about light and color in aquatic environments that you should know if you are going to make color work for you. The principal factors to assess are the depth to be fished, the clarity of the water, and the intensity of the light.

Research and conventional thought tell us that as light passes through water its intensity is reduced. This applies vertically as well as horizontally and is further influenced by the clarity of the water. As light intensity is reduced, red and violet are the first to lose their distinctive hue, followed by brown; ultimately these appear black. Blue and green retain their hue much longer, though they fade and don't appear the same shade. Fluorescent counterparts remain visible at greater depths and distances, with fluorescent chartreuse being especially visible. No less an authority than the United States Navy, after testing the visibility of colors at various depths in saltwater, concluded in a report that "fluorescent colors have been shown to be much more effective than regular paints of the same color under almost all conditions of underwater viewing." The Navy also found that background contrast—dark water, sandy or vegetative bottom, and so forth—significantly affected visibility of all colors and that different times of the day produced different results. Fluorescent orange, for example, was most visible early in the morning, but less so later, whereas fluorescent green exhibited the reverse pattern (fluorescent chartreuse was not tested); the Navy report concluded that this effect had more to do with contrast against background colors than with differences in brightness.

These tests relate only to human vision and perception, however. The color preferences of bass vary widely according to a researcher who studied the reactions of largemouth bass to color. He used a light meter to record light transmittance values under clear, stained, and muddy water conditions at specific times of the day and under clear and overcast sky conditions. One of his findings was that the most visible color doesn't necessarily contrast with the background, but the way light disperses in the water is very important. If you have plankton or debris or sediment, these can have different effects on the scattering of light, either reflecting or refracting it, and this seems to modify things so that the consistency of background contrast is not always critical.

Surprisingly, his research showed that fish in muddy water can perceive color at greater distances—up to 4 feet—than had previously been thought. Their range of vision was a maximum of 10 to 12 feet in stained water and up to 40 feet in the clearest water. Anglers who almost always fish under clear water conditions can attest to the ability of fish like salmon and trout to see lures from a great distance, which may account for the fish-catching productivity of brightly flashing, highly reflective silver and chrome spoons and plugs. It is common to catch fish that have not been spotted below the boat on sonar equipment; when attracted to the lure, the fish are far enough away that they are outside the cone angle of the transducer.

Another of his findings was that each color of the spectrum is either camouflaged or highly visible at some time during the day; in other words, colors fade in and out depending on the conditions of the environment. This makes sense if you consider the biological interaction between a predator and prey fish such as shad, minnows, or sunfish, for example. If those forage organisms were highly visible all the time to predators, their population would be limited. But they're not always visible. They're camouflaged a large part of the time. Only sometimes are their particular color patterns highly visible.

Another finding was that certain colors used in combination seemed to be especially attractive. Many anglers can attest to this, whether using different colors of prism tape on spoons or using combined paint colors on their plugs. It is no accident that the hands-down favorite spoon color pattern for northern Canada fishing, for example, is the so-called Five of Diamonds, which is five red diamond shapes on a yellow background. Decades

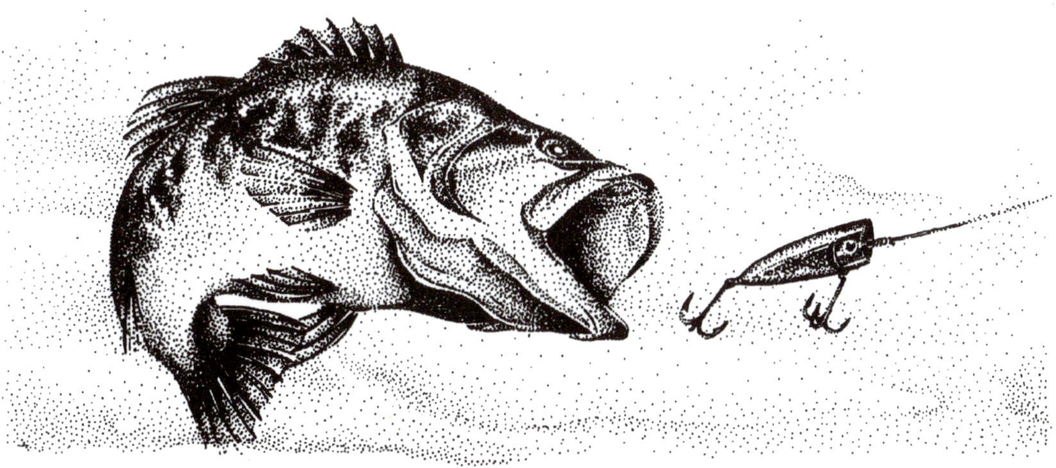

ago before the world of lures and colors exploded, red and red-and-white lures were vitally important to anglers. Surely anglers then thought that those colors were especially visible to fish. Today not only do we have a greater range of available colors, we even have lures that emit light when there is little or no natural light available. These are phosphorescent and chemiluminescent products, intended for use under low-light conditions. Early morning, evening, night, and dark cloudy days lend themselves to the use of light-emitting lures or colors, as does fishing in very deep water. Anglers have used chemiluminescent light sticks inside plugs to catch lake trout and salmon at night, in early morning, and in deep-water downrigger fishing. Although this strategy has been moderately productive, phosphorescent lures, which have to be exposed to a light source, seem preferable because they are more subtle; however, they are less convenient because they need repeated exposure to light.

Some famousfishing waters hold dubious dam distinctions: the Grand Coulee on the Columbia River is the world's longest concrete dam; the Oroville on California's Feather River is the tallest dam in the United States.

Phosphorescent lures have been available for a long time. Phosphorescent paint is used on the exterior of these lures (although you can add phosphorescent tape to conventionally painted lures). You hold phosphorescent lures close to a light source, such as a lantern or spotlight, to "charge" them up. The charge lasts for roughly 20 minutes, after which you have to recharge the lure. This system is good for those who are casting and can recharge lures periodically between casts, but it isn't as convenient for trollers who have to bring lines in to retrieve lures for recharging.

L

The matter of lure color and color visibility is an especially interesting subject for trollers because they are usually passing by fish fairly quickly and often don't have a chance to make repetitive presentations. The fish are in all likelihood striking out of hunger and reflexive instinct, as opposed to being aggravated or coaxed, and the fish's abilities to hear and see prospective prey seem to be particularly important aspects of foraging. If you adhere to the theory that fish won't strike trolled lures that they can't see, then you must play the color game fastidiously. Trout and salmon trollers, for instance, fish with some of the strangest lure colors and color combinations imaginable, and thus perhaps play to the fish's sense of vision more than many other trollers, although big-game anglers using offshore trolling lures are not far behind in this department.

You can alter lure colors, especially on spoons, if you keep a supply of colored prism tape with you. This tape is sold in sparkle and reflective versions, in sheet form or precut into various patterns, including lightning bolt, ladderback, angled strips, and more. You can completely cover an old color with a new one, or add a strip of color to a lure to enhance it. Before putting on the tape, it's best to keep a lure in the sun or in your pocket for a while to warm it up (in cold weather or when fishing cold water) so that the tape will adhere better.

You should consider visibility as an important aspect of all lure fishing and should realize that on occasion it can be the paramount factor causing a fish to be attracted to your lure, but that it is usually is not the sole factor. A combination of factors, including the action of the lure, its speed, its color, the manner in which it is fished, and the place in which it is fished, all contribute to success.

LURE MAKING

Nearly every generic type of commercially manufactured lure on the market got its start as someone's experimental creation. Since the first angler tried to pull fish out of the water, people have been making tools to catch fish. Nowhere has there been more devotion to making such tools than in the arena of lures. Many of the most successful lure manufacturing companies in the world started with a homemade or handmade creation that was crafted for the purpose of catching fish and that eventually turned into a business. Even today you can buy lures that were made in someone's garage workshop and are sold to tackle stores on a limited or regional basis.

Tinkering with lures has fascinated anglers for generations. Some of this tinkering leads to no more than making modifications *(see: lure modifying/repairing)*, but some leads to actually making lures, not with the intention of starting a commercial enterprise (although it can happen), but with the intention of expanding an interest in angling into a hobby where lures or rigs are made for personal use. Many fly anglers create their own flies and poppers *(see: flycasting tackle)* and get a lot of pleasure out of this craft, and they enjoy the satisfaction of taking fish on artificials that they have created. From a creative standpoint, making lures is akin to tying flies but obviously much different in terms of process and materials.

Although few people have access to some of the more sophisticated raw-material components of certain lures (imported woods, hi-tech plastics, sophisticated molding materials, machinery, etc.), it is possible to acquire suitable materials and components that will allow you to make or assemble lures that catch fish. Obviously, some lures are easier to make than others, and what you make will likely reflect the kinds of fishing you do and the species you pursue. A river steelhead and salmon angler is going to need spoons and spinners, for example, whereas a reservoir crappie angler is going to need a lot of small jigs. If you fish in places (where it is common to lose a lot of tackle (like brushpiles and other cover, or swift-flowing rivers and streams) then making your own lures not only has a hobby element but a practical one in that you're likely to lower your average cost for terminal tackle items.

Practicalities. The following information will help you get started in lure making. Don't be put off by the list of tools or supplies; a good way to economize is for fishing buddies or members of a club to get together on acquiring some of the materials as well as the bulk supplies. Obviously you should always be careful when working with tools; here, you should be especially careful when you are heating and pouring plastics or metals. These substances not only can cause a bad burn but also can produce undesirable fumes. Using the appropriate protective devices (a breathing mask, glove, eyewear, smock, etc.) is a good idea; proper ventilation is also necessary. Be attentive to issues concerning the use and disposal of lead, since you're likely to work with lead for jig heads, sinkers, and spinnerbaits. If lead is prohibited for terminal tackle use, you may not be able to acquire material for melting and pouring, and whatever old lead that you possess may have to be disposed of properly.

Make sure that you use quality components and those of appropriate size, length, strength, etc. The components must be able to stand up to the anticipated use and to the pressure that will be brought on the terminal tackle. Big, strong fish can decimate components; even good-quality components will split or break if they are too weak for the line strength or the drag tension. Some lures will come apart after being victim to only a few fish because the wire or the hook hangers or other components were not heavy enough. Obviously the quality of paint and the finish that you give will be important, especially for wooden lures, which can soak up water and become unbalanced. The proper paint and finish will help guard against this.

If you'll be making a lot of lures, remember to keep a junkyard of old lures and parts. The components from discarded lures (lips, hook hangers, screws, etc.) can be useful when making or modifying lures. You might get some useful parts from old and cheap throwaways at grab bag bins and flea markets.

Finally, remember that the success of many, if not most, lures, whether they are commercially made or homemade, is dependent upon their action in the water. When you make your own lures, you have to constantly check to see that they work right in the water; if they don't have the correct action, chances are they will not be fish catchers. So keep tinkering with each lure until it does work like it's supposed to.

Tools

Tools for making lures vary widely with the type of lure. In many cases only a few tools are required. Do not buy tools until you have a need for them. Some general suggestions are as follows.

Pliers. Standard pliers can be used to bend wire, hold lure parts, and perform general-purpose tasks.

Round-nose pliers. These are used for making the round eyes on various rigs and lures.

Split-ring pliers. These slim-jawed, long-nose pliers have a tooth on one end of the jaw for easy opening of split rings, and are ideal for changing free-swinging hooks on lures.

Molds. Aluminum or metal molds for molding jig heads, certain spoons, and sinkers are readily available from several companies. Most are hinged, two-piece styles for use with molten lead. There are also plastic molds for making plug and fly rod popper bodies; they use a special two-part plastic mix that works quickly and easily. Both two-part and open-face molds are available for melting PVC plastic and molding soft plastic lures.

Wire formers. Several types of wire-forming tools are available for making different bends in wire as required with various rigs, spinners, spinnerbaits, and buzzbaits. Instructions are supplied with these easy-to-use tools.

Wire cutters. Wire cutters are necessary to cut wire and finish wire-formed lures. Side-clipping wire cutters that can make a flush cut are best; because they have no bevel along the outside edge of the cutting blades, they can cut very closely to eliminate a protruding tag end.

Snips. Various types of snips can be used to cut sheet metal if you're making spinner blades and spoon blanks from scratch. The best of these are so-called aviation snips, which have compound leverage and are designed for cutting through thicker-gauge metals than what can be cut with standard sheet metal snips.

Carpentry tools. For making plugs from wood blanks, consider tools such as back saws, coping saws, drills, drill bits, carving knives, rules, rasps, files, sandpaper, and emery boards. Some of these, such as files, rasps, and emery boards, are also a must when making certain lures, for example, when the metal on spoons must be smoothed or the seam edges on jig heads sanded.

Brushes. Small plastic-handled disposable brushes are a must for painting and also for coating with clear protective finishes.

Scale netting. This is necessary for putting a scale-pattern finish on lures; it's available from hobby sources and from fabric shops (where it is known as tulle).

Supplies

Lure-making supplies are available from specialty mail-order merchandisers and also from some tackle shops. Some of the items you may need include the following:

Spinner blades. These come in several different shapes, many sizes, and many metallic and painted finishes. They are primarily used in making spinners and spinnerbaits, and sometimes they are attachments on other lures.

Buzzbait blades. Buzzbait blades are like large, wide propeller blades and are designed to be used singly or in tandem (counter-rotating) on the buzzbait shaft. Many finishes, styles, and several sizes are available.

Spinner bodies, beads, and other parts. Beads of different size are used for the bodies of some spinners and are available in many colors of plastic and in solid brass and nickel-plated brass. Odd-shaped bodies are also available in plastic, brass, and nickel-plated metal. Other necessary parts include clevises to hold the blade and allow rotation on the shaft, and colored plastic sleeves to fit over hooks.

Spoon blanks. Spoon blanks are available in many sizes, finishes, and shapes for easy spoon assembly. To complete the lure, you need only add hooks with split rings by using split-ring pliers or add a split ring at the head of the lure for line fastening. Blanks for lipless thin-metal baits, also called blade baits, are sometimes available without hooks, similarly to spoons.

Wire forms. Wire forms for spinners come in straight shafts, with an eye wrapped on one end and with a loop fastener for hanging hooks on the finished lure. Wire forms for jigging spoons and lead tailspinners are made to be molded into the lead lures, leaving an exposed hook hanger(s) and line tie. Those for spinnerbaits and buzzbaits are made in the required shapes and designed to be slipped onto a hook and molded into the head of the lure.

Spinnerbait, buzzbait blanks. These blanks come painted or unpainted; the former requires painting the head, and both require adding blades and skirt to complete.

Plug blanks. Different styles of plug blanks are available, both painted and unpainted. Most have molded-in hook hangers and require only hooks, attached with split rings, to complete. Some wood blanks require hook hangers and lure screw eyes to add hooks and line ties and to hold propellers.

Jig heads. Molded, unpainted jig heads are used as they are and rigged with grubs or worms, but they can also be painted and wrapped with skirt material to make hair jigs.

Hooks. Hundreds of styles, sizes, and finishes of hooks are available for all types of lure making. The most common are treble hooks for crankbaits, large single hooks for spinnerbaits and buzzbaits, and bent-shank jig hooks for molding jigs.

Propellers, lips, hook hangers, plug fittings. Hook hangers, propellers, screw-in lips, and other plug fittings make it easy to complete hard baits.

Skirt material. Plastic and rubber spinnerbait and buzzbait skirt material can be obtained in bulk or in completed form ready for use, often from good tackle shops. Other material for dressing jigs and hooks includes hackle, marabou, natural fur, synthetics, and stranded flash materials in any combination or color; these are available from tackle shops, mail-order houses (especially fly tying suppliers), and craft shops.

Various Colorado (left) and Indiana (right) blades are used for making spoons, spinners, and assorted bait rigs.

Thread. Thread is needed for wrapping tails and skirts on jigs and hooks. Use the 2/0 size for small lures, A for medium lures, and D for large lures.

Liquid soft plastic. Milky-looking liquid plastic is used to make new soft plastic lures and is available from some tackle shops and mail-order houses.

Liquid plastic additives. Hardener, softener, color, and scent may be mixed in the liquid soft plastic to effect the feel, look, or smell of the finished lure.

Plastic for foam-bodied lures. Two-part foam plastic is available to make polyurethane bodies for plugs and popping bugs.

Spinners

Spinners are among the easiest of lures to make, since they require no special skills and no painting. The necessary parts include spinner wire, clevises, blades, bodies or beads, and hooks. Usually the spinner wire is 0.030 in diameter and available straight, with a wrapped eye or with a hooked loop eye. The wrapped eye is often best for standard spinners, since it eliminates having to make a line-tie eye. Use wire several inches longer than the intended spinner to give yourself some working room. Clevises come in folded or stamped styles, with stamped best for spinners. Get the right size to allow shaft clearance with the blades chosen. Shaped bodies in metallic and painted finishes or metallic or plastic beads make up the bodies of spinners. Bodies and beads can be mixed in a lure. Treble hooks are standard on most spinners, but you can use doubles or singles also. Choose the right size, based on experience or comparison with commercially made spinners.

Begin making the spinner by slipping a clevis into the hole on a blade and then sliding the wire shaft through the clevis. Make sure that the concave side of the blade faces the shaft. Then slide on a small metal bead to serve as a bearing for the rotating clevis. Add a body or series of beads as desired. Most bodies are sized to end at the lower end of the blade.

At this point, use pliers to make a right angle bend in the wire, leaving clearance for the wire wrap and also clearance for the turning clevis. The right angle is to position the eye in the center of the wire. Usually a clearance of about $^{1}/_{4}$- to $^{3}/_{8}$-inch is about right. Use round-nose pliers to complete a wrap; then slide on a treble hook. At this point, the eye will be complete, with the excess wire at right angles to the main spinner shaft. Hold the spinner eye and hook with pliers; then wrap the excess wire two turns around the spinner shaft. Use flush-cutting wire cutters to remove the excess wire.

Many variations, sizes, and colors of spinners can be made using this basic, simple technique.

Spinnerbaits

Spinnerbaits are almost as easy to make as spinners, although they can be more time-consuming if you mold your own bodies by using wire forms and hooks. You can also purchase the parts needed, which include the body/wire form, skirts, spinner blades, clevises, beads, split rings, and swivels. With a wire/painted body form, begin cutting the upper shaft to the length you desire for attaching the blades. Then use round-nose pliers to form an incomplete eye in the end of the wire. Separately, use split-ring pliers to connect a spinner blade and small swivel to a split ring. Slip the other eye of the swivel onto the partially completed eye on the end of the shaft, and close the eye with pliers.

Skirts are held in place by friction, fitting over the collar of the molded lead body. Slide the skirt over the collar to complete the lure. If the lure is unpainted, paint the body before adding the skirt *(see: lure modifying/repairing)*. To make your own bodies, follow the instructions that come for making jigs.

It is also easy to make in-line spinnerbaits (where the blades are on the main shaft). For this, the instructions are the same as for a spinnerbait with an overhead arm, but prior to making the eye in the wire, slide on a clevis holding a blade (concave to the rear) and a few small beads to separate this forward blade from the blade added to the end of the wire. Then complete as with the other lure.

Buzzbaits

Buzzbaits are similar to spinnerbaits except that they're designed to be used on the surface, the blades are different, and the body shape is often slightly flattened. To make buzzbaits, you'll need the wire/body form, skirts, buzz-style blades, and pop rivet-type bearings.

Assembly is easy. First slide a single buzz blade onto the upper straight shaft. Then add a small bearing sleeve, and use pliers to make a sharp right-angle bend in the wire close to the end. Add a skirt by sliding it onto the collar on the rear of the body. That's all there is to it. Variations can include two blades, which should be counter-rotating (they are sold and described that way), with a bearing bead or two between them for separation (you don't want the blades to hit and lock) and easy spinning, and a choice of plastic or metal blades. Plastic is harder to find, but if you've saved the plastic blades from older commercially manufactured models, you can adapt them.

If the lure is unpainted, you have to paint the body before adding the skirt *(see: lure modifying/repairing)*. To make your own bodies, follow the instructions for making jigs.

Spoons

Spoons can be simply assembled from the basic

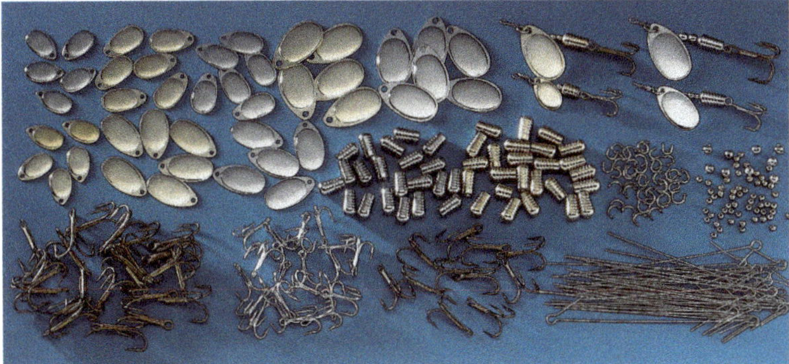

These are the components for making spinners.

components, or you can go the extra distance and make them from scratch.

To assemble spoons with free-swinging hooks, you'll have to obtain appropriate blanks, which are the spoon bodies without any parts or hooks. Many sizes, styles, and finishes (metallic and painted) are available. You also need split rings and hooks. Treble hooks are traditional on most spoons, but you can use singles or doubles as the circumstances may warrant; lightweight trolling spoons are popular in single-hook versions, and some places actually require the use of single hooks on lures. To assemble, use split rings and split ring pliers to connect the hole in the rear of the blank to the hook eye. Then use the same technique to add a split ring as a line tie to the forward hole in the blank. The same process, incidentally, is used for lipless thin-metal baits, or blade baits.

To make lightweight spoons from scratch, you can buy sheet metal from hobby shops and use heavy snips to cut out shapes that you wish to try. To shape the blade, hammer it on a scrap of wood until satisfied with the shape and appearance. Then use a drill or drill press to make a small hole ($^1/_{16}$ inch to $^1/_8$ inch) through each end.

You can make fixed-hook spoons (like weedless spoons) by drilling an additional hole in the center of the blank and then turning up (toward the concave side) the tail end of the blank with the hole. Thread a hook through the hole in this bend, and

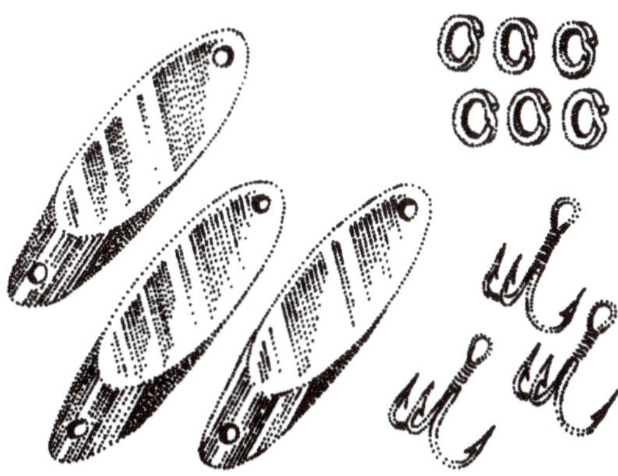

Casting spoons can be assembled from readily available bodies, hooks, and split rings.

put a bolt or pop rivet through the hook eye to the hole in the center of the blade. Because of the size of hook eyes, this is usually possible only in large spoons. Small fixed-hook spoons can be made by soldering the hook to the concave side of the blade, although some finishes and metals are difficult to solder.

Other variations are to drill small holes on each side of the tailing edge of the spoon and use small split rings to attach tiny willowleaf spinner blades for added flash.

Jigs

Jigs are essentially a leadheaded hook that has various head shapes and that is dressed with some material (perhaps a body of hair, feathers, soft plastic, or a combination of these). The term "jig" technically refers to the entire lure in its dressed form, whereas leadhead refers to the lure without body dressing, and bucktail refers to a lure with a hair body. However, these terms are often used interchangeably, especially leadhead and jig *(see: jig).*

Making completed or dressed jigs can be simple if you use premolded leadheads; these can be obtained in unpainted or painted versions in virtually any style or size. Making any type of jig can be more involved if you do the actual leadhead molding.

Molding leadheads. To mold jig heads onto hooks, you need the proper molds (which are the forms into which you pour the molten lead), the right size and style of jig hooks (which are often specific for each mold), any additional required attachments, a pouring ladle, a source of lead heat, heavy gloves, and a sturdy work area. Safety is essential for working with lead. Make sure that the work area is sturdy and large enough and that there is proper ventilation to protect from lead fumes. Do not eat or smoke during this activity (lead can be transferred to your body this way), and make sure that pets, young children, or other distractions aren't present.

Use a strong pot or ladle to melt the lead, and use an old stainless steel teaspoon to strain off any dross or slag floating on the surface. Begin by pouring lead into the mold *without a hook in the mold cavity.* The purpose of this is to heat the mold so that you get complete jig heads. These initial moldings, usually deformed as a result of contacting the cold mold, can be remelted. Once the mold is hot enough (all cavities fill completely), add the jig hook to the mold, close the mold, and rapidly pour the lead into each sprue hole. Allow it to cool for a few minutes; then open the mold to remove the hot leadheads. Continue the process to make up a batch of leadheads. Later use wire cutters to remove the sprue particles from the leadheads. Once the leadheads have cooled, they are ready for painting and/or dressing.

An ideal way to make leadheads is to try to pour a season's supply of leadheads at one sitting, with the aid of a partner and several molds. One person can be responsible for pouring the molds; the other for emptying the poured molds and refilling them with hooks.

Dressing. You can tie a hair, feather, or synthetic tail to an unpainted head and then paint the head and the thread wrap at the same time, or you can tie onto a painted leadhead and wrap it with an appropriate color wrap, sealing that for protection with a clear finish. For painting details, *see: Lure Modifying/Repairing.*

To tie a skirt of hair, feathers, or synthetics onto a leadhead, you need a vise or locking pliers to hold the hook, skirt material, and tying thread. Skirt material can be bucktail, calftail, saddle hackles, or material known as Ultra Hair, Super Hair, FisHair, etc. Tying thread can be size 2/0 for small jigs, size A for medium jigs, and size D for very large jigs.

To tie a skirt onto a leadhead, the hook has to be held securely, point up. Fly tying vises are ideal, although you can use a small hobby vise or hold the hook in locking pliers that in turn are clamped into a bench vise. With the hook horizontal, use fly tying techniques to tie down the thread and skirt materials. For this, begin by wrapping the thread around the collar or hook shank, wrapping over previous wraps to secure the thread. Then lay bundles of fur, synthetics, or feathers onto the collar and wrap over with thread. This can be done in one bundle or by wrapping several bundles in place to get different colors/materials or a thicker tail. Clip any excess material in front of the thread wrappings. Continue to wrap to make a neat, tight collar of thread, and tie off using a whip finish, such as that used on a rope end to prevent unraveling. Seal and protect the wrap by dipping the head and thread wrap into paint (if not previously painted) or coat with a clear epoxy, fly tying head cement, or clear fingernail polish *(see: fly tying).*

Some leadheads are fished with soft tails, most of which are made of plastic. To put these on a jig, simply slip the soft body (lizard, worm, shad, grub, crayfish, etc.) onto the hook. Most anglers wait until they're on the water to decide which soft body, or at least which color, to put on the jig. And many anglers add a soft body to a jig that has already been dressed with a hair or synthetic tail.

Sinkers

Sinkers can be molded using the same techniques as used for making jig heads. Molds are available for making all sizes and types of sinkers. The same safety and procedural considerations must be followed as for jig heads. You can even make sinkers with special features, such as egg sinkers, worm weights (slip sinkers), and split shot, by using core rods and inserts supplied with the molds. Sinkers do not require hooks, but some require swivels (bass casting), wire forms (walking sinkers), or wire eyes (pyramid, dollar, others). Insert these into the mold before pouring, using the same procedure as the one used for hooks when making jig heads.

Some sinkers such as worm weights are painted; most are not.

Soft Plastic Bodies

Soft plastic bodies can be made through a molding technique similar to that for molding sinkers and jig heads. For this you need the liquid plastic, plastic color, plastic scent (if desired), a melting pan, and one- or two-piece soft plastic molds. Allow plenty of work space and good ventilation.

To mold soft plastic bodies by using an open-face, or one-piece, mold, first melt the liquid plastic on the stove, setting heat very low to prevent burning. Next add color and scent according to the manufacturer's directions. Continue melting and stirring to mix the color and scent. Once the mixture is molten, carefully pour the liquid plastic into each cavity of the open-face mold, filling but not overfilling. Place the mold horizontally in a shallow pan of water to cool. After the lures are cured, remove them from the mold but keep them in cool water for additional curing. Since this process takes a few minutes, it is best to work with a partner and with several molds on a rotation basis.

With two-part molds, secure the mold according to the manufacturer's instructions. Fill the mold reservoir with liquid plastic; then use the mold plunger to inject the liquid plastic into the mold cavities. Allow it to cool in water before opening; repeat.

Plastic Plugs, Bugs

If you don't want to mold your own bodies, you can obtain premolded and prepainted bodies for topwater plugs and crankbaits; these have built-in hook hangers and only require assembly with hooks, using split rings and split-ring pliers.

Some plastic lure bodies are available in unpainted halves, which require gluing and painting. The halves are glued together with cyanoacrylate glues (so-called super glues) or with ketones such as nail polish remover. Often these are not painted externally and are clear so that you can insert Mylar sheeting or prism material for simulated scales or paint the inside prior to gluing.

Molding plastic bodies. There are molds for making good plastic-bodied fly-rod bugs, topwater plugs, and diving crankbaits. They are two-part molds that are easily secured and unlocked, and they're designed to take wire form hook hangers. To mold these lures, you need polyethylene molds, two-part polyurethane plastic, mixing rods, and mixing cups. Most of the fly-rod bug molds make from four to eight lures. The plug molds make one or two at a time, so it helps to have several molds and work on a rotation basis.

Begin by using the supplied jig form to bend the lure wire into the line tie/hook hanger shape. Spray the mold cavities with mold release or nonflavored no-stick cooking spray. Place the completed wire form into the mold and close it, using the locking pins to secure it. Pour out equal amounts of the two-part plastic on separate surfaces, and put them into a common mixing cup. Mix rapidly because you have only 35 seconds until the mix starts to foam and to form the lure. Pour rapidly into the sprue holes in each mold. Do *not* completely fill the mold cavity, since the foam expands to 20 times the original volume. (The amount in the mold cavity can be easily seen through the translucent sides of the plastic mold.)

Set the mold aside for about a half hour; then unlock the mold and carefully separate the two sections to remove the completed lure. Set the completed lure aside for 24 hours to completely cure. Finish by painting *(see: lure modifying/repairing)* and adding split rings and hooks.

You can also add color to the plastic (one-part only, then mix) to make solid-colored lures. Popping bugs are not made with the wire form but by using kinked-shank popper hooks.

Wooden bodies. Shaped wooden bodies can be purchased and require only painting and assembly, using lure-size screw eyes and other fittings. Most premade bodies are of topwater design, such as simple cigar shapes or torpedo shapes, to which one or more propellers can be added. These are best painted before assembly.

Assembly will require small screw eyes for the hook hangers and line tie, along with hooks, any propellers desired, etc. Split rings generally are not used, since the hooks can be attached directly to the screw eye. Even though these bodies are made from relatively soft woods, use a small-diameter pilot drill to make a hole in the wood to take the screw eyes. It also helps to brush the screw eye with bar soap for lubrication when inserting it. Screw eyes come in both open and closed styles, with the closed type used for the line tie and the open type used for hooks. Insert the screw eye almost completely into the pilot hole, add the hook, close the screw eye, and then make the last few turns to completely insert the screw eye. When adding propellers, allow some play and clearance for the propeller to turn.

Wood-bodied lures can also be made by using a wood lathe or by carving with appropriate tools. When using a lathe, use all pertinent safety practices associated with the lathe, including wearing safety goggles, removing ties and loose clothing, rolling up sleeves, and removing jewelry. Since only straight bodies can be made, most lathe-produced bodies are for various topwater lures. It is possible to attach a metal or plastic lip to some straight wooden bodies and make them into shallow or medium divers.

If you intend to make a lot of bodies on a lathe, first make one, paint and assemble it, and then use it to be sure that the shape, size, and action are what you wish. If so, make a cardboard template of that shape for producing more on the lathe.

Carving is necessary to make good diving plugs. This begins with a blank or block of wood. The

Some species of lungfish, especially those of the African genera Protopterus, are able to breathe air and burrow in a dormant state away from the water until seasonal rains come.

best woods generally available are poplar, basswood, and cedar, which can be cut from planks obtained at craft wood shops. The ideal sizes for most freshwater plugs are about $1^1/_2$ inches square by 4 to 6 inches long; blanks for saltwater are usually about 2 inches square by 6 to 8 inches long.

Before carving, decide on the shape of the plug and make a life-size template to use in drawing the shape onto the plug blank. Draw center lines down each side of the plug blank. Then use your template to trace the shape of the plug. Realize that you will usually need two templates, one for the top/bottom view or shape of the plug and the other for the side or profile of the plug.

After drawing the lines, begin by removing wood outside of the lines. There are two ways to do this. One is to mount the blank in a vise and use a coping saw to cut out the outlines to reduce the amount of carving necessary. To do this, use the scrap cut-out material as a "frame" to hold the blank. This allows cutting on all four sides. The other way to do this is to use a carving knife to cut out the shape, working on one side at a time. Do not carve randomly on the plug, since the working template lines will be removed early, leaving you with no guides as to shape or size. Carving along first one side, then the opposite, then retracing the lines on the cut sides for final cutting, makes the carving easier and the results more accurate.

After the plug has been carved or sawn into a rough rectangular shape, use a carving knife to round off the sides. Once it is roughly shaped, use a wood rasp to further round the body, followed by successively finer grades of sandpaper. Finish with the finest-grade sandpaper available; then drill pilot holes for the line tie and hook hanger screw eyes. Paint as described elsewhere and finish assembling.

Lure and Bait Rigs

You can make an endless variety of bait and lure rigs by using assorted terminal tackle attachments, single-strand wire, braided wire, and nylon mono-filament line. In making any rigs, be sure to use components that are equal or appropriate in size and strength. There is no point in using 200-pound-test wire with a tiny snap, or a huge snap with light 18-pound-test wire.

Learn the best possible connections for each type of component. For single-strand wire, it is possible to make a tight wrap around a hook, snap, or swivel by using a wire former. Another possibility for single-strand wire is the Haywire Twist *(see)*. For braided wire, use leader sleeves, properly crimped in place with crimping pliers. Finely braided multistrand wire allows you to tie standard knots.

Do not use more components than necessary. For example, to put a hook on a wire trace, don't use snaps, swivels, or split rings; connect the hook directly to the wire. To make the hook interchangeable, add a snap. To make it interchangeable and swiveling, use a snap swivel at the end of the wire.

Bait or lure rigs such as this free-sliding-sinker rig (left) and drop rig (right) are quickly made from components.

Most rigs can be figured out easily by comparing them to commercially manufactured versions or by planning the parts necessary and the method of connecting them. Many types of rigs are possible once you have the components and the simple skills required to make the necessary connections. Some typical rigs and rigging follow.

Single- and two-hook bottom rigs. These are easily made in nylon monofilament by tying one or two in-line dropper loops for the snelled hook

Snelled-hook freshwater bait rigs such as these are easily assembled from spinner blades, plastic beads, and leader material.

attachment, tying a loop at the top for the line tie and adding a large snap at the bottom for sinker attachment.

If using braided wire, make the same arrangement, using leader sleeves to make the extensions to hold snelled hooks and the line tie and sinker snap attachments. Single-strand wire can be used by making tight or Haywire Twists for the various attachments.

Skirted trolling rigs. Nylon monofilament, braided wire, or single-strand wire can be used for skirted trolling rigs, which are also called hoochies. To provide weight and to keep the vinyl skirt from sliding down the rig, attach a lead sinker to a wire form, with an eye at each end of the wire, the rear eye fastened to a short bead chain leader ending with a single hook.

Slip the vinyl skirt over the end of the wire so that it snugs down on the egg sinker. The bead chain leader and rig must be long enough for the bend of the hook to meet the tail of the vinyl skirt. Another solution is to connect the hook to the wire or mono, thread tri-beads (available at craft shops) onto the line, and then add an egg sinker and the vinyl trolling skirt. Finish with a split ring or loop for attaching to the line.

Fishfinder rig. These surf rigs (which are also good for baitfishing for carp and catfish) are basically a sliding sleeve over the line, with a sinker attached to the sleeve. They can be easily made using nothing more than a large snap swivel and no sleeve, or using a large swivel through holes drilled in the side of a thin PVC sleeve (available at hobby shops), with the split ring holding a large snap-swivel rig.

A simple skirted trolling rig, sometimes called a hoochy, can be made from a vinyl or plastic squid body attached to a heavy leader.

See: Lure; Lure Modifying/Reparing; Lure Tuning.

LURE MODIFYING/REPAIRING

Anglers who use lures eventually accumulate a large collection that represents a sizable investment. Maintaining that investment requires only common sense and a few minutes of care periodically. Many lures that survive repeated fishing efforts are still serviceable with a little bit of care, and others can be made more useful or effective through various modifications. Most lure modifying or repairing is easily done on nonfishing days or during the off-season or, most often, slack times while fishing.

Of course, many lure-modifying activities take place on the water, usually in response to existing circumstances or as a way to stimulate a response by targeted species that are proving evasive. Making existing lures more attractive to fish is the ultimate purpose of all lure-modifying activities, and the ability to modify some lures on the spot to suit fishing conditions is an advantage that shouldn't be overlooked.

Whenever you modify a lure, you're always trying to figure out how to make it look or work better, and you are inevitably pondering the bigger question of what makes any lure work. Whatever answer you get is bound to make you a better angler.

Naturally, many lures are certifiable fish catchers right out of the box and often need no modification to be productive. Some lures that are otherwise effective can be made even better by making certain changes. Others can benefit from alterations because they simply don't work right or because the circumstances dictate an alteration. Fortunately, lures of all types can be repaired, modified, or otherwise refurbished. Some repairs and modifications are specific to certain lures; others are common to all lures. A table of general suggestions for repairs and modifications is contained later in this section, while specific activities follow.

To help with any modifying and repairing efforts, it's a good idea to hold onto lure parts that can be used for modifying and repairing other lures in the future. Don't discard the hooks unless they're corroded or deformed. Retain the split rings, screws, old lips, etc. And when you have lures that don't work as is, hang onto the bodies if there's a chance you could dress up another lure with them or could resurrect them with some alterations.

Refinishing

Most lure refinishing is elective; anglers choose to take an existing lure and do something to give it a different look. That might be painting or polishing, or sprucing up the lure with a marker, tape, or glitter.

Deciding when to refinish a lure is subjective. Some anglers refinish a lure because the circumstances require a new look. Some anglers simply do a cosmetic touch-up on a lure that has seen heavy use. Obviously the painted finish on lures can become chipped, scratched, cracked, and damaged. This will vary with the lure, since some finishes adhere very well to certain lures but not to others. Paint chips off leadhead jigs, for example, relatively easily. Minor scratches and paint loss are not likely to be a problem in effectiveness, particularly for larger lures with more color on their bodies. However, some metal-bodied lures lose their appeal if they are tarnished, and they may need to be refinished to regain their luster.

Liquid painting. Liquid paints are used for most lure painting. The first step in this activity is proper preparation of the area to be finished. If possible, first remove all the hooks. This is easy on some lures, especially those with free-swinging hooks, and makes it safer to handle them. It is impossible with certain lures, like buzzbaits, spinnerbaits, some spinners, and fixed-hook spoons, but many of these have large hooks that are less dangerous than the small trebles of other lures.

Wash the lure in a warm soapy bath and scrub with an old toothbrush. Once clean and dry, examine the lure finish. If the paint is peeling and flaking, try to remove as much as possible with your thumbnail or a razor blade. Once this is done, or if it is not possible, roughen the finish with fine sandpaper or steel wool to provide some grip to the remaining finish so that the new coat stays on.

If some parts of the old finish are intact and others flake off, it might be difficult to repaint the lure without ending up with an uneven or mottled-looking surface. A possible solution is to paint the bare areas with white paint, let them cure, and roughen as described. Several coats might be necessary to build up the bare area to the level of the remaining paint.

When painting metal surfaces, such as spoons or spinner blades, scrub them with steel wool to slightly roughen the surface. If the surface is corroded, scrub it with steel wool and a powder abrasive cleanser and then clean and dry thoroughly. Paint it after masking any hooks, line ties, weedguards, or similar attachments.

Types of paints vary widely. One basic rule is to stick with sealers, undercoats, paints, and clear overcoats from the same manufacturer to avoid any possible chemical reaction between different paint formulations. The best paints are those that have a glossy finish. Types of paints can include enamel, lacquer, acrylic, epoxy, and powder. Of these, epoxies are the most durable, but they are often not available in small containers for hobby use. They are also two-part products that require mixing (just like the glues), but they may not be as shiny as other paints. Enamel, lacquer, acrylic, and similar paints are available in small containers from hobby and art supply stores and through tackle shops and mail-order companies. All of these are easily applied. Acrylics are especially good since they are bright, durable, and allow a water cleanup.

If you are painting new lures or lures in which all the paint has flaked off, you'll need to use a sealer or base coat first. This is particularly true with wooden plugs, which are porous, but it is important as a base for any lure. Sealers, labeled as such, are available for any of the aforementioned paints. In place of a sealer, or as a base coat over existing old paint, use white, since it will allow the brightness of overlying paints to come through. This is particularly important for fluorescent paints.

Application methods for sealers, base coats, and finish coats include dipping, brushing, and spraying.

Dipping. Dipping is ideal for those lures that are easy to handle, can be dipped into a paint container without affecting the rest of the lure, and can be hung up to dry. For example, dipping would be difficult with spinnerbaits or buzzbaits because you can't dip them without painting either the wire form or the hook. Lures that are good for dipping include topwater plugs, various swimming and diving plugs (with the hooks removed), jigs, and spoons. Dipping does require a container into which the entire lure (or the part to be painted) can be dipped. Hobby shops sell small 1/4-ounce paint containers that many lure makers like to use for painting lures, but the containers are too small to use for dipping anything but tiny jigs.

Thin paints, or paints thinned deliberately, are best for dipping because they are not as likely to cause runs and sags. You can dip one lure at a time or a whole rack of identically hung lures. To dip a rack of lures, you will need a trough or long pan to hold paint. Whether dipping a rack or one lure at a time, withdraw the lure(s) from the paint slowly so that excess paint can run off and drip back into the container. Hang the lures on a rack, and periodically blot the bottom with a paper towel or cotton-tipped stick to prevent an accumulation at this point.

Dipping is effective when you want an even application of paint in one or two colors. It is possible to make two-tone painted lures, such as a red head/white body topwater plug, by first dipping the body completely in white paint, letting it cure, then partially dipping it into red paint, letting it again cure, and finishing with a complete dip into a clear finish coat.

You can also dye some lures by dipping them, or parts of them, into a dye solution. Dyes are available in small jars and in various colors. Small lures can be dipped into them, but most often dyes are used with soft-bodied lures, particularly for coloring the tails of worms, grubs, and fish bodies.

Brushing. Brushing is best for spinnerbaits, buzzbaits, blades and bodies on spinners, and similar lures where dipping isn't possible. It also works for adding additional colors, such as contrasting bars, to a lure. Brushing will not yield professional results, but the fish usually don't care. Some paints have built-in brushes or felt tips in the caps, although disposable brushes are also ideal for this. When brushing, fill the brush with paint and then

L

brush over the prepared unpainted area. Avoid repeated brush strokes over the same area, particularly with fast-drying paints such as some acrylics. Hang up the lure to dry.

On-the-water paint brushing can be accomplished by applying colored nail polish to a lure. You can easily add an eye, dots, diamonds, stripes, or bars, and the polish dries quickly. Clear nail polish makes a good finishing coat for other painting.

Spraying. Spraying will create beautiful results in terms of color shading, patterns, scale finishes, and similar effects, but on the small area of lures it does waste paint. Canned aerosol enamels and lacquers are typically used for spraying, although other paints can be used with professional-style airbrush equipment. Airbrush equipment is relatively expensive and requires extensive cleanup after painting.

Careful spraying, whether with canned paints or airbrush equipment, requires quick passes of the sprayer to paint the surface without leaving a heavy buildup of paint that will run. Spraying is best for those lures that do not have any attachments or parts that should remain unpainted. Plug bodies are ideal for this. Jigs, spinnerbait bodies, and buzzbait bodies all should have the wire or hooks masked (use masking tape) to protect from the spray paint.

Easy professional-looking results can be obtained by spray painting a base coat of white and then coating the belly of a crankbait yellow, the side silver, and the back black. The result is a professional-looking lure, with the paint colors gradually feathering from one to the other.

Variations require more time but are possible. One is to spray a base coat of paint on the sides, wrap the side with scale netting (available in fabric shops as tulle), and spray a second color to give a scale effect. Templates are easy ways to make individual patterns. To get a smooth finish, don't allow the template to touch the lure. Possibilities include spraying through a coarse comb for a vertical-bar perchlike finish and making templates that will allow you to spray spots, gill plate shapes, stripes, and similar patterns.

To avoid painting anything other than the lure, spray outside on a calm day or spray into a painting box made from a large cardboard carton, open on one side only and lined with cotton batting, sponges, or strips of cloth to catch excess paint.

Keep in mind that, in a pinch, you can spray paint a lure with fast-drying paint and use it within minutes to catch fish. Anglers have literally used an aerosol can of paint (especially fluorescent yellows and ranges) to quick-color a lure that is the right size, shape, and action for the fishing but not the right color. Being careful not to get the paint on your clothing or equipment, you can grip the lip with a pair of needle-nosed pliers, hold the can nozzle the right distance from the lure, and make a fast pass over both sides (remove the hooks first to keep paint off them). Give it a few minutes to air dry, add an eye with a marking pen if desired, put the hooks back on, and you're set. This may not look very professional, but it often doesn't have to. If you like what you've got, then later put a clear finish coat over it to preserve it.

Whether you use one or all of these painting methods, there is no end to the possibilities that you can create. Making a lure that is very lifelike or unique may have the benefit of giving the user more confidence; it also may help because it is unlike the commonly used lures or colors often presented by other anglers. Be careful about getting carried away, however. Remember that forage fish all have a light belly, dark back, and red gills, and are not completely dark or light. The color of the water and the habits of the target species will greatly determine the alterations you make. Lures that will be worked fairly quickly, for example, generally need mostly the proper shading rather than a lot of detail. These might need only a stripe along the side instead of more intricate patterning, including a representation of eyes and gills. However, a lure that is worked more slowly, especially in clear water where the fish's vision is accentuated, may benefit from the extra detailing.

Powder painting. Powder paints allow you to put durable hard finishes on lures easily and quickly using a completely different painting process. Because the lure must be heated in a flame, powder painting is possible only with metal lures, such as spinnerbaits, buzzbaits, spinner blades and bodies, jigs, weedless spoons, jigging spoons, and blade baits.

In all cases, the lure must be heated and then dipped into the powder paint. This is a powder, not liquid, and was originally designed for commercial electrostatic painting of appliances, machinery, and other objects where paint is deposited by electric charge and then baked on.

In appearance, the paint is almost like a talcum powder, but it comes in colors so that various colors or color combinations are possible. The advantages are that the paint is relatively cheap, there is no waste or shelf life or storage problems, and it "dries" instantly. And as with liquid paints, you can mix colors. Yellow and blue can be mixed to make green, white and red to make pink, red and blue to make purple, etc. Powder paint is readily available from some tackle shops and many mail-order companies.

Heat sources can include a cigarette lighter, alcohol lamp, propane torch, or electric heat gun (like the kind used to strip paint). The painting steps are simple. Hold the lure with pliers in a heat source for a few seconds until hot. Then rapidly dip the lure into the powder paint, completely cover it with paint, and remove it from the powder. Done properly, the chalky-looking powder paint will turn glossy and smooth, looking like the best possible paint job. As soon as the lure cools, it is ready to fish or to finish if other assembly or additions are required.

Frog-imitating lures have been around a long time; in 1910 Shakespeare sold the Rhodes Mechanical Swimming Frog, with rubber body and flexible kick-back legs.

The right amount of heat is the key to powder paint, and experimentation is a must. Controlling the heat is particularly important with leadhead lures, since too much heat will melt the head, ruining the lure. Try for a few seconds first and check the results. If the paint does not adhere completely, reheat and try again. This is possible at least several times. If the paint covers completely, but looks powderlike rather than glossy, wave the lure through the heat to melt the powder and remove it from the flame while it glosses over. To do this, you must have a "clean" flame; this procedure will not work with a cigarette lighter because carbon will build up on the lure.

Don't overheat the lure. Overheating causes the paint to build up too much or to bubble. If the paint fills the line tie (hook eye) of the lure, as often happens with jigs, use a heated wire to clean out the paint. Once the paint is cool, you can also drill out the paint with a small drill bit or hobby rotary tool.

It is also possible to make several colors, such as a jig head first dipped in yellow and followed by a partial dipping in red, to make a yellow body/red head lure. Glitter can be added to the lure after the first coat and then protected with a clear coat. The clear coat looks powdery white, but after melting, it cures to a clear finish.

For even more durability, bake the finished lures in a standard kitchen oven. Hang the lures on a wire rack, make sure that they do not touch, and bake for 10 to 15 minutes at 250° to 300°F. Hang blades for spinners, buzzbaits, spinnerbaits, and metal lure parts on S-shaped hangers made from paper clips.

Powder paints are obviously best on a new lure that doesn't have old paint on it, but these paints can be used to repaint an older lure if excess paint is removed and if the flame is not so hot that the heat burns the old paint. For best results with an old lure, remove the old paint completely by using tools or paint remover and then repaint.

Polishing. The metal surfaces of spoons, spinner blades, and the like can become tarnished or corroded, but you can restore the original finish with polishing. For badly corroded lures, first polish with steel wool and then with abrasive cleanser. Metal polishes such as silver polish and brass polish also work well. If the surface is still discolored, consider painting with metallic-finish paints.

Glitter coating. A simple way to spruce up a worn-out looking lure is to coat it with glitter. In the past, only coarse-style glitter was available, but today's lure refinishing kits use microglitter, which is far more attractive. Glitter is also available from craft stores.

There are two ways to use glitter. One is to coat the lure with a clear finish coat and, while it is wet, shake on glitter. You can use several different colors of glitter, such as silver on the belly of a crankbait, red on the sides, and black on the back. Once the initial coat cures, add a second clear coat to protect the glitter finish.

A second method is to mix glitter into a liquid clear coat of thin epoxy finish or urethane; use a disposable brush to paint the lure body with this mix. You can, of course, put glitter only on certain parts of a lure—sides, vertical bars, or horizontal stripes—using either of these two methods.

Taping. Adhesive tape also provides refinishing possibilities for lures. Tapes is best used on flat or almost flat lures such as spoons and spinner blades; however, with proper trimming and application, it can be placed on almost any lure.

Tape is available in sheets for customizing, in various small precut patterns and shapes, and in rolls. There is a wide range of plain, glitter, metallic, and prism colors. Tape can be used for the entire side of a lure body, for strips shaped like a bar, or for smaller designs that are simply meant to add a dash of pizzazz.

The key to the most efficient use of tape is to first cut it into the proper shape and then apply it to a dry, warm lure. If you are applying tape outside in cold weather, tuck the tape and the lure in your pocket or under your armpit for a few minutes to warm them up; you'll get better adhesion this way. When you're using tape at home, you can cut with scissors; onboard a boat, you may have to make due with utility scissors on an all-purpose tool or even a sharp knife. Keep in mind that the rounded shape of plugs makes them difficult to refinish with tape; smaller angled strips are best here, and the edges will probably peel up in time. To keep the tape from peeling off on any lure, consider covering it with a clear finish coat.

Marking. Permanent felt-tip markers are also handy for refinishing or modifying lures. Various designs and patterns can be marked on any lure. The result will not be glossy like paint, but this is a quick easy way to change lures. There are wide- and thin-point markers, and the style depends on the lure and detailing necessary.

A red or black broad-tip marker may be all that you need to make some fish-catching adjustments to plugs, including eyes, gills, stripes, and bars. However, a light color can be used to make a plug belly more pronounced. Most people use markers to detail hard lures, but markers can also be used on soft plastics. Here, a finer point is usually better. With soft plastics, you can use a marker to work on the body, tail, claws, or legs. A little bit of orange or chartreuse, for example, on the extremities of some soft plastics can be very effective.

Additions

One of the most important ways to alter the appearance of lures is to add something to them. The addition might be a hook, rattle, skirts, or eyes. Naturally the appropriate addition depends on the type of lure and the target fish. Lures used for bass and pike are probably the most appropriate for additions.

Eyes. Eyes that wear or come off lures, or lures

that don't have eyes, can be improved with the addition of eyes or by changing to larger, more visible eyes. General theory suggests that eyes are an important triggering signal to fish when they are attacking prey and that large visible eyes on lures, particularly those simulating baitfish, are important.

You can add eyes to lures in a number of ways, but the most common is simply by painting. Eyes can be painted on any lure. This is easily done by making small eye-painting tools from nails or pins having different-size heads. Stick a short length of dowel into the end of the pin or nail to make a handle. Touch the head of the tool to the surface of the paint; do not submerge it. Then touch the tool to the lure where you want the eye. Two- and three-tone eyes are possible by using tools with three different head sizes, allowing each coat to dry before applying the next. Typically colors are light for the outer ring and dark or contrasting for the pupil. You can also paint eyes on lures by using a marking pen or a brush.

Another option is to use ready-made eyes that can be applied onto lures. Craft stores are good sources, and you can buy stemmed plastic eyes there. Select an appropriate size, and apply the eyes by removing the stem with side-cutting wire cutters and gluing the eyes in place with epoxy or a "super" glue. Don't cut off the stem, however, if you plan to apply the eye by drilling a hole in the lure for the stem.

Perhaps an easier method is to use adhesive tape eyes, which are made in various sizes and colors and are very easy to apply. For a different look, you can glue on doll's eyes, which have movable pupils, most of which are black although some are colored. The various eye types are available from tackle shops, mail-order companies, and craft stores.

Skirts. Skirts of rubber, silicone, LumaFlex, and similar synthetic materials are easily added or replaced on spinnerbaits, buzzbaits, and jigs by taking off the old one and slipping on a replacement. Many of the skirted lures have a collar, with a small bump at the tail end to keep the skirt from sliding off. If the fit is tight, lubricate it with saliva. If you wish the skirt to be permanent and it has a tendency to slip, add a little CA glue once the skirt is in place.

Tying new or replacement hair skirts is similar to, but simpler than, tying flies. To do this for new lures or when repairing old lures, begin by holding the lure or lure part in a vise or in vise-grip pliers held in a bench vise. Dressings are easily tied on hooks for spinners and other lures, jig heads, spinnerbaits, and buzzbaits. Use size 2/0 thread for small hooks and heads, size A for medium-size lures, and size D for large heads and dressings.

Begin by wrapping the thread around the jig collar or hook shank and then wrapping over the thread to secure it in place. Make a half dozen more wraps, and clip the excess thread. Now tie down a bunch of tail material. Tail or dressing material can include hackle, marabou, bucktail, calftail, synthetics, stranded flash material, or a mix of these in any color combination. Place each bunch on in turn, wrap tightly, and clip excess material in front of the wrap. Once all the material is wrapped in place and clipped, continue wrapping; tie off with a whip finish. This is the same as the finish used to whip the end of a rope and consists of wraps around the standing thread and the dressed area that are finally pulled tight after a half dozen wraps. Do two of these, clip the thread, and then protect with a coating of paint, clear nail polish, fly tying head cement, or epoxy rod finish. When using the thick epoxy, rotate until the epoxy cures to prevent sags and drips.

Trailer/stinger hooks. Trailer hooks, also known as stingers, are often added to spinnerbaits and buzzbaits, and sometimes to spoons and spinners. Special trailer/stinger hooks are made for this and are usually labeled as spinnerbait hooks because of their prevalent use on these lures. Ideally, they must have an eye that is large enough to slip over the existing hook.

There are several ways to hold the trailer hook in position on the main hook, the primary one being to place a small piece of soft vinyl or rubber tubing over the eye of the stinger hook and then to run the point of the main hook through the tube-cover trailer hook eye. The tubing keeps the stinger hook in proper alignment on the bend of the main hook. Often such tubing is included in packs of stinger hooks, but it can be obtained from medical supply stores or from pet stores that sell aquarium supplies (small-diameter filter tubing) and cut to length. An alternative is to use a button of discarded soft plastic worm in place of the tubing. Slip the button over the eye of the stinger hook; then slip this onto the end of the main hook, as with the tubing.

Another option is to attach a soft grub or worm as a trailer and attractor in the style of a Texas rig. Bury the eye of the hook into the head of the worm,

Changing hooks and blades and adding trailers are among the simplest lure modifications.

and slip the trailer/stinger combination onto the main hook. The Texas rig also keeps the stinger hook weedless.

Soft bodies added to main lure hooks are common trailers and are often an important element of a given lure's fish-catching effectiveness. Single and twin curl-tail trailers, for example, are staple additions to spinnerbaits, and many anglers will not fish these lures without such a trailer. Choose one that is proportionate to the size and weight of the main lure. Snipping off a portion of the forward section of the soft body may keep it the right length and distance for the lure.

These bodies, as well as chunk or strip pork trailers and split-tail eels, provide more action to the lure and also more bulk, which translates into weight for casting distance and into buoyancy for a slower rate of fall. Using soft trailers provides the option of either matching the lure color or offering a complementary or contrasting one.

Trailer blades. Many lures can benefit from placing a spinning blade as a caboose. Actually it may look more like a fast-moving tail. A rapidly spinning blade certainly offers flash and sometimes a visible attack marker for predators. Various sizes and styles of blades can be used to enhance some lures. Small Indiana or Colorado blades, for example, are good on smaller lures, including little jigs and spoons. Larger models are effective behind a trolling lure, especially the metal-headed lures preferred for high-speed offshore use. As with other applications, willowleaf styles tend to work best for fast use, and rounder styles for slower fishing.

No matter what type you employ, it's necessary to make a good connection via a ball bearing swivel. The spinner blade does no good if it doesn't spin easily. You need a ball bearing with a ring large enough to fit over the barb of the hook and onto the bend; you can put a small piece of tubing (as mentioned with trailer hooks) over the swivel ring before putting it on the hook, which will keep the blade in place and away from other parts of the lure.

On some spoons, particularly weedless models, you can add a spoon on an in-line wire form with or without beads, and attach this to the front of the lure. The spinner revolves while the spoon wobbles, and the spinner produces extra action even when the lure retrieve is stopped and the lure sinks. The combined product has some flash as well as the traditional wobble, and it may be more productive than the unaltered version.

Rattles. Rattles can be added to virtually all lures. Plain cylindrical "worm" rattles are available in different sizes and are made of glass, plastic, and aluminum. Some are available with extra sleeves and eyes for attaching to line and lures.

Affixing the rattle to the lure is the main trick. Using a rattle with a soft lure is easy, since the rattle can be inserted into the body of the lure. It is possible to glue rattles into holes drilled in the bodies of plugs or crosswise on the lips of plugs. It is also possible to use a dab of silicone sealant for this purpose, as well as electrical tape.

A rattle can be attached to the hooks of most lures, but it must be small in comparison to the hook in order to avoid impeding the gap, the hooking ability, or the action. You can also fix a rattle to topwater plugs, crankbaits, lipless plugs, and jigging spoons, and to upper and lower spinnerbait arms, buzzbait arms, weedless spoon weedguards, spinner bodies, jig hooks (under the skirts), and the wire rigging of skirted trolling lures. However you choose to attach the rattle, make sure you test the lure before fishing it to see that the action is proper. Making an addition can affect the swimming action of some lures; generally, the larger the lip on a plug, the less affect it will have.

Light sticks. Small chemiluminescent light sticks—the glow-in-the-dark tubes that are often used around Halloween—can be used to add a glowing presence to some lures. Like rattles, they can be attached to various lures, including the body of some spinners, the blades of some spoons, and inside certain hard and soft lures. A few lures are made with holders to grab these sticks, but most need some form of temporary attachment that doesn't hinder the lure action. Unlike a rattle, the light stick has to be bent and shaken to activate the chemicals inside, which produce a bright light for a full day or longer; the stick has to be replaced when it has lost its glow.

Plastic-bodied plugs can be modified to incorporate a small ($1^1/_2$ inches or less) light stick, producing an effect that few commercially made lures can offer. These sticks fit snugly inside many plugs without affecting the action. To install a light stick, drill a hole that is the same diameter as the light stick and then insert the activated stick into the body.

This modification can be made to many plastic plugs, especially diving plugs, crankbaits, and minnow imitators. You may have to sacrifice a lure or two when you first experiment because you need to determine the best place and angle to drill the hole. Generally the best spot is on top at the rear, a location that has no adverse effect on the action or diving depth of most lures, in part because it doesn't promote water resistance.

If you hold the plug up to a very bright light, you can usually see the interior configuration—plastic-bodied plugs are essentially hollow—and approximate the best place to drill. The hole should be made at an angle so that the top of the light stick will just barely protrude. Although not absolutely necessary, putting the plug in a block vise to secure it may help you drill a more precise hole. Use a drill bit that conforms to the size of the light stick; the stick should fit snugly into the lure. With the hole made, don't push the light stick completely into the cavity of the lure; it is very difficult to extricate. If it does go in too far, enlarge the hole and impale the head of the stick with a sharp, strong needle to pull it out.

When you're ready to use one of these modified lures, activate the light stick and insert it into the plug. If the fit is tight, water might not seep into the cavity. If water does get in, it will make the lure heavier and the action of the lure may be affected; simply shake out the water. You can also seal the opening with silicone sealant. Dab the silicone around the top of the stick, give it a few minutes to harden, and you're set. When you want to replace the stick, peel off the sealant and pull out the stick. If the light stick is stuck in the hole, jab the point of a hook into the stick and pry it out.

Try translucent or light-colored plugs for this modification. Dark lures won't allow much of the light stick's glow to come through, and transparent lures may provide too much of a glow. You may want to scrape the paint off a dark plug; some have an undercoat of bone or light gray color, which gives a nice glowing effect. A possibility is to get a transparent plug and then apply a paint finish that will react well to the neon-green light of the stick.

Most light sticks, incidentally, are neon- or chartreuse-green in color, but they may be available in other colors, including red. These small light sticks can also be placed inside some soft-bodied lures like jerkbaits, adding a different dimension to them for night fishing.

Weights. Anglers have long been adding weight to lures for various purposes. Plugs, in particular, have been subject to such modifications, either to increase their overall heft for distance achievement or more likely to affect their balance or buoyancy. Soft plastic lures are also modified with weight to make them sink faster or to swim in a certain way when retrieved.

Plugs. With plugs, the main objective today in adding weight is to affect their buoyancy by making them sink, usually slowly, or suspend once they've been retrieved to a given level. The idea is to keep them in the strike zone longer and prevent them from immediately bobbing up toward the surface. Most floating/diving plugs float at rest, dive when retrieved, and then fairly quickly bob back toward the surface when the retrieve is halted; neutral-buoyancy lures, however, remain at their diving depth or rise or sink very slowly, behavior that imitates the way that baitfish stay at a particular level when they stop moving.

Anglers have put lead wire and split shot on their hooks to try to achieve neutral buoyancy, and this method does occasionally work. However, there is a tendency for any object on the bare hooks of plugs to adversely affect the action of that lure, so this is not a good solution for most plugs.

When fewer suspending lures were available from manufacturers, anglers strategically inserted small weights into wooden floating/diving plugs to achieve neutral buoyancy. This is still possible, but it is a somewhat delicate operation that requires getting things just right to achieve desired results without impairing lure action. Most people prefer to buy plugs that suspend or to use pliable adhesive weights.

Judiciously adding adhesive pieces of lead to floating lures can make them rise slowly or suspend.

You can turn ordinary small wooden crankbaits and small- to medium-size wooden minnow-imitating plugs into neutral-buoyancy lures. Take some BBs or similar-size split shot and a short length of thin, but relatively stiff, wire. Put the lure on its side and, using a drill bit the size of the shot, drill a hole in the lure's midline between one-third and one-half the way down from the head, approximately in the location of the balance point of the lure. Place several shot side by side in the hole, pinch them with pliers so they don't stick out the side, and test for buoyancy. You may need to drill another hole and insert more shot. The object is to get the lure to barely rise (or to not rise at all) when submerged. When you're close to achieving this, punch the wire crossways through the lure. Test for buoyancy again, and punch another piece of wire through if necessary. Snip the wire so that it is just shorter than the width of the plug, and use a pick to push the wire inside the lure. Let the lure dry overnight; then give it several coats of lacquer. You might want to put a little quick-drying epoxy in the hole before inserting the shot.

Adding interior weight is useful only for wooden lures, and only for some types and styles. It cannot be done on all wooden lures. However, virtually any plug that is used under the surface, whether a shallow runner or deep diver, plastic or wood, can be modified with the application of exterior adhesive weight. This kind of weight doesn't ruin the lure and requires just a little bit of experimenting.

These adhesive weights, which are known as SuspenDots or SuspenStrips, are placed on dry floating/diving plugs little by little and tested in the water until the proper effect is achieved. They can be removed at any time if the angler no longer wishes the lure to sink or suspend.

The process starts by adding either strips or dots to the lure. The best placement locations, especially for large-bodied plugs like crankbaits, is either beneath the bill or on the forward section of the belly near the front hook hanger. You have to make sure that the location is the pivot point of the lure, so that the action isn't affected. The adhesive dots and strips (one strip equals two and a half dots in weight) are exact increments of weight, so once you have established the proper number and placement of these on a given lure, you can be reasonably sure that the weight will be the same for identical lures. And you can add parts of these by cutting them.

You can also alter the suspending angle of a given lure according to adhesive placement. To make it suspend more vertically (which might be desirable in timber cover), focus the weight on the front of the plug; to make it suspend horizontally, place it farther along the belly. You can also add weight to the tail section of a lure for the purpose of making it cast better. Some plugs, when cast with light line or in windy conditions, tend to tumble because they're light in the tail, which can cause the line to catch on the hooks. Putting some weight on the tail can make such a lure easier to cast and less troublesome.

Soft lures. The major addition or modification to soft lures is either coloring (by dipping) or adding rattles. However, large soft lures like heavy-body worms and jerkbaits may be modified by putting some weight into them. This is most appropriate for jerkbaits, some of which are packaged with stick- or nail-like lead weights that can be split into different lengths and inserted into the soft lure.

A good tactic is to weight these soft lures in the forward part of the tail section (the forward part of the rear half). The weight changes the retrieval motion so that a quick snap rather than a short sweep is used to work them. But it also lets the lure drop backward when slack is given, rather than float in the same spot or settle down, an action that can trigger otherwise reluctant fish to strike.

The weights shouldn't be placed too far back in the tail, or the movement of the lure will be adversely affected; keep the weights at least $1^1/_2$ inches from the end of the tail. From two to four weights can be added for 6- to 8-inch jerkbaits, usually being placed just aft of the middle. The number will vary with the type of soft lure; those with more dense tails can accommodate extra weight. For deep water, use more; for shallow water, use less. For jerkbaits with a thick belly section, insert the stick weight from the belly straight up and one-half to two-thirds of the way toward the back. For jerkbaits with a thin belly section, insert the stick weight from the back straight down and halfway toward the belly. Snip the ends off so there is no protrusion from the soft plastic.

You can also modify soft jerkbaits by putting a short piece of flexible wire into the head and bending it so that, when retrieved, the lure keeps working to one side rather than darting to and fro, or regularly swims upward or downward when jerked.

Weedguards. The hooks of some lures can be made mostly or partially snag- and weed-free by making various modifications. Spinnerbaits, for example, may benefit from spanning a rubber band from the line tie eye to the hook barb. It is also possible to make the blade weedless by removing it, straightening the wire, adding 1 inch of the end of a clutch-type ballpoint pen (to serve as a shield over the swivel), and then reassembling the blade to the wire.

Most weedless adaptations to lures exist with these enhancements made as part of the original manufacturing, usually using wire or stiff nylon brushlike guards ahead of hook points and fabricated into the lure construction. Heavy jigs and casting spoons are the primary examples. Making existing nonweedless lures snag-free usually requires some workshop tinkering, using stainless steel wire, wrapping thread, and glue. It's difficult to work with multihooked lures and treble hooks, so single hooks lend themselves best to this modifying. The right wire size is important because the final weedguard needs to be strong enough to resist objects yet not impede hooksetting. In essence, this is accomplished by extending the wire from the hook eye to the hook point, aligning a short foot of the wire on the forward bottom of the hook shank, wrapping this tightly with thread, and applying glue to the finished wrap. For more information, *see: Weedguard.*

Lips/bills. Most plug lips are made of plastic and are molded or epoxied into the head of the plug so that they can't be removed. Perhaps you have some old lures sitting around that aren't being used; the parts might be useful on another type of lure, especially older models with metal screw-on lips. If you can locate any of these lips, or are able to purchase metal lips from component suppliers, you can make serviceable lures that have no lips, or repair lures that have lost lips.

For example, you may be able to take a surface stickbait that has a nice body but unimpressive action and make a good shallow-water wobbling plug out of it for bass fishing. For starters, you may need to remove the rear hair-covered treble hook and replace it with an undressed treble. Then, to make it swim, unscrew the small, curved metal lip from an old lure, center it on the stickbait under the head, and screw it on. The combination of a line tie at the nose and a new small lip causes the lure to wobble wide and dive only a few inches below the surface. Use it to fish just over the top of barely submerged vegetation.

Since the line-tie is not connected to the lip, you don't need to worry about the strength of the lip-holding screws. This is an especially important point, since there can be a lot of tension on the line-tie connection. Adding a metal lip or bill to a plug is generally best when the line-tie location is on the head of the lure.

Changes

Replacing hooks. Free-swinging hooks on lures are easily replaced when the originals become rusted or damaged or when you need to switch sizes, styles, or finishes.

Most hooks are easily replaced using split rings, which are commonly employed to attach the hooks to many lures, especially plugs and spoons. The easiest way to replace these hooks is with split-ring pliers, available in several styles and sizes, but always with a tooth at the end of one long jaw to open the split ring. The easiest one-step method of replacement is to open the split-ring with the pliers and then start the old hook onto the split-ring. Once there is enough room, add the eye of the replacement hook. Use the split-ring pliers to grip the ring as you work both hook eyes around the circumference of the ring. The advantage of this method is that you're removing the old ring and adding the new one in the same step, saving time and stress on the ring. If your efforts open the gap on the ring, it may no longer be serviceable for the strength of line you're using, so be attentive to the condition of the split ring; it can become a weak link between the rod and a fish.

If you're replacing treble hooks, note that, in addition to various sizes, styles, and finishes, they come in regular and short-shank lengths. Short-shank lengths can be used to adjust for the additional separation from the lure body caused by the addition of the split ring. Make sure that you choose the right type of treble for lure repairs and modifications.

You can also modify the way a plug works by using a different size of treble hook. Switching manufacturer-supplied treble hooks with slightly larger sizes is a common change. Putting large hooks on a floating minnow plug, for example, will change its buoyancy and may make it into a very slow sinker, or at least cause it to rise upward more slowly when twitched in a stop-and-go fashion beneath the surface. Putting a larger hook on the rear of some surface lures (chuggers and poppers, for example) may make the tail sit lower in the water, raising the head and producing sharper noises and creating more splash. And a larger treble on the front of some diving plugs may help them to run deeper.

Notice that the word "may" has been used with each of these examples. Many plugs, especially smaller ones, are very finely balanced by the manufacturer; putting just slightly larger, and thus heavier, hooks on them can alter the action. You have to test the lure in the water after each change to make sure that it will still have the right inherent action.

Some types of hooks, most notably the popular Siwash or salmon style hook, can be found in open-eye versions as well as closed eye. The open-eye type can be slipped over a split ring (or wire eye), and the eye can be closed by pressing with heavy-duty pliers. This avoids having to thread the hook through a split ring. If you're using double hooks, their parallel shanks make it easy to slide the hooks into place on a hook hanger.

Replacing hooks, especially using single hooks in place of trebles, is an overlooked facet of lure modification that has bearing not only on lure action and fishing success, but also on safety, conservation, and catch-and-release issues. For more information about this aspect of lure modifying, as well as on modifying and changing hooks in general, *see: Hook.*

Segmenting wooden plugs. Anglers constantly talk about the importance of lure action in catching fish; and to the human eye, the belly-dancing action of a jointed plug is about as good as it gets. The trouble is that jointed plugs are expensive for commercial lure manufacturers to make; it's almost like producing two lures. Jointed plugs are vastly outnumbered on retail store racks by unjointed or one-piece models. Fortunately, anglers who are handy with tools and have a home workshop can make single- or double-jointed modifications to otherwise good-running, commercially made one-piece wooden plugs.

One-piece wooden lures can be segmented by carefully cutting through the body with a fine-toothed hacksaw. Cut back all sides on an angle to allow for a wide wobble between segments, put a sufficiently long-stemmed wire loop into both segments, and use slow-curing two-part epoxy to anchor the wire. Unfortunately, you'll have to sacrifice a lure or two in order to get the hang of this. Make sure that the epoxy will hold at least 30 pounds of pulling strength, more if you're likely to use heavier line. You have to segment the lures in the right areas to achieve optimum swimming action; only experimentation will teach this. Give the exposed raw wood several coats of black (or matching) epoxy paint, and cover it with clear lacquer to seal the wood.

This segmenting is particularly worthwhile with small and large diving plugs as well as with minnow-

People handy with basic tools can make enticing, unique fish catchers by segmenting one-piece wooden lures.

Table of Common Modifications and Repairs

Lure Type	*Modifications*	*Repairs*
Plugs	Repaint Refinish with tape or marker Add eyes Add rattles Add split rings Add larger or different propellers Remove propeller(s) Shave, scrape, or trim plastic bills Sand popper lips	Replace hooks Repaint or refinish Reglue or refasten bills Replace damaged propellers
Casting/Trolling Spoons	Paint or add tape Add spinner blade to hook Add rattles Put tail on free-swinging hook Add plastic trailer to hook	Repaint or refinish Add line-tie split ring
Spinners	Repaint Add glitter or tape to blades Tie hair skirt to the hook Add rattles Cup blade with pliers to change speed	Reform wire or clevis Replace hooks Refinish blades As a final repair, cut the main wire shafts to assemble new spinners
Spinnerbaits	Repaint body and/or blades Add plastic trailer and/or stinger hook Add rattles Add crimp-on weight to hook shank for deep fishing Change blade(s) Change skirt; trim length to avoid short strikes Make hook/blade weedless Strengthen open line-tie by bending it into a loop	Repaint body or blades Replace blades Replace skirt
Buzzbaits	Repaint body or paint blades Replace skirt Add plastic trailer and/or stinger hook Add rattles	Repaint body Replace skirt Replace damaged blades
Jigs	Repaint body Add or improve eyes Replace skirt Add grub or worm trailer Glue a grub or shad body onto a bare hook leadhead Add stinger hook Add rattles	Repaint body Replace skirts
Weedless Spoons	Paint or add tape Add weight via rubber core sinker on lower arm or main hook Make weedless with soft plastic body on hook point Add plastic trailer to hook Add spinner blade to tail Add spinner on shaft to head Add rattles	Bend weedguard back into position Repaint or refinish
Jigging Spoons	Add spinner blade to tail Put tail on free-swinging hook Repaint or refinish Add rattles	Replace hook Repaint or refinish Add line-tie split ring
Lipless Crankbaits	Paint or refinish Replace blades Add rattles Add small rear spinner blade	Replace hooks Repaint
Soft Lures	Add rattles Add interior weight/light stick Dip into colored dye Rig tail hook on worm Rig with hooks, propeller, and beads	Trim excess parts, long arms, pincers Remelt and remold

imitating lures. Large-lipped plugs that create a lot of pulling resistance are especially forgiving when it comes to segmenting and usually allow a lot of leeway. The smaller the lip, the more critical it is to segment properly and the easier it is to go awry, especially if you need to retrieve or troll the lure quickly.

Adapting cut plugs. Cut-plug style trolling lures for salmon and steelhead fishing are different than a lot of other lures and pose a special problem for light-line users when the plug body separates from the rigging and rides up light line. Anglers using noodle rods or other light tackle with 2- through 6-pound test have a lot of strain on the line when a good fish is on, and the sliding of the cut plug up the line can nick the line and cause it to break. To avoid this, put a small tube in the middle of these lures, one that fits snugly so it won't separate from the plug. Some anglers use a piece of air-conditioner tubing wrapped in masking tape; others use a glass insert and ream the hole in the head of the plug to a size that will accommodate the insert.

When using jointed-style cut plugs, try putting a split ring between the joints to give the lure a wilder wobble. However, if you do this, be sure that the split ring is strong enough to take heavy strain.

Remelting soft plastics. Rather than discarding old soft plastic lures, you can save and remelt them to make new lures *(see: lure making).* In addition to getting more mileage out of these, remelting has the advantage of helping to keep these long-lasting plastics out of the environment.

Save old soft plastics and sort them by color. If a lure has several colors in it, cut and separate the parts by color. About once a year, melt down each color separately in an old cooking pan, using a very low heat to prevent burning (to avoid breathing in fumes, consider wearing a nose and mouth mask). The molten soft plastic can then be used to fill soft plastic lure cavities to make new lures, or poured into containers (like old plastic ice cube trays) to make "ingots" of colored soft plastic that can be melted down later for making new lures.

See: Buzzbait; Jig; Lure; Lure Making; Plug; Spinner; Spinnerbait; Spoon.

LURE RETRIEVER

A device used to free a lure snagged in deep water.

See: Unsnagging.

LURE STORAGE

There are a host of versatile ways to store terminal tackle. Traditional portable storage systems evolved from wooden to metal to rigid plastic boxlike containers with pivoting, compartmented trays. They are known as tackle boxes, and plastic models are still available today. However, the realm of items in which to hold tackle has vastly expanded to a potpourri of storage systems, many suited to specialized applications, and with an accent on individual traylike plastic utility boxes of varying size stored within soft-sided carriers or satchels.

Plastic boxes are by far the most popular today because they are easy to care for and come in a great range of designs. However, a few metal boxes, particularly small, pocket-size aluminum models used to store flies, can still be found, and even some wooden ones. Leather, suede, nylon, and cloth tackle satchels or wallets are also in use, as well as flexible, foldable tackle systems made of dense sailcloth with compartments covered by vinyl. For all but a relatively few anglers (those with big offshore boats and plenty of space), the one common denominator in tackle storage is portability. Most tackle boxes also have in common something that wasn't available with older boxes: movable compartment dividers that allow you to fashion the number and size of storage compartments to suit your needs.

Tackle boxes. The traditional style of tackle box comes in trunk, hip roof, and drawer configurations. A trunk box has one or more trays that pivot up and back together to reveal a large open well at the bottom of the box. These were once the standard but are now rare, partly because the support brackets lacked durability. Hip roof boxes are similar, though they have two sets of trays that open out to face each other; they are also less common today, though more prevalent than the trunk box. The drawer box is the most popular style among larger boxes and has trays that slide out rather than pivot on a bracket; this type usually has more compartments for storage than trunk or hip roof designs and may allow for bulk storage in bottom or top wells.

The type of box to use largely depends on the amount and size of objects that you need to store. Typically most anglers outgrow small or intermediate boxes and purchase more boxes or larger ones as they accumulate tackle and/or their fishing interests expand. Many people who do a lot of angling and/

This display represents some of the box, tray, and satchel possibilities for lure storage.

or who fish for various species keep several boxes or storage systems, often organized by lure types or tackle-by-species.

Double-sided plastic tackle boxes with see-through lids were very popular in the late 1980s and early 1990s, and still have devotees. Some have an over/under tray arrangement in which one or two latches (preferably two) open to reveal a lower storage well; only the upper tray has a see-through lid. Other versions are accessed from the top and bottom via separate latches. These boxes have see-through lids on both sides, which have a tendency to become scratched and cracked or broken more so than the over/under model. Both styles have movable compartments, hold a surprising amount of gear, and can be readily stowed or stacked on top of one another. Some boxes are geared toward specific types of storage needs, such as big lures, and possess features (a rack to hold spinnerbaits, for example) that accommodate this. Compartments are usually wormproof, which means that soft lures will not disintegrate in them; older plastic boxes caused the components of soft-plastic lures to break down, and the lures became unusable blobs.

When you're considering the purchase of a rigid tackle box such as these, check to see whether the box is watertight and has channeling to prevent water from entering the interior, and whether the latches are strong and allow snug closure. Some boxes are designed to prevent accidental spillage (even tipping) in case the latch is left open and the box picked up. Look for a good-quality hinge-pin arrangement in the back rather than one that is part of the molded box; the hinge-pin will last longer. A good handle is critical, too. Large handles aid in carrying and exchanging, but if they stick out too much from the box, they may get in the way. A recessed handle is desirable where boxes will be stacked or objects placed on top of them.

Utility boxes and soft carriers. The biggest change in tackle storage over the past decade has been a trend toward use of opaque-see-through utility boxes of various sizes, stored in soft-sided carriers. These lightweight utility boxes are handleless one-level polypropylene trays, usually with movable compartments, with varying exterior and depth dimensions. Anglers may purchase a good quantity of these, store items by category or application needs, and mix and match boxes in the carriers as their situations require.

Soft carriers, called bags and satchels by some, exist in all types of configurations to accommodate these boxes. The better models are made of waterproof ripstop nylon, and some have a waterproof bottom; others are water resistant. They have zippered access, with front or top tray loading, and most have a shoulder strap as well as top handle. The amount of terminal gear and the number of lures that can be stored in some models is very impressive, especially those with side compartments for small trays and pouches or holders for tools and spools and other miscellaneous items.

Other storage. Not all storage is as formal as a large tackle box or satchel-utility box system. Wading anglers who are mobile need something that can be worn instead of toted. A fishing vest is a multipocketed and compartmented tackle storage system that is worn over shirt or jacket and predominantly used by flycasters and river and stream anglers. Full-length versions are standard, but shorter models are used by deep-water waders and float-tube anglers. Both have many pockets, some designed especially to hold specific items (reel spool or sunglasses), and are intended for the storage of many small items; they even include a pouch in the back for small fish. Alternatives to vests are rigid chest boxes, soft chest packs, and soft fanny packs, which may not hold as much but are the utmost in light portability.

See: Vest, Fishing.

LURE TUNING

See: Tuning Lures.

LUXEMBOURG

This small country in western Europe is bounded by France, Belgium, and Germany. At 2,586 square kilometers it is smaller than the state of Rhode Island, and is largely a plateau comprising the upper basins of the Sauer (Sûre) and Alzette Rivers. Although tourism is important to the country, Luxembourg attracts relatively few visiting anglers, and its modest fisheries resources are highly regulated and similar to those in larger adjoining countries with more numerous and extensive watercourses.

Brown trout, grayling, pike, and various coarse species inhabit most of the rivers of Luxembourg, as well as its small ponds and reservoirs. Large pike reportedly exist in reservoirs along the upper Sauer, as do trout and charr.

Ponds in many villages and towns are accessible to anglers who purchase a permit, and a state license provides fishing access to the public water along the middle Sauer between the mouth of the Alzette River at Ettelbruck and the mouth of the Our at Wallendorf, Germany. Regulations vary with respect to seasons, methods, and equipment for both public and private waters.

M

MACHACA *Brycon guatemalensis.*
The machaca is a member of the Brycon genus of the Characidae family, which has some 800 species, most occurring in Central and South America.

The machaca inhabits lakes and streams in southern Mexico, Honduras, Nicaragua, Costa Rica, and Panama, and possibly in other Central American countries. It is mainly herbivorous as an adult but is caught on small plugs and jigs by anglers. Like most characins, it is equipped with an adipose fin, and it is silvery overall and has a small mouth. The common catch is 1-pounder, but this fish often reaches several pounds in weight. The all-tackle world record is a $9^1/_2$-pound Costa Rican fish. In general body shape and appearance, it is similar to a fellow Brycon, the matrincha *(see)* of Brazil. More than one species may be called by this name.

MACKEREL
Mackerel are members of the Scombridae family, which includes tuna *(see)* and numbers some 50 species in 15 genera.

Mackerel and tuna are both mainly schooling fish of the open sea. They provide sport virtually wherever they are found, and they contribute significantly to commercial fisheries, because they are good to eat. And all are good fighters as well; larger mackerel can rip line from a reel with tremendous speed, and some even take to the air on occasion.

Like tuna, mackerel are especially streamlined. The body is literally a spindle, with a pointed head and a much-tapered tail. The large caudal fin is lunate (crescent-shaped). Mackerel are much smaller than tuna overall, but they are just as speedy, displaying swift attacking speeds. Some of these fish have slots into which their spinous dorsal fins fit; this adaptation further reduces friction and enhances their speed. The spiny and soft-rayed dorsal fins are separate, and the soft-rayed dorsal fin is matched in size and shape by the anal fin directly beneath it. Following each fin is a series of finlets, the number varying with the species. In all species, the scales are extremely small or lacking. Most tuna and mackerel are ocean blue or greenish on the back, grading to a silvery shade on the sides and the belly. Some notable exceptions do occur, however.

Angling techniques for mackerel vary to some extent with locations and species. Trolling rigged baits and lures, and fishing baits from a drifting or anchored boat, are predominant methods. Casting plays a minor role, and then typically when chumming attracts the fish close to a boat. Surf and shore fishing are seldom productive, except for a few smaller coastal species.

See: Kawakawa; Mackerel, Atlantic; Mackerel, Cero; Mackerel, Chub; Mackerel, Frigate; Mackerel, King; Mackerel, Narrowbarred; Mackerel, Pacific Jack; Mackerel, Pacific Sierra; Mackerel, Spanish; Offshore Fishing; Wahoo.

MACKEREL, ATLANTIC *Scomber scombrus.*
Other names—mackerel, common mackerel, Boston mackerel; Arabic: *scomber;* Danish: *almin- delige, makrel;* Dutch: *gewone makrel;* French: *maquereau;* German: *makrele;* Italian: *lacerta, macarello;* Japanese: *hirasaba, marusaba;* Norwegian: *makrell;* Portuguese: *cavalla;* Spanish: *caballa;* Swedish: *makrill;* Turkish: *uskumru.*

Like other members of the Scombridae family, the Atlantic mackerel is a fast-swimming, school-

A string of Atlantic mackerel, caught on a multihook rig, from Long Island Sound, New York.

Atlantic Mackerel

ing, pelagic species that garners both significant recreational and commercial interest. It is known as a feast-or-famine fish; sometimes it is almost completely absent, and at other times it is plentiful in swarming schools. A delicious fish with an abundance of protein, vitamins, and minerals, it has a pleasing oil content. The flesh is firm-textured with a distinctive, savory flavor. Mackerel are available in markets whole or filleted, usually fresh but sometimes frozen, and smoked or salted.

Identification. Atlantic mackerel have smooth, tapering heads, streamlined bodies, and brilliant coloration. An iridescent greenish blue covers most of the upper body, turning to blue black on the head and silvery white on the belly. These brilliant colors fade somewhat after capture but still distinguish these fish. The skin is satiny and has small, smooth scales. The tail is forked. Another distinguishing characteristic is the series of 23 to 33 wavy, dark bands on the upper part of the body, extending to a moderately prominent lateral line. There are two fins on the back, one spiny and one soft, followed by a number of small finlets. There are also finlets present on the under surface of the body near the tail.

Size/Age. The average length for adult Atlantic mackerel is 14 to 18 inches, and the average weight is $1^1/_4$ to $2^1/_2$ pounds. The maximum observed size in recent years has been about $18^1/_2$ inches and weighing about 3 pounds. The all-tackle world record is a 2-pound, 10-ounce fish caught in Norway. The maximum age is roughly 20 years.

Distribution. Occurring in the North Atlantic Ocean, the Atlantic mackerel ranges from Labrador to Cape Hatteras, North Carolina, in the eastern region; and from the Baltic Sea to the Mediterranean and Black Seas in the western Atlantic.

Habitat. The Atlantic mackerel is pelagic, preferring cool, well-oxygenated open-ocean waters.

Life history/Behavior. Atlantic mackerel native to the western Atlantic coast comprise two populations rather than one vast, homogeneous stock as once supposed. The southern population appears offshore in early April, advancing toward Virginia, Maryland, and New Jersey to later spawn off the coast of New Jersey and Long Island. In late May, the northern group enters southern New England waters for a short period and mingles with the southern stock. The northern population soon moves north again to spawn off the coast of Nova Scotia and in the Gulf of St. Lawrence in June and July. These spring movements are probably triggered by water temperatures, and they generally provide the most angling opportunity and result in the greatest harvest.

As autumn approaches, fish that summer along the Maine coast begin to migrate southward toward Cape Cod and, after October, disappear off Block Island. The northern population returns through the Gulf of Maine in November or early December and vanishes off Cape Cod. Both groups winter between Sable Island off the coast of Nova Scotia and Cape Cod in waters generally warmer than 7°C. This annual disappearance, sometimes overnight, has puzzled people for years, and over the years it has given rise to many far-fetched stories.

Atlantic mackerel are moderately prolific, but many factors affect survival of the young. The eggs are released wherever the fish happen to be, leaving adverse winds to push eggs or small fry into areas where their chances of survival are slight. This behavior, combined with predation of large as well as young mackerel, results in a curious pattern of either superabundance or scarcity.

Food. The diet of Atlantic mackerel consists of fish eggs and a variety of small fish and fry.

Angling. Finding mackerel is the necessary element in catching them. Anglers typically locate the fish on sonar equipment or by observing slicks on the surface; when this fails, private boats follow charter and party boats (which do a brisk business in mackerel fishing when this species is available), and otherwise look for clusters of boat activity. Most fishing occurs in near-shore environs or in large bays.

A good deal of mackerel fishing is done with a rig that consists of several small tube lures attached at 1-foot intervals to a main leader and weighted with a heavy (3- or 4-ounce) diamond jig. Because mackerel are midwater fish, it's important to present the bait at the right level. Most anglers find this level by dropping their rig to the bottom, then slowly working it back up in increments, pausing and jigging as they do this. Once they catch fish, they return their rig to the same level. When the fish are not too deep, jigs and flies are also effective, and sometimes chum is used to attract and hold the fish near the boat.

See: Inshore Fishing; Mackerel.

MACKEREL, CERO *Scomberomorus regalis.*

Other names—cero, spotted cero, king mackerel, black-spotted Spanish mackerel; French: *thazard franc;* Portuguese: *cavala-branca;* Spanish: *carite, cavalla, pintada, sierra.*

A popular gamefish in tropical waters and a member of the Scombridae family, the cero mackerel is a pelagic species that also has commercial interest. It is considered excellent table fare and is marketed fresh, smoked, and frozen. Offshore anglers may use the cero mackerel as rigged bait for larger predatory species.

Identification. The cero mackerel is iridescent bluish green above and silvery below, with rows of short, yellow brown spots above; there are also yellow orange streaks and a dark stripe below, which runs the length of the body from the pectoral fin to the base of the tail. The front of the first dorsal fin is bluish black and has 17 to 18 spines and 15 to 18 gill rakers on the first arch. The pectoral fins are covered with small scales. The cero mackerel differs from the king mackerel *(see: mackerel, king)* and Spanish mackerel *(see: mackerel, Spanish)* in the pattern of its spots, which are rather elongated and arranged in lines instead of being scattered; the cero mackerel also has a lateral line that curves evenly down to the base of the tail, which further distinguishes it.

Size. The all-tackle world record cero mackerel weighed 17 pounds, 2 ounces. This species usually weighs less than 5 pounds.

Distribution. Found in tropical and subtropical waters in the western Atlantic, cero mackerel range from Massachusetts to Brazil; they are common to abundant throughout the Florida Keys, the Bahamas, the Antilles, and Cuba.

Habitat. A nearshore and offshore resident, the cero mackerel prefers clear waters around coral reefs and wrecks, and is usually solitary or travels in small groups.

Spawning. These fish spawn offshore in midsummer.

Food. Cero mackerel feed mainly on small schooling fish, such as sardines, anchovies, pilchards, herring, and silversides, as well as squid and shrimp.

Angling. As with most mackerel fishing, fast trolling while looking for baitfish is a good way to find ceros. Trollers can catch them on small feathers and baits, but the best sport is on light tackle and in casting small silver spoons and white jigs. They also hit surface swimming plugs, chuggers, and shallow-running plugs. Ceros have sharp teeth, so a wire leader is essential.

See: Mackerel.

MACKEREL, CHUB *Scomber japonicus.*

Other names—common mackerel, tinker mackerel, Japanese mackerel, Pacific mackerel, Spanish mackerel, scomber, smaach; Afrikaans: *makriel;* Arabic: *baljeh;* French: *hareng du Pacifique, maquereau blanc, maquereau espagnol;* Greek: *koliós;* Hawaiian: *opelu palahu, saba;* Italian: *cavallo, lanzardo, scombro macchiato;* Japanese: *honsaba, masaba;* Portuguese: *cavala, cavalinha, sarda comun;* Spanish: *caballa, cachorreta, macarela, salmonete, verle;* Turkish: *kolyoz;* Vietnamese: *cá thu Nhât-bán.*

This small member of the Scombridae family is commercially cultured in Japan and used in Chinese medicine. In addition, it is a good food fish and is marketed in many different ways.

Identification. The chub mackerel has a bluish or greenish back with roughly 30 irregular black bars that dissolve into a series of dusky spots near the lateral line. The pectoral fin has a black spot, and there are usually five finlets behind the dorsal and anal fins. The first and second dorsal fins have a large space between them, and the entire body is scaled. The chub mackerel is similar to the frigate mackerel *(see: mackerel, frigate),* which also has 30 irregular bars on its back, except that it has scales all

M

Cero Mackerel

over its body; the frigate has scales only in corselets around the pectoral fins.

Size/Age. The chub mackerel usually grows to 20 inches and 2.2 pounds, although it has been reported to 2 feet and 6 pounds. The all-tackle world record is a 4-pound, 12-ounce fish taken off Mexico in 1986. They can live for 9 to 10 years.

Distribution. Found in the Atlantic, Indian, and Pacific Oceans, chub mackerel occur in warm and temperate transition waters and adjacent seas. In the eastern Pacific, they occur from Alaska to Cabo San Lucas and are most abundant between Monterey, California, and southern Baja California. In the western Atlantic, they extend from the Gulf of St. Lawrence to the Florida Keys and Cuba, and also from Venezuela to southern Brazil. Chub mackerel are apparently absent from Indonesia and Australia.

Habitat. Chub mackerel inhabit inshore and offshore waters at the surface, schooling by size in the company of other species of fish, including small bluefin tuna. Huge schools sweep along the eastern Pacific coast in the summer and fall. In the western Pacific, chub mackerel are said to move into deeper areas of Asian waters to remain inactive during the winter season.

Spawning behavior. A female chub mackerel may produce 1 million pelagic eggs.

Food. Chub mackerel feed on copepods and other crustaceans, as well as on small pelagic fish and squid.

Angling. Like other mackerel, chub mackerel are preyed upon by tuna, marlin, sharks, and other fish. Anglers use them as cut- or whole-rigged bait for these species. They are not a significant target of sportfishing, but some anglers pursue them on a variety of baits, flies, and small lures.

See: Mackerel.

MACKEREL, FRIGATE *Auxis thazard.*

Other names—bullet mackerel, frigate tuna, leadenall, mackerel tuna; Arabic: *deraiga, sadah;* French/Danish: *auxide;* Italian: *tombarello;* Japanese: *hira sóda, soda-gatsuo;* Malay/Indonesian: *aya, baculan, kayau, selasih;* Portuguese: *judeu;* Spanish: *barrileto negro, melva;* Swedish/Norwegian: *auxid;* Turkish: *gobene, tombile.*

Frigate mackerel are an abundant member of the Scombridae family and hold an important place in the food web, especially as a forage fish for other species. They are commercially significant and marketed fresh, frozen, dried/salted, smoked, and canned.

Frigate Mackerel

Identification. The color of the frigate mackerel is dark greenish blue above and silvery white below. It has 15 or more narrow, oblique, dark wavy markings on the unscaled back portion of its body. There are eight dorsal finlets and seven anal finlets. It resembles the tuna family more than the mackerel with its more lunate than forked tail; as with all mackerel, however, its first and second dorsal fins are separated by a wide space.

Size. The average frigate mackerel weighs less than 2 pounds and is less than 20 inches long. The all-tackle world record is a 3-pound, 1-ounce fish taken off Australia.

Distribution. Frigate mackerel are cosmopolitan in warm waters, although there are few documented occurrences in the Atlantic Ocean. They are subject to periods of abundance and scarcity in particular areas.

Habitat. A schooling species, frigate mackerel inhabit both coastal and oceanic waters.

Food. Frigate mackerel feed on small fish, squid, planktonic crustaceans, and larvae.

Angling. There is little angling interest in this species, although it may be used as bait for other species.

See: Mackerel.

MACKEREL, KING *Scomberomorus cavalla.*

Other names—kingfish, giant mackerel; French: *maquereau;* Portuguese: *cavala;* Spanish: *carite, carite lucio, carite sierra, rey, serrucho, sierra.*

The largest mackerel in the western Atlantic, the king mackerel is a prized gamefish and an important commercial species, with millions of pounds of fish landed annually. A member of the Scombridae family, the king mackerel has firm meat, most of which is sold fresh or processed into steaks. Smaller quantities are canned, salted, smoked, and frozen. It may be ciguatoxic *(see: ciguatera)* in certain areas, however.

Identification. The streamlined body of the king mackerel is a dark gray above, growing silver on the sides and below, and there are no markings on the body, although the back may have an iridescent blue to olive tint. Most of the fins are pale or dusky, except the first dorsal fin, which is uniformly blue; the front part of this fin is never black, which distinguishes it from the Spanish mackerel *(see: mackerel, Spanish)* and the cero mackerel *(see: mackerel, cero).* Other distinguishing features include the sharp drop of the lateral line under the second dorsal fin, as well as a relatively small number (14 to 16) of spines in the first dorsal fin and a lower gill rake count, which is 6 to 11 on the first arch. Young king mackerel may be mistaken for Spanish mackerel because of the small, round, dark to gold

King Mackerel

spots on the sides, but these fade and disappear with age.

Size/Age. Averaging less than 10 pounds in weight, the king mackerel is usually 2 to 4 feet long and weighs up to 20 pounds. It reaches a maximum length of $5^1/_2$ feet and a weight of 100 pounds. Females grow larger than males. The all-tackle world record is a 90-pound fish taken off Florida in 1976. This species is believed to reach 14 years old, but those older than 7 years are rare.

Distribution. In the western Atlantic, king mackerel range from Massachusetts to Río de Janeiro, Brazil, including the Caribbean and the Gulf of Mexico, although they are only truly abundant off southern Florida. Two separate populations are suspected, one in the Gulf of Mexico and one in the Atlantic. In the eastern central Atlantic, they have been found around St. Paul's Rocks.

Habitat. King mackerel are primarily an open-water, migratory species, preferring warm waters that seldom fall below 68°F. They often occur around wrecks, buoys, coral reefs, ocean piers, inlets, and other areas where food is abundant. They tend to avoid highly turbid waters, and larvae are often found in warm, highly saline surface waters. A schooling species, king mackerel migrate extensively and annually along the western Atlantic coast in schools of various sizes, although the largest individuals usually remain solitary.

Life history/Behavior. Male king mackerel become sexually mature between their second and third years, and female fish between their third and fourth years. They spawn from April through November, and activity peaks in late summer and early fall. A large female may spawn 1 to $2^1/_2$ million eggs.

Food. King mackerel feed mainly on fish, as well as on a smaller quantity of shrimp and squid.

Angling. As with other mackerel, the primary chore in catching kingfish is finding them, and anglers can invest long hours looking for these fish. A lot of trolling is done in an effort to locate them, although once located, these aggressive fish can be readily caught in smaller sizes; the biggest fish are more difficult to come by.

Fishing methods include trolling or drifting either deep or on the surface using strip baits, lures, or small whole baits, as well as casting lures and live baits. Balao, mullet, jacks, herring, pinfish, menhaden (pogies), blue runners, ladyfish, croaker, and Spanish mackerel are among the baits used; the largest baits are preferred for bigger mackerel. Spoons, feathers, jigs, and plugs prove effective under various conditions, as do such combinations as feathers and strip baits and skirted strip baits. Chumming works well to attract and hold these fish; at anchor, this method can provide opportunities for fly tackle. Some anglers use extensive amounts of freshly ground chum while trolling.

Many anglers land larger fish by trolling with multiple (two or three) bait rigs, rigs of mullet on feathers, spoons, or live fish slowly in the boat's wake. Another effective big kingfish offering is a large plain spoon pulled deep with a planer.

A weakfish from the northern New Jersey shore.

M

Downriggers are used in conjunction with live baits, and live fish may also be run near the surface on kites. Deeper fishing produces large individuals when there are plenty of mackerel, as the large ones are below the crowd.

The best months for fishing off North Carolina and Virginia are May and October, whereas winter and early spring are best off South Florida. Many kingfish are caught off inlets and passes, as these areas are important for producing baits, which follow the rising tide in and the falling tide out. Inshore areas with breaks in the bottom depth or with contours are good spots for slow trolling, especially if they hold abundant bait.

Kingfish make a long and powerful run, rest, and then repeat the performance. Now and then a fish will leap from the water. To avoid overpowering the fish and pulling the hook out of its mouth, a rod with a soft tip is helpful.

See: Inshore Fishing; Mackerel; Trolling.

MACKEREL, NARROWBARRED *Scomberomorus commerson.*

Other names—barred mackerel, doggie, commerson's mackerel, giant mackerel, kingfish, king seer, seer, serra, snook, barracuta; Afrikaans: *katonkel, koning-makriel;* Arabic: *chanaad, kanaad, khabbat;* Bengali: *champa, matia;* Cantonese: *kau yue;* Fijian: *walu;* French: *coros prêtre, tanzard;* Indian languages: *chumbum, konam, mah-wu-leachi, yellari;* Japanese: *yokoshima;* Malay/Indonesian: *iyot, luding, tenggirri;* Philippine languages: *tangigi, maladyong;* Spanish: *carite estriado;* Swahili: *nguru, nguru-mtwane;* Thai: *insi, thu insi.*

The narrowbarred mackerel, a member of the Scombridae family, is an important commercial species throughout its range and also a prominent gamefish. Its flesh is of excellent quality, marketed in various ways, and it is also used as whole bait, strip bait, or chum. Individuals caught off the east coast of Queensland, Australia, have been associated with toxic poisoning *(see: ciguatera).*

Identification. The narrowbarred mackerel is so called because it has many irregular, vertical wavy bars on its sides, which increase as the fish grows. The first dorsal fin has 16 to 17 moderate or low spines, the second has 16 to 19 rays followed by 8 to 10 finlets, and the anal fin has 17 to 20 rays, also followed by 8 to 10 finlets. The lateral line dips below the second dorsal fin. The body is more compressed than that of the similar wahoo *(see),* and there are three to six gill rakers on the first arch, whereas the wahoo has none.

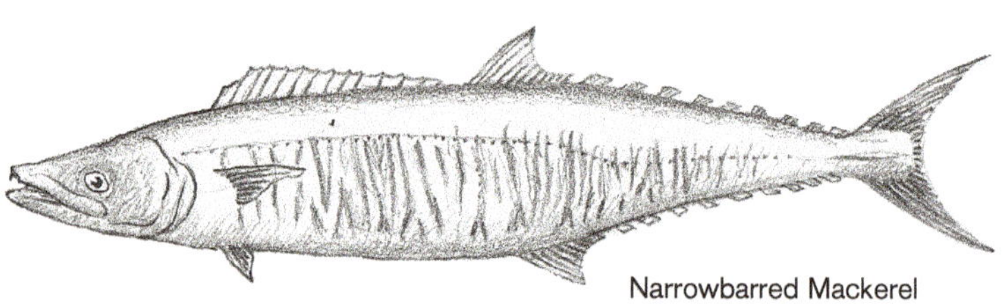

Narrowbarred Mackerel

Size. The all-tackle world record is a 99-pound fish taken off South Africa in 1982.

Distribution. Inhabiting tropical and warm temperate waters of the Indian and Pacific Oceans, narrowbarred mackerel occur from the Red Sea and South Africa to southeastern Asia, north to China and Japan, and south to southeastern Australia. Some populations have immigrated to the eastern Mediterranean Sea through the Suez Canal. In the Atlantic Ocean they are reported from St. Helena.

Habitat. A pelagic and migratory species, narrowbarred mackerel are found in shallow waters, over dropoffs and gently sloping reefs as well as in lagoons. They migrate extensively, but it is thought that permanent resident populations exist in certain areas. They form small schools, although larger fish usually travel alone.

Food. Narrowbarred mackerel feed mainly on small pelagic schooling fish like anchovies and sardines, as well as on flyingfish, squid, and shrimp.

Angling. Although not known to many Western anglers, the narrowbarred mackerel is a highly rated gamefish that sounds often, runs hard and fast, and occasionally leaps. Fishing methods include surface or deep-trolling with squid, mullet, sauries, flyingfish, garfish, and strip baits, as well as with artificial trolling lures. Live-bait fishing near reefs with these and other natural baits is also productive. The best fishing is at dawn or dusk and at high or low slack tide.

See: Mackerel; Offshore Fishing.

MACKEREL, PACIFIC JACK *Trachurus symmetricus.*

Other names—horse mackerel, jack mackerel, jackfish, mackereljack, scad; Spanish: *charrito, chicharro.*

Not a true mackerel but a member of the Carangidae family of jacks, the Pacific jack mackerel is marketed fresh, smoked, canned, and frozen.

Identification. The body of the Pacific jack mackerel is somewhat compressed and elongate, with a tail that is as broad as it is deep. It is metallic blue to olive green on the back, shading to silver on the belly. Its last dorsal and anal soft rays are attached to the body, or rarely separated from the fins, and the sides are covered with enlarged scales. The Pacific jack mackerel bears a resemblance to the Mexican scad, but the enlarged scales distinguish it, as do the last, attached rays of the dorsal and anal fins. On the Mexican scad, the rays are isolated finlets.

Size/Age. The Pacific jack mackerel can weigh 4 to 5 pounds and live 20 to 30 years.

Distribution. In the eastern Pacific, Pacific jack mackerel range from southeastern Alaska to southern Baja California, extending into the Gulf

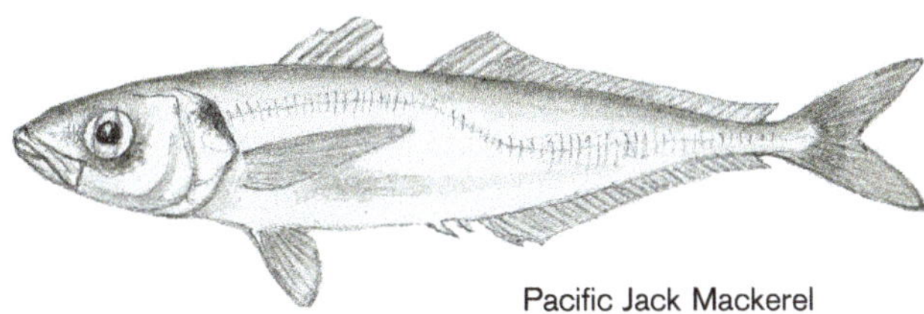
Pacific Jack Mackerel

Pacific Sierra Mackerel

of California, Mexico. They are also reported from Acapulco, Mexico, and the Galápagos Islands.

Habitat. Pacific jack mackerel are often found offshore in large schools; adults are found up to 500 miles from the coast and in depths of up to 150 feet. Young fish school near kelp and under piers, whereas larger fish often move offshore or northward.

Spawning behavior. Sexual maturity comes early for Pacific jack mackerel. Half of females are ready to spawn at age 2, and all fish spawn by age 3. Spawning takes place from March through June over a considerable area, from 80 to more than 240 miles offshore.

Food and feeding habits. Pacific jack mackerel feed on small crustaceans and fish larvae, as well as on anchovies, lanternfish, and juvenile squid.

Angling. Younger jack mackerel do not feed extensively on anchovies, do not readily bite on a baited hook or lure, and thus are a much less common addition to the catch of anglers, although they are a common commercial catch. They can be jigged, however, on small feathered hooks and frequently are used as baits for larger gamefish.

See: Jacks.

MACKEREL, PACIFIC SIERRA *Scomberomorus sierra.*

Other names—Pacific sierra; Spanish: *macarela, serrucho, sierra, verle.*

The Pacific sierra mackerel is an abundant fish in the Pacific along the coasts of Mexico and Central America. A member of the Scombridae family of mackerel and not to be confused with the Atlantic sierra *(Scomberomorus brasiliensis),* which occurs only in the Atlantic, the Pacific sierra mackerel is an eastern Pacific fish that is excellent to eat. It is marketed fresh and frozen. It resembles the Spanish mackerel in appearance, and the all-tackle world record is an Ecuadorian fish of 18 pounds caught in 1990.

Pacific sierra mackerel extend from La Jolla in Southern California south to the Galápagos Islands and to Paita, Peru. They have recently been reported from Antofagasta, Chile. A schooling species, Pacific sierra mackerel are found in surface coastal waters and over the bottom of the continental shelf. Thought to spawn close to the coast, they feed on small fish, especially anchovies.

See: Mackerel.

MACKEREL, SPANISH *Scomberomorus maculatus.*

Other names—Atlantic Spanish mackerel; Portuguese: *sororoca;* Spanish: *carite, pintada, sierra, sierra pintada.*

The Spanish mackerel is a popular gamefish and a good food fish of the Scombridae family. It is also of significant commercial interest, and whole fish are frequently used as bait for big-game fishing.

Identification. The slender, elongated body of the Spanish mackerel is silvery with a bluish or olive green back. There are 16 to 18 spines in the first dorsal fin, 15 to 18 soft rays in the second dorsal fin—with 8 to 9 finlets behind it, and 13 to 15 gill rakers on the first arch. The lateral line curves evenly downward to the base of the tail. The Spanish mackerel resembles both the cero mackerel *(see: mackerel, cero)* and the king mackerel *(see: mackerel, king),* but it has bronze or yellow spots without stripes; the cero mackerel has both spots and stripes of bronze or yellow, whereas the king mackerel has neither. The Spanish mackerel lacks scales on the pectoral fins, which further distinguishes it from both the cero and the king mackerel, which have scales on them. Also, the front part of the first dorsal fin on the Spanish mackerel is black, whereas it is more blue on the king mackerel, and the second dorsal fin and pectoral fins may be edged in black.

Size/Age. The Spanish mackerel grows to 37 inches and 11 pounds, averaging $1^1/_2$ to 3 feet and 2 to 3 pounds. The all-tackle word record is a 13-pounder taken off North Carolina in 1987. Fish older than five years are rare, although some have been known to reach eight years.

Distribution. In the western Atlantic, there are two separate populations of Spanish mackerel: one in the Gulf of Mexico and the other along the main western Atlantic coast. The former extends from the Gulf of Mexico throughout Florida waters to the Yucatán, and the latter extends from Miami to the Chesapeake Bay and occasionally to Cape Cod. They are absent from the Bahamas and the Antilles, except around Cuba and Haiti, but are abundant around Florida.

Habitat. Occurring inshore, near shore, and offshore, Spanish mackerel prefer open water but are sometimes found over deep grassbeds and reefs, as well as shallow-water estuaries. They form large, fast-moving schools that migrate great distances along the shore, staying in waters with temperatures above 68°F; these schools occur off North Carolina in April, off the Chesapeake Bay in May, and off New York in June, returning south in winter.

M

Spanish Mackerel

Spawning behavior. Spanish mackerel spawn offshore from April through September. Females release between a half million and $1^1/_2$ million eggs, and the larvae grow fast to reach lengths of 12 to 15 inches after the first year. They are able to reproduce by the second year.

Food and feeding habits. Spanish mackerel feed primarily on small fish, as well as on squid and shrimp; they often force their prey into crowded clumps and practically push the fish out of the water as they feed.

Angling. Casting, live-bait fishing, jigging, and drift fishing are all employed to catch this abundant fish, and a variety of lures—including metal squids, spoons, diamond jigs, and feather lures—are all effective. Bucktail jigs are particularly good, especially when retrieved rapidly with an occasional jerk of the rod tip to impart a darting motion. When fish are plentiful, small jigs may be rigged in multiples behind a single line. Minnows and live shrimp are the best natural baits. Light, 6- to 10-pound, spinning tackle provides excellent sport.

After the fish have been located and several hooked, boats make tight circles to stay with the school. Because Spanish mackerel migrate close to land, they are caught from small craft inshore, as well as from larger boats, and by anglers on piers, bridges, and jetties.

See: Inshore Fishing; Mackerel.

A Spanish mackerel from the Arafura Sea near the Cobourg Peninsula, Australia.

MACKINAW

A term for lake trout *(see)*.

MADAGASCAR

Located in the Indian Ocean and separated from Mozambique on the western African continent by the Mozambique Channel, Madagascar was once part of the Gondwana continent, which connected Africa and Asia. After these landmasses separated, Madagascar stood as the fourth largest island in the world, and it is situated in one of the most productive fishing spots in the world.

Known for its unique and superb fauna and flora, Madagascar's landscape has the diversity of high mountains, dry plains, and tropical forests. Its shoreline is dotted with coral reefs, separated only by passages that become long underwater canyons, and by small islands around which fishing is particularly productive. Most of the prominent Indo-Pacific gamefish species thrive here, including black marlin, blue marlin, sailfish, dolphin, wahoo, kingfish, African pompano, amberjack, sharks, grouper, tuna, snapper, jacks, and more. An abundance of sailfish and the lack of fishing effort make this a top site for Pacific sails, as well as a developing fishery for big black marlin.

Madagascar's fishery focuses on three productive centers on Nosy-Be, a small island ideally situated between the northwest coast of Madagascar and the Mozambique Channel and a one-hour flight from the capital city of Antananarivo. The centers include the Italian-owned Marlin Club, the French-owned Sakatia Club, and the locally owned Centre de Pêche Sportive de Madagascar (CPSM). The latter is the oldest center and has not only a small fleet of well-equipped sportfishing boats, but also a boat maintenance and tackle repair facility. It features a fixed beach camp that enables anglers to overnight in remote areas closer to the fishing grounds. Their eight-tent, 16-person beach camp, Terres Rouges, is situated on the northern side of Nosy-Be and can be reached only by boat. The beach camp was built by CPSM because quality accommodations were lacking on Nosy-Be (tourism in Madagascar commenced only in the early 1990s); the facilities now existing on the island, in the main Nosy-Be town of Hellville, are a one-hour boat ride from the major fishing grounds, but they are only a 15-minute run from the beach camp.

The grounds around Nosy-Be are not only diversified but also unexploited. Fishing is good year-round and peaks during the dry season, from April through October. From January through March, occasional rains are common, but the fishing remains good, especially for marlin. More black marlin than blue marlin are landed here. Blacks are most abundant from April through August but are also caught from September through January. As of 1998, the biggest black taken was a 750-pounder, but in 1997 a fish estimated at 900 pounds was hooked and lost. Some striped marlin have reportedly been caught as well.

The sailfish season usually begins around the first week in June and continues through September, but fish are occasionally caught in mid-March. In early October, the Varatraza, a local wind from the east, pushes out the bait for about three weeks, and the sailfish depart. At the end of October the bait returns, along with fewer sailfish, which stay until January. At the height of the season, many sails are raised, and in the best of times in the late 1990s, boats experienced 20 strikes in a half day of fishing.

Although some good boats are available in Madagascar, sportfishing is just developing. It is likely, however, that this could be a hotspot in the future.

MADTOM

The madtom is a member of the catfish *(see)* family, Ictaluridae, often referred to as bullhead catfish. Although the larger members of the catfish family have gained notoriety as sportfish, commercial fish, or food fish, the secretive and diminutive madtom escapes public attention.

These are little-known fish with interesting lifestyles. Madtoms are important links in the food webs of many streams, making it possible for large predators such as bass, wading birds, and water snakes to benefit from the stream's vast energy, represented by larval insect production. They are also a unique natural resource to North America's small streams and are endemic to the continent north of Mexico. The 40 species belonging to the family Ictaluridae occur naturally in the United States and Canada, and 27 are madtoms.

Like other members of the Ictaluridae family, madtoms possess stinging venom in their dorsal and pectoral spines. The venom originates from cells of the skin sheath over the pectoral fin. The toxicity of the venom varies but approximates that of a bee sting, although every person reacts differently to being stung.

Identification. Madtoms are recognized by their unique adipose fin. Non-madtom catfish have a fleshy fin protruding from their back just ahead of the caudal fin. The adipose fin of a madtom is continuous with the caudal fin.

Madtoms belong to the genus *Noturus,* which is divided into three subgenera, *Noturus, Schilbeodes,* and *Rabida,* each with its own distinct appearance. The *Schilbeodes* are dull colored, generally brown or yellow brown. The *Rabidas* have colorful markings with many bands and saddlelike pigmentation. There is only one species in the subgenus *Noturus,* the stonecat *(Noturus flavus).* The stonecat *(see)* possesses the plain appearance of the *Schilbeodes;* however, no other madtoms match this species in size. Stonecats exceed 7 inches as adults and may reach 12 inches in some locations.

There are several tricks to identifying madtoms. Identifying the river where a madtom was collected is the first step to identification. Because most madtom species are limited in distribution (often within one or two states or even one river), many species can be quickly excluded, depending on location. If the madtom possesses body markings, these can be used to determine its species, as the pigmented patterns of each species are distinct.

Other traits used to identify madtoms include their toothpatch, lips, and pectoral spine. On the roof of a madtom's mouth is a toothpatch used for crushing prey. On the stonecat, there are lateral extensions on the ends of the toothpatch. Some, such as slender and freckled madtoms, have differences in their lips. The slender madtom has lips that meet equally, whereas the top lip of the freckled madtom protrudes beyond the bottom lip.

Black Madtom

Another differentiating trait is the pectoral spine. Many madtoms possess spines that are unique in their structure, some possessing many saw-like teeth and some having none. The tadpole madtom has a smooth, straight pectoral spine, whereas the northern madtom has a sharply curved spine with sawlike teeth on both the front and back sides.

Size. Fish size is often correlated with the life history and reproductive strategies a species possesses. Larger fish are often immune to predation as adults; this is not generally so for madtoms, which have a small adult body size. Nevertheless, madtoms avoid predators by virtue of their nocturnal lifestyle, hard spines that artificially inflate their body size when erected, cryptic coloration, and use of cover.

Even so, their chance of survival from year to year may be low. Fish size is often correlated with maximum age, and madtoms are no exception. Larger madtoms live longer. Body size is often an indication of energy stores available for egg production, and therefore will be indicative of the number of eggs each female will produce per spawning season. Because madtoms spawn few eggs relative to other fish, they must invest heavily in each egg to ensure its survival.

To give their young an advantage, madtom females lay large eggs, which provides more energy for embryo growth, allowing young madtoms to hatch at a much larger size and decreasing their chances of being eaten. Madtoms also provide parental care, maintaining a stable and optimum growing environment and protecting the eggs and small, young madtoms from predators.

Madtoms exhibit a range of lifestyles related to body size. At one extreme the stonecat may reach 12$^1/_2$ inches in length, produce 200 to 500 eggs per female, spawn perhaps three or four times in its life, and live six or seven years. At the other end of the spectrum, the least madtom barely reaches 2$^1/_2$ inches, produces about 30 eggs, lives maybe two years with luck, and spawns probably once in its lifetime.

Habitat. Most anglers are probably unfamiliar with madtoms because they tend to be nocturnal, hiding under rocks, logs, and undercut banks during the day. Also, their body markings and color patterns (or lack of, depending on their preferred habitat) help camouflage them from the peering eyes of birds, water snakes, and anglers. Most madtoms prefer the cool, clear water of smaller streams, but some species are adapted to living in lakes, large streams, or muddy rivers. Where aquatic vegetation and beaver dams exist, madtoms take full advantage of their numerous niches.

Most madtoms have strong habitat preferences, and thus use unique habitats. The stonecat primarily inhabits small to large rivers with rubble or boulders and lakes with gravel bars. In contrast, the black madtom prefers vegetation over gravel or sand in the clear moving water of springs, creeks, and small rivers. The margined madtom prefers rocky riffles with fast moving water in small and medium-size rivers. Different species are even known to prefer rocks of specific sizes for cover. Because madtoms are choosy about their homes, they often have problems dealing with the degradation of their preferred habitats.

Food. Madtoms are crepuscular feeders, which means they feed mostly at dusk and dawn. As insectivores, they primarily feed on a diet of midge larvae, mayfly larvae, caddisfly larvae, and crayfish. Most madtoms are not as picky about their food as their housing and will eagerly devour any available prey. Madtoms generally consume smaller amounts of stonefly, beetle, black fly, dragonfly, alder fly, and fish fly larvae. An occasional small fish (such as lamprey larvae), spider, or zooplankton has also been found in their stomachs. When placed together, large adult madtoms have consumed small juvenile madtoms of the same species.

Reproduction. Madtoms start spawning about mid-April and finish spawning in mid-July. Like most fish, the commencement of spawning and the length of the spawning season depend heavily on water temperature. Madtoms usually begin spawning after the water temperature has reached 64°F, and stop spawning after water temperature exceeds 81°F. During the spawning season, adults are sexually dimorphic, which means males look different from females.

Madtoms construct nests to rear their young and provide post-spawning protection. A nest consists of an area with a pebble or gravel substrate that has been cleared of silt and debris.

Most madtoms prefer to nest under rocks; however, the speckled madtom and others have been known to nest in discarded beverage cans or bottles.

Although madtoms are small fish, they have relatively fewer and larger eggs compared to species that do not exhibit parental care. Madtom eggs may be up to 0.2 inches in diameter; they are adhesive and stick to the substrate and each other. Generally, a short time after laying the eggs, the female leaves the nest and parental duties to the male. Eggs hatch in eight to ten days, depending on water temperature. After approximately 21 days of parental care, the male parent will leave the young madtoms on their own.

Threats. More than two-thirds of all madtom species have been listed as threatened or endangered by various agencies in different states. The main threat to madtoms is the degradation or destruction of stream habitats. Madtoms are particularly vulnerable because their naturally small distributions may not provide sufficient refuge for undisturbed areas useful for recolonizing impacted areas. Activities that increase stream temperature and erosion rates are especially significant, as many madtoms depend on cool water for spawning and silt-free nests for juvenile survival. Protecting madtoms, therefore, means protecting small and medium sized rivers.

Madtoms have gained recognition as bait for bass fishing and as an aquarium fish. Because of the problems associated with naturally small and disjunct populations, and because many threatened or endangered madtoms are protected through state and federal laws, anglers and aquarists should exercise caution in the collection of madtoms. Check with local fisheries biologists to make sure that collecting madtoms is legal and that madtom populations in local streams can support such activities.

Another problem with using madtoms as bait is introduction of non-native fish into streams *(see: exotic species)*. Many anglers return unused live baits to the stream before surrendering for the day. However, this may inadvertently introduce non-native fish into new rivers, possibly leading to the elimination of a different madtom species or another fish altogether.

See: Catfish; Madtom, Brown; Stonecat.

MADTOM, BROWN *Noturus phaeus.*

The brown madtom is a widely distributed and relatively common member of the madtoms *(see)*. This diminutive catfish may be used in bait fishing for bass, and is prominent in moderate to fast flowing water.

Identification. Brown madtoms are dull colored. The upper body possesses a chocolate brown or yellowish-brown tint. The ventral side is pale. Juvenile brown madtoms, especially those collected in complex leaf debris or vegetation, may be black. These fish will adjust the intensity of their body color to simulate shades of their surroundings. The upper lip of the brown madtom protrudes beyond that of the lower lip, and the rear of the pectoral spine has six saw-like teeth.

Size/Age. Male and female brown madtoms grow at the same rate but males reach a larger overall length because they live longer. The largest individual collected to date was a male that measured 6 inches in total length. Females live at least three years while males may live four or five years. The total length of three-year-old fish ranges from 3.9 to 5.1 inches.

Distribution. The brown madtom has a fairly wide distribution covering the following areas: Mississippi River tributaries in Kentucky, Tennessee, Mississippi, and Alabama; Tennessee River tributaries in Tennessee and Alabama; the Gulf Slope in the Sabine River drainage of Louisiana; and Bayou Teche drainage in Louisiana. It has also been reported in the Ouachita River drainage in Arkansas, probably introduced with other baitfish. In areas where brown madtoms are collected, they are usually abundant.

Habitat. This species is usually abundant in springs and small streams where areas of vegetation exist, in accumulations of debris, and underneath undercut banks. Madtoms in one stream in northern Mississippi preferred undercut banks to all other types of cover. Brown madtoms can be found in moderate to fast flowing water over small gravel or coarse sand.

Brown Madtom

Food. Brown madtoms exhibit crepuscular feeding, with peak feeding activity following sunset and just before sunrise. The diet, similar to other madtoms, is primarily composed of midge larvae, caddisfly larvae, and crayfish.

Reproduction. Spawning, as determined in northern Mississippi research, took place from May through July.

See: Catfish; Madtom.

MAGGOT

Soft-bodied insect larva, especially of the housefly, bluebottle fly (or blowfly), and greenbottle fly. Fly larvae, also known as waxworms, are natural baits used when fishing for coarse fish *(see)* and in ice fishing *(see)*. Maggots are commonly fished in their natural white color but may be available in a darker dyed form; they are hooked through the blunt end or through the midsection. Pupated maggots, known as casters, are also used for coarse species and are fished with the hook buried inside.

MAGNUSON ACT

See: Fishery Conservation and Management Act.

MAHIMAHI

See: Dolphin, Common.

MAHSEER

Mahseer are a fish of mystery and are little known to the angling and scientific community in the Western world. References to this species, even in comprehensive natural-history books on fish, are either lacking or merely mention the mahseer as an Asiatic cyprinid that attains huge sizes. Mahseer are well known in their endemic range, however, and collectively are the largest and most important species for sportfishing within that range, particularly in India *(see)*.

Species

The name mahseer itself is evidently derived from the Sanscrit word *mahasaul,* which is derived from

M

Tor Mahseer

mahasalkalin, meaning "a fish with large scales." Mahseer belong to the huge Cyprinidae family of minnows, which includes carp and their many relatives. For many years, mahseer were classified by taxonomists under the genus *Barbus,* and thus called large-scaled barbels, a nickname that has stuck even though these fish have been reclassified.

The exact number of mahseer that exist is still a bit vague, but at least six species are described under the genus *Tor.* Several of these are the largest of the cyprinid clan. They include the following species.

The putitor mahseer *(Tor putitora).* Also known as the yellow-finned mahseer, common Himalayan mahseer, golden mahseer, and Himalayan salmon, this is the leviathan of the clan. In India it has been reported to attain a length of 2.7 meters. The males reach a weight of 190 kilograms or 418 pounds, and females achieve 220 kilograms or 484 pounds. Modern catches do not reflect fish even approaching this size, however, and contemporary records in some literature indicate a maximum of 132 pounds. It has a high food value and occurs in southern Asia in Afghanistan, Pakistan, India, Nepal, Bangladesh, Bhutan, and the Himalayas.

The tor mahseer *(Tor tor).* Also known as the red-finned mahseer, the golden mahseer, the thick-lipped mahseer, in Bengali as *mohashol,* in Burmese as *nga-dauk,* and in Nepali as *sahar sor,* the tor mahseer can grow to a length of 1.7 meters and a weight of 100 kilograms or 220 pounds. Contemporary records indicate a maximum size of 167 pounds, and a 95-pounder caught in 1984 from India's Cauvery River is registered as the all-tackle world record. It occurs in Pakistan, India, Bangladesh, Nepal, and Bhutan. This is the species most commonly referred to simply as "mahseer."

The mosal mahseer *(Tor mosal).* Also known as the copper mahseer, the mosal mahseer can grow to 1 meter in length. It is found in Himalaya and Burma.

The khudchee *(Tor khudree).* Also known as black mahseer and yellow mahseer, khudchee are found in India and Sri Lanka and grow to 450 millimeters and 22.6 kilograms.

The mussullah *(Tor mussullah).* Also known as the high-backed mahseer, the mussullah grows to 1.5 meters and nearly 90 kilograms.

The jungha *(Tor progenius).* Also known as the jungha of Assamese, this species is found in India and grows to 150 centimeters and nearly 90 kilograms.

Another species that is lumped in with mahseers because of its large scales is the bokar *(Acrossocheilus hexagonolepis).* Also known as the katli, bokar of Assamese, and katli of Nepalese, this species may grow to 11 kilograms and occurs in India, Bangladesh, Nepal, Burma, the Malay Peninsula, Thailand, and China.

Traits and Angling

In general terms, the characteristics of species in the genus *Tor* are an elongate and moderately compressed body with a small head and prominent snout, a strongly curved inferior or subinferior mouth, a protractile upper jaw, lips that are thick and continuous at the corners of the mouth, two pairs of barbels, large scales (on giant specimens, as large as the palm of a hand), a full lateral line, and pharyngeal teeth for crushing food.

Although mahseer are described as omnivorous bottom feeders, most species primarily consume aquatic plant matter, algae, insects, and mollusks. Some, and presumably large individuals, are also piscivorous.

Mahseer primarily inhabit rivers but also occupy the still waters of lakes and canals. The backwaters of rivers, the junctions of rivers, the mouths of tributaries, eddies, and the heads and tails of pools are their favorite habitats. Some species travel up tributaries to spawn, whereas others migrate up a main river; this activity occurs at the onset of the rainy season, and the fish return downriver after the rainy season. In the hilly sections of Indian rivers, the best fishing time is August and September. The rainy season is usually a poor time; turbid water, late spring, early fall, and the lowland sections of rivers all improve the chances of taking large fish.

Large mahseer are powerful fish that can make determined runs in big rivers. They are not flashy fighters, but, similar to their carp brethren, they are powerful and strong. Larger fish have extremely powerful jaws and can do crushing damage to a person's fingers. These fish take many kinds of natural food, but paste baits are especially preferred. Various spoons are also effective. Light to heavy tackle is used, depending on the size of fish targeted.

See: India.

MAINE

Most people associate angling in Maine with images of landlocked salmon or wild brook trout in remote ponds and lakes surrounded by spruce-covered shorelines. Although those attributes remain applicable, the Pine Tree State's abundant waters offer a great deal more, both in freshwater and marine environs.

On the inland front, brown trout, smallmouth and largemouth bass, togue (lake trout), pickerel, and panfish attract residents and nonresidents alike to Maine's 2,500 lakes and ponds and 37,000 miles of rivers, as well as to its untold miles of streams and brooks. The largest state in New England, Maine offers varied terrain and angling opportunities, meeting a wide range of tastes. Indeed, some Maine bass waters would make a Floridian feel at home, and a few brown trout streams resemble pastoral Hampshire chalk streams. Between these extremes are rushing, tumbling rivers, immense lakes, mountain ponds, true limestone streams, and much more.

On the maritime front, Maine's 3,500 miles of rocky coastline—offering innumerable bays, coves, tidal rivers, a sprinkling of beaches, and thousands of rugged islands and ledges—combines with an ecologically diverse sea floor to provide an ideal environment for several dozen gamefish and food fish species. The cold, clear water of coastal Maine is among the cleanest in the United States. Maine's saltwater sportfishery is lightly exploited when compared with that in more populated states to the south. Still, angler participation has increased in recent times, and the value of the recreational fishery has grown considerably. The populations of cod, pollock, haddock, hake, and other bottom dwellers—long the saltwater species for which Maine has been known—are dwindling, however, and are in a troubled state. Angling for these species has been supplemented and in some cases overshadowed by the pursuit of bluefin tuna, various species of sharks, as well as striped bass, bluefish, and mackerel.

Freshwater

Although Maine's once-fabulous northwoods brook trout fishery has declined in response to the growing network of logging roads, brown trout fishing in the southern half of the state is steadily improving, with some browns weighing over 10 pounds. Two- to 4-pounders raise few eyebrows, and 12- to 14-inch fish are routine. Southern and central Maine have brown trout fishing galore in places, some of it world-class, thanks to landlocked salmon, smallmouth and largemouth bass, and striped bass. These gamefish take the pressure off nonindigenous browns.

Mainers love the landlocked salmon, which accounts for its designation as the Pine Tree State's official fish. A smaller landlocked version of the lordly Atlantic salmon, these fish fight with fast runs and high acrobatic leaps that endear them to anglers. Residents and nonresidents prize these landlocks above all and turn—among coldwater species—to brown trout as a distant second choice.

Most of Maine's smallmouth and largemouth bass live in the southern half of the state, near population centers, and offer world-class angling. Until recently, many residents considered these species "trash" fish and concentrated their efforts on salmonids or sea-run striped bass. Their attitude has changed, and more residents are turning from salmonids to black bass or stripers. Anglers routinely catch 16-inch black bass in Maine, and they have a chance to take 4-pound smallmouths and 5-pound largemouths on any cast.

One highly appealing feature of Maine's bass fishery is the profusion of small ponds in pristine settings with little shoreline development. Smallmouths over 7 pounds and largemouths over 10 pounds are possible, particularly in smaller ponds avoided by folks with big, fast boats that require elaborate launching ramps. Bass waters with cartop boat launches are seldom fished, and strict regulations keep the bass population strong in larger waters, despite increasing pressure.

Togue have few followers in Maine, so double-digit specimens can hit a lure on any outing. A 10- to 15-pound togue would make any angler happy, but 20-plus-pound togue are also occasionally caught. And the chance, however remote, exists to take a 30-pounder. Because some Maine waters have too many togue, fisheries biologists have instituted liberal bag limits. This practice allows landlocked salmon and baitfish, especially smelt, to proliferate. Even in waters originally populated by native togue (spread across the state) and brook trout, salmon are far more popular, which has inspired management programs to favor landlocks.

Pickerel and panfish such as white and yellow perch, sunfish, black crappie, and horned pout (bullhead) produce fast fishing for youngsters and anglers who want to eat their catch without hurting the more valuable salmonid and bass resources. Although white perch are actively pursued (their white, flaky meat is prized table fare), pickerel and panfish are generally underutilized in Maine; prolific fishing pressure has put a minimal dent in the populations of these species.

Maine was once a popular destination for

Atlantic salmon anglers, but many formerly prominent Atlantic salmon rivers have dwindled to runs so small, they are not worth fishing. Indeed, this species is experiencing hard times in the Pine Tree State, and restoration efforts are far from bearing fruit.

Southern Maine. In general, Maine waters are sterile. In southern Maine, however, lakes, ponds, rivers, streams, and brooks are richer in nutrients, so fish grow faster. Southern Maine waters therefore produce quality brown trout, landlocked salmon, and largemouth and smallmouth bass. Each year, anglers land 10-plus-pound browns, and on rare occasions 20-pound browns, in this region. Four-pound smallmouths and 5-pound largemouths excite plenty of anglers every season, and some take larger fish. A 7-pound smallmouth or 8- to 10-pound largemouth is possible.

Lakes and ponds produce fast action for brown trout and landlocked salmon shortly after ice out, normally in mid-April. Surface fishing peaks in May and begins to peter out in June; only trollers working the depths with downriggers or lead-core lines linger. Knowledgeable trollers find action all summer. In September, waters cool, and browns and landlocks come to the surface again. Hundreds of Maine waters offer October and November fishing to open-water anglers, but the fall season is strictly catch-and-release for salmonids and bass.

Top spots for giant browns are Square Lake and Mousam Lake, both in the towns of Shapleigh and Acton. These waters produce 10-plus-pound browns most years. Square occasionally yields a 20-plus-pound brown, making this a rare but possible accomplishment.

A classic river for browns is the Saco, particularly around Steep Falls. The Little Ossipee from Newfield to Ossipee Falls, and Pleasant River in Windham, are designated for catch-and-release and host brown trout and brook trout aplenty. Most are pansize, but the opportunity for bigger trout exists.

Sebago, Maine's second largest lake and the deepest in New England (maximum depth 316 feet), holds a smorgasbord of fish, but landlocked salmon, togue, and smallmouths attract the most attention. Sebago is nationally famous for its salmon; the scientific name for landlocks, *Salmo salar sebago,* is derived from this lake. Salmon prowl near the surface of Sebago from ice out in mid-April to early June before descending to deeper water. In September, cool weather brings salmon to the surface again. Today, 4-pound landlocks are a typical trophy salmon from this famous lake, a far cry from a documented 22-pound, 8-ounce landlock caught in 1907. Togue have come on strong in Sebago since a controversial stocking program introduced them in the 1970s. Tributaries to Sebago, such as the Crooked and Songo Rivers, have runs of landlocked salmon in May and again in September, offering top fly fishing action.

Coves around this huge water offer anglers the best smallmouth action in southern Maine, and 3- to 5-pound specimens keep Sebago bass anglers returning. The shallows produce panfish action for white perch and black crappie.

North of Sebago, and in the same drainage, is a cluster of large ponds and lakes that have bass galore. Raymond Pond in New Gloucester routinely yields 3- to 5-pound smallmouths and largemouths each season. Beautiful Crescent Lake in Raymond holds 3- to 5-pound smallmouths and largemouths; 6- to 8-pound largemouths are rare but available. Thomas Pond in Casco has similar fishing and the added attraction of pickerel in the 4- to 5-pound range. Few Maine anglers bother with this toothy predator, so it is an underutilized resource. Moose Pond in Denmark has produced largemouths in excess of 11 pounds; this is a rare catch, of course, but the lake clearly offers big bass. Thompson Lake offers giant smallmouths—at least one documented smallie weighed 8 pounds.

In truth, it would be difficult to find a pond or lake in southern Maine that doesn't have one species of bass, or both. Another plus for this region is myriad streams with brook trout, some holding native fish.

Central Maine. Central Maine has been a great success story for fisheries biologists, beginning with the brown trout fisheries in the Kennebec River between Skowhegan and Augusta. Biologists for the Maine Department of Inland Fisheries and Wildlife tout this large river as one of the best brown trout waters in the Northeast. Fish up to 20 inches are routine; in recent years, at least one documented brown of 30 inches fell to an angler using a dry fly, which is remarkable. Rainbows up to 20 inches make this section of the river even more interesting. June, early July, and September are top months, but people catch fish year-round.

Farther east, the St. George River flows from St. George Lake in Liberty to the ocean in Thomaston. On the way, this small freestone river slides through woodlands, pastoral farm country, and small villages with church steeples. In shallow riffle sections, browns average 8 to 10 inches, but the St. George flows through several ponds before reaching the Atlantic. Near the inlets and outlets, browns run from 10 to 18 inches, but the occasional larger fish does exist. May and early June are prime months to hit the river sections near the ponds.

Damariscotta Lake in Jefferson routinely produces 4-pound browns, and this water improves each year, thanks to intensive management. China Lake in Vassalboro grows browns up to 4 pounds, and larger specimens in years when baitfish thrive.

The ponds along the St. George River have black bass, but a 3- to 4-pound smallmouth would be a trophy here, and a 5-pound largemouth would cause a stir. Central Maine does have world-class bass waters, though. Top bets are Cobbosseecontee Lake just west of Augusta; Androscoggin Lake in Leeds; Webber and Threemile Ponds in Vassalboro;

and China, Windsor, and North Ponds in the Belgrade Lakes. These waters hold plenty of 3- to 4-pound smallmouths and 4- to 5-pound largemouths. Fish grow bigger here, though; 6- to 8-pound largemouths are always possible, and smallmouths of 6 pounds and larger live in these waters. This area also has small remote and semiremote bass ponds that provide solitude and perhaps the trophy of a lifetime. As in southern Maine, few ponds and lakes in central Maine lack bass.

Farther northeast, just above Bangor, the Penobscot River between Milford and Lincoln has arguably the best river smallmouth fishing in the world. Here the river flows over a gravel bottom, and water depths are generally up to 4 feet. Fish average 13 inches, and 3-pounders are common. Anglers do take the occasional $5^1/_2$-pound smallmouth. Islands dot this river in Greenbush and Argyle, the top spot on the river for this species.

Long Pond in the Belgrade Lakes is one of Maine's three top trophy landlocked salmon waters. Four-pounders won't impress many Long Pond regulars because this water gives up 6- and 7-pound salmon every year, and larger specimens are possible. St. George Lake in Liberty routinely produces salmon up to 4 pounds. Ice out in central Maine occurs in mid-April, and salmonids stay near the surface into June. After spending the summer in the depths, they surface in September.

Long Pond also has a good northern pike population, the result of illegal stocking in the 1980s, as pike are not indigenous to Maine. This species has flourished here and attracts crowds. Sabattus Pond in Greene has pike, too, also illegally stocked. Mainers love this new, exotic species.

Waldo County, in the eastern section of central Maine, offers excellent fishing for brook trout. Nearly every brook holds native brook trout, and the ones flowing into the ocean have sea-run brook trout, colloquially called "salters." The time to fish for salters is in April, when spring waters run high, drawing trout from their estuarine environment. Small brooks hold 8- to 10-inch specimens, but rivers like the Passagassawakeag in Belfast have a May run of fish in the 1- to 2-pound range. In general, large waters have later runs.

Down East. Washington County, which contains West Quoddy Head—a small peninsula that is the easternmost point of land in the U.S.—has landlocked salmon and smallmouth bass fishing that attract anglers from around the world. Smallmouths run smaller here than in southern and central Maine, but most of the bass lakes and ponds have little development, and many have no shore dwellings, just forests. The more remote waters lie in pristine country where anglers might not see another person all day.

Although anglers won't take trophy salmon here as readily as in other parts of Maine, trophy specimens do swim in these waters. West Grand and East Grand Lakes are two of Maine's best salmon lakes. These are huge waters with enough coves and peninsulas for anglers to find seclusion. West Grand lies north of the village of Grand Lake Stream, and East Grand is on the Canadian border. Ice out is in late April or early May, and landlocks cruise near the surface until June, when summer heat drives them deeper. They come back to the surface in September. Both lakes also hold bass and togue.

Grand Lake Stream is one of Maine's premier landlocked salmon streams, and fly anglers congregate there in May, early June, September, and early October. This is also one of the few opening-day hotspots in Maine. When fishing season begins on April 1, ice and snow still cover the state, but salmon that have spent the winter in the pool below the dam provide April Fool's Day action.

Top bass waters in Washington County include Third Machias Lake in the Machias lakes chain just west of Grand Lake Stream village. Fifteen-inch smallmouths are average, and 4-pounders are possible. Meddybemps Lake near Calais, and Big Lake west of Princeton, have similar-size smallmouths and attract bass anglers from across the nation. Junior Lake just northwest of West Grand Lake has smallmouths that average 15 inches, but 6-pounders are possible.

The St. Croix River has smallmouths galore that average 13 to 15 inches, but a 4-pounder doesn't surprise St. Croix regulars. This river has fast-water sections that look like salmonid habitat, but parts of the St. Croix look as "bassy" as any water in the country.

Washington County has myriad brooks, and most of them have brook trout. Because the many dozens of lakes and ponds attract the majority of anglers, many brooks are underfished. This is a wonderful place to catch native brookies in secluded woodland settings. Also, brooks and small streams running into the ocean offer sea-run brook trout in early April.

Most Down East bass waters also boast excellent pickerel fishing, with 4-pound catches somewhat common. Many bass waters support white perch, and this area provides Maine's best angling for this species.

Rangeley Lakes. This region attracted wealthy New York City anglers in the mid-1850s, and they caught giant brook trout for 50 years, some weighing as much as 12 pounds. Eight-pounders were possible on any outing. Anglers decided to stock landlocked salmon in the Rangeley Lakes in 1873, and this species flourished. One documented specimen in 1905 weighed $18^1/_2$ pounds. Landlocked salmon, land development, and fishing pressure, however, helped end the era of giant brookies. Today a 4-pound brook trout is a trophy. Larger specimens are possible but rare.

Nevertheless, Rangeley Lake now ranks as one of the three top spots in Maine to catch trophy landlocked salmon. Indeed, the chance always

M

The Guinness Book of Records lists the largest freshwater fish as the rare pla buk or pa beuk, found only in the Mekong River and tributaries. The largest was 9 feet $10^1/_4$ inches long and weighed $533^1/_2$ pounds.

Many of Maine's waters, including Fish River Lake shown here, have notable salmon and trout fisheries.

exists to catch an 8-pounder. Four-pound landlocks surprise no one, and 2-pounders are average. Nearby Mooselookmeguntic and Cupsuptic Lakes, just west of Rangeley Lake, have smaller salmon, and a 3-pound fish would be a good catch. The action in general is better in these two lakes, however, than it is in Rangeley.

Ice out occurs late in this northern, mountainous region, often in mid-May. Trout and salmon stay near the surface through May and most of June, so surface trolling lasts longer than in southern Maine. Fish drop deeper in summer and return to the surface in fall.

Trout and salmon swim upstream here in June and September, when rain brings fresh water rushing down the Kennebago River, the Cupsuptic River, or smaller streams running into the Rangeley Lakes. These are excellent targets for fly anglers. September runs attract anglers from across the nation to cast flies at brook trout weighing 4 pounds and more, and at salmon that weigh from 4 to 8 pounds.

Moosehead Lake region. Moosehead Lake is Maine's largest lake, spreading over 74,890 acres and extending more than 34 miles in length. With the exception of two small villages (Greenville and Rockwood) on the south end, shoreline development is nonexistent, so the setting is classic northern Maine.

This lake has landlocked salmon, brook trout, and togue, and most anglers troll for these species. Brook trout run up to 4 pounds and occasionally larger, but a 16- to 18-inch brookie is a good fish. Salmon have never run large in Moosehead Lake, and 14- to 16-inch fish are average. Moosehead is a togue lake, although landlocks were introduced about a century ago. The togue average 18 to 20 inches, but 20-pounders are possible on rare occasions.

Ice out on Moosehead occurs in early to mid-May, and high water from the spring melt draws salmon, brookies, and even togue up or down the rivers in this region, including the Moose River, the sprawling East Outlet of the Kennebec River, and the tiny Roach River. These rivers also have September runs of salmon and brookies, and fly anglers hit these waters hard due to abundant fish and a spectacular remote setting. Catching togue in rivers is highly unusual in the U.S.

When anglers head to the Moosehead Lake region, they often think of Moosehead Lake itself; yet, the region stretching from Jackman to the west and over toward Millinocket to the east has an incredible 236,000 acres of water and 4,200 miles of rivers, streams, and brooks—most all of it salmonid habitat.

East of Moosehead lies a cluster of ponds, many of them regulated for fly fishing only. Roads go to a number of these ponds, but some are remote. There are seven Roach ponds that run into Moosehead and attract salmonid anglers, and the Nahmakanta region, a state-owned tract of wilderness, has many more blue-ribbon trout ponds and streams. West toward Jackman is more of the same, with dozens of trout ponds, many remote. Anglers are hard pressed to find waters in this area without brook trout. Togue lakes are also numerous.

Baxter region. The endless ponds in Baxter, northwest of Millinocket, and the remote and semiremote ponds on paper company lands north of there, hold brook trout; in many instances, special regulations exist to protect the fishery. Baxter State Park waters are heavily regulated and routinely produce native brookies in the 12- to 14-inch range and larger. Nesowadnehunk Lake just west of Baxter, and Munsungan and Millinocket Lakes north of Baxter, are three of the best spots in Maine for stillwater brook trout in a remote setting. They routinely produce 2-plus-pound brookies.

The rugged West Branch of the Penobscot River, below Ripogenus Dam just south of Baxter State Park, has a national reputation as a landlocked salmon river and is the best spot in Maine for river landlocks. Four-pound fish are common. The lower section of Nesowadnehunk Stream also has salmon, many of them running up from the West Branch. A private road parallels the Penobscot River, but lower Nesowadnehunk Stream is remote, offering only a foot trail.

Waters in this region peak in late May and June and again in September. The high elevation and northern latitude help keep waters cool all summer. In addition, northern Maine receives as much as 60 more days of rain than does southern Maine. In short, summer fishing can be spectacular.

Much of Maine's north country belongs to large corporations that allow access for a minimal fee. This is truly a sportsman's paradise, and one of the nation's best examples of big business accommodating the public's recreational needs.

Aroostook County. Much of Maine caters to tourists, but a large section of Aroostook County is an agricultural area, worked mostly by potato farmers, with few sporting camps and motels. This should not discourage anglers, though, because the region offers brook trout, landlocked salmon, and brown trout in different settings, ranging from remote boreal forests to pastoral farmlands and, surprisingly, true limestone waters.

Three major limestone waters—Prestile Stream, Meduxnekeag River, and parts of the Aroostook River—lie in eastern Aroostook, right in the middle of potato country. They flow through a limestone belt and hold fat trout that feed voraciously on myriad caddis- and mayflies. This is limestone fishing at its best, with little pressure.

Prestile Stream and the Aroostook River harbor brook trout and the occasional Atlantic salmon, although the latter is rare. Meduxnekeag has browns and brookies. These main rivers can produce small trout in the 8- to 10-inch range all day, discouraging folks who are after bigger fish. When dusk comes, though, a 2- to 3-pound brook trout is possible, and the Meduxnekeag has 20-inch browns and larger. Best of all, every brook running into these primary rivers has trout. Often, even the smallest of brooks has trout that are 12 inches or larger, even during summer.

Southwest of Fort Kent near the Canadian border is a state-owned township colloquially called the Red River, or Deboullie Lake, region. This tract of public land has several blue-ribbon brook trout ponds that lie in remote woods. Trout average 10 to 12 inches, but Black Pond holds 4-pound brookies. Island, Denny, and Galilee Ponds have the typical Maine brookies running from 8 to 12 inches, but the occasional 16-inch fish livens a day. Deboullie has landlocked salmon, brook trout, and the rare blueback trout, which is a landlocked arctic charr. June brings heavy hatches on these waters.

In northeastern Aroostook, the Fish River chain of lakes and the thoroughfares between them offer anglers excellent opportunities for trophy landlocked salmon and brook trout. Late May, June, and September promise the best fishing, but in the north country, abundant summer rains keep fish active throughout the season. Eagle, Square, Cross, Mud, and Long Lakes are huge waters, and the latter is one of the three best spots in Maine for trophy landlocks. Fly anglers hit the thoroughfares between these waters each June and September and catch salmon that average 2 pounds; 4- to 5-pound specimens don't raise an eyebrow. Brookies around 16-inches are common, but 4-pound trophies are possible.

Saltwater

Historically, most recreational fishing in Maine has been conducted on party and charter boats targeting cod, pollock, haddock, hake, and other bottom dwellers. Several thousand pounds of fish was not an uncommon day's bounty for a boatload of 20 anglers from the 1950s through the 1970s. As groundfish stocks in the Gulf of Maine plummeted in the 1980s due to commercial overfishing, the number of larger deep-sea passenger boats declined proportionately, but a few continue to operate, and catches can still be good. Many charter boats began to pursue bluefish during this period, a species that had resumed its annual summer migrations north into Maine waters in 1973 following a 51-year hiatus. Today, most offshore charter boats, and a large and growing fleet of private sportfishing and commercial craft, focus their efforts on giant bluefin tuna. Fishing for blue, mako, and porbeagle sharks has become increasingly popular, but most of the catch is tagged and released.

Inshore recreational saltwater fishing in Maine has centered around the plentiful Atlantic mackerel for nearly a century. Mackerel thrive all along the state's coastline from late spring through fall, and thousands of residents and summer visitors enjoy light-tackle sport with these accommodating little gamesters. Striped bass fishing, both as an activity and as an industry, has burgeoned since the early 1990s, when seasonal bluefish populations began to recede. Anglers quickly turned their attention to bass, which became plentiful enough to attract thousands of new sportfishing participants and to fuel many new coastal guide services, charter boats, outfitters, and tackle shops. In the late 1990s, some 75 percent of Maine's nearly 300,000 residents and visiting saltwater anglers primarily targeted striped bass.

The Downeast coast. The upper half of the state's rugged shoreline, from Penobscot Bay to the Canadian border, is referred to as the Downeast coast, as old-time sailing ships from Boston often ran downwind on an easterly course to get there. Despite a tremendous area of seemingly prime habitat for a number of game and food species, sportfishing pressure is extremely light here due to a short summer season, fewer striped bass and bluefish than in the southern waters of the state, and a corresponding dearth of party and charter boats.

Groundfish, including cod, pollock, cusk, and haddock, are available all along this section of Maine's coast, in water depths from 60 to well over 300 feet. Experienced anglers seek out the rocky humps and ledges that rise from the sea floor and around which these bottom feeders congregate. They send down 8- to 24-ounce chrome-plated diamond or Norwegian-style jigs attached to sturdy 30- to 50-pound-class outfits. Natural baits such as sea clams, squid, and mackerel chunks also work well, especially for haddock and cusk, but may attract dogfish—small sharks regarded as pests. Party boats specializing in bottom fishing can be found in Eastport, Jonesport, Bar Harbor, and Rockland. These normally provide half- or full-day trips.

Atlantic mackerel are available from mid-June through September in bays and harbors virtually everywhere Downeast, ranging from "tinkers" of 6 to 10 inches up to "clubs" approaching 2 pounds. They are taken on small pieces of bait, tiny diamond jigs, or trolled multihook feather or tube rigs, and it's not uncommon to catch several dozen in an hour when the fish are schooling. Fly fishing for mackerel is popular in many areas, and any small streamer dressed with a bit of Mylar for added flash will produce.

Cod was the first species established as a state fish. There has been a life-size wooden carving of the "sacred cod" hanging in the Massachusetts state house since 1784.

Anglers pursue striped bass in the tidewaters of numerous rivers along the Downeast coast, notably the Penobscot, although a good amount of local knowledge as to specific areas and stage of the tide is necessary for consistent success. Bluefish migrated north annually to this region of the coast during the 1980s but were scarce in the 1990s, as stocks have diminished; populations of menhaden, a prime forage species for blues, have likewise decreased.

The Midcoast. The stretch of shoreline from Penobscot Bay south to Casco Bay, referred to as the Midcoast, offers very good fishing. The Camden-Rockland area has launch ramps for private boaters seeking mackerel and groundfish, and Thomaston, at the navigable head of the St. George River, provides access to both Penobscot and Muscongus Bays. Island-studded Muscongus Bay, as well as the Medomak River that empties into it, see comparatively little sportfishing pressure, although mack-erel, groundfish, and striped bass are available during the summer months. Johns Bay, on the eastern side of Pemaquid Point, holds plenty of mackerel and can host fair numbers of bluefish in the 6- to 15-pound range in summer, along with stripers in the Johns River.

M

The Damariscotta River, just west of Johns Bay and separated by Rutherford Island, is comprised of channels, estuaries, and mud flats and is navigable as far upriver as the town of Damariscotta on Route 1, where there is a public launch facility. Although not as heavily fished as rivers to the south, the Damariscotta provides fine striped bass action, including 50-plus-pounders, for small-boat anglers. The river is dotted with thousands of lobster trap buoys, however, which can make fishing difficult in some sections.

Boothbay Harbor, just around the corner from the mouth of the Damariscotta, is the northernmost destination for serious saltwater sportfishing on the East Coast. A bustling summer resort as well as an important lobstering port, the Boothbay region is home to a number of guide, charter, and party boats, along with a half-dozen marinas that accommodate private boats. The most popular offshore area is a plateau-like expanse of bottom 200 to 350 feet deep. Called The Kettle, it is situated 10 miles south of Seguin Island. Jigging produces good numbers of cod, pollock, cusk, hake, and other groundfish; trolling or chumming can produce giant bluefin tuna between 200 and 1,000 pounds from mid-June through September. Anglers also land blue, mako, and porbeagle sharks on The Kettle and in adjacent deeper waters. Inshore fishing for mackerel, striped bass, and bluefish is productive in most of the Boothbay area's bays and around the islands.

The Sheepscot River, the western boundary of the Boothbay region, is one of Maine's coldest waterways year-round, yet it never freezes over. Bluefish are taken on trolled plugs at the river's wide mouth, known as Sheepscot Bay, and striped bass are caught all the way up to the town of Wiscasset on Route 1 and several miles beyond. The beach at Reid State Park on the western shore of the mouth offers good striped bass fishing for surf casters, especially in late summer and early fall.

The Kennebec River. Once polluted by industrial discharge many miles upriver, the Kennebec once again hosts populations of Atlantic salmon, striped bass, sturgeon, and shad thanks to stringent environmental laws. Home to a world-class, small-boat sportfishery for stripers that has expanded steadily since 1990, the Kennebec annually yields thousands of bass each summer from the river's mouth all the way to the Edwards Dam in Augusta some 35 miles upriver, as do the waterways connecting the Kennebec to the Sheepscot River. These include the Sasanoa River with its Upper Hell Gate, Hockomock Bay, the Cross River, and Lower Hell Gate. Live baits, plugs, jigs, and flies all produce stripers in the Kennebec system, and much of the best fishing occurs during the outgoing tide. Launch ramps are available at Bath, Phippsburg, and Hallowell (on the Kennebec), and at Wiscasset (on the Sheepscot). A number of licensed striper guides operate out of these towns as well as Boothbay Harbor and ports in Casco Bay.

Popham Beach, on the western shore of the mouth of the Kennebec, is a popular and easily accessed surf fishing spot for stripers and blues. The coastline around the corner and stretching southwest to Small Point, which is mostly sand beach dotted with rocky islands and ledges, is good striper territory and can be worked from shore or boat. Seguin Island, 2 miles offshore, is surrounded by deeper waters that produce bass and bluefish on trolled swimming plugs.

Casco Bay. Casco Bay is the watery backyard of Portland, Maine's largest city. Bounded by Cape Small to the east and Cape Elizabeth to the west, the bay is 18 miles wide at the mouth and extends nearly the same distance inland. Studded with islands and shoals, Casco Bay waters and the rivers that empty into it—notably the New Meadows, Harraseeket, Royal, and Presumpscot—provide good fishing for striped bass, bluefish, mackerel, and groundfish during the warm-weather months. Blues are landed almost anywhere, especially on swimming plugs trolled around the ledges in the outer bay, which include Temple and Lumbo Ledges, Halfway Rock, Bulwark Shoal, and Alden Rock, yet they will often chase baits up onto the shallow mud flats along the northwest side of the bay from Portland to Brunswick. Each of these rivers holds striped bass from June through September, as do many of the islands and ledges. Cod and pollock prefer the underwater humps from 50 to 150 feet deep in the outer portions of the bay, and anglers take them on jigs or baits. Numerous marinas and launch ramps exist along the bay's perimeter, and the area boasts more than a dozen guide, charter, and party boats that target groundfish, stripers, and blues. Sharks and bluefin tuna are available in South Harpswell and the greater Portland area.

The Southwest coast. The southwest coast, stretching from Casco Bay to Kittery, offers excellent fishing.

The Spurwink River, which marks the southerly border of Cape Elizabeth just below Portland, provides good action for striped bass in the summer and is a favorite among flycasters. Adjacent Higgens Beach is one of Maine's top surf fishing spots and yields some of the largest striped bass taken in the state each year. Crescent-shaped Saco Bay, home of famous Old Orchard Beach, is bounded on the south by Biddeford Pool and the mouth of the Saco River, an excellent striped bass river that can hold bluefish as well. Public launch ramps and access to the shore are available in the Camp Ellis area.

The 5-mile stretch of coast from Biddeford Pool down to Cape Porpoise offers good inshore fishing for stripers, blues, and mackerel. Kennebunkport, a mile up the Kennebunk River, is home to several deep-sea party boats. Perkins Cove at the town of Ogunquit, some 10 miles down the coast from Kennebunkport, hosts a small fleet of party, commercial, and pleasure boats. York Harbor, 7 miles farther downcoast, provides good access to Boon Island and its adjacent ledges 6 miles offshore, where action for bluefish, bottom fish, and bluefin tuna is good.

All of the ports along the southwest coast are jumping-off spots for Jeffreys Ledge, which ranges from 20 to 30 miles offshore and stretches southwest from Kennebunkport to Newburyport in Massachusetts. Jeffreys is the most popular and heavily fished offshore ground off the southwest coast and consistently yields good catches of cod, pollock, haddock, bluefin tuna, and sharks. Other bottom-fishing and tuna grounds farther east in the Gulf of Maine, including Platts Bank and Cashes Ledge, are accessed from these ports as well.

The Piscataqua River, the natural border between Maine and New Hampshire, provides fine striped bass fishing from May through October; live baits (mackerel, menhaden, pollock, and eels) are especially productive on larger fish. Bluefish roam the Portsmouth Harbor area at the river's mouth and the outer shoreline, and bass, blues, groundfish, and tuna are taken around the Isles of Shoals, a cluster of rocky islands 7 miles offshore. Anglers who land stripers on the Piscataqua should be aware that size and possession limits for striped bass in Maine and New Hampshire may differ. Fish landed from the Maine riverbank fall under Maine regulations, and vice versa.

MAINTENANCE

See: Tackle—Care, Maintenance and Repair.

MALAŴI

By African standards, the 45,700-square-mile landlocked country of Malaŵi in the southeastern corner of central Africa is small, but an impressive 30 percent is covered by water, primarily by Lake Nyasa. Formerly known as Lake Malaŵi, Nyasa is the third largest lake on the African continent, and the twelfth largest freshwater lake in the world.

Malaŵi does not offer the abundant game and wildlife viewing opportunities available in some African countries, and fewer international tourists visit Malaŵi. Yet, with lush green hills, spectacular mountain ranges, lofty plateaus, and abundant bird life, as well as Lake Nyasa, Malaŵi has varied attractions, and many Africans are attracted in particular to the sandy shores of Nyasa. Nevertheless, fishing opportunities for the traveling angler, especially the international visitor, are modest.

This is unfortunate and ironic, because crystal clear Lake Nyasa, which is 567 kilometers long and up to 80 kilometers wide, has more endemic species of fish than any other lake in the world. Accounts of the number of species vary from 200 to 500, and some biologists suggest that even these numbers are conservative.

Although Lake Nyasa is touted in tourism literature as an angler's paradise because of its multitude of fish species, the greatest portion of these are small aquarium fish and members of the Cichlidae family, including many varieties of mbuna rockfish and assorted tilapia. The tilapia, and other coarse fish—including vundu (African catfish growing to 30 kilograms), tsungwa (growing to 2 kilograms), and mpasa, or lake salmon (a member of the carp family growing to 3 kilograms)—although valued as table fare, are not compelling gamefish, nor are they especially attractive to international anglers. Mpasa are strong fighters, however, and are caught in some of the 14 rivers that feed the lake, most notably Bua, Luweya, Lufira, and North Rukuru. Tigerfish are also reputed to be in the lake, which has hosted light-tackle fishing tournaments.

Many thousands of people living around Lake Nyasa rely on it for commercial or subsistence fishing, and, although angling opportunities are minimal, visitors can enjoy snorkeling, whereby they can observe great schools of small, colorful cichlids. Boats are available for hire at lakeside hotels, but good information on where to fish is lacking. Because of its size and great depths, Nyasa can get very rough in windy weather.

M

There are other possibilities in Malaŵi, however, including river tigerfishing and rainbow trout angling, both in or near the Shire Highlands south of Lake Nyasa. The highlands include Mount Mulanje, central Africa's highest peak at 9,849 feet.

Tigerfish are concentrated in the lower Shire River, which exits Lake Nyasa and eventually merges with the Zambezi River in Mozambique. The lower Shire plunges through chasms, and tigerfish up to 7 kilograms favor the rapids and eddies below Kapichira Falls. Access from Chikwawa can be rugged in the wet season, necessitating a 4-wheel-drive vehicle. The lower Shire is wide here, and a boat is generally necessary. The dry season (May through November) brings optimal fishing conditions.

Not far to the east and northeast, mountain streams and lakes are stocked with rainbow trout. Anglers can fish rivers on the lower slopes of the Mulanje Mountains, or on the Chambe and Lichenya Plateaus. In the Zomba Plateau, rainbows thrive in many streams, as well as in Lake Mulunguzi. Streams and lakes in Nyika National Park also contain trout. Licenses from either the park or forestry offices are required, only fly fishing is permitted, and the period from September through April is recommended.

Numerous reservoirs of various size exist here, and reportedly some on the tea estates in Mulanje and Thyolo have been stocked with largemouth bass. The rainy season is from November through March, and it can be humid between December and February, although evenings are cool in the colder altitudes.

M

MANGROVES

A tropical to semitropical treelike plant (genus *Rhizophora*) found in tidal conditions in salt marshes, muddy swamps, lagoons, and estuaries. Mangrove forests are found in eastern North America (Florida and the Caribbean), eastern South America, West Africa, Southeast Asia, and Australia.

Able to extract freshwater from their saline environment, mangroves grow with their roots in the water to heights of 30 to 40 feet, and have edible fruit. Three different mangroves—red, black, and white—are most commonly known, and all occur in Florida.

Red mangrove trees suggest big green millipedes walking on the water, their prop roots desperately grasping the bottom. Their long, arrowlike seed pods hang vertically, with the seed at the bottom. Black mangrove trees have pencillike roots and usually occupy slightly higher elevations upland from the red mangrove. White mangroves occupy the highest elevations farther upland than either the red or black mangroves.

Mangrove systems help purify the water in estuaries by filtering runoff; they provide breeding and nesting areas for many marine animals and birds, prevent shoreline erosion, and buffer inland areas from storm winds and tides. Mangrove thickets offer so much protection from the elements that boaters facing a hurricane emergency may take their boats far up mangrove creeks for shelter.

The waters beneath mangroves are used as nurseries by many important fish species. As the leaves die and decay, they become food for the community of animals living on the bottom. Snook, jacks, snapper, sheepshead, grouper, small jewfish, and barracuda hide and forage through the tangles of roots. Tarpon prowl the channels just outside the mangroves. Juvenile tripletail are seen lying on their sides, floating alongside and resembling mangrove leaves. Occasionally, mangroves growing in slightly brackish water harbor largemouth bass.

Anglers in shallow-draft boats drift along mangrove shorelines, tossing surface plugs and flies as near the roots as possible, to draw fish out from concealment, and then work hard to keep hooked fish from getting back into the roots.

MANITOBA

In a country with wall-to-wall fishing opportunities, Manitoba stands second to no Canadian province. It offers diverse species and notable locations that run the gamut from metropolitan catfish to tundra trout. The tourism literature calls this province an angling paradise, a lofty description not without merit.

One of Canada's heartland provinces, Manitoba is sandwiched between Ontario and Saskatchewan on its east and west, and Minnesota/North Dakota and Nunavut Territory on its south and north. Within its boundaries is a landmass of 251,000 square miles, slightly smaller than Texas. Despite its central North American location, Manitoba is a maritime province: Its northern boundary straddles Hudson Bay and Nunavut Territory at the 60th parallel. There, Churchill is Canada's only arctic seaport, with 63 frost-free days, ocean-sailing vessels, and saltwater fishing for arctic charr.

Fifteen percent, or 39,000 square miles, of Manitoba's landmass is water. It boasts 100,000 freshwater lakes and 75 species of fish. With these abundant resources, it is no wonder that many anglers, residents and nonresidents alike, visit its waters, many with hopes of catching a trophy fish.

Through the Manitoba Master Angler program, a province-supported initiative to recognize notable catches, trophy fish have been recorded since 1960. Today some 10,000 trophy fish among 28 species are registered annually, the most popular being northern pike, lake trout, walleye, channel catfish, brook trout, whitefish, and smallmouth bass. Other species in the province, and with varying constituencies, are arctic charr, arctic grayling, black crappie, brown trout, bullhead, burbot, carp, freshwater drum (silver bass), goldeye, kokanee, largemouth bass, mooneye, muskellunge, perch, rainbow trout, rock bass, sauger, splake, sturgeon, tullibee, and white bass.

Manitoba is a world leader in progressive fish management, with aggressive catch-and-release programs and legislated mandatory use of barbless hooks. In fact, barbless hooks are mandatory throughout the province, for all species of fish. More than 75 percent of the trophy fish caught and recorded in the Master Angler program are released to fight again. A tape measure and camera are standard equipment.

Manitoba consists of three distinct geologic regions. Mesozoic shale covers the southwest portion; Paleozoic limestone extends through the north-central portion; and Precambrian granite extends outward in a northwesterly direction to the Hudson Bay Coast and beyond the provincial boundaries.

The Mesozoic region is typified by small shallow lakes in the agricultural belt. Through control of water levels in rivers, these lakes have become great producers of northern pike, walleye, and stocked trout.

The Paleozoic region contains large, relatively shallow lakes that are excellent producers of walleye, sauger, whitefish, and white bass. Lake Winnipeg, the seventh largest freshwater lake in North America and covering an area of 9,398 square miles, is an excellent example of this type of lake. Two other very large lakes of Paleozoic limestone are Lake Winnipegosis, which covers 2,086 square miles, and Lake Manitoba, which has a surface area of 1,817 square miles.

In general terms, the best angling waters are in the Precambrian shield country to the north and northeast, which is typified by fertile deep lakes and countless rivers. Gods Lake, Island Lake, and Big Sand Lake are good examples of this type of Precambrian granite.

Provincial Parks

Whiteshell Provincial Park. With an area of 672,334 acres, Whiteshell is Manitoba's largest park. The northern boundary is the Winnipeg River; the eastern boundary is the Manitoba/Ontario border; and the Trans-Canada Highway traverses the park to the south. The park is characterized by numerous lakes, rivers, and rugged Precambrian shield terrain, with a forest of spruce and fir, intermixed with aspen, poplar, and poorly drained tamarack or black spruce fens and bogs. Fishing is superb here, and in most Whiteshell waters, targeted species include northern pike, walleye, lake trout, whitefish, smallmouth bass, lake sturgeon, goldeye, mooneye, and sauger.

The Winnipeg River to the north, which became very prominent in the 1700s when it was an important fur trade route, is one of the great fishing rivers of Manitoba. Rising in Lake of the Woods and sweeping in a giant arc across the northern limit of Whiteshell Provincial Park, the river starts at Eaglenest Lake at the Ontario border, which is noted for large northern pike, trophy walleye, and scrappy smallmouth bass. At Seven Sisters, the river broadens to form a series of lakes: Natalie, Sylvia, Margaret, Eleanor, Dorothy, Nutimik, and Lac du Bonnet. It then drops through a series of cataracts and bays to join Lake Winnipeg. There are seven fishing lodges and five provincial campgrounds on this series of lakes, and fishing is consistent for northern pike, walleye, smallmouth bass, and sturgeon. The area is a paradise for wildlife, and it offers a variety of hiking trails, canoe routes, and archaeological sites.

Anglers fish primarily from boats, which are available from numerous camps. Walleye thrive in rapids and fast-moving waters. Northern pike prefer quiet bays, weedbeds, and waters near rapids. Smallmouth linger around deep, rocky ledges, and sturgeon feed on the bottom near large rapids or falls. Pike run from 5 to 10 pounds, but occasional 15- to 20-pounders exist. Walleye run from 2 to 7 pounds, and smallmouth average 2 pounds. Sturgeon vary from 10 to 80 pounds; Manitoba's record is 126 pounds. Anglers practice all methods of fishing, but spoons, spinners, and jigs are the most popular offerings. Sturgeon are taken on dead baits or minnows. Goldeye are landed with wet and dry flies.

The largest entirely artificial reservoir in the United States is Lake Mead, an impoundment of the Colorado River in Nevada.

The rest of Whiteshell Park stretches along Highway 307, which runs north to south and connects a large quantity of lakes with many facilities. Although family cottages dominate most of the lakes, good fishing is available throughout the season. This is ideal country for a family vacation, and the more adventurous angler can take a canoe trip to many backwoods areas, including the Mantario Wilderness. Mantario was set aside for hiking, canoeing, and fishing, and no motorized craft are allowed. The fishing is excellent, especially for northern pike, walleye, and smallmouth bass.

Nopiming Provincial Park. A little farther north of Whiteshell Provincial Park is Nopiming Provincial Park, a new wilderness area. *Nopiming,* an Anishinabe word meaning "entrance to the wilderness," is set in the Precambrian shield country east of Lake Winnipeg and is accessible only via an isolated gravel road from Provincial Trunk Highways 304 and 314. Rock and water are the prominent features of the park.

Because of its relative isolation, Nopiming Provincial Park has excellent fishing. Walleye, northern pike, lake trout, and smallmouth bass abound in the many lakes and rivers in the area. Only three lodges exist in the park, but campgrounds are available throughout. The main campgrounds are at Tulabi Falls, Black Lake, Beresford Lake, and Quesnel Lake. Backcountry camping is also allowed, and the area offers exceptional road-accessible canoeing. Notable canoe routes are Seagrim Lake, Rabbit River, Bird River, and Manigotagan. Excellent walleye thrive in Black, Quesnel, Manigotagan, Gem, and Bird Lakes.

Northern pike exist throughout Nopiming, and noteworthy smallmouth bass are caught in Shoe and Tooth Lakes.

Atikaki Provincial Park. The vast area north of Nopiming Provincial Park, between Lake Winnipeg and the Ontario border, is accessible only by air. This region offers excellent sportfishing, and lodges are scattered throughout the park. The northern portion is known as Atikaki Provincial Wilderness Park. *Atikaki* means "county of the caribou," and roughly 350 woodland caribou range in or near this park, which was designated as a wilderness zone in 1985.

The boreal forest and Precambrian shield make this park a true and typical Manitoba wilderness for canoeing and trophy angling. Notable lakes are Aikens, Sasaginnigak, Dogskin, Amphibian, Family, and Moar. All are excellent for northern pike and walleye, with Aikens also having lake trout. Lodges, as well as outpost camps, are available at some of the smaller lakes.

The Interlake District

A large area ranging from farmland in the south to coniferous forest in the north lies between Lake Winnipeg and Lakes Manitoba and Winnipegosis. The northernmost two-thirds of this area is sparsely settled and has few roads, making it a natural home for wildlife. The region supports many worthwhile angling spots, and although these places are widely scattered, all can be reached via Highway 6, which runs north out of Winnipeg and parallels the eastern shore of Lake Manitoba.

The Narrows of Lake Manitoba, 130 miles north of Winnipeg via Highways 6 and 68, is renowned for large walleye, jumbo perch, silver bass (drum), and common carp. Forty miles north of Ashern, Lake St. Martin and the Fairford River offer good northern pike and walleye action. A new road, Provincial Trunk Highway 513, which runs off Highway 6, has opened a new area at Dauphin River on Lake Winnipeg, where the walleye action is superb. Northern pike to 15 pounds are also common.

At Grand Rapids, 250 miles north of Winnipeg on Highway 6, is a large hydroelectric generating station connecting Cedar Lake to Lake Winnipeg. Cedar Lake is a large body of water renowned for huge northern pike. Fish exceeding 25 pounds are common, and some in the 30-pound class have been taken. Cedar Lake is part of the Saskatchewan River, which flows from the Alberta Rockies and empties into Hudson Bay, and also has excellent walleye and whitefish angling. The 14.2-pound Manitoba record whitefish came from this system. Some of the best local walleye and northern pike fishing is in the vicinity of Waterhen.

Gods Lake/Gods River Area

Gods Lake/Gods River. The Gods Lake/Gods River country of northeastern Manitoba has long been famed for trophy lake trout, brook trout, and northern pike. Located 365 miles north of Winnipeg and serviced by four lodges with all-weather landing strips, Gods Lake itself is 65 miles long and 20 miles wide, and provides superb fishing. Lake trout average 6 to 12 pounds, with many exceeding 20 pounds; northern pike average 6 to 16 pounds, with some in the 30-pound class; and brook trout average 3 to 5 pounds, with many in the 7- to 9-pound class. Walleye and whitefish are also present.

Single barbless hooks are mandatory for brook trout fishing in the Gods and Island Rivers, and only one brookie over 18 inches can be kept. Spoons and large spinners are popular for lake trout and northern pike, and small spinners and flies for brook trout. Jigs can be especially effective on all species at certain times in the summer, and fly fishing is most effective in July, when insects are hatching. Even large whitefish can be taken when fishing for brook trout on the river.

Gods River water is very clear and fast, with many shallows and rapids, and navigation here is recommended only for skilled canoeists. The brook trout in these waters are brilliantly colored, large, and naturally strong because of the fast-moving water. They are famous throughout the continent and live up to their hard-fighting reputation. These are native, wild fish who deposit their eggs in early September on gravel beds in slack waters behind islands and along boulders in the main river itself. Early in the following summer, the fry inhabit warmer quiet waters along the banks and enjoy a plentiful supply of aquatic insects. The young fish triple in size during the brief midsummer and adapt to hiding and feeding among rocks in deeper and faster water. Trophy brookies over 20 inches or 4 pounds are about 6 years old, and their diet includes minnows as well as insects. These brook trout do not retire into Gods Lake itself, but live in the big river year-round.

Other waters. Several other great fisheries have been developed near Gods Lake, most notably Knee, Molson, Edmund, Bolton, Gunisao, Utik, and Silsby Lakes. All are serviced by lodges and have better-than-average northern pike fishing.

Knee Lake lies 400 miles north of Winnipeg and is 45 miles long, with a width of up to 5 miles. The lake comprises numerous islands, bays, and reefs, which create ideal structure, and therefore, some of the finest fishing habitat in North America. Utik, Bolton, Silsby, Gunisao, and Edmund are smaller but produce excellent trophy northern pike, along with fast action for walleye and whitefish.

Trophy northern pike are the predominant species in these waters. They average 8 to 18 pounds, and many are in the 20- to 30-pound category. Anglers can expect good fishing throughout late June, July, and August. The timing of ice out can affect the catch in the early season, but northern pike are always available in shallow bays or near the spawning beds in rivers.

Gunisao Lake is noted for trophy walleye and is probably the best trophy walleye lake in Manitoba. It is 16 miles long and has approximately 75 islands that provide extraordinary walleye habitat, as well as sheltered fishing in all weather.

The Far North

Because the Precambrian shield runs in a northwesterly direction up to and including the 60th parallel, the far north has developed into a unique and marvelous fishery. This area of sand eskers and treeless tundra creates a vacation destination with the freshest, cleanest air and trophy fishing that Manitobans say is second to none. Sites with fully developed lodges, complete with all-weather landing strips, are Nueltin, Nejanilini, North Knife, and Big Sand Lakes, and the North Seal River chain.

Nueltin Lake. Nueltin Lake is 800 miles north of Winnipeg, straddling both the 60th parallel and the borders of Manitoba and Nunavut Territory. Shaped like an hourglass, the lake is 125 miles long and up to 35 miles wide. The southern third lies in Manitoba and is heavily tree-lined with stunted spruce and tamarack. The northern part of Nueltin is only 380 miles from the Arctic Circle and is situated in nearly treeless, flat, and lichen-covered tundra where caribou are occasionally seen.

Nueltin is as remote as one can get in Manitoba, with wild, unspoiled beauty, countless islands and bays, many incoming rivers, and plenty of sandy beaches where you might see the tracks of a moose, wolf, fox, or bear if not the animal itself. Granite outcroppings are the only breaks in the barren land.

The lake is cold and deep, and therefore supports huge lake trout and trophy northern pike. There are no walleye this far north, but the added attraction is grayling up to 4 pounds, which can be caught in the frigid, fast-flowing streams and rivers that feed into Nueltin, especially around Nueltin Narrows. Lake trout in the 30- to 50-pound class live in Nueltin, as do northern pike in the 15- to 30-pound range. There is one main lodge on this enormous body of water, but it is open only 10 weeks each year, starting with ice out in mid- to late June, and there are outpost camps at Windy River and Nueltin Narrows as well as access to other area waters.

Nueltin has benefited from an enlightened lodge-instituted trophy-only policy that was begun in 1977 and subsequently changed to a catch-and-release-only policy (with the exception of a shore lunch fish). As a result, Nueltin lays claim to being the first catch-and-release lake in North America and, along with requiring the use of only single barbless hooks, the first to ensure that it will have preserved long-lived trophy fish for generations to come. As a result, 20-pound pike and 40-pound lakers go back into the water, as do 5- and 15-pounders, and a steady increase has occurred in the number of trophy specimens caught and released at Nueltin.

Nueltin Lake has some of Canada's best lake trout fishing; this is a 35-pounder.

The Manitoba Master Angler program is testimony to the lake's great pike and lake trout fishing, even though two-thirds of Nueltin lies in Nunavut Territory, and trophy fish caught in those waters aren't registered in this government program. In effect, Nueltin would dominate the stat sheet far more than it usually does were this not so.

Lots of fish, even pike and lakers of enormous size, are an honest-to-goodness possibility for any angler, even those who are moderately skilled. The biggest laker taken to date weighed 56 pounds, and bigger ones have been lost.

Nueltin lends itself to various angling techniques. For big lake trout, trolling is undoubtedly the best tactic, especially in the main part of the lake. Early in the season, however, when the ice is still receding, the bays and river inlets with open water offer the best chances for huge fish, with possibilities for light-tackle angling as well as casting and jigging. Spoons and large jigs are the best lures, and DeBartok Rapids and Sealhole Lake are two prime locales.

For pike, the period from mid-June (when the camps open) through early July offers the most action, with plenty of fish in shallow water that are eager to strike surface lures, spinnerbaits, and weedless spoons cast into the shore in the backs of countless bays. Good pike and lake trout fishing are available throughout the season.

Nearby and accessed from Nueltin's camp by floatplane is Kasmere Lake, which has similar species to Nueltin and which has only been fished by the occasional fly-in day angler. Minimal fishing effort, however, has already tabbed the lake as a hotspot for big pike. A new lodge was built on Kasmere in 1999.

Big Sand Lake. Big Sand Lake is 525 miles north of Winnipeg and 200 miles west of Hudson Bay. It is the headwaters of the South Seal River, and supports fishing for trophy northern pike plus lake trout, walleye, and arctic grayling. There is one lodge on the lake, which opened in 1988, and outpost camps exist on Leclair, Wood, Wolf, Otter, and Jordan Lakes. The serenity of the location coupled with incredible trophy fishing opportunities is enough to excite even the most experienced angler.

Big Sand Lake is 50 miles long and has produced northern pike in excess of 35 pounds. It is not uncommon to catch 100 or more pike per day, and good opportunities abound for fish up to 20 pounds. Cabbage weeds flourish in bays and along points and deep shorelines, creating great habitat for these sulking predators.

Walleye are plentiful at Big Sand as well, and can be caught in abundance even close to the lodge near the outlet of Katimew Lake, one of many tributaries to Big Sand. The lake is not known for huge walleye, but there are many in the 3- and 4-pound class, readily caught on crankbaits and jigs.

The lodge practices a strict no-kill (except small fish for shore lunch), barbless-hook-only angling policy. Once commercially fished by the Indians, Big Sand Lake has been off limits to commercial ventures for some time, and only sportfishing is practiced today. Good-size grayling (3-pounders) inhabit the South Seal River, which is a pleasant two-hour boat ride from the lodge.

North Seal River. The North Seal River system is another fish factory, one that has been newly developed for anglers. It comprises a series of lakes on the North Seal River chain and includes Chatwin, Minuhik, Egenolf, Blackfish, Nicklin, Steven's, Maria, and Burnie Lakes. Located 700 miles north of Winnipeg, the North Seal River watershed has opened a new remote fishery dominated by the Robertson Esker, a stunning geographical formation of sand dune and rock some 300 miles long.

Formed by a subglacial riverbank, Robertson Esker gives shape and character to the region. Rising above the land, then falling below the water, the esker has become an area where rivers become lakes and lakes revert to rivers. Sandbars, rocky shoals, and fast-flowing rivers add up to excellent fishing for northern pike, lake trout, grayling, and walleye. A main lodge, several mini lodges, and outpost camps service the system.

The Northwest

The so-called northwest portion of Manitoba is actually the central region north of the 53rd parallel. All but a small portion of this section of the province is in the Precambrian shield country. It is a very popular destination for visiting anglers and has many facilities. Although this renowned area is several hundred miles north of the international boundary, paved highways make this easily accessible in all weather.

The Pas, Flin Flon, Thompson, and Lynn Lake are significant centers and have daily air and bus service. Clearwater, Cormorant, and Athapapuskow Lakes are probably the most famous, with Rocky, Reed, Kississing, and Cranberry Lakes following close behind.

Clearwater Lake is astonishing for its crystal clear waters with visibility to a depth of 40 feet. The lake itself is 15 miles long and 15 miles wide, and ranges from 80 to 100 feet in depth. Because of this depth, ice out is always late at Clearwater—usually not until the first week of June. Lake trout, northern pike, and whitefish are frequently taken by trolling or vertical jigging with heavy spoons. The average lake trout is 3 to 5 pounds, but many trophies of 15 to 25 pounds have been landed. Northern pike are available from 10 to 20 pounds, and whitefish run 3 to 5 pounds. Cormorant Lake is just a little farther to the northeast and is accessible by gravel road. This is an excellent walleye and northern pike fishery, with many bays and islands for protection.

The balance of the lakes in this area are all accessible by road, and all provide excellent northern pike and walleye fishing. There are lodges at each of the lakes and many campgrounds in the area, making this an excellent family vacation destination. Lake Athapapuskow held the world's lake trout record of 63 pounds for almost 30 years. Even today, at least one or two trophy fish in the 35- to 40-pound range are caught in Athapapuskow every year.

The Southwest

Manitoba's southwest also offers some fishing opportunity, although most of the lakes are relatively small and shallow. Stocking programs, especially in the Duck, Porcupine, and Turtle Mountains, have given these areas new life. Such exotic species as kokanee salmon, splake, brook trout, brown trout, and rainbow trout are among the fish stocked here. Muskies have been successfully stocked in Line Lake in the Duck Mountains, and northern pike and walleye inhabit most of these waters.

The southwest contains two of Manitoba's largest southern rivers: the Red, which originates in the United States, and the Assiniboine, which runs east and north from Saskatchewan. Both are excellent producers of some 12 to 15 fish species, particularly giant channel catfish, trophy carp, and walleye, along with bullhead, freshwater drum, sauger, northern pike, white bass, sturgeon, perch, tullibee, goldeye, mooneye, black crappie, and rock bass.

Several man-made structures, including Lockport Dam, the Portage Diversion, and Shellmouth Dam, have created reservoirs and lakes that have become meccas for bank and boat anglers. Although only a few lodges exist along the rivers, ample facilities are nearby.

Red River. The Red River is unquestionably one of the best bets in North America for large walleye, producing an awe-inspiring number of specimens weighing 10 pounds or more. These fish are migrants from Lake Winnipeg.

Generally dirty and roily, especially in spring

and early summer, the Red River flows northward in farm country from the Dakotas through southern Manitoba and into Lake Winnipeg. The hotbed of big-fish activity is in Manitoba, in the Selkirk area just north of the city of Winnipeg and below the Lockport Dam. Big walleye, however, can be caught anywhere in the river. They fall for a variety of presentations, with slow trolling one of the more reliable techniques for newcomers to this waterway.

October, when a tremendous run of big walleye migrates out of Lake Winnipeg, is the best time to fish. The run starts in mid-September, when the water cools and the north winds blow. Incidentally, the Winnipeg River, which is about 60 miles from Lockport, is another good producer of walleye. It does not seem to hold as many large fish, but its walleye are more aesthetically appealing, sporting an emerald green coloration in the fall. Winnipeg River fish are locally called greenbacks.

Actually, all walleye here are called "pickerel," and most local anglers fish with so-called pickerel rigs, which sport a long-shanked bait hook for a nightcrawler and a small spinner blade. Drifting and stillfishing with live bait or jigs tipped with bait is also popular. Some anglers, mostly visitors from the U.S., troll with plugs, and this method merits attention as well.

The Red River is also known as one of the premier spots in North America for giant catfish. In Manitoba, the Red dominates the Master Angler citation list, and rates among the best places to pursue 20-pound or better specimens. The huge cats are almost exclusively taken on baits, predominantly chicken liver or gizzard shad chunks, fished along the bottom. Several other rivers in this area also offer good catfishing.

MANTA

See: Rays and Skates.

MAPS

The word "map" is frequently used by anglers to convey several different products. Technically, a map details land features, and a chart details water features. Topographic maps depict land features in great detail but do not provide subsurface details about water. They may help some freshwater anglers locate places worthy of fishing (ponds or river backwaters, for example) but are of no value from a hydrographic standpoint. Navigational charts, on the other hand, and underwater contour maps depicting hydrographic information, provide little information about land areas but significant detail regarding depth, obstructions, and navigational aids. When used in conjunction with a compass or a GPS, they help you maintain course, especially in fog, low-light conditions, or at night.

Every angler who fishes a large or unfamiliar body of water should have a good map or chart of that place and use it in conjunction with sonar. The best and most detailed of these are navigational charts, which exist for virtually all bodies of water that are deemed by federal agencies as navigable. This includes coastal waters and large inland waterways but does not include many bodies of freshwater. Maps that are not navigational charts but that do show underwater detail usually contain a notice that they are not to be used for navigational purposes; nevertheless, depending on the degree of detail, they can be of general navigational value and an important source of information to anglers.

Maps and charts that show underwater contours and hydrographic features can help you navigate without getting lost or possibly running into obstructions, and can help you find areas that may provide good fishing. Maps that are studied at home, prior to on-the-water fishing, often allow anglers to devise a plan and avoid haphazard fishing, which is especially useful when time is limited.

Navigational charts (and topographic maps) are produced by American and Canadian federal agencies and are available at some sporting goods stores, marinas, and major-city map stores. Dealers usually stock local area charts and maps and can order others for you. To order maps yourself, obtain a map index from the appropriate government agency. United States topographical maps are produced by the U.S. Geological Survey; navigational charts of U.S. waters are distributed by the National Oceanic and Atmospheric Administration, Distribution Division; Canadian topographic maps are distributed by Natural Resources Canada, Ottawa; navigational charts of Canadian waters are produced by the Canadian Department of Fisheries and Oceans, Hydrographic Section, Ottawa.

Order maps long before you expect to depart on a trip. Remember that the larger the scale, the

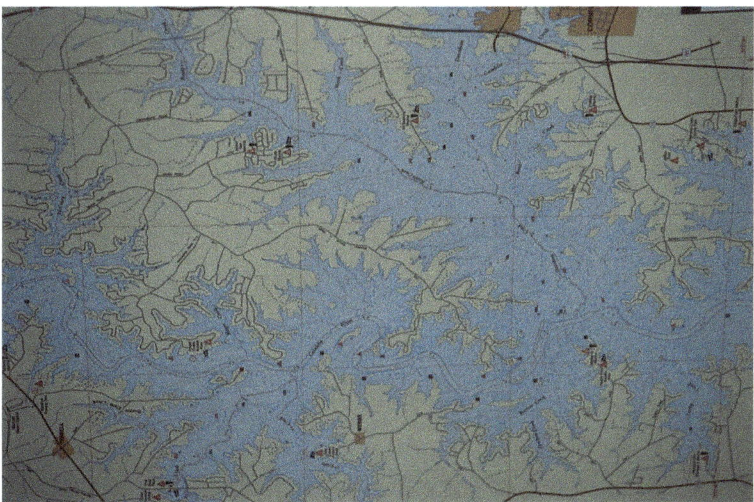

A compressed map of a large reservoir depicts submerged river and creek channels as well as access sites and relative depths.

M

more detail is provided. Other maps of big waters may be available from jurisdictional agencies such as the Corps of Engineers or the Tennessee Valley Authority (TVA), although their maps are rarely detailed enough to give you more than general information.

Maps supplied by private firms are often geared to anglers' interests and provide a good deal of underwater contour information. Their size and scale will determine how helpful they are as boating and fishing aids. Many useful maps can be found at tackle shops, sporting goods stores, and marinas near popular waterways. In addition, state freshwater fisheries agencies often have contour maps (ranging from large-scale to reduced size on an 8$^1/_2$-by-11-inch sheet of paper), particularly for smaller lakes and ponds, and you should check with these agencies for such availability.

Not all of the information on underwater contour maps or navigational charts is totally accurate or complete, and anglers must use good judgment when using them, but these products are substantial aids to anglers who know the habits of their quarry and its habitat and can identify areas that are likely to be productive. This is particularly so where big lakes are concerned and where it would take an inordinate amount of time to explore. Moreover, once you've had success at finding fish, you may refer to a map to locate other areas that may be similar.

The features of an underwater contour map or navigational chart are evident once you've read the symbols index. Navigational charts especially should be studied, because many aids to navigation are identified.

It's a good idea to store maps in a large, clear, sealable plastic pouch or to treat them with a waterproofing material to help them last in marine environments. Color coding the different contour levels or marking certain areas with indelible markers is also worthwhile.

See: Navigation.

MARGATE, WHITE

See: Grunts.

MARGIN

The edge of a body of water, especially stillwaters such as ponds or lakes. This is a European term, coincident with margin fishing, which refers to short-range, or close-in fishing efforts.

MARGIN FISHING

A term for fishing the edges of ponds and lakes for carp *(see)* by using long rods and dappling the surface with a bait when cruising or basking fish are attracted there.

MARIANA ISLANDS

See: Portugal.

MARICULTURE

The raising of marine fish or shellfish under some controls, usually for the purpose of commercial sale. Ponds, pens, tanks, or other containers may be used. Feed is commonly used. This term is often used synonymously with, and secondarily to, aquaculture, which is a more generic term that encompasses cultivation of fish in freshwater environs as well as in saltwater. Fish farming (as well as oyster farming, shrimp farming, etc.) is another term used to describe mariculture operations; and a marine hatchery may be a form of mariculture, although hatcheries operated by government agencies usually release fish before commercial harvest size is reached, and usually raise them for the purpose of supplementing sportfishing stocks. Private hatcheries may raise fish to be sold for private stocking efforts or for commercial sale to food processors, fish markets, and restaurants.

See: Aquaculture; Hatchery.

MARINA

An establishment along the water where boats are kept and where varying services and supplies are available. Marinas usually have mooring docks in the water and provide dry storage on trailers or on ground supports or inside closed buildings; they may offer boat and engine repairs and servicing. They may sell or rent boats as well as supply drive-up fuel and fresh water. Some marinas have a store where various provisions, including ice, navigational charts, and sometimes bait and fishing and boating equipment, are available.

Marinas are usually occupied by recreational boats and provide seasonal, long-term, and/or temporary dockage. They often have a boat launch, and some have a heavy-duty facility for hauling large vessels out of the water.

MARINE

Pertaining to the sea and saltwater environs from the open oceans to the high-water mark and into estuaries; also used to refer to seawater or saltwater.

MARINE RADIO

A general term for radiotelephones used in boats, primarily applied to VHF radios.

See: Communications.

MARKER BUOY

Not to be confused with channel- or shoal-marking buoys *(see)* anchored as strategic aids to navigation, marker buoys are small portable floats, usually attached to a heavy weight, used by casting and trolling anglers to temporarily mark the location of such underwater hydrographic features as channels, dropoffs, shoals, points, and bars in mid-depth waters.

Most marker buoys are nothing more than plastic floats, usually brightly colored for easy spotting, attached to heavy weights by strong line. They are tossed in the water at a specific site, the weighted line drops to the bottom of the water, and the float marks the spot. The float is retrieved later along with the line and weight wrapped around the float. Flat markers are better than round, barbell versions because the former are more resistant to the effects of current, wind, and waves. Round markers can be blown quite a distance from the site they are supposed to identify, which does not happen with the square, flat marker buoys.

Marker buoys are frequently used in conjunction with sonar equipment. Most big-lake and saltwater anglers, and most deep-water trollers, don't use marker buoys because they roam so widely in search of fish, because the buoys aren't functional in really deep water, or because placement of the buoys could interfere with fishing. However, marker buoys can be effectively used by boaters on small- to medium-size bodies of water who are looking to define specific and relatively shallow underwater structures or contours for casting, vertical jigging, or trolling; and by those who may be trolling to locate schools of fish that they will stop and cast to.

MARLIN, BLACK *Makaira indica.*

Other names—Pacific black marlin, giant black marlin, silver marlin (Hawaii), white marlin (Japan); Arabic: *kheil al bahar;* Indonesian: *layaran, mersuji, suji;* Japanese: *kurokawa, shirokajiki;* Portuguese: *espadim negro;* Spanish: *aguja negra, marlín negro.*

The astonishing power of the black marlin, combined with its immense size—it rivals the blue marlin *(see: marlin, blue)*—make it one of the most sought-after fish in the sea. A member of the Istiophoridae family of billfish, the black marlin is renowned for its inspiring fighting qualities and its spectacular jumps as it struggles to escape. It challenges anglers from all parts of the globe.

The meat of the black marlin is firm and white and brings a high price on the commercial market. It is prized in Japan, where it is eaten as sashimi, but banned in Australia's State of New South Wales because of the threat posed by high mercury and selenium levels.

Identification. The black marlin is the only marlin, regardless of size, whose pectoral fins are rigid and cannot be folded flat up against the body without breaking the joints. The pectoral fins also have an airfoil shape, whereas those of other marlin are flat. The ventral fins are extremely short, almost never exceeding 12 inches in length. The first dorsal fin is retractable and fits into a groove along the back; it is proportionately the lowest of any billfish, usually less than 50 percent of the body depth. The leading edge of the second dorsal fin sits slightly in front of the second anal fin. The lateral line, which is rarely visible in adults, is a straight double row of pores.

Its body is laterally compressed, rather than rounded—much more so than in the similar-size blue marlin, and the upper jaw is elongated in the form of a spear. Dorsally, the body is a dark slate blue, but this coloring changes suddenly to a silvery white below the lateral line. Light-blue body stripes are usually visible on live marlin, especially when the fish is excited; these fade after death. Slight variations in color cause some specimens to have a silvery haze over the body. In Hawaii this has led to the name "silver marlin" (once thought to be a separate species). The name "white marlin," applied in Japan, refers to the color of the meat rather than the external color of the fish, and should not be confused with the white marlin *(see: marlin, white)* species.

Size. The black marlin has been known to reach a length of 15 feet; the long-standing all-tackle world record was caught off Cabo Blanco, Peru, in 1953 and weighed 1,560 pounds. The Australian national record is a fish of 1,439 pounds, taken off Cairns in 1973. Australia consistently produces the largest specimens today, particularly specimens exceeding 1,000 pounds. Although exceptions exist, giant

Black Marlin

black marlin are larger than giant blue marlin taken on rod and reel. This may be because large black marlin are more accessible and more often occur within the range of sportfishing vessels. Japanese longline fishermen contend that giant blue marlin taken far out at sea beyond the range of sportfishing boats are larger than giant blacks. Marlin exceeding 300 pounds are almost always females; a 500-pound male is a rarity.

Distribution/Habitat. This species appears to be confined to the tropical and subtropical waters of the Indian and Pacific Oceans. In tropical areas, distribution is scattered but continuous in open waters, and denser in coastal areas and near islands. Occurrence is rare in temperate waters. A few stray black marlin travel around the Cape of Good Hope into the Atlantic, moving up the southwest coast of Africa until they reach the Ivory Coast. Some have been known to cross the ocean from there, traveling in a southwesterly direction as far as Río de Janeiro, Brazil, or in a northwesterly direction as far as the Atlantic coasts of the Lesser Antilles. Such excursions, however, are exceptional and very rare. Little is known of the migrations of this pelagic species, but they do not appear to be extensive except in unusual cases.

In Australia, black marlin extend from the east coast of Tasmania in the south to Cape York in the north, and from the west coast of the Gulf of Carpentaria to Albany in southern Western Australia. They are rarely seen along the South Coast of Australia. The principal recreational fisheries are off North Queensland and New South Wales. They prefer the warm ocean currents along the edges of the Great Barrier Reef, but also migrate into the cooler waters off the coast of New South Wales.

A black marlin is about to be released near Isla Coiba, Panama.

Life history/Behavior. The black marlin is an oceanic, highly migratory, pelagic fish that is generally found no deeper than 75 meters. The fecundity of the black marlin is high, with estimates running to more than 220 million eggs for large females. In Australian waters, spawning takes place in the northwest region of the Coral Sea between October and December, and in the Timor Sea until March. No research has yet determined if the eggs are released at once, or in batches throughout the season. The larvae have been identified in the northwest Coral Sea off northwestern Australia, and off Lizard Island in North Queensland. Some adult fish and juveniles, on both the eastern and western coasts of Australia, migrate southward in summer. The large fish tend to stay close to the edge of the continental shelf, which, along the Great Barrier Reef, can be within a few hundred meters of the outer edge. In New South Wales waters, smaller specimens are taken within 100 meters of the rocky coastline.

Food. Large black marlin feed primarily on scad mackerel, frigate mackerel, trevally, squid, tuna, and mackerel tuna. Smaller fish are known to feed on herring, kahawai, pilchards, squid, scad and frigate mackerel, and others.

Angling. In Great Barrier Reef waters, the most productive fishing is from October through December, which coincides with the black marlin's spawning time. This is when the big females are present.

Most big black marlin are taken by anglers trolling dead or live whole fish, but methods of trolling with lures—using both soft- and hardhead lures, and live-bait fishing—are increasing in popularity as techniques and lure designs improve. All methods require careful consideration of many varied factors, including water temperature (15° to 30°C), time of day, weather conditions, moon phases, location of bait schools, and empirical knowledge.

When trolling natural dead or live baits, anglers in the Great Barrier Reef fishery of North Queensland use gamefishing tackle from 6 kilograms to 60 kilograms and baits up to and often in excess of 10 kilograms in mass, and work in waters to 30 fathoms. Hook size and type (straight, not offset), wire type and strength, knots, doubles, leaders, and swivels must be immaculate in their presentation.

Where big baits are used in the heavy line classes, only two rigs are normally deployed, clipped to outriggers. In light-line classes, more rigs can be fished. Baits are rigged so that they skip and swim naturally without spinning. The most popular trolled bait in Great Barrier Reef waters is the scad mackerel (known familiarly as "scad"), perhaps because of its ready availability and the documented successes with it. Other baits are tuna and bonito.

Trolling with lures is highly successful, and in many instances it is favored over baits because of its effectiveness and the no-mess ease and speed with which the lures can be used. Trolling speeds, lure shape and color (both head and skirt), lure size, distance behind the boat, whether fished from outriggers or not, line-weight-to-lure ratio, and number of lures out are but some of the vital considerations upon which success hinges.

In the lighter line classes (6 to 15 kilograms), both small, natural live baits, and strip baits taken from larger mackerel and tuna, are used successfully. Teasers are towed to attract the marlin to these baits and are brought inboard when the marlin has sighted the baits. Drift fishing with live baits is sometimes practiced, but more often than not sharks find the baits before the marlin do.

Much importance is placed on the competence of the boat's skipper, whose skills in controlling and positioning the boat for maximum assistance to the angler are critical to a successful outcome.

Australian anglers have an opportunity to fish in a unique manner for black marlin; that is, they can fish from land. On March 6, 1979, a rock angler using 10-kilogram line landed a 64-kilogram black marlin along the south coast of New South Wales. This was the first recorded land-based marlin capture in Australian waters. In 1986, a record black marlin weighing 110 kilograms was taken on 10-kilogram line from the rocks in the same general area.

The favorite bait for the land-based angler is the frigate mackerel, which is abundant in these waters. Bridle rigging, as for boat fishing, is the proven method of bait presentation. Basic tackle is a medium- to fast-taper 2.5-meter rod with roller guides, and a finely tuned big-game reel with sufficient line capacity (using 10- to 24-kilogram line) to cope with the stripping runs of the marlin.

Assisted by current and offshore winds, which take them away from the rocks, baits are supported by balloons or polystyrene foam attached to leaders that break away from the main line when the fish strikes. Land-based anglers usually fish in pairs for safety reasons and for gaffing purposes; gaffing from a rock platform can be a dangerous and difficult operation requiring the assistance of another party. Long-handled gaffs to 6 meters, or sliding gaffs attached to heavy cord and designed to slide down the line, are favorites.

See: Big-Game Fishing; Billfish; Offshore Fishing.

MARLIN, BLUE

Makaira nigricans and Makaira mazara.

Other names—Atlantic blue marlin, Pacific blue marlin, Cuban black marlin; French: *espadon, makaire bleu;* Japanese: *makajiki, nishikuro;* Portuguese: *agulhao preto;* Spanish: *abanco, aguja azul, castero, marlín azul.*

A blue marlin is revived off Chub Cay in the Bahamas.

A premier member of the Istiophoridae family of billfish, the blue marlin is one of the foremost big-game species worldwide. Some taxonomists believe that the blue marlin that occurs in the Atlantic and Indo-Pacific Oceans are closely related but separate species. They identify *M. nigricans* as an Atlantic-only species and *M. mazara* as the species occurring in the Pacific and Indian Oceans. Others treat the two populations as subspecies, *M. nigricans nigricans* and *M. nigricans mazata.*

The blue marlin has exceptional size and strength, and is a powerful, aggressive fighter. It runs hard and long, sounds deep, and leaps high into the air in a seemingly inexhaustible display of strength. Because of these characteristics, and because it is more widespread than other marlin, the blue marlin is arguably the most popular and sought-after by anglers. Intensively pursued commercially in many parts of its range, it is overexploited. The flesh is pale and firm and makes excellent table fare, especially when smoked. In the Orient it is often served as sashimi or in fish sausages. Blue marlin are seldom eaten in North America, and the vast majority caught by anglers are released after capture, and many of those released are tagged.

Identification. The pectoral fins of blue marlin are never rigid, even after death, and can be folded completely flat against the sides. The dorsal fin is high and pointed (rather than rounded) anteri-

Blue Marlin

orly, and its greatest height is less than its greatest body depth. The anal fin is relatively large and also pointed. Juveniles might not share all of these characteristics, but the peculiar lateral line system is usually visible in small specimens. In adults it is rarely visible unless the scales or skin are removed. The lateral line of a Pacific blue marlin is a series of large loops, like a chain, along the flanks. The lateral line of all Atlantic blue marlin is a reticulated network that is more complex than the simple loops of Pacific specimens. The vent is just in front of the anal fin, as it is in all billfish except the spearfish, and the upper jaw is elongated in the form of a spear.

The back is cobalt blue and the flanks and belly are silvery white. There may be light-blue or lavender vertical stripes on the sides, but these usually fade away soon after death, and they are never as obvious as those of the striped marlin *(see: marlin, striped)*. There are no spots on the fins. Small blue marlin are similar to white marlin *(see: marlin, white)*, but the blue has a more pointed dorsal fin at the anterior end, more pointed tip on the pectoral and anal fins, and lacks dorsal fin spots.

Size/Age. The blue marlin is the largest marlin existing in the Atlantic Ocean. Elsewhere, it is capable of growing to sizes that equal or exceed those of the black marlin *(see: marlin, black)*. Japanese longline reports indicate that the blue marlin is the largest-growing member of the Istiophoridae family. It apparently grows larger on average in the Pacific Ocean, where decades ago one commercially caught specimen reportedly weighed 2,200 pounds, and an angler-caught specimen (which did not qualify for world-record status) weighed 1,800 pounds. The all-tackle world record for Atlantic blues is a 1,402-pounder caught in 1992 at Vitoria, Brazil; the all-tackle world record for Pacific blues is a 1,376-pounder caught in 1982 at Kona, Hawaii. The giants are all females, as male blue marlin rarely exceed 300 pounds. Most blue marlin encountered by anglers range between 150 and 400 pounds. Blue marlin are believed to live for more than 15 years, although fish exceeding 10 years of age are uncommon.

Distribution/Habitat. This pelagic, migratory species occurs in tropical and warm temperate oceanic waters. In the Atlantic Ocean, it is found from 45° north to 35° south latitude, and in the Pacific Ocean from 48° north to 48° south latitude. It is less abundant in the eastern portions of both oceans. In the Indian Ocean, it occurs around Ceylon, Mauritius, and off the East Coast of Africa. In the northern Gulf of Mexico, its movements seem to be associated with the so-called Loop Current, an extension of the Caribbean Current. Seasonal concentrations occur in the southwest Atlantic (5° to 30° south latitude) from January through April, in the northwest Atlantic (10° to 35° north latitude) from June through October, in the western and central North Pacific (2° to 24° north latitude) from May through October, in the equatorial Pacific (10° north to 10° south latitude) in April and November, and in the Indian Ocean (0° to 13° south latitude) from April through October.

Life history/Behavior. The life history of the blue marlin is poorly known. The full extent of its oceanic wanderings, as well as its open-sea spawning activities, are unknown. These fish are found in the warm blue water of offshore environs, usually over considerable depths and where there are underwater structures (for example, canyons, dropoffs, ridges, seamounts) and currents that attract copious supplies of baitfish. They are usually solitary.

Food and feeding behavior. Blue marlin feed on squid and pelagic fish, including assorted tuna and mackerel, as well as dolphin. They feed on almost anything they can catch, in fact, and they feed according to availability rather than selectivity. Because they require large quantities of food, they are scarce when and where prey is limited.

Angling. Fishing methods for blue marlin include trolling large whole baits such as bonito, dolphin, mullet, mackerel, bonefish, ballyhoo, flyingfish, and squid, as well as various types of artificial lures and sometimes strip baits.

See: Big-Game Fishing; Billfish; Offshore Fishing.

MARLIN, STRIPED *Tetrapturus audax.*

Other names—striper, marlin, Pacific marlin, Pacific striped marlin, barred marlin, spikefish, spearfish, New Zealand marlin, red marlin (Japan); Arabic:

kheil al bahar; French: *empéreur;* Hawaiian: *a'u, nairagi;* Japanese: *makajiki;* Portuguese: *espadim raiado;* Spanish: *agujón, marlín, marlin rayado, pez aguja.*

Widely distributed in the Pacific Ocean, the striped marlin is the most prevalent marlin in the Istiophoridae family of billfish, the most common Indo-Pacific billfish species, and a prized catch of anglers. It is well known for its fighting ability and has the reputation of spending more time in the air than in the water when hooked; lacking the overall size and weight of the blue marlin *(see: marlin, blue)* or the black marlin *(see: marlin, black),* it is more acrobatically inclined. In addition to making long runs and tail-walking, it will "greyhound" across the surface, performing up to a dozen or more long, graceful leaps. It is caught fairly close to shore in appropriate waters.

The striped marlin has red meat and is the object of extensive commercial fishing efforts, primarily by longlining. Many people throughout its Indo-Pacific range hold its flesh in high esteem, and it is rated best among billfish for sashimi and sushi preparations. Heavy fishing pressure has resulted in reduced stocks, however, as is true of all billfish.

Identification. The body of the striped marlin is elongate and compressed, and its upper jaw is extended in the form of a spear. The color is dark or steely blue above and becomes bluish silver and white below a clearly visible and straight lateral line. Numerous iridescent blue spots grace the fins, and pale-blue or lavender vertical stripes appear on the sides. These may or may not be prominent, but they are normally more prominent than those of other marlin. The stripes persist after death, which is not always true with other marlin. The most distinguishing characteristic is a high, pointed first dorsal fin, which normally equals or exceeds the greatest body depth. Even in the largest specimens, this fin is at least equal to 90 percent of the body depth. Like the dorsal fin, the anal and pectoral fins are pointed. They are also flat and movable and can easily be folded flush against the sides, even after death.

Striped marlin have scales, fins on the belly, and a rounded spear, which set them apart from swordfish, which have no scales or ventral fins and a flat bill; from sailfish, which have an extremely high dorsal fin; and from spearfish, which do neither the long spear on the upper jaw nor the body weight of the larger marlin.

Size. The largest striped marlin on record is a 494-pound fish caught in New Zealand in 1986; in the United States the largest known is a 339-pound California fish. They are common from under 100 pounds to roughly 200 pounds.

Distribution/Habitat. Found in tropical and warm temperate waters of the Indian and Pacific Oceans, the striped marlin is pelagic and seasonally migratory, moving toward the equator during the cold season and away again during the warm season. It has been occasionally found on the Atlantic side of the Cape of Good Hope. Striped marlin are especially abundant in the southern Pacific Ocean, where New Zealand produces most of the largest specimens.

In the eastern Pacific, the striped marlin ranges as far north as Oregon but is most common south of Point Conception, California. It usually appears off California in July and remains until late October. The best California fishing locality is in a belt of water that extends from the east end of Santa

A striped marlin caught off Malindi, Kenya.

M

Catalina Island offshore to San Clemente Island and southward in the direction of the Los Coronados Islands. The waters around the Baja Peninsula, Mexico, are especially known for striped marlin, which are particularly abundant off Cabo San Lucas.

Life history/Behavior. The life history of this species is poorly known. Striped marlin are found in the warm blue water of offshore environs, usually above the thermocline. They are mostly solitary but may form schools by size during the spawning season. They are usually present where there is plenty of forage.

Food and feeding habits. The striped marlin is highly predatory, feeding extensively on pilchards, anchovies, mackerel, sauries, flyingfish, squid, and whatever is abundant. The spear of the marlin is sometimes used for defense and as an aid in capturing food. Wooden boats frequently have been rammed by billfish, and in one instance the spear penetrated $18^1/_2$ inches of hardwood, $14^1/_2$ inches of which was oak. When it uses its bill in capturing food, the striped marlin sometimes stuns its prey by slashing sideways with the spear rather than impaling its victim, as some believe.

Angling. Fishing methods for striped marlin include trolling whole fish, strip baits, or lures, and fishing with live baits. Most striped marlin are taken by trolling 8- to 12-inch skirted offshore lures. Blind strikes are the rule, but a fish spotted on the surface can occasionally be tempted to strike if lures are trolled past it, or if live baits are cast to it.

Spotting, stalking, and casting or trolling to surface-located stripers is an exciting possibility, as the fish are often visible in favorable conditions. Surface stripers may be "tailers," which are free-swimming fish with their sickle-like tails exposed; "sleepers," which are inactive fish with their dorsal and tail fins sometimes exposed; "jumpers," which are simply unhooked free-jumping fish; and "feeders," which are fish actively feeding along the surface. Different methods may be employed depending on the disposition of the fish. Lob-casting live baits to surface fish works well but requires considerable effort. Once a striped marlin is located, the angler should cast a bait in front of and beyond the marlin, and then reel the bait back toward the fish. Strikes usually result from properly presented live baits, of which Pacific mackerel is the favorite.

These fish are often fickle, and areas where they congregate may change each year. Savvy anglers concentrate on temperature breaks and converging currents in areas with plentiful baitfish and clean blue water.

See: Big-Game Fishing; Billfish; Offshore Fishing.

MARLIN, WHITE *Tetrapturus albidus.*

Other names—spikefish, Atlantic white marlin; French: *espadon;* Italian: *marlin bianco;* Japanese: *nishimaka; nishimakajiki;* Portuguese: *agulhão branco, espadim branco;* Spanish: *aguja blanca, aguja de costa, blanca, cabezona, marlin blanco, picudo blanco.*

The smallest of the four marlin in the Istiophoridae family of billfish, the white marlin is a top-rated light-tackle gamefish and an active leaper. It is the most frequently encountered marlin along the East Coast of the United States, where it is almost exclusively released (often tagged) after capture. There is an active commercial fishery for the white marlin in many parts of its range, however; the flesh is of good quality and is especially tasty when smoked.

Identification. The body of the white marlin is elongate and compressed, and its upper jaw extends in the form of a spear. In overall appearance, the white marlin is generally lighter in color and tends to show more green than do other marlin, although it may at times appear to be almost chocolate brown along the back; the flanks are silvery and taper to a white underbelly. Several light-blue or lavender vertical bars may show on the flanks, especially when the fish is feeding or leaping. Some specimens have a scattering of black or purple spots on the first dorsal and anal fins.

Its most characteristic feature is the rounded, rather than pointed, tips of the pectoral fins, first dorsal fin, and first anal fin. Some specimens apparently vary from the norm in that the dorsal and pectoral fins may be more pointed; the anal fin is more consistently rounded than the other fins. The first dorsal fin resembles that of the striped marlin in that it is usually as high or higher than the greatest body depth. It differs from that of the striped marlin *(see: marlin, striped)*, or any other marlin, in that both margins are convex. The flat, movable pectoral fins can easily be folded flush against the sides of the body. The lateral line is visible and curved above the pectoral fin but is otherwise straight.

Size. The largest rod-and-reel-caught white marlin is the all-tackle 181-pound, 12-ounce world record, taken off Brazil in 1979. Fish to 8 feet in length are common throughout their range, although white marlin can attain a length of 10 feet. The largest specimens are caught in Brazilian waters. Off North America, the white marlin is prominent in offshore waters off Maryland, North Carolina, and Florida.

Distribution. The white marlin occurs throughout the Atlantic Ocean from latitudes 45° north to 45° south in the west, including the Gulf of Mexico and the Caribbean Sea, and from 45° north to 35° south in the east. A few eastern strays have been recorded in the western Mediterranean and off France.

Life history/Behavior. Although this pelagic and migratory species usually favors deep-blue tropical and warm temperate (exceeding 27°C) waters, it frequently comes in close to shore where waters aren't much deeper than 8 fathoms. It is normally found above the thermocline, and its occurrence varies seasonally. It is present in higher latitudes

in both the Northern and Southern Hemispheres during the respective warm seasons. It is usually solitary but sometimes travels in small groups, the latter tendency reflecting feeding opportunities. Spawning occurs in the spring, with both sexes reaching maturity at around 51 inches in length. Females are capable of producing many millions of pelagic eggs.

Food and feeding behavior. White marlin feed on assorted pelagic fish and squid, concentrating on whatever is most abundant at a given time and place; this especially includes sardines and herring. It may use its bill in capturing food, stunning its prey by slashing it sideways and then turning to consume it. It also captures prey without using the bill as a weapon. The actual feeding habits of individual fish are not well known, but on a few occasions white marlin have been observed balled up in a small group herding baitfish for feeding purposes. This trait is believed to show cooperative hunting instincts, which also exist at times in other pelagic species.

Angling. White marlin can be caught by trolling with small whole or strip baits as well as with small spoons, feathers, or any of a variety of other artificial lures. Live-bait fishing with squid, ballyhoo, mullet, bonefish, mackerel, anchovies, herring, and other fish is also effective in specific situations. A good deal of successful northwestern Atlantic fishing employs whole rigged small- and medium-size ballyhoo. These are usually fished undressed (without an accompanying colored skirt) and trolled offshore in 100 to 1,000 fathoms over specific underwater contours and where there are surface temperature changes and color breaks, both of which tend to concentrate baitfish. Aficionados use outrigger lines and flatlines, as well as teasers, and fast speeds—around 6 knots. Tackle is often in the 20- and 30-pound conventional range, and anglers may keep spinning or levelwind outfits handy with a rigged bait for fish spotted within casting distance of the boat (often when the boat is idle or just getting started). Trolled baits taken by whites are dropped back on a 3- to 10-count, to give the fish a chance to get the bait in their mouth before the angler sets the hook.

A white marlin, hooked off Bimini in the Bahamas, makes an effort to throw the hook by coming to the surface.

Due to their size and activity, white marlin make good candidates for fly rodders, provided the fish are numerous and can be teased into casting range. Anglers fishing for whites often encounter other pelagic species, inviting a chance at larger blue marlin *(see: marlin, blue)*. For blues, it's best to have a larger bait or lure, on a heavier outfit, ready to employ in the trolling spread.

See: Big-Game Fishing; Billfish; Offshore Fishing.

MARSH

A freshwater marsh is wet or periodically flooded treeless land, usually characterized by grasses, cattails, or other freshwater-tolerant plants. Although some scientists might make a narrow definition differentiating a marsh from a wetland *(see)*, they are virtually the same.

A salt marsh is flat land with grasses and possibly shrubs subject to overflow by saltwater during high tide. Salt marshes are generally quiet areas and vary in size, although some bays may contain thousands of acres. An important component of estuaries *(see)*, salt marshes receive food organisms and detritus with the incoming tide, and send detritus and waste materials into the estuary with the outgoing tide. They help filter impurities and nutrients from the water and also hold shorelines in place. Mussels, crabs, snails, killifish, and many other small and medium-size fish use the salt marsh and are preyed upon by larger fish, some of which also spawn here; the young of many species grow up in tidal marshes, making them vitally important nurseries.

In a salt marsh, sportfish are caught on sandbars or in the deeper water behind sandbars, on the downstream side of points, around mussel beds, at undercut banks and along banks with steep dropoffs at high tide, in deep channels at low tide, in holes and troughs, on sand flats at high tide, and along the edge of a flat. The inlet, especially if it narrows, is a good spot, as are funneling points, like channels underneath bridges and between land points.

See: Inshore Fishing.

MARSHALL ISLANDS

See: Micronesia.

MARYLAND

With trout streams in the west, bass in the restored Potomac River, a restored striped bass population in Chesapeake Bay, and marlin in the Baltimore Canyon, Maryland holds many and divergent fishing possibilities. This befits a state with the Allegheny Mountains and Piedmont Plateau among its topography, and half its landmass consisting of coastal plain.

The fact that Maryland ranks 42nd in size among the United States may be reflected in its freshwater fishing opportunities, as there are no large natural lakes, and the Potomac and Susquehanna Rivers are of prime importance, but it is certainly not reflected in its saltwater opportunities, especially the inshore and tidal interface areas, which are influenced by the expansive reaches of the Chesapeake Bay. Most of the eastern half of the state drains toward the Chesapeake Bay; the bay is largely responsible for the 3,190 miles of tidal shoreline that exists in Maryland, although Maryland's Atlantic coast is formed by a narrow barrier that establishes three bays.

Naturally, the primary angling quarry in the Free State is striped bass, locally called rockfish. However, speckled trout, bluefish, weakfish, flounder, red drum, black drum, white perch, and other species draw near-shore interest; white marlin, blue marlin, tuna, sharks, dolphin, and wahoo are the major offshore interests. These are complemented in freshwater by smallmouth and largemouth bass, crappie, bluegills, northern pike, walleye, brook trout, brown trout, and rainbow trout. Few anglers are able to take advantage of all this bounty, but there's certainly plenty to choose from.

Freshwater

Conowingo Reservoir/Susquehanna River. The 4,000-acre Conowingo Reservoir in Hartford County is the largest impoundment in Maryland. It backs up the Susquehanna River behind Conowingo Dam on U.S. Route 1. Boat ramps are available, and outboard motors are permitted. Some areas of the reservoir have a rocky bottom that can eat up a prop or lower unit, so caution is advised.

Striped bass and hybrids are available and give the unsuspecting angler plenty to handle. The hybrids run smaller than their purebred cousins, as is normal, but what they give up in size, they more than make up for in spirit.

Striped bass are more common in the tailrace below Conowingo Dam, which is the continuation of the Susquehanna River and shortly flows into the Chesapeake Bay. Anglers land them from the catwalk and from the shoreline, or by wading in the river. Boaters using special prop guards work the rocky waters just below the tailrace, and cast or troll small swimming plugs.

Smallmouth bass exist in good numbers farther down the Susquehanna near Port Deposit, along the rocky shoreline. Largemouth bass are taken less than a mile farther down the river.

The entire area from Havre de Grace and Perryville to the Patapsco River flowing out of Baltimore holds plenty of white perch, striped bass, catfish, and largemouth bass. These fish will move up and down the bay and river as saltwater intrusion moves in and out. Saltwater reaches its highest level in late summer, especially during periods of drought. At this time, bass and other freshwater species may be concentrated in the headwaters.

Tidewater bass fishing is also found along the eastern and western shores of the bay. The Chester River from Millington to Kings Town is very good bass water. Runs of white and yellow perch in the spring attract legions of anglers to the Millington area, where a small shad dart tipped with a minnow is the favored bait.

The Wicomico River in Salisbury is a good spot for tidal largemouth fishing. The remains of old docks and sunken boats are the most likely hiding places for these fish. Crankbaits and plastic worms or lizards are popular offerings.

Potomac River. The Potomac River forms most of the western boundary of Maryland, and its tributaries drain most of the western half of the state. Restored to better health after years of abuse and neglect, the Potomac provides important recreational opportunity today, especially for bass anglers, and some of this is available right at the doorstep of the nation's capital.

On its western shore the restored Potomac River provides excellent fishing for bass in sight of America's most famous monuments. Largemouth bass are numerous from the capital down to the Route 301 bridge. The dense vegetation growing

M

in the feeder creeks and over the flats near the Woodrow Wilson Bridge hold tremendous numbers of largemouth bass. The vertical walls that line the shorelines in Washington, and the numerous docks along the Virginia side of the river, are equally good locations for largemouth. Crankbaits work well around the docks and vertical walls; spinnerbaits and plastic worms draw strikes in the thick weeds. Striped bass mingle with largemouths but are governed by strict seasons and bag limits.

Smallmouth bass, which were introduced to the Potomac watershed in the mid-1800s, are primarily abundant from the capital north. Fishing from float boats or canoes and by wading the shallows produce good catches. Crankbaits or plastic lures that imitate small minnows or crawfish work very well, madtoms are the favored live baits, and streamers are most effective for flycasters.

Good areas to float and fish for smallmouths exist around Knoxville, Harper's Ferry, Sandy Hook, and Brunswick. It's possible to use boats up to 16 feet long with small motors, although you must be careful around rocks; a propeller guard, used by many river veterans, is advisable.

There are many access sites for the Potomac River. Boat ramps at Edwards Ferry and the C & O Canal Aqueduct near Dickerson in Montgomery County provide access to the upper Potomac. A boat ramp on the Anacosta River at Bladensburg Road can be used by shallow-draft boats. A better access site for fishing in D.C. is found on the Virginia side near National Airport. Areas south of D.C. are accessed from ramps at Tantallon on Piscataway Creek, Marshall Hall Road in Piscataway National Park, Sweden Point in Smallwood State Park, and Friendship Landing Road on Nanjemoy Creek.

Deep Creek Lake. Located near McHenry in Garret County in the far western part of the state, Deep Creek Lake provides a wide range of warm- and coldwater fishing opportunities. Largemouth and smallmouth bass are available, the former more common in shallow, weedy areas or around boat docks or piers, and the latter more common on rocky bottoms, steep dropoffs, and points. Other prime warmwater species include pickerel and northern pike. Brown trout, brook trout, and rainbow trout also call Deep Creek Lake home, providing what biologists call two-story fisheries.

Deep Creek Lake has access via a boat ramp, cartop boat launch site, and a fishing pier; various facilities are available at Deep Creek Lake State Park on the east side of the lake.

Prettyboy and Loch Raven Reservoirs. Prettyboy and Loch Raven Reservoirs provide a total of 3,900 acres of fishable water close to the major urban complex of Baltimore/Washington, D.C. Loch Raven is located off Route 146, whereas Pretty Boy is farther north at the junction of Routes 25 and 111. Both sites offer largemouth and smallmouth bass, crappie, sunfish, perch, and carp. Loch Raven additionally offers pickerel and northern pike.

Both reservoirs supply the Baltimore area with drinking water, so regulations require that only electric motors be used. Due to the size of these lakes, it can take a good deal of electric power to cover all the fishing areas. Boat ramps and cartop launching are available at both lakes, and Loch Raven has boat rentals.

Bass anglers flock to Prettyboy and Loch Raven, but other available species draw legions of fans. The crappie run in the spring sees boat anglers working underwater brush piles, with a fair number of people lining the roadway bridge. Large carp inhabit Loch Raven as well, and they may readily feed on the surface in summer, when locusts emerge from their shells and fall into the water. This provides some surface action for anglers; the better the locust crop, the better the sight fishing.

Other sites. Garrett County has excellent trout fishing sites, with the Youghiogheny River offering more than 29 miles of fishable water. Brook, brown, and rainbow trout are available upstream of the Route 42 bridge at Friendsville. Special management areas are located along the river, where regulations stipulate fly fishing or catch-and-release only. This is a long stretch of water with plenty of room for everyone, but anglers must respect the rights of property owners who have granted public access.

Eastward in Allegany County, Rocky Gap Lake in a state park of the same name is a 250-acre impoundment with largemouth and smallmouth bass, walleye, crappie, channel catfish, brown trout, and rainbow trout. The rainbows are governed by special fishing regulations. Boaters must use electric motors, but launch sites are available for trailers or cartop craft. Boat rentals and a fishing pier are available, and the adjoining state park, which is 5 miles east of Cumberland, offers various facilities.

The Beaver Creek Watershed near Hagerstown covers 8 miles of trout streams holding brown and rainbow trout. The watershed is accessible upstream of Route 68, which is south of Hagerstown. Here, too, the rainbow trout fishery is governed by special regulations.

Greenbrier Lake, in Greenbrier State Park on Route 40 near Interstate 70, has largemouth bass, crappie, and bluegills. It also harbors rainbow trout, but the availability is seasonal and governed by special regulations. Boats can be powered by electric motors only; launch sites for cartop and trailered boats, and rental boats, are available.

Saltwater

Chesapeake Bay. This large inlet of the Atlantic Ocean is aptly referred to as Maryland's greatest natural treasure. The bay in its entirety is America's largest estuary, and its 46 principal rivers and streams drain 64,000 square miles in six states. About 1,725 square miles and 123 linear miles of the bay are in Maryland, and its exceptional num-

Nova Scotia biologists report that about 1 in 10 young Atlantic salmon survive to become smolts, which migrate to sea; in many rivers fewer than 1 in 25 survivors will return to spawn.

ber of tidal shorelines and tributaries make it one of the most important nursery grounds in North America for various aquatic resources.

Among those resources is a plethora of saltwater fish that are accessible from many sites. The population of each species may vary from year to year, but the quality of the angling is uniformly good.

Saltwater fish may venture as far up the bay as the mouth of the Elk River or the Susquehanna Flats when late-summer droughts enable saltwater intrusion to reach this area. This is not a consistent condition, and the Chesapeake Bay Bridge is normally the northern boundary for most saltwater species—except striped bass, which, being anadromous, inhabit the bay year-round, all the way to the base of the Conowingo Dam.

The town of Rock Hall is named for striped bass, which are locally known as rockfish, and a few charter boats operate from this location to pursue these admired fish. Most upper-bay stripers are taken on trolled bucktails, tube lures, or spoons. When the fishing is good, anglers find schools of breaking fish on the surface; then light tackle and small jigs can provide plenty of activity.

Rock Hall Harbor and the Chesapeake Bay are accessible from two area boat ramps and from two fishing piers, one on Sharp Street and one at the junction of Bayside Avenue and Walnut Street in Rock Hall.

Various notable angling locations are farther down the Eastern Shore in or near Kent Island, which is surrounded on the north by the Chester River and on the south by Eastern Bay. Kent Narrows separates Kent Island from the mainland and offers boat ramps, marinas, and a small charter boat operation. A pier at Matapeake State Park is open for fishing and produces good numbers of white perch and striped bass.

The mouth of the Chester River on the back side of Love Point can produce striped bass, croaker, white perch, spot, and small blues. The water depth falls off from a few feet to 25 to 30 feet, and action centers along this dropoff.

A very steep edge runs along the bay side of Kent Island down to Bloody Point. The bottom drops from several feet to 117 feet at the deepest part along this edge. Trolling for stripers is good here in the spring and fall, with bluefish prevalent in the summer. Anglers who work the bottom find croaker, spot, trout, and flounder, catchable on squid, cut baits, and jigs.

Directly across the Bay from Kent Island is Annapolis. Anglers here find access at Sandy Point State Park and head to the pilings of the Chesapeake Bay Bridge for striped bass. Casting bucktails or live eels is the favored technique. Trolling with bucktails, tube lures, or spoons, and drifting with live eels are proven methods for stripers at Dolly's Lump, Hackett Point Bar, or Tolly Bar. Spot, croaker, weakfish (also called gray trout, or trout, locally), white perch, and flounder are taken by bottom anglers using squid, bloodworms, or cut menhaden.

The South River and West River possess numerous marinas and boatyards, and the heavy boat traffic does not improve fishing. The area between Thomas Point and Curtis Point, however, where both rivers empty into the bay, holds fair numbers of striped bass, bluefish, croaker, spot, and trout.

Chesapeake Beach is a small town on the western side of the bay with access to particularly productive areas. The big fleet of charter boats that operates from Chesapeake Beach fishes for a variety of species from spring into the fall. Striped bass and bluefish are the primary targets and are usually taken by anglers trolling with bucktails, spoons, and tube lures. Chesapeake Beach charter captains have a system for trolling six or eight wire lines from a narrow deadrise boat that instills envy in those who cannot run more than three lines without getting at least two tangled.

The boats out of Chesapeake Beach run as far north as Holland Point Bar or the Old Gas Buoy, and as far south as the Gooses and Calvert Cliffs. There is a sharp drop at Calvert Cliffs, where the bottom falls from 5 to 50 feet along an edge that runs south to Cove Point. Stripers and blues stack up along this structure, especially in the spring and fall.

During the summer, small blues, weakfish, flounder, and croaker become more numerous, and the fishing shifts to bottom bouncing with squid, bloodworms, and cut fresh fish. During warm weather the boats may run to the Eastern Shore, where this type of fishing is more productive.

The Choptank River is east and south of Chesapeake Beach, and boasts good fishing all the way up to Cambridge. An old bridge over the river here has been turned into a fishing pier, and it can be especially productive for striped bass and white perch. The channel edge running from Cambridge to Tilghman Island is a good area to fish for stripers, blues, and weakfish. At times, any of these fish will chase baits on the surface; then, small bucktails and spoons are very effective.

Tilghman Island has been a fishing hotspot for many years. Boats pass out to the bay through Knapps Narrows in search of striped bass, bluefish, weakfish, flounder, and black drum. The drum are caught near Popular Island on peeler crab in late spring and early summer. These fish weigh 40 to 80 pounds and give upper-bay anglers a chance to tangle with a real saltwater monster.

Trolling with bucktails, spoons, or tube lures is the most common method for catching blues, striped bass, and weakfish. Bottom-fished peeler crab is the primary method for taking flounder, weakfish, and croaker.

The Little Choptank River holds striped bass in shallow, sheltered water. Casting bucktails or bottom fishing with peeler crabs will catch stripers along with some weakfish, flounder, and small blues. Boat ramps are located on Ragged Point Road and Taylors Island Road; these respectively access Brooks Creek and Slaughter Creek, which empty into the Little Choptank.

The Honga River, Fishing Bay, and Tangier Sound meet at Hooper Strait and funnel gamefish and baitfish into this area. The edge of the deep channel running down the Honga River is a good location for weakfish and striped bass. Bottom fishing with peeler crabs is the most popular technique here, but a bucktail tipped with a peeler crab will often catch weakfish or stripers.

Fishing Bay is a wide yet shallow body of water with excellent summertime fishing for weakfish and small blues. The ever-popular peeler crab is the preferred bait for weakfish, too; spoons and bucktails attract bluefish. Anchoring in Hooper Straight and soaking peeler crabs on the bottom will produce a mixed bag of weakfish, spot, croaker, flounder, and bluefish. Trolling around Hooper Light with spoons and bucktails is good for bluefish and striped bass.

Charter boats and a boat ramp are located at the marina at the junction of Routes 336 and 335; there are several other ramps in the area. Crisfield is the last town on the Maryland side of the Eastern Shore with access to the bay, and it has a large charter fleet and many facilities.

Boats leaving Crisfield head into Tangier Sound for weakfish, blues, croaker, spot, and striped bass. To the south, the same species, and speckled trout and red drum, inhabit the waters along Pocomoke Sound. In summer, boats anchor along the edge of the channel in Tangier Sound where the bottom drops almost straight down from a few feet to more than 100 feet. Weakfish move up this wall in the evening to feed on soft crabs hiding in the shallows. Anglers intercept them by soaking peeler crabs on or close to the edge. They use the same technique throughout Tangier and Pocomoke Sounds.

Point Lookout marks the entrance to the Potomac River and access to fishing hotspots in the middle sector of Chesapeake Bay. Solomon's Island on the Patuxent River just north of Point Lookout has a charter boat fleet, launch ramps, and many amenities. The deep harbor promises good fishing for weakfish, striped bass, croaker, and spot. The shoals between Drum Point and Hog Point are good trolling areas for stripers and blues.

Charter boats running out of Smith Creek near Ridge, and from the St. Mary's River, carry patrons past Point Lookout into the bay. A boat ramp and fishing pier in Point Lookout State Park offer access to the good fishing.

Chumming is the most widely used method for catching weakfish, bluefish, and striped bass. Boats anchor on the Middle Grounds, where they grind up fresh or frozen menhaden to create an oily chum. Even small private boats carry a portable grinder to make fresh chum. Once the fish are in the slick, small pieces of menhaden are dropped into the current. The action can be fast and exciting.

Big-game species are prime attractions for Maryland's offshore fleet, which often ventures out to the canyons.

Atlantic Ocean. Maryland's coastline along the Atlantic Ocean is only 31 miles long, but it packs a wallop that is disproportionate to its size.

From the coastline, the Atlantic is accessible only through the inlet at Ocean City. Just over 100 miles from Washington, D.C., and 120 miles from Norfolk, Virginia, this is a popular site for vacationers as well as anglers. At one time Ocean City billed itself as the white marlin capital of the world, and it still sees some impressive numbers of these elusive billfish. Today almost all billfish, including white marlin, are released, as anglers realize these fish are too valuable to catch only once.

The big boats that sail out of Ocean City in pursuit of marlin, tuna, dolphin, and wahoo must run 50 to 70 miles east to the region where the warm blue water of the Gulf Stream meets the edge of the continental shelf. Baltimore Canyon, Poor Man's Canyon, and Norfolk Canyon traditionally produce the best action. Most fishing occurs over the 50-fathom curve, and more often than not out at the 100-fathom curve. Some captains pull rigged ballyhoo, mackerel, or squid, while others use trolling lures.

The best concentration of white marlin hereabouts is usually from mid-August through mid-September, although whites show up as early as the beginning of June. The major tournaments are scheduled in early September, to coincide with peak fishing, when the marlin are migrating southward. The fish have averaged in the 55- to 70-pound range in the past. These numbers won't break any records, but if the fish are pursued with light tackle, they provide the best of sport.

Closer to the beach, tuna, big bluefish, and sharks inhabit the shoals. Jack's Spot is one of the better locations. Chumming and chunking produce most of the tuna and sharks, whereas trolling spoons is a primary technique for big blues. Ocean

City once had the 30-pound line-class record for bluefin tuna, and yellowfins are often found in the 30- to 90-pound class. Some monster bigeye have come into Ocean City, including a number of past or present world records, the best of which is the all-tackle and 50-pound line-class Atlantic bigeye, which weighed a mammoth 375½ pounds.

Behind Ocean City, the shallow waters of Isle of Wight and Assawoman Bays hold good numbers of flounder, weakfish, and croaker. Jetty anglers take small blues, striped bass, and weakfish out of the inlet, and boaters cast to the submerged south jetty.

Surf casters work the entire coast from Ocean City to the Virginia line. Most of Assateague Island National Seashore is open to four-wheel-drive vehicles that have the proper equipment and permits. Surf fishing is best in the spring and fall, when the fish bite and the bugs don't. King whiting, croaker, blues, red drum, weakfish, and striped bass are caught on an assortment of lures and baits.

MASSACHUSETTS

The Commonwealth of Massachusetts may rank only 44th in size among U.S. states, but one wouldn't know that from an overview of its fishing opportunities. Striped bass, tuna, cod, Atlantic salmon, brook trout, and yellow perch are among the fish that have long been associated with the Bay State, and although each has had its peaks and valleys, sportfishing for these and myriad other species reaches into every sector of this heavily populated state.

From its prominent Atlantic islands to its seaboard lowlands, Massachusetts' 192 miles of coastline and 1,519 miles of tidal shoreline reflect the prominence of the sea and its fisheries past and present. Indeed, a codfish still hangs in the statehouse here. In the upland hills and valleys, trout and salmon—equally traditional New England staples—present a diversity of opportunity that in many cases is found shoulder-to-shoulder with bass and such imports as northern pike and muskies.

Rivers and streams, brooks and ponds, reservoirs and lakes, tidal waters and estuaries, coastlines and bays, inshore and offshore—it's all here.

Freshwater

Rivers. A number of the Bay State's rivers, and some of the brackish ponds and estuaries, are not only loaded with warmwater and coldwater fish species, but lunkers from the salt as well.

This fresh and salt double dipping includes striped bass up to 50 pounds, some of which have been taken 100 miles inland.

The Connecticut River, which travels from northern New England across Massachusetts, and the Merrimack River, which meets the Atlantic at Newburyport, are the primary rivers for anadromous species. They not only provide stripers in the spring but also American shad and blueback herring, as well as Atlantic salmon.

Salmon, of course, began to disappear after the construction of dams and the advent of industrial pollution in the 1800s. Before then, it was said that one could "walk across the Connecticut and Chicopee Rivers on the backs of the salmon." Those days will never be seen again here, but some remnant of this abundance may occur if federal and state Atlantic salmon restoration efforts prevail.

With respect to numbers of returning fish, these efforts have produced moderate results at best. The bright light, however, has been the discovery of spawning salmon in the Connecticut and its feeder streams. These fish must be released, but at some future date perhaps fish could be kept if there is a major breakthrough in numbers of returning fish.

Now that rivers are cleaner, and fish lifts and ladders have been constructed, it is encouraging to observe the fish migrating farther north. Salmon and shad, in fact, have once again made their way upstream through Connecticut and Massachusetts and into Vermont.

American shad are abundant not only in the Connecticut and Merrimack but also in the North and Palmer Rivers. They are also being established in the Charles and Taunton River Basins. Labeled "the poor man's salmon" in this state, shad are caught on darts and other small colorful lures, as well as on flies during their spring migration.

Among the Bay State's rivers, the Connecticut stands out for its diversity, offering the aforementioned species as well as such standbys as bass, trout, pickerel, pike, catfish, carp, and crappie, and some walleye. Giant sturgeon are present but rarely landed, and an occasional alligator gar is encountered in the backwaters or oxbows.

Crossover fishing isn't limited to the large rivers. Both migratory striped bass and resident largemouth bass are taken side by side in freshwater on the Bass River in Yarmouth, more than a mile upstream at the first bridge.

Two rivers that draw serious anglers and beginners alike are the Deerfield and Swift. These wind through the mountains of the Berkshires and the rolling hills of the Connecticut Valley, the Swift being fed by Quabbin Reservoir. The fishing is excellent because of continuous trout stocking, and the scenery is equally commendable.

Similarly, the Westfield River and its branches are heavily stocked with trout, and sections of this waterway also wind through mountains, providing valley fishing where a solitary experience can be enjoyed. The Millers, Green, Chickley, and Cold are streams in the Western and Valley Districts that also offer heavy trout fishing in a wildlife-rich area, and on many stretches there is solitude for the day. A great number of feeder brooks offer an excellent combination of well-stocked rainbow and brown trout, as well as a few native brookies.

Elsewhere, the Nashua, Shawsheen, Concord, and Ipswich Rivers offer trout, bass, pickerel, pike, and plenty of panfish. Even the once-polluted

Housatonic in the Berkshires, and the Charles of Boston fame (the longest river wholly within Massachusetts, incidentally), have cleaned up their act and offer angling opportunities.

Coldwater lake fisheries. Atlantic salmon captured in the Connecticut and Merrimack Rivers and used as brood stock in the anadromous salmon restoration program are replaced each spring with new returning spawners, because it was discovered that the larger holdover brood stock did not provide as many eggs as the smaller fish of each new spring. Thus, one of the best-received fish-stocking programs in the state was started, and now holdover specimens are released into a number of ponds each spring and fall. Brood salmon between 5 and 25 pounds have been released in various ponds statewide. Many of these locations also have trout, and anglers fishing for 1-pound rainbows can find themselves battling a salmon up to 35 pounds, as the stocked fighters grow quickly.

Landlocked Atlantics are taken both in open water and under the ice in much the same manner as trout, mainly by stillfishing with live baits or a variety of cast or trolled lures, flies, and streamers. Favored artificial offerings for casters and trollers often have the blue, green, and silver coloration of herring. Ice anglers must drill large holes, as the big salmon rarely fit through the standard ice hole. They mostly take large live shiners on tip-ups or on a jigged perch eye or rainbow smelt.

In the Northeastern District, the main lakes that receive brood stock each year are Forest Lake in Methuen, Baddacook Pond in Groton, Lake Saltonstall in Haverhill, Pleasant Pond in Wenham/Hamilton, Lake Cochituate's middle and north ponds in Framingham/Natick/Wayland, Hopkinton Reservoir in Ashland/Hopkington, and Lake Pearl in Wrentham.

In the Southeastern District, they include Little and Long Ponds in Plymouth, and Cliff and Peters Ponds in Brewster. In the Central District, they include Wallum Lake in Douglas, Whalom Lake in Lunenburg/Leominster, Comet Pond in Hubbardston, Lake Quinsigamond in Worcester, and Webster Lake in Webster.

In the Connecticut River Valley District, these include Lake Mattawa in Orange, Five Mile Pond in Springfield, and Congamond Lakes in Southwick. In the Western District, they include Laurel Lake in Lee, Onota Lake in Pittsfield, Otis Reservoir in Otis, and Goose Pond in Lee/ Tyringham.

In addition to these Atlantic salmon brood stock plantings, landlocked salmon are also stocked in Quabbin Reservoir. Sockeye (kokanee) salmon have been stocked in Onota Lake in Pittsfield and Laurel Lake in Lee, where little or no reproduction was noted and only rare catches are recorded.

The state plants rainbow, brown, and brook trout in all the major coldwater lakes and ponds. More than a half-million pounds go out each year, with the greatest number in the spring and a moderate amount in the fall. More than 50 percent of the fish are a foot or longer when planted, and 25 percent are 18 inches or larger. Hundreds of 2-foot-long trout are surprise plants throughout the state. Many trout are also stocked by sporting clubs.

Massachusetts' biggest body of fresh water, Quabbin Reservoir has a diverse fishery.

Very few waters have native trout populations, so lake stocking is primarily a put-and-take activity, not one that supplements native fish. Whereas most of the state gets heavy trout angling pressure, many of the trout ponds on Cape Cod are underfished, and as a result their inhabitants can grow to truly lunker size. Brackish waters such as Mashpee/Wakeby Ponds in Mashpee and Sandwich offer up large fish.

Sea-run brown trout, known as salters, were introduced into Cape Cod streams—the Mashpee, Quashnet, Coonamessett, and Childs—to supplement the small but holding native brook trout salties. They provide a challenge to fly and ultralight-gear anglers.

Tiger trout are a favorite of Bay State anglers and are also stocked in all the major coldwater lakes and ponds. These showy hybrids put up a strong fight, but when not actively feeding they can be finicky and require great patience from an angler. They take bright streamers and flies and small lures.

Rainbow smelt, which are an eating favorite of both humans and predators, are common in southeast coastal streams, while landlocked populations exist in Quabbin Reservoir, Onota Lake in Pittsfield, Lake Quinsigamond in Shrewsbury, Littleville Reservoir in Huntington, Higgins Pond in Brewster, and Long Pond in Plymouth.

Warmwater lake fisheries. Most of Massachusetts' trout ponds and lakes are two-story fisheries, supporting warmwater species in addition to trout and/or salmon. The primary warmwater fish are crappie, smallmouth bass, largemouth bass, chain pickerel, yellow perch, white perch, suckers, pumpkinseed, bluegills, white catfish, channel catfish, and horned pout (bullhead). There are two special stocking programs for several of the more predacious fish not normally found in this state,

M

and these have met with well-publicized success.

One is for the tiger muskie, the nonreproducing cross between a muskie and a northern pike. These fast-growing eating machines can hit the 30-pound class in relatively few years. First stocked to reduce the number of runt-size panfish, they soon became one of the state's top freshwater quarries due to size and fighting ability. Many tiger muskies are released by successful anglers until they reach top-end trophy size.

The important muskie waters in Massachusetts include A1 Site and Chauncy Pond in Westboro, Cheshire Reservoir in Cheshire, the Chicopee River in Ludlow, Cochituate Lake in Framingham, Cook Pond in Fall River, Desmond Pond in Rutland, Hamblin Pond in Barnstable, Hampton Ponds in Westfield, Indian Lake in Worcester, Mascopic Lake in Tyngsborough, Maseapoag Lake in Sharon, McCleod Pond in Colrain, Monoponsett Pond in Halifax, Nippenicket Pond in Bridgewater, Norton Reservoir in Norton, Otis Reservoir in Otis, Pontoosuc Lake in Pittsfield, Quannapowitt Lake in Wakefield, Red Bridge Impoundment in Ludlow, Rohunta Lake in New Salem, Sabbatoa Lake in Taunton, Spy Pond in Arlington, and Webster Lake in Webster.

Northern pike were introduced into Massachusetts waters and are stocked in all the tiger muskie locations mentioned, as well as other waters. These have also proven popular with open-water and ice anglers, and some dandy catches have been made through the ice.

Waters that possess pike but not tiger muskies include Attitash Lake in Amesbury, Lake Buel in Monterey, Buffumville Reservoir in Charlton, the Charles River in Natick, Cheshire Reservoir in Cheshire, the Concord River in Concord, Dark Brook Reservoir in Auburn, East Brimfield Reservoir in Sturbridge, Forge Pond in Granby, Hamilton Reservoir in Holland, Lashaway Lake in East Brookfield, Leverett Pond in Leverett, Manchaug Lake in Sutton, Massapoag Pond in Lunenburg, North Spectacle Pond in New Salem, Onota Lake in Pittsfield, Quaboag Pond in Brookfield, Silver Lake in Wilmington. Snipatuit Pond in Rochester, South Watuppa Pond in Fall River, Wequaquet Lake in Barnstable, Whitehall Reservoir in Hopkinton, and Winnecunnet Pond in Norton.

The first baitcasting reels were made by Kentucky watchmakers in the early nineteenth century; the first multiplying reel was reportedly produced in 1810.

Walleye were stocked in the state until 1960, and only small populations persist in the Connecticut River in Northfield and Turners Falls, where reproduction is fair to good. There are a few walleye in Lake Chauncy in Westboro, Quabbin Reservoir, and the Assawompsett Pond system. Incidentally, Assawompsett, which is a 2,400-acre "pond" in Lakeville, has some historical significance. Here, a white man was murdered by Indians while fishing in the 1670s, and this precipitated King Philip's War.

Bass waters. In Massachusetts, the size of the pond does not dictate the size of the bass; both smallmouth and largemouth lunkers inhabit big waters, like the Connecticut River and Quabbin Reservoir, and small no-name farm ponds alike.

Among the better-known bass waters are Ashland Reservoir in Ashland, Ashumet in Mashpee and Falmount, Auburn Lake in Auburn, Barehill in Harvard, Big Alum in Sturbridge, Billington Sea in Plymouth, Buffumville Reservoir in Charlton, Canton Reservoir in Canton, Chebacco Lake in Hamilton, Chequaquet in Barnstable, Congamond in Southwick, Cook in Fall River, Cranberry Meadow in Spencer/Charlton, Dark Brook Reservoir in Auburn, Dayville in Huntington, Dudley in Wayland, Dunham in Carver, and East Brimfield Reservoir in Brimfield.

Also, East Waushaccum in Sterling, Flint in Tyngsboro, Fort Meadow Reservoir in Hudson/Marlboro, Fresh in Plymouth, Glen Echo in Charlton, Goose in Tyringham, Great East in Acton, Great Herring in Plymouth, Hamilton Reservoir in Holland, Indian in Worcester, Jamaica in Boston, John's in Mashpee, Knop's in Groton, Lackey Dam in Uxbridge/Sutton, Attitash in Amesbury/Merrimack, Lake Boone in Hudson/Stow, Lake Chauncy in Westboro, Lake Cochituate in Natick/Framingham, Lake Mirimichi in Plainville/Foxboro, Lake Monomonac in Winchendon, and Littleville in Huntington.

Also, OxBow in Easthampton, Pearl in Wrentham, Lake Quinsigamond in Worcester, Lake Sabbatia in Taunton, Long in Brewster, Long in Lakeville, Manchaug in Sutton/Douglas, Mascuppic in Tyngsboro/Dracut, Mashpee/Wakeby in Mashpee, Massapoag in Sharon, Monponsett in Halifax, North in Hopkinton, Norton Reservoir in Norton, Onota in Pittsfield, Putnamville Reservoir in Danvers, Quaboag in Brookfield, and Sampson's in Carver.

Also, Santuit in Cotuit, Shirley Reservoir in Lunenburg, Singletary in Sutton/Milbury, South Watuppa in Fall River, Stockbridge Bowl in Stockbridge, Tispaquin in Middleborough, Upper Mystic in Winchester, Webster in Webster, Whitehall Reservoir in Hopkinton, Whittins in Whittinsville, Wickaboag in Brookfield, Winthrop in Holliston, Long in Lakeville, and Lower Mystic in Arlington.

Reservoirs. Quabbin Reservoir, located in the Connecticut River Valley District, is the state's main water supply and, at 28 miles long and 25,000 acres, its largest and best-known lake. The better part of five towns were covered by damming feeder rivers, and the area offers the closest thing to wilderness fishing in the state. Quabbin attracts anglers from several New England states for bass, trout, pickerel, and panfish, but to have success there with any regularity, one must study lake maps and talk with locally experienced anglers and bait shop owners.

This closely controlled reservoir opens to the public in April and closes in October, the exact dates often depending on weather and water conditions. There are several access gates for boaters and shore anglers.

Quabbin has a population of self-sustaining lake trout, some of which reach the 20-plus-pound class. These are a major draw, especially in early spring, and are caught in waters accessed from Gate 8 near Pelham (off Route 202), and from Gate 31 in New Salem (off Route 122). Both areas offer boat launch facilities as well as boat and motor rentals. Numerous walk-in gates along Routes 202, 122, and 32A provide shore fishing opportunities.

Lake trout are caught at Quabbin on trolled or stillfished live or dead shiners, and large trolling rigs with a variety of lures. After ice out they are often near the surface and can be caught from shore or boat. As the weather warms, veterans here switch to free-swimming live baits, weighted with a barrel sinker and fished on the bottom.

Landlocked salmon in the 2- to 5-pound class are also plentiful in the Gate 8 portion of Quabbin. They are primarily caught on wobbling spoons and streamer flies.

Gate 43 in Hardwick is the third main gate and also offers boat launching and rentals. This site accesses one of the sections of Quabbin that is well known for bass (another is the area near Gate 31), although these fish are plentiful throughout the reservoir and respond to the entire line of presentations. Discovering an old streambed or a submerged stone wall can lead to excellent bass action.

Largemouths to 6 pounds and smallmouths to 4 pounds are regular catches. Many Quabbin bass anglers practice catch-and-release even though the population is self-sustaining and healthy. Anglers seeking good-eating fish can tie into a healthy population of white perch in the vicinity of Gate 8.

Although Quabbin is the major reservoir draw, smaller Wachusett Reservoir in the Central Wildlife District offers a self-sustaining lake trout population and has produced many state-record fish in the past. The highlight is superior smallmouth bass fishing.

About an hour west of Boston, Wachusett is an old reservoir, impounded in 1908. It is 8½ miles long and has 37 miles of shoreline. It receives water from the Quinnapoxet and Stillwater Rivers, as well as via an aqueduct from Quabbin. Wachusett has produced state-record brown and rainbow trout and white perch in the past, has an abundant rainbow smelt population, and is especially favored for bass and trout in the spring. Controlled access is provided by means of gates, and the lake is open from ice out in April through November. Only shore fishing is permitted, however, so the bulk of trout activity takes place in April and May, when the water is cold and the fish are most accessible.

Saltwater

New Hampshire border to Cape Ann. Extending from the New Hampshire border to the Merrimack River, Salisbury Beach offers surf fishing for large striped bass beginning in June, with nighttime, dawn, and dusk trips producing best in summer. Bluefish are also caught here, close to shore from July through September, although numbers are down from years past. Boat anglers score during the day by trolling or chunking deep around dropoffs, ledges, and other structure just offshore. From April on, Atlantic mackerel gather near the surface over ledges, wrecks, and lumps. Cod and pollock are available in near-shore waters from late fall through April, then move to offshore structure during the warmer months.

Moving south, the Merrimack River offers a wealth of fishing options. American shad begin migrating upstream to their spawning grounds in late April/early May. They readily hit small shiny spoons and flies, and can weigh up to 9 pounds. Although not a dependable catch, hickory shad can spice up river action throughout the season. Another spring option is Atlantic mackerel. The larger specimens weigh up to 5 pounds and are caught near the mouth of the river beginning in April. Tinker mackerel will often stay in the area through the summer, providing a ready source of bait for bluefish and striped bass anglers. Look for schools dimpling the surface over prominent bottom structure.

Stripers of all sizes can be caught virtually anywhere inside the river, from the Joppa Flats to the bridges and jetties and along the grassy banks. Nighttime fishing is especially productive in summer, when big bass move into the shallows to feed close to shore. Deep-drifting bait at the river mouth account for lots of big stripers and the occasional bluefish, even during midday hours. Strong currents at the mouth of the Merrimack demand extreme caution for both shore and boat anglers.

Boaters launching from the river have ready access to the Isles of Shoals (actually in New Hampshire waters) to the northeast. The deep, rocky shoreline of these scenic islands holds lots of big stripers due to an abundance of baby pollock, mackerel, and other baitfish. Jumbo bluefish also cruise the chilly waters in summer, and can be taken on trolled swimming plugs and chunk baits fished near the rocks.

Plum Island, which begins at the Merrimack's south jetty, is a classic barrier island that has long been famous among surf casters seeking stripers and blues, plus the occasional cod or pollock, along the ocean shore. Nowadays, early-season beach access is limited because of efforts to protect the endangered piping plover, but good fishing still exists. Boat anglers do well during the day by trolling jigs, plugs, and spreader bars on wire line in deeper water, or by drifting baits at night over sandbars. The southern tip of the island, known as Sandy Point, is a particularly productive spot due to strong currents that sweep bait in and out of Plum Island Sound.

The Parker River and the labyrinth of tidal creeks that meander through the expansive salt marshes behind Plum Island hold white perch and striped bass, including some surprisingly big specimens. Schoolie bass provide fast action all along the grass banks for fly and light-tackle anglers, especially at night, dusk, and dawn.

Just south of the Parker, the Ipswich River offers plenty of calm, sheltered water and a meandering estuary with good striper fishing all along its length. The rocks just outside the mouth of the river produce good striper fishing for wading anglers. To the east is Castle Hill, where stripers are taken right along the shore. Castle Neck (Crane's Beach) offers good striper and bluefish action early and late in the season for shore anglers, before the summer crowds and boat traffic all but eliminate any chance of daytime fishing. The bass and bluefish grounds in 20 to 30 feet of water off Castle Neck produce well for trollers during summer. Boaters often score big fish at night by drifting baits near the bottom.

The Essex River begins at the eastern end of Castle Neck. Flounder are caught here over shallow, mud-bottomed areas in spring and fall. Beautiful Essex Bay comprises a broad expanse of protected tidal creeks, sand flats, and deep holes, making it a perfect spot for anglers in small boats, canoes, and even kayaks. Look for stripers cruising the flats on a rising tide. Work the marsh banks at night, and the deeper pockets and channels during the day.

At Cape Ann, the coast begins to take on a distinctly New England appearance, with rocky headlands plunging into cold Atlantic swells. Striped bass are found all along this rocky coast; the key is to present baits, lures, and flies in the foaming water along the base of the rocks, where bait is tumbled in the wash. Fishing the bottom with fish chunks and live eels is another productive method, especially for those seeking big bass. Bottom anglers can also score with cunner, small cod, and pollock by fishing baits over rocky zones. Flounder can be taken over a mud bottom. A mile or so off Halibut Point, the Dry Salvages serve as a rocky oasis that holds cod, pollock, cunner, mackerel, striped bass, and blues. The same applies to Thacher and Milk Islands.

During summer and fall, bluefin tuna occasionally move in close to Cape Ann, in some years just a few miles from shore. Cape Ann also offers a short run to the productive bluefin grounds of Jeffreys Ledge. Traditional hotspots on Jeffreys include The Cove, New Scantum, and The Fingers. The ledges also offer decent bottom fishing for pollock, cod, and haddock.

The offshore waters hold good numbers of sharks, including blues, makos, threshers, porbeagles, and browns. Shark anglers seek their quarry by setting up long chum slicks over prominent underwater structure and around offshore temperature breaks.

Cape Ann to Boston Harbor. The rugged, scenic shoreline from Cape Ann to Boston, also known as the North Shore, is an inshore angler's paradise, especially for those seeking striped bass. Myriad protected coves offer shelter for small boats, and the clear, cold water keeps gamefish active during the hot summer months. Mackerel appear along the North Shore in April, taking up station around such inshore structures as jetties, ledges, and wrecks. Flounder, tomcod, and small pollock are available to anglers working baits along a muddy bottom. Deeper ledges, wrecks, and hard-bottom areas hold bigger cod, pollock, and cunner. These fish move closer to shore from late fall through spring, whereas in summer they're commonly found in depths ranging from 60 to 180 feet.

The near-shore waters of Gloucester and Rockport host excellent striped bass fishing, and numerous spots provide shore anglers with action. Farther along the coast, the coves, islands, and promontories around Marblehead and Manchester-by-the-Sea provide a spectacular backdrop to any striper trip. Flies, plugs, spoons, soft plastics, and bait all produce. Bluefish cruise here, too, but not in the numbers of years past.

The granite ledges and numerous islands (such as Cat, Bakers, Eagle, and Great Misery) from Magnolia to Nahant provide a sanctuary for all kinds of prey species, from eels and silversides to crabs and lobsters, all of which serve as food for big striped bass. The key is to focus on any sort of rocky structure, but note that marinas and docks serve as prime striper hangouts. Small boats are ideal for this type of fishing, as a lee shore is almost always available. The Danvers River in Beverly also holds a large population of stripers throughout the summer that shouldn't be overlooked by small-boat and shore anglers.

Boston area. Boston Harbor is rapidly shaking its reputation as one of the country's most polluted and fishless waters. The rugged, scenic islands (such as Spectacle, Lovell, Long, Georges, the Brewsters, Gallops, and Peddocks) that lie scattered about the mouth of the harbor offer the same type of great fishing opportunities as the North Shore. Better still, the Harbor Islands have received national park status, and there are plans to make them more accessible to visitors.

Mackerel are crowd-pleasers in the early spring, whereas groundfish such as tautog, tomcod, cunner, and small pollock can be taken by bottom anglers among the numerous wrecks and rocky zones. Beginning in late May/early June, hordes of school-size stripers make their appearance, and are often seen busting on the surface around the harbor islands, especially at dawn on a dropping tide. Bigger bass are available from June through October. Chunking with baits; drifting live eels; trolling spreader bars, tubes and plugs on wire line; and retrieving big flies on fast-sink lines all produce keepers. These techniques also produce action with slammer blues throughout summer and early fall.

Keeper bass can even be caught in downtown Boston! Each season, big fish are taken off Logan Airport, the New England Aquarium, and in front of the Charles River locks during the spring herring run.

Just south of Boston are Quincy, Hingham, and Dorchester Bays, once known as the country's most productive winter flounder grounds, but now depleted by overfishing. Flounder are still caught here, however, particularly in the spring, and indications are that these waters might again host a healthy population of flatfish.

The Neponset River, which feeds into Dorchester Bay, features a classic New England estuary often overlooked by anglers because of its proximity to Boston. Nevertheless, it serves as sanctuary and nursery to many types of baitfish and crustaceans, which in turn attract striped bass. Anglers enjoy prime light-tackle and fly fishing all along the river's grassy banks. White perch and winter flounder are other Neponset residents.

Offshore offerings. Rising from the middle of Massachusetts Bay some 30 miles due east of Boston, Stellwagen Bank is readily accessed by anglers from both the North and South Shores. This popular piece of bottom structure, which rises from roughly 180 feet to a peak of 90 feet, acts as a giant fish factory, attracting an enormous range of gamefish. The bank's plankton- and nutrient-rich waters produce huge shoals of sand eels, butterfish, and whiting, which sustain a resident population of cod, pollock, flounder, hake, and other bottom fish. Mackerel are thick in the upper levels of the water column. Although it's considered an "offshore bank" by many anglers, Stellwagen also attracts huge striped bass and bluefish, which can sometimes be seen feeding on the surface. And even if the fishing's slow, there are plenty of whales to keep things interesting.

Starting in July, big-game anglers keep an eye out for the arrival of bluefin tuna on the bank. Stellwagen also draws its share of sharks, among them blues, makos, and threshers. Sharkers who want to stay clear of all the activity on the bank seek out temperature breaks farther offshore. The basic method is to set out a long chum slick, which draws the fish to the hooked baits, or within casting range.

Boston to Cape Cod Canal. The towns of Quincy, Hull, and Hingham offer quick access to the many inshore ledges and islands in and around Boston Harbor, which hold big bass and bluefish beginning in June. Atlantic mackerel arrive in April and provide light-tackle action around jetties, wrecks, and underwater structure. Winter flounder are available to bottom fishermen drifting sandworms in protected harbors and coves in early spring and fall. Farther south, off Cohasset, Stellwagen Ledges in 60 feet of water may serve up small cod, tautog, and pollock from late fall to early spring, with striped bass and bluefish taking up residence for the summer. Also in summer, large cod and pollock are targeted over deeper wrecks out in Massachusetts Bay.

The South Shore is a prime area for those who like to fish bait chunks and live eels for big stripers and blues, especially at night. Fly anglers enjoy good success by working large "slab-type" flies around rocky areas washed by swells.

Scituate's three cliffs have long been known to produce great striper action for both surf and boat anglers. The North River, which flows into the Atlantic between Scituate and Marshfield, is another important waterway for sportfishing. Shad arrive in May, followed shortly by hordes of schoolie stripers. White perch are also available, providing early-season sport for light-tackle anglers who fish small jigs, flies, and pieces of worm. Bigger bass hit the river in June and often cruise along the grassy banks at night. Mackerel can be jigged outside the jetties in April and May. The mouth of the North River is always a good spot to fish chunks and eels for big bass and blues, but anglers should use caution in this heavy-current spot, especially at night.

Duxbury Bay, Plymouth Harbor, and Kingston Bay are prime bass territory, including areas of shallow, sandy flats where stripers can be sight-fished with fly tackle and light spinning gear. Winter flounder are available inshore in spring and fall but move to deeper water in summer.

Summer bottom anglers out of this area pursue cod, pollock, flounder, and big tautog around the deep wrecks in Massachusetts Bay, which serve as oases on an otherwise featureless bottom. These wrecks often hold chopper bluefish in summer. Expect these bottom fish to move into shallower areas as the waters cool in late fall.

Some 15 miles out from the Duxbury/Green Harbor area, Stellwagen Bank serves up everything from cod and pollock to striped bass and bluefish to sharks and giant bluefin tuna during the course of the season. Serious sharkers go beyond the bank and establish chum slicks near temperature breaks. Their targets are blues, makos, and threshers.

From Plymouth to Sagamore, the coast is mostly beach, save for scattered rocky outcroppings. Mackerel schools move through in April and May, with some good-size fish swimming within reach of small boaters. Striped bass are caught from shore all along this stretch of coast, with sandbars, deep holes, and rocks producing action, especially at night. Daytime trollers score by using wire line to present tubes, jigs, and umbrella rigs along contour lines. Come fall, schools of bluefish and bass often mix together on the surface, chasing baitfish on their way south; diving birds may point the way to some great topwater action.

Cape Cod: Sandwich to Provincetown. The east end of the Cape Cod Canal serves up small cod and pollock action in early spring and late fall, as well as through the winter for those willing to tough it out. Mackerel gang up around the jetties and near-shore structure in April, and the

According to The Guinness Book of Records, the largest piranha in captivity weighed 3 pounds 6 ounces and died of self-inflicted electrocution; it chewed through the heating cable in its tank.

Surf anglers fish for striped bass and bluefish off Cape Cod.

first striped bass are close behind. The jetties and the power plant outflow (just inside the canal) are good spots to cast for stripers and bluefish throughout the season.

The Cape Cod Canal itself is a fantastic and famous fishing spot, especially among striped bass fanciers. While boat fishing is not permitted in the canal, shore anglers line the riprap banks, casting jigs and plugs to the stripers and blues that often chase baitfish to the surface during slack water. Chunks of mackerel and live eels fished on the bottom also take their share of fish. Best fishing takes place at night and dawn, when boat traffic is minimal.

Moving onto the Cape, Scorton Creek in Sandwich is a great striper spot, and even holds schoolies throughout the winter. Fish are landed well back into the creek and all along its grassy banks, making it a great spot for shore anglers, as well as those in small boats and canoes. Scorton also boasts a population of sea-run trout, which are available during winter. Sandwich Harbor offers good wade fishing for stripers and blues, especially at night, but anglers should use caution when working along the bars, which are subject to strong currents.

Barnstable Harbor offers more protected striper fishing for fly and light-tackle anglers, from the east end of Sandy Neck well back into the marshes. Look for schools busting under diving birds, especially in June and September/October. The harbor also yields good catches of flounder, both blackbacks and fluke. Look for the latter around sandy areas washed by strong currents.

Sandy, gently sloping flats run the length of the inner arm of the Cape, offering great sight fishing for stripers and even bluefish from June through September. Casting to big stripers is possible as they cruise through water just a few feet deep. Bluefish arrive in June and are taken through September. Wire-line trollers tow umbrella rigs along the deeper contours for bass and blues with good success. Cod and an assortment of other bottom fish, along with big bluefish, are available over the deep wrecks in Cape Cod Bay. Billingsgate Shoal off Wellfleet is a famous fishing spot, producing everything from fluke to stripers to bluefish because of the fast currents that sweep baitfish over the raised bottom. The channel leading into Wellfleet Harbor is another good place to fish for the same species.

The shallows from Barnstable to Provincetown are thick with sand eels through the summer, which attract fluke, bluefish, and stripers. Good spots to fish include the mouth of inlets and any pockets, rocks, or near changes in bottom composition. Casting lures and flies along the edge of grassy or weedy patches often draws strikes from bass hiding in the darker zone.

Cape Cod: Provincetown to Falmouth. Provincetown Harbor produces world-class fluke fishing, especially in September, with bluefish and stripers mixing into the catch. Turning the corner and heading down Cape Cod's Outer Beaches, you'll find Race Point, long a mecca for surf anglers on the trail of trophy bass. Boat anglers do well by drifting bait or trolling spreader bars and parachute jigs near the bottom on wire line and downriggers. During the day, deep holes, troughs, and rocky areas are prime places to drift eels or troll with deep-diving plugs and umbrella rigs.

The coastline from Race Point to Nauset Inlet, once a bastion of beach-buggy subculture until access was severely restricted, still produces many huge striped bass and bluefish from June through October for those willing to hike the strand. At night, stripers often move into the surf zone to feed just a few feet from shore.

Hardy anglers can take cod and pollock on bottom baits from late fall through early spring, before these fish move to deeper zones for the summer. Nauset Inlet off Chatham is well known for huge stripers, yet it can be a dangerous place for both boaters and surf casters because of the fierce currents that flow in and out of Pleasant Bay. The bay itself harbors lots of big bass, which often hold in pockets on the grassy bottom and cruise the shallows after dark.

Jutting into the ocean south of Chatham is Monomoy Island, another famous landmark that's surrounded by great fishing. Bearses and Pollock Rips lie off the island's east end and southern tip, respectively. Both shoals are swept by strong currents, making them great places to catch stripers and blues. Experts drift eels and live pogies (menhaden), or use wire line to fish jigs and spreader bars down deep.

This is also the northernmost range of the so-called summer migrants—bonito, false albacore, and Spanish mackerel—which arrive in late summer and depart in early October. The miles of shallow sand flats along Monomoy's western shore offer phenomenal sight-casting opportunities for anglers seeking striped bass and bluefish from June to September.

Good striper and bluefish action are enjoyed all along the Cape's south side, from Chatham to Falmouth. The Bass River in Hyannis is one of the first spots on the coast to produce schoolie stripers, with bigger bass available from June through October. Hyannis Harbor sees big bluefish in June, and again in late August and September. Blues are also encountered on the sand flats close to shore off Cotuit and Osterville in June. As the waters warm, the big blues move out to the rips like those at Succonesset and Horseshoe Shoals, although small "snarbor" blues may provide fast action in the shallows through the summer.

This stretch of coast is prime territory for bonito, false albacore, and Spanish mackerel from late July through September. Pods of these fish typically cruise the beaches or gang up around the mouths of saltwater ponds and bays, such as Green Pond, Great Pond, Eel Pond, Waquoit Bay, Osterville, and Popponessett Bay. These spots also hold stripers and bluefish, although summer action is generally best at dawn and dusk. Anglers profit from great schoolie action inside the ponds and harbors throughout the season, even during midday. Fly and light-tackle anglers can score by simply working streamers, jigs, and spoons around the numerous dock pilings.

The waters between the Cape and "The Islands" (Martha's Vineyard and Nantucket) are rife with shoals and rips that hold blues, bass, bonito, false albacore, and fluke throughout the season. These spots are especially productive during the hot summer months, when inshore areas quiet down during the day. Most of the aforementioned species are occasionally caught on or near the surface, especially at dawn and dusk, but most of the time you'll need to get baits and lures down deep to score.

Woods Hole in Falmouth offers prime access to great fishing along the scenic Elizabeth Islands chain and Vineyard Sound. Woods Hole's rocky rips can be a great spot to fish for stripers, especially at first light, although the swift currents and summer boat traffic demand constant vigilance on the part of the helmsman. In August, the rocky ledge extending from Nonamesset Island into Vineyard Sound is a perennial hotspot for bonito and false albacore. Small-boat anglers enjoy good action with stripers by throwing plugs and flies all along the shores of the Elizabeths. Early morning and late evening yield the best results, but be sure to keep an eye out for rocks. June is a good time to cast and retrieve live eels in the shallows for stripers, especially around Cuttyhunk Island. Famous Sow and Pigs Reef off the tip of Cuttyhunk is filled with scary boulders, but many anglers think the payoff with big bass is worth the risk.

The powerful currents that sweep through each of the cuts, or "holes," between the islands tumble all kinds of baitfish, making them vulnerable to bluefish, bass, bonito, and albacore. While schoolies and occasionally keeper bass will chase baits on the surface, usually around slack tide, the biggest fish normally hug the bottom. Wire-line trollers do well with parachute jigs, tubes, and plugs through the holes, while bait dunkers often chunk at anchor or drift with eels and pogies. Fluke fishing is quite good around the mouths of the holes, while rocky outcroppings and wrecks on the Buzzards Bay side of the Elizabeths hold good numbers of tautog, big scup, and the occasional black seabass for bottom anglers.

While fishing along the Elizabeths, keep an eye out for birds working over busting fish in Vineyard Sound and Buzzards Bay. Bluefish, bonito, or false albacore are often below them.

Martha's Vineyard and Nantucket. For many anglers, Martha's Vineyard and Nantucket represent the promised land of inshore fishing, boasting hotspots too numerous to list. The Vineyard is famous for its shore and surf fishing for striped bass, bluefish, bonito, and false albacore. The numerous saltwater ponds (for example, Tashmoo, Menemsha, Lagoon, Tisbury Great Pond) around the island provide shelter for numerous prey species and offer protected fishing for both shore and small-boat anglers. On outgoing tides, predators from bass to bonito line up at the inlets to intercept baitfish being flushed out of the ponds. On the island's west shore, Tashmoo Pond hosts scads of schoolie stripers in June, and outgoing tides produce well, especially at night. Bluefish often lurk outside the jetties, too.

Moving south, anglers score with big stripers by working plugs, flies, and jigs around boulders in Lambert's Cove and off Cedar Tree Neck and the Brick Yard. Menemsha Pond hosts a big run of herring in May, producing some of the season's first action with really large bass. Farther down, between Menemsha and Gay Head, Lobsterville Beach and Dogfish Bar provide wade-fishing access for anglers after blues, bass, bonito, and albacore. The rocks in front of the famous Gay Head cliffs and Squibnocket make these spots prime territory for big stripers.

The island's exposed, wave-pounded south shore produces huge fish each season for surf casters, who patrol the beach in four-wheel-drive vehicles looking for diving birds over breaking fish. Night fishing can be especially good here, with stripers and blues feeding close to the beach. Big brown sharks move in along the south shore during summer, and some adventurous anglers have even taken them from the shore. The big rip that forms off Wasque Point on the very southeast tip of the island serves as a magnet for everything from bass to bonito, making it a crowded spot in summer.

Along the east coast, Cape Pogue, Chappaquiddick Point, Edgartown Light, Big Bridge, Little Bridge, East Chop, and West Chop are all productive shore spots. It's worth noting that the Vineyard also offers some decent sight casting for stripers and blues on the sand flats, such as

In June 1903, the New York City firm Abercrombie & Fitch, calling itself "The World's Headquarters for Fishing Tackle," advertised its first catalog; it contained 160 pages and cost 3 cents.

M

those off Cape Pogue, Edgartown (Middle Flats), Dogfish Bar, and inside Tashmoo Pond.

Bonito and false albacore fever grips the island from late July to mid-October. Some perennial hotspots for these fast and frequently finicky fish are Vineyard Haven, the entrance to Cape Pogue Bay (The Gut), Lobsterville Beach, Menemsha Pond, Tashmoo Pond, Hedge Fence Shoal, Edgartown Light, and Wasque Point. Expect Spanish mackerel and bluefish to join in the fray at times.

For boat anglers, the numerous shoals surrounding the Vineyard are particular attractions. Lucas Shoal and Middle Ground in Vineyard Sound produce outstanding catches of summer flounder (fluke), stripers, blues, and, in summer and early fall, bonito and albacore. Three nautical miles northeast of Vineyard Haven, Hedge Fence is another excellent spot for all the above species, as is L'Hommedieu Shoal, another 2 miles beyond Hedge Fence.

Bait and wire-line anglers on the trail of trophy bass often visit areas like Devil's Bridge off Gay Head, Squibnocket Point, Wasque Shoal, and the Hooter Buoy at the end of Muskeget Channel. Big bluefish are caught in these spots, too.

Like Martha's Vineyard, Nantucket is surrounded by phenomenal fishing. Surf anglers cruise the sandy beaches from June through October, looking for blitzes and haunting hotspots such as Great Point, Sankaty Head, Smith Point, the harbor jetties, and Eel Point. The rip-filled waters off Nantucket hold big bluefish throughout the summer, when mainland hotspots fizzle. The waters off Tuckernuck Island and the nearby shoals (for example, Old Man, Great Point, Pochik, Rose, and Crown) give up numerous keeper bass and chopper blues, especially for anglers who jig deep with wire line. Flycasters and surface pluggers can score big blues here all season.

Nantucket is a fantastic spot to chase bonito and false albacore in late summer and early fall. Smith Point, Eel Point, and Nantucket Harbor are good spots to try, as well as the rips. And on calm, sunny days, anglers stalk striped bass and bluefish on the shallow sand flats of Madaket Harbor and Tuckernuck Bank, as if sight fishing for bonefish on tropical flats.

Bait-rich Nantucket Shoals to the east also holds big striped bass down deep, as well as cod and pollock. Deep wrecks in this area provide oases for some of the biggest cod and pollock still found in New England.

Southeast of the islands, offshore species like yellowfin tuna and white marlin may show up on traditional grounds like The Fingers, The Star, The Dump corners, and The Claw in July, August, and September, although there are no guarantees. The key is to look for the arrival of warm Gulf Stream water curling in from the canyons. Some trollers locate the action by trolling along the 20-fathom edge until they find a concentration of baitfish or a temperature break. Those willing to make the long run to the edge of the continental shelf can troll or chunk for blue and white marlin; bigeye, yellowfin, and albacore tuna; wahoo; and big mako sharks.

Buzzards Bay. The entrance to Buzzards Bay has numerous ledges and wrecks that offer great bottom fishing, especially in early spring and mid- to late fall. Spots like Mishaum Ledge, Coxens Ledge, Hen and Chickens, and Negro Ledge all hold big tautog, seabass, scup, and winter flounder. From May through November, these ledges are magnets for stripers and bluefish. Trollers using wire line and tube-and-worm combos score big by working along the rips that form over these rocky rises.

Along the eastern shore of Buzzards Bay, numerous points, coves, creeks, and harbors hold schoolie bass throughout the season. The best action occurs in June and October, when bass often chase baits on the surface. Look for schools of blues feeding in shallow zones from Memorial Day through early July, providing fast surface action. Summer fluke fishing is good along sloping shorelines in 10 to 40 feet, and muddy zones hold winter flounder in May and November.

The strong currents flowing back and forth between Cape Cod Bay and Buzzards Bay make the western end of the Cape Cod Canal a great spot to fish throughout the season. Schoolie bass usually chase baitfish on the Mashnee Flats or in front of the Massachusetts Maritime Academy, and bigger fish lurk in the depths around Hog Island, Wings Neck, and the "Old Canal" channel. The Mashnee Flats, Onset Harbor, and the tip of the Stony Point Dike give up lots of fluke during the warm months, and scup and tautog are caught near riprap "islands" and rocky patches. From mid-August through September, bonito and false albacore arrive in the upper bay. Good spots to look for them include the entrance to Onset Harbor, Scraggy Neck, Toby's Island, the Maritime Academy, and near the tip of the Stony Point Dike.

The Wareham and Weweantic Rivers at the head of Buzzards Bay hold white perch and loads of small bass in season, with the occasional lunker to keep things interesting. Herring enter the rivers in May, making this one of the best times to score a keeper. Bluefish arrive in this area near Memorial Day and provide prime plugging action through June as they gorge on squid. The big fish depart by July, but small (1 to 5 pounds) "snarbor" blues may linger through the summer. In August and fall, menhaden (pogy) schools sometimes become trapped in coves and harbors along the western shore of the bay, providing fast-paced action with "gorilla" bluefish. Bird Island's rocky shallows and the boulders off Butler Point are prime spots to cast for bass and blues throughout the season, especially at dawn and dusk. During summer, when hot weather chases striped bass to deeper water, drifting eels and trolling tubes around Nyes Ledge, Cleveland Ledge, Great Ledge, and Wilkes Ledge often produces big fish. Shallower rocky spots like Bird Island Ledge, Dry Ledge, Sippican Neck, and the Bow Bells hold tautog, flounder, and scup in the early spring and fall, and are good places to fish the bottom for bass in June, particularly at night.

The rocky shallows along Aucoot Cove and Converse Point off Marion are great areas to toss a plug or fly for stripers. Bluefish move into the waters around Ram Island in June. Apponagansett Bay in South Dartmouth often sees late-season bluefish blitzes. Barney's Joy Point, Gooseberry Neck, and Mishaum Point feature lots of rocks that attract big bass throughout the season, although careful boat handling is necessary. Try working big, slow-swimming surface plugs and huge streamer flies around these shores for big bass at first light. Live eels and pogies should produce similar results. Sandy, sloping beaches like Horseneck and Demerest Loyd provide good fluke fishing in spring and fall. For sight fishing, try poling, drifting, or wading the sand flats on an incoming tide; you're bound to see stripers and even blues looking for a meal, especially in June.

The Westport River near the Rhode Island border offers miles of protected water for stalking stripers in small boats and from shore. At dawn, watch for schoolies busting baitfish along the edges of the marsh grass; bigger fish cruise the same shallows at night, looking for eels and crabs. The mouth of the Westport is a great place for shore anglers to fish plugs and baits at night. Bonito and false albacore often chase baits outside the river mouth from August through mid-October.

Westport is a great jumping-off spot for boaters, since it offers easy access to the Elizabeths, Martha's Vineyard, Buzzards Bay, and eastern Rhode Island.

Saltwater Species Overview

Winter flounder (blackbacks) Found year-round in all state waters. Inhabits shallow, mud-bottomed bays, harbors, and estuaries during May and in mid- to late fall.

Summer flounder (fluke) Most common around Cape Cod, the Islands, and in Buzzards Bay. Prefers sand or mud bottoms with good current flow. Peak season runs from May through October. Available in shallow water (10 to 30 feet) early and late in season, but may seek deeper areas (40 to 60 feet) in midsummer.

Tautog (blackfish) Available year-round. Most common from Cape Cod south, particularly in Buzzards Bay. Inhabits rocky bottom, ledges, and wrecks. Peak fishing from April through June and from October through December, when present in fairly shallow water. Seeks deeper zones in summer.

Black seabass Most common in waters south of Cape Cod, including Buzzards Bay. Inhabits wrecks, reefs, and ledges. Found in deeper water (30-plus feet) through summer. Frequently found on same grounds as cod, pollock, tautog, and other bottom dwellers.

Atlantic mackerel Available in cold Atlantic waters beginning in April. Most common from Cape Cod Bay north in summer. Large schools gather near surface around near-shore structure (wrecks, jetties, ledges) and over offshore banks.

Cod and pollock Available year-round in all waters except Buzzards Bay. Small fish move into near-shore areas (20 to 60 feet) from late fall through early spring. Usually inhabit wrecks, rocky bottom, shoals, and deep banks. Larger fish found on deeper (60-plus feet) wrecks and banks.

Scup (porgy) Available year-round in inshore waters. Most numerous south of Cape Cod. Inhabits rocky areas, docks, piers, and wrecks.

White perch Available year-round in salt marshes, estuaries, and tidal creeks.

Striped bass Enters inshore waters south of Cape Cod in April and departs in late November. Enters waters north of Cape Cod in May and departs in October. Inhabits shallow flats, rocky coastlines, estuaries, tidal creeks, shoals, ledges, wrecks, channels, and high surf.

Bluefish Available in waters south of Cape Cod from early June into late October. Available north of Cape Cod from late June through October. Inhabits flats, surf, shoals, wrecks, ledges, offshore banks, and channels. Big fish most numerous inshore early and late in season. Moves to deeper, colder water in summer.

Bonito Available in waters south of Cape Cod from late July to mid-October. Found along beaches, shoals, and inlets.

Little tunny (false albacore) Available in waters south of Cape Cod from mid-August through mid-October. Found along beaches, shoals, and inlets.

Spanish mackerel Available in inshore waters south of Cape Cod from late July through October. Found along beaches, shoals, and inlets.

Bluefin tuna Available from July through November. Schools gather over deep banks, ledges, and shoals, although also encountered in open water.

Yellowfin tuna Found in offshore waters (120-plus feet) south of Nantucket and Martha's Vineyard. Availability dependent upon influx of warm Gulf Stream water. May first show in July.

Sharks (blue, mako, thresher, brown, porbeagle) Available in offshore waters from July through October. Found over deep banks and around temperature breaks.

White marlin Found in offshore waters (120-plus feet) south of Nantucket and Martha's Vineyard. Availability dependent upon influx of Gulf Stream water. May arrive in July and depart in September.

MATCHING THE HATCH

An expression for the selection and use of artificial flies that exactly, or as closely as possible, mimic the look, size, and behavior of naturally occurring

aquatic insects. The origin of this expression is in fly fishing, and principally used when angling with dry flies for trout; however, the principle of imitating the existing prominent natural forage for any species at any point in time is common to all methods of angling and may be generically referred to as matching the "hatch."
See: Hatch.

MATE

A person who assists the captain on a charter boat *(see)* or party boat *(see)*. The chores of a mate are usually broad, from netting or gaffing fish to tying up fishing rigs, preparing bait, filleting fish, cleaning up the boat and equipment, and much more. The mate usually performs all the chores necessary for fishing, with the exception of running the boat (and sometimes may assist with this as well). Generally, it is the captain's job to pilot the boat, locate fish, and constantly keep the boat in position to maximize angling effort.

Some large charter boats have two mates, and party boats always have at least one mate, sometimes two or more; on party boats they may also be called deckhands. Small boats that are operated by a fishing guide *(see)*, and some charter boats (usually those in freshwater that are in the 20- to 25-foot range), do not have a mate; in these instances the guide or captain does all of the necessary chores. When trolling is involved, passengers must assist in holding the steering wheel (maintaining the boat's course), which sometimes works out well and sometimes does not. The absence of a mate under certain conditions may lead a small-boat skipper to keep unproductive lures in the water or stay in one place unnecessarily long instead of making the effort to change lures or places.

Often the quality of the fishing experience is directly related to the ability of a mate to do important chores, and sometimes to the speed with which they are done. Demeanor and effort are important as well. Good mates make a big difference in some outings and should be rewarded with an appropriate gratuity for the services rendered.

In some places and situations, one of the qualifying requirements for obtaining a captain's license is demonstrating experience on a fishing boat for hire, and having been a mate for a certain length of time fulfills this.

MATRINCHA

Other name—Portuguese: *matrinxã.*

The matrincha is a member of the Brycon genus of the Characidae family. There are reported to be some 800 species of Brycons, most in Central and South America. "Matrincha" is the English-language name for a Brazilian fish known as *matrinxã* and is identified in some literature as *Brycon hilarii.* Brazilians say that it is closely related to a

A matrincha from the Cururu River, Brazil.

similar species known as *jatuarana.* Both are characins. They are superb gamefish on light tackle and provide delicious table fare. Few anglers are familiar with either fish, although more have encountered the matrincha.

Identification. The matrincha has a stout, rounded body with a small head, a high dorsal fin that is centered on the body, an adipose fin, and a broad, squared tail. Its coloring is silvery to bronze and dark across the back; the pelvic and caudal fins are dark.

Size. The maximum attainable size of the matrincha is uncertain, although Brazilian literature indicates that it may reach 31 inches and 11 pounds. The world record is 7 pounds 5 ounces, and 3- to 4-pounders are common. The *jatuarana* is said to be darker and reaches a maximum weight of 17 pounds.

Distribution. In Brazil, the matrincha reportedly occurs in some sections of the states of Amazonas, Acre, Pará, and Rondônia. The São Benedito River in southern Pará, and its tributaries, have been good fisheries for this species, but the full range both in Brazil and elsewhere is uncertain.

Habitat/Behavior. A schooling species, the matrincha is found in small groups in clear rivers during the dry season. It reportedly occurs in large schools prior to the flood season, when spawning takes place in the whitewater of large rivers. During the high-water season, they scatter into the flood lands.

Food. The matrincha is believed to be omnivorous, consuming fruit, seeds, plant matter, and small fish as season and water stages dictate.

M

Angling. Most anglers encounter this species in low clear water, where the fish cluster in small groups and are fairly skittish. They are caught below rapids and in the head of runs or pools but are easily spooked or moved off after being fished for a while. They are also caught from under trees and logs along riverbanks.

Although large lures—such as those meant for peacock bass—may occasionally catch a matrincha, smaller offerings, such as spinners, spoons, and jigs, are better. Matrincha are good targets for light-tackle fishing with spinning and fly gear, and their broad profile allows them great purchase in rivers. This results in a strong fight not unlike that experienced with American shad, including impressive aerial displays. Spinning tackle with 6- to 10-pound fine-diameter line is the best equipment.

MAURITANIA

The Republic of Mauritania is a large country within the Sahara Desert in northwestern Africa whose coastline bisects the Tropic of Cancer and fronts the eastern Atlantic Ocean. Although numerous gamefish exist along Mauritania's coast, there is limited sportfishing.

The Sport Fishing Club of Nouadhibou was created by the promotional office of the airline company Air Afrique in 1973. Anglers began to test the Baie de l'Etoile (Star Bay), and a newly constructed Fishing Centre was inaugurated in 1977. By 1998, about 350 angling tourists from throughout Europe annually passed through the Air Afrique Nouadhibou Fishing Centre. An international fishing competition at this site brings together more than a hundred anglers from 10 nations each year.

The courbine, or meagre (in the drum family), is the premier fish in Mauritania. The Fishing Centre reports that between 300 and 350 of these fish, with a mean weight of 40 kilograms, are taken annually. The record is a 63-kilogram specimen. At the centre, anglers catch 30 to 35 tons of fish of various species annually, 60 percent by surf casting from the beach; they catch the remainder by trolling and drifting.

Surf casting produces other species with regularity, including bluefish, skipjacks, spotted seabass in great quantities, garrick, snapper, guitarfish, hammerhead sharks, tope, and various jacks. Anglers land many red and gray sea bream and grouper by bottom fishing and with light-tackle casting. The season is year-round, with a light increase in October, November, and December.

The Mauritanian government, in cooperation with Air Afrique, has reserved a portion of sea that is 25 kilometers long and 5 kilometers wide in the Bay of Levrier, which contains Star Bay. The purpose is to reserve a site exclusively for sportfishing and to prohibit commercial fishing.

MAURITIUS

The 720-square-mile island of Mauritius is just north of the Tropic of Capricorn at 20 degrees south latitude, and about 535 miles east of Madagascar in the Indian Ocean. This locale places it in the migratory crossroads of many pelagic fish species and brings them close to the island itself. The big blue marlin is the foremost angling attraction.

In the Western world, many people are better acquainted with the dodo bird than with Mauritius. That large, goofy-looking, nonflying bird with the hooked bill was one of many fascinating creatures and remarkable flora that Dutch explorers found on Mauritius when they arrived at the end of the sixteenth century. Mauritius was then uninhabited, which no doubt caused Mark Twain to comment that God had modeled heaven after this island.

Mauritius is densely populated today and has become a booming tourist destination. Although known to the jet set and among the European and South African big-game fishing community, the independent sovereign British Commonwealth nation of Mauritius is little known to North American anglers, and is often described as a "new discovery." It is only "new" because it is so far away to so many. Tourism has become an important industry, however, and a half million visitors journey to Mauritius annually, many of them to enjoy beautiful beaches, to dive on extensive coral reefs, and to surf.

The 206-mile-long coastline of Mauritius is almost entirely surrounded by coral reef, and within a mile of shore the ocean drops to more than 2,000 feet. The Indian South Equatorial Current washes around these islands, and with current pushing bait and gamefish upward at these and associated volcanic islands and seamounts, opportunities to catch fish exist year-round.

As mentioned, marlin are the premier gamefish in Mauritius. Outstanding action can be had for either blue or black marlin, although the former clearly shine here because they are especially large.

More than two dozen Pacific blue marlin granders—fish weighing more than a thousand pounds—have reportedly been caught in Mauritius waters since people took note of such things. A 1,100-pound blue caught off Le Morne in February 1966 remained an all-tackle world record until 1982. And in November 1984, a 1,430-pound blue marlin was taken here on 130-pound tackle; unfortunately, it did not qualify as a world record because it struck two lines at the same time. Nonrecord granders were caught in the 1990s, and a 950-pound blue caught off Le Morne in December 1994 established a women's line-class world record.

In 1989, a fish just under the 1,376-pound world record (Hawaiian) was taken. Naturally, anglers land many smaller blue marlin in Mauritius, with an average weight of roughly 350 pounds. The availability of so many big blues, however, has fueled speculation that the next all-tackle world record, and possibly the first rod-and-reel blue marlin over 1,500 pounds, may come from Mauritius.

As for black marlin, they run large on average, although no fish caught here has yet contended with the granders of other locales. Nevertheless, fish up to 700 pounds have been landed, and black marlin here consistently average in the 300- to 500-pound range, providing plenty of excitement. A catch of a 300-pound blue and a 300-pound black on the same day is theoretically possible (though unlikely), and gives great fodder to the imagination.

The prime time for marlin is from October through March—the spring and summer seasons in Mauritius, and the peak of the tourist trade. Good catches of both blues and blacks occur throughout the year, however, and some striped marlin enter the catch at times. Offshore trollers fish from large, well-equipped sportfishing vessels and use live baits, mainly bonito and skipjack tuna, but also lures.

A particularly pleasant aspect of Mauritian big-game trolling is that it can be done within minutes of shore. A nine-hour fishing day involves little running and a lot of angling—one covers a great deal of potentially productive water in the course of a day.

Most of the Mauritius sportfishing fleet is harbored near the southwestern or northwestern sections of the island, respectively, at Black River and the Le Morne Peninsula; some originate out of Grand Baie on the east coast. Many marlin are caught off the southwestern area of the island, offshore but in sight of the Le Morne Peninsula, where the dropoff from reef to great depths is sharp and an upwelling draws schools of baitfish to the surface. The fishing is concentrated from the dropoff to about 7 miles offshore.

Closer inshore, one might encounter such other billfish as striped marlin and sailfish. Neither of these are considered abundant in Mauritius waters, but specimens to 240 and 80 pounds, respectively, have been recorded, and these two fish are taken from time to time each year.

Several species of tuna are abundant in this area of the Indian Ocean. Yellowfin tuna are found all year long, and the most and biggest fish, up to 240 pounds, are caught in March and April.

Skipjack tuna are especially prevalent all season. Mauritius holds the all-tackle world record, which is shared by two 41-pound fish, and has established numerous other line-class and fly-rod skipjack world records. An abundance of skipjack makes for light-tackle and fly-rod opportunities that are seldom explored here.

Dogtooth tuna, which inhabit tropical reef waters, are plentiful as well. Mauritius holds the 50- and 80-pound line-class world records for this species; a 224- and a 230-pounder, respectively, were caught off Le Morne.

Wahoo, small dorado (dolphin), barracuda, and a variety of sharks, plus such reef fish as grouper, are other gamefish possibilities. The Mauritian record for wahoo is 125 pounds, but these fish are usually landed at one-third that size. The best action is from September through January. Anglers land dorado year-round.

Sharks are fairly abundant, although they don't pose the big-game fighting problems—mutilated billfish—that occur in other marlin hotspots. Mako sharks grow quite large, and a world-record 1,115-pounder caught by a boat from Black River in November 1988 is the largest mako taken on sporting tackle. Hammerhead, tiger, and blue sharks are available too, and a 400-pound blue from Mauritius holds an International Gamefish Association (IGFA) line-class world record.

Mauritius is roughly comparable in size to Maui in the Hawaiian Islands. It is ringed by a coral reef, and inshore the waters are calm, gorgeous, and conducive to all manner of water sports, with warm lagoons, soft powder-sand beaches, and tropical greenery. The interior landscape includes thick forests, waterfalls, gorges, mountains, and lush vegetation; there are several small lakes and streams originating in the highlands, but freshwater fisheries are undetermined.

The climate of Mauritius is tropical and generally humid. In the summer months, from November through March, the coastal temperature varies from 73° to 90° F. The rainy season occurs from January through March, and cyclones may occur between November and February.

MAXIMUM SUSTAINABLE YIELD

The largest average catch that can be taken continuously from a stock under average environmental conditions. Maximum sustainable yield is different from optimum yield, which is the recreational and/or commercial harvest level for a species that achieves the greatest overall benefits, including economic, social, and biological considerations.

See: Fisheries Management.

MAYFLIES

Mayflies are members of the scientific order Ephemeroptera, a term derived from *ephemera*, meaning short-lived, and *ptera*, meaning wing. They are the best-known aquatic insects *(see)* and include approximately 700 species, all of which have aquatic larvae and a relatively short-lived terrestrial adult stage. Their life cycle consists of egg, nymph, and adult stages, with most of this being in the nymph, or immature, form.

The larval development period depends on species and local climate but can last from two weeks to two years. Because of the large numbers of different species and varying life cycle times, mayfly larvae can be observed in a healthy stream at any time of year. They can be found in a variety of habitats, including exposed rock surfaces in fast current or buried in soft bottoms. Generally, they are confined to streams with high levels of dissolved oxygen and good water quality.

Nymphs range from barely visible in size up to $1^1/_2$ inches, feed on algae or plant debris, and are timid creatures until the eve of their emergence. They may be flat-bottom clingers, soft-bodied burrowers, torpedo-shaped swimmers, or cylindrically shaped crawlers.

When mature, the nymph loses its timidity and becomes active. It may make several trips to the surface and back to the bottom. Some swim to the surface and immediately pop out of their nymphal skin, or case, and fly away. Some struggle to get free of the case. Some fall to the surface several times before they are able to fly away. In streams, trout have a limited opportunity to feed on the adult, but they take advantage of it, and this makes a great opportunity for the dry fly angler. Most fishing opportunity is in the nymphal stage.

The first adult stage of the winged insect is called a dun, or subimago. When the dun molts, or sheds its skin, it is sexually mature and is called a spinner, or imago. It mates in the air, and females then fly down to the water's surface to lay their eggs. Both males and females die shortly afterward. Some females repeatedly dip their abdomen into the water while sustaining flight. Others land on the water, drift with the current, and lay their eggs at rest. Some species actually submerge to lay their eggs. Young nymphs soon emerge from the eggs.

Single species often all hatch into a terrestrial stage in a very short period of time, and huge numbers may be observed emerging from the stream or as a swirling mass above it. This occasion is widely referred to as a hatch.

Mayfly larvae are mostly distinguished by these characteristics: platelike, filamentous or feathery gills along the abdomen; three (sometimes two) long hairlike tails on the abdomen (the tails may appear webbed), which extend from the body at the same level; three pairs of segmented legs (six legs in total) on the middle section of the body; a usually flattened body; and one claw at the end of each leg. Adult mayflies have large, upright wings that are sail-shaped.

Mayfly larvae may be distinguished from stonefly larvae by the presence of platelike or feathery gill

Mayfly

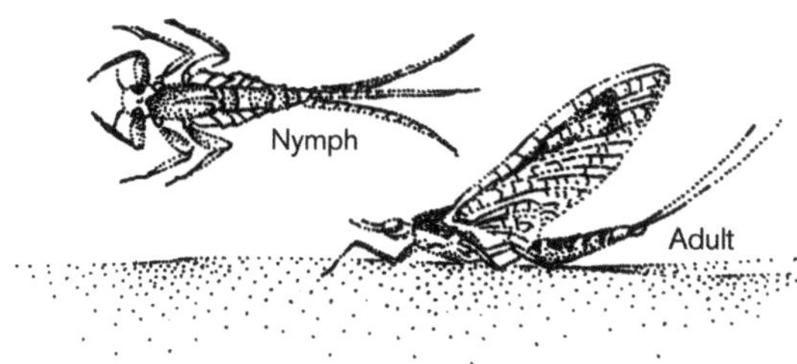

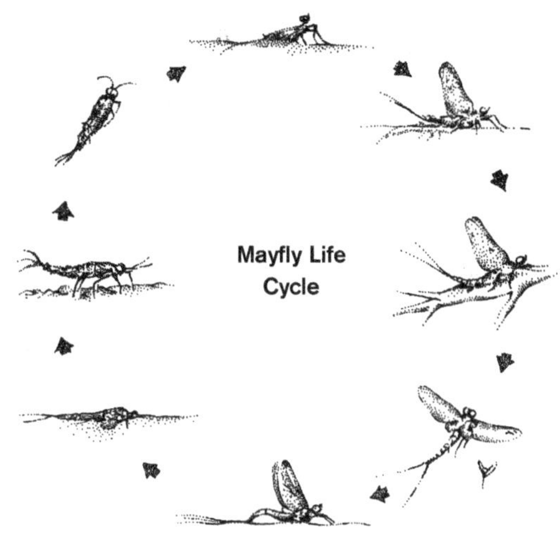

tufts along the sides of the abdomen. In addition, mayfly larvae usually have three hairlike tails and very short antennae (usually shorter than the head length).

Damselfly larvae can also be similar to mayfly larvae, except damselfly larvae have no gills on the sides of their abdomen and they have three broad oar-shaped tails (these are the damselfly larvae's gills) that extend from the back end of the damselfly in a tripod formation. Mayfly larvae have tails that extend from the back end of the abdomen all in the same plane with (parallel to) the ground.

MEAGRE *Argyrosomus regius.*

Other names—croaker, salmon bass, shadefish; French: *maigre commun;* Italian: *bocca d'oro;* Spanish: *corvina.*

The meagre is a large member of the Sciaenidae family (drum and croaker) common to the eastern Atlantic. An important food fish, it is prominent in commercial trawl fisheries and is also a target of anglers.

It occurs in the eastern Atlantic, from Norway to Gibraltar and south to the Congo, including the Mediterranean and the Black Sea, and migrated into the Red Sea via the Suez Canal. It generally inhabits inshore and shelf waters, close to bottom, but is also found at mid- and surface levels when foraging on schools of baitfish.

The meagre is commonly found to 60 inches in length, but it is reported to attain a maximum of 78 inches in length and a weight of 284 pounds. The all-tackle rod-and-reel record is a 105-pound, 13-ounce specimen caught in 1986 in Mauritania.

Meagre spawn inshore during spring and summer. Young fish may enter estuaries and coastal lagoons; adults and juveniles migrate along coastlines and from inshore to offshore environs in response to changes in water temperature.

MEALWORM

The larva of a meal beetle, also called a mousie, used to tip the hook of a small ice fishing jig or placed on a small bait hook.

See: Jig; Maggot.

MEASURING FISH

Fish are measured in various ways and for a variety of reasons. The simplest kind of measurement and the most common reason for measuring involve fish that the angler wants to keep; such fish need to be measured for length to comply with existing laws pertaining to that species. Many species of fish, especially those in freshwater, cannot be kept by anglers unless they meet certain length requirements. How to measure fish in accordance with applicable laws, and the reasoning behind this, is detailed in other entries *(see: fisheries management; regulations)*.

Another common reason for measuring involves large fish that will be kept by an angler who desires to know the weight. This information may be simply for personal gratification, for submission in a contest, or for the sake of claiming a record. Although measuring can also include taking length and girth measurements (which are required for world-record certification), it especially involves the weighing of a fish. Many types of spring and digital scales are available and can be carried with anglers. The accuracy of these varies widely, not to mention that they are often used when a boat is unsteady and moving with wind or waves—a condition that tends to allow the fish to surge on the scale. Some spring scales, however, especially the brass tube Chatillon models, are so accurate that they can be calibrated well enough to pass official weight-inspection tests and may actually be certified for use in record keeping. For record establishment, it is absolutely necessary to have a fish weighed on a scale that has been recently certified for accuracy. Most weighings of fish are performed on scales at stores (grocery, meat, and produce scales), at fishing lodges or camps, at marinas, and at fishing clubs. For conscientious anglers who catch fish that are large but not record class, even ordinary pocket or tackle box scales should be checked periodically against known weights so that their degree of accuracy can be determined.

Estimating Weight

Weighing on the water can be harmful to big fish, because they may be out of the water for a long time and held in a position that doesn't support their internal organs well (being hung by the mouth); thus, for really large fish that are to be released, weighing may be harmful or may not be practical. Weighing fish that will be released is specifically not recommended by some fisheries agencies and, as a practical matter, it is good to minimize handling of a fish for all purposes, weighing included *(see: catch- and-release)*.

Large fish that are released and not weighed, however, are often subject to speculation—even outlandish guessing—regarding the actual live weight. For many years, anglers and fisheries biologists have been working on ways for people to reasonably determine weight based upon length and/or on length and girth measurements. No single table or formula applies to all species, owing to the vast differences in body shapes that exist. And no method has been totally perfect time after time, but there are ways to come close enough to knowing the live-released weight for most fish.

In all cases you need to know the length. To make measurements, use a soft tailor's tape measure or a piece of marked cord or thin-diameter rope that will not shrink and is marked at regular intervals. In a pinch, you can measure small fish by spreading your fingers and using the distance from pinky to thumb. Another emergency measure is to use your fishing rod, aligning the butt with the tip of the fish's jaw. Still another is to cut nylon line off the reel and cut it to the exact length (and girth) of the fish.

Tables. The best way to get a quick, on-the-spot idea of the fish's weight without having to do multiplication and division (what if you have no pen?), and when you have forgotten to stick a calculator in your tackle box, is to refer to a table. In some of the finest lakes in northern Canada, where lake trout must be released unharmed and people catch huge specimens, all boats are equipped with a waterproof length-girth-weight table, affixed to the seat or gunwale, that can be instantly referenced as soon as a tape measure (also supplied) is wrapped around and along the trout.

An increasing number of freshwater fisheries agencies are publishing weight estimation tables for the most popular and common species in their jurisdiction; these are correlated to total length only (no girth) and are based upon the average weight for fish of that length in that jurisdiction. One of the best of these tables, offered by Pennsylvania, is a waterproof, pocket-size booklet covering 16 freshwater fish, which also has instructions for photographing and releasing the catch. Tables for use in saltwater with billfish are appearing, although these are specific to regions rather than being worldwide.

Formulas. Formulas have long been developed in freshwater and saltwater for using length and girth to estimate the weight of a fish, and these have been evolving since the days (at least the 1940s) when a formula for fish with a cylindrical body shape was applied to all fish, although this didn't take into account especially elongate or round species.

The following formulas, published by the Minnesota Department of Natural Resources, take body shape into account:

Walleye *Length*^{3} ÷ 3,500 (*length* × *length* × *length* ÷ 3,500)
Pike *Length*^{3} ÷ 2,700
Sunfish *Length*^{3} ÷ 1,200
Bass *Length*^{2} × *Girth* ÷ 1,200
Trout *Length* × *Girth*^{2} ÷ 800

The formula for pike is not accurate when applied to large, heavy muskies (it makes them far too large), although some people use *Length* × *Girth*^{2} ÷ 800 for these fish (which is also above the actual weight by a small amount). Very heavy specimens of any species are often tough to fit into these formulas because their bellies tend to become distended, and fish of equal lengths can have much different thickness (just as every human being that is 68 inches tall doesn't weigh the same, even though there are average weight charts).

Formulas and tables are based on averages using standard-size fish up to large-size fish, but seldom extraordinary sizes of fish (because there are so few extraordinary fish). So these formulas are guidelines, not absolutes. The difference between an estimated 39-pound fish and an estimated 42-pound fish is really minor in the overall scheme of things unless a record is involved, which likely means killing the fish anyway; and the main purpose is releasing the fish unharmed.

Likewise, in saltwater, determining the weight of virtually all released billfish species is mostly an estimate. The same is now true for tarpon, since almost no tarpon are actually killed and weighed and many people fishing for them have no real experience in weighing tarpon of any size, let alone of all sizes. Eyeball estimates are usually well off the mark, generally being higher than the fish actually weighs (as determined by actual weights when tagged fish are recovered and actual weights are compared with estimated weights).

The old formula of *Length* × *Girth*^{2} ÷ 800 is still used by some people for billfish and other saltwater species, but this is as much off the mark as it is close; some people divide by 900 for species that are very long and thin-bodied, like wahoo, king mackerel, and barracuda. Some private parties and some research groups or fisheries agencies have developed a formula or created preliminary tables that convert length to weight, but these have been calculated for fish in specific oceans and regions of oceans (you can't compare Pacific sailfish to Atlantic sailfish, for example, since the former are much larger on average than the latter).

With catch-and-release fishing being more prominent, it's likely that existing tables and formulas will be refined and that ways to estimate weights for other species will be developed. Spreading your hands apart doesn't suffice any longer.

See: Records; Tagging.

MENDING

Mending is an important and basic line-manipulating skill used by fly anglers to effect a proper presentation and/or drift of a fly without drag. Drag is the influence of current on a fly that inhibits it from drifting in a free manner as if it were a natural insect. A drag-free drift is highly desirable and often necessary for all, or as much as possible, of the presentation, and certainly for the period when the fly is in the likely zone where a fish lies. In some situations a drag-free drift is possible for only a few seconds before the current grabs the line and pulls the fly downstream too fast.

To avoid or minimize drag on the fly, an angler must maneuver the line in such a manner that the fly floats unhindered with the current. It is usually the effect of converging current, or of currents that operate at different speeds, that causes the fly line to flow either faster or slower than the fly and pull on it, either dragging it across the surface if it's a dry fly, or up- or across-current if it's a nymph.

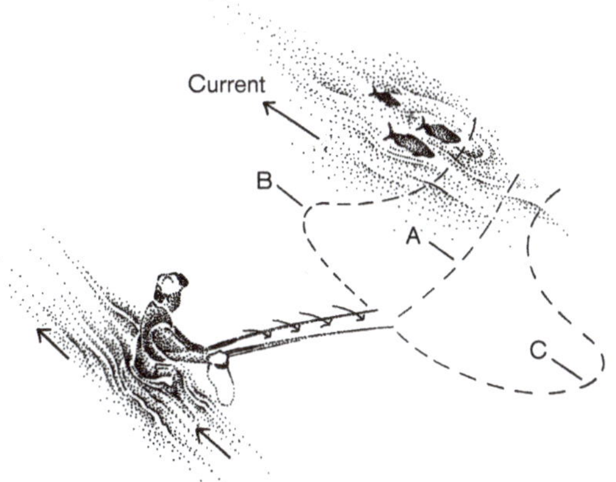

When a fly line is laid across current (A), a strong midstream flow will catch the belly (B) and place unnatural drag on the fly. This can be countered by mending line that is already on the water. After making the initial cast (A), use your rod to pick up the belly of the line and drop it upstream (C), which permits a drag-free float of the fly that lasts long enough for it to drift naturally to the fish.

There are various methods of mending the fly line to prevent or postpone the current from dragging the fly. This mending is accomplished by throwing additional slack into the line; most often slack is thrown into the belly of the line when the line is already on the surface, but it may also be accomplished in other ways and in a variety of situations, some of which are briefly described here.

On-water mends. A standard mend on a cast made quartering upstream is performed the moment the fly and line are on the water; the angler lifts the rod quickly and flips the belly and forward part of the line upstream. This is best done with some slack line hanging between the reel and the stripping guide on the rod. If the cast is long, the forward part of the line may be mended several times to lengthen the drift. This tactic can also be employed to lift the line a few inches above the surface to get it over an object, like a rock, in the current. The objective is not to move the fly from the path of its normal drift, but to extend the length of a natural drift.

A series of roll casts or tip rolls of the slack line is also another way of mending a small amount of line, and is especially useful when you're already well into a drift and need to extend it but cannot with an upstream mend, which would in itself pull on the floating fly. Stripping some slack off the reel and feeding it out will also give the drift a little more mileage.

A variation on this technique would be throwing a mend downstream when you're casting across slow-moving water and placing your fly in swifter current. Flipping the line downstream allows the fly to float naturally and faster and then meet up with the pace of the line.

In-air mends. Mending can also be accomplished by manipulating the fly line and leader in the air at the end of the forward cast but before the line contacts the water. This is done in several ways that throw slack into the line, resulting in the term "slack line casts."

One way to do this is to drop the rod tip from a vertical position to one side and then return it to the vertical position while the forward cast is in progress and before it lands. In essence, this action forms a curve in the line and is thus called a curve cast; it can be accomplished upstream or downstream.

Another version, sometimes called a reach cast, is done by reaching upstream with the rod while the line is in the air and then laying the line on the water. In a similar fashion, slightly overpowering the cast and stopping the line so that the fly stops in midair and bounces a bit backward, then letting the line fall to the surface, creates a series of curves in the line on the water. This is called an S-cast, or S-curve. In all of these maneuvers, further mending can be accomplished without creating drag by sending slack out in a tip roll, which is an abbreviated roll cast. A version of this for short drifts in quick water, or pocket water *(see)*, is called a pile cast. It is accomplished by casting high above the target spot, stopping the cast abruptly, and dumping the line on the water. This action piles up the line closer to the fly and allows a short drag-free float.

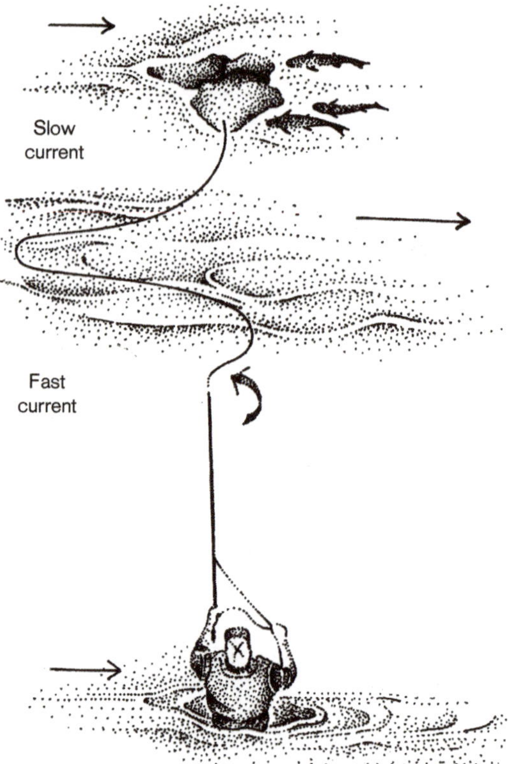

When making a presentation across a fast, narrow flow of water, you can avoid instantaneous drag on a fly by making an upstream curve cast. Here, as the forward cast nears completion, the angler throws an upstream in-air curve in the line, which deposits most of the belly into the fast current, allowing the fly to float for a short distance drag-free in the slower current.

MENHADEN, ATLANTIC *Brevoortia tyrannus.*

Other names—pogy, bunker, bughead, bugfish, fatback, menhaden, mossbunker; Danish, Finnish, Norwegian, Polish, Swedish: *menhaden;* French: *menhaden tyran;* Spanish: *lacha tirana.*

A member of the herring family, the Atlantic menhaden is a hugely important commercial species; greater numbers of this fish are taken each year by commercial fishermen than of any other fish in the United States. Although it is marketed fresh, salted, canned, or smoked, the Atlantic menhaden is mainly used for the production of oil, fertilizer, and fish meal. Excessive fishing of the species has caused population declines.

Identification. The Atlantic menhaden has a deep and compressed body, a big bony head, and a large mouth with a lower jaw that fits into a notch in the upper jaw. It also has adipose eyelids, which make it appear sleepy. It has a dark blue back, silvery sides with an occasional reddish or brassy tint, pale-yellow fins edged in black, a dark patch on the shoulder, and two or three scattered rows of smaller spots.

Size. The Atlantic menhaden can reach a length of $1^1/_2$ feet.

Distribution. This species occurs in the western Atlantic Ocean from Nova Scotia to the Indian River in southern Florida. In the northern regions, it is primarily known as bunker.

Habitat. Atlantic menhaden inhabit inland tidal areas of brackish water and coastal saltwater. They migrate in and out of bays and inlets, and are found inshore in summer. Some populations move into deeper water in winter.

Atlantic Menhaden

Life history/Behavior. Atlantic menhaden form large and very compact schools consisting of both young and adult fish; this makes them vulnerable to commercial fishermen, some of whom use spotter planes to locate the schools and direct commercial vessels to the fish, which are then encircled.

Menhaden have distinct seasonal migrations—northward in April and May, and southward in early fall. Spawning occurs year-round, although not in the same locations at the same time. For example, because high water temperatures are detrimental to breeding, the peak spawning season off the southern coast of the U.S. is October through March. Egg estimates run in the tens of thousands to hundreds of thousands. They are free floating and hatch at sea. Once hatched, the offspring are carried into estuaries and bays, which serve as sheltered nursery areas in which young Atlantic menhaden spend their first year. The fish mature between their first and third years.

Food and feeding habits. Using long filaments on their gills, Atlantic menhaden filter zooplankton and other small plants and animals out of the water.

Angling. Although there is no angling for menhaden, they are widely used as baits for such species as mackerel, Atlantic bonito, bluefish, striped bass, and sea trout, as well as other species. When menhaden schools are located, specimens may be snagged for use as live baits, or taken with a cast net, the latter being productive at night when the fish are attracted to lights; chunks are commonly used for hook baits and for chumming.

Like all herring, live menhaden are difficult to keep alive. The water has to be kept cool and well aerated, and a circular well is a must. Live fish can be hooked through the lips or the back behind the dorsal fin, and they are drifted or slowly trolled, usually without weights. Because whole live menhaden are large, anglers must give gamefish time to swallow the fish before setting the hook.

MESOTROPHIC

Moderate nutrient levels. A mesotrophic lake is one that is intermediate between oligotrophic *(see)* and eutrophic *(see)* lakes, with moderate levels of nutrients and capable of supporting both coldwater and warmwater fisheries in different portions. Lake aging goes through a process from oligotrophic to mesotrophic to eutrophic.

METAL LURE

In a strict sense, a metal lure is any artificial lure that is all or mostly made of metal. Today this is primarily spoons, spinners, and jigs. Lures are usually cate-gorized by their type or function, rather than the material that they are made from, since there is so much overlap in the use of materials. Thus, it is uncommon today to refer to a lure as a metal lure. However, in an antiquated sense, a metal lure is an old and collectible item that was made of metal or that had mainly metal components, created in the early days of artificial lure making. Perhaps the oldest ancestor of today's plugs, for example, is the Phantom Minnow, an English lure with metal head, metal fins, three treble hooks, and a silk body, first crafted around 1800; this lure existed at a time before metal spoons or spinners and before wooden plugs.

See: Antique Fishing Tackle.

MEXICO

Mexico has been a great draw for anglers, especially those from the United States, for many years and continues to provide surprises, with new hotspots being discovered periodically in inland bass fishing, offshore billfishing, and flats fishing. A large country, Mexico is blessed with an exceptional amount of coastline on the Pacific, the Gulf of Mexico, and the Caribbean, but it lacks significant water reserves inland.

Much of Mexico's saltwater fishery is explored through established sportfishing operations, and because some areas of both coasts have minimal access, they have not been thoroughly investigated for angling potential. Opportunities for self-guided exploration exist for the adventurous angler, although this is most reasonable for those fluent in Spanish. The farther one gets from the more popular tourist sites, the less likely it is that the locals will speak English. The language difference is one factor that probably keeps most northern-based anglers from fishing on their own in Mexico, particularly in the most southerly areas of the mainland. In addition, certain areas of the country present security concerns for self-guided travelers.

Nevertheless, hot bass fishing lakes; striped marlin off Cabo San Lucas; Pacific sailfish off the western mainland; Atlantic sailfish at Cancún and Cozumel; and tarpon, permit, and bonefish along many areas of the Yucatán coast present world-class opportunities.

Freshwater

Mexico does not have the abundant inland angling opportunity or diversity that characterizes most U.S. states and all Canadian provinces. Its freshwater fishing pales in comparison to its saltwater opportunities, and yet many people equate Mexico with fantastic largemouth bass angling.

To understand freshwater fishing in Mexico, it

helps to know a few things about the country as a whole. Mexico is a large nation with varied terrain and climates. Although about half of Mexico is a dry plains plateau, and a continuation of the plains of the southwestern U.S., it has high peaks, canyons, mountain ranges, valleys, and coastal plains. It has relatively few sizable rivers and almost no large natural lakes. Most of the rivers aren't navigable, and many are in the valleys and canyons of mountain regions. The longest river is the Rio Grande, or Rio Bravo del Norte, which runs along the Mexican–U.S. border. It has been identified as one of the most polluted waterways in North America.

Although Mexico is generally arid and warm, its climate varies with altitude and has some bearing on Mexico's fisheries, particularly in the winter in those locations subject to high-mountain (that is, coldwater) runoff. Some areas have very low average annual rainfall and are subject to drought, which may continue for years, whereas others are subject to peaks and troughs in temperature and precipitation.

The largest lakes are artificial, having been formed by dams that were primarily constructed by federal engineers for irrigation, hydroelectric power generation, or both. There are perhaps 50 of these waters in various parts of the country; many of them are in the northwestern region in the foothills of the Sierre Madre Occidentals. Some were constructed as long ago as the 1930s, although the majority were formed in the last four decades. Some were constructed as recently as the mid-1990s, and undoubtedly others are likely to be created in the future, although the rate of large, new-water creation slowed to a near halt in the late 1990s. These lakes are usually full of brush and trees; some are literally flooded forests, and catching large, strong fish from them can be a challenge.

Sportfishing in freshwater is not a tradition for Mexicans. Most resident fishing efforts in this country have long been directed at subsistence or commercial activities, using handlines or nets. Few Mexicans have had the means to obtain modern angling or boating equipment, and even today only a small percentage of residents fish for sport in freshwater.

As mentioned, there is considerable interest in freshwater fishing in Mexico among nonresident anglers, mainly from the U.S.; approximately half of these come from Texas, Oklahoma, and Louisiana, and their interest focuses almost entirely on black bass, *negra lobina.*

Rainbow trout are said to be indigenous to Mexico, presumably in the higher and cooler western mountain region, from the northern part of the state of Durango toward the southern part of the state of Sonora, and a species of golden trout was identified in a small area there. Still, there is no identifiable fishery for trout.

Catfish are present in many Mexican lakes, and some species are likely indigenous. Although federal authorities have stocked channel cats in some waters, neither angling nor commercial fishing for this species has caught on. Lake Comedero has many catfish, as does Lake Oviachic.

Most of the predominant fish in Mexican lakes are the result of planned or unplanned introductions. Mojarra and largemouth bass were among the first species introduced, dating back to at least the 1930s. Mojarra, common to Central America, were replaced in the early 1980s by tilapia, which were introduced by the federal government. The high-protein tilapia have no sport value, but the planting has been very successful, providing a thriving commercial fishery. They have also become a food source for bass, but this is an unintentional benefit of their introduction. Tilapia are plentiful in many lakes; on hot days in some waters, it is possible to see thousands of these fish milling about near the surface, feeding on minute organisms. Tilapia are prolific, and in some Mexican lakes they spawn three times in a season. Nevertheless, they have been overfished by netters in certain lakes, and, although not eliminated, reduced to small sizes.

Crappie are present in Lake Novillo in the state of Sonora. Bluegills are present here, too, as well as in other waters. Both species are believed to have been introduced by Americans with homes on the lake, as a means of providing food fish for introduced largemouth bass. Some lakes have gar and some carp, but many lack rough fish species entirely. Most have threadfin shad and gizzard shad, although in northern waters the threadfin shad are subject to die-off during extreme cold weather.

There are no known peacock bass in Mexican waters, although rumors suggest that they were placed in Lake Baccarac in the mid-1980s; none are known to have been caught. Peacock bass purportedly would not attain large sizes in Mexico and would succumb to extreme cold swings, although the southernmost region of the country, in and around the state of Chiapas, might be conducive to this species.

In some lakes in the southernmost regions of Mexico the fisheries are unknown, unpublicized, and undeveloped. These areas have long been politically unsettled; operators interested in exploring the region and possibly setting up fishing camps have been dissuaded for safety and security reasons. This is true in some other areas as well.

Mexico does have some natural lakes, called *lagunas,* but few hold largemouth bass or have notable fisheries for this species. Bass anglers have focused their attention over the years on impoundments (known as *presas,* or reservoirs), primarily on newer ones as they first became accessible, and, in a few instances, on older ones. Larger impoundments and lakes with bass include, but are not limited to, Lakes Angostura, Novillo, Macuzari, and Oviachic in Sonora; Dominguez, Hidalgo, Baccarac, Mateos, Ocaroni, El Salto, Comedero, and Huites in Sinaloa; Aguamilpa in Nayarit; Palmito and Tortuga in Durango; Chapala in

Jalisco; Pátzcuaro in Michoacán; Malpaso and Angostura in Chiapas; Miguel Alemán in Oaxaca; several small lakes near the city of Tampico; Guerrero, Españole, and Azúcar in Tamaulipas; Cochillo in Nuevo León; Don Martín in Coahuila; Boquilla and Granacia in Chihuahua; and Falcon and Amistad on the Texas border.

The federal government constructed most of the larger man-made lakes, but some are cooperative ventures with power companies. The construction of western reservoirs in the foothills of the Sierra Madre has been extremely successful. These lakes were intended to provide water for irrigating fertile lands among the coastal plains and valleys along the Sea of Cortez and to help grow food products to feed Mexicans. These goals were achieved and resulted in the exportation of food to other countries, especially the U.S. These efforts have produced hard-currency benefits.

Largemouth bass have been stocked throughout Mexico at least since the 1930s, and they have been transplanted and introduced widely. How the bass got into some Mexican waters is open to speculation. Americans were evidently involved, often deliberately introducing bass both with and without the blessing or knowledge of Mexican authorities.

Northern-strain largemouths were the only known bass in Mexican waters until the late 1970s. At that time, the results of stocking pure Florida-strain largemouths in American waters that did not previously have this species, especially in California and Texas, were becoming evident; Mexico seemed like another suitable location for these fish.

Around 1977, fishing camp operators arranged for the state of Florida to donate 30,000 pure-strain Florida bass fingerlings to the Mexican state of Tamaulipas. These were placed in rearing ponds there, grown to 8 or 9 inches, and then introduced into Lake Guerrero. Until those fish matured, huge largemouth bass were not known in Mexico.

Since then other lakes, in the states of Sinaloa and Sonora, have been stocked with Florida bass, many with the assistance of Mexican officials. Naturally, some of the fish that have been moved from one place to another are second- or third-generation Florida bass, and in some cases have crossed with northern-strain largemouth. Baccarac, Comedero, El Salto, Huites, and Oviachic are some of the impoundments that hold these fish, in addition to Guerrero.

Anglers have caught very big largemouth bass (from pure Florida stockings), including a confirmed 17-pounder from Guerrero. Rumors suggest that bigger fish have been caught, including some 18-pounders from Guerrero and a 19-pounder from Baccarac, but these reports are clouded with suspicion of netting. Two 18-pounders were reportedly caught by commercial fishermen in Comedero in 1997, and it is likely that bass of this size or larger have been caught by netters in Mexico.

Because some Florida bass have grown to more than 10 pounds in just $3^1/_2$ years, some people speculate that newly created western Mexico lakes, which have ample forage and which are not netted, have the potential to grow a bass exceeding the long-standing 22-pound, 4-ounce world record.

Veterans of the Mexican bass fishing scene have watched a succession of boom-and-bust lakes develop. The boom is usually due to the typical pattern that envelops new lakes with good forage and bass populations—quick-growing bass that are aggressive and uneducated. Their feistiness is due in part to a fat torso. This results in high numbers of fish caught per boat or angler on a daily basis. The mantra of camp owners and operators in Mexico has historically involved numbers; 100 bass (or more) a day is the calling card for legions of anglers who could not experience such fishing on their home waters in their wildest dreams.

The bust has followed within a few years (sometimes as few as two or three), when either the average size or the number of fish has dropped. These changes are often blamed on local netting, which has certainly contributed to the problem (as has spearfishing). Even lakes officially designated as sportfishing-only lakes have lost that status in just a few years, and netting or poaching crept into the picture.

Netting, both illegal and legal, is practiced sooner or later on virtually all Mexican lakes. Tilapia are primarily pursued, but other species are sought after too, including the abundant largemouth bass, even though Mexico's congress passed a law in 1994 that protects these fish and prohibits them from being the target of commercial fishing. The law has not been well enforced, however. In a country with many poor people, and where it is difficult to convey to local residents and to public officials the value of fishing-oriented tourism, netting is virtually inevitable.

Netting is not the only problem. For various reasons, many of the once awesome and highly touted hotspots become mediocre or average fisheries, or fisheries with ample bass but few medium or large specimens, or fisheries that have ample but hard-to-catch bass. As new lakes age, they mature, creating an ecologically based retreat from their former productivity. Furthermore, many Mexican impoundments, especially mountain lakes, are subject to extreme fluctuations, which adversely impact a maturing population of bass. The bass may go deeper, and the population may become oriented to the security of deep water, which makes them more difficult to locate and catch.

Two of the biggest problems with Mexican lakes are drought and fluctuating water levels. Lowland impoundments are prone to drought and may be very low for many years. Some went dry and had to be restocked when they were refilled.

The water level in mountain lakes can vary dramatically. In late 1997, for example, Lake Huites,

If there are fish in the depths of Russia's Lake Baikal, it will take a lot of line to reach them; Baikal is 5,371 feet deep and has seven times the volume of Lake Superior.

then touted as one of the greatest bass lakes in North America, was dropped at a rate of $2^1/_2$ to 3 feet a day for weeks in anticipation of predicted precipitation from El Niño. The lake was down about 120 feet from full pool and still falling when, just after Christmas, a freak heavy snow fell in the upriver mountains, quickly melted, and caused the reservoir to rise 47 feet over $2^1/_2$ days. Neither of these circumstances was beneficial to the fishery, even though the lake was new and chock-full of largemouths.

Unstable water levels, which are generally unusual in closely maintained American waters and which cause havoc with bass, are a normal occurrence on most Mexican lakes. In irrigation lakes, the water level normally drops; unless the water falls too fast, there is no need for concern. Rising water, however, can cause bass to withdraw for long periods; it may take three to four weeks—preferably with the water high and stable—before they become active again.

Ironically, although many people think of Mexican bass lakes as conducive to shallow fishing and surface action, this is often not the case, except in new lakes that are full, or when a lake has experienced stable conditions for a long period. In mountain lakes, bass have a tendency to stay deep, perhaps due to the often falling water, and, of course, they become harder to catch when they stay deep.

The age of Mexican bass lakes varies, and some of the older lakes, including Guerrero, Baccarac, Oviachic, Palmito, and Novillo, have windows of opportunity, primarily around spawning time, during which some anglers will catch enough fish to be happy. When conditions on these lakes are ideal, the angling will be good. Unfortunately, it may not be good every year at the same time, or it may be good for just a short period, or it may be downright poor for several years and then revive.

M

Before and during the spawn are the preferred times for largemouth bass fishing in Mexico. Spawning season varies with altitude and location. Bass in mountain lakes normally spawn between mid-March and early April; those in the flatland lakes spawn in January. Some lakes that are just $1^1/_2$ hours apart have spawning seasons that are months apart. October and November can be good months as well, and sometimes provide the best fishing, although this may vary from year to year due to other conditions.

The lack of summertime anglers is one element that skews the fishing results in Mexico. In fact, January through March is preferred by many visiting anglers because of poor weather and fishing conditions at home, because it is usually warm in Mexico at this time, and because the fish are usually shallower and more accessible. Many camps are closed between May and September.

The catch-and-release ethic has produced a dramatic change in Mexico's bass fishery, one that came about only in the early to mid-1980s. Previously, visiting anglers commonly kept excessive numbers of bass of all sizes, especially in the lakes that could be reached by car. Guerrero, one of the most accessible lakes, was particularly vulnerable, and thousands of pounds of largemouth bass were hauled away from Guerrero in freezers in the back of pickup trucks by people who thought there was no end to this resource and for whom no limits had been established (and some of these anglers complain today about Mexicans netting fish!). This lake, and other drive-in lakes in northern Mexico, were seriously hurt by such actions. Voluntary and involuntary limits, a changing ethic, and the realization of the damage incurred on some lakes eventually resulted in changed attitudes and practices. For many mountain lakes, where access is difficult, their isolated location made them secure from excessive sportfishing, although not from legal or illegal netting. There, the greater problem may be that eventually the fish will become smarter after being caught.

It is hard to be definitive about the prospects for Mexico's bass lakes, as they are continually changing. New lakes offer many more fish than some anglers could get at home, bass that are much easier to catch, and a better climate. So January through March will probably always be peak periods for most anglers. When people have to work hard to catch only 15 or 20 bass a day, however, the yield does not warrant the expense. In fact, when bass fishing productivity drops below a standard of about 40 quality fish per boat per day, and the chances of landing an 8- to 10-pound bass diminish, the better camp operators look for greener pastures, even though this type of action would be a terrific day on almost any bass lake elsewhere in North America.

A person visiting Mexico on a self-guided vacation, with plenty of time to spare and bringing a boat to fish from (likely a cartop boat), can probably find acceptable bass fishing in many lakes that do not have established fishing camps. The very mention of netting in a lake is enough to keep foreign visitors away, but that may not necessarily imply that the fishing is awful (although it probably means that large specimens are unlikely). Even if the lakes are netted, there's a good chance they will have plenty of smaller bass (2 to 5 pounds) that are unsophisticated and very susceptible to angling, as virtually no one will have been tossing lures at them. Moreover, at least one lake that is netted for tilapia—El Salto—was producing large bass as recently as 1999, in part because the lone camp operator there instituted a successful clothes-for-bass program designed to encourage netters to release bass.

Keep in mind that bass exist in many Mexican waters that are not among the more well known or currently popular sites. A traveler with time and a boat can cheaply sample many waters that don't draw tourists or are not prominent on road maps.

Lake Guerrero. Lake Vicente Guerrero is in the state of Tamaulipas, about 175 miles south of Brownsville, Texas, and about 20 miles from Victoria. It covers about 100,000 acres when completely full, is loaded with brush and timber, and has many flats, islands, and creekbeds.

Lake Guerrero's history is typical of many Mexican bass lakes. It was formed in 1971 and was not supposed to be fishable for several years, but five incoming rivers filled the new reservoir quickly, flooding farmlands, ranches, roads, and the village of Padilla. Half-submerged at full pool, Padilla's church was a dramatic and frequently used photographic backdrop for anglers posing with their catch.

Throughout the 1970s, Guerrero provided what some considered the greatest bass fishing in the world. If you could make even a feeble cast, with virtually any lure you could catch a bass. The early game was to fish for many small bass and lots of 4- to 7-pounders. In the clear shallows, anglers could see a fish coming to strike a lure from 8 or 10 yards away. At times, three to five bass, each weighing perhaps 5 pounds, would follow a hooked brethren to the boat. It was, in essence, the ultimate bass fishing experience, one that would be repeated on many other newly created reservoirs in the decades that followed.

These experiences were nearly the ultimate in freshwater fishing excess. For at least a decade, with the exception of a ban on live bait, this was a no-holds-barred catch-and-keep fishery. The larger bass disappeared first, although hordes of small fish remained. Then the population of small bass dwindled, the anglers dwindled, and the camps closed. A prolonged drought drew Guerrero down drastically. Some camps, once at water's edge, were left a mile or more from the shrunken lake, and Guerrero was declared finished. Nearly a decade later, big bass began to show up, thanks to the planting of Florida-strain fish. The lake experienced a rebirth, and the anglers returned.

The big bass were not the 7-pounders of years past, but fish weighing more than 10 pounds. Fifteen- and 17-pound specimens, and reputedly some larger, were caught in the early 1990s. Guerrero was a gold mine once again, this time for lunkers. But this fishery also peaked, perhaps because the original pure-strain fish passed on, but the lake still produces 10-pound fish today.

One reason for Guerrero's resurgence in the mid- to latter 1990s was a prolonged drought in Tamaulipas, which kept the lake 25 feet below normal and roughly half full for about a decade. These conditions produced a stability that is unusual for Mexican impoundments. Experienced anglers have had good success in Guerrero in recent times, some fishing methodically in deep water; those with lesser skills have experienced varied results. Being present when the fish are active, which is often hit-or-miss, can provide a lot of action. February and March, when the fish usually spawn, are favorite times for many Guerrero veterans. Some of the best big bass fishing has occurred in midsummer at night, although large fish are caught in all seasons.

A 10-pound largemouth is landed at Lake Guerrero, long known for its bass fishing.

Due to a shifting clientele, the availability of replica taxidermy mounts, new government harvesting restrictions, and a generally improved conservation ethic, there is a much better attitude toward releasing big bass. These days, 3- and 4-pound fish are plentiful, and some monsters do inhabit these waters. How Guerrero's bass fishery will develop in the future, however, is anybody's guess.

Lake Huites. Lake Huites stands in sharp contrast to Lake Guerrero for many reasons. It was not impounded until 1994; it was first stocked with pure-strain Florida largemouth bass; it is a mountain lake situated in the remote Sinaloan foothills; and for anglers it was a catch-and-release fishery when it first opened to fishing in 1997. Like Guerrero and other Mexican lakes, however, especially highland impoundments, it is subject to extreme fluctuations, and netting started soon after the first spinnerbaits hit the water.

All 240 people from the village of Techobampo, as well as those from two other villages, were relocated in 1994 when a dam on the Río Fuerte was completed and a new impoundment—built for irrigation and hydroelectric power—started to fill. That dam also backed up the Chinipas River, a serpentine watercourse that flows into Huites from rugged peaks near renowned Copper Canyon. Barranca del Cobre, Mexico's larger and deeper version of the Grand Canyon, is a nearby scenic wonder with a maximum depth of more than 6,000 feet.

Southwest of canyon country, on the outskirts of the Sierra Madre Occidentals, Lake Huites is 22 miles long and covers 30,000 acres when full. It is so remote that most of the first guides employed at fishing camps there had never seen a boat or outboard motor before, and the nearby villages

Lake Huites in the western mountains is one of Mexico's newest bass fisheries.

got electricity only once the dam was built. The drive from Los Mochis, 18 miles of which follows a winding, rutted, neck-wrenching burro trail, takes more than three hours.

It is extremely still in the narrow sections of the lake, especially on the Chinipas. Boats travel through chasms so steep that the sun doesn't penetrate until midmorning. Overhead, huge boulders hang on precipices hundreds of feet up, and every osprey that flies by has a fish in its talons. Below, the tips of 40-foot-tall trees barely reach the water's surface, and the bass might pull your fishing rod into the water if you don't hold onto it.

Adventurous American anglers, showing the tenacity of burros themselves, flocked to Huites for stupendous largemouth bass fishing action. Florida-strain largemouths, planted in 1994, grew quickly, producing football-shaped bass with small heads and a large girth, and a hot chili pepper disposition.

Landing these dynamos is not guaranteed and is always a challenge. Flooded *au natural,* Huites is loaded with trees and brush, and the bass linger along the shorelines amidst this protective cover. When the fish strike a lure, they dive for the nearest wood, often a multilimbed cactus, and either break the line or achieve freedom when an exasperated angler is unable to extract them.

There were so many bass in the early days at Lake Huites, losing half the fish that struck your line was not a problem. In fact, the bass often congregated in spots, usually off points near deep water. These areas produced so much action, anglers didn't have to search all over this expansive water to find them, a rarity in most U.S. bass lakes. When unusual cold spells hit Huites, or when extreme changes in water level occur, however, the fishing can be off for a while.

The effects of tilapia (and possibly bass) netting and of angling pressure, as well as the ultimate size potential of Huites' bass, remain to be seen. The peak for this fishery, at least in terms of giant bass, could be yet to come.

Other lakes. Although Huites has been the latest darling of the avid visiting bass angler, other lakes in the northwest still have a following. All of them have never-ending brush and tree cover, remote locations, waters that are quiet and virtually empty when compared with lakes in the U.S., and they are surrounded by beautiful mountain scenery. They are characteristically long and relatively narrow, with steep shorelines that are often protected from wind. Many are usually clear, at least by most standards, and are replete with rocky points, coves, and many bassy nooks. When the water level changes, these lakes present a whole new look.

Lake Comedero, also known as Lake José Lopez Portillo, is a 30,000-acre impoundment that was stocked with northern-strain largemouths in 1985. Located about 45 miles southeast of Culiacan, this was a tremendous fishery in the early 1990s, and still has a following. In recent times it has not produced massive catches, but it does have big fish potential. Sportfishermen have caught bass to 15 pounds here, and in 1997 local commercial fishermen allegedly caught two 18-pounders.

Lake El Salto was another hot lake shortly after it opened in 1990. This 24,000-acre timber-studded lake was stocked with 200,000 Florida-strain bass in 1985 when it was filling. About $1^1/_2$ hours from Mazatlan in the Sinaloan mountains, El Salto quickly forged a reputation for 8- to 10-pound bass and plentiful small fish but no midsize specimens. Soon, the large fish appeared to be gone, leaving only small bass. El Salto had a large number of netters, and after just a few years it was written off by anglers.

However, in 1998, a deluxe lodge was built by a prominent outfitter, and visiting anglers once again started catching a lot of bass in the 10-pound class, with some up to 14 pounds. In December 1998, El Salto produced a lake-record 14-pound, 3-ounce bass, and a newly implemented conservation program to discourage netting of bass makes some think the lake could be ripe for a 20-pounder. In 1994, a 16-pound, 3-ounce bass was found dead in El Salto; it had choked to death with a tilapia wedged in its throat. As of the spring of 1999, El Salto's reputation as a big-bass lake had been reclaimed.

Lake Baccarac near Los Mochis opened to fishing in 1984. A 35,000-acre impoundment on the Sinaloa River, and also known as Lake Bacubirito, it has produced some huge Florida-strain largemouths, including a reputed 19-pounder around 1994, and was drawing anglers throughout the late 1990s.

Lake Oviachic, better known as Lake Obregon, is both an old lake and a new lake. This 30,000-acre impoundment on the Yaqui River was originally impounded in the 1950s. The lake went dry in the early 1980s, was refilled and restocked with northern-strain largemouth bass in 1990, and took on a new life. Although it hasn't produced trophy-caliber bass, the 27-mile-long lake is known for an abundance of action. Muddy water from upstream releases (out of Lake Novillo), however, can turn the fish off.

Lake Novillo, a 25-mile-long impoundment below the convergence of the Moctezuma and Yaqui Rivers, has drawn people since the early 1970s, but it has not been a prime spot for visiting anglers in recent times.

All of these lakes are subject to changes, some of which happen almost overnight. Due to their remoteness, it is difficult to maintain current information on their status. Some turn on briefly when rainfall or clearing water occurs. Some turn off quickly due to other factors. As mentioned in the introductory section, when the fish are not actively hitting in the shallows of these mountain lakes, they must be pursued deep.

Many claims are made about the quality of the fishing in Mexican waters; it takes some legwork to procure reliable information from those who have fished them recently, or from local operators and their representatives. Almost without exception, each of the lakes mentioned has at one time been called the greatest bass fishing lake in Mexico. Be advised that superlatives are thrown about easily here.

Large spinnerbaits and large plastic worms are the standard fare for Mexican bass, incidentally. It may be necessary to use $^1/_2$-ounce sinkers with the worms. Big jigs, jigging spoons, and surface plugs get some play, too. Anglers should be prepared to shuttle from their accommodations to the lake, especially in the mountainous west and when the water levels are low. You may have to take a camp van or bus to reach the water.

Saltwater

Baja. Situated immediately south of the California border, the Mexican states of Baja California Norte and Baja California Sur constitute a great expanse of angling territory. This large area offers remarkably limited opportunities for freshwater anglers; a few trout in the mountains near Ensenada are one exception. Understandably, most of Mexico's angling action occurs in saltwater.

Unlike other parts of Mexico, Baja California is separated from the mainland by a large gulf called the Sea of Cortez. With this inland sea to the east, and the Pacific Ocean to the west, the 760-mile-long Baja Peninsula is virtually surrounded by water, and the Baja presents tremendous fishing opportunities along both coasts. Boaters experience the best action, but excellent shore fishing opportunities exist on the Pacific side as well.

The more-developed towns have fishing fleets and cater to traveling anglers, especially those interested in blue-water species. Mexico offers significant opportunity to the adventurous angler with plenty of leisure hours; learning where to fish for the most rewarding and desirable species takes time, much of it spent traveling unpaved roads. If this potential appeals to you, learn Spanish, rent a van, load it with fishing tackle, get a map of the Baja, and start fishing when the road meets the water.

To cover in detail every fishing nook and cranny of this close to 2,000-mile coastline would require volumes. So, the following is only a review and offers a summary of the major species available, and the places and seasons to pursue them. We'll begin in the north, on the Pacific side of the Baja, and work south to Cabo San Lucas, then north along the Sea of Cortez to the fishing village of San Felipe. Many of the fish landed around the Baja are nomadic, and the water conditions may vary little from place to place. As a result, the species and techniques noted bear repeating.

Tijuana to San Quintín. Along the Pacific Ocean near the California border from Tijuana to Ensenada, surf anglers can expect to catch barred perch, corbina, and various croaker by using natural bait, small jigs, and soft-bodied grubs. Farther from shore, on local reefs, are rockfish and lingcod, as well as kelp bass, barracuda, and bonito.

Offshore, pelagic blue-water species include albacore, striped marlin, bluefin tuna, yellowfin tuna, and yellowtail. The best action for these larger open-water fish occurs during summer and fall, and at other times in years when the warm water lingers.

Many of the same gamefish inhabit the waters farther south, but here they are generally more abundant. There is less pressure on these species, as access is difficult for surf anglers and only larger fishing boats are able to cruise the longer distances required to ply these waters.

San Quintín to Guerrero Negro. From San Quintín south to Guerrero Negro, the offshore fishing is excellent, offering good numbers of bluefin, yellowfin, and bigeye tuna. These species are caught during summer and fall. Dorado and yellowtail are common too. Because of the distance from good ports, few private sport boats ply these waters. Anglers fishing from long-range boats that depart from San Diego dominate this fishery.

For shore-based anglers who want to work the surf zones of this region, the only access to beaches is via unpaved dirt roads, mandating the use of a four-wheel-drive vehicle. But anglers who brave the tough road conditions will find hard-fighting gamefish, among them white seabass and corvina, and excellent surf fishing for barred perch and corbina.

Anglers who travel out to the beaches must be completely self-sufficient, bringing all the necessary camping items, food, water, fuel, and fresh or frozen bait. Artificial lures such as metal jigs and soft-bodied jigs work well for many species, but bait is necessary to catch big white seabass consistently. Squid is especially favored because it is tough, relatively inexpensive, stays on the hook, keeps well on ice, and attracts all of the aforementioned species.

Guerrero Negro to Magdalena Bay (Mag Bay). Not far offshore in the waters off Guerrero Negro are numerous pinnacles and reefs, plus a few islands, that provide food and cover for hungry gamefish. Here, anglers fishing from long-range boats can expect some tuna, as well as dorado, yellowtail, white seabass, and black seabass. Close to shore in nearby estuaries are cabrilla, grouper, and some snook. In the surf line, croaker, corbina, corvina, and white seabass will take baits and lures.

Farther south at Mag Bay are several offshore banks that attract schools of gamefish. Some of the more well known ones are Uncle Sam, Thetis, and Potato Banks, and they provide excellent tuna and wahoo action. In the fall, at times, large numbers of striped marlin and big sailfish can be seen pounding schools of bait, providing excellent nonstop action.

Inside Mag Bay is a huge network of channels lined with mangroves. The best access here is by small boat. One can launch at the small town of San Carlos and head out to these channels, which hold a large variety of fish. Snook, cabrilla, grouper, corvina, halibut, Sierra mackerel, and pargo will eagerly grab lures and baits.

Magdalena Bay (Mag Bay) to Cabo San Lucas. Offshore anglers who head south of Mag Bay will still catch marlin, dorado, and yellowfin tuna, but not always in the same quantities as when fishing over the productive banks. Shore-bound anglers will find it tough to access the surf, because only a few unpaved roads head out to the Pacific Coast. Those who make it to the beaches will find the standard fare: croaker, corbina, corvina, surfperch, cabrilla near rocks, and white seabass.

North of Cabo San Lucas, offshore anglers will pass over the Goldengate Banks, which produces good action for marlin, dorado, yellowfin tuna, black seabass, grouper, and pargo. South of here by 20 miles or so, anglers will pass over the Jaime Banks just before reaching Cabo. Here, striped marlin fishing in winter and early spring can be fabulous.

The southernmost tip of the Baja, known as Cabo San Lucas, is world famous for billfish. Large numbers of striped marlin invade the waters near Cabo from about the first of the year into early spring. At that time, nearby Jaime and Goldengate Banks host large numbers of striped marlin in the 90- to 150-pound range.

Here, marlin feed on extensive schools of mackerel that forage near the banks. Striped marlin are receptive to trolled marlin lures and are especially fond of live bait. Live mackerel are the most common baitfish, but small green jacks, locally called *caballito,* are key menu items. Large yellowfin tuna, some exceeding 200 pounds, also cruise these banks at this time of year. A handful of anglers out of Cabo target big tuna and are rewarded with good numbers of 200- to 275-pound yellowfins.

As the season progresses into summer, fishing for the larger blue and black marlin improves, and peaks in the fall, when major tournaments, such as the renowned Bisbee and Gold Cup, are held. The larger marlin are hooked on trolled jigs and large live baits such as skipjack, small dorado, and football-size yellowfin tuna. Although marlin are the main target in this area, wahoo, dorado, roosterfish, and school yellowfin fishing are especially good inshore.

Northeast of Cabo San Lucas, toward the Sea of Cortez, is the town of San José del Cabo. This former small fishing town has grown rapidly, with new hotels and golf courses springing up along the landscape. The fishing is particularly good here, and anglers work the nearby Gordo Banks for all the important billfish, and also enjoying some good reef fishing for grouper and pargo. The spring and summer months see good numbers of wahoo grabbing trolled lures and baits on the Gordo Banks. Large cruisers from Cabo San Lucas will fish this area, as will numerous 20- to 25-foot local center-console *pangas.*

East Cape to La Paz. The area known as the East Cape covers roughly the waters northeast of Cabo San Lucas, from Punta Frailles to the southern end of Cerralvo Island near La Paz. This is a popular area for anglers because of consistently great fishing. Several fishing resorts thrive here, offering well-equipped fishing fleets comprised of both cruisers and *pangas.*

This region is a great producer of striped, blue, and black marlin during the spring and summer. But other blue-water residents such as swordfish, yellowfin tuna, dorado, wahoo, and sailfish will be among the catches.

Closer to shore, roosterfish, jack crevalle, and ladyfish inhabit the waters along the beaches and the edges of rock formations. At nearby reefs, leopard grouper, pargo, triggerfish, African pompano, and a few amberjack are available.

La Paz to Loreto. The waters near La Paz provide ample fishing opportunities. During the winter and early spring, large schools of yellowtail frequent the offshore reefs and islands. Large grouper and large pargo are also available here. In the offshore waters near La Paz, striped, blue, and black marlin provide action during the summer months.

As one travels farther north, to Loreto, yellowtail become a primary offshore target, along with do-rado, school tuna, and sailfish. Anglers land an occasional marlin as well.

Loreto to Bahía de los ángeles. Like most areas in the Sea of Cortez, the waters from Loreto to Bahía de los ángeles provide anglers with ample opportunities to stretch their lines. The region is interspersed with numerous rock reefs and small islands. Yellowtail abound during the late winter and spring, when they grab jigs and live baits. Grouper and cabrilla inhabit the reefs along with several species of pargo.

Offshore, yellowfin tuna appear in summer, as do schools of hungry dorado. Billfish will show up as well, and the occasional striped marlin and sailfish are taken. Loreto is a favored destination not only because the fishing is excellent, but also because the town is conveniently located near a large airport, allowing anglers quick access from all of the western states.

From Loreto north toward Bahía de los ángeles and the islands in the Cortez Midriff, action focuses on the current rip lines boiling near small islands and reefs. This is great habitat for schools of baitfish, because currents around the islands concentrate plankton, which baitfish—like sardines—love. Among the baitfish are such hungry predators as bonito, Sierra mackerel, grouper, cabrilla, and hordes of yellowtail. Anglers can produce excellent action using live baits and by casting jigs to yellowtail ranging from 10 to 30 pounds.

Bahía de los ángeles to San Felipe. North of Bahía de los ángeles, the schools of yellowtail begin to thin out and anglers target cabrilla, Sierra mackerel, grouper, and other near-shore species. At the northern end of the Sea of Cortez is the small town of San Felipe, a popular site for anglers from Arizona and California, especially in winter, when temperatures here are warm and balmy.

This particular region differs from the rest of the Baja because of tremendous tidal influences. Between high and low water the tide drops 20-plus feet. Anglers here normally do not pursue the bluewater glamour fish but are content with many types of croaker, including corbina, yellowfin croaker, shortfin corvina, white seabass, and orangemouth corvina. One type of croaker once common to this area is now close to extinction. Called the *totuava,* this fish reportedly reached up to 200 pounds, but due to overfishing and changes in habitat it is now a rare, protected catch that must be released.

Farther offshore, anglers can expect good numbers of Sierra mackerel. These slim silver torpedoes range from 2 to 5 pounds and take a variety of metal jigs and small tuna feathers. A short wire leader is required when fishing for Sierra because they have a well-developed set of sharp teeth that will sever both monofilament line and careless fingers. Along with the Sierras are small bonito and skipjack.

Pacific mainland coast. The western mainland shore of Mexico is most renowned for its beaches, cruise ship landings, and such popular sun-and-fun spots as Acapulco, Mazatlán, and Puerto Vallarta. There is much more, however, including excellent angling and many miles of lightly fished or unfished waters, from the northern reaches in the Sea of Cortez south to the open waters of the Pacific. Although the fisheries along some sections of this coast have been influenced by commercial fishing activities (longlining affecting billfish and tuna, and netting affecting inshore species), some areas have rebounded due to new regulations, and the fisheries in other areas have varied due to the changing effects of warm currents, El Niño in particular.

The entire western mainland coastline has a diversity of pelagic, bottom, and inshore species, including such popular quarry as Pacific sailfish, striped marlin, Pacific blue marlin, black marlin, dolphin, yellowfin tuna, roosterfish, cubera snapper, and corvina among many others, pursued from big charter boats, little skiffs, long wooden *pangas,* or surf and shore. Moreover, the adventurous can have much of the best angling with little, if any, competition.

Sails here are caught within a few miles of shore. Blue marlin are caught a few miles farther out and typically weigh in the 150- to 300-pound range, although larger fish, including a line-class world record, have been caught. Billfish are present year-round, but the best chance of scoring is during the winter months.

Dolphin (dorado) are perhaps the foremost quarry, being swift, able jumpers and great table fare. They are especially abundant from summer through fall in the northern reaches of the Cortez, although they generally move southward as the season progresses. In the fall, smaller school fish wander into shallower water and provide light-tackle opportunities. These dolphin range from a few pounds to 40 or 50 pounds. The larger ones are usually caught in the heat of summer, and live mackerel, if available, are the preferred local bait, although trolling is done as well.

Many line-class world records for the popular roosterfish have been set in the Sea of Cortez. Cubera snapper and assorted bottom fish, including massive grouper and seabass, are abundant all along the coast in rocky locales. Overshadowed by the more glamorous species, but still possessing qualities that endear it to anglers in the know, is the corvina. These weakfish-like creatures are perfect for small-boat and inshore anglers who prefer to work the bays, estuaries, and surf-line rips. They are caught in several subspecies, and although they can grow larger, corvina range from 3 to 15 pounds.

The favored, accessible locales for sportfishing along the western mainland are—from the north—Kino Bay, Guaymas, Topolobampo, Mazatlán, Puerto Vallarta, Ixtapa/Zihuatanejo, and Acapulco. Some of these, especially Mazatlán and Acapulco, are popular tourist sites with large sportfishing charter fleets and tend to attract vacationers who want to spend a day fishing offshore for dolphin or sailfish *(pez vela).* Consequently, these areas do not typically attract serious anglers. In fact, the best angling destinations, albeit without the best

Bombay Duck is a term for a marine lizardfish abundant in the Ganges Delta and the Arabian Sea. Also called bummalo, this ordinarily small fish is split, boned, sun-dried, and used as a condiment.

boats and facilities, are the smaller towns farther south along the coast that don't attract large numbers of tourists and where, in some cases, visiting anglers can launch from a beach in a *panga.* Puerto Escondido and Huatulco, for example, are more than an hour south of Acapulco and offer excellent fishing for adventurous travelers. These areas were lightly explored until the 1990s.

The Pacific mainland coastline of Mexico is extensive, and a good map will reveal its many inlets, points, bays, and estuaries. Some of the estuaries wander inland, miles from the sea, and many are mangrove-lined, offering opportunities for snook, corvina, snapper, and jacks, especially in the winter. These sites promise light-tackle action for the inshore angler no matter what the weather or water conditions offshore. Snook and snapper prefer the edges of these areas, and anglers usually land them by casting to cover. Jacks and corvina linger around the mouths of inlets and estuaries and prefer cast spoons and jigs.

Five red diamond shapes on a yellow background is a top spoon pattern for fishing in northern Canada. The so-called Five of Diamonds first appeared on a Thompson spoon in 1950.

The northern section of this coast is within the confines of the Sea of Cortez and offers quarry similar to that found along the Baja Peninsula. Kino Bay is close to various islands that attract diverse species; Tiburon is especially notable. Topolobampo, near Los Mochis, lies both north and south of a bay- and inlet-studded coast, with an abundance of explorable inshore water.

Guaymas, which is easily reached by highway from Nogales, Arizona, was a billfish hotspot in the mid-twentieth century, suffered from commercial fishing, then enjoyed a renaissance in the early 1990s, when sailfish, all three species of marlin, plus yellowfin tuna, wahoo, and dolphin were caught offshore from San Carlos Bay. Greater numbers of billfish and tuna congregate here when warmer currents are present, and summer through fall has been the best period. Good reef fishing can be had within a few miles of the bay; grouper, red snapper, triggerfish, cabrilla, and yellowtail are among the species anglers pursue. Surf fishing for pompano, corvina, and mackerel was once very popular but has waned and is showing no signs of a revival.

Just below the Tropic of Cancer and at the southern end of the Cortez, Mazatlán has scores of well-equipped charter boats, and although some light-tackle inshore fishing is possible, the focus is primarily offshore. Mazatlán is known for producing sailfish year-round, but the prime period for these fish, called *pez vela,* is from June through September. This is also a good period for large dolphin. Two line-class world records were established in this port in the past; one specimen weighed a phenomenal 83 pounds, 6 ounces. Blue marlin and black marlin are landed from May through December, and striped marlin are present from December through May. Swordfish, tuna, roosterfish, and red snapper are among the other species caught here.

Farther south and nicely situated in the Bay of Banderas, close to deep water, Puerto Vallarta has many of the species found in Mazatlán. Sailfish are prevalent from May through December, tuna from September through March, wahoo from September through December, and marlin from August through December. Although not known for snook, in 1997 Puerto Vallarta's surf produced a snook that could have been a new world record had it been weighed on a certified scale; the fish hit 63 pounds on a truck scale.

The adjacent villages of Ixtapa and Zihuatanejo, which lie north of Acapulco, receive minimal sportfishing attention because they are small and out-of-the-way. Nevertheless, the area is a growing resort destination and offers good sailfish action. As of the late 1990s, sailfish could still be pursued at reasonable prices. A roosterfish line-class world record was established here, and the local bounty also includes yellowfin tuna, blue marlin, black marlin, dolphin, jack crevalle, skipjacks, and Sierra mackerel. December through April is the primary period for offshore fishing, but billfishing can be spotty. With no shelf nearby to concentrate fish, trolling efforts are geared to hooking up with migrants, which may be plentiful or hard to locate. Even in poor times, some sailfish are raised and/or caught. Inshore fishing has been lightly explored here.

The same is true of the coast from south of Acapulco to the border with Guatemala. A close look at a map reveals substantial shoreline but a lack of reasonable access. Yet various small villages dot the area, so there is clearly much to be explored.

Huatulco, for example, is a small village east of Puerto Angel and west of Salina Cruz in the state of Oaxaca. It was unheard of until a resort facility sprang up there in the late 1980s. Although the community has grown into a small tourist destination, it is still unlikely to be found on most maps. Situated on the edge of the Gulf of Tehuantepec, and not far from the Middle America Trench, with associated dropoffs and several seamounts, Huatulco is nicely positioned to receive a warm northerly flowing current, and this brings with it a bounty of baitfish as well as lots of sailfish, plus marlin, yellowfin tuna, and dolphin.

Although the inshore opportunities are unexplored, the sailfishing is so good that poorly equipped anglers, even first-timers, have explored a few miles offshore in *pangas* and hooked up with a number of Pacific sails. When the area was first fished in 1990, *pangas* were the only game in town. Later, at least one modern sportfishing operation with a well-equipped boat established itself. This area could become one of Mexico's top billfishing destinations.

The nine bays around Huatulco are noted for numerous beautiful, soft sandy beaches. Anglers have landed sailfish at the outskirts of the bays and within 2 miles of the beach. Although the fish are present year-round, the best season is from late spring through summer; some days in this period see 20 or more sails raised, and the size is fairly large on average, many in the 125-pound range. Blue and black marlin are both caught here, predominantly in winter and early spring. A 750-pound black was reportedly caught in August of 1996, and blue marlin have been landed to about 500 pounds.

With all of these sailfish, light-tackle opportunities are excellent. It will be necessary to bring your own equipment, especially fly or light-tackle gear, if you expect to hire a local *panga* (which can be done economically). They may have heavy tackle and a limited amount of terminal gear; tackle is not available locally.

Gulf of Mexico. The eastern coast of Mexico fronting the gulf contains many of the species found throughout the coastal areas of the gulf from Florida through Louisiana and Texas, but these waters have been seriously affected by commercial fishing, much of the region is populated and of moderate interest to tourists, and it is lightly visited by traveling anglers. Better and more accessible fisheries exist both to the north, in Texas waters, and to the south along the Caribbean at the Yucatán Peninsula in Mexico and in Central American countries.

Tarpon, snook, redfish, seatrout, jewfish, mackerel, barracuda, snapper, jack crevalle, and grouper are among the species that inhabit the coastal areas from Matamoras and Laguna Madre south to the Bay of Campeche; the more popular species like snook, tarpon, and redfish are endemic to numerous bays and estuaries, especially those with moderate-size rivers. The Pánuco River at Tampico was once a hot tarpon spot, particularly in April; Laguna de Tamiahua, south of Tampico, was a top seatrout spot; and farther south the area around Tuxpan was noted for tarpon, snook, and many other species. Offshore reefs in this region, from just north of Tampico to just south of Tuxpan, are noted for a variety of species, and tarpon and snook are known to inhabit the rest of the coast, at Alvarado, for example, and the eastern region of the state of Tabasco.

To the west, in the eastern state of Campeche, Laguna de Terminos was a top North American tarpon site from the mid-1950s to the mid-1970s. Little has been heard from this area in recent times, but all sizes of tarpon thrived here, including fish reportedly to 190 pounds. Winter produced difficult fishing for tarpon, but the late spring and summer months, from June through August, brought the best tarpon action, although the heat makes this the least comfortable season.

Located between Ciudad del Carmen and Isla de Aguada, the lagoon spans 60 miles and is fed by five rivers, of which the Candelaria is the most significant. An extensive network of jungle creeks, mangrove swamps, and flats exist here, with one major pass to the shallow Campeche Bank on the coast. Snook were a prominent catch in the past, and other species in the lagoon complex or along the coastal shore included jack crevalle and permit in summer, as well as seatrout, barracuda, ladyfish, kingfish, grouper, jewfish, and more.

Yucatán Peninsula. The Yucatán Peninsula is one of the foremost archaeological regions of the world and the home of numerous Mayan ruins. Estimates suggest that several hundred years ago up to 4,000 Mayan canoes on trading missions navigated regional waters at any one time—such was the thriving, ancient Mayan culture. Today, the watercraft of this area are more modern, their numbers far less, and their activities quite different.

Geographically, the low, flat Yucatán Peninsula is to the country of Mexico what the point is to a fishhook. And, even considering the excellent fishing at Mexico's westernmost region around the Baja Peninsula, the Yucatán can arguably be called the country's leading edge for anglers. Jutting into the sea, and bounded by the Gulf of Mexico to the north and the Caribbean to the east, the Yucatán is so fortuitously situated that it is blessed with some of the finest inshore and offshore angling in the world.

Most of the Yucatán's fishery centers along the coast of Quintana Roo, a state that comprises the eastern region of the peninsula. At the northeastern corner, Isla Holbox offers good fishing for tarpon and has recently become more accessible through the addition of new facilities catering to anglers. Small tarpon are available year-round, but late spring and summer are reportedly the best times for tarpon in the 70- to 100-pound range, and larger tarpon are present. Snook inhabit these waters, as do bonefish, jack crevalle, and some permit.

Better known are the highly touted fisheries nearby to the southeast at Isla Mujeres, Cancún, and Cozumel, and farther south at Boca Paila and Ascension Bay. There is year-round fishing on all of the Yucatán flats, but the favored time to visit is from late fall through spring, which coincides with the popular tourist season, although a cool spell then could diminish flats success. The summer and fall are good times here as well, and less visited.

Cancún/Isla Mujeres. The offshore fishing at the tip of the Yucatán Peninsula—which doesn't in fact take place very far offshore—centers around the islands of Cancún and Isla Mujeres. They lie adjacent to the Yucatán Channel, which separates Cuba and Mexico and is dominated by strong northward-flowing currents that funnel baitfish and pelagic species along the tip of the Yucatán Coast.

As a result, the sailfish population is extraordinary—as good as anywhere in the Atlantic. It is so good, in fact, that the best days witness multiple hookups, with glowing reports of not just two, but even three and four of these high-dorsal-finned creatures at a time. White and blue marlin add to this already incredible fishery, and the whites are so plentiful at times that they, too, can be a source of multiple strikes or hookups.

Anglers land the white and blue marlin around the 100-fathom curve off Cancún and Isla Mujeres, which is just a few miles offshore. Whites are typically taken a bit shallower, however, and sailfish shallower still. Most of the fishing occurs directly offshore or to the northeast or southeast. Arrowsmith Bank, less than 20 miles to the southeast of Isla Mujeres, is another hotspot, although good fishing close to the island often dissuades anglers from making the run.

There is no real shelf or quick dropoff around Isla Mujeres and Cancún, but an upwelling of sorts exists out in the 100-fathom water, where currents sweep by. This area is productive for dolphin and marlin, and attractive to baitfish.

It is the presence of prodigious schools of baitfish, especially in the spring and early summer, that makes the waters off the northern tip of the Yucatán such an attractive area for billfish, especially sailfish. It is routine to find sailfish balling bait, so trolling methods commonly involve looking for such activity and fishing with bait. Dorado, bonito, and other fish find the bait schools, too, and sometimes make it harder to focus on just the sailfish, but facing too many eager and hard-fighting creatures is one problem most anglers can cope with.

Lots of activity makes this a hot place to try fly fishing, although when the sailfish are ganging up on bait, a fly may not turn their heads. Unquestionably, the light-tackle fishing, using spinning rods and 8- to 20-pound line (these sailfish average 40 to 50 pounds) is great. The best period for billfish and dorado is in the spring. Other species you might catch while trolling for sailfish and white marlin include wahoo, kingfish, and blackfin tuna; grouper, cubera snapper, mutton snapper, and jack crevalle are hard-fighting inhabitants of local reefs and inshore environs.

The big news inshore are the glamour species: bonefish, and plenty of them, plus tarpon, snook, and permit. None of these fish run to giant sizes here, but they are so readily available that experienced anglers say catching one is almost a sure thing.

A hooked sailfish leaps in front of a boat near Cozumel.

Some of this action occurs less than an hour's drive from Cancún. This resort city, which was just a small village of a few hundred people in the mid-1970s, was carved out of the mangrove coast by the government and made into a Mexican Riviera. An image of what the fishing used to be like on the Cancún flats is close by, however, especially at Isla Blanca lagoon, 20 miles to the north. There are extensive flats here, as well as numerous coves, bays, mangrove islands, and other fishable locales up the coast, most of them lightly explored and generally reached via a 7-mile-long dirt road. A boat trip requiring some 20 minutes to the area around Cabo Catoché follows.

Bonefish, mostly in small groups, and permit are plentiful on the flats. Snook and tarpon (in the 20- to 30-pound class, and a few larger) are in good supply around the mangrove islands, shores, and inlets. All of these species are sought after by boaters (wading is hard on the flats, most of which are very soft), stalking and sighting fish to cast to—the most exciting of all inshore angling pursuits. A grand slam of all four of these highly coveted species is quite possible on spinning gear, and remotely possible on a fly (you'd have to get the permit first, always the most difficult chore). Tarpon and snook fishing here is good all season, but it's best from May through August, a time that is also good for other species.

Cozumel. Long before the Spanish conquest, Cozumel was a pilgrimage site for Mayan worshipers of Ixchel, the fertility and moon goddess. There is perhaps irony in this; today, many anglers make a different sort of pilgrimage to this well-known Caribbean island because its waters are so fertile, and they often do so around the time of full moon. Atlantic sailfish—the premier quarry and found more abundantly here than in most other locales worldwide—begin their migration off this island around the time of full moon in March. The sailfish actually show up in numbers (some can be caught all year long) in February and really get cooking in March, peaking from then into June.

Cozumel is 33 miles long and 9 miles wide and situated off the east-central coast of the Yucatán Peninsula. The accessibility of Cozumel, which is a prime fun-and-sun tourist destination that is easily reached from the United States, has attracted large numbers of anglers in private boats, as well as tourists, looking for a one-day venture in hopes of catching their first sailfish. Cozumel is *the* place to do that, and also *the* place to catch sails on a fly rod as well as on light spinning tackle and on casting tackle. Cozumel is also an excellent place for a realistic chance at a multiple hookup, a grand billfish slam (white and blue marlin plus sailfish in a single day), or a super grand slam (the other three billfish plus swordfish).

Cozumel's offshore fishery has held up well for years, sometimes raising double-digit numbers of fish. In the best of times on a *slow* day off Cozumel, you might catch three or four sailfish (this would be a good day almost anywhere else). Dolphin, kingfish, bonito, and blackfin tuna are also in the offshore mixed bag, sometimes in good numbers and sizes (dolphin especially), although they are usually an incidental catch in billfishing.

Trolling at Cozumel predominantly takes place in the 12 miles of deep water that separates the island and the mainland; in fact, this is where most offshore trolling occurs, often close to the Yucatán near Playa del Carmen in 10 to 60 fathoms of water. Sailfish apparently migrate northward with the strong current, coming from the open waters of the Caribbean and working their way up the coast past Cozumel, passing the head of the peninsula at Isla Mujeres and Cancún, and then moving into the Gulf of Mexico.

The Caribbean is deep here, with well over 100 fathoms of water between mainland and island. There is a sharp drop from 10 to 60 or so fathoms near the mainland, and this is the zone that is heavily worked. Up the coast, the bottom rises to a bank and is not nearly as deep close to shore.

Baitfish are abundant along this area, especially off several coves south of Playa del Carmen, and sailfish, migrating through in groups, are obviously drawn to them. Boats trolling and zigzagging north-south along the mainland edge frequently encounter pods of these billfish and experience multiple hookups. After such an encounter the savvy skipper may run north a fair distance and then troll southward with the hope of engaging other fish from that pod.

Anglers also encounter white marlin in along the mainland shoals and edges, sometimes catching them in the same locales as they do sailfish. Blue marlin, however, are more likely to be caught farther offshore and over deeper water, typically in the channel, which has some irregular bottom structure.

Less attention is devoted to reef and flats fishing in Cozumel, and the area has not been publicized for this. Although bonefish are abundant along the Yucatán flats on the mainland, they are not as abundant at Cozumel because the island has little shallow water. The island does harbor some bonefish and permit, however, and although this may not be a world-class fishery, it is good enough to provide a very pleasant day, especially if you don't favor big-water fishing, or a heavy blow comes up that keeps big boats off the water, or you just want to take a spinning or fly rod in tow and poke around. These bonefish and permit are in and near a small lagoon at the south end of the island, and in one at the north end. The fish aren't big in either locale, but the setting is pristine and peaceful.

The reefs around Cozumel are another matter entirely. Rated among the world's finest for diving, they are the island's main draw after angling. Palancar Reef, which surrounds Cozumel, is one of the world's largest coral reefs. and its edges yield big grouper, red snapper, and other bottom fish, as well as the occasional dolphin and kingfish.

Southern flats and bays. World-famous shallow-water light-tackle flats fishing exists along southeastern Quintana Roo. The shoreline drops off sharply just south of Cancún and doesn't offer flats fishing, but south of Tulum— the most visited of all Mayan archaeological sites—are tarpon, bonefish, permit, snook, and assorted other species. This is the region in and around the Sian Ka'an Biosphere Reserve, a 1.3-million-acre region with tangled mangrove swamps, vast tropical forests, and isolated swampy beaches. Netting is prohibited in the preserve, and the number of local inhabitants is minimal, leaving the fish undisturbed and plentiful. Boca Paila, Ascension Bay, and Espiritu Santo Bay are the main fishing areas, and facilities are available at each location.

As with the flats to the north at Isla Holbox, the fish are not generally large, although some huge permit have been caught here, including 40- to 50-pounders on fly tackle. Catching the grand slam species (tarpon, bonefish, and permit) or super grand slam (plus snook) in a day is a realistic goal, especially at Ascension and Espiritu Santo Bays. Indeed, this may be the foremost place in the world to achieve these accomplishments.

Bonefish and permit are the stars here, both often traveling in large schools on the flats. Tarpon mostly inhabit the mangrove backwaters, and range from small specimens up to 70 and 80 pounds. The snook run to 20 or 25 pounds but are generally less numerous than the other species. Big barracuda, plus sharks and jacks, also frequent these waters. Although some flats can be waded, most are soft and muddy, making poling and casting from boats the standard angling method.

Boca Paila is roughly two hours by auto from Cancún and was originally fished in the early 1970s by anglers taking a long boat ride from Cozumel and camping on the beach. Protected from prevailing winds and boasting many easily reached flats, Boca Paila has the mother lode of small bonefish and has long been renowned for its plentiful permit. Tarpon, snook, and barracuda, as well as various reef species, are also targeted here.

Much the same can be said for vast Ascension Bay as well, 25 miles south of Boca Paila and with a cornucopia of mangrove islands, channels, flats, and creeks. Other fish encountered here include jack crevalle, cubera snapper, and large barracuda. Large permit cruise the flats at Ascension Bay, as do big schools of bonefish ranging from 1 to 5 pounds. There are tarpon in the mangrove areas and also in some landlocked lagoons accessible via a rugged dirt road.

Espiritu Santo Bay is roughly 15 miles south of Ascension Bay and less known and visited. Loads of flats and mangrove lagoons exist in this large area, too, and a barrier reef parallels the shoreline and crosses in front of the mouth of the bay. Huge permit and ample schools of bonefish inhabit the flats, and small tarpon favor areas near mangrove shores, between the reef and shoreline, and the lagoons.

MICHIGAN

Michigan is a state of outdoor fanatics. And with a combined 2 million resident and nonresident fishing licenses sold annually, angling ranks as a big facet in the state's immense tourism and recreational matrix.

Two factors account for the wild popularity of fishing here. First, with more big-water coastline than Florida and Oregon combined, plus 11,000 inland lakes and 3,000 rivers, Michigan has as much and as varied sportfishing as any other state, and far more than most. The St. Clair River alone has 90 species of fish, more than a dozen of them sought by anglers. Gull Lake near Kalamazoo has 52 species and is probably the only place in the world where you'll hear locals complain about "nuisance" Atlantic salmon that prey on the fish anglers really want to catch, bluegills!

The second factor is that Michigan has something many states lack but which is just as important to anglers as fish: widespread access to virtually all of those waters through some 9 million acres of publicly owned land.

Michigan's fisheries are primarily coolwater and coldwater, and the state has three distinct climatic and geographic zones.

The Upper Peninsula (UP) is a continuation of Ontario's Laurentian shield country, where a thin layer of soil over rocky outcroppings grows trees and not much else. Winter comes early, stays late, and brings arctic conditions. Fishing here usually means brook trout on the inland streams, smallmouth bass and pike in the smaller lakes, and salmon in the Great Lakes.

The northern Lower Peninsula, a gigantic sand and gravel pile left behind by the glaciers and that also doesn't grow much but trees, gets almost as cold as the Upper Peninsula, especially the central highlands. But winter starts a couple of weeks later, spring comes a couple of weeks earlier, and a network of fast-flowing rivers provides much of the best trout water in the state. This zone also offers magnificent smallmouth bass and northern pike fishing, both inland and in the Great Lakes; plenty of walleye, sunfish, perch, and smelt in inland lakes; and anadromous brown trout, steelhead, and Pacific salmon (mostly chinooks) in Lakes Michigan and Huron. The northern waters of the latter two lakes also provide especially fine carp fishing, in waters so clear that fly- and spinning-tackle fans stalk 20- to 30-pound carp like oversize bonefish and can often see their quarry coming at 200 yards.

From Saginaw Bay south, the climate is much milder. Snow and below-zero temperatures occur each year, but they're generally confined to midwinter, and by March anglers are out in boats while enthusiasts in the northern parts of the state are still ice fishing. There are few trout streams here but lots of bigger, warmer rivers with excellent concentrations of smallmouth and largemouth bass and pike. The area is dotted with lakes teeming with crappie, sunfish, perch, and bass.

The state has shoreline on four of the five Great Lakes: Superior, Michigan, Huron, and Erie. The principal gamefish in all the big lakes is the chinook salmon, which was imported from the Pacific in 1968, a couple of years after the state's Department of Natural Resources (DNR) first stocked the Platte River on Lake Michigan with coho salmon. Chinooks grew large and plentiful for a couple of decades, and a state record of 46 pounds, 1 ounce was set.

An outbreak of bacterial kidney disease in the early 1990s drastically reduced the chinook populations in Lakes Michigan and Huron, especially the former. Better disease control in the hatcheries and increased care in selecting eggs from returning fish at weirs have brought the salmon back to excellent levels, and with increased emphasis on stocking lake trout, brown trout, and steelhead, it's common for anglers to boat five-fish limits comprised of three or four species in a morning.

Cohos also inhabit all four lakes, but these smaller and more acrobatic fish are most common in Lake Michigan. They don't hang around Michigan waters much, however, and make a big annual circle of the lake, spending the summers largely off Indiana, Illinois, and Wisconsin. Thus, chinooks are the primary salmon stocked today.

Steelhead are another immensely popular fish with trolling anglers, and whereas there is some evidence that the first rainbows stocked in Michigan rivers 100 years ago included sea-run subspecies that reached the Great Lakes, all of the rainbows there today are anadromous, although most come from stock that hasn't been in saltwater for generations.

Before the salmon, there were lake trout—both the fat and the lean species. The lean was far preferred, and it was virtually wiped out by the 1940s due to overfishing, pollution, and the arrival of parasitic lamprey eels. The fat trout, which lives deeper, didn't come as close to extirpation, but their numbers were also decimated.

Today, lakers are making a comeback in most of the Great Lakes, with the exception of northern Lake Huron. The U.S. Fish and Wildlife Service determined that lake trout once again reached a self-sustaining level in much of Lake Superior in 1997, and stocking has produced good populations in Lake Michigan. Ironically, the lake trout that provided eggs for the restocking were mostly descendants of Lake Michigan fish that had been planted in a lake in Wyoming before World War II. Evidence of the well-being of these fish is seen in the Michigan record laker, a $61^1/_2$-pound fish caught in 1997 in Lake Superior. It is reportedly the largest lake trout ever caught in the U.S.

Trolling, with crankbaits in spring and spoons throughout the summer, is the principal method of catching Great Lakes salmonids in Michigan. The introduction of the downrigger vastly increased the catch of salmon and lakers in summer, when the fish run deep. Previous to that invention, anglers usually fished wire line, which required far more laborious cranking to wind 200 to 300 feet back onto the reel. Another major breakthrough was the sideplaner board, which dramatically increased the catch of walleye and steelhead by covering more water and positioning the lures away from the boat.

Pacific salmon are one of the primary tourist attractions and economic mainstays of many small towns on the Great Lakes, supporting hundreds of charter boats and tackle shops. Yet many people believe that the DNR has bestowed the salmon fishery with an importance far out of proportion to its economic value and its overall place in the Michigan fishing picture. They argue that far more people spend far more time fishing inland lakes and streams that get short shrift from the DNR, which spends the bulk of its fish hatchery dollars on Great Lakes salmonids.

In the fall, the salmon run up dozens of streams and provide wonderful sport for pier anglers and wading anglers miles from the big water. The primary limiting factors are hydroelectric dams on most rivers, but a new licensing agreement between the federal government, the state, and the hydroelectric companies has regulated water flows through the dams and should improve salmon spawning conditions downstream.

In fact, although trout anglers have generally fought for removal of these dams where possible, in a few instances they objected to the dams' removal because they feared that allowing salmon and steelhead to run up a stream like the Au Sable would decrease populations of resident brown trout.

Steelhead make their runs mostly in the winter and spring, although the number of summer-run fish is increasing. Steelies often use the same lies as salmon, but smart anglers know that when the salmon are in the streams, fishing a spawn sack below the salmon redds can prompt a smashing strike from a holdover rainbow.

Expecting Michigan walleye anglers to get excited about angling elsewhere is like carrying coal to Newcastle. If you were to name the five great walleye grounds in the world, Michigan accesses three of them: Saginaw Bay on Lake Huron, Little Bay de Noc on Lake Michigan, and Lake Erie. Many inland lakes also abound with walleye, and plants by walleye clubs in places like Whitefish Bay on Lake Superior are expected to spawn new world-class fisheries within a few years.

The involvement of these clubs in running ponds under the aegis of the DNR has been of immeasurable value in improving and preserving the state's walleye populations. Showing enlightened self-interest, the clubs use volunteer labor to produce fish more cost effectively than a state or commercial hatchery can, and the benefits accrue directly to club members.

Michigan's numerous Great Lakes tributaries are noted for salmon, trout, and steelhead fishing.

Inland, Michigan has thousands of miles of trout streams, ranging from mile-wide major rivers like the St. Marys to creeks you can step across but that can still hold big browns. The grayling that filled rivers in the northern Lower Peninsula before the turn of the century are just a memory, but imported brown, rainbow, and brook trout replaced them everywhere.

A small population of grayling still live in Neff Lake 10 miles west of the town of Grayling, the last survivors of a failed attempt to reintroduce Montana grayling in the 1980s.

Grayling is the city where Michigan's angling industry began, with Chief David Shopenagon, a revered Indian guide, teaching the craft to white disciples like Rube Babbit before the turn of the century. There were virtually no trout streams in the Lower Peninsula before about 1880. These were the days of the grayling, and the old chief and his fellow guides led sports from across the U.S. and Europe on expeditions that yielded hundreds of fish a day (and sometimes sent thousands of salted fish in barrels to Chicago, New York, and Detroit).

The wretched excess started the grayling's decline, but the nails were pounded into the coffin by the lumbering industry, which literally hacked down every tree in northern Michigan that was

M

worth cutting. When the loggers were finished, in many areas stump fields that stretched from horizon to horizon were all that was left. Chemicals and sawdust from lumbering operations were poured willy-nilly into the streams, the loss of the forest canopy raised their temperatures, and by the 1920s this fish was extinct.

But anglers abhor a vacuum as much as nature, and it wasn't long before they began dumping trout into streams that were virtually empty of a top-rank predator. Browns were introduced to the Pere Marquette in 1883 (one of the first plantings in the U.S.), rainbows shortly thereafter in several rivers, and brook trout from the Upper Peninsula were spread to every creek and rivulet that flowed near a railroad line.

The brook trout has been adopted as the official state fish, and its range has spread from its original Upper Peninsula habitat to the southernmost regions of the state. But many people think that a better choice would have been the scrappy smallmouth bass, which was not only native everywhere in the state but today commonly reaches the 4-pound mark.

Michiganders like to boast that their state has more registered boats—about 900,000—than any other, something to be expected in a state populated by fishing fanatics. While bigger boats are required for the rougher water of the Great Lakes, inland-lakes fishing tends to be more of a tin-boat activity. Small aluminum boats in the 10- to 14-foot range, rigged with small outboards, are ideal for launching on many lakes and rivers where the ramps are dirt or grass and the path to them is a narrow forest two-track.

Although these offer some good fishing, the larger specimens of most species are found in the big Great Lakes waters and their bays. As a result, Michigan has some impressive rod-and-reel gamefish records. These include an 11-pound, 15-ounce largemouth bass; a 9-pound, 4-ounce smallmouth bass; a 17-pound, 3-ounce walleye; a 47-pound, 12-ounce muskellunge; a 39-pound northern pike; a 32-pound, 10-ounce Atlantic salmon; a 9-pound, 8-ounce brook trout; and a 26-pound, 8-ounce rainbow trout.

Commercial fishing for game species was virtually ended by the state in the 1970s, but a federal judge ruled that native Americans could still carry on commercial fisheries for salmon, lake trout, and whitefish. This ruling has led to an ongoing conflict between anglers and Indian commercial fishermen, with the former accusing the latter of overharvesting the resource, and the latter accusing the former of attempting to wriggle out of legal obligations. The conflict is greatest in places like Grand Traverse Bay and northern Lake Huron, where the nets of tribal anglers tend to be concentrated in the same small areas where anglers fish.

The present agreement between the state and Indian tribes runs out in the year 2000, and many observers think that the recognition of several new tribes by the federal government in the 1990s, all of which have claimed fishing rights, will make the problem even more difficult to resolve.

Upper West Coast

A couple of fly anglers once made a bet on who could get the most chinook salmon hookups in one day on the Pere Marquette River. Some of the takes were only headshakes that lasted seconds, but the winner recorded 126 strikes over 10 hours, and landed and released 23 salmon that ranged from 8 to 25 pounds. The "loser" had 94 strikes and landed 21 fish.

No one ever planted chinooks in the "P-M," as Michigan anglers refer to this big stream that runs 150 miles from its headwaters to Ludington on Lake Michigan, about halfway up the western shore of the Lower Peninsula. But some of the fish planted in nearby streams in the 1960s and 1970s strayed there and created the finest self-sustaining run in the state, averaging about 40,000 fish each fall.

Anglers from other states are often amazed to learn that Michigan has better Pacific salmon fishing, both in streams and in the Great Lakes, than most of the Pacific regions where these fish originated. The runs in rivers like the St. Joseph, Grand, Big and Little Manistee, Pere Marquette, Platte, and Betsie usually begin in late August, peak in late September, and trickle off through October, but genetic drift appears to be creating summer runs.

In the rivers, anglers catch salmon and steelhead on a variety of flies (including Woolly Buggers, nymphs, and egg flies), spoons, and spawn. The steelhead runs continue off and on throughout the winter, usually peaking in March and April, just before the inland trout season opens.

What has really kicked up the success rate of Michigan anglers is a locally developed technique called light-line nymphing. The angler uses a fly rod and reel, but instead of traditional fly line, the reel is spooled with the synthetic running line normally used as backing.

The leader is about 10 feet long, and the 18-inch tippet (normally 6 to 10 pounds) is tied to a three-way swivel, with a point fly on the end of the tippet and a second fly on a dropper from the swivel. Weight in the form of split shot in a slinky (a thin fabric tube filled with three to eight shot) is clamped onto another dropper off a barrel swivel about a foot above the top fly.

By adjusting the amount of shot for the water depth and current flow, anglers can flop the flies into the water, and the "tick, tick, tick" of the shot bouncing along the bottom ensures them that the flies will pass by the fish just at eye level.

Anglers run light-line rigs through deep holes where they know large numbers of fish concentrate. Although the fish are almost always hooked in the mouth, some critics say this is merely a form of legal-

M

ized snagging for fish, which constantly open and close their mouths while holding over the bottom.

Offshore in the Great Lakes, as mentioned earlier, the salmon have rebounded from the decimation caused by bacterial kidney disease a decade ago. Today they are the most abundant species in the daily mixed bag landed by charter boats. The catch also commonly includes steelhead, lake trout, and brown trout up to 10 pounds.

The primary forage fish is the alewife, which apparently reached the Great Lakes from the Atlantic with the construction of the first shipping canals in the nineteenth century, and by the 1950s these fish constituted the primary biomass of the four lower lakes. But the decimation of lake trout populations by pollution, lamprey eels, and overfishing enabled alewife populations to explode, and many people can remember days in the 1960s and 1970s when summer algae blooms consumed so much dissolved oxygen in the water that the alewives died off in the millions and washed up on the beaches, leaving stinking windrows of rotting fish 2 feet high.

Salmon were introduced to Lake Michigan by the Michigan DNR in 1966, primarily to control the alewife population. In the early 1970s, coho numbers exploded in response to a virtually unlimited food supply, and the wait to launch boats at ramps was sometimes measured in hours during the wildest days. By the early 1990s, the Pacific salmon had proven so successful that biologists said alewives were on the verge of becoming an endangered species in Lake Michigan.

Coho and chinook numbers stayed very high through about 1990, until the outbreak of bacterial kidney disease knocked the salmon back and caused another, smaller, alewife boom. For a few years, boat operators reported seeing occasional rafts of dead alewives floating on the surface, skinny fish that apparently couldn't handle the twin stresses of spawning and starvation. But a salmon comeback and increased numbers of other salmonids by 1995 apparently resulted in at least a temporary balance of power that satisfied both the alewives and the predators.

Steelhead fishing is outstanding on Lake Michigan. These anadromous rainbows support an important summer charter boat fishery that usually requires skippers to run 15 to 20 miles offshore. The steelhead boats fish the scum line, a region where upwelling currents and prevailing winds concentrate enormous numbers of ants, bees, butterflies, caddisflies, houseflies, and other terrestrial insects that are carried offshore by the return flow of upper-level winds that fill in the low pressure created over the lake by the daily breezes.

This rich food source in turn concentrates steelhead from all parts of the lake, and biologists estimate that more than a million of the big rainbows spend the summer in this one patch in the middle of northern Lake Michigan.

Large boats venture onto Lake Michigan from many ports.

Incredibly, anglers routinely catch 10- to 15-pound steelhead 20 miles from shore that have nothing in their stomachs but bugs, whereas steelhead taken inshore have stomachs filled with smelt, alewives, and other forage fish. This is an eye-popping lesson in the biomass of insects carried offshore by the lake-breeze weather machine.

The coastline of the northwestern Lower Peninsula has fine smallmouth bass populations wherever rocky bays exist. Both arms of Grand Traverse Bay are excellent, and the annual return of the smallies to spawn on the shallow rock reefs at Waugoshance Point off Wilderness State Park on the Lower Peninsula's extreme northwestern tip draws thousands of anglers who come just to catch and release the fish before the season officially opens (often as many as 80 fish a day, ranging from 12 to 19 inches).

Southern Lake Michigan ports like Grand Haven and St. Joseph once were renowned for party boats that returned to shore with perch that were so big, they looked like small walleye. But something has happened to the perch population, which has fallen off by as much as 80 percent. While biologists are investigating the problem as a Great Lakes–wide phenomenon, it is most evident in Lake Michigan, and scientists suspect it is largely the result of competition for food with a host of exotic invaders at all levels of the perch's life cycle.

Upper East Coast

Salmon and steelhead fishing continue to be good to excellent in Lake Huron, but sea lamprey levels were so high by 1998 that the Michigan DNR said they were killing virtually every lake trout before it became old enough to reproduce.

The problem results from a fantastic explosion of lampreys from the St. Marys River and some biological similarities between the two species. Both sea lampreys and lake trout like water temperatures below 45°F, and both concentrate off the shoreline on reefs in the fall and winter—the trout to spawn on the deep reefs and the lampreys to prepare for their spawning run up nearby rivers. Having lampreys and lake trout in close proximity in high densities results in extremely high predation of the latter by the former.

Biologists hoped that new lamprey control programs scheduled through 2005 would alleviate the problem, but some Michigan DNR biologists insist that it is a waste of time and money to stock lake trout in northern Lake Huron until it has been proven that the controls will work.

In addition to salmon, the primary species sought along the Lake Huron shoreline of the Upper Peninsula is perch, and even here there were problems. Perch numbers were declining, as they had been for five years throughout most of the Great Lakes, and local anglers believe that an exploding cormorant population was largely responsible. Although cormorant numbers have increased remarkably over the past 15 years, their daily feeding requirements show that they cannot account for such a drastic reduction in perch.

The Guinness Book of Records lists the sailfish as the fastest fish based on speed trials in which one sailfish peeled off 300 feet of line in 3 seconds, equal to 68 mph.

A bit farther south, along the Lake Huron shore of the northern Lower Peninsula, the fishing for chinook salmon and steelhead is usually very good. But many anglers say that an even better fishery is the big, lake-run brown trout population planted off Alpena and other ports in the area. As fat as a football and often twice as long, these fish are powerful fighters, albeit not as spectacular leapers as their close cousin, the Atlantic salmon, and they are also wonderful table fare.

Because of the emphasis on salmon, anglers here tend to overlook the exceptionally good walleye fishing, which consists mainly in trolling crankbaits in early spring, and spoons through the summer.

From the mouth of the Au Sable River at Oscoda, anglers can fish for salmon, steelhead, and walleye by trolling out through the pier heads or casting from the rocks and jetties. The lower reaches of the Au Sable, below a dam that blocks upstream passage of fish, is a popular place for steelhead anglers pulling plugs from downstream-drifting boats.

The Singing Bridge area near Oscoda was once the scene of fantastic smelt runs, but this species, too, has declined dramatically throughout the Great Lakes since the late 1980s. Introduced to the Great Lakes less than 100 years ago, smelt ran up every creek and river on spring nights just after ice out, often in such numbers that people could reach into the water and pull out silvery fish by the handful.

Smelt are among the tastiest of fish, either headed, gutted, and deep-fried or simply tossed whole into the hot fat, which some gourmands claim is the only way to prepare them. A night of smelt dipping was once a Michigan spring ritual from the balmy shores of Lake Erie to the icy beaches of Lake Superior. A father could take his small children to a creek that ran onto a beach, turn them loose with a long-handled dipnet, and head home within a couple of hours, transporting 10 gallons of smelt in the trunk and sleeping kids in the back seat.

But those runs have largely failed to materialize in recent years in most of the Great Lakes. Today's smelting often means catching two or three fish at a time rather than two or three dozen, and biologists say it may reflect the Great Lakes' vastly increased numbers of smelt-gobbling big predators, from salmonids to walleye.

Lower West Coast

Here, too, salmon—cohos in the spring and chinooks through the summer—are the dominant species for offshore anglers. The original Great Lakes salmon plants were far to the north in Platte Bay, but the DNR stocked descendants of those fish in the St. Joseph River, the major stream in southeast Michigan, through the 1970s, and continued to stock chinooks into the 1990s.

The most productive fishing isn't from a boat but from the river pier heads. Anglers casting spoons and spawn start the year with steelhead and big brown trout just after ice out; walleye, flathead catfish, and channel catfish are the summer quarry; and salmon are the ticket in the fall. Smallmouth and largemouth bass are usually caught at any time.

The offshore waters at this southern end of Lake Michigan warm much earlier than do the northern waters (which in some years never crack the 40s, even in midsummer). The cohos move south along the Michigan shoreline and provide angling activity through early June, after which they continue their annual migration through Indiana, Illinois, and Wisconsin waters, where they spend most of the summer before heading straight across the lake to the mouth of the Platte in fall.

But the chinook are found offshore all year, and although the key to catching them is always to find the cool water they like, in southern Michigan they often tend to be more concentrated simply because there's less cold water to inhabit.

Whereas Michigan coho salmon primarily provide fishing for anglers in other states, the huge numbers of Skamania steelhead planted by Indiana have been a boon for southwestern Michigan anglers. The silver rockets are an offshore fishery all summer, and rivers like the St. Joseph now get both spring, summer, and fall runs of steelhead originally planted by both states. The fish that run in late winter and early spring usually weigh roughly 5 pounds, but summer-run steelhead are regularly caught into the midteens.

The most overlooked fishery here is probably the big brown trout inhabiting the waters just offshore (the state record, incidentally, is 34 pounds, 6 ounces). They can be taken within a long cast of shore in April, and even in the heat of summer are usually found along reefs and bottom structure in 60 to 90 feet of water, less than a mile offshore along most of this shoreline.

M

The area is speckled with hundreds of inland lakes that have good public access and are stocked by the DNR. One of the most interesting is Gull Lake, where some anglers complain because the state has stocked it with landlocked salmon. These anglers would prefer to catch panfish, and they say that when they catch landlocks, the salmon usually have sunfish in their stomachs.

But many other lakes are stocked with sunfish, and some have excellent populations of hybrid sunnies that run to 10 inches and will put a healthy bend in a light fly or spinning rod. This is also Michigan's best largemouth country, with a climate that sees spring arrive a month before it does in the northern regions, fall last a month later, and winter temperatures moderated by the prevailing westerly winds off the relatively warm waters of huge Lake Michigan (although most of the four Lower Great Lakes usually freeze in a normal winter, parts of Lake Michigan often remain open).

Lower East Coast

An angler's heaven, Saginaw Bay holds prodigious numbers of big walleye, perch, and bass in its inner reaches, and chinook salmon, steelhead, and lake trout where its green, turbid waters meet the clear seas of open Lake Huron. On a fall day, a person can hunt ducks in the morning, fish in the afternoon, and hunt with a bow or gun for deer in the evening until sunset.

But Saginaw Bay can also be rough, and each fall usually brings a tragedy or two, when small-boat owners disregard the warning signs and are overwhelmed by big seas and icy water as the wind starts to howl.

The south shore of the bay is laced with myriad canals and creeks that provide bank fishing opportunities as well as havens for boaters when the weather turns stormy. The canals are the best areas to pursue perch and panfish, and in spring they hold impressive numbers of carp that are the subject of a controversial weekend bowfishing tournament. The critics object to what they call a senseless slaughter of fish; many of the archers post scores that are measured in the tons of carp killed.

If small-lake anglers want to get a grasp of the size of Lake Huron, they need only realize that Saginaw Bay, some 60 miles long and 30 miles wide, is larger than most other lakes in the U.S. except the five Great Lakes. And yet Saginaw is not the biggest of Lake Huron's bays. That honor goes to Georgian Bay on the Canadian side.

Saginaw Bay is known nationally for its fabulous walleye fishery. During the spring spawning run in April and May, anglers routinely cull 7-pounders, and 40 or more pounds of walleye are often boated in just a couple of hours. Walleye fishing continues through the winter, and ice anglers on snow machines can rival summertime anglers in productivity on a sunny winter weekend.

South of Saginaw Bay, the shoreline has a paucity of streams and offers few places of refuge for boaters. The section from the mouth of the bay south to Port Huron at the head of the St. Clair River sees mostly salmon trolling, with a few steelhead, walleye, and brown trout mixed in.

The Upper Peninsula

"Nine months of winter and three months of poor sledding" is how locals often describe the climate of this 350-mile-long witch's finger, bordered on the north by the world's largest freshwater lake, Superior, and on the south by enormous Lakes Michigan and Huron.

This is the area many Michiganders think of when they talk about "Up North," the place they go to get away from it all. Yoopers, the residents of the UP, refer to Lower Peninsula denizens as "trolls," because they live below the Mackinac Bridge that connects the two landmasses.

The hills and second-growth forests of the UP make up a third of Michigan's 57,000 square miles, but they are home to only about 300,000 of the state's $9^1/_2$ million residents. And that's why fishing is still so good in the thousands of lakes and beaver ponds and hundreds of creeks and rivers that fill every low spot. After the logging companies cut down the virgin forests at the end of the last century, and usually abandoned the land afterward to avoid paying taxes on it, the resulting economic bust cleared out much of the population.

Although mining and logging continued as the major industries, there were few enough people that the landscape was able to recover from the worst excesses. Today, about 2 million acres of the UP are owned by the state or federal government and another 2 million acres are in Conservation Forest Reserve, which gives the lumber and mining companies a tax break if they keep the lands open for public recreation.

Lake Superior offers excellent chinook salmon trolling from ice-out until freeze-up. Charter boats are available at various ports, including Munising, Marquette, and Ontonagon. Covering more than 31,000 square miles and stretching 350 miles in length, Superior is larger than some states. It is also home to America's least-visited national park, Isle Royale, located near the western end of the lake, some 40 miles off the nearest Michigan shoreline and accessible by ferry from Houghton and Copper Harbor on the Keweenaw Peninsula, or via a 30-minute airplane ride from those ports.

Some 44 miles long and 8 miles wide, Isle Royale boasts several large lakes of its own that have excellent brook trout and pike fishing. The island's shorelines are the site of runs of coaster brookies, inland equivalents of the anadromous salter brook trout that run to the ocean off New England.

Another unusual angling opportunity in the UP is lake trout fishing at Stannard Rock, 40 miles off Marquette. A seamount rises from depths of 600 feet to within 60 feet of the surface, and anglers

Little Bay de Noc provides some of North America's top walleye fishing.

who make the long and often rough trip out are rewarded by lakers up to 40 pounds that hang out along the upper slopes and take cast spoons.

Each fall, coho and chinook salmon run in the Rock, Sand, Carp, and numerous other Upper Peninsula rivers, and both summer- and winter-run steelhead strains are found all along Superior's shoreline, although spring offers by far the best angling. Although this is the biggest water on the Great Lakes, it is also the coldest and the least rich; salmon and steelhead here tend to run slightly smaller than those caught in Lakes Michigan and Huron.

Salmon is the glamour species along the UP's southern shore on Lake Michigan as well. Nearly all of these are chinooks that average about 12 pounds, but Little Bay de Noc, near the town of Escanaba, shares with Lake Erie and Saginaw Bay a fabled reputation for walleye, both in number and in size.

Needless to say, these waters also harbor excellent smallmouth fishing just about anywhere an angler can find submerged rocks, and when the smallies come to spawn on the inshore reefs in spring, it's common for wading fly and spin anglers to take 50 a day on artificials. Although the majority are under the 14-inch legal limit, enough 18- to 20-inchers hit to bring many anglers back year after year.

From the Brule River on the Wisconsin border on the west to the St. Marys River on the Ontario border to the east, the UP is the land that John Voelker made famous in books written under the pen name Robert Traver. A former Marquette County prosecutor and state supreme court justice who owned a fishing cabin at Frenchman's Bend, Voelker especially loved the native brook trout thronging hundreds of UP streams, which ranged from yard-wide rivulets to springtime brawlers with Class V rapids.

Brook trout are still the primary stream species here, and many UP anglers know of a creek where they can take 15- to 19-inch "specks." Many of the streams are fishable with fly tackle, although others are so brushy that they are more suitable for the worm-dunking techniques described in "The Big Two-Hearted River" by UP brook trout aficionado Ernest Hemingway.

Hemingway often fished here as a young man when his family owned a summer home on Walloon Lake in the northern Lower Peninsula. And proving that he was as savvy an angler as he was a writer, if you follow the route that Hemingway has young Nick Adams take in "The Big Two-Hearted River," you'll arrive not at that stream but at the Fox near the old logging town of Seney.

The mouths of many streams on the Lake Superior watershed offer excellent spring fishing for steelhead, and fall sees chinook salmon run in the same waters. While fly fishing is effective using Woolly Buggers, Black Stonefly Nymphs, and local patterns, most anglers prefer to cast spoons.

This region is famous for phenomenal smallmouth bass fishing too. Craig Lakes State Park and Lake Michigamme are well known, but anglers who explore the back roads and forest two-tracks with a canoe or a small rowboat atop their vehicle will find access to literally hundreds of fish-rich lakes and ponds that may not appear on most maps.

Tremendous angling is available to anyone who visits Porcupine Mountains Wilderness State Park on the Lake Superior shore in the western Upper Peninsula. This 100-square-mile roadless area was slated to become a national park, until World War II claimed all of the federal budget, and the state bought it. Its myriad lakes, rivers, and creeks abound with pike, smallmouth bass, and brook trout, and often all three.

The Porkies, as the locals call this mountain region, offer backpacking anglers walk-in sites where they are unlikely to see another angler for two or three days at a time, but the wilderness cabins scattered throughout the hiking-trail system are always booked months in advance.

At the opposite end of Lake Superior is the St. Marys River. To fish the famed rapids here, take a fly or spinning rod in one hand, a heaping measure of courage in the other, and wade very, very carefully through the labyrinth of rocks and whitewater below the locks.

The area's incredible rainbow trout fishing was praised in print already in the 1930s; if anything, the angling is even better today. Not only are there wonderful steelhead runs (with the fish averaging 8 to 10 pounds), the river also hosts runs of chinook, coho, and pink salmon, and anglers fishing the rapids sometimes catch all four salmonid species in one afternoon, along with a walleye or whitefish or two for good measure.

Below the mile-long stretch of rapids, the river broadens and slows and offers superb angling for walleye, smallmouth bass, and muskellunge, the latter largely ignored by the locals. Another interesting fishery is the Atlantic salmon run cre-ated by a stocking program that Lake Superior State University runs at the big hydroelectric plant.

Raised in old penstocks, the Atlantics return each summer to their release site, and can be seen holding in the fast currents of the crystal clear water a few feet from the generating plant. Like all Atlantics, they show a maddening disregard for everything that boat and bank anglers throw at them, but every now and then someone hooks and lands one of the silver devils up to 20 pounds. Biologists have recovered tags from St. Marys' Atlantics that were caught in Lakes Huron and Michigan, some 250 to 300 miles away.

In northern Lakes Michigan and Huron, anglers have discovered a wonderful new sport in sight fishing for 20- to 30-pound carp. They employ the same fly fishing and spinning techniques as for bonefish, redfish, and tarpon on saltwater flats. The water on these shallow Great Lakes flats is so clear, anglers can spot cruising carp against the bottom at 200 to 400 yards. Enthusiasts must wade or fish from poled boats for this extremely spooky quarry.

Although this type of fishing exists virtually anywhere in the Great Lakes that has a bottom covered with fist-size rocks (which shelter the insect larvae and crayfish the carp feed on and yet don't get roiled by wave action), the best sites are mostly on the Upper Peninsula shorelines of Lakes Michigan and Huron. Among the hottest of the hotspots are the Garden Peninsula and associated islands, several bays just west of the gigantic Mackinac Bridge, and the stony flats around Les Chennaux Islands at the eastern end of the UP.

The favored tackle is an 8-weight fly rod or a 7-foot spinning rod that casts a 6- to 8-pound line. The fish are extremely shy and sensitive to any line slapping on the water, a lure cast too close, or even the reflected flash of a rod.

The lures are similar to those used in stream fishing for smallmouth bass: small rubber-tailed jigs for spin anglers, and No. 6–8 dark Woolly Buggers, Stonefly Nymphs, and crayfish patterns for flyrodders. This is a summer fishery, and the carp usually come out of deep water onto the flats by about 9 A.M. as the sun warms the shallows. They cruise and feed actively for a few hours and then spend the afternoon lazing by the dozens in a protected bay before returning to the deep water in the evening.

Anglers who have worked out their patterns either pole a boat along a shoreline or stake out a point of channel on a stony flat, where the fish move through on routes that are as predictable as a train.

It's common for anglers to catch and release 10 to 20 of these powerful fighters a day. The average is about 15 pounds, and it's interesting that most anglers will catch a dozen fish weighing more than 20 pounds for every one under 10 pounds.

Another exciting and gustatorially rewarding form of fly fishing that may be unique to northern Michigan is the midsummer whitefish binge on mayflies. Commercial netters or ice anglers usually pursue these Great Lakes whitefish. But when they dimple the surface like brook trout during the brown drake and hexagenia hatches on the Great Lakes in July, they're suckers for almost any spent-wing dry fly in sizes 4 to 6.

These whitefish average about 5 pounds, but they run to 10 pounds, and when a big whitefish decides to use its slab-sided body against a 6-weight fly rod and a 5-pound tippet, the angler is in for a long fight. But a trip for a day of whitefish angling during the hatches is well worth it, because many people consider the whitefish the best-tasting species in freshwater, and summer whitefish binges are also common on many inland lakes in the UP.

Anglers can get the same opportunity with the Menominee, the smaller round whitefish that's sometimes called a lake herring. Running to about 2 pounds, they also will feed on hatching mayflies, but not with the predictable annual regularity of the bigger lake whitefish.

In the mid-1990s, anglers trolling the St. Marys landed what appeared to be three world-record pink salmon in a week. These fish didn't just break the existing record of 8 pounds; at 11 and 12 pounds, they demolished it. Taxonomic evaluation established that the fish were not purebred pinks but a hybrid between a pink and a chinook, and locals soon adopted the term "pinook" to describe them.

Pinks got into the Great Lakes supposedly by accident in the 1950s. Canadian scientists wanted to introduce them, but the American states involved in the Great Lakes stocking project did not. Fisheries technicians supposedly dumped a few thousand fry into Lake Superior, theorizing that they would never survive spawn.

Forty years later the little humpbacks are not only thriving, they now run in the St. Marys every year rather than in alternating years, the pattern they follow in most places. This frequency is attributed to genetic drift, and now that anglers have reported catching stray pinks in many Lower Peninsula streams that have salmon runs, the fish are expected to eventually establish themselves there.

Famed for its gamefish production, the St. Marys also harbors the scourge of the Great Lakes, the sea lamprey. More of these parasitic eels are spawned in the St. Marys than in all other Great Lakes tributaries combined.

In the 1990s, lampreys rebounded to the pandemic levels at which they virtually wiped out lake trout in the Great Lakes in the 1950s and 1960s. Ironically these anadromous eels are even more susceptible to pollution than brook trout, and by cleaning up rivers, humans have given the eels more and better places to spawn. The eels have reached such high levels in northern Lake Huron that they kill virtually every lake trout before it reaches maturity. And with a shortage of lake trout to feed on, the eels began preying in greater numbers on salmon and whitefish.

This problem has been compounded by the size and huge flow of the brawling St. Marys rapids, which made conventional chemical and mechanical lamprey treatment techniques ineffectual. But biologists believe that they will gain control of the eels through a program that uses a new chemical that is toxic to eels but not to other creatures, and sterile male eels that are released into the river to mate with females who subsequently produce sterile lamprey eggs.

Urban Area Fisheries

Detroit. Most muskie lakes don't give up one 48-inch fish in a year, but at least six Lake St. Clair anglers caught and released muskies between 48 and 52 inches in one day in the summer of 1997. Incredibly, they weren't fishing for muskies; they were drifting worm harnesses on 6- to 10-pound line for walleye. And if that's not startling enough, summer isn't the best time to catch big muskies here. The experts say that if you want a really big fish, troll traditional foot-long muskie lures in October when the monsters are trying to put on fat for the winter.

Angling-club records show that not only are Lake St. Clair's muskies bigger today than at any time on record, there are a lot more of them. It's common for muskie tournament boats to catch and release 15 to 20 fish a day, and all within view of the skyscrapers of America's fifth largest city.

Muskie fishing is almost a religion for some anglers on these waters, where trolling shallow lures within yards of the boat was perfected. The $4^1/_2$ million residents of Greater Detroit live on the edge of what is probably the finest urban fishery in the world, and certainly in the U.S. Lake St. Clair, which lies about 2 miles east of Detroit, is a shallow bowl about 40 miles across, an aneurysm between the St. Clair and Detroit Rivers, which carry water from Lake Huron 60 miles north of the city to Lake Erie 30 miles to the south.

Painted to resemble fish, two "Heddon Fish Planes" composed the world's first air freight company, Heddon Aviation, started in 1920; they delivered Heddon fishing lure orders.

Anglers who fish here should buy both Michigan and Ontario licenses. The best walleye fishing is usually on the Canadian side of these waters, and the best angling for other species crosses the unmarked international boundary line as weather and bait movement dictate.

The spring walleye run is remarkable. About 3 million walleye spawn in the Thames River on the Ontario side of Lake St. Clair. Most of these fish come up the Detroit River from Lake Erie, and self-described Detroit River rats think they've been cheated if a March or April outing doesn't provide a bunch of 6-pounders in a couple of hours, with an excellent shot at an 8- to 10-pound wall hanger. And even after the spawning run ends, anglers can count on catching 2- to 7-pounders most of the rest of the year. Jigging early in the year and drifting crawlers or trolling crankbaits later in the spring are the usual methods.

Walleye and muskies draw so much attention that most locals virtually ignore other fisheries that approach world-class status. When a national bass tournament was held on this system in the mid-1990s, the top 10 anglers had 20 smallmouth bass apiece that averaged $2^1/_2$ to 3 pounds. One angler practicing for that tournament caught and released about 60 smallmouths in one afternoon, fish that averaged more than 3 pounds.

Lake St. Clair has some largemouths, but more are found in Detroit River backwaters that have the structure and habitat bucketmouths prefer. An excellent smallmouth fishery exists in the Detroit River in the heart of downtown. A favorite spot is around the pilings in front of the 800-foot glass tower of the Renaissance Center.

Like most major cities, Detroit has hidden its riverfront behind concrete cliffs of office towers, commercial buildings, and moldering warehouses. But the city has built a new fishing pier, there is access to the river behind many of the commercial sites, and local anglers are beginning to take advantage of the city's excellent bank fishing for walleye, smallmouths, white bass, and carp.

Steadily clearing waters throughout the St. Clair River–Lake St. Claire–Detroit River system (thanks to zebra mussels) have resulted in steadily increasing populations of smallmouths and other sight feeders. There are even excellent numbers of northern pike, an extremely unusual occurrence in waters that have big muskie populations. Pike and muskies have a relationship similar to that between wolves and coyotes; in this case, the northerns hold the upper hand. Pike eggs hatch roughly three weeks before the muskie eggs; when the muskie eggs do hatch, they are just the right size to provide a meal for the pike fry, so it's rare to find fishable numbers of both rapacious species in the same lake.

Lake St. Clair also maintained good perch populations in a period when these little cousins of the walleye were on the decline in the rest of the Great Lakes system, and offers plenty of bluegills, white bass, catfish, and carp.

A local secret brings specialist anglers each spring to the St. Clair River a few miles upstream from Lake St. Clair. Fishing mostly after dark and before dawn, they drift 4-inch minnows and round gobies for Great Lakes sturgeon that occasionally exceed 50 pounds. While most sturgeon species elsewhere are in serious decline, the Great Lakes fish are holding their own, especially in Lake St. Clair, although it has been years since any have lived long enough to match the 200- to 300-pound specimens caught at the turn of the twentieth century. The fish are plentiful enough that anglers are catching and releasing several a night, and they are allowed to keep one fish over 50 inches per season.

An overlooked resource is the Huron River, best known for the riffles that hold smallmouth bass and rock bass. But it also has stretches with brown and rainbow trout, and lakes with excellent populations of catfish, panfish, and northern pike.

This stream flows through Ann Arbor, home of the University of Michigan, where canoe liveries offer excellent access to the fishery. In spring and fall, anglers concentrate at the Flat Rock Dam near the river mouth to catch steelhead in March and April, and chinook salmon in September, but the DNR and anglers' groups are raising money for a series of salmon ladders that will enable the anadromous species access to upstream stretches.

Saginaw/Bay City/Midland. These three cities share more than the Statistical Metropolitan Sales Area. In addition, they are on the Tittibawassee–Saginaw River drainage, which offers hundreds of thousands of urban residents angling that matches some wilderness opportunities. This is especially true in spring, when walleye mass in the rivers to prepare for spring spawning.

The Tittibawassee also features a huge spring sucker run that attracts thousands of worm dunkers, and both it and the Saginaw are home to large numbers of big channel cats, crappie, and largemouth bass.

Just outside these cities lie the Shiwassee Game Refuges, a 15,000-acre complex of marshes, sloughs, and creeks where five significant rivers come within a few hundred yards of each other. This is a wonderful small-boat fishery; it is shallow and includes hundreds of miles of protected waterways that hold excellent numbers of largemouth bass, pike, panfish, and carp.

Grand Rapids and Lansing. One of the best steelhead holds in America doesn't have a location. It has an address.

The Grand River in downtown Grand Rapids, Michigan's second biggest city, has spring and summer runs of big rainbows. Commuting motorists idling in traffic can glance down from a bridge or high-rise building and see an angler playing a leaping trout. Visiting anglers have no trouble locating fish. They just look for the gaggles of local anglers working the broken water in front of the art museum or upstream from the Sixth Street Bridge.

And Grand Rapids anglers can drive just 20 minutes and find themselves wading an excellent trout stream, the Rogue River, which runs just north of town and supports a fine fishery despite the intense angling pressure.

Other quality fisheries near Grand Rapids are the Thornapple and Flat Rivers, which hold enormous numbers of smallmouth and largemouth bass. Anglers access both streams by wading or from a canoe, and both cater to those who fish with light spinning tackle or fly rods.

The Grand River is Michigan's longest, and improvements in water quality and fish ladders have resulted in salmon runs through the center of the state capital, Lansing, 68 miles upstream from Grand Rapids, and in tributaries on the Michigan State University campus. A new riverwalk in downtown Lansing, just a long cast from the state Capitol building, is popular with lunchtime anglers, many of them in suits and ties, and a local tackle shop has started an enormously popular rough fish tournament that sees anglers vie for the biggest carp, sucker, and bullhead, just like their counterparts in England.

The Grand also has excellent populations of smallmouth bass in riffle sections, and largemouth in the backwaters along its entire length, but the Portland State Game area a few miles downstream from Lansing has wadeable water that is among the best for both. And it's a great place to catch channel catfish up to 10 pounds, which often smack plugs being cast for smallies.

The owner of a Lansing fly shop has developed a new sport that is gaining in popularity and respect. He sight fishes with 2- and 3-weight rods and No. 20 to 28 nymphs for the various sucker species in the Grand. It's a highly specialized form of angling, and it takes time to develop the knack of hooking the fish, with skilled anglers often outfishing the more ham-handed 20-to-1.

Lake Erie

At the time of The Toledo War, when Michigan and Ohio almost came to blows, most people figured Michigan lost because Ohio kept control of most of western Lake Erie, whereas Michigan had to settle for the then howling wilderness of the Upper Peninsula as compensation. But 150 years after the state militias laid down their arms, hordes of Ohio anglers make the cash registers of UP tackle shops jingle, and Michigan still has access to Lake Erie and what is unquestionably the finest walleye fishery in the world.

Michigan's share of the shallowest, warmest, and second smallest Great Lake is a 50-mile stretch of shoreline between Monroe and the Ohio border in the extreme southeast corner of the state. That's more than enough, because only 20 miles to the south is Ohio's Maumee River, which each spring sees an annual walleye spawning run that averages an incredible 10 million fish. Any angler who wants the experience of catching a batch of smaller fish within two hours and then spending the rest of the morning culling 8-pounders needs to visit these waters in spring, just after the run.

The sonar screens in the western basin of the lake are black with post-spawn walleye for miles off the shorelines, and although these fish are usually in a neutral mood, their numbers are so fantastic that 10 minutes of trolling puts a crankbait in front of so many fish, a strike is almost guaranteed.

Michigan anglers launch from ports like Luna Pier and Monroe, but those who fish here regularly also carry a license for Ohio, which lets them work the waters around the Bass Islands and Put-in-Bay, and Ontario, giving them access to Pelee Island and the Canadian shore.

And although the walleye is king (or queen, in the case of the 8- to 12-pound spring giants), western Lake Erie, which has a deeper basin than its eastern counterpart, also has excellent populations of 10- to 15-pound steelhead, coho salmon of similar size, and chinooks that average 12 pounds and run to 20.

Smallmouth and largemouth bass and northern pike offer excellent fishing along the Lake Erie shoreline and offshore shallow reefs. Most anglers prefer to cast jigs or crankbaits. Yellow perch continue to hold their own here despite a general decline in the rest of the Great Lakes.

Despite its size, Erie is the shallowest of the Great Lakes, averaging 40 feet and having a maximum depth of 210 feet. It is also the warmest, routinely exceeding 70°F in midsummer. One of the great ironies is that most of the walleye in its waters today were restocked from outside sources after overfishing and pollution destroyed the original stocks by the 1960s. In fact, the walleye subspecies found here, called the blue pike by local anglers, is now thought to be extinct.

Inland Northern Lower Peninsula

On warm, muggy nights in late June, when bats and whippoorwills swoop above the silky currents of trout streams and fly anglers in most parts of the country are climbing out of the water, tens of thousands of anglers set out for the rivers in northern Michigan. They usually try to reach their selected spot while they can still see well enough to wade safely, and then wait patiently and hopefully for something that many of them think about all year: the hex hatch. The night-hatching *Hexagenia limbata* is the nation's biggest mayfly, and it can appear in such incredible numbers that huge cannibal brown trout that normally wouldn't even dream of feeding on a surface fly lose all sense of caution and go on a nightly mayfly binge.

The Au Sable and Manistee Rivers in north-central Michigan have the best-known hex hatches (the flies usually start the hatch downstream and work up toward the headwaters over a two-week period). But hexes, often referred to by locals as the Michigan caddis, can be found virtually everywhere in the state, even on Lake St. Clair near Detroit, where the locals curse the "Canadian soldiers" that can gather under street lights in such numbers that cars skid on the greasy patches created by their crushed bodies.

Hexes are maddeningly unpredictable, but as a rule the hatch usually starts after midnight and can consist either of a smattering of flies lasting 10 minutes or a blizzard hatch that goes on for two hours. The spinners can return to the water anytime from dark to dawn, and anglers often observe two peaks of activity during the night, switching from hatcher to spinner imitation as needed.

The fish can be just as schizophrenic as the insects. Sometimes a fantastic hatch or spinner fall will fill the air and water with hexes, yet not a fish rises. Experts say this usually occurs in the first few days of the hatch, when the fish haven't yet keyed on the big flies, and near the end of it, when they are so stuffed with food that they don't need to eat.

Hex anglers usually fish No. 8 to 12 imitations, although the bodies of the flies are only about $1^1/_2$ inches long at a maximum. The usual routine is to locate undercut banks and bends that have good habitat for big trout, listen for the "gloop" sound of a feeder, and then stare into the darkness until eyes accustomed to the gloom can spot the rising fish.

Sometimes anglers come back to work the same monster night after night, and these two weeks probably see more trout over 20 inches taken from these waters than the rest of the season combined, largely because of the hex hatch but probably also because so many anglers are out fishing at night. The biggest confirmed fish taken on a dry fly during the hatch is a 10-pound 8-ounce brown landed near Grayling.

The forests of northern Michigan have largely grown back, albeit different forests than the horizon-wide stands of enormous white pines that once covered the landscape. The Au Sable, one of the most storied trout streams east of the Rockies, fell on hard times again in the 1980s and 1990s. With sewage, phosphates, and other pollutants removed, underwater plant growth declined dramatically, and many anglers say that a lack of plants to feed insects and hide fish is the reason that the population of trout over 8 inches has declined, although baby fish are still plentiful.

The state plans two long-term experiments to fix the problem. One involves increasing the amount of "large woody debris," (such as fallen trees). The other involves grinding up oak and maple leaves and dumping them into the river in an effort to enrich and improve the chemistry of the river bottom. Some scientists believe that decades of mismanaged timbering operations resulted in the gradual impoverishment of the river's ability to sustain large amounts of insect life.

That's not to say that this fishery is poor. A declining Au Sable is still a better trout stream than many that are still in their prime. The spring Hendrickson hatch, which usually coincides with the opening of trout season, still produces excellent dry fly fishing for 12- to 18-inch brown trout. Many anglers prefer to fish the Manistee, which flows west to Lake Michigan, even though its headwaters lie within 10 miles of those of the Au Sable, which flows east to Lake Huron.

One of the most popular ways to fish both streams is from an Au Sable riverboat, which is somewhat of a cross between a canoe and a bateau. Between 18 and 23 feet long, and 3 to 4 feet wide, this boat was designed to separate two fly anglers, with the anglers at the front and the guide at the rear. Instead of a paddle, the guide usually steers the boat with an ash pushpole. The boat's speed downriver is controlled by dragging chains and by increasing the amount of chain let out as the current gets stronger.

Another hatch that causes fish to go wild is the gray drake hatch on the Pere Marquette, usually in mid-June. This river gets regular stockings of brown trout (many anglers have fought against similar stockings on the Au Sable). When the gray drakes get going, it's common for flycasters to take 10 or more 12- to 16-inch browns in an evening, and most anglers say that by the time the fish reach that size it's impossible to tell stocked trout from those born in the stream.

Relicensing the hydroelectric dams resulted in agreements between the states, federal government, and utility companies that have provided better-regulated water flows. As a result, a marvelous brown trout fishery has developed in the Manistee below Tippy Dam, where anglers routinely catch stream-resident browns that run from 3 to 8 pounds. Most of these fish are taken on spawn or plugs, but fly anglers take a few on streamers.

The northern Lower Peninsula abounds with smaller streams that hold excellent populations of brook and brown trout, nearly all of them dependent on natural reproduction. Most of these streams have healthy populations of aquatic insects that start popping out with the little black stonefly hatches in April, just in time for the traditional last-Saturday trout opener, and continue through a sequence of caddisflies, stoneflies, and mayflies that almost always sees the season close before the hatches end. Indeed, on streams with extended seasons, Indian summer can bring excellent dry fly fishing on Blue-Winged Olives, tiny Tricorythodes, and white mayfly patterns well into October.

The area also has hundreds of lakefront resorts, ranging from mom-and-pop cabins to world-renowned lodges, which offer excellent fishing for walleye, smallmouth bass, and panfish. Among the best lakes in this region are Leelenau, Mullet, Burt, Cadillac, Mitchell, Walloon, Fletcher Floodwaters, Houghton, and Higgins.

Ice Fishing

In many Michigan lakes more fish are taken through the ice in winter than from open water the rest of the year. Even southern Michigan is far enough north that anglers can count on six weeks to two months of ice fishing, and one of the best spots is Lake St. Clair's Anchor Bay near Detroit. A hotspot for spearing pike, it's best known for marvelous winter perch and panfish production.

Houghton Lake, in the north-central part of the Lower Peninsula, hosts the annual Tip-Up Town Festival every winter, an event that has outgrown its ice fishing roots to become a snowmobile festival that sees as many as 8,000 machines a day zipping across the ice. The quarry here is perch and northerns, but driving 10 miles farther to Higgins Lake produces excellent opportunities to fish for lake trout, rainbows, and smelt, the latter usually being taken deep on small minnows. If you've never caught a 10-inch smelt on a light rod from 60 feet of water, you're in for a real surprise.

This far north and inland, ice fishing usually starts in December and ends in March (in the UP it can last until May). Walleye, perch, and sunfish are the primary rod-and-reel targets. Pike anglers mostly use tip-ups and spears.

Another spearing target through the ice is the sturgeon, in Black Lake. Because they are allowed only one sturgeon 50 inches or larger per season, many anglers save their efforts for winter, when they can spend hours staring through a green hole in the ice, waiting for the few seconds when the big, dark shape attacks the spearing decoy.

Trout and salmon are caught year-round on inland lakes not designated as trout lakes, and ice fishing probably accounts for the primary harvest of splake, which often is found in less than 3 feet of water once the ice is on.

The Exotics Problem

The captain of a research vessel was standing on the bridge wing of his ship in Saginaw Bay when he saw something beneath the hull near the stern. Alarmed, he ran back, leaned over the side and realized that he was looking at the bottom of the rudder 15 feet below, a new experience in waters that used to be so murky one couldn't see more than a yard beneath the surface.

The reason Saginaw Bay and the rest of the Great Lakes are clearing so rapidly (approaching almost tropical clarity in some areas) is the zebra mussel, a dime-size, filter-feeding bivalve from the Baltic that reached the lakes in the ballast tanks of oceangoing ships about 20 years ago. Without natural enemies, the zebra mussel population exploded, reproducing at a rate that researchers say is 1,000 times greater than in their home waters.

The mussels quickly caused problems by coating and clogging city and industrial water-intake pipes and other underwater structures, but, for anglers, the short-term results of the infestation have been largely positive. What the long-term results will be, no one knows. While the clear waters over tropical reefs appear to teem with life, scientists and anglers know that the richest freshwater fishing grounds are usually in murky waters, living soups that can sustain much larger biomasses.

Some biologists believe that because the mussels feed by filtering tiny organisms from the water, they will compete directly with juvenile gamefish and forage fish for food, or indirectly by removing that food from the water column by excreting it as waste in a form that is unusable by the small fish or the even tinier creatures that the small fish eat.

In the eastern basin of Lake Erie, water clarity had reached a point by 1998 that biologists were worried it could no longer sustain the massive forage base needed to feed the huge numbers of

Minnesota has more boats per capita than any other state in the United States and claims more shoreline than California, Florida, and Hawaii combined.

salmon, steelhead, and walleye. Given the rate at which the mussels were spreading, they were concerned that the trend would eventually be repeated even in the vastly greater volumes of Lakes Huron and Michigan.

But for the present, the clearing waters in most places have improved weed growth and populations of sight feeders like smallmouth bass, pike, and muskellunge. The clearer water resulted in a decline in the walleye population in Lake St. Clair near Detroit, but anglers learned to change fishing methods, and many walleye still inhabit the deep, dim channels of the nearby St. Clair and Detroit Rivers.

Another major concern is the continued arrival of exotic species to the Great Lakes in the ballast of seagoing ships. The European ruffe, a perch relative of no angling value but with an enormous appetite for gamefish eggs, showed up in Duluth Harbor at the extreme western end of Lake Superior in the early 1990s. Within five years it was the predominant species in the harbor, but at first it spread only slowly along the northern shoreline of the lake, a few miles a year. Then scientists discovered ruffe in the harbor at Alpena, Michigan, on Lake Huron, about 500 miles to the southeast. It became evident that Duluth ruffe had been transported to Alpena in the ballast of the freighters that carry cement between the two ports.

More than 100 exotic plants and animals have been documented in the Great Lakes over the past 100 years, and most of them arrived in the past three decades. Some of them, like the spiny water flea, have so far been little more than a nuisance to anglers; but others, like the zebra mussel, are considered an economic threat to water intakes and other underwater structures, and the ruffe and round goby could be major threats to sportfish.

Michigan, with a share of four of the Great Lakes, is at the center of the effort to solve the exotics problem, but most scientists believe that these species will continue to arrive until the federal government devises an enforceable solution affecting ships entering the lakes from other countries. Ironically, exotic species here also include the salmon and steelhead that have become the glamour attractions of Great Lakes sportfishing.

MICROFILAMENT *(Line)*

See: Line.

MICRONESIA

Micronesia is a substantial grouping of islands in the North Pacific Ocean, east of the Philippines *(see)* and north of the island of New Guinea, and stretching from just north of the equator to about the 20th parallel. In Greek, *Micronesia* means tiny islands, and indeed this region contains some 2,000 islands (mostly coral atolls and islets) that are spread out among the Northern Mariana Islands, the Marshall Islands, Guam *(see)*, Kiribati *(see)*, the Caroline Islands, and Nauru. The largest island is Guam, and it is followed in size by Babelthuap in the Republic of Palau, which is part of the Carolines; both are volcanic in origin.

The Northern Marianas are a U.S. commonwealth and include approximately 16 coral and volcanic islands, the major ones being Saipan, Tinian, and Rota. The Caroline Islands are much larger in overall size, consisting of many hundreds of islands, islets, and atolls, with the principal subdivisions being the states of Chuuk (formerly Truk), Pohnpei (formerly Ponape), Kosrae, and Yap, all of which are in the independent Federated States of Micronesia, and the Republic of Palau, which is a U.S. Trust Territory. The independent Marshall Islands consist of 34 atolls and coral reefs that are divided into the Ratak and Ralik Chains; Kwajalein is the largest atoll, and Bikini the most renowned.

Hardly anyone can tell you where Micronesia is, let alone which islands it comprises or what the angling situation is. Sportfishing is still virtually unknown in this part of the world, and although the true potential here has yet to be determined, it appears to be vast. Many parts of Micronesia are essentially untapped and virgin by modern standards, although they still bear the scars of World War II and subsequent nuclear testing actions. This is especially true of the Marshall Islands, which were subjected to devastating nuclear bomb and megabomb testing and ensuing radioactive fallout.

Bikini Atoll in the Marshalls consists of 36 islets that surround a lagoon that is 21 miles long and 11 miles wide. Atomic tests were begun here in 1946. A megabomb that was detonated in 1954 produced radioactive fallout on the ocean and islands for great distances around Bikini. Although concerns regarding radioactive contamination of the soils and plants on islands in the region existed into the late 1990s, resettlement of Marshallese to some islands has occurred, and attempts at surface restoration of the atolls are underway. The long-term effect on marine life has been much more favorable, and dive camps have been established at some, including Bikini.

Divers are more likely than anglers to have visited Micronesia's coral reefs, and they have reported tremendous marine life, including in and near the Marshall Islands. A 1997 *National Geographic* expedition to Rongelap Atoll, which is about 100 miles east of Bikini and was the recipient of 1954 fallout due to westerly winds, found no visible scars from nuclear radiation to the atoll's coral reef and aquatic life, and described it as "an Eden for fish."

The Caroline Islands have been explored by a few anglers, especially around Chuuk and Pohnpei. Lagoons, reefs, dropoffs, channels, and varied interesting terrain exist here, much of which has never seen sportfishing activity. Likewise, Bikini Atoll, where flats, coral reefs, and nearby deep blue water produced a potpourri of species, was visited only in the late 1990s.

Given the location of the Micronesian atolls in the Pacific, it seems billfish might be plentiful here. Marlin haven't been aggressively targeted by the few anglers who have plied these waters; encounters have been largely accidental, in part because there are few proper boats available and in part because only so much ground can be covered by a few vessels in a limited period of time in such a vast area. When a big-game sportfishing boat was brought to the Caroline Islands in the late 1980s as part of a touring mother-ship operation, however, anglers on board caught more than a dozen billfish in several weeks, including both sailfish and blue marlin. The biggest of the latter nearly hit 500 pounds. Reportedly, these were the first sport-caught billfish in Micronesia. Blue marlin have also been landed more recently off Bikini Atoll and are accompanied by virtually all the pelagic species found throughout the central Pacific, including dolphin, wahoo, and assorted tunas, some in terrific numbers.

The coral reefs, atoll channels, and lagoons abound with sportfish, a full listing of which is still to be completed. Angling reports from these virgin waters have been replete with unabated action; clearly, a bountiful light-tackle fishing paradise exists. Large barracuda, yellowfin tuna, dogtooth tuna, bigeye tuna, bluefin trevally, wahoo, mahimahi (dolphin), kawakawa, rainbow runners, and the usual assortment of grouper, snapper, and sharks are caught close to the atolls.

Flats in the region also contain bonefish, as well as several species of trevally, various snapper, and an assortment of other species. The coral atolls are hard and wadeable, and they are plentiful not only throughout the Marshall Islands, but also in all of Micronesia. As more and better flats become known and accessible, this region will offer among the best flats fishing in the world.

With so few boats and so few anglers currently exploiting these waters, the better locales throughout the vast area of Micronesia have yet to be fully identified.

MIDGES

Midges belong to the scientific order Diptera, a term that is derived from *di,* meaning two, and *ptera,* meaning wing, owing to the presence of just two wings. These aquatic insects are much smaller than many other aquatic insects and are often overlooked, but they are extremely abundant and important food sources for fish in shallow areas of streams, lakes, and most vegetated areas. Two-winged insects represent a broad group of organisms, including deerflies, mosquitoes, blackflies, no-see-ums, and tiny insects that are commonly called gnats in North America or buzzers in Great Britain, but the major food is represented by midges (all midges belong to the genus *Chironomus* and are called chironomids) and secondarily by the larger craneflies. The larvae of these insects are most important as trout food.

Midge

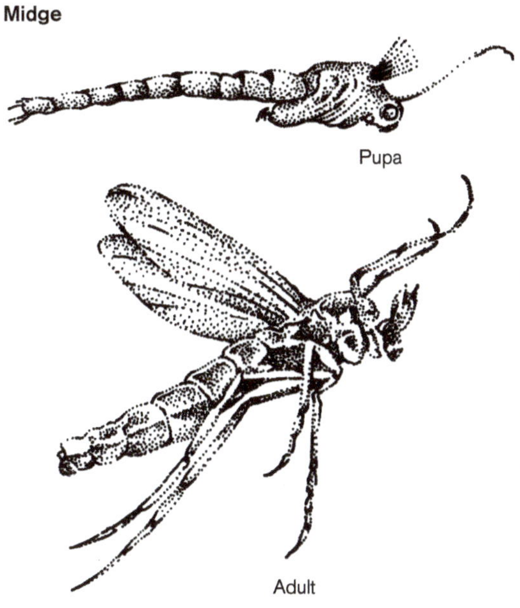

The life cycle of these insects is similar to caddisflies *(see)* and consists of egg, larva, pupa, and adult stages, with most of this being in the wormlike or grublike larva stage. Midge larvae, which are only $^1/_8$ to $^1/_2$ inch long, burrow into bottom muck or cling to bottom debris, and are widely consumed by trout. After several months, the larva turns into an actively moving pupa, the preadult form that it maintains for several weeks until it matures and swims to the surface. Just under the surface, it hatches into a winged adult, a process that takes enough time to attract the attention of fish, which consume the metamorphosing pupae and emerging adults in large numbers. This activity presents excellent fishing opportunity to fly anglers, who must correctly represent the appropriate stage and size and color of insect species, as well as fish their imitation naturally just beneath the surface. Adults look like mosquitoes, and after emerging they sit on the water surface, where they are preyed upon. When they leave the surface, they often appear in such swarms that they are a nuisance, although they do not bite.

Craneflies are two-winged insects that are less common than midges, but as adults are larger and sometimes very prevalent along stream banks, where they dance over and along the water, becoming a target for trout. Their larvae is also longer than midge larvae, ranging up to 3 inches long and looking very wormlike (they may be called water worms), but their pupae are terrestrial.

See: Aquatic Insects.

M

MIDWATER

In or near the middle layer of water. This term is generally used by biologists to describe the habitat of fish that are not surface or bottom (benthic or demersal, respectively) dwellers.

MIDWAY ATOLL

The coral atoll of Midway consists of Eastern and Sand Islands, situated near the geographic center of the Pacific Ocean and about 1,300 miles northwest of Honolulu, Hawaii. A strategic air and naval base during World War II, Midway was closed to the public and utilized by the United States Armed Forces until September 1993. It is now under the jurisdiction of the U.S. Fish and Wildlife Service, and Midway Atoll National Wildlife Refuge is the first remote island refuge open to the general public in the Pacific.

The Fish and Wildlife Service entered into a public-private partnership to provide refuge operations and support, as well as opportunities for public education and enjoyment. Sportfishing, as well as diving and eco-touring activities, have been conducted at Midway since the late 1990s to benefit overall operations. Anglers practice catch-and-release, except for record fish and consumption.

Essentially a virgin fishery, although similar to that of Hawaii for most pelagic species, the waters around Midway are productive and provide diverse opportunities. Species that were caught in the earliest explorations of the waters around Midway include blue marlin, black marlin, striped marlin, sailfish, bluefin tuna, yellowfin tuna, mahimahi (dolphin), wahoo, giant trevally, bluefin trevally, kawakawa, amberjack, rainbow runners, and grouper. A handful of giant trevally line-class records have been set here, and this species is especially prevalent; 50- to 60-pounders are common and some reach 100 pounds.

A 600-foot dropoff exists just a few miles from the reef, and this is where most big-game fishing has so far occurred. Although 400-pounders have been common, specimens to 850 pounds have been recorded, and expectations for larger fish are realistic.

This area is likely one that will receive much more attention in the future. Several well-equipped sportfishing boats operate here, with experienced crews and opportunities for both inshore and offshore fishing. Accommodations are comfortable, and there's wildlife viewing to be enjoyed as well.

MIGRATION

A regular journey made by a particular species of fish, on an annual or lifetime basis, usually associated with propagation patterns but also associated with the seasonal availability of food. Most migrations are mass movements and involve travel over a particular route, usually at the same time annually. Migration is not to be confused with the relocation of fish because of pollution, sedimentation, storms, or the temporary relocation of food sources. Anglers, for example, often refer to fish as making migrations from deep water to shallow water to feed, an action that is really a localized movement. The periodic movement of fish in a water body is not necessarily a migration, although the movement of a fish species to and from breeding grounds (such as walleye in spring moving from a spawning river back to the main lake) is a migration.

Migrations occur in various species and in both freshwater and saltwater. All freshwater fish that move from lake or river environs to a tributary in order to spawn will migrate to and from the spawning grounds at or around the same time each year. All anadromous *(see)* and catadromous *(see)* fish undertake spawning migrations, the former from saltwater to freshwater and the latter from freshwater to saltwater, also around the same time annually. Pelagic *(see)* ocean species migrate from winter to summer grounds, both for spawning and for food procurement, also around the same time annually. Migrations occur in north-south, south-north, offshore-inshore, and inshore-offshore patterns, and in combinations of these (some sea organisms migrate up and down in the water column). Some fish migrations cover great distances, even thousands of miles, and some are extremely short, perhaps just a short distance up a river.

Water temperature is an important factor in the migration of many gamefish. Although they may appear in a certain area at about the same time each year, their arrival, and in some cases departure, does not occur until specific water temperatures are established or no longer exist. This is usually what makes the migratory arrival of a given species earlier or later than usual, as well as the departure.

Homing instincts are not fully understood, but it is known that the chemical difference in specific tributaries is what allows anadromous species such as salmon to return to their river of birth as adults to propagate. They receive the chemical imprint of their birth water as smolts prior to migrating out to sea.

The migratory habits of many freshwater and saltwater species are important to anglers, even if they are not fully understood, because these habits dictate the appearance and availability of the species. It is when many species of fish are undertaking their spawning migrations, like American shad and the various salmon, that they are most accessible. Likewise, when many pelagic species are following schools of pelagic baitfish, such as herring, their location can be better defined, and thus they become more accessible. When factors that change the presence or abundance of baitfish (like a temperature change) occur, the predators will follow, meaning that anglers should be trying to find the food and should be fishing in places where the primary food sources are most abundant.

Milkfish

MILKFISH *Chanos chanos.*

Other names—salmon herring; Afrikaans: *melkvis;* Fijian: *yawa;* French: *chano, thon;* Hawaiian: *awa;* Japanese: *sabahii;* Philippine languages: *bangos, banglis, bangolis, bangris, banglot;* Tahitian: *tamano;* Thai: *pla nuanchan;* Vietnamese: *cá măng.*

A herring-like fish, the milkfish is very important in the Indo-Pacific, where it is used widely for food. The fry are collected from rivers and used for stocking ponds, where they are raised to juvenile status and eventually marketed fresh, smoked, canned, and frozen.

Identification. Looking somewhat like a large mullet or a tarpon, the milkfish has a streamlined and compressed body, large eyes, and silvery metallic coloring. It also has a small, toothless mouth, a single spineless dorsal fin, and a large forked tail fin.

Size/Age. The milkfish can reach 5 feet in length and a weight of 50 pounds, and live for 15 years. The all-tackle world record is a 24-pound, 8-ounce Hawaiian fish.

Distribution. In the Indo-Pacific, milkfish occur from Japan south to Australia, west to the Red Sea and South Africa, and east to Hawaii and the Marquesas Islands; in the eastern Pacific, they occur from San Pedro, California, to the Galápagos Islands.

Habitat. Adults travel in schools along continental shelves and around islands where there are well-developed reefs and where temperatures exceed 20°C. Milkfish flourish in water as hot as 32°C.

Life history/Behavior. Milkfish spawn in shallow, brackish water, and a single fish may produce 9 million eggs. These float on the surface until they hatch, and the new larvae enter inshore waters two to three weeks after hatching. Older larvae settle in coastal wetlands during the juvenile stage, occasionally entering freshwater lakes, and older juveniles and young adults return to the sea to mature sexually.

Food and feeding habits. Milkfish larvae feed on zooplankton, whereas juveniles and adults eat bacteria, soft algae, small benthic invertebrates, and sometimes pelagic fish eggs and larvae.

Angling. Not readily caught on rod and reel, milkfish are usually an incidental catch for anglers.

MINIMUM LENGTH LIMIT

A restriction pertaining to the minimum size of fish that may be kept; the restriction prohibits anglers from keeping fish that are less than the specified length. A minimum length limit is the shortest length of a fish, and it is determined by measuring the fish with a ruler. There are several methods of measuring fish, and the appropriate method is often specified in applicable fishing regulations brochures.

A minimum length limit is a legal game regulation established by the fisheries agency with jurisdiction over the location being fished, and enforced by fish and wildlife conservation officers.

See: Measuring Fish; Slot Limit; Fisheries Management; Regulations.

MINNESOTA

Sportfishing is more than recreational pursuit in the Land of 10,000 Lakes; it is a way of life. About 1.4 million fishing licenses are sold in Minnesota every year, and about one in four residents own a fishing license. Every year on the second weekend in May, an estimated 1 million people participate in the general fishing opener, a day regarded more as a celebration of spring than the beginning of the fishing season. Sportfishing tourism is among the top five industries in the state.

With its bounty of water and its northern forests, Minnesota has come to epitomize the northwoods fishing experience. The phrase "going up North"—a standard in Minnesota vernacular—means piling into the family car for a weekend at the cabin, usually to fish for walleye, northern pike, bass, or panfish. Perhaps the most enduring postcard image of Minnesota is that of a canoe floating serenely on a remote northern lake, its occupant holding a fishing rod.

But Minnesota offers much more than northwoods lakes. The Minneapolis–St. Paul metropolitan area boasts one of the nation's largest and most diversified urban fisheries. Twin Cities lakes are populated with trophy muskies (in excess of 30 pounds), feisty walleye of all sizes, unlimited numbers of panfish, and largemouth bass up to 7 pounds. Lake Minnetonka, which is within sight of downtown Minneapolis, became the darling of competitive bass angling in the mid-1990s, in part because it yielded catches of bass with an exceptional average weight of 4 pounds.

Lake Superior, the world's largest body of freshwater, abuts the far northeastern edge of Minnesota; this deep and cold lake is home to chinook and coho salmon, two species of rainbow trout (steelhead and Kamloops), and a burgeoning lake trout population.

Minnesota also contains the headwaters of the Mississippi River. As the river winds south from Itasca State Park, it develops into a world-class fishery for smallmouth bass and walleye, even in the urbanized stretches within Minneapolis and St. Paul. The renewed fishery there is due to dramatic improvements in water quality.

The St. Croix River, a federally designated wild and scenic river, supports thriving numbers of

A one-third-inch-long clam, collected at 12,350 feet in the ocean, was estimated by scientists to be over a century old.

smallmouth bass, walleye, crappie, and muskies. Several other major river systems—notably the Minnesota, St. Louis, and Rainy Rivers—are established walleye fisheries.

For trout lovers, the southeast corner of the state offers hundreds of miles of streams full of browns, brookies, and rainbows. Inland streams along Lake Superior's North Shore hold native populations of brook trout, while dozens of northern inland lakes supply anglers with brook, rainbow, and lake trout. Minnesota enjoys a large and growing population of fly fishing enthusiasts, despite the state's obsession with walleye, the official state fish.

For true trophy seekers, Minnesota has some of North America's finest muskie waters; indeed, two fish exceeding 50 pounds in 1996 came close to bumping off the 54-pound state record. Large northern pike are also found in select trophy waters.

In the winter, anglers turn their attention to ice fishing, which is a story unto itself. Some lakes support entire communities of heated fish houses. Minnesota is also the birthplace of the modern portable ice fishing shelters that have revolutionized the way many anglers spend their winters.

More than 1 million acres of roadless forests and nonmotorized lakes are at the disposal of backcountry anglers in the Boundary Waters Canoe Area Wilderness. Most canoeists regard a Boundary Waters trip incomplete without a sizzling meal of fried walleye.

Unheralded but equally important are the dozens of lesser rivers, hundreds of smaller prairie lakes, and thousands of farm ponds—there are actually 15,292 lakes and nearly 15,000 miles of rivers and stream in the state—that provide opportunities for all manner of warmwater species.

M

Species Overview

The fisheries in many of Minnesota's lakes, particularly those in the central and northern regions, are so diversified that it is possible to catch all of their prime species in the same day. The following information applies to nearly all of these lakes.

Walleye. Spring and early summer are best suited to fishing for walleye throughout Minnesota. These fish are typically oriented to shallow-water structures such as sand and gravel bars, rocky points, dropoffs, and shallow bays. The universal lure for walleye at this time of year is a jig and minnow, the latter being a shiner or a fathead. Jig sizes vary depending on how deep they are fished, but generally a $^1/_8$- or $^1/_4$-ounce size is sufficient. The minnow is impaled through the head, cast, and slowly bounced across the bottom. Walleye always attack the jig-minnow combination during its falling motion.

Leeches and nightcrawlers become the baits of choice as summer progresses. Anglers favor using them under a slip float, usually over or near shallow structures such as rockpiles and reefs. They can also be trolled slowly using a variety of live-bait rigs, or threaded on a jig and cast. Crankbaits and stickbaits also come into play later in the summer; they are typically trolled in shallow water (3 to 15 feet) for more aggressive fish. In the fall, walleye return to the shallows, where anglers land them on all manner of live-bait rigs. Throughout Minnesota, walleye fishing is done using light- to medium-weight spinning equipment rigged with 6- or 8-pound-test monofilament.

Some of the more popular walleye lakes in north-central Minnesota are Gull, Pelican, Mille Lacs, Leech, Winnibigoshish, Osakis, the Whitefish Chain, Ottertail, Cass, Cut Foot Sioux, and Fish near Duluth.

Northern pike. Aggressive and plentiful, northern pike are often considered a nuisance by walleye anglers. However, they are a popular species when walleye are not biting. Most pike weigh between 2 and 8 pounds, but trophy lakes can yield specimens larger than 20 pounds. Pike are caught most of the year, even in the warmest summer months. They are often taken incidentally on jig-minnow combinations, but anglers serious about catching large pike use large crankbaits, spoons, or large sucker minnows suspended under a float or a bobber.

Most lakes in the central and northern region harbor northern pike, but truly large pike are found in Mille Lacs, Leech, and Winnibigoshish. To grow large, pike need a prey base of tullibee or cisco, a rough fish found generally in larger lakes. This is not to say some smaller lakes don't produce the occasional lunker.

Largemouth bass. Bass inhabit most shallow, weed-filled lakes. Starting early in the summer, spinnerbaits are popular lures. So are jigs tipped with plastic grubs and pork rind. The universal plastic worm is a particularly popular lure in Minnesota, with many variations in colors and sinker sizes. Crankbaits are effective in the summer, as bright sun drives bass deeper. Some of the more notable Minnesota bass lakes are Le Homme Dieu, Gull, the Chisago Chain, and numerous waters in the Detroit Lakes area.

Smallmouth bass. Smallmouth are more plentiful in the lakes of northeastern Minnesota, but one of the most important smallmouth fisheries cuts through the heart of the state. The Mississippi River boasts smallmouths in good numbers and sizes up to 23 inches in length. The best stretches of the river lie between Brainerd and Elk River, sections of which have special regulations to promote trophy fishing.

Most anglers float the Mississippi River in small boats or canoes. Minnow-imitating lures are popular baits, as are jigs tipped with minnows. The river has become a popular destination for fly anglers, who have success with poppers and wet flies.

Crappie. Crappie are plentiful in central and northern Minnesota, but most anglers keep their top spots a blood secret. The best crappie lakes are those that are lightly fished; otherwise, word of good crappie fishing spreads quickly and the tasty panfish fall prey to overfishing. The best crappie fishing occurs in late April and early May, when the fish congregate in shallow, dark bays to feed on insects and small minnows. The most common fishing technique is to employ a small minnow fished under a slip bobber. A tiny jig lends color and extra weight.

Central and Northern Lakes Region

Minnesota's central and northern lakes region represents the core of the state's walleye, northern pike, panfish, and bass fisheries. The region could be roughly defined as that north-south area between St. Cloud and Bemidji and extending from Detroit Lakes east to Duluth. Sportfishing permeates the economy of this region; every town, no matter how small, has at least one bait shop.

North-central Minnesota is dominated by several large lakes: Mille Lacs (132,000 acres), Leech (111,000 acres), and Winnibigoshish (58,000 acres). These shallow, hard-bottomed lakes are ideal walleye factories. Within this area lie hundreds of other lakes ranging between 500 and 20,000 acres. This is the heart of Minnesota's vacation country; resorts, lodges, and summer cabins dot the shorelines here.

Lakes in this region share many similarities. Most are multispecies lakes, although walleye are the primary target. A few are stocked with walleye, but most have naturally sustaining populations. Bass and panfish are the second-most sought-after species, followed by northern pike and yellow perch.

Lake Mille Lacs. This is Minnesota's most treasured walleye lake and one of the finest such fisheries in the nation. Bowl-shaped, shallow—few spots exceed 30 feet; and measuring a grand 132,000 acres, Mille Lacs is ideally suited for producing walleye. Consequently, scarcely a foot of this lake's shoreline isn't occupied by a resort, lodge, private cabin, or launch service. In the winter, hundreds of ice fishing houses, ranging from shanties to palatial cabins with televisions and hot tubs, crowd onto the lake, creating small ice fishing villages complete with plowed roads. Nearly a half-million pounds of walleye (none are stocked) are pulled from Mille Lacs in an average season.

In recent years the lake has earned a deserved reputation for trophy muskies, northern pike, and smallmouth bass. The lake's emerging muskie population has specimens pushing 40 pounds; pike can range from small "hammer handles" to 20-pounders; and smallmouth as big as 7 pounds have been caught. When nothing else is biting, jumbo perch can fill an angler's stringer in the summer and winter. Many people believe that Minnesota's next state-record muskellunge will come from Mille Lacs. It is not uncommon for anglers to see 20 or more of these fish in a day and, if they are lucky, land one or two. Most cast heavy jerkbaits, surface lures, or bucktails.

Despite these riches, the walleye is king on Mille Lacs, and for many Minnesotans the pursuit of these fish borders on obsession. A typical "keeper" walleye ranges between 1 and 4 pounds, but fish in excess of 8 pounds are not uncommon, with a few 11- to 12-pounders taken each year. In the late 1990s, courts allocated portions of the Mille Lacs walleye fishery to Chippewa tribes, which has resulted in different sportfishing regulations almost on a yearly basis.

Despite its rather plain appearance, Mille Lacs can be a challenging lake. The bottom is composed of a variety of substrates—sand and mud "flats" and rocks—and walleye linger in these areas depending on the season and time of day. Jigs tipped with minnows or leeches are a primary bait for walleye, fished either over shallow rocks and sand, or over the lake's famous mud flats. Live-bait rigs are equally successful, as are crankbaits trolled over the rocks. The bulk of the walleye are caught in May and June; in the summer, the fish head for deep water.

Because the lake is huge, a good-size boat (16 feet or larger) and a map are recommended. Heavy winds can produce big waves and make the lake unfishable. Fishing launches are popular, and scores of guides call Mille Lacs home.

Leech Lake. Like Mille Lacs, Leech Lake near the town of Walker is a fine walleye fishery, in terms of numbers of fish and their size. Walleye fishing is best in the early summer and again in the fall, but savvy anglers are able to find them in deeper waters all summer long.

This huge, many-armed lake, however, is perhaps most famous for its muskie fishing. In the 1950s, during a period of warm, stagnant summer weather, the lake's muskies went on a "rampage." Anglers caught so many that they filled wheelbarrows. Black-and-white photos from the era show anglers standing next to racks bulging with dozens of large muskies.

The lake's reputation continues. In 1996, an Iowa angler caught a muskie weighing 52 pounds, the state's largest in several decades. Fish in excess of 40 inches are not uncommon. Muskies bite all summer, but the prime angling occurs in September and October, when the fish aggressively chase bait. Popular lures are bucktails, jerkbaits, and topwater plugs.

Northern Border Lakes

Lake of the Woods. This huge lake straddling Canada claims the title "Walleye Capital of the World," a moniker shared by a half-dozen other major walleye fisheries in the nation, including Minnesota's own Lake Mille Lacs. Suffice to say that Lake of the Woods is a formidable walleye lake. Because it is 55 miles wide at its greatest point and covers 65,000 miles of shoreline, it appears on most national maps and occupies that distinctive knob of northern Minnesota that protrudes into Ontario. It is home to a substantial resort and lodge community accessible through the towns of Baudette and Warroad. Another geographical aberration called the Northwest Angle—accessible only through Canada or across the lake—supports numerous fishing resorts.

Lake of the Woods offers walleye and sauger in both good numbers and size. The end of commercial fishing gave the fishery a much-needed boost. Photos on resort walls tell the story: smiling groups of anglers posing with catches ranging from 1-pounders to 12-pounders. The prime periods are late May and June, and the early fall, when walleye stay shallow and succumb to a variety of live-bait rigs and jigs. Otherwise, downriggers and crankbaits have emerged as a prime summer technique for deep-dwelling walleye. Locating prime underwater structure, such as reefs and sandbars, is key to catching Lake of the Woods walleye.

Ice fishing is another big attraction at Lake of the Woods. Resorts employ specially designed tracked vans, hovercraft, and amphibious vehicles to travel far out on the lake, where ice houses provide heated fishing environments. An estimated 84,000 anglers visit Lake of the Woods to ice fish every winter. Air service is also available for winter and summer anglers wanting access to resorts on distant Oak Island.

Large muskies inhabit Lake of the Woods, although dedicated muskie chasers will fish both Minnesota and Ontario waters. Lake of the Woods arguably offers an angler's best chance to land a 50-plus-inch muskie in the United States. Muskies are caught from mid-June through the fall, but August may be the best month; the fish can be active and shallow then, and may strike surface lures. Some trolling is done here, but most muskie anglers favor casting, as shallow water, rocky reefs, and submerged weed growth are bountiful.

Big pike are also plentiful; many are caught through the ice early in the winter. Largemouth bass exist in some areas of Lake of the Woods, but the lake is a haven for smallmouths, which, though not huge, offer abundant and relatively shallow action all season. With 14,000 islands in this gigantic and confusing body of water, anglers will find numerous rocky nooks to work.

Other large border lakes. Island-studded Rainy Lake lies on the Minnesota-Ontario border near International Falls. It is an enormous lake with a resurgent walleye population. It is also a first-class smallmouth bass and crappie lake. Portions lie within Voyageurs National Park, which is one of the nation's few water-based national parks. Special permits aren't needed to fish in the park, and backcountry camping opportunities are numerous and scenic. With many reefs and shallow rocks, Rainy Lake is a tricky lake to navigate, but the scenery and sportfishing are well worth the visit. A lake map is recommended. Houseboats are a popular means of seeing and fishing the lake; several local companies rent them.

Lake Kabetogama is the next water east of Rainy Lake. It, too, lies within Voyageurs National Park and is a reputable walleye fishery. Smallmouth bass are fewer here. Like Rainy, it hosts a thriving resort industry. The next lake, Namakan, is another fine walleye fishery.

Boundary Waters Canoe Area Wilderness

The 1-million-plus-acre Boundary Waters Canoe Area Wilderness is a gem in America's wilderness system. Located in northeastern Minnesota along the Canadian border, this sprawling network of pristine lakes and rivers is completely roadless and open to nonmotorized boats only, although a handful of border lakes allow outboards of 25 horse-power or less. Tens of thousands of canoeists flock to the Boundary Waters every season, making it the most heavily used wilderness in the nation.

Boundary Waters offers superb backcountry fishing for walleye, northern pike, smallmouth bass, lake trout, and stream trout, but novices should do their homework before planning a trip. Fishing success varies greatly from lake to lake and season to season. Most veteran anglers plan circuitous canoe routes that include stops at prime fishing lakes, which enables them to fish a variety of lakes while enjoying new scenery. Otherwise, a common strategy is to set up a base camp on a prime fishing lake and take day trips from there.

Either way, this takes planning and research, so it is advisable to hire a guide for a first trip. With literally hundreds of lakes and routes to choose from, novices can easily waste time on unproductive waters.

Two time periods offer the best fishing: late May through June, and September through October. In the spring and earlier summer, walleye and bass still roam the shallows, typically in such areas as rocky points, bays, river inlets and outlets, and shallow reefs. Lake trout and stream trout also inhabit the shallows. Once summer arrives, most species head for deeper reefs and rocky structures where they can still be caught, but only by those who know where these specific structures lie. Likewise in the fall, walleye, bass, and lake trout move back into shallow areas. For fishing and scenery, fall is a particularly spectacular season in which to visit the Boundary Waters.

Because most Boundary Waters fishing is done from canoes, camping and fishing gear must be lightweight to ensure feasible portages. A well-conceived fishing outfit should include a medium-weight spinning rod and reel; a minimum selection of crankbaits, spoons, and spinners; and terminal tackle for live-bait rigs. Minnows, nightcrawlers, and leeches are the natural baits of choice.

Several large lakes are famous Boundary Waters fisheries. They include Basswood, which is the home of the state-record northern pike, and Saganaga, Seagull, Gunflint, and the Minnesota portions of Crooked and Lac La Croix Lakes. Saganaga, which has depths to 240 feet, is the deepest Minnesota Lake. Walleye and smallmouth bass are the target species, but northern pike are also found in most Boundary Waters lakes. Lake trout inhabit only the deeper lakes, and stream trout are available in state-designated trout lakes.

The Boundary Waters are accessible through major entry points in Ely, Grand Marais, and the Gunflint Trail. Special permits and fees are required to enter the wilderness; reservations must be made well in advance. Numerous outfitters, guides, and well-stocked tackle shops are available at major entry points. A number of popular guidebooks serve as valuable tools for planning a fishing trip.

Prairie Lakes and Rivers

As one heads south from northern Minnesota, the state slowly transitions from northern spruce and pine forests to central hardwoods and then to farmland and prairies. A steady dose of farmland greets the traveler south of Interstate 94. This region maintains a remarkable number of thriving fisheries.

Big Stone Lake, located in extreme western Minnesota, rates as one of the state's best walleye fisheries. It is actually a dammed portion of the Minnesota River that straddles the South Dakota border. As a border lake, Big Stone opens earlier than other lakes and offers superb walleye fishing. Just up the road, Traverse Lake is considered another good walleye lake.

Farther downstream is Lac qui Parle Lake, one of the state's least-known walleye meccas. Nearby Artichoke Lake is another sleeper walleye site.

Several counties west of Lac qui Parle is Kandiyohi County, which is home to three fine walleye lakes: Green, Diamond, and Big Kandiyohi. Farther south, the lakes surrounding Mankato are renowned for their bass fishing. Lake Tetonka, located farther west near the town of Waterville, is home of the state-record largemouth bass.

Lake Superior

The recovery of Lake Superior's lake trout fishery is one of the great ecological success stories of this century. Attacked by invading sea lampreys, lake trout were nearly wiped out of the lake in the 1950s. But by the 1960s, federal and state biologists had devised ways to control lampreys and, buoyed by stocking programs, lake trout began a slow recovery in Lake Superior waters of Minnesota, Wisconsin, and Michigan.

While the lake trout recovery was underway, fisheries managers in Minnesota and the other states tried experimental stockings of Pacific salmon, subspecies of rainbow trout, and even Atlantic salmon. For the most part, these fish thrived; through the 1980s, Lake Superior became a menagerie of big gamefish, sating the appetites of anglers seeking large salmonids and giving rise to a huge charter boat industry.

That success story was tempered significantly in the 1990s, at least in Minnesota waters of Lake Superior. Runs of chinook salmon and steelhead declined significantly, and the state's Atlantic salmon stocking program was discontinued. Coho stocking also ceased. Meanwhile, lake trout became more abundant than ever.

Along the Minnesota portion of Lake Superior, anglers still catch salmon, but in fewer numbers. Steelhead anglers still ply the waters of the Knife, French, and other rivers, but the fishery is catch-

Minnesota's renowned Boundary Waters offers winter fishing via dogsled team access and summer fishing via canoe-portage access.

and-release only for wild stocks. (The nonnative Kamloops strain of rainbows are still relatively plentiful and can be kept.) Lake trout now make up the bulk of the catch, including specimens up to 20 pounds and even a rare 30-pounder.

Minnesota's portion of Lake Superior's shoreline is stunning in its beauty, and it is relatively undeveloped. The North Shore starts in Duluth and ends at Canada's border. The lake is clear, cold, and dangerous to those who don't know its moods. A large boat (20 feet or more) is recommended, although locals often use deep-V inland boats as small as 16 feet. A small fleet of charter boats still operates out of the Duluth harbor.

Downriggers are a popular tool for pursuing salmon and trout in Lake Superior. Anglers employ a variety of plugs and spoons, which can be moved with downriggers through varying depths and according to water temperatures. Anglers often search shallow reefs and use heavy jigs for lake trout. Shore casting is also popular, using spoons and plugs. Steelheaders ply the rivers in the spring with spawn sacks and flies.

Lake Superior's inland streams and lakes. Tumbling out of the rugged North Shore ridges are numerous streams and creeks that harbor native brook trout. These streams are remote and overgrown with brush; they offer a challenge to anglers willing to explore the backcountry. Most of the trout are small—a 15-incher is a trophy—but these streams are beautiful and relatively untouched by the angling hordes.

Likewise, numerous inland lakes in Lake and Cook Counties offer fishing for rainbows, larger brook trout, lake trout, and splake. The Gunflint Trail, which heads northwest from Grand Marais, provides primary access to many of these backcountry lakes. Trout are typically caught all season long, but the prime periods are spring and fall.

Southeast Bluff Country

The landscape of southeastern Minnesota departs dramatically from the rest of the state. As the prairies approach the Mississippi River, they rise to form rolling, oak-studded hills, scenic valleys, and limestone bluffs. From theses highlands bubble hundreds of miles of creeks and streams that eventually empty into the Mississippi River. Southeastern Minnesota—a region that includes Fillmore, Houston, Winona, Olmsted, and Wabasha Counties—has a strong resemblance to New England, with small farming communities, narrow winding roads, and big red barns. It's a beautiful part of the Midwest.

It is also trout country. Brook, rainbow, and brown trout make their home in streams and rivers, some of which are stocked by the Department of Natural Resources (DNR). Most, though, support wild browns or brookies. When the trout season opens in mid-April, anglers pursue trout that range from 6 inches to several pounds. Occasionally, browns in excess of 5 pounds are caught in deeper pools.

The streams are too numerous to name, but most belong to two major watersheds: the Whitewater and the Root River systems. Some streams are small enough to jump across; others, such as the main stem of the Root River, can handle canoes and small, flat-bottomed boats. The DNR publishes a comprehensive map of designated southeast trout streams, which are accessible through easements and at road and bridge crossings. Finding a place to fish isn't difficult, but intrepid anglers must take the time to seek permission from private landowners to access pools away from the crowds.

Bait anglers can get by with a simple nightcrawler, hook, and split shot. Others rely on a variety of small in-line spinners and small crankbaits, whereas fly anglers typically employ Elk-Hair caddis, Bead-Head Pheasant Tails, Blue-Winged Olives, Tricos, and other small mayfly imitations. Fly hatches can sometimes be quite heavy through the late spring and summer, offering fly anglers terrific opportunities to fool trout with their own creations. In recent years, fly fishing in the southeast region has become popular; local tackle shops, even in small towns, often stock good selections of popular patterns.

Smallmouth bass are an overlooked species in the southeast. Fly anglers with surface poppers can have terrific action throughout the summer; otherwise, small crankbaits and surface plugs work with spinning gear. Bass up to 19 and 20 inches are available.

The Twin Cities

The state-record tiger muskie came from Lake Calhoun, just a mile from downtown Minneapolis. Portions of the Mississippi River in St. Paul provide such a wealth of walleye that regulations require catch-and-release only. Lake Minnetonka regularly yields bass over 5 pounds, and a recent state-record crappie came from Coon Lake in the northern suburbs. These are a few examples of the superb fishing opportunities found in and around the Twin Cities.

The Twin Cities muskie population is a result of an intense state stocking effort. Prime lakes include Calhoun, Harriet, Independence, Owasso, Bald Eagle, Cedar, and Rebecca. The best fishing typically occurs from midsummer through fall. Casting heavy lures is the main technique, but trolling is also effective.

Pool 2 of the Mississippi River, which is below the Ford Dam in St. Paul, is one of the most popular open-water winter fisheries in the state. Catches of 50 or more walleye in a day are not uncommon. Sauger are also plentiful. Most anglers use jigs and minnows; crankbaits are more effective for trolling the river's rocky shores in the summer. Walleye up to 10 pounds are caught regularly.

Many people regard Lake Minnetonka as one of the best largemouth fisheries in the nation, not because it holds extremely large fish (7 pounds is about the maximum because of the short growing season) but because it produces large numbers of fish in the 2- to 5-pound range. Jigs adorned with plastic bodies and tails, soft-plastic worms, and crankbaits are among the more popular baits. Ironically, the invasion of a fast-growing exotic weed, Eurasian milfoil, is credited with bolstering the lake's bass population. Lake Minnetonka is also a good walleye and muskie lake.

Other popular Twin Cities bass lakes are Lake Waconia, Demontreville and Olson Lakes, Big Marine, and Forest Lake.

Quality panfish opportunities are plentiful in the Twin Cities, too. Coon Lake is famous for its crappie, as is Minnetonka. White Bear Lake holds good crappie and sunfish populations, as does Lake Phalen, Lake Harriet, and Prior Lake. Popular walleye lakes are White Bear, Prior, Calhoun, Harriet, Phalen, Forest, and Bald Eagle.

Mississippi River, Southern Reaches

Once it leaves the Twin Cities, the Mississippi River winds its way south along the Wisconsin-Minnesota border through scenic river towns such as Hastings, Red Wing, Lake City, Wabasha (the setting for the popular movie "Grumpy Old Men"), and Winona. Walleye and sauger are plentiful throughout the system. Spring and summer fishing in the stretch from Hastings to Red Wing is superb. Anglers focus their efforts around wing dams—sub-surface structures that jut into the river. Red Wing is another well-known walleye and sauger fishery virtually year-round. Anglers congregate near the dam on warm days in the winter; catches of 50 to 100 fish daily are not uncommon. Jigs and minnows, live-bait rigs, and crankbaits are preferred offerings.

The river widens and forms Lake Pepin near Lake City. Pepin is another reputed walleye fishery, and white bass are also popular here. Anglers track schools of white bass by following feeding gulls. Both predators key on migrating schools of baitfish. Backwaters of the river provide fast northern pike action in the spring.

MINNOW

More than 2,000 species constitute the minnow, or Cyprinidae, family of freshwater fish, making it perhaps the largest family of fish. "Minnow," "shiner," and "dace" are three names commonly associated with members of this family, which also includes carp *(see)* and chub *(see)*.

Minnows occur in Africa, Asia, Europe, and North America. Although this family attains its greatest diversity in Asia, it is the largest family of freshwater fish in North America, where more than 300 different species occur. The greatest diversity in North America exists in the southeastern United States, but minnows are widely distributed throughout North America—from Alaska to southern Mexico—and often represent a large proportion of species within regional fish faunas.

Minnows are used extensively as bait by anglers; keeping them lively in a proper well or container is especially important.

Well-known genera of native North American minnows include *Campostoma* (stonerollers), *Cyprinella* (satinfin shiners), *Gila* (Gila chub), *Luxilus* (highscale shiners), *Lythrurus* (smallscale shiners), *Nocomis* (chub), *Notropis* (true shiners), *Phoxinus* (redbelly dace), *Pimephales* (bluntnose minnows), *Ptychocheilus* (squawfish), and *Rhinichthys* (dace).

Identification. Minnows are characterized by a single dorsal fin, abdominally located pelvic fins, soft fin rays, cycloid scales, and a set of bones connecting the inner ear to the swim bladder. This last attribute is known as the Weberian apparatus and enhances the ability of minnows to detect sound.

Minnows do not have teeth in their mouths but instead grind food with pharyngeal teeth located in their throat. Males of many minnow species have keratinized bumps known as tubercles on their head, body, and fins. Tubercles may facilitate body contact during spawning, or they may be used in aggressive interactions between males. The large tubercles of chub and stonerollers have earned these species the nickname "hornyheads" among many anglers.

Even for ichthyologists, exact minnow species can be especially difficult to identify. Some useful characteristics include breeding coloration, location of tubercles on nuptial males, pharyngeal tooth counts, mouth shape, anal fin ray counts, various scale counts, and the presence or absence of barbels. Knowledge of species distribution aids in identification, especially when two similar-looking species have nonoverlapping ranges.

The best approach to minnow identification is to obtain a regional guide to fish containing both dichotomous keys and illustrations. Many excellent guides are available and can usually be obtained from university libraries, natural-history museums, and specialty bookstores.

Habitat. The ecological habitats of minnows are as diverse as the family itself. Minnows occur in creeks, streams, rivers, swamps, ponds, lakes, and impoundments. The majority of minnow species, however, occur in flowing waters and do not fare well in impoundments.

Food and feeding habits. Most species feed on aquatic insects, crustaceans, and detritus, but a few are specialized for feeding on algae or plankton. Larger species, such as chub in the genus *Semotilus,* or squawfish, prey on other fish.

Size/Age. The body size and life span of minnows vary widely. Adults of most minnow species are less than 100 millimeters long and live for two to five years. One of the smallest species is the blackmouth shiner *(Notropis melanostomus),* which may not exceed 37 millimeters in length. At the opposite end of the spectrum is North America's largest native minnow, the Colorado squawfish *(Ptychocheilus lucius),* which has been recorded to reach a total length of 1.8 meters and a weight of 45 kilograms. Minnows in this genus may live for more than 10 years.

Life history. Minnows exhibit a variety of life history attributes. The breeding season can be as short as one month, or last throughout the year. Many species reproduce between March and August, probably because warmer water temperatures are more conducive to the production of gametes and survival of larvae. Accordingly, the length of the breeding season is generally longer for species occurring in lower latitudes.

The number of eggs produced (or fecundity) by female minnows varies both within and among minnow species. In general, larger females can produce more eggs. The flagfin shiner *(Pteronotropis signipinnis),* for example, matures at lengths under 30 millimeters and releases an average of 32 eggs per clutch. In contrast, the giant Colorado squawfish *(Ptychocheilus lucius)* may produce around 20,000 eggs. Total fecundity is often underestimated because many minnows produce multiple clutches of eggs within a single spawning season. Aquarium-held bannerfin shiners *(Cyprinella leedsi),* for example, may release up to 228 eggs every 3 to 10 days. Multiple clutch production may ensure that individuals from at least one clutch survive, especially in stream environments where rapid changes in physical conditions can impact the survival of larval or juvenile fish.

Mature egg sizes in minnows range from about 0.6 millimeter to 2 millimeters in diameter. Species exhibiting territorial behavior or occurring in fast-water habitats generally produce the largest eggs. For example, the central stoneroller *(Campostoma anomalum)* is a territorial species that produces 2-millimeter eggs. In contrast, the cherryfin shiner *(Lythrurus roseipinnis),* a species characteristic of slow-flowing Gulf of Mexico coastal-plain streams, produces eggs that average 0.77 millimeter in diameter.

Spawning behavior. The reproductive behavior of North American minnows is fascinating and complex. Substantial variation in reproductive behavior exists within the family, but species can be grouped into a few general categories.

Broadcasting species scatter their eggs over plants, gravel, or the nests of other species and then abandon them. Broadcasters can spawn as pairs in which males clasp individual females, or as large groups in which it is less clear which males fertilize which eggs. The broadcasting strategy is used by the majority of species for which spawning behavior is known.

Crevice spawning occurs in many species of satinfin shiners and in the California roach *(Hesperoleucus symmetricus).* Males guard territories around the crevices associated with rocks and logs. Males and females swim next to each other alongside the crevice, and the female deposits eggs into it. Males may deposit sperm during solo runs along the crevice or while swimming with the female. Although no post-spawning parental care occurs in these species, fertilized eggs situated within the crevice are well protected from predation.

Pit, pit-ridge, and mound building all involve manipulation of the substrate by territorial males for the construction of spawning nests. Eggs laid within these types of nests may suffer lower mortality rates because of the presence of territorial males (which may deter egg predation), partial or full concealment within the substrate, and better aeration as a result of the hydraulic properties of the nest. The widely distributed striped shiner *(Luxilus chrysocephalus; see: shiner, striped)* is a pit spawner.

Eight species within the highscale shiners, as well as stonerollers, dig circular spawning pits in gravel with their snouts and mouths. More than one male may attempt to fertilize a female that swims over the pit.

Pit-ridge nests are constructed by chub in the genus *Semotilus.* Gravel is piled at the upstream portion of the nest upon completion of the initial pit. After spawning, males cover the eggs with gravel and dig another pit downstream of the just-formed ridge. The ridge can approach 2 meters in length as the male continues to bury the eggs from each spawning act. The pit-ridge nest of the fallfish *(Semotilus corporalis)* is the largest nest known among fish.

Mound building occurs in eight species of chub and cutlips minnows *(Nocomis* and *Exoglossum* species). As with pit-ridge nesters, the eggs are covered by the male after fertilization.

The ornate shiner *(Codoma ornata),* the pugnose minnow *(Opsopoeodus emiliae),* and the bluntnose minnow are egg clusterers. Eggs are laid in a single layer on the underside of a flat object. In addition to guarding the cavity, male bluntnose minnows increase survivorship of the eggs by removing fungused eggs with their mouths and fanning the egg mass. Male bluntnose minnows also rub the eggs with their nape, which may spread protective mucous layers over them.

Nest-associating minnows include roughly 25 species that spawn over the nests of other minnows, and about 10 species that spawn on sunfish nests. Most nest associates are categorized as broadcasters, but some species of highscale shiners and stonerollers can build pits or spawn over the nests of other species.

Value. Minnows are extremely important ecologically. They transfer energy throughout aquatic ecosystems by converting their detrital, algal, and microorganismal diets into fish flesh that can be eaten by larger fish. They are also an important food source for birds and other wildlife. Minnows serve as hosts to freshwater mussel larvae *(glochidia),* which attach to fish gills in order to disperse and complete early development. Many mussel species require a particular fish host, so the decline of certain minnow species may result in the decline and possibly the extinction of certain freshwater mussels.

Nest-building minnows are sometimes referred to as "keystone species" because their presence has a strong effect on many other species in aquatic communities. These nests not only provide spawning habitat for many other minnows, but the large number of eggs deposited in them may also be consumed by other species of fish and stream invertebrates.

Minnows are sought after and eaten by many anglers. In addition, they are used as bait and constitute a large proportion of the natural forage base upon which freshwater gamefish depend. Examples of species that are commonly fished for and eaten include chub of the genera *Nocomis* and *Semotilus,* the peamouth *(Mylocheilus caurinus),* the Sacramento blackfish *(Orthodon microlepidotus),* stonerollers, squawfish, and carp. Many of these species are taken with flies or artificial lures, and put up a good fight when caught with light or ultralight tackle.

Almost all minnow species are suitable for use as bait. Species such as the golden shiner *(Notemigonus crysoluecas)* and the fathead minnow *(Pimephales promelas)* are widely sold as bait because they are easy to culture in large quantities. Anglers can easily collect other species from streams by using a small seine net, but they should be familiar with state regulations before doing so.

Because of their abundance and broad range of body sizes, minnows are important forage items for many game species. Given their wide distribution throughout North America, the introduction of nonnative forage fish is usually unnecessary and potentially harmful to native fish.

Beyond their value to anglers, minnows contribute much to humanity. Many naturalists enjoy observing minnows in nature and keeping them in aquariums. Minnows that are sensitive to pollution can be monitored by aquatic biologists and used as indicators of stream health. The diverse lifestyle of minnows makes them ideal subjects for both education and research in biology, ecology, and evolution. Finally, the diversity of minnows makes them a significant component of aquatic biodiversity.

Conservation. Many species of North American minnows are endangered, threatened, of special concern, or thought to be declining by aquatic biologists. As of the early 1990s, 10 species were thought to be extinct and nearly 70 were listed as needing some form of legal protection. One group of minnows, the blackline shiners, is especially sensitive to habitat change and thus highly imperiled. Imperiled species in this group include the pugnose shiner *(Notropis anogenus),* the blackchin shiner *(Notropis heterodon),* and the bridle shiner *(Notropis bifrenatus).*

Other groups of minnows characterized by a high degree of imperilment include the satinfin shiners *(Cyprinella* species*),* minnows in the genus *Dionda,* and chub in the genus *Gila.* Examples of imperiled minnows from these genera are the turquoise shiner *(Cyprinella monacha),* the Devils river minnow *(Dionda diaboli),* and the Borax Lake chub *(Gila boraxobius).*

Imperiled minnows occur all over North America, but a high proportion of declining species occurs in the southwestern U.S. and northern Mexico. Causes of decline include chemical pollution, sedimentation, channelization, changes in flow regime, impoundments, introduced species, and general degradation of aquatic habitats.

A large threat to minnows and other fish is competition for food and other resources from introduced species. Introduced minnows can also transmit diseases to native fish and other aquatic life. Minnows are easily introduced outside their native range when they are transferred long distances in anglers' bait buckets. In addition, many bait shops sell nonindigenous minnows. To solve this problem, anglers could collect their own baits from the water they plan to fish and discard the unused baits in the same location. Alternatively, anglers can demand that local bait dealers stock only native minnows, and fisheries managers can monitor bait suppliers. Enforcement of water-quality regulations and the protection and restoration of aquatic habitats is also important.

See: Minnow, Fathead; Shiners; Shiner, Common; Shiner, Emerald; Shiner, Golden; Squawfish, Northern; Stoneroller, Central.

The production of baitcasting or levelwind reels began in 1810 when watchmaker George Snyder, President of the Bourbon County Anglers Association, built the first Kentucky reel.

MINNOW, FATHEAD *Pimephales promelas.*

Other names—minnow; French: *tête de boule.*

The fathead minnow is a small, hardy, and widely cultivated member of the Cyprinidae family of minnows that is commonly used as bait, and it is an important forage species for gamefish. It is also commonly used in toxicity studies.

Identification. The fathead minnow has a stubby, deep, compressed body with a short head that is flat on top. The snout is blunt. The mouth is small and slanted and possesses pharyngeal teeth. The body is generally dull in color, being dark olive or gray above and fading to muted yellow to white below. The scales become larger toward the tail and smaller toward the head, and the lateral line curves downward and is incomplete. There is a dark spot at the middle of the anterior dorsal rays, the caudal rays have dark outlines, and the leading edge of the pectoral fins is black. There is also a stout half-ray at the front of the dorsal fin. There are no barbels, but breeding males develop tubercles on the snout and become darker.

Size/Age. Fathead minnows average $1^1/_2$ to 3 inches long, and grow to only 4 inches. Most die in their third year.

Distribution. This species ranges widely (in part through introductions) across North America, from Quebec to the Northwest Territories and south to Alabama, Texas, and New Mexico, as well as in Mexico. It is most common in the Great Plains and scarce in mountainous regions.

Habitat. Fathead minnows prefer ponds and pools or slow-moving water in streams, creeks, and small rivers. They can tolerate muddy water and are occasionally found in roadside ditches.

Spawning behavior. Fathead minnows have an extended spawning period, from late spring into summer. It commences when the water temperature exceeds 60°F. They are nest spawners, often creating nest sites under floating or suspended objects or beneath logs or stones, generally in 1 to 3 feet of water. Males create the nests, herd the females into them, and guard the nest until the eggs hatch; several females may deposit eggs in one nest site, and the adhesive eggs hatch in six to nine days.

Food. The diet of fathead minnows is mostly algae, as well as bottom detritus, zooplankton, and insect larvae.

Angling. The fathead is a hardy minnow and widely used as a bait by anglers. It is raised commercially and sold not only to bait shops but also for stocking in ponds as forage for gamefish. Because of their small size, fathead minnows are consumed as forage by many species.

See: Minnows.

Fathead Minnow

MINNOW PLUG

A floating/diving plug that is minnow-shaped and mostly fished on or just beneath the surface.

See: Plug; Surface Lure.

MINNOW TRAP

See: Trap.

MISSISSIPPI

Mississippi anglers do not lack for places to fish. The Magnolia State offers not only large reservoirs, but also a number of large and small river oxbows on the Mississippi and Yalobusha Rivers, several impoundments on the Tennessee-Tombigbee Waterway, 21 publicly managed smaller lakes, and literally hundreds of miles of float fishing opportunities on several large creeks.

All told, some 175 different freshwater fish species have been identified in the state's waters. The most popular for anglers by far are largemouth bass, black crappie, white crappie, channel catfish, flathead catfish, blue catfish, bluegills, and redear sunfish. Other well-known species are also present, however, including smallmouth bass, pure-strain and hybrid striped bass, and sauger.

The southern portion of the state offers the added bonus of brackish water conditions where anglers may catch several common saltwater species, including redfish, flounder, and speckled trout. Farther offshore, easily reached barrier islands provide excellent small-boat and wading opportunities for additional species like Spanish and king mackerel, cobia, red snapper, and an occasional tarpon. Yet farther offshore, charter skippers search for billfish and dolphin.

Because of the state's generally warm climate, fishing is popular year-round. In the larger reservoirs, anglers use a variety of artificial lures for bass, but prefer live baits, primarily minnows and earthworms, to take crappie and sunfish.

Large Reservoirs

The best known of Mississippi's large reservoirs is Ross Barnett, a 30,000-acre impoundment of the Pearl River near the capital city of Jackson. The lake features a distinct mixture of open water, shallow grassbeds and flooded stumps, and winding river channel. Depending on the time of year and the type of water being fished, bass anglers often do well with spinnerbaits, topwater and shallow-running spoons, and plastic worms rigged weedless but weightless that are worked through stumps and over vegetation.

The spring months traditionally rank as the best time for crappie on Ross Barnett, and anglers use both live minnows as well as $^1/_8$- and even $^1/_{16}$-ounce hair jigs, sometimes tipped with a minnow, around stumps and timber along the Pearl River channel south of State Highway 43.

Other major impoundments wholly within Mississippi include Lakes Arkabutla, Sardis, Enid, and Grenada. All are old and basically shallow flood-control lakes, but at times each produces fine fishing action for several species, particularly bass, crappie, and catfish. The four lakes are located along a north-south line near Interstate Highway 55 between Memphis, Tennessee, and Grenada, Mississippi, and draw many anglers from western Tennessee.

Arkabutla is the northernmost of these four lakes; because it muddies quickly after a rain, it is best known for its blue and flathead catfish populations. Likewise, crappie fishing can be excellent at Arkabutla, particularly farther up the lake's two main tributaries, the Coldwater River and Hurricane Creek. Live minnows fished under floats work best for crappie here, whereas cat anglers prefer homemade baits concocted from a variety of foods like beef or chicken livers.

Crappie are also the primary attraction at Sardis Lake, but bass anglers do well in spring and fall, when the fish tend to move shallow on gravel banks and points. Major tributary creeks that have gained reputations for both species include Clear, Toby Tubby, Hurricane, Greasy, and Big Spring, all of which feature a variety of cover and structure.

Enid Reservoir, approximately 20 miles south of Sardis, is, like Sardis, an excellent crappie lake. In 1957 Enid produced the current 5-pound, 3-ounce world-record white crappie; heavier-than-usual crappies, generally referred to locally as "slabs," are caught each spring. The primary technique is working small hair jigs in 3 to 4 feet of water around brush and stumps, but plastic jigs and live minnows are also popular. When the fish are deeper than 5 or 6 feet, anglers here often use longer fly rods rigged with small spinning reels and light monofilament line, as the longer rods offer more precise depth control of lures or baits. Another technique is to cast a minnow or jig with a bobber and begin reeling it back. Periodically the retrieve is stopped to allow the bait or lure to sink slowly, and this is when strikes often occur.

At maximum pool, which is 64,000 acres, Grenada Lake is the state's largest reservoir. Autumn brings crappie anglers to the lake by the scores, but throughout the rest of the year anglers stay busy with largemouth bass, white bass, and channel catfish. A popular summer fishing technique is slow-trolling with live minnows, a tactic that often catches bass in addition to crappie.

In the northeast corner of the state, the Tennessee River makes a brief swing through Mississippi on its way from Alabama into Tennessee. This part of the river is impounded as Pickwick Lake, and, as in the Alabama portion of the lake, it produces excellent smallmouth fishing. Two significant tributaries, Yellow and Indian Creeks, flow into the lake from Mississippi, and both are well-known hotspots.

Mississippi's best smallmouth—a 7-pound, 15-ounce specimen—came from Yellow Creek. Spinnerbaits slow-rolled near deeper brush and over rocky points do well on smallmouth much of the year, but many anglers here have learned to drift small plastic grubs in the current on 6- or 8-pound line. In fall, large topwater plugs also produce well. In winter, walleye and sauger are also present, both of which are usually caught on $^1/_2$-ounce and heavier jigs crawled slowly along the bottom over rocky banks.

Near Meridian, Okatibbee Lake is a smaller impoundment but one that provides top action for bluegills, particularly in Twitley Branch and Gin Creeks. Special fish attractors have been constructed in various parts of this 3,800-acre lake, and these provide good places to try for crappie.

Tennessee-Tombigbee Waterway Lakes

The U.S. Army Corps of Engineers created a number of lakes along its 234-mile-long Tenn-Tom Waterway project between Pickwick Lake and the Gulf of Mexico, including several in Mississippi. Among these are Aberdeen, Columbus, and Aliceville, the last of which is shared with Alabama. Although the Tenn-Tom Waterway itself is essentially a 300-foot-wide barge canal, the lakes themselves provide extensive backwater areas for fishing.

In most Southern backwater areas, vegetation is common because the water is generally shallow. Stumps and standing timber are also present, especially at Columbus Lake, which, while making small-boat navigation occasionally difficult, provides excellent habitat for fish. Bass over 10 pounds have been taken from several of these Tenn-Tom lakes, usually in spring on spinnerbaits, buzzbaits, and shallow-running minnow-imitation plugs.

Mississippi River Oxbows

Anglers can choose from literally dozens of small to fairly large oxbow lakes of the Mississippi River, formed when the silt-laden river changed course and isolated a curve. Sometimes the oxbows are completely separated from the river; at other times they are open at one or both ends, and size can vary from less than 100 to several thousand acres. Most oxbows usually include an abundance of standing timber like willows and/or cypress trees, and they tend to have distinct deep-water channels as well as shallow-water flats.

Among the largest and best known Mississippi River oxbows are Tunica Cut-Off in northern Mississippi near the city of Tunica, DeSoto Lake near Clarksdale, and Lake Ferguson near Greenville. All three offer 2,500 or more acres of bass, crappie, and catfish action. Sunfish, particularly bluegills, are also present in most oxbow lakes and provide hours of entertainment for anglers armed with a simple cane pole and a bucket of small minnows.

Largemouth bass as well as striped bass are targeted by many anglers here. The stripers are taken with large topwater lures, jerkbaits, and heavy plastic grubs, whereas largemouth anglers often flip $^1/_2$-ounce jigs or soft-plastic lures around the cypress trees.

Game and Fish Commission Lakes

Over the past several decades, the Mississippi Department of Wildlife, Fisheries, and Parks has constructed 21 small public fishing lakes totaling 5,111 acres throughout the state. Ranging in size from 12 to 1,200 acres, these mini-impoundments are designed to provide fishing opportunities in areas where previously there were none. They are heavily stocked annually with largemouth bass, catfish, and sunfish to provide optimum enjoyment, and at least one of the lakes, Waller, has produced bass over 11 pounds. Neshoba County Lake is well known for its crappie population.

The lakes are open daily on a fee basis, and small aluminum boats may be rented on site. All boat operation is restricted to trolling speed only. Concession stands selling licenses, tackle, and limited picnic supplies are also available on each lake.

Float Fishing Streams

Mississippi offers a number of excellent streams for quiet float fishing, including Black Creek, a portion of which has been protected as a National Wild and Scenic Stream. Highway bridge crossings offer excellent put-in/take-out points for lengthy trips; one popular Black Creek float begins at U.S. Highway 98 east of Hattiesburg and continues to U.S. Highway 11, a distance of about 12 miles. Other Black Creek float trips are available in the Desoto National Forest south of Hattiesburg.

Another popular waterway for canoe and jonboat anglers is the Bogue Chitto River south of Brookhaven. Many different trip options are available on this stream, which actually leaves Mississippi and flows through lower Louisiana all the way to the Gulf of Mexico. The Pearl, Leaf, and Chickasawhay Rivers also offer scenic floats through the southern portion of the state.

On all of these waterways, anglers find both largemouth and spotted bass, crappie, warmouth, a variety of sunfish, and channel catfish. Most use lighter spinning tackle with down-size lures like spinnerbaits, crankbaits, and topwater plugs to fill a stringer. In some areas fly fishing is popular but can be difficult because of low, overhanging branches. Overnight camps are frequently set up on river sandbars, and here anglers bait bottom rigs with doughballs or homemade "stinkbaits" for catfish.

Gulf Coast

Because several important rivers, including the Pearl, Pascagoula, and Biloxi, flow into the gulf along the 90-mile-long Mississippi coast, anglers have the chance to fish brackish water, where largemouth bass and channel bass may hit on successive casts. The Biloxi and Pascagoula areas, especially, offer dozens of miles of winding rivers, secluded bays, and small bayous for this type of fishing.

Inshore saltwater opportunities in St. Louis Bay near Pass Christian as well as Biloxi Bay offer protected fishing for flounder and other shallow species. Offshore the coastline is also somewhat protected by a string of small, separate islands—Grand, Cat, Ship, Horn, and Petit Bois—which together form the federally controlled Gulf Islands National Seashore. These islands offer good surf, wading, and small-boat angling for speckled trout, flounder, bluefish, and redfish. Still farther offshore the Chandeleur Islands are nationally famous for redfish and trout action; anglers can charter boats or planes in Gulfport to take them to the islands for trips lasting one to several days.

Biloxi, Gulfport, Ocean Springs, and Pascagoula all support charter fleets that regularly comb gulf waters for mackerel, snapper, dolphin, grouper, tripletail, and other species. Many skippers have created private artificial reefs just offshore for red snapper. Bottom fishing and trolling are popular around the area's many old oil platforms and artificial reefs. In the blue water 50 to 100 miles out, sailfish and blue marlin are taken during the summer months by many of these charter boats.

MISSOURI

The angler looking at a map of Missouri might suppose that two mighty rivers, the Missouri and the Mississippi, provide a lot of fishing. They don't. Both suffered such severe navigation development that the immense fishery they once represented is today a fragment of its former self. Nevertheless, Missouri offers abundant angling for a landlocked state, and this potential is fairly diverse, thanks to 13 large reservoirs, thousands of smaller reservoirs, and many rivers and streams.

The quality of the state's gamefishing is largely due to an excellent conservation agency. The Missouri Conservation Department, which for several decades has been the best-funded and best state conservation agency in the nation, has used scientific research to develop and maintain healthy fish populations in most of the state's waterways.

The largemouth bass ranks first with both resident and nonresident anglers in the Show-Me State, and it is followed closely in popularity by crappie. Next, in descending order, come catfish, sunfish, white bass, smallmouth bass, walleye, sauger, and, surprisingly, trout. Missouri even has muskellunge, which are stocked in two of the state's reservoirs, and includes among its fish populations in certain waters striped bass, hybrid stripers, paddlefish, freshwater drum, and carp.

Most people coming to Missouri to fish do so in one or more of the larger reservoirs. Many also come to fish and float the streams of the Ozarks. A smaller number pursue trout, primarily rainbows and, in a few places, browns, stocked in water kept cold by either spring discharges or deep-reservoir discharges, usually referred to as tailwaters.

Major Reservoirs

Missouri's important reservoirs are primarily in the southern half of the state. These vary in size but generally support a great deal of recreational activity. They are subject to some water-level fluctuation, as they are also used for generating power and controlling floods. They're listed here in order of total acreage, which is not necessarily an indication of fishing prominence, which can vary.

Lake of the Ozarks. This sprawling, twisting mid-Missouri reservoir is about 35 miles southwest of Jefferson City, nearly midway between Kansas City and St. Louis, and is at the heart of Missouri's biggest and most developed vacation area. Lake of the Ozarks is a 59,520-acre reservoir originally built for power generation but now little-used for that purpose. Much of its acreage is subject to intense use from all manner of boaters, and the lake is ringed with houses and boat docks. Those docks, in fact, provide the primary cover for bass and therefore the main fishing action for largemouths.

Lake of the Ozarks is deep, clear, and beautiful, particularly in the lower end, which is more like a typical highland impoundment. The lake becomes progressively more stained as you head to the upper sections, especially in the Osage and Niangua arms. It has an excellent number of largemouth bass, and has been known for many of these in the 3- to 5-pound range. It also has good numbers of white bass, crappie, and catfish, as well as paddlefish (a state-record paddlefish—134 pounds, 12 ounces—was snagged in the Niangua arm in 1998). Many of the biggest bass are caught in late winter, prior to the spawn, and April and May are especially good for quantity.

Truman Lake. Located in west-central Missouri and west of Lake of the Ozarks, Truman Lake, also known as Harry S Truman Reservoir, is a 55,600-acre U.S. Army Corps of Engineers flood-control and recreation reservoir on the Osage, Grand, and Pomme de Terre Rivers. With 958 miles of shoreline, it has countless coves, sloughs, and embayments along the main lake as well as in the many creek and river feeders.

Truman is unlike many other Missouri reservoirs in that it does not contain great depths or clarity. The water is predominantly muddy or stained, and the average depth at normal times is just 15 feet. It contains good populations of largemouth bass, white bass, crappie, bluegills, and catfish, as well as burgeoning walleye and striper numbers.

The flooded timber of Truman Lake provides challenging cover to fish for bass.

The tailwater below Truman Dam, which forms the upper reaches of the Osage Arm of Lake of the Ozarks, is an excellent place to fish when water flow is heavy.

Bull Shoals Reservoir. Straddling the Arkansas-Missouri line in the deepest part of the Ozarks, Bull Shoals is a 45,440-acre Corps of Engineers flood-control and recreation reservoir on the White River. It has 740 miles of shoreline, most of it rocky bluffs and ledges. Like other mountain waters, it is extremely clear and deep, and sometimes difficult to fish, yet it is annually considered one of the best lakes in Missouri. Bull Shoals is favored over its neighboring reservoir, Table Rock, by many anglers because it doesn't get as crowded with other boaters, due to fewer amenities and houses on the lake and a more remote location.

Bull Shoals is known for excellent largemouth bass, smallmouth bass, and spotted bass fishing, as well as renowned tributary runs of white bass in the spring. Crappie, bluegills, catfish, and walleye, as well as some rainbow trout in the lower end, round out most of the fishing, and there's good striped bass angling as well. The cold water in the White River below Bull Shoals Dam provides some of the country's best trout fishing.

Table Rock Reservoir. Located in far southwestern Missouri near Branson, this is a popular lake for varied recreation, yet one that annually supports excellent bass fishing. A highland reservoir with deep structure and rocky shoreline, Table Rock is 70 miles long and covers 43,100 acres at conservation pool. Viewed on a map, Table Rock is serpentine, with countless nooks, crannies, and bends that befit its location in the up-and-down Ozark hills.

Though it was impounded in the 1950s, Table Rock continues to produce good fishing for largemouth bass, spotted bass, smallmouth bass, white bass, and crappie, and also holds catfish and paddlefish. A lot of deep fishing is done here, and angling can be good throughout the year. Winter fishing for spotted bass and largemouths is good, and larger specimens tend to be caught from February through April.

Lake Stockton. About 51 road miles northeast of Springfield in the Ozarks of southwestern Missouri, Lake Stockton is a 25,000-acre Corps of Engineers flood-control, power, and recreation reservoir on the Sac River that was fully impounded in 1971. It contains good populations of largemouth bass, walleye, and crappie, and is considered by many an overlooked body of water. Smallmouth bass, white bass, bluegills, and catfish are also present. Smallmouths aren't abundant, but they have been of good size; the lake produced a state-record 7.2-pound smallmouth in 1994.

Ultraclear water often makes this lake hard to fish. That water clarity makes it a favorite with divers, however. It is also popular with sailors, who take advantage of its preponderance for wind. Being somewhat like a prairie lake, Stockton does not benefit from the protection of hills, as other Missouri impoundments do, so it is prone to wind at all times, especially early in the year.

Norfork Lake. Straddling the Arkansas-Missouri border, Norfolk is a 22,000-acre Corps of Engineers flood-control and recreation reservoir on the North Fork River. Only a small segment of the lake actually extends into Missouri.

Norfolk contains good populations of largemouth, smallmouth, spotted and white bass, crappie, bluegills, and catfish, as well as a good population of striped bass, which are maintained through annual stocking by Arkansas. It is an extremely clear, deep reservoir that is sometimes tough to fish. Cold water from Norfork Dam provides some of the country's best angling for large brown trout in the lower North Fork River in Arkansas.

Mark Twain Lake. Located in northeastern Missouri between Perry and Monroe City and about 30 miles southeast of Hannibal, this is an 18,600-acre flood-control and recreation reservoir on the Salt River. Pretty, and with many protected coves, Mark Twain Lake was created in 1984, making it one of the newer reservoirs in this state. The lake contains good populations of black bass, white bass, crappie, bluegills, and channel catfish, but also has flathead catfish and walleye.

Smithville Lake. Located about 20 miles north of Kansas City in northwestern Missouri, Smithville Lake is an 8,040-acre Corps of Engineers reservoir impounded in 1980 for flood control and recreation. Despite intense fishing pressure, the lake has produced good fishing, in part owing to an abundance of weeds and flooded timber, and in part to 175 miles of shoreline fishing opportunity. Largemouth bass are the mainstays here, but the lake also has crappie, bluegills, and catfish. March through May are good times to beat the crowds and garner largemouths.

Pomme de Terre Reservoir. A 7,820-acre Corps of Engineers flood-control and recreation reservoir on the Pomme de Terre River, this lake is situated in western Missouri south of Truman Lake and northeast of Lake Stockton, and about 60 miles from Springfield. It has good populations of largemouth bass, white bass, crappie, bluegills, and catfish, and Missouri's best population of muskellunge. Despite being small, Pomme de Terre has been ranked among Missouri's best bass fishing waters, and it has had less angling pressure than this state's better-known and larger reservoirs. Fall and winter are top bass periods.

Wappapello Reservoir. This southeastern-Missouri impoundment is 15 miles north of Poplar Bluff, with major access on the southern part of the lake around the town of Wappapello. A Corps of Engineers flood-control impoundment, Wappapello has 7,200 acres at normal summer level, and is narrow, shallow, pretty, and relatively easy to fish. It usually provides good crappie fishing all winter, and is one of the state's best early-spring fishing spots.

Thomas Hill Reservoir. A 4,500-acre reservoir built to provide cooling water for a coal-fired power plant, Thomas Hill is roughly 30 miles northwest of Moberly. It has a good population of catfish of all sizes, some largemouth bass, and a good population of white crappie. The best fishing usually occurs in the winter, especially around the hotwater outlet in Brush Creek Cove.

Long Branch Lake. Although it often doesn't get the credit, Long Branch is one of the best big-bass waters in Missouri. Situated near Macon in Mark Twain's area of northeast Missouri, Long Branch is a 2,400-acre Corps of Engineers flood-control lake that is not heavily fished. It has a good population of channel catfish of all sizes, a good population of largemouth bass, including fish larger than 6 pounds, plus many small crappie and carp. It is frequently muddy because of siltation in the watershed.

Lake Taneycomo. Near Branson in far southwestern Missouri, Taneycomo is a 1,730-acre hydroelectric and recreation reservoir on the White River, sandwiched between Table Rock and Bull Shoals Reservoirs. Cold water from Table Rock Dam makes this small lake hospitable for rainbow and brown trout, which are stocked frequently by state fisheries personnel. Narrow, protected, and more river than lake in its upper half, Taneycomo provides some of the best trout fishing in mid-America.

Clearwater Reservoir. Situated in southeastern Missouri about 150 miles south of St. Louis, Clearwater is the smallest of Missouri's major reservoirs and sometimes difficult to fish because of superclear water. A 1,650-acre Corps of Engineers flood-control and recreation reservoir on the Black River, it contains good populations of largemouth bass, spotted bass, white bass, crappie, bluegills, and catfish.

Smaller Reservoirs

In one count made several decades ago, Missouri was found to have some 200,000 ponds and small lakes. The biggest and best of these for public fishing are impoundments either owned or managed by such government agencies as the Missouri Department of Conservation (MDC), the U.S. Forest Service, and the Division of Natural Resources (the state park agency), or by individual counties and municipalities.

The MDC manages or shares management of nearly three dozen of these reservoirs, which range in size from less than 100 up to 300 acres. Fishing in these impoundments varies from pretty good to excellent, primarily with warmwater species. These reservoirs exist all over the state, and information about them is available from the MDC.

Streams

The streams of the northern half of Missouri are prairie-like in character. Access can be difficult, but access sites have been developed on many. Catfish are the primary species caught from these streams.

The primary stream fishing interest in Missouri exists in the Ozarks, a river-carved uplift covering much of this state south of the Missouri River and extending into Arkansas. Ozark Mountain streams, which draw many out-of-state anglers, are gentle, clear, and crooked, which makes for perfect canoeing water. The rocky bluff banks provide habitat for smallmouth bass, which are highly prized among Missouri anglers, although the primary species is the goggle-eye (rock bass).

Most Ozark streams are not floatable, being too small to be passable most of the year. These "wading streams" represent a good many areas to fish, but it isn't easy to find them or get access because almost all of them flow through private land. Fishing on them can be tough because of the small size and clarity of the water. But so pretty and pleasant is a float on these streams that catching a fish, even a small one, is a bonus.

A brief description of the most important float streams in the Ozarks follows. Access to these is easy because they are all served by liveries, which provide both canoes and transportation to and from the river. All an angler has to do is show up.

Meramec River. About 100 miles of this fine stream is considered canoe water. The best floats and most of the liveries are in the upper third of the Meramec, from Missouri Rt. 8 near St. James to Meramec State Park near Sullivan. Many stretches as far down as St. Louis County are optimal for fishing and floating.

Huzzah and Courtois Creeks. Pretty little tributaries of the Meramec, the Huzzah and Courtois offer excellent floating when they have enough water. The most dependable floats are the lower 12 miles of the Huzzah and lower 18 miles of the Courtois. Some of the liveries on the Meramec offer floats on these creeks.

Bourbeuse River. The Bourbeuse is a gentle, crooked little stream with some attractive stretches. Not all sections are served by canoe liveries.

Big River. A long tributary of the Meramec, the Big River features sporty riffles spaced between long, slow holes. Fishing is surprisingly good. Not all stretches are served by liveries.

Black River. This beautiful Black River is extremely popular with St. Louis-area floaters. The best floating is in the 13 miles below Lesterville. On the three forks above Lesterville, canoeing is fun only when water flow is sufficient. Below Clearwater Lake the Black is somewhat slower and better known for its fishing.

Current River. The Current is the most famous of Missouri's float streams. About 135 miles of this stream, which with the Jacks Fork forms the Ozark National Scenic Riverway, is considered float water. From Montauk for the first few miles downstream the flow is sometimes not adequate for canoeing. Below Doniphan the river broadens and slows. Canoe liveries rent canoes only within their districts.

Jacks Fork River. The beautiful Jacks Fork River, which is part of the Ozark National Scenic Riverway, offers the best floating in Missouri when it has enough water. Only the 13 miles below Alley Spring are floatable all summer. The stretch above Alley, when floatable, is not for beginners.

Big Niangua River. The Big Nianqua is within an easy drive of Lake of the Ozarks. About 44 miles, from Williams Ford to Mill Creek, is considered canoe water. The most popular floats are those above and below Bennett Spring State Park, near Lebanon.

Gasconade River. Known more as a fishing stream than a canoeing stream, the Gasconade nevertheless has many stretches rewarding to the canoeist. Over most of its 300 miles, though, the Gasconade spaces its sporty stretches between long, slow holes. The best canoe water is the 150-mile section between Competition, near Lynchburg, to the Paydown access, near Vienna. Some stretches are not served by canoe liveries.

Big Piney River. A long, gentle tributary of the Gasconade, the Big Piney is scenic in its upper and middle stretches and is worth floating and fishing all the way through Fort Leonard Wood to the Gasconade above Jerome.

North Fork River. Clear, cold, and beautiful, the North Fork has few long holes and many

M

According to The Guinness Book of Records, the ocean sunfish (Mola mola) produces up to 300 million eggs at a single spawning.

sporty stretches with spectacular scenery. Flowing through rugged, remote segments of the deep Ozarks, it eventually joins Bryant Creek and becomes Norfork Lake just north of the Arkansas border. About 29 miles, from Twin Bridges to Tecumseh, is prime canoe water in all but the driest summers.

Bryant Creek. A tributary of the North Fork, Bryant Creek is smaller, more crooked, and less popular, but almost as beautiful. Only about 17 miles, from Hodgson Mill to the North Fork, is considered year-round float water.

Eleven Point River. Eleven Point, a national scenic river administered by the U.S. Forest Service, flows through some of the most rugged and remote country in the Ozarks. For several miles it forms the western border of the famed Irish Wilderness. The best floats are from Greer Spring to Riverton. Inflow from Greer nearly doubles the size of the river. The stretches above Greer are floatable only during wet weather.

Other Waters

The Missouri River provides relatively little fishing in Missouri and is not a pleasant place to be, thanks to channelization done for navigation between 1950 and 1980. The river is a flop for navigation because it is so swift and narrow. Its fishing is primarily for catfish with some crappie, bass, and carp fishing in the small remaining backwaters.

The Mississippi in Missouri, too, is channelized and provides limited sportfishing. Above St. Louis, the pools behind navigation dams provide some slack water and some angling opportunity. The most notable fishery in the Mississippi is for sauger in the raceways below the dams at Winfield, Clarksville, and Saverton. The fishing is good only in winter, when the freeze-up in northern states clears the river and limits its flow.

Trout fishing in Missouri is essentially found in three venues. One is Lake Taneycomo, previously described. Another is the four trout parks: Maramec Spring, Bennett Spring, Montauk Spring, and Roaring River. These public parks provide put-and-take fishing for rainbows stocked daily in major spring branches. The third trout fishing possibility is the dozen or so small spring branches both public and private; four have small populations of self-sustaining rainbows, and the rest are stocked.

MODULUS

A measure of how effectively a material resists deformation. Modulus can also be considered a measure of how quickly a material recovers after being flexed. This term is used in conjunction with tensile, which means to place a material under a tension load, and is often used by fishing rod manufacturers in describing rod blank properties. A high-tensile-modulus material, for example, is one that has a stiff structure and a high stiffness-to-weight ratio.

This is an overused and often misunderstood word in fishing rod manufacture. Modulus alone is not an indicator of the quality of a rod, since many other factors, including the amount and quality of the resin, the taper design, and the wall thickness of the blank, affect action and performance.

See: Rod, Fishing.

MOJARRA

Mojarra are members of the Gerridae family of tropical and subtropical saltwater fish. Roughly 40 species are in this family, some of which also occur in brackish water and a few rarely in freshwater. They are small and silvery and have a protractile mouth. The upper jaw of the mojarra fits into a defined slot when the mouth is not extended, or "pursed." When feeding, the mouth is protruded and directed downward. The dorsal and anal fins have a sheath of scales along the base, and the gill membranes are not united to the isthmus. The first, or spiny, dorsal fin is high in front, sloping into the second, or soft-rayed, dorsal. The tail is deeply forked.

Most mojarra are less than 10 inches long. They are important for predator species and are used as baits by some anglers. Some species are observed in schools on sandy, shallow flats.

The spotfin mojarra *(Eucinostomus argenteus)* is abundant in the western Atlantic off the coast from New Jersey to Brazil. It occurs in the eastern Pacific along the coast from Southern California to Peru. The yellowfin mojarra *(Gerres cinereus)* is common in Florida and the Caribbean.

Yellowfin Mojarra

MOLD

A preshaped form into which molten lead or plastic is poured for making sinkers, weights, and soft-plastic lure bodies by hobbyists; molds for hobby use may be purchased from large tackle retailers or mail-order suppliers. Molds are used in the commercial manufacture of many fishing and boating products, including lures, terminal tackle, fishing reels, boat hulls, and many other items.

MOLLUSK

A group of freshwater and saltwater animals with no skeleton and usually one or two hard shells made of calcium carbonate. This group includes the oyster, clam, mussel, snail, conch, scallop, squid, and octopus. Mollusks may be used as bait when angling, but they are not targeted by anglers or deliberately sought with sporting equipment.

MONGOLIA

Sandwiched between Siberian Russia and northern China, Mongolia is a large country about the size of western Europe. It has a small population of 2.4 million that is 40 percent nomadic. It encloses the Gobi Desert and is distinguished geographically by Inner Mongolia, which is the area between the Gobi Desert and the Great Wall of China on the south, and Outer Mongolia.

Tourism is not well developed; it opened to Westerners only in 1990. Nevertheless, opportunities for adventurous anglers exist in unusual places for various species, including grayling, pike, whitefish, lenok, several species of sturgeon, and, especially, taimen, the world's largest salmonid. Dry fly fishing is said to be excellent in the northern regions of Mongolia, where ultraclear water offers superb sight fishing conditions. Taimen there range from 27 to 66 inches in length; they can be caught in the 30- to 40-pound range and may weigh from 60 to 100 pounds. Lenok, which are a brown trout look-alike, range from 2 to 8 pounds.

Mongols are generally hunters, not anglers, and fish is not part of their diet, so there is little to no subsistence, commercial, or recreational angling for fish by natives. When they do fish for taimen, Mongols use heavy trotlines that are baited with meat, or they use lures made of marmot or sheep skin and that look like rodents.

Mongolia's geographic location causes its rivers and streams to be located in or course through the Arctic, Pacific, and Central Asian drainage basins.

The Arctic Basin contains about one-fourth of Mongolia's landmass and is comprised of the Selenge River and its tributaries, which flow northerly and across the Russian border into Lake Baikal; the Shishkhed River west of Lake Hovsgol; and the Bulban River in Khovd Province. There are 25 species here, including sturgeon, burbot, northern pike, lenok, perch, and whitefish.

The Pacific Basin, which is in the northeastern region and contains about 11 percent of the country's landmass, includes the Onon, Uldz, Kherlen, and Khalkhin Gol Rivers. These flow easterly and merge with Russia's Amur River. The area harbors 41 species, including sturgeon, grayling, taimen, carp, and whitefish, and possibly pike, Dolly Varden, and charr.

There is no ocean drainage for the remaining 64 percent of Mongolia's territory, which blends into the vast closed Central Asia drainage basin. In the northwest, this area includes saline Uvs Lake, which is Mongolia's largest lake by surface area, as well as Khar Us, Khar, and Khyargas Lakes. In the central region, it includes the Gobi Altai Mountains and the Valley of the Lakes between the Khangai Mountains. Only five species have been identified here, among them grayling.

There are reportedly more than 4,000 lakes in Mongolia, most of them freshwater. Thirty percent of the lakes are found in the mountainous regions. Lake Hovsgol is the 14th largest lake in the world, the deepest lake in Central Asia, and the largest in Mongolia by water volume. There are nearly 100 tributaries to Hovsgol, but just one outflow, the Egiin River, which runs southeast to the Selenge River. Siberian grayling and lenok are the major sportfishing attractions among nine species of fish in this lake, which is said to be one of the purest large bodies of freshwater in the world.

Mongolian lakes experience a large swing in climatic conditions. They become warm in the summer, peaking in July and August; the temperature drops markedly in September and gradually until mid-November. Lakes are thickly frozen from late November until late May or early June.

There are some 1,200 rivers and streams in Mongolia with a total length of 70,000 kilometers. The rivers generally start to warm up in late April and rise in temperature until July. In August they gradually decrease until November when they freeze. All of the rivers freeze, and stay frozen for between 140 and 180 days. Late summer is reportedly a prime time for taimen sight fishing, as this is when the rivers are at their lowest and clearest stage, although the best chances for catching large individuals at this time may be at night; smaller fish are reportedly plentiful during the day in some locations in August.

Opportunities to fish in this wild and rugged country are provided by several adventure travel agencies.

See: China.

MONKFISH

A common name for the goosefish *(see).*

MONOFILAMENT (LINE)

See: Line.

MONTANA

Montana's fisheries are vast and varied, as befits a state that ranks fourth among the 50 United States in land area, encompasses 1,490 square miles of inland water, and contains a plethora of rivers, some of which progress eventually to the Gulf of Mexico and the Pacific Ocean. These are among the most heralded trout flows in North America. Though piscatorially associated with various trout, the Treasure

M

State also has warmwater fishing opportunities, and provides anglers with great choice in fishing experiences due to a large land area, a low population density, and a broad diversity of water types.

These waters include 26 sizable rivers and their attendant tributaries, at least 10 mountain ranges and wilderness areas offering breathtaking alpine angling opportunities in streams and ponds; 30 large lakes and reservoirs; and nearly a hundred smaller lakes.

As a headwaters state, Montana features pristine waters that are born in mountain snowmelt and grow from unnamed trickles and streams to celebrated rivers and lakes. The headwaters of both the Missouri and Columbia Rivers, for example, begin high in the mountains, and there are many others along the Continental Divide, which runs through Montana from Canada and Glacier National Park in the north to Idaho, Wyoming, and Yellowstone National Park in the south.

As is true in other places, fishing in Montana may be approached by type of water, targeted species, or location. In general, warmwater fisheries are east of a north-south line running from the Canadian border to just west of Billings, and coldwater fisheries are west of that. Both fisheries exist in some bodies of water, however, and the various geographic regions of Montana are delightfully distinct, offering different fishing experiences.

No matter where or when an angler fishes in Montana, the time of year and weather conditions play a major role in determining success. For example, many Montana rivers experience huge runoffs in late spring to midsummer, which can affect how to fish a particular river. Factors like snowmelt in the spring, or irrigation on some rivers in the summer, could suggest that another time of year or a different site be selected.

Tourism is among the leading industries in the state, so visitors can expect to be treated cordially in Montana, and tackle shop owners are more than happy to offer sound advice on local conditions.

Species

The cutthroat trout is Montana's state fish, and although it is native to the state, it is gone from much of its original territory. The Westslope cutthroat is native west of the Continental Divide and in some of the drainages located east of the divide, where it is referred to as the upper Missouri cutthroat. Yellowstone cutthroat are native to the Yellowstone River drainage. The cutthroat also goes by the names blackspotted, red-belly, native, and flat cutthroat. It inhabits cool, clear mountain streams and lakes. The cutthroat is similar to a rainbow trout but has a red slash on its lower jaw. There are crosses between the different cutthroat species and between cutthroats and rainbows, all of which are difficult to identify. Cutthroat trout in Montana are roughly 10 inches long but may grow to 18 inches.

Rainbow trout are found throughout Montana but are native to the Kootenai River drainage in the northwest. Montana rainbows typically average 12 inches but may reach 24. Brown trout are an introduced species most common in the lower reaches of fairly large streams and also found in reservoirs or lakes that have suitable tributaries for spawning. Browns here are often 13 inches long but seldom longer than 24 inches.

Brook trout were also introduced to the state and inhabit small spring-fed streams and ponds. Widespread in clear, cold streams and lakes, and frequently found in high-mountain beaver ponds, they are often 9 inches in length but seldom more than 16 inches.

The golden trout, also introduced, exists in fewer than a dozen high-mountain lakes in southern and southwestern Montana, whereas numerous lakes have golden-rainbow hybrids or golden-cutthroat hybrids. The golden trout does well in the harsh conditions of high-mountain lakes and streams as well as in clear, cold lakes at lower elevations. Golden trout routinely are 10 inches but seldom bigger than 18 inches.

The bull trout is native to Montana and was called the Dolly Varden until 1978, when the primarily inland form of the fish was designated as a separate species—the bull trout. The fish does best in large, coldwater streams but also inhabits smaller streams and lakes that have a tributary to ascend to spawn. Bull trout routinely are 16 inches long and may get as big as 36 inches. Their numbers are dwindling in Montana.

The lake trout is native in Elk, Twin, St. Mary, and Waterton Lakes and is also known as mackinaw. Inhabiting deep, cold lakes and reservoirs, this species averages 22 inches but may grow to 40 inches.

The kokanee is a landlocked sockeye salmon that was introduced to the state. It inhabits cold, clear lakes and reservoirs and ascends streams to spawn. Kokanee are found in the far northwestern region, at three or four sites in central Montana, and in Fort Peck Reservoir in northeastern Montana. The typical size is 11 inches, but the fish may reach 18 inches.

Native mountain whitefish are found throughout the western third of the state and in the streams of the mountainous portions of southern Montana. It is common in medium-size and large, clear, cold rivers and some lakes and reservoirs. Whitefish are common at 12 inches and may reach 20 inches.

The arctic grayling, also known as the Montana grayling, is rare in the lower 48 states, but they are found in certain areas of Montana. Historically, the fish is a stream species but now mostly inhabits mountain lakes where it has been planted. The upper reaches of the Big Hole River in southwestern Montana, as well as a few mountain streams in northwestern Montana, can yield grayling. Grayling normally are 10 inches long but may reach 18 inches.

Northern pike are native to the St. Mary River drainage but are also found extensively throughout eastern, north-central, and northeastern Montana. They are prevalent in some far northwestern waters. The fish is common at 20 inches but may grow to 45 inches.

The shovelnose sturgeon is a large-river and reservoir fish that can tolerate turbid water. Native to Montana and also known as hackleback, this fish has a snout shaped like a shovel. It is similar to the pallid sturgeon. The shovelnose commonly is 32 inches long in Montana but can reach 41 inches.

Paddlefish are native to Montana and thrive year-round in Fort Peck Reservoir and in the tailwater below Fort Peck Dam. In the spring, these fish spawn upriver in the lower reaches of both the Missouri and Yellowstone Rivers. They commonly grow to 60 inches, but some 72-inch specimens have been caught.

Channel catfish are native and are found in many reaches of the Missouri and Yellowstone River systems. A 17-inch channel cat is common, but they seldom exceed 30 inches. Black bullhead were introduced and are found in creeks, rivers, and farm ponds of eastern Montana, as well as in a few lower areas of far northwestern Montana.

Burbot, also known as ling, are native to Montana and are a popular species. Found in large rivers and cold, deep lakes and reservoirs, burbot are commonly caught at 20 inches long, and they sometimes attain 30 inches.

All of the various sunfish and perch in the state were introduced. Largemouth bass inhabit the eastern third of the state and a small portion of northwestern Montana, which is at lower elevation. Smallmouths favor isolated stretches of the Bighorn, Musselshell, Yellowstone, Milk, and Tongue Rivers, and Fort Peck, Homestead, South Sandstone, and Tongue River Reservoirs. Both species are regularly 11 inches long but can grow to 18 inches.

Pumpkinseed may be found in some of the same waters as smallmouth bass; bluegills are in only about a dozen or fewer areas in eastern Montana; green sunfish are present in some far southeastern waters; rock bass are in the Tongue River; crappie are in the Bighorn, Stillwater, and Yellowstone Rivers, Fort Peck Reservoir, Lake Elwell, and portions of the Missouri River above Fort Peck Reservoir.

Yellow perch, which are a favorite panfish with Montana's ice anglers, are available throughout the eastern third of the state, a large portion of northwestern Montana's lower-elevation waters, and the Missouri River and its tributaries. Eight-inch perch are most common, and they occasionally reach 15 inches.

Walleye are found in the Bighorn, Marias, Milk, Missouri, Stillwater, and Yellowstone Rivers, in Lake Elwell, and in Fort Peck and Canyon Ferry Reservoirs. Sixteen-inch walleye are common, and occasionally 30-inchers are taken. Canyon Ferry has produced some 19- and 20-pound walleye.

A brown trout comes to the net of a Montana fly angler.

Sauger, also called sand pike, are prevalent in all of the walleye waters and in the Tongue River in southeastern Montana. They range from 13 inches all the way up to an occasional 24-incher.

Northwest Region

Flathead Lake/Flathead River. Flathead Lake is the largest natural freshwater lake west of the Mississippi River and a particularly scenic Montana destination. Its surface encompasses more than 125,000 acres, and its shoreline covers 185 miles. Fishing is a prime draw, but the highly accessible lake is also heavily used by sailors, powerboaters, cruise boat enthusiasts, and the like, which makes for a lot of summertime activity.

Nevertheless, Flathead is known for trout, salmon, perch, and whitefish angling. Lake trout to more than 40 pounds have been recorded, as have bull trout of 26 pounds. The deeper waters between Melita and Wild Horse Islands, in Skidoo Bay north of Finley Point, and in the vicinity of Angel Point south of Lakeside on the west shore, are prime laker territory.

Kokanee salmon are found in Flathead also, especially in Big Arm and Elmo Bays; off the islands in the Narrows at the north end of Polson Bay; and in Skidoo, Blue, Yellow, and Woods Bays. At least a dozen public access points beckon around the lake.

The Flathead River is part of a system unique to Montana. The North, Middle, and South Forks converge to form the Flathead River, which eventually flows into Flathead Lake. Fishing any of the forks is more of a sightseeing trip than a fishing expedition. The forks run out from the wilderness and are spectacular rivers, but they are low on nutrients and support marginal populations of fish. Most of the fish live in Flathead Lake and run up the river to spawn. All three rivers are spotty at best for cutthroat and bull trout.

The Kootenai River. The Kootenai is rainbow trout water, and what's left of the river in Montana—Libby Dam flooded the upper half—produces some lunkers. Anglers occasionally land cutthroats, which probably were washed over the dam, and bull trout. A population of white sturgeon frequents the river, but their numbers are scarce and their fate is uncertain.

Anglers using baits, lures, and flies can all do well on the Kootenai. Fly anglers might be advised to try the waters between Libby and Kootenai Falls, known locally as "the Rocks." The river from Libby Dam to Libby and from below Kootenai Falls to the old Troy Bridge has some fine holes and would be good territory for bait and lure users.

Lake Koocanusa. Lake Koocanusa, created by damming the Kootenai River above its confluence with the Fisher River above the town of Libby, is entirely surrounded by national forest land, but access is challenging because the surrounding terrain is steep and boat launch sites are scarce. The reservoir is subject to large water-level fluctuations because of the dam. At 95 miles long, the reservoir is huge but narrow. Kokanee salmon, cutthroat trout, rainbow trout, and bull trout are present, as are whitefish and burbot.

Lake Mary Ronan. A 1,500-acre lake, Mary Ronan is west of Flathead Lake and northwest of the town of Dayton, and sustains a rainbow trout population. The lake is closed to angling during the spring spawning season but opens in May. Public access is good on the east side of the lake.

McGregor Lake. This scenic 1,500-acre lake is roughly 30 miles west of Kalispell on U.S. 2 and offers good fishing for lake trout. It is planted with rainbow, and there are decent numbers of brook trout and yellow perch. The lake is a popular ice fishing destination.

Swan Lake. Just off State Highway 83 near the town of Swan Lake, at the north end of Swan Valley, this 2,500-acre lake is roughly 10 miles long and a mile or so wide. It offers excellent fishing for rainbow, cutthroat, and bull trout, as well as kokanee salmon, perch, northern pike, and sunfish. Swan Lake once had a sizable bass population, but these fish have dwindled. Both the inlet and the outlet of the lake are typically productive.

Though only a fraction of its rivers are well known, Eastern Canada has over 400 salmon rivers, the greatest such resource in the world.

Whitefish Lake. Whitefish Lake is just northwest of the town of Whitefish and offers cutthroats, bull trout, lake trout, and whitefish. The lake also has a good population of northern pike.

The Yaak River. The Yaak is located in arguably the most remote corner of Montana. A tributary to the Kootenai, it produces nice rainbows and cutthroats. The river above Yaak Falls is fairly gentle and accessible by road, whereas the area below the falls is mostly canyon and tough to get to.

Eastern Region

Bighorn River. The Bighorn River, which flows from Yellowtail Dam to the Yellowstone River near Custer, is one of the best big-trout fisheries in Montana and gives up some mighty browns and rainbows. For much of the year, water temperatures in this tailwater fishery are moderate, and the water is rich in nutrients from the area's limestone streams. The Bighorn is clear, and sunlight helps moss and weeds grow on the bottom. It all adds up to good habitat and great growth rates. Browns in the river operate on a boom and bust cycle, depending on the most recent drought, which in a severe year can de-water the river, raise water temperatures, and cause brown trout mortality. Rainbows, once planted in the river, have become a stable population and no longer need to be planted.

The Bighorn is a large river but in a few spots anglers can wade across. It flows through Crow Indian Reservation, and anglers should be aware that tribal lands are off-limits to anglers. Be attentive to stream access laws and stay within the high-water mark on the stream. Because of access limitation, the best way to fish the Bighorn is from a boat.

Dry flies and nymphs work well on this river, depending on conditions, and streamers can be deadly. Those who use spinning gear take many fish, but this method can be tricky when moss and weeds are heavy, typically from late spring to early autumn.

Bighorn Lake. Bighorn is a 70-mile-long reservoir situated in a red-walled canyon and was created by damming the Bighorn River. The lake is home to brown and rainbow trout, crappie, largemouth bass, sauger, walleye, yellow perch, burbot, and channel catfish. It is surrounded by the Bighorn Canyon National Recreation Area south of Billings at the Montana-Wyoming border. State Highway 313 leads to the lake, but only two public access sites exist on the Montana end of the lake, and one of those is reached by road from Wyoming.

Fort Peck Reservoir. Fort Peck is one of the nation's best walleye fisheries, but it has not experienced the angling pressure seen at other lakes and reservoirs in the upper Midwest. It is home to some 40 species of fish, including channel catfish, crappie, lake trout, northern pike, sauger, smallmouth bass, yellow perch, and an occasional rainbow trout.

Formed by Fort Peck Dam on the Missouri River, the reservoir covers roughly 250,000 acres and stretches more than 130 miles through the Missouri Breaks, a rugged and unforgiving landscape. This is gumbo country, and those who drive into the area must either be ready to leave in the face of threatening weather, or be prepared to stay until the clay dries out after a rain.

Access to the reservoir is through a handful of boat launches and campgrounds around the huge reservoir. Naturally, a body of water this large is best fished by boat.

Nelson Reservoir. The 4,500-acre Nelson Reservoir is 15 miles northeast of the town of Malta, close to U.S. 2. Northern pike, walleye, and yellow perch offer great fishing from April through about November. The fishing slows down in midsummer, but late spring and early autumn are productive.

South-Central Region

The Yellowstone River. This is hallowed fishing ground. Born in Wyoming's high country, the Yellowstone flows through Yellowstone National Park before entering Montana. The upper reaches of the river are nurtured by the pristine waters of the park and a nearby wilderness area. The river is particularly special because its 670 miles of unimpeded flowage makes it the longest free-flowing river in the continental U.S.

Along its route from Yellowstone National Park to Billings, the river holds native cutthroat, rainbow, and brown trout. Momentous occasions on the river include the caddisfly hatch in late spring, the salmonfly hatch in late June or early July, and exceptional hopper fishing in late summer.

The upper Yellowstone runs through Montana's Paradise Valley where, for a fee, anglers tired of the big river can test their skills on the educated trout of the area's crystal clear and famous "spring creeks."

Tributaries to the Yellowstone are the Boulder, Shields, and Stillwater Rivers. Angling on the upper Yellowstone can be challenging. Cutthroats dominate the upper reaches of the river, and there is deep water through Yankee Jim Canyon. Below the canyon the river widens, and a few islands appear. Bank fishermen can do well here, and brown trout are the dominant species.

The river, which has been heading north thus far, turns east several miles below Livingston at what is known as the "big bend." Below Livingston, the water is classic fly water. The river uses several channels from year to year. From Springdale to Columbus, the "middle Yellowstone" is underfished but remains excellent trout water.

Perhaps on the Yellowstone as much as any other river in Montana, knowing where to fish is crucial. It takes several trips to the river to become familiar with it.

At Columbus, the river begins to change to a warmwater fishery, and the change continues until below Billings. The trout give over almost completely to such warmwater species as catfish, sauger, paddlefish, and walleye. There are smallmouth bass in the river, too, along with burbot and northern pike. Channel catfish are most prevalent from Huntley downstream, and smallmouths are most common from Forsyth downstream.

Southwest Region

The Beaverhead River. The Beaverhead River meanders for some 45 to 50 miles as the crow flies, from where it begins south of Dillon at the Clark Canyon Reservoir to Twin Bridges, where it joins the Big Hole. Good habitat makes this an excellent fishery for big rainbow and brown trout, but the river is among the toughest in Montana to fish.

Access is one problem. Because of the thick streamside willows that hang over the steep banks, the river is tough on the wading angler. Those who fish from boats do better, but the river is swift and tricky, and tensions with landowners run high.

The upper stretch of the Beaverhead, from Clark Canyon Dam to Barretts Diversion, winds through a narrow, rocky valley. The lower river courses through a wide valley. Unlike some of Montana's other classic trout streams—which have riffles, pools, and runs—the Beaverhead is a slick river that belies its swift nature.

The upper portion of the river is a favorite for outfitters and guides, but the lower portion of the Beaverhead is much less heavily fished. Fishing suffers below Dillon, where the river loses it clarity. Irrigation draws off some of the water in summer, and the habitat in general declines.

Most of the fishing on the Beaverhead is with heavy, weighted flies, although dry flies can be productive. Bait users do well in the high turbid waters of spring runoff, and lure users have success in summer and fall.

The Big Hole River. One of Montana's blue-ribbon trout streams, the Big Hole River is classic water. It flows for 150 miles through one of the state's most picturesque high-mountain valleys and joins the Beaverhead River at Twin Bridges.

Rainbows and browns inhabit the lower river, but the brown trout don't get much above where Fishtrap Creek joins in. State fisheries biologists have found a number of 5-pound browns above the village of Divide, and a 20-pounder was taken during electroshocking just below Divide. Big Hole's potential seems clear.

Cutthroat trout, brook trout, and limited numbers of grayling populate the higher reaches of the Big Hole. The grayling has a tough time holding its own against some of the other introduced species, and is primarily located in high-mountain tributaries and the river itself, from Wisdom to Jackson. Grayling are a catch-and-release species.

Cutthroat, too, did not compete well and are now only a small portion of the Big Hole's fishery. But the brookies do well and are relatively easy to catch in the river's upper reaches and tributaries.

Like the Beaverhead, the Big Hole is hit hard by irrigation, and in extremely dry years is practically de-watered. In some years the river has been closed to fishing.

One of the hottest times on the Big Hole is the spring salmonfly hatch that runs up the river for about three weeks in June. That is perhaps the busiest time on this great river, but there is good fishing before that hatch, too.

Fishing is best by boat during spring runoff and the salmonfly hatch, but later in the year, after July, a wading angler can fish the river well. Fly anglers are in the majority on the Big Hole. Lure anglers will not do as well there as on other Montana rivers.

Portheus, a fish that resembled the modern tarpon in appearance, lived in the times of the dinosaurs and grew to be 14 feet long.

Clark Canyon Reservoir. Clark Canyon Reservoir, which is about 20 miles south of Dillon near Interstate 15, gives up big trout. There is ready access to the water and camping, and boat launches are available. The reservoir covers roughly 6,500 acres and was formed by damming the Beaverhead River. It is primarily home to rainbows, but these waters also contain brown trout and burbot. The reservoir offers good fishing year-round and is particularly popular with ice anglers from southwestern Montana.

The Gallatin River. The Gallatin River is born in the northwest corner of Yellowstone National Park, then grows up along a 100-mile race to where it joins the Madison and the Jefferson Rivers to create the Missouri River near Three Forks. Along the way, the river provides a variety of water from the easily accessible but small-stream-like Upper Gallatin to the not-so-accessible and slower-moving lower river. In between is Gallatin Canyon, which is classic riffle-pool trout water. For most of the way from the park boundary to the mouth of the canyon, the river is followed by a highway, offering numerous public access points.

There are no dams on the Gallatin, and spring's high water means great fishing for anglers using bait. High water comes in mid- to late May and subsides near the end of June.

Cutthroats are prevalent in the upper reaches of the stream, and brown trout are more common in the lower, slower water. In between are brookies near the mouths of feeder streams, and rainbows throughout the main stream. The East Fork of the Gallatin meanders through private land just west of the town of Bozeman and offers primarily good brown trout fishing. Access can be difficult, however.

Spinners, bait, dry flies, and nymphs all work on the Gallatin, another Montana river with a reliable salmonfly hatch beginning early in June.

Georgetown Lake. This 6,000-acre high-mountain lake about 20 miles west of Anaconda is as heavily fished year-round as any lake in the state. Georgetown Lake is shallow, but the grassy bottom provides great habitat for kokanee salmon and rainbow trout. The lake is easily accessible, as State Highway 1 follows it for much of its northern shoreline. This is an extremely popular destination for ice anglers from Butte, Anaconda, and Missoula.

Jefferson River. The Jefferson is unlike the other two rivers—the Gallatin and the Madison—that come together to form the Missouri River. Gentle and deep, Jefferson River flows a little more slowly. Born when the Big Hole and the Beaverhead come together just north of Twin Bridges, it is made up of long slow stretches interrupted by short riffles. This makes for superb brown trout water, and there are occasional rainbows. The slow water also makes for an abundance of undesirable species like carp, chub, and suckers, however, and also for plenty of whitefish.

The Jefferson is a tough place to be a trout during long, hot summers because of heavy de-watering due to irrigation. But autumn on the Jefferson, as on most other southwest Montana streams, can be a magical time.

The Madison. The Madison is probably the most heavily fished river of the trio that come together at Three Forks to make up the Missouri River, and with good reason: It is classic dry-fly water; the river has comparatively high numbers of fish; and it is all situated in spectacular scenery.

The Madison originates in Yellowstone National Park where the Firehole and the Gibbon Rivers meet, then flows about 100 miles to where it joins the Gallatin and the Jefferson. There are two sections. The upper river, from Quake Lake to Ennis Lake, is one long riffle. Where the stream flows through Beartrap Canyon, the lower river contains some of the wildest water in Montana. Below the canyon, the river widens and slows for the rest of its 30-mile trip to the Three Forks area.

The upper Madison is catch-and-release only, and fishing is restricted to artificial flies. A few stretches are closed to fishing altogether. Access to this part of the river is good because it is followed closely by roads.

Madison Meadows is the section from the Highway 289 crossing to the confluence with the Gallatin and the Jefferson. This stretch is about 20 miles long and is bordered mostly by private land. Fishing here is marginal during warm months but good during the winter.

The Ruby River. The Ruby River is a tributary of the Beaverhead and hard to access in its lower reaches. Expect to encounter some fee fishing, although several access sites have been achieved through a coalition of landowners, state officials, and anglers. The river flows into the Beaverhead above Twin Bridges. Fishing is good above Ruby Reservoir for foot-long rainbows, but, again, access is tricky. The river originates on national forest land, where the access is better and the stream is good for neophyte anglers.

Western Region

The Blackfoot. The Blackfoot River gained notoriety with the release of Hollywood's version of the novel *A River Runs Through It.* But the Blackfoot River today is not the same as it was in the past. Logging has contributed siltation to the river, and a sizable body of gold ore located above the town of Lincoln keeps the threat of mining hanging over the headwaters.

Still, the Blackfoot runs for roughly 100 miles from its beginnings on the western slope of the Rocky Mountains to the lumber mill town of Bonner, where it joins the Clark Fork River. The river offers deep-forest stream banks and open-meadow stretches. There are campsites and frequent access points along the river, which has largely escaped subdivision to date.

Cutthroats are prevalent in the river above Lincoln, but this stretch of water has small numbers of fish and the habitat is poor. Below Lincoln the fishery improves rapidly, as more tributaries pour into the river. The free-flowing Blackfoot is ripped with logjams, and the water is home to some fine brown trout, plus brookies, rainbows, cutthroats, and a few bull trout. Rainbows dominate the river from where the North Fork enters.

Floating the Blackfoot can be tough, especially above Johnsrud Park, but from there on the river settles down and is manageable.

The Bitterroot River. The Bitterroot River is born high in western Montana and runs north following the Bitterroot Range to its confluence with the Clark Fork River in the town of Missoula. The valley was among the first to be settled in Montana, and settlement continued well into the late twentieth century with the subdivision of many Bitterroot Valley farms and ranches. Logging, too, contributes to the decline of the fishery, but in spite of closed access and siltation, the Bitterroot River still is one of Montana's better trout streams.

The Bitterroot mostly gives up rainbows and brown trout, but brookies, cutthroats, and bull trout are present, too. The river holds a surprise or two: northern pike, thanks to illegal plants, and largemouth bass inhabit some of the slower backwater stretches.

Flies, nymphs, lures, and bait all work well on the river, which, depending on the time of the year and condition of the water, is noted for its clarity. Spring runoff is dramatic and, until that ends, the water will be cloudy. Irrigation also hits the river hard, and when that happens, most anglers head upstream.

The river offers dynamite dry fly fishing before the spring thaw raises water volume and turbidity. Runoff is generally in late May and June.

The Clark Fork River. The Clark Fork River is still making a comeback from the sad heydays of mining in the Butte area and smelting in the Anaconda area. But the river, which flows on to exit the state at Huron, where it is a mighty river indeed, provides a wide variety of water.

Silver Bow Creek and Warm Springs come together below a mining company's settling ponds just upstream from the burg of Warm Springs to form the Clark Fork. From there to Garrison Junction the river is home to mostly brown trout. Among the hottest water on the upper Clark Fork is that section from Gold Creek to Drummond. Trout numbers are poor until Rock Creek dumps in, and then the numbers are good to Milltown Dam. The Blackfoot River joins the Clark Fork here, but from this point until below the town of Missoula, the fishing is usually poor.

When the Bitterroot and the Clark Fork come together, the fishing changes. Browns give way to rainbows. There is outstanding fishing on the Clark Fork from Missoula to Superior, if you can find it. The fish seem to congregate in particular areas, and the water in between is lackluster. This is a river that demands to be known before it gives up its good fish.

Rock Creek. Rock Creek is a tributary of the Clark Fork River, but the similarities are few. One of Montana's blue-ribbon trout streams, Rock Creek is roughly 50 miles long and has a road running beside it. The stream is classic trout water, with riffles, runs, and pools; it supports rainbow trout, brown trout, cutthroats, brook trout, and bull trout.

Like the Big Hole, Rock Creek experiences a tremendous salmonfly hatch beginning in early June.

Some of the land is private, but access points exist along most of the stream, including a number of U.S. Forest Service campgrounds along the upper and middle reaches. Rock Creek receives some of the heaviest pressure of any stream in Montana.

North-Central Region

Lake Elwell. Lake Elwell is a 17,000-acre reservoir created by Tiber Dam on the Marias River and located southwest of Chester in Liberty County. The lake is relatively deep at about 150 feet and offers a truly good walleye fishery. It also yields an occasional burbot and rainbow trout, and regularly produces perch and pike.

Fresno Reservoir. Created by a dam on the Milk River, Fresno Reservoir is about 10 miles west of Havre and is easily reached from U.S. Highway 2 by county road. The reservoir encompasses about 6,000 acres and is used for irrigation, so the water level can fluctuate. The lake provides northern pike, perch, and walleye fishing. There have been plan-tings of trout and bass, but few anglers report taking these species.

Lake Frances. Just southwest of the town of Valier, Lake Frances is a 5,500-acre lake on the Dry Fork of the Marias. The lake is home to burbot, perch, pike, rainbow trout, and walleye, and it provides good ice fishing. Trout are becoming less common here.

The Missouri River. The Missouri River wears many faces in its long, long run from Three Forks to Fort Union, where it is joined by the Yellowstone just after it leaves the state of Montana.

For the trout angler, the truly fine water is a 90-mile stretch from below Holter Dam to just above the town of Cascade. This section is rated a blue-ribbon trout stream because of its big browns and rainbows. But with greatness comes fame, so this stretch of river is heavily fished. Outfitters who once would have touted the Bighorn as Montana's best river, now bring their clients to the Missouri. The river can be a busy place.

Trout fishing declines at about the town of Cascade, where the river runs deeper and slower. Where the Smith River dumps into the Missouri, trout numbers fall off substantially. This area of the river does offer some walleye fishing, however.

Downstream, the complexion of the Missouri

changes even more, and although trout are present, most anglers go after walleye, sauger, perch, catfish, or burbot.

The Smith River. The Smith River was the first river in Montana to be regulated for use by floaters and campers. The floatable portion of this little river is only about 60 miles long, yet it receives some of the highest use of any stream in the state. A permit system is in place, and roughly 80 percent of these permits are going to local or nonguided anglers; 20 percent is set aside for guided floaters.

The river is a quality fishery for rainbows in its upper reaches, and brown trout in the middle to lower stretches. But angling pressure, like floating pressure, is heavy on this river.

Stream Access

According to state law, the public may access waters within Montana for recreational use within the "ordinary high-water mark." The high-water mark is the line where water is present for "sufficient periods to cause physical characteristics that distinguish the area below the line from the area above it," such as soil and vegetation. The ordinary high-water mark does not encompass flood plains. This applies to stream-related recreational use such as fishing, swimming, boating, and hunting, and it is important for all anglers to understand.

In Montana there are two classes of streams: Class I and Class II. Class I streams are those that have been declared navigable or that support commercial use and include most of the state's largest rivers. Class II streams are not navigable but support stream-related recreation.

Anglers do not need permission from landowners for use of water between the ordinary high-water mark and the stream. But anglers should get permission from the landowner to cross private land.

You may camp within the bed and banks of Class I streams if it is necessary for recreational use and occurs out of sight or more than 500 yards from a dwelling. Camping closer requires landowner permission. You may not camp on Class II waters.

Anglers and boaters may portage around barriers above the ordinary high-water mark but only in the least intrusive manner. Barriers are defined as artificial obstructions in or over water that totally or effectively obstruct recreational use. Montana's stream-access law does not speak to portages around natural barriers.

MOOCHING

The most common technique for catching salmon in Pacific Northwest coastal waters is "mooching." Mooching involves the use of bait and is practiced in a way that includes a bit of drifting and subtle trolling. There are a number of ways to mooch; the differences revolve around the size of bait used, the speed of the boat, and the strength of the tackle. A lot of mooching is done in areas where there is current—in rivers as well as in coastal areas where tides and eddies are prominent.

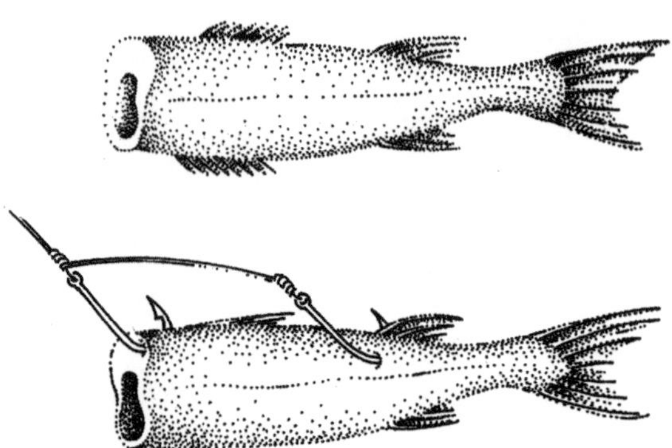

Plug-cut herring, shown here, mooch well if the proper cutting angle is achieved on the bait, and the hooks are correctly placed.

For mooching, anglers use herring, sometimes live, sometimes freshly killed and fished whole or cut, and sometimes fished as thawed/treated/cut bait. Cut bait is preferred in most areas, but the angle of the cut is important because it influences the speed of the roll as the bait is drifted or trolled. An angled cut is made behind the gills by the pectoral fin; the innards are pulled or routed out. Snelled salmon hooks in two- or three-hook rigs are used. Positioning the hooks is important and varies according to the number of hooks used, size of the bait, and the speed of the roll desired. In any case, the lead hook is impaled through the head, inserted inside the cavity behind several ribs and hooked out through the top of the bait.

Tackle consists of a long rod, generally $10^1/_2$ feet, and a reel capable of holding several hundred yards of line. In some locales, notably British Columbia, anglers are partial to so-called "mooching reels," which are 1:1 direct-drive devices akin to large fly reels. Levelwind reels and fly reels are also used. The latter are used with lighter line, shorter rods, and smaller bait when smaller fish, especially coho salmon, are abundant.

Fairly heavy sinkers, from 2 to 6 ounces, are used; these are keel-shaped and fished several feet above the bait. A barrel swivel is used a few feet ahead of the sinker, and the length of the leader from swivel to bait is roughly equal to the length of the rod.

Boat control is very important in this type of fishing, whether drifting or trolling under power. Tides, wind, and swells dictate positioning, but the object is to achieve a proper roll of the bait, as well as to keep it in the most advantageous locations. When trolling, or "motor mooching," the boat operator frequently (in some cases constantly) puts the tiller-steered motor in and out of gear, and sometimes may go backward a short distance to maneuver.

Although some strikes are vicious and result

in instant hookups, many are soft—the fish may bump the bait—and the angler has to pay out line quickly to give the fish time to get the bait well into its mouth without feeling resistance. Most fish are hooked just inside the mouth and can be released without harm if that is desired.

MOONEYE *Hiodon tergisus.*

A member of the *Hiodontidae* family, the mooneye is a close relative and very similar in appearance to the better known goldeye *(see).* It is most important as forage for assorted predator species. Its flesh is soft and bony and of no human food value, and it is not a target of anglers, although it may occasionally be an incidental catch and can be consumed after smoking. Though often called a herring or shad, it is neither.

Identification. The mooneye is a small fish whose compressed body is deep in proportion to its length and is covered with large, loose scales. Dark blue to blue green over the back, it is silvery on the sides and tapers to white on the belly. It has a small head and a short, bluntly rounded snout with a small terminal mouth containing many sharp teeth on the jaws and tongue.

The color of its eyes and the position of its anal fin distinguish it from the goldeye. The iris of the large eyes of the mooneye are silver colored (unlike the gold-colored iris of the goldeye). The mooneye's dorsal fin begins before the anal fin (the goldeye's begins opposite or behind its anal fin). The mooneye can be distinguished from the gizzard shad by not having a dorsal fin ray projection.

Size/Age. Mooneye are slightly larger on average than goldeye and are often found to be 2 pounds in weight, although their maximum attainable size is uncertain. They may live at least 10 years.

Distribution. Endemic to North America, mooneye occur in the St. Lawrence–Great Lakes region (except Lake Superior), the Mississippi River drainage, and the Hudson Bay basin from Quebec to Alberta, and southward to the Gulf of Mexico. Mooneye are also present in Gulf Slope drainages from Mobile Bay, Alabama, to Lake Pontchartrain, Louisiana.

Habitat. Mooneye inhabit deep, warm, silty sections of medium and large rivers, the backwaters of shallow lakes connected to them, and impoundments.

Spawning behavior. Mooneye spawn in the spring, moving up tributary rivers or streams.

Food. This species feeds on plankton, insects, and small fish. Small mooneye are preyed upon by large predators, including walleye, pike, catfish, and salmon.

Angling. Though seldom the target of angling effort, mooneye can be caught on flies and on natural bait that are impaled on small hooks and suspended below a light float. Light spinning and fly tackle is used. Mooneye may be fished live or as cut bait for other species, notably catfish.

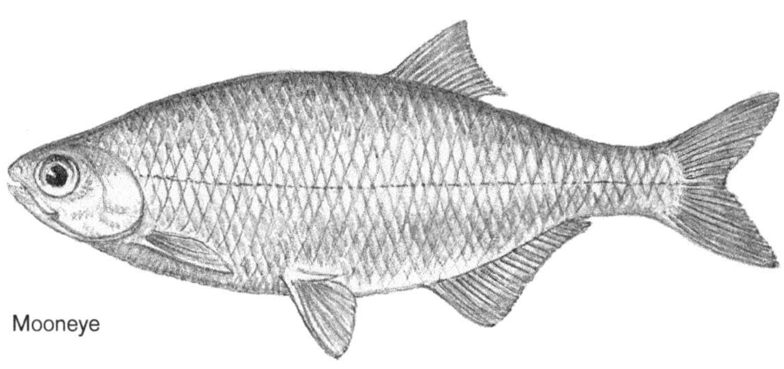
Mooneye

MOONFISH, ATLANTIC *Selene setapinnis.*
MOONFISH, PACIFIC *Selene peruviana.*

Other names for Atlantic moonfish—French: *lune;* Portuguese: *corcovado, galo verdadeiro, peixe-galo;* Spanish: *corcobado, jorobado, lamparosa.*

Other names for Pacific moonfish—horsefish, Peruvian moonfish, pug-nosed shiner, blunt-nosed shiner; Spanish: *caraja, jorobado, pez luna.*

Small members of the Carangidae family of jacks and not well known to anglers, moonfish are a good food fish and are commercially marketed fresh and salted/dried.

Identification. Similar to the lookdown *(see),* Atlantic and Pacific moonfish are shiny, silvery, and platelike, but their bodies are more elongated. They have the similar steep head profile, but it is more concave than in the lookdown. Another difference is that the front rays of their dorsal and anal fins are not elongated. The young Atlantic moonfish has an elongated black spot on its midside, and the Pacific moonfish has a black spot at the upper edge of the operculum.

Size. Moonfish may reach 10 to 12 inches in length.

Distribution. The Atlantic moonfish occurs in the western Atlantic from Nova Scotia to Mar de Plata, Argentina, including the Caribbean Sea and the Gulf of Mexico. The Pacific moonfish occurs in the eastern Pacific from Redondo Beach in Southern California and throughout the lower Gulf of California to Peru, but is usually rare north of Baja California, Mexico.

Habitat. Bottom-dwelling species, moonfish usually form schools and inhabit inshore waters of up to 50 to 60 meters in depth. Young Atlantic moonfish are found over muddy bottom in bays and river mouths, whereas young Pacific moonfish may be found near the surface.

Food. Moonfish feed on small fish and crustaceans.

Angling. *See: Inshore Fishing; Jacks.*

MOON PHASE

See: Solunar Tables; Tides.

MOORING

A place where a boat is kept at anchor. A boat is said to be moored when securely anchored or when tied to a dock, pier, or other structure.

MOROCCO

For most people Morocco means heat, bazaars, and Casablanca, but for many European anglers this country on the northwest corner of the Sahara Desert is an idyllic backdrop to diverse and breathtaking fishing.

Situated on the northwestern tip of Africa, Morocco is separated from the rest of the continent by the towering Atlas Mountains and the Sahara. Its coastline faces the Atlantic Ocean on the east, and the Mediterranean Sea on the north. Morocco's climate, geography, and history are all more closely related to the Mediterranean than to the rest of Africa, and visitors are often struck by the odd sensation of having not quite reached Africa. In the north on the Mediterranean coast, fine beaches, lush highland valleys, and evocative old cities like Marrakech, Fez, and Meknes reinforce this impression. This Mediterranean character melts away as one moves south and east, into and over the starkly beautiful ranges of the Atlas Mountains.

The climate in Morocco is reliably dry, although a small amount of rain does fall between November and March. Temperatures vary considerably by season and locale. Whereas the southern and southeastern desert regions can reach extremely high temperatures during the hot summer months, the higher altitudes of the mountains are cool during summer evenings and freezing in winter.

Due to these extremes of climate, Morocco offers many hotspots both for saltwater and freshwater fishing. In fact, it is possible to fish for white marlin on deep-blue ocean waters, and the following day catch largemouth bass on a placid mountain lake.

Although angling locations are plentiful, sportfishing facilities are scarce. In 1999, there were only two local professional sportfishing operators for both saltwater and freshwater: Sochatour (71 Avenue des FAR, Casablanca 01, Morocco; phone: 212-2-314694 or 212-2-314719; fax: 212-2-314699), and Louis Champeaux (phone: 212-2-206401). There is a European sportfishing operator in Great Britain, The Best of Morocco, Ltd. (Seend Park, Seend, Wiltshire SN12 6NZ; phone: 0380-828533). It is necessary to bring your own fishing equipment.

Saltwater

The Moroccan coastline offers wide sandy beaches as well as a number of interesting rocky shorelines. The diversity of fishing in this fascinating country is great, particularly around Dahkla and Agadir (for surf casting) in the deep south, and around Casablanca (for deep-sea fishing) in the northwest.

Near Morocco's southern border, Dahkla is washed by the cool Canary Current and offers some truly breathtaking scenery and sea fishing. From high above fossil-rich cliffs the view is absolutely beautiful: mile upon mile of white-gold sand and a seabed that drops away beyond the third or fourth breaker into deep water. It is a completely unspoiled and virtually unfished haven.

The best prospects for angling are from the end of May until September, when stingrays, shovelnose rays (guitarfish), jacks, snapper, bluefish, garrick, grouper, sharks, bream, and a variety of different species of bass are plentiful.

One particular fish, the courbine (or meagre; in the drum family) moves close inshore in good numbers during June and July. Fish between 30 and 80 pounds are commonly caught at this time of year. The best baits for this giant fish are squid, cuttlefish, and octopus (known locally as *calamar, choco,* and *poulpe*). All are available at the local market in Dahkla.

Facing the Atlantic Ocean at about the same latitude as Bermuda, the thriving seaport metropolis of Casablanca sits in the northwest corner of Africa, a temperate, agriculturally rich region that bulges toward nearby Spain just across the Straits of Gibraltar. Though Casablanca's fame was made in the movies, the white marlin grounds near this city have won it a different kind of recognition. Since 1987, the clear blue waters off Mohammedia, a suburb 12 miles north of Casablanca, have gained international fame through the consistent exploration and world-record-setting catches of skilled French and American skippers and anglers.

White marlin are found from 8 to 35 miles off Mohammedia Marina's docks, depending on the shifts in the warm currents that converge off this coast. Anglers troll rigged needlefish or mackerel where the surface temperature rises abruptly from about 70° to 77°F, as this is where schools of white marlin and sometimes swordfish are found chasing skipjack tuna. The best season for white marlin runs from August through mid-November. In the same months it is also possible to troll or drift with live baits in inshore waters for amberjack, snapper, grouper, bluefish, garrick, and tuna.

Freshwater

In the southeast, Morocco's mountain ranges yield to the desolate expanse of the Sahara. The rivers that flow down this side of the Atlas support long, narrow, and lush river valleys that resemble linear oases and are dammed to form beautiful lakes.

Within easy driving distance of Morocco's ancient city of Marrakech are three large reservoirs, each one with good to excellent sportfisheries. Twenty miles south of Marrakech is the Lalla Takerkoust Dam, which hosts a prolific stock of carp. Forty miles north of the city is El Massina Dam, home to a big population of largemouth bass. Twenty miles east of Marrakech is Ait Aabel, which boasts the best fishing of the three. Fed by the Tessaout River, Ait Aabel is huge, wild, and secluded, and has been stocked with largemouth bass, which are abundant. They are especially found among the massive boulders at the base of the dam, where shore anglers have an opportunity to catch them.

Going afloat (boats are hired through the two local operators) enables the angler to explore the steep-sided gorges of the rivers that help fill Ait Abel during the winter rains. The changes in depth along the course of this flooded canyon are tremendous and keep the sonar on the fishing boats bobbing up and down like a yo-yo. The greatest concentrations of bass are around sunken trees, bushes, rocky outcrops, and ledges.

MOSQUITOFISH *Gambusia affinis affinis.*

The mosquitofish is a member of the large Poeciliidae family of livebearers, which is closely related to killifish *(see)* or cyprinodonts, differing from them mainly in bringing forth their young alive rather than laying eggs.

Also known as the North American topminnow or the western mosquitofish, this species is famous as the number-one scourge of mosquito larvae. Although there are other larvae-eating species of fish, the mosquitofish tolerates salinity and pollution levels that would kill most other species, and it produces up to 1,500 young in its lifetime.

Native to the southeastern United States, the mosquitofish has been introduced to suitable warm waters around the world since 1905, when it was experimentally introduced to Hawaii and virtually eliminated mosquitoes. It has been transplanted to the southwestern U.S., the Caribbean, Central America, Europe, and the Middle East, and coldwater strains have gone to Canada, Russia, and the northern U.S., among other areas. All of this has made *Gambusia affinis affinis* the widest-ranging freshwater fish on earth (other species of mosquitofish have not been as successfully introduced).

Female mosquitofish are about 2 inches long, and the males are only half as large. As with other species of livebearers, the anal fin of the male is modified to form an intermittent organ for introducing sperm into the female. A mature female may produce three or four broods during one season, sometimes giving birth to 200 or more young at a time. When she is carrying young, the female becomes obviously plumper and develops a large black area on each side just in front of the anal fin. This fish is easily raised in aquariums and is not sensitive to temperature variations, but it does not adjust well to living with other fish.

Although it has been highly effective at controlling malarial mosquitoes, the mosquitofish is not a panacea. Mosquitofish larvae cannot survive without water (as mosquito larvae can), they do not control mosquitoes in places with abundant surface

Mosquitofish

vegetation to hide mosquito larvae, they may consume the young of forage and game species, and they can have adverse effects on indigenous fish species.

MOTOR, ELECTRIC

An electric motor is one of the most important and useful items that any boating angler can have. An electric motor, called a "trolling" motor by most of the angling fraternity, allows you to maneuver and position your boat in the proper angle for casting and to make the type of presentation that is required for the fishing circumstances, all as quietly and carefully as possible. An electric motor could most appropriately be called a maneuvering motor or a positioning motor because its main purpose is keeping anglers who cast from a boat in position to make more and better presentations, and thus fish effectively.

Electric motors essentially take the place of oars and sculling paddles, but they are quieter and interfere less with fishing activities. They can be used in trolling but are primarily used for positioning while casting. Electric motors are predominantly used by freshwater anglers, especially bass and walleye anglers; saltwater usage has been less widespread, in part because of difficulties in keeping electronic equipment that is exposed to corrosive elements in working order. However, this is changing. Manufacturers have vastly improved the corrosion resistance of motors meant for saltwater use. Previously, many motors used in saltwater were beefed-up versions of freshwater motors, but now they are specifically designed for the harsh salt environment, having stainless steel and corrosion-resistant parts, tighter seals, improved torque, remote-control operation, and more power.

All electric motors are battery powered. Some run off a single 12-volt battery; others require 24 or 36 volts. Still others have the capability of running off either one or two 12-volt batteries. Not all electric motors are alike. Some are more powerful; some more battery efficient. The amount of energy (designated as amperes, or amps) consumed by electric motors varies, and this figure, when known, will tell you how many hours of continuous use you can get out of a battery at varied speeds. Modern electric motors are much more efficient at consuming and conserving battery power than in the past. However, it is a fact that the heavier the boat and boat load, the more power, or thrust, is needed.

As a rule, to position a boat effectively in wind

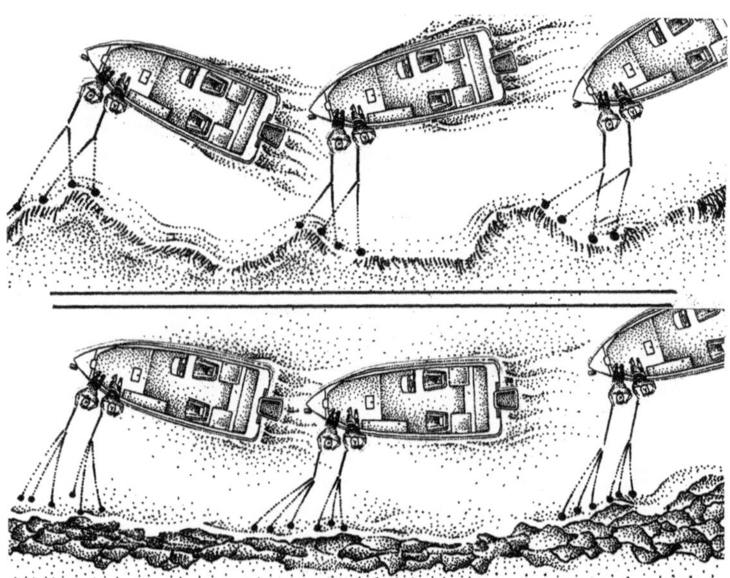

Electric motors are primarily used for getting and maintaining position for good casting presentations. Paralleling a ragged shoreline (top) and steep bluff (bottom) as depicted here allows two bass anglers to cover the area well, sometimes overlapping casts.

and/or current, you will need at least a pound of thrust for every 100 pounds of gross boat weight (including yourself and companions). Thus, if the gross weight is 2,000 pounds, you'll need an electric capable of delivering at least 20 pounds of thrust at full power. If the wind and current conditions tend to be particularly bad in your area, you might even need 50 percent more thrust, or a 30-pound thrust electric in this example.

An important factor to consider is how much fishing is done in areas of substantial current or wind; both of these drain the reserves of a battery quicker than calm-condition operation. Saltwater operation, in general, is more demanding than freshwater, partly because a lot of power is needed to combat currents and wind, and partly because saltwater casters may have to do a bit of moving to keep up with quickly moving and widely roaming fish. Boat weights, wind and current demands, and angler interest have consistently pushed electric motor manufacturers into offering more powerful products, and if batteries ever improve to provide more power over extended periods, there will be a new race for greater thrust.

On most fiberglass and on many aluminum boats in freshwater, the electric motor is mounted permanently on the bow, with the bracket support installed on the bow port to put a little weight on that side and counterbalance the console and driver weight on the starboard side. On small boats such as rowboats and jonboats, electric motors can be mounted on the front or back. Boats move with greater ease when pulled rather than pushed, so many anglers prefer bow mounting; plus, with bow mounting, they can see where they're headed and know when to avoid objects. Bow mounting is preferred for casting to cover and working along specific edges, but a single motor (you can't put two on the bow) may not have the power needed in open water conditions.

Saltwater anglers, particularly those who use flats boats, are most likely to employ one or two long-shafted transom-mount motors, which are operated either manually or by remote control. They prefer transom mounting because it is close to the stern poling platform and does not require lowering into the water, making motion and noise that might spook fish. Two transom motors provide the gusto to follow quickly moving fish, which cannot be done by poling; however, maneuverability, especially in wind is tougher with transom operation.

Some anglers, especially guides and tournament anglers, put bow and transom-mount motors on their boats, using either or both when conditions warrant. However, numbers and power aren't always in the best interests of the angler, because no electric motor is completely quiet. Some anglers firmly believe that certain fish, under certain conditions, are attuned to electric motors and are turned off or alarmed by the sounds that they make. This is especially true in clear water and on exposed flats, and in the shallows.

Small boats usually require only a single 12-volt electric motor, though you can employ more than one motor at a time. Some anglers who fish in places where gas outboards are prohibited rig up two or three electrics in unison, and some manufacturers have units specifically for this application. Small-boat electrics feature a turnscrew-clamp transom mount, which makes them adjustable and removable. With some, you can leave the bracket installed and remove the rest of the motor. Some of these models can also fit on the front of a small boat, but it pays to first check out your boat and then see whether the motor you like will fit the design of your bow.

Permanent-mount electrics are used on conventional bass boats and large craft and can be operated manually or remotely, depending upon the unit. Most remote units are operated via a foot-control pedal on the bow deck; some have merely a long electric cord, and some are totally remote controlled, operated by a wireless touch pad or by voice command. The latter types eliminate the hindrance of wires and cable, and have become increasingly popular in both freshwater and saltwater. Completely remote units operate by radio frequency control and by air pressure (pneumatic) control. Some of the remote models can be operated from 200 feet away from the boat, meaning that in gentle flats conditions, anglers can get out of the boat and walk along the flats, keeping a low profile, while the boat stays an unobtrusive distance away, ready to be called closer when needed.

For years, many anglers shunned cable-controlled bow-mount electric motors because they were prone to cable or foot-lever pad breakage.

These items have improved, but they aren't foolproof, and when a cable breaks or the foot control malfunctions, you're out of commission. Moreover, some people struggle with the actual movement of the foot control because it isn't smooth, isn't situated well on their boat, or, as is the case with some long-cable remote motors, is hard to operate and unresponsive. You can run the foot control when standing or seated.

Manual models do not have a foot control pedal or cable running to the motor and are steered by turning a fixed handle or a handle extension device. They are mostly operated by hand but may be maneuvered with your foot or knee, although you have to be properly balanced to do this. Manual bow-mount motors are relatively easy to steer, but they are poor in rough water, in sharp turns, or in reverse because you have to physically turn the motor around, which can mean reaching out over the boat. They're usually operated from a standing position, are less prone to breakage, and are best for agile people.

One important feature to look for in an electric motor is a breakaway bracket; this device allows the shaft of the motor to slip back should the motor collide with an immovable object. This feature will save you from having bent shafts and damaged lower units, and will prevent extraordinary stress on the mounting bracket when objects are struck head on. Another important consideration is the length of the shaft. Big boats and boats that will be used in rough water conditions require a long-shaft motor so that the prop will grab properly and, in the case of manual models, so that the control handle is at an accessible height (although there are accessory devices that attach to the upper shaft and extend upward to make manual control easier.

Another important feature is a good armature and easy-release/take-up system for getting into and out of the water with minimum effort. Different motors vary greatly in this regard. There are also automatic devices for raising and lowering bow-mounted electric motors.

Batteries and Chargers

With an electric motor you'll also need one or more batteries, plus a means of recharging the battery. An electric motor does not automatically recharge the power source, and in the course of a full day's fishing, you may drain the energy of a battery considerably. With pulse modulation, good electric motors today don't drain a battery as much as they did in the past, and depending on the fishing circumstances, you may be able to get two or three days out of a battery without recharging it. But you'll still need a battery charger.

The best products for powering electric motors are deep-cycle batteries. Deep-cycle batteries are often called marine batteries, but not all "marine batteries" are deep-cycled, so you should check to be sure that the batteries you obtain for electric motor use are deep-cycle products. These are constructed with special plates that allow them to be regularly drawn down and recharged; standard batteries are not meant to do this and do not have nearly the life of deep-cycle batteries when used for electric motor operation.

Deep-cycle batteries for electric motors are rated by size or amp-hours as well as by voltage. Make sure you get the right voltage for your motor's needs. Amp hours are the amount of amperage that a battery can consistently produce over a 20-hour period. A size 24 battery yields typically 60 to 70 amp hours, and a size 27 might yield 70 to 85. Batteries may also have a marine cranking amp rating, which is the amps it produces for 30 seconds at 32°F, and reserve capacity, which is the number of minutes during which a battery will produce 25 amps. For maximum performance, get the highest-amperage batteries you can, plus a high-amp-capacity battery charger with multiple features. For starting the outboard motor, you don't need a deep-cycle battery. A conventional automotive battery will do, but opt for a non-deep-cycle marine battery. However, if you want to reduce weight in your boat, then you can use one battery for all electrical needs, and it should be capable of being repeatedly drawn down and recharged.

In 1999, an empty two-piece cardboard box for a lure called the "Michigan Life-Like Minnow," which was manufactured in February 1908 by A. Arntz of Muskegon, Michigan, sold at auction for $2,600.

Remember that the batteries are the lifeline to your boat's operation. Clean the terminals and connections regularly for good contact. Signs of a weak battery include low electric motor propulsion, weak sonar signals, low temperature gauge readings, low tachometer and speedometer readings, and weak fuel gauge indications.

Batteries on a full charge last longer, so keep your charge level high at all times, even through the winter. It is best to recharge a deep-cycle battery as soon as possible after it has been drawn down. Staying in a weakened condition can damage the plates and promote a shorter life. If you are charging directly to a battery, you can use the clamp-type terminal connectors, being sure to place the positive and negative wires properly and keeping the battery compartment ventilated. If your boat is wired for automatic charging, you need an adaptor that is attached to your charger's lead wires and that merely needs to be plugged into the boat receptacle with the system switched into the charging mode. There are also onboard automatic battery chargers that can be wired into the system; these will charge the batteries by themselves, shut off when charged, and monitor the battery status to recharge as necessary.

Checking open-cell batteries used to be done by monitoring the acid levels in the cells and filling them with distilled water. Their charging state was checked with a hydrometer. That system has been rivaled by popular maintenance-free sealed liquid acid and gel batteries. The technology and performance of the sealed liquid acid battery is much the same as its open-cell predecessor, but the sealed gel battery theoretically allows less liquid dissipation.

You cannot check the amount of electrical energy left in a sealed battery with a floating hydrometer. You must resort to more sophisticated means in the form of electronics, which allows you to monitor the amount of remaining charge via a dash-mounted gauge. This type of electronic hydrometer works by accurately measuring the battery's voltage, and translating that number into percent of charge remaining. Some instruments will display total amp hours withdrawn from the battery at any time, as well as the precise battery voltage, and even the rate at which the current is being withdrawn.

The total lifetime of your battery depends greatly upon the charger you use. Some batteries are more sensitive to excessive charging voltage than others, and if you have an onboard-charging system but an unregulated output alternator, you can damage a battery, especially a gel version. Overcharging increases the internal temperature of the battery, which accelerates destruction of its positive plates and results in reduced storage capacity and battery life.

The ideal AC charger for a maintenance-free battery is not the old standard type that reverts to a trickle when full charge is reached, because constant current can cause damage. A charger should be capable of automatically not exceeding safe voltage levels for either gel or liquid acid batteries, and should shut off when the charging cycle is complete.

Some of the more sophisticated electric motors, such as this bow-mounted unit on a bass boat, provide remote cableless operation.

If you must charge two or even three batteries at the same time with a single charger, you're going to need at least a 20-amp heavy-duty model. You can safely charge two or even three in parallel, provided they are all equally discharged. Otherwise, connecting them in parallel will result in the battery(ies) with the higher charge trying to recharge the battery(ies) that is lower, and enough heat could be generated in the connecting wires to start a fire. Obviously, if you use those batteries connected in parallel at all times, then they will always all have exactly the same state of charge.

One way of keeping batteries alive for long periods and keeping them capable of accepting full charges is to use pulse technology maintenance products. These somewhat help prevent sulfation of the battery plates. When crystallized sulfate molecules build up on the lead plates, they prevent full recharging, which leads to more sulfate buildup and eventually to a dead battery. Pulse technology is a system that discharges a pulsating DC current into the battery, removing sulfates from the plates and, if used continuously, preventing them from returning. Some models are connected to solar panels that permit full-time pulsation and that are capable of maintaining batteries at all times, even when they are not being used (in a boat, recreational vehicle, etc.). Products with pulse technology have been used by the military for various applications, and in recent years these products have spread to recreational and consumer automotive applications. Extending battery life for several years is possible with such systems and has obvious economic benefit; helping to reduce the disposal of (toxic) batteries also has environmental benefits.

It is important to note that in typical lead-acid batteries, the failure to routinely monitor and replace battery-consumed water results in irreversible plate damage. In sealed maintenance-free batteries, the user has no opportunity to monitor water level to minimize plate damage and maximize battery life. Newer low-maintenance batteries exist that have an oil-water mixture that serves to retain water and minimize its loss, yet also allows for the addition of more water to maintain proper fluid levels and to keep the plates covered.

Batteries are the lifeblood of the electric motor. Frequent use of an electric motor battery means that the battery constantly goes through the process of being charged (often overcharged), then drained at varying levels of discharge, and often neglected before or during charging again; and all of this happens over a wide range of time and temperatures. Obviously batteries have to take a lot. Although battery technology has improved, it has not kept pace with angling needs. Batteries are also the main thing that is holding up the further development of electric motors for fishing. Smaller batteries with increased life and with much greater power are needed for the demands that anglers put on their motors.

Maneuvering Tactics

Speed and position are the key elements to fishing effectively and to properly running a boat with an electric motor. It takes a little practice to learn how to pilot a particular boat with a particular motor, especially to learn how to control it along and around places that you cast to. The strength of the motor, the weight of the occupied boat, and the conditions encountered determine how best to run the motor. Eventually, dealing with constant on/off operation and directional maneuvering becomes second nature.

In one sense, maneuvering a boat with an electric motor is similar to driving a car around town, where you alter speed frequently and manipulate the steering wheel constantly. However, it is also unlike driving a car because you have no brakes to slow down and no pavement or lane markers to easily follow, and you are more susceptible to being blown off course.

Maneuvering a boat with a bow-mounted motor, which pulls the boat bow-first, is a bit different from maneuvering with a transom-mount motor, which pushes it bow-first. The latter is harder to use in the wind, because the bow gets shoved by the wind and the boat quickly slips off course, requiring constant correction.

In small, light boats with a transom electric you would do well to fish stern-first to better control positioning. You can turn the motor around and run it with handle facing away from you, or you can rotate the head so that the handle faces the bow but the motor pulls away from the stern.

Under calm or near-calm conditions, maneuvering a boat is relatively easy. You'll get plenty of casts in, and you can keep the boat positioned properly for long periods of time. When underway, the main issue is selecting the proper speed to allow you and companions ample opportunity to make presentations in desired places.

The stronger the wind, the harder this becomes. Often it is not beneficial to manipulate your boat with the wind. Even with the motor set on the slowest possible speed, you're likely to blow past desirable fishing locations quickly. Fishing fast is seldom productive, except perhaps when chasing schooling surface-feeding fish. When white bass or stripers are on top and moving, for example, you need to quietly stay with them and rapidly get lures amongst them.

When casting to specific places, such as weedbeds, points, mangrove edges, rocky shorelines, etc., you generally need to make an accurate cast and a measured retrieve, sometimes more than once, which cannot be done properly in a poorly controlled boat. Running the boat into the wind at a speed that keeps you in the right place for the right casts is necessary. It is now possible to run a well-charged battery hard all day without killing it, so there is no battery-power-saving excuse for not bucking the wind.

Sometimes the wind comes crosswise at your boat, and this is especially difficult to counter when you're casting to a particular shoreline or weed edge. Head into and across the wind, and keep up speed to maintain position. In this situation, and some others, it may be advantageous for a companion to move to the front of the boat to fish. Doing so minimizes concern for where the back of the boat is positioned, and both anglers will have equal opportunity to make good presentations.

Running the boat properly and fishing effectively at the same time is not very difficult except in the wind or when navigating through heavy vegetation or timber. At all times you have to anticipate where the boat is headed and simultaneously observe what is coming up to cast to. You have to be on top of the boat position at all times, not wait, for example, until you've drifted close to cover to adjust position. Getting close to cover, incidentally, is all right when the water is murky, but not when it's clear. And, of course, this may still depend on the species. Using an electric motor on high power in shallow water is likely to spook most species of fish, even if the water is murky.

Another consideration in boat positioning is the depth below your boat, as well as the depth where you're casting and retrieving. It is often desirable to keep your boat positioned in a certain depth of water. Let's say, for example, that you're fishing crankbaits along a moderately sloping shoreline and that there's a sharp break to deeper water at 10 or 12 feet, which is where most bass are being caught at the time. That break may be 70 feet from shore, which is where you might situate the boat if you were casting close to the bank. By studying your sonar as you fish, you see that if the boat is in 25 feet of water, you can cast your lure into the shallows where it is 4 or 5 feet deep and retrieve the plug through the 12-foot range and then on out to the boat in an effective manner. So you slowly keep following that 25-foot contour, and if you notice a change in contours—such as a hump or extended point—you immediately maneuver the boat accordingly so that you keep your casts and lures in the proper places. This is fishing effectively.

MOTOR, TROLLING

A common term for electric motors, which are used rarely for trolling but mostly for maneuvering boat position while fishing, especially when casting.

See: Motor, Electric.

MOUSIE

See: Mealworm.

MOZAMBIQUE

Mozambique is a large and lengthy country in southeastern Africa with 2,470 kilometers of coastline on the Mozambique Channel of the Indian Ocean. It has had a checkered saltwater sportfishery in the latter decades of the twentieth century, owing to civil strife and a poorly developed infrastructure—a situation common to many developing African nations. Freshwater sportfishing is virtually unknown, and the entire coast, stretching from the southern border with South Africa to the northern border with Tanzania, possesses some of the least-explored coastal fishing in the world. Saltwater gamefishing was outstanding in the past, although lightly pursued with both primitive equipment and primitive vessels. It has the potential to be a great attraction in the future.

Saltwater

Inhaca Island, Paradise Island, Bazaruto, Pomene, Xai Xai, and Tofo are all names that stir distant memories for some anglers and fuel a desire to return and fish the magnificent coast of Mozambique. Those memories, however, date back to before 1970.

Early in the 1970s, a fierce war put an end not only to Portuguese colonialism (the country became independent in 1975), but also to public fishing along this unspoiled stretch of African coast. Twenty years of civil war followed, and for most of that time Mozambique was closed to all but a very limited number of foreign diplomats who managed to fish the waters adjacent to the capital city of Maputo, at the extreme southern tip of the country.

In more recent times, a few intrepid anglers have visited the smattering of islands that exist off this coast. These islands are separated from the mainland by 20 miles of tidal flats, a fact that deterred rebel forces from approaching the islands and protected the small band of loyalist soldiers guarding their sovereignty. Reports filtered out about fantastic fishing, with some indication that the years of inactivity had resulted in regeneration of this coast. Some anglers believe that all that is needed now is boats, fuel, and accommodations to draw anglers in droves, possibly creating one of the world's foremost big-game centers.

The heaviest giant squid ever recorded weighed $2^1/_5$ tons and had one tentacle that measured 35 feet long.

Before the early 1970s, Santa Carolina, or Paradise Island, as it was commonly known, was southern Africa's answer to Cairns of Australia, Kona of Hawaii, and Cabo Blanco of Peru—all famed for their big marlin. Situated in the huge bay within the Bazaruto archipelago, it was a prime port for anglers to take advantage of pelagic fisheries opportunities brought about by the close southerly flow of the warm Aghulas Current coursing through the Mozambique Channel between the mainland and Madagascar.

Big black marlin, many over 1,000 pounds, were then boated from craft barely suitable for big-game fishing. Single-diesel-engined tubs with jury-rigged fighting chairs and makeshift outriggers were on the brink of giving way to modern sportfishing boats when the civil war commenced. At that time, other billfish included Pacific blue marlin, striped marlin, Pacific sailfish, and swordfish. Black marlin were the main quarry, with special emphasis placed on late in the season, when larger catches were registered, especially at Bazaruto (south of Beira).

Today, a band of ardent anglers and scuba divers, mainly from South Africa, journey to the lower Mozambique coast to make use of the rustic lodges and campsites built there, and they use high-speed 18- to 23-foot craft powered by dual outboards.

An abundance of king mackerel, wahoo, barracuda, dorado, bonito, and small tuna can be caught, but it is angling for sailfish and marlin that will spearhead the future redevelopment of the angling infrastructure of the area. With a current lack of big boats, a chicken-and-egg situation exists; the full potential of the Bazaruto archipelago, as well as the rest of the lengthy coast, will be realized only when fully equipped offshore charter craft make their appearance.

Some fishing efforts have indicated that a viable sailfish resource still exists here, but the full extent of this is unknown. Concerns exist about conserving fisheries resources here, because the region has a prevailing lack of protein and food, and local fishing crews, such as they are, need financial persuasion to release captured species, particularly large specimens like billfish.

Beach anglers have opened up new horizons along the white sandy shores of the islands. Prior to the war, a limited number of anglers fished from a few of the rocky promontories that stretch out into the ocean at the extremities of numerous bays and coves. Often they caught an abundance of gamefish, the main one being giant trevally.

At present, shore-based anglers—fishing from sand spits and channel edges—seek ocean predators as they await the vast array of food being swept out of the bay off the seemingly endless sandbanks and through the gaps between islands. Using lures, freshly netted sardines, or live bait, anglers question the need to take a craft to sea to access the diversity and quantity of fish. An ample supply of fish has even made fly fishing—a technique that is altogether new in this part of the world—more promising. It is possible that bonefish on the shallow flats will be targeted eventually, opening up a new vista of opportunities for light-tackle angling. Decades ago, huge bonefish, including specimens from 18 to 23 pounds, were reportedly landed around coastal Mozambique, although the status of this fishery is uncharted today.

With peace, government stability, and a vastly improved road system, the Mozambique coast is becoming a popular spot for South African anglers. The mystique of primitive Africa combined with excellent fishing either from shore or in modern high-powered craft (though small) makes this a unique experience, and the day may come when exploration of the entire coast and offshore waters unveils terrific treasures.

Freshwater

As primitive as the coastal fishery is, the inland fishery is even more so. Mozambique has numerous rivers and lakes, and the status of their fisheries is relatively unknown today. Forty percent of the country is comprised of coastal lowlands, but westward in the interior the land rises to low hills and plateaus, with mountainous regions in the west and north. It is purely speculative to suggest that the higher reaches may contain trout; however, some regions border highlands that do possess rainbow trout, especially in Malaŵi *(see)*.

The rivers are likely to contain some of the same species found in neighboring countries, possibly including tigerfish. It is reasonable to expect that these can be found in the Zambezi River, as the Zambezi is a hotbed for tigerfishing upriver in Zimbabwe. There, after exiting Lake Kariba, it flows into extreme western Mozambique, where it forms a large lake behind Cabora Bassa Dam, which on a map appears to be slightly smaller than the 180-mile-long Kariba. The Zambezi flows southeasterly from here to the Indian Ocean, widening considerably in its lower sections. The lake and the river in Mozambique almost certainly possess tigerfish, vundu, and tilapia, as well as other species, although the size of the fish and extent of the population are completely speculative.

Other significant rivers with unknown fisheries resources include the Ruvuma, which forms most of the northern border with Tanzania, and the Limpopo, which is in the far south and flows from South Africa into Mozambique and through a large delta before reaching the sea near Xai Xai. Numerous other rivers and tributaries flow from the highlands.

In addition to Cabora Bassa, Lake Nyasa forms part of the Malaŵi border, as do Lakes Chilwa and Chiota, although the fisheries of the latter are unknown. A short stretch of the Shire River, which in Malaŵi is known to have tigerfish, flows in Mozambique before entering the Zambezi River.

MUDDING

The behavior of bottom-feeding fish in shallow water, especially the bonefish, which creates a mud trail as it roots while feeding, often with head down and the upper lobe of its tail out of the water.

MUDLINE

The edge created in a large body of water by the influx of turbid current, usually a river. The mudline is obvious at the river mouth and for a variable distance (depending on the volume of incoming water and big water current) along the shore near the river mouth. The clearer edge of the mudline is attractive to some species of gamefish.

MULLET

Mullet are members of the Mugilidae family, a group of roughly 70 species that range worldwide in shallow, warm seas. A few species live in freshwater and some are reared in ponds. All are good food fish, especially in smoked form, although smaller ones may be too bony to eat. Mullet roe is considered a delicacy. Mullet are important food fish for many predator species, and anglers use them alive or dead, in chunks or strips, as baits.

Identification. The striped mullet *(Mugil cephalus)* is bluish gray or green along the back, shading to silver on the sides and white below. Also known as the black mullet, or fatback, it has indistinct horizontal black bars, or stripes, on its sides; the fins are lightly scaled at the base and unscaled above; the nose is blunt and the mouth small; and the second dorsal fin originates behind that of the anal fin. It is similar to the smaller fantail mullet *(M. gyrans)* and the white mullet *(M. curema)*, both of which have a black blotch at the base of their pectoral fin, which is lacking in the striped mullet.

Fantail mullet have an olive green back with a bluish tint, shading to silvery on the sides and white below. Its anal and pelvic fins are yellowish; there's a dark blotch at the base of the pectoral fin; the mouth has an inverted V-shape; and the second dorsal fin originates behind that of the anal fin.

The white mullet, also known as silver mullet, is bluish gray on the back, fading to silvery on the sides and white below. It lacks stripes; small scales extend onto its soft dorsal and anal fins; there's a dark blotch at the base of the pectoral fin; and the second dorsal fin originates behind that of the anal fin.

Size. The striped mullet may reach a length of 3 feet and weigh as much as 12 pounds, although the largest specimens have come from aquariums. Roe specimens in the wild are common to 3 pounds, but most striped mullet weigh closer to a pound. The fantail mullet is small and usually weighs less than a pound. The white mullet is similar in size to the fantail.

Distribution. The striped mullet is cosmopolitan in all warm seas worldwide and is the only member of the mullet family found off the Pacific coast of the U.S. The fantail mullet occurs in the western Atlantic in Bermuda, and from Florida and the northern Gulf of Mexico to Brazil. The white mullet is found in the western Atlantic in Bermuda and from Massachusetts south to Brazil, including

Striped Mullet

M

White Mullet

the Gulf of Mexico; in the eastern Atlantic from Gambia to the Congo; and in the eastern Pacific from the Gulf of California, Mexico, to Iquique, Chile.

The Brazilian mullet *(M. brasiliensis)* is prevalent in the southern Caribbean southward along the South American coast. Common species off the coasts of Europe and Africa and in the Mediterranean are the thick-lipped mullet *(M. chelo),* the thin-lipped gray mullet *(M. capito),* and the golden mullet *(M. auratus).* Some common species in Indo-Pacific waters include the 3-foot-long blue-tail mullet *(Valamugil buchanani),* which is found in Indonesia, Micronesia, Melanesia, the Mariana Islands, and southern Japan; and the 2-foot-long fringelip mullet *(Crenimugil crenilabis),* which occurs in the Red Sea, along the East Coast of Africa, and from southern Japan to Lord Howe Island, Australia. A freshwater mullet *(Myxus petardi),* called pinkeye, occurs in Australian coastal streams and migrates downriver to spawn in estuaries.

Life history/Behavior. Mullet are schooling fish found inshore in coastal environs. Many, but not all, species have the unusual habit of leaping from the water as they race along in schools. Some have stiff bodies when they jump, and fall back into the water with a loud splat, which usually draws the attention of people nearby; most newcomers to mangrove coasts think these leaping fish are a sporting species or are being pursued by gamefish, although this is often not the case.

Theories as to why mullet jump abound: to escape predators, remove parasites, coordinate spawning migrations, aid respiration, and so forth. Some research has supported the respiration theory. Research on striped mullet showed that the fish uses the upper portion of the pharynx for aerial respiration, obtaining air by jumping or holding its head above the water. The research showed that the jumping frequency of this species seemed to be inversely related to dissolved oxygen concentration. The less oxygen, the more often the fish jumped. Biologists say that the upper pharyngeal cavity of the striped mullet can hold about 2 percent of the fish's body volume, and could supply oxygen for at least five minutes. This would enable the fish to feed in waters with a low oxygen concentration. If this fish can obtain air by sticking its head above the surface, however, why does it jump?

Adult striped mullet migrate offshore in large schools to spawn; juveniles migrate inshore at about 1 inch in size, moving far up tidal creeks. Fantail mullet spawn in near-shore or inshore waters during spring and summer, and juveniles occur offshore. White mullet spawn offshore, and the young migrate into estuaries and along beaches.

Food and feeding habits. These mullet feed on algae, detritus, and other tiny marine forms; they pick up mud from the bottom and strain plant and animal material from it through their sievelike gill rakers and pharyngeal teeth. Indigestible materials are spit out. In most species, the stomach is gizzard-like for grinding food.

Angling. Mullets do not ordinarily take hooked baits or lures, but anglers may pursue them for use as bait by snagging them with small treble hooks (cast into schools). They are commonly captured by cast net. Occasionally they are caught on flies or doughballs or even wads of algae; when hooked, they fight gamely.

MULLOWAY *Argyrosomus hololepidotus.*

Other names—southern meagre, jewfish, silver jewfish, river kingfish, butterfish, soapy, kob (South Africa); French: *maigre du sud, maigre africain;* Italian: *bocca d'oro.*

The mulloway, because of its size and the availability of the waters it inhabits, is a much-sought-after prize among both shore-based and boat anglers, especially in Australia. A rather slow-moving fish that exhibits an initial burst of great power when hooked, it is considered a straightforward fighter with few, if any, nasty habits. Small mulloway, known as soapies, are short on reputation as table fish, hence the name, but adults are excellent fare, and the species is commercially valuable.

Identification. The mulloway has a body coloring that varies from bluish gray to bronze green on top. It is silvery below. Fish taken at night, however, can be a silvery color all over. A row of prominent pearly spots extends along the lateral line. There may also be a large black blotch at the base of the upper margin of the pectoral fin, although this is sometimes missing. The caudal fin is rounded, and the long dorsal fin—consisting of a spined section and a rayed section—extends from just above the pectoral fin to the "wrist" or caudal peduncle. The teeth are short and sharp within a large mouth, the inside of which is bright orange.

Size. This fish is known to grow to more then 70 kilograms and a length of 2 meters in some parts of its range. In Australian waters, the largest mulloway recorded by rod and reel weighed 43.7 kilograms. This species can live for at least 30 years, with 6-year-olds weighing about 8 kilograms. Juveniles, or soapies, weigh up to 2 kilograms and are around 50 centimeters long. Most mulloway taken by anglers in Australia weigh less than 10 kilograms.

M

Distribution. This species occurs along the western and eastern coasts of Africa to Australia, including Oman and the east coast of India. It ranges around the southern half of Australia from North West Cape in Western Australia, across the southern portion, and up the East Coast to as far north as Bundaberg in Queensland.

Habitat. Small mulloway tend to remain in estuaries, where they are found in schools. As they grow, they spread out into bays and inshore waters, frequenting coastal reefs, ocean beaches, and rocky shores. In flood conditions, they congregate around river mouths to feed on thousands of small fish that are washed into the sea.

Life history/Behavior. Fecundity is unknown, and larvae have not been identified, but juveniles as small as 5 centimeters have been found in rivers along Australia's East Coast. They grow rapidly, increasing in length by about 2 centimeters per month. Spawning probably takes place in summer. As they mature, mulloway are inclined to become solitary, moving along the coast from river to river, along coastal beaches, and up into the estuaries when searching for small fish.

Food and feeding habits. Mulloway feed on various fish species, including mullet, garfish, bream, luderick, leatherjackets, common mackerel, pilchards, and yellowtail (scad). They also eat sand crabs, prawns, and worms. They are especially fond of giant beach worms *(Australonuphis),* which they may identify by smell. These worms grow to more than 2 meters in length and are found along the Australian coast.

Angling. In Australia, every recreational angler aspires to catch a big mulloway (30 kilograms or more), but the majority must be content with smaller specimens to roughly 10 kilograms. The most popular method is to fish the ocean beaches, points, and river entrances using surf fishing tackle, and a minimum of 200 meters of line testing 15 kilograms or more. Boat and estuary anglers prefer shorter, stout boat rods, and some estuary anglers use heavy handlines. Offshore anglers will target reefs and wrecks surrounded by a sandy bottom. Hook sizes vary from 5/0 to 10/0.

Baitfishing is the first choice except where mulloway are feeding on small fish washed into the sea at flooding river entrances, which makes large surface lures and poppers effective. Surf anglers normally use strip baits of mullet, bluefish, bonito, or tuna flesh, or dead whole baits of pilchards and garfish rigged on ganged 5/0 hooks. While waiting for the sun to set before fishing for mulloway, surf anglers fish for bluefish to be used as bait; fresh fillets of bluefish are certain to attract mulloway moving along a surf beach. Where they can be caught, the giant beach worms are likely to take priority over other baits.

Mulloway travel well up into estuaries and are often taken 10 kilometers from the ocean. Within estuaries, anglers land small individuals at all hours of the day. The large, old specimens are almost invariably taken at night, usually during the two hours on either side of the change in the tide. Estuary mulloway respond well to fresh prawns, bloodworms, small squid, and small live mullet and yellowtail, in addition to the other baits mentioned.

Fishing in estuaries with soft-plastic lures and minnow plugs has increased in popularity during daylight hours, and is sometimes effective when fishing under bridge lights that have attracted small baitfish. Occasionally, a small mulloway is tempted by a trolled metal spoon meant for bluefish.

The initial run of a hooked mulloway can be long and powerful, often stripping 100 meters of line from the reel. Skilled anglers make no attempt to stop the fish during this run. Instead, the strike is registered when the run stops and the fish swallows the bait, as evidenced by recognizable head shaking. The subsequent fight becomes a test of stamina, drag control, and patience on the part of the angler.

Fly fishing for mulloway is rarely practiced, although a fly presented to schooling mulloway can be just as effective as any surface lure.

MULTIFILAMENT *(Line)*

See: Line.

MULTIHOOK RIG

Using multiple hooks on bottom fishing rigs is a standard process, and it is usually accomplished with two, and occasionally three, hooks separated vertically off the main fishing line. However, in gathering baitfish for sportfishing purposes in saltwater, the term "multihook rig" has come to mean a string (half a dozen or so) of small fine-wire hooks on a single rig. These have variously been known as quill rigs, fish catchers, lucky joes, and other terms; most are handmade and tedious to tie. In recent years, a small variety of such rigs have been commercially manufactured, by far the most common and popular of which is the Sabiki rig, a Japanese creation used to catch pilchards, herring, goggle-eyes, cigar minnows, mackerel, and an assortment of baitfish.

These rigs are employed in situations where it is impractical to use a cast net *(see)* to gather bait (usually because of depth or current), and they feature six hooks on small leaders that branch off a main line. Each hook on the rig is dressed with a small trimmed piece of iridescent dried material (often fish skin or shrimp), and many also have a small luminescent paint bead head, which can be charged under light to glow. The branch line is lighter than the main line, and the components of the rig may vary depending on the application.

These rigs are fished with or without chum, and in water that varies from 10 to 15 feet deep to many hundreds, provided that schools of baitfish have been located. In some cases, the baitfish are attracted

Multihook (Sabiki) Rig

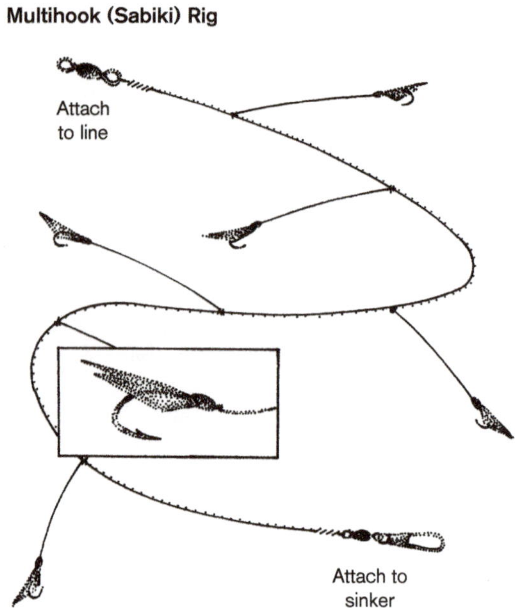

by chumming; in others, large schools are pinpointed with sonar before the rig is lowered. Heavy sinkers, attached to a swivel at the bottom of the rig, are used to get the rigs down and help keep the bait from getting tangled in the rig when retrieved. The rig is jigged in short motions, and when a fish grabs hold, it is held still for a few seconds to allow the wriggling caught fish to attract its brethren. Multiple catches are common.

Fish should be removed from the bottom hooks first, working up the rig and being careful not to get impaled on the super sharp points. A small hook extractor will help in unhooking. To store the rigs, use a rectangular piece of cardboard with notches cut in the middle of each end; wrap the main line over the notches and clip each branch hook off to the side of the board.

MULTIPLYING REEL

A revolving spool reel with multiplying action as opposed to single action, that is, a reel whose spool revolves more than one time for every turn of the handle. Single-action reels are those that have essentially a 1:1 retrieve ratio, where one turn of the crank causes one turn of the spool; multiplying reels have a greater than 1:1 gear ratio, where one turn of the crank causes more than one full turn of the spool.

The term "multiplying reel" or "multiplier" began at the turn of the nineteenth century and is generally associated with American craftsmen who fashioned the famous Kentucky Reel, which was the forerunner both of today's baitcasting reels and of other revolving spool reels in which the spool turns at a greater than 1:1 ratio. Before that time, the only reels available were single-action revolving spool versions, primarily employed for storing and retrieving line. Throughout the nineteenth century and well into the twentieth century, the term "multiplying reel" was in common use; today, it is used only when referring to antique tackle.

See: Antique Fishing Tackle; Baitcasting Tackle; Conventional Tackle; Flycasting Tackle; Kentucky Reel; Single-Action Reel.

MUMMICHOG

See: Killifish.

MUSKELLUNGE *Esox masquinongy.*

Other names—maskinonge, muskallonge, mascalonge, muskie, musky, 'lunge, silver muskellunge, Great Lakes muskellunge, Ohio muskellunge, Allegheny River muskellunge, spotted muskellunge, barred muskellunge, great muskellunge, great pike, blue pike, etc. Occasionally, it is referred to as a "jack" in some areas.

The muskellunge is the largest member of the Esocidae family of pike. Its name is derived from the native Indian word *maskinonge,* which has had numerous interpretations. Among them are deformed pike *(mashk kinonge);* ugly fish *(mas kinonge);* and large pike *(mas kenosha).* Unlike its blood relative, the northern pike *(see: pike, northern),* which has circumpolar distribution, the muskellunge is strictly a North American species, native to central and eastern North America. Although it is bodily pikelike and does occur in some of the same waters, it is vastly different in behavior and abundance (or lack thereof). It is one of the world's foremost gamefish by virtue of its size, strength, and predatory habits, and also by virtue of its contrary nature. The muskellunge is one of the most difficult freshwater sportfish of North America to willfully catch, and its habits and feeding behavior are as, or more, difficult to understand than those of any other freshwater species, including the most highly touted and lowly populated Atlantic salmon. Although a devoted coterie of anglers fervently pursues muskellunge, these enthusiasts are a fraction of the total angling populace, most of the rest of whom do not have the opportunity to catch this species or prefer more dependable or more abundant species.

Although the range of the muskellunge has expanded through stocking efforts, this fish is abundant only in portions of its range. It has not been pursued commercially for many decades, but the number of large individuals has declined since the 1960s as a result of many environmental factors, especially habitat destruction and alteration that has affected spawning and predator-prey relationships, as well as the capture and killing by anglers of many of the largest individuals. The voluntary release of muskies has increased since the mid-1980s, and today muskie fishing is mostly a catch-and-release endeavor, especially among devotees of this fish. The flesh of a muskellunge is white and flaky and of excellent quality, but many anglers

Muskellunge

have never tasted it and have no need to because there are equally good table fish available among more abundant species like walleye and northern pike, one or both of which are usually found in the same environs as the muskie.

Identification. Like other species belonging to the *Esox* genus, the muskellunge has an arrow-like body that is long and sleek. A single soft-rayed dorsal fin is located very far back near the tail. The pelvic fins are located relatively far back on the belly, about halfway between the pectoral fins and the tail, instead of directly under the pectoral fins. The mouth is large, with the maxillae reaching back at least to the middle of the eyes, and it is broad like a duck's bill, but full of teeth.

The coloration and markings on muskellunge are highly variable but usually consist of dark markings on a brownish or green background. There are numerous dark, vertical bars that may appear as vermiculations or spots, and sometimes the body has no markings. The northern pike, by comparison, has light-colored, oblong or kidney-shaped spots against a darker body, and the chain pickerel *(see: pickerel, chain)* has a unique chainlike pattern on the sides, although the spaces between the "links" of the chain may be seen as large oblong spots, depending on one's point of view. The grass and redfin pickerel look much more like the muskie in their markings, but they grow only to roughly 15 inches in length.

The muskie can also be distinguished from other *Esox* species by both cheeks and the gill cover, which are usually scaled only on the top half. In the pickerel, the cheeks and gill cover are fully scaled; in the pike, the cheeks are fully scaled, but the gill cover is usually scaled only on the top half. Another distinction occurs in the number of pores under the lower jaw. In the muskie there are 6 to 9 pores along each side (rarely 5 or 10 on one side only). In the northern pike there are 5 along each side (rarely 3, 4, or 6 on one side only). In the pickerel, there are 4 along each side (occasionally 3 or 5 on one side only).

The variable markings and colorations of muskellunge have lead to identity confusion over the years, and at one time it was believed that there were at least four species or varieties of muskellunge, but these patterns occurred throughout the range of the muskellunge, and subspecies are no longer recognized. An exception is the tiger muskellunge *(see: muskellunge, tiger),* a sterile hybrid resulting from the breeding of true muskellunge and northern pike parents.

Size/Age. Muskellunge are among the largest North American fish dwelling entirely in freshwater. Although reports suggest the existence of fish from 80 to 100 pounds that were netted, speared, or otherwise encountered (including scales from an angler-lost St. Lawrence River fish that a biologist verified as being from a muskie that he estimated at 100 pounds), there is no hard verification of any muskie weighing more than 70 pounds. Even some of the known 60-pounders are subject to doubt. The former all-tackle world record and current New York State record muskellunge is a 69-pound, 15-ounce fish that was caught in 1957 in the St. Lawrence River. This fish has been disputed, however, and a slightly smaller and previously caught 69-pounder from Wisconsin has replaced it. Thus, 70 pounds stands as the maximum known size for muskellunge. Most muskellunge encountered by anglers weigh between 7 and 15 pounds and are less than 40 inches long; specimens exceeding 20 pounds are not uncommon, but it is extremely hard to come by one weighing more than 30 pounds. Very few in excess of 40 pounds were caught throughout the 1990s, and most released fish are not weighed; their size is measured by estimated or actual length in inches. They have been known to live between 25 and 30 years, and many fish live for 15 years, although the average life span is closer to 8 years.

Distribution. The muskellunge is endemic to eastern North America. It is native to the Great Lakes, Hudson Bay, and Mississippi River basins from southern Quebec to the Red River of the North in Manitoba, and extends south in the Appalachians to Georgia and west to Iowa. It has been introduced (including the hybrid version) widely to Atlantic coast drainages as far as southern Virginia, and elsewhere in the southern and western United States, although its representation in many of these areas is minor.

Habitat. Muskellunge live in medium to large rivers and in lakes of all sizes, although their preferred

Muskellunge/Barred Variation

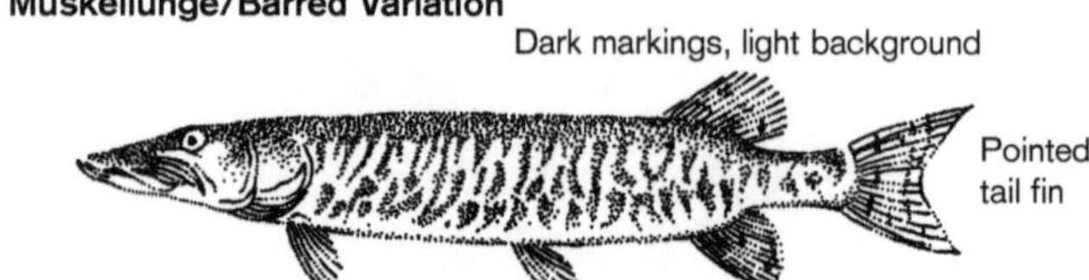

Muskellunge/Spotted Variation

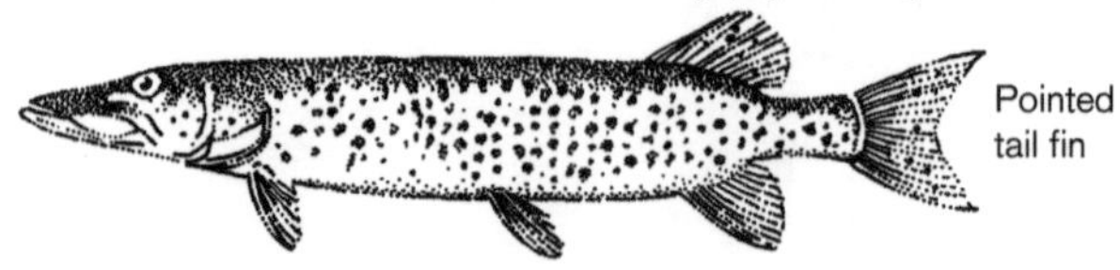

Muskellunge/Clear Variation

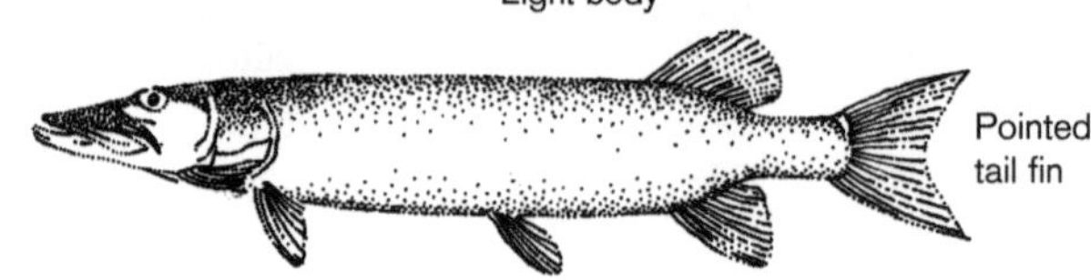

Tiger (Hybrid) Muskellunge

Subtle distinctions differentiate the four variations in muskellunge coloration and marking.

habitat is cool waters with large and small basins or both deep and shallow areas. They are found in waters no more than 75 acres in size, as well as in enormous waters like Lake of the Woods, Ontario; Lake St. Clair, Michigan; or the St. Lawrence River.

They rarely venture far from cover and favor shallow, heavily vegetated waters less than 40 feet deep, but they sometimes inhabit deep water that lacks vegetation but offers ample prey.

Life history/Behavior. Muskies spawn in the spring in 1 to 3 feet of water, in shallow bays covered with vegetation. This occurs just after ice out, and when the water temperatures are between 49° and 59°F. They are broadcast spawners and disperse the fertilized eggs randomly. The eggs sink to the bottom but are not as adhesive as northern pike eggs. Their spawning season usually occurs after the northern pike's in areas where the two species coexist. On rare occasions, a hybrid tiger muskie *(see: muskie, tiger)* results, but this situation also causes small northern pike to mature before small muskies do, making predation on the muskies more likely.

Muskie eggs usually hatch in 8 to 14 days, and within 10 weeks the young may be 4 to 6 inches long. Females grow larger than males at all ages, and both reach sexual maturity in three to five years.

Food and feeding habits. The muskie is a solitary fish that tends to stay in the same area, lurking opportunistically in thick weedbeds and waiting for prey. It is seldom a wandering, roaming fish, although it may migrate from deep to shallow environs to feed. Its diet is varied, with a preference for larger, rather than smaller, fish, as the muskie is well adapted to capturing and swallowing fish of considerable size. Yellow perch, suckers, golden shiners, and walleye are among its favorite foods, but it also consumes smallmouth bass and many other fish, as well as the infrequent animal (duck, muskrat, and the like).

Angling. Muskellunge are generally harder to catch than any other freshwater species. They are unpredictable, even for those who constantly seek them. Sometimes, and in some waters, they are not as difficult to catch as the oft-quoted "fish of a thousand casts" or "fish of 100 hours" clichés suggest. This is especially true of smaller individuals, and an extremely small number of people catch these fish with some degree of consistency. Generally, however, muskie fishing requires hard work, many hours on the water, and a great deal of patience—and there are no guarantees. Muskie fishing is the one form of freshwater angling (Altantic salmon angling runs a close second) in which merely glimpsing the quarry is a feat. A "follow"—when a muskie is visually observed as it trails a lure to the boat—is as meaningful as tossing a horseshoe close to the peg.

Muskies generally lurk in or near places where they can lie relatively concealed to ambush forage fish, so anglers must seek places that provide feeding opportunities. Muskies are large fish that have big mouths that strike big lures, perhaps because they are prone to eating big fish. A 15-inch walleye isn't imposing to a 40-inch muskie; muskies position themselves in strategic locations that attract prey large enough to make an ambush attack worthwhile. The nature of the cover, the depth of water around the cover and nearby, and the presence of current determine which places are better than others. Following are prime locations to concentrate on.

Submerged vegetation. Muskies are attracted to the edges of vegetation, particularly to the breakline where weeds end and deep water begins, and to corners, pockets, or other irregular contour features of weedbeds. In the fall they move away from dead and decaying vegetation, and anglers should look for them in whatever green and healthy weeds exist.

Points of land. Whether they extend from the shore or from islands, points are natural impediments to fish movement and serve as attractants to prey and predator alike. Concentrate on points with a long underwater slope adjacent to deep water, especially if they break sharply from 10 feet off to 20 or 25 feet, or those that have some form of heavy vegetation around their perimeter, or those with rockpiles on the underwater breaklines.

Shoals, bars, submerged islands. With or without a hard bottom or vegetation, these structures attract baitfish and gamefish, making them reliable feeding areas.

Confluences. Near and just below a warmwater discharge, feeder creek, or other tributary is a prime place to seek muskies. In the fall, for example, the immediate area near a warmwater discharge is affected and may be attractive to forage fish and muskies. Where a tributary meets a major flow is a promising locale as well, especially in summer, when the tributary may be dumping cooler and more oxygenated water into the main flow.

Current. A point or shoal that is washed by a strong current is a promising place to find muskies. A locale where strong current can bring baitfish washing by, or which retards the movement of weak, crippled, or wounded fish, is also a top spot. Back eddies, slicks, and current edges are worth a look, too.

Although muskies may inhabit deep water, most fish are taken in less than 30 feet of water; depths of 15 to 30 feet are the norm. In many places, they hold in much shallower water. Most casting anglers catch muskies in depths between 5 and 15 feet; trollers usually catch them in depths ranging from 8 to 30 feet.

Casting and trolling both have devotees, partially by law (trolling for muskies is not legal in a few places) but mostly by traditional preference. Trolled lures are fished on fairly short lines, as there is seldom much reason to put out more than 75 feet of line. Muskies are not spooked by boat noise, and some trollers catch them right in the prop wash, within 10 to 25 feet of the boat and just a few feet below the surface.

The primary advantage of trolling for these fish is the ability to cover a lot of territory on large bodies of water, although heavy vegetation on some waters hinders trolling efforts. Also, trollers don't see fish that might follow their lures, but casters often do. Muskies will pursue a cast-and-retrieved bait right to the boat, occasionally striking at boatside but more often vanishing. This activity shows an angler where a fish is located; good muskie casters remember all of the places where they have caught and seen fish on their favorite waters, and they continue to visit those places regularly. The choice of whether to cast or troll should be based on your own interests and abilities as well as the habitat and angling situation.

Muskie lures don't have the diversity of lures intended for other fish. And although no sure-fire lure exists, there are some contenders. Large jigs, jerkbaits, a few surface plugs, bucktail spinners, and assorted diving plugs are the common lures; bucktails are the runaway favorites for casting, followed by jerkbaits. Some anglers land muskies on large jigs or surface plugs, but it's best to focus on bucktails and diving plugs until you've become proficient.

A muskie, tagged in the dorsal fin, is about to be released at Lake of the Woods, Minnesota.

Bucktail spinners (weighted in-line spinners heavily dressed with bucktail hair over one or two treble hooks) are mainly used in shallow- to mid-depth casting, over the top of submerged cover and along the edges of shallow submerged cover. They are seldom used for trolling. They are manufactured in a host of color combinations, but black is the hands-down top muskie producer. If you're new to casting for muskies, start with a black bucktail around cabbage beds.

Among diving plugs, shallow-running minnow-style baits account for many catches. Anglers use them around the edges of weedy habitat and sometimes retrieve them over the top of deeply submerged vegetation.

Deeper-diving plugs are both cast and trolled. A good tactic with a deep-diving plug is to reel it down until it hits vegetation, then stop the retrieve (which allows the lure to float upward), then reel it in a few feet until you hit vegetation, then stop, and so forth. This action is similar to that of a jerkbait except that the lure is far more enticing when retrieved. Deep-diving plugs are better than other lures for casting around reefs and points and quick-current edges that don't tend to accumulate vegetation. Shallow, medium, and deep divers all have trolling applications. Five- to 8-inch-long plugs are customary for this, preferably in single- or double-jointed versions, but also in unjointed models. Popular muskie plug colors include black, black-and-white, chartreuse, silver-and-black, and yellow, plus perch, walleye, bass, and muskie patterns, but there is no clear favorite.

No matter what lure you tie on, the way you use your boat and equipment to cope with the conditions can be a factor in your success. Drift along the side of, rather than through, prime habitat. This permits many casts around an area without alarming any fish. An electric motor is just as beneficial to a muskie caster as it is to a bass angler, primarily for precise boat control and positioning. Sonar can be a substantial aid, too, for achieving proper boat positioning over areas likely to hold muskies.

Most muskie anglers use heavy tackle. Twenty-five to 40-pound line and a stiff rod is standard, but some anglers are successful with 12- to 20-pound line and a 6-foot fast-action baitcasting rod. Muskies fight well but not laboriously, although they can provide spectacular jumping action. They are noted for being hard to drive a hook into, and for escaping from anglers who thought they had a well-hooked fish. Repetitive hook setting and sharp hooks, as well as low-stretch lines, can be advantageous. The muskie's formidable dentures make a steel leader and sharp hooks advisable.

See: Pike.

MUSKELLUNGE, TIGER *Esox masquinongy x Esox lucius.*

Other names—tiger muskie, norlunge, nor'lunge, hybrid muskellunge.

A member of the Esocidae family, the tiger muskellunge is a distinctively marked hybrid fish produced when true muskellunge *(E. masquinongy)* and northern pike *(Esox lucius)* interbreed. This occurs when the male of either species fertilizes the eggs of the female of the opposite species. This is not a common occurrence in the wild but has happened naturally in waters where both parent species occur, making it an unusual and prized catch.

The tiger muskie was believed to be a separate species until scientists succeeded in crossing a northern pike with a muskellunge, thereby discovering the tiger muskie's true origin. Deliberate crossbreeding of these species in hatcheries by fisheries managers is now much more common than natural hybridization, and tiger muskies have been stocked in many waters where neither parent occurs naturally. Fish culturists prefer to cross a male northern pike with a female muskellunge because the eggs of the muskie are less adhesive and don't clump as badly in the hatching process.

Populations of introduced tiger muskies are naturally self-limiting because this hybrid is sterile and cannot reproduce itself. Its numbers can therefore be controlled over time. It also grows quickly and is aggressive, making it an excellent catch for anglers.

The tiger muskie has a distinctive look and should not be confused with the true muskellunge, which has been called a tiger muskie in some areas. In most respects, notably in size and appearance, the hybrid is very much like the true muskellunge, and anglers hold the naturally occurring hybrid in higher esteem than the true muskie because of its rarity, its beautiful markings, and its game nature. The true muskie may have either bars or spots on the sides or no markings at all, but it is rarely as strikingly beautiful as the tiger muskie, which has dark, wavering tigerlike stripes or bars, many of them broken, that are set against a lighter background.

As is true with many hybrid fish, the body of the tiger muskie is slightly deeper than that of either comparable-length parent. The cheeks and jaws are usually spotted, with 10 to 16 pores existing on the underside of the jaws. The tips of the tail are more rounded than in the true muskie, and the fins have distinct spots. In very large specimens, the fins, especially the tail fin, appears to be much larger than for a comparable true muskie.

Naturally occurring tiger muskie in excess of 30 pounds are extremely rare, and most have come from Wisconsin lakes. A 51-pound, 3-ounce fish, caught in 1919 at Lac Vieux Desert on the Wisconsin/Michigan border, is the all-tackle world-record tiger muskie. For a time, it was thought to be a true muskellunge and thus held the world record for that species.

Methods of fishing for tiger muskies are no different than those for true muskies. Naturally occurring tiger muskies are caught incidentally by anglers fishing for true muskellunge or other fish species. Introduced muskies are caught both as targeted and incidental catches. Most are released alive, particularly those of natural origin.

See: Muskellunge.

Tiger Muskellunge

Conversion Charts

THE SYSTEM OF WEIGHTS AND MEASURES USED IN MOST COUNTRIES AND IN ALL SCIENTIFIC work is the International System of Units (SI), which is commonly referred to as the metric system. A notable and influential exception to this is the United States, where the general public, and non-scientific publications, use the U.S., or U.S. customary, system of weights and measures. Throughout the *Ken Schultz's Fishing Encyclopedia & Worldwide Angling Guide*, there is a liberal use of both metric and U.S. customary weights and measures without parenthetical conversions to equivalent weights or measures. Some anglers, especially those who travel widely and those who pay close attention to world-record fish weights and fishing line classifications, are accustomed to both systems, which are often found mixed at boat docks, fish camps, and tackle shops throughout the world. The following information is provided to help the reader make the conversion from one system to another.

U.S. To Metric Conversion Formulas

When You Know . . .	*Multiply By . . .*	*To Determine . . .*
Inches (in)	25.4	Millimeters (mm)
Inches (in)	2.54	Centimeters (cm)
Inches (in)	0.0254	Meters (m)
Square Inches (sq in)	645.0	Square Millimeters (sq mm)
Square Inches (sq in)	6.45	Square Centimeters (sq cm)
Square Inches (sq in)	0.00064	Square Meters(sq m)
Feet (ft)	30.5	Centimeters (cm)
Feet (ft)	0.305	Meters (m)
Feet (ft)	0.0003	Kilometers (km)
Square Feet (sq ft)	0.093	Square Meters (sq m)
Fathoms (fath)	1.827	Meters (m)
Fathoms (fath)	0.0018	Kilometers (km)
Yards (yd)	0.914	Meters (m)
Square Yards (sq yd)	0.836	Square Meters (sq m)
Statute Miles (mi) (5,280 ft)	1.61	Kilometers (km)
Nautical Miles (n mi) (6,020 ft)	1.852	Kilometers (km)
Square Miles (sq mi)	2.56	Square Kilometers (sq km)
Miles per hour (mph)	1.61	Kilometers per hour (kph)
Knots per hour	1.84	Kilometers per hour (kph)
Acres	0.405	Hectares
Ounces of Weight (oz)	28.3	Grams (g)
Ounces of Weight (oz)	0.0283	Kilograms (kg)
Ounces of Fluid (fl oz)	29.6	Milliliters (mL)
Pounds (lb)	454.0	Grams (g)
Pounds (lb)	0.454	Kilograms (kg)
Pints (pt)—U.S.	0.473	Liters (L)
Pints (pt)—Imperial	0.568	Liters (L)
Quarts (qt)—U.S.	0.946	Liters (L)
Quarts (qt)—Imperial	1.14	Liters (L)
Gallons (gal)—U.S.	3.79	Liters (L)
Gallons (gal)—Imperial	4.55	Liters (L)
degrees Fahrenheit (°F)	0.555 (after subtracting 32)	degrees Celsius (°C)

Metric To U.S. Conversion Formulas

When You Know . . .	*Multiply By . . .*	*To Determine . . .*
Millimeters (mm)	0.039	Inches (in)
Centimeters (cm)	0.394	Inches (in)
Centimeters (cm)	0.0328	Feet (ft)
Square Centimeters (sq cm)	0.155	Square Inches (sq in)
Meters (m)	39.37	Inches (in)
Meters (m)	3.281	Feet (ft)
Meters (m)	1.09	Yards (yd)
Meters (m)	0.547	Fathoms (fath)
Square Meters (sq m)	1.2	Square Yards (sq yd)
Kilometers (km)	3,279.0	Feet (ft)
Kilometers (km)	1,093.0	Yards (yd)
Kilometers (km)	546.0	Fathoms (fath)
Kilometers (km)	0.621	Statute Miles (mi)
Kilometers (km)	0.545	Nautical Miles (n mi)
Square Kilometers (sq km)	0.386	Square Miles (sq mi)
Kilometers per hour (kph)	0.621	Miles per hour (mph)
Kilometers per hour (kph)	0.545	Knots per hour
Hectares	2.47	Acres
Grams (g)	0.035	Ounces of Weight (oz)
Grams (g)	0.002	Pounds (lb)
Kilograms (kg)	35.2736	Ounces (oz)
Kilograms (kg)	2.2	Pounds (lb)
Milliliter (mL)	0.034	Fluid Ounces (oz)
Liters (L)	2.11	Pints (pt)—U.S.
Liters (L)	1.76	Pints (pt)—Imperial
Liters (L)	1.06	Quarts (qt)—U.S.
Liters (L)	0.880	Quarts (qt)—Imperial
Liters (L)	0.264	Gallons (gal)—U.S.
Liters (L)	0.22	Gallons (gal)—Imperial
degrees Celsius (°C)	1.8 (and add 32)	degrees Fahrenheit (°F)

Table Of Metric and U.S. Equivalent Line Strengths

Metric	*U.S. Customary*	*Metric*	*U.S. Customary*
1 kg	2.2 lb	10 kg	22.0 lb
2 kg	4.4 lb	15 kg	33.0 lb
3 kg	6.6 lb	24 kg	52.8 lb
4 kg	8.8 lb	37 kg	81.4 lb
6 kg	13.2 lb	60 kg	132.0 lb
8 kg	17.6 lb		

Table of Fish Weights

Metric	*U.S. Customary*	*Metric*	*U.S. Customary*
1 kg	2.2 lb	60 kg	132.0 lb
2 kg	4.4 lb	70 kg	154.0 lb
3 kg	6.6 lb	80 kg	176.0 lb
4 kg	8.8 lb	90 kg	198.0 lb
5 kg	11.0 lb	100 kg	220.0 lb
6 kg	13.2 lb	200 kg	440.0 lb
7 kg	15.4 lb	300 kg	660.0 lb
8 kg	17.6 lb	400 kg	880.0 lb
9 kg	19.8 lb	500 kg	1,100.0 lb
10 kg	22.0 lb	600 kg	1,320.0 lb
20 kg	44.0 lb	700 kg	1,540.0 lb
30 kg	66.0 lb	800 kg	1,760.0 lb
40 kg	88.0 lb	900 kg	1,980.0 lb
50 kg	110.0 lb	1,000 kg	2,200.0 lb

www.ingramcontent.com/pod-product-compliance
Lightning Source LLC
LaVergne TN
LVHW060636110826
845147LV00018B/993
9781684427703